STUDENTS LOVE THE BOOK OF KNOWLEDGE!

"A-List helped me improve my scores with their unique approach and easy to learn techniques...Thank you so much A-List for making my goals into a reality! You're the best!"
–Marcelle B.
Accepted into NYU

"I loved my experience with A-List... I couldn't be more appreciative of all the help that A-List has provided for me, and would strongly recommend A-List to any future SAT or ACT takers!"
–Evan S.
Accepted into University of Pennsylvania

"A-List prepared me for both the SAT and ACT better than I thought imaginable...I recommend A-list to anybody trying to get a great score."
–Adam G.
Accepted into University of Florida

"Working with A-List helped me to realize my potential in standardized testing, and gave me the confidence I needed for the college process and the future... A-List taught me skills that have tremendously improved my comprehension, writing and general intelligence. I give A-List an A+!"
–Alex B.
Accepted into Northwestern University

"My scores jumped way up after A-List."
–Sam V.
Accepted into Bowdoin College

"I was given the necessary materials in order to raise my SAT/ACT score. I felt confident and prepared walking into the test."
–Lindsay P.
Accepted into Tulane

"My experience with A-List was incredible. The program offered me specific advice to help me excel on the SAT—tips and strategies that I do not think I could have done without. The materials A-List provided me with were extremely helpful. I found A-List's Book of Knowledge concise, entertaining, and easy to understand. Working with A-List was the best gift my parents could have ever given me."
–Madiha S.
Accepted into Harvard University

STUDENTS LOVE THE BOOK OF KNOWLEDGE!

"A-List helped me improve my scores with their unique approach and easy to learn techniques. Thank you so much A-List for turning my goals into a reality! You're the best."

—Marcelle R.

Accepted into NYU

"I loved my experience with A-List... I couldn't be more appreciative of all the help that A-List has provided for me, and would strongly recommend A-List to any future SAT or ACT takers!"

—Lynn S.

Accepted into University of Pennsylvania

"A-List prepared me for both the SAT and ACT better than I thought imaginable. I recommend A-List to anybody trying to get a great score."

—Adam C.

Accepted into University of Florida

"Working with A-List helped me to realize my potential in standardized testing, and gave me the confidence I needed for the college process and the future. A-List taught me skills that have tremendously improved my comprehension, writing and general intelligence. I give A-List an A+."

—Alex B.

Accepted into Northwestern University

"My scores jumped way up after A-List."

—Sam V.

Accepted into Bowdoin College

"I was given the necessary materials in order to raise my SAT/ACT score. I felt confident and prepared walking into the test."

—Lindsay R.

Accepted into Tulane

"My experience with A-List was incredible. The program offered me specific advice to help me excel on the SAT—tips and strategies that I do not think I could have done without. The materials A-List provided me with were extremely helpful. I found A-List's Book of Knowledge concise, entertaining, and easy to understand. Working with A-List was the best gift my parents could have ever given me."

—Madiha S.

Accepted into Harvard University

A-LIST
THE BOOK OF KNOWLEDGE SAT

2ND EDITION
TEACHER MANUAL

A NOTE ABOUT THE SOLUTION MANUAL

This book contains the full text of *The Book of Knowledge SAT 2nd Edition*, along with notes and explanations for all practice problems.

For quick reference, answer keys alone are available in Appendix D at the back of this book.

This book contains additional pages providing answers and explanations inserted next to the drill or exercises.

None of the above-described material appears in the student edition.

Note that pagination in this book corresponds with the student edition. Pages with teacher notes are unnumbered.

■ Table of Contents

Introduction to the SAT   5

Evidence-Based Reading and Writing

Introduction to Evidence-Based Reading and Writing   23

Reading
- » Introduction to Reading   31
- » Reading Techniques   37
- » Reading Question Types   65

Writing and Language
- » Introduction to Writing and Language   111
- » Standard English Conventions: Conventions of Usage   119
- » Standard English Conventions: Sentence Structure   163
- » Standard English Conventions: Conventions of Punctuation   189
- » Expression of Ideas   211

Math
- » Introduction to Math   233
- » Math Techniques   257
- » Math Fundamentals   279
- » Heart of Algebra   309
- » Passport to Advanced Math   333
- » Graphing   357
- » Problem Solving and Data Analysis   379
- » Additional Topics in Math   407

Essay
- » Essay   449

Appendices
- » Appendix A: Writing Drills   475
- » Appendix B: Math Drills   481
- » Appendix C: Summaries   513
- » Performance Logs   519

▦ Table of Contents

Introduction to the SAT

Evidence-Based Reading and Writing — Introduction to Evidence-Based Reading and Writing 25

Reading
- Introduction to Reading 31
- Reading Techniques 32
- Reading Question Types 65

Writing and Language
- Introduction to Writing and Language 111
- Standard English Conventions: Conventions of Usage 119
- Standard English Conventions: Sentence Structure 167
- Standard English Conventions: Conventions of Punctuation 180
- Expression of Ideas 211

Math
- Introduction to Math 235
- Math Techniques 257
- Math Fundamentals 260
- Heart of Algebra 309
- Passport to Advanced Math 333
- Graphing 357
- Problem Solving and Data Analysis 379
- Additional Topics in Math 407

Essay
- Essay 449

Appendices
- Appendix A: Writing Drills 479
- Appendix B: Math Drills 481
- Appendix C: Summaries 515
- Performance Tips 519

■ Introduction to the SAT

Welcome to the SAT! This book will show you everything you need to conquer the test. We'll run through the content you need, show you tricks and shortcuts specific to SAT-style questions, and warn you about traps and common mistakes. This book is the product of the sum total of A-List's expertise, combining the knowledge gained from hours of research into actual SAT questions with the practical experience of successfully increasing countless students' scores.

The SAT has recently undergone some radical changes starting in 2016. This of course means that there isn't a very long track record of real tests in the new format, and consequently not as much data we can analyze. Since everything is still relatively new, there's still a chance the College Board (the people who make the SAT) might surprise us. We've combined the information that has been released with our knowledge of and experience with the SAT's history to get a firm grasp of what will be expected of you. As more information is released and more tests are given, we'll continue to update our materials to make deeper analysis of past tests and firmer predictions about what your test will look like.

I. FORMAT

The SAT is composed of 4 sections (called "tests"), plus an optional 5th, presented in this order:

Section	Part	Number of Questions	Time	Description
EVIDENCE-BASED READING & WRITING (EBRAW)	1. Reading Test	52 questions	65 min	5 passages, each with 10–11 questions on reading comprehension
	2. Writing & Language Test	44 questions	35 min	4 passages, each with 11 questions on grammar, usage, and style
	TOTAL	**96 questions**	**100 min**	
MATH	3. No calculator	20 questions	25 min	15 multiple-choice questions 5 Student-produced response questions (Grid-ins)
	4. Calculator OK	38 questions	55 min	30 multiple-choice questions 8 Student-produced response questions (Grid-ins)
	TOTAL	**58 questions**	**80 min**	
ESSAY	5. Essay	1 essay	50 min	**Optional.** One 1–4 page essay.
	TOTAL	**154 questions**	**3 hours**	
	with essay	154 questions + 1 essay	3 hours 50 min	

A few general notes about the format:

- All multiple-choice questions have four choices, ABCD.

- Some questions on the Math Test are not multiple-choice questions. These are called the "Student Produced Response Questions" or "grid-ins" for short. Students must produce their own responses and bubble them into the answer sheet.

- **The SAT does not take off points for wrong answers**. This means that random guessing will not count against you. A wrong answer counts the same as a blank.

II. SCORING

Scoring on the SAT is unnecessarily complicated:

- On each of the two sections—Evidence-Based Reading & Writing and Math—you will get a **section score** from **200 to 800**.

- These two section scores will be added together to give you a **total score** from **400 to 1600**.

- For each of the three tests—Reading, Writing, and Math—you will get a **test score** from **10 to 40**.

The section scores and test scores are the most important ones. This is confusing. Let's explain.

In general, scores are calculated by taking the number of right answers (the "raw score") and translating that score into a final score using a special scoring table. Each test has its own unique scoring table in order to adjust for slight difficulty differences among tests: a harder test will be slightly more generous about awarding points.

The Evidence-Based Reading and Writing *Section* (we'll call it EBRAW) is made up of two parts called *Tests*, as we saw in the table above. For each of these tests, you add up the number of right answers and use a special table to find your Test Score, 10 to 40. Then you add your Reading Test score and Writing Test score, multiply by 10, and that's your EBRAW Section score. So say you got a 23 on the Reading Test and a 25 on the Writing test. Add them together and multiply by 10 to get a 480 on the EBRAW section.

$$23 + 25 = 48 \qquad 48 \times 10 = 480.$$

The Math works the other way around. The Math *Section* is also made up of two parts (calculator and no-calculator), but you don't get separate scores for those parts. The Math *Section* is the Math *Test*. You add up *all* your Math correct answers on both sections and use a special table to find your Section score, 200 to 800. Then you divide by 10 and divide by 2 to get your Math Test score.* You get an 800-point score *and* a 40-point score for the same set of 58 questions. Why? Who knows! Symmetry, I guess?

---

* Or just divide by 20.

Other scores

Would you like some more scores? Here are some more scores!

You will also get **subscores** showing your performance on different types of questions within a test. *Also*, you will get some **cross-test scores** showing your performance across different sections. These are also calculated using scoring tables.

Type	Scale	Tests Included	Name
Subscore	1–15	Reading and Writing	Words in Context
			Command of Evidence
		Writing	Expression of Ideas
			Standard English Conventions
		Math	Heart of Algebra
			Passport to Advanced Mathematics
			Problem Solving and Data Analysis
Cross-Test Score	10–40	Reading, Writing, and Math	Analysis in Science
			Analysis in History/Social Studies

- You get subscores that are solely on Writing and Math Tests, but you get no subscores solely for the Reading test.

- The Words in Context and Command of Evidence scores cover questions from two tests, Reading and Writing, but are not "cross-test scores". They are "subscores" and are on the 1–15 scale.

If you choose to take it, you'll also get three scores for your Essay, each on a scale from 2 to 8.

Test	Scale	Name
Essay	2–8	Reading
	2–8	Analysis
	2–8	Writing

To sum up:

Type	Quantity	Scale
Total Score	1	400–1600
Section Score	2	200–800
Test Score	3	10–40
Subscore	7	1–15
Cross-Test Score	2	10–40
Essay subscore (*optional*)	3	2–8
Total	**18 scores**	

That's a lot of scores.

Yep.

Do I care about all these scores?

Probably not! All of this only matters inasmuch as it helps you get into college. So you should only care about scores if colleges care about scores. This scoring system is still relatively new, so many colleges haven't figured out themselves how to use these numbers.

- The most important ones are the Total Score and Section Scores. These are the ones on the old 800 point scale that colleges are familiar with. If admissions officers look at anything, they'll look at these.

- Next most important are likely the Test Scores, since they differentiate how well you did on the Reading and Writing Tests, which test very different skills.

- Third would be the Essay subscores: if you took the essay, these scores are the only ones that show your performance.

Everything else is up in the air. It's possible that colleges look at them, but they may very well ignore them.* That's not to say they won't be useful. Those breakout scores can be helpful for *you* in your own analysis of your performance. They can help you figure out what kinds of questions you did well or poorly on, so you'll know what to work on before the next time you

---

* Would colleges just ignore information? Sure! When the SAT introduced the Writing section in 2005, a lot of schools weren't sure how to interpret it or whether it was useful at all, so they just ignored it altogether.

take the test.

Point values

As we said, each test has a different scoring table. On one test, a raw math score of 29 might correspond to a final math score of 520. But on another, a raw score of 29 gives you a final score of 540, and a raw score of 27 gives you a 520.

This is done in order to adjust for differences in difficulty among different tests. No two tests are exactly the same, so it's inevitable that any given test will be slightly easier or harder than another. If the test is easier than normal, its scoring table will be a bit harsher; if it's harder, the table will be more lenient. This way, the test is *standardized*—scores will be comparable no matter which actual test you took.

But the differences between scoring tables aren't very drastic. Therefore, we can get an approximate sense of how much each question is worth on your actual final score.

Question Type	Points Per Question	
	Section Score (200–800)	Test Score (10–40)
Reading	6 pts	0.55
Writing		0.65
Math	10 pts	0.50

How can this table help you?

- This table shows the **value of each question on your score**. On average, getting one Reading question right adds about 6 points to your final EBRAW score. One Writing question also adds about 6 points. One Math question adds about 10 points to your Math section score.

- Math questions are worth almost twice as much as Reading and Writing questions because there are fewer Math questions. 58 Math questions go into your Math section score, but 98 total Reading and Writing scores go into your EBRAW section score. If more questions are contributing to the same number of points, each will be worth less.*

---

* In fact, the Writing questions are worth *slightly* more than the Reading questions because there are fewer Writing questions. In reality, Reading questions are worth about 5.5 points and Writing about 6.5 points (that's just the Test score's point value times 10), but they're close enough to call them both 6 for our purposes.

- You can use this table to figure out how many more questions you need to get a **target score**. Divide the number of points you *want* by the questions per point to see how many questions you need.

  For example, say you've currently got a 540 on the EBRAW section and you want a 600. You want 60 more points on your score. 60 ÷ 6 = 10, so you'll need to get about 10 more questions than you're getting now. Remember: that's 10 more questions *total* across both Reading and Writing. So getting 5 more question on each would do the trick.

- Furthermore, this can give you a sense of how your mistakes are actually affecting your score. It can **quantify your mistakes**. On any given test, you can count up the number of questions you missed *that you should have gotten right*.* Multiply by the values in the table above to see what you should have scored on that test.

  For example, say you got a 520 on a Math Test and you missed 3 Plug-In questions, 2 Backsolve questions, and made 3 RTFQ mistakes.[†] That's 8 questions you should have gotten right: 8 × 10 = 80 points. You should have gotten another 80 points on this test, so you should have gotten a 600. [‡]

A few cautions about these numbers:

- Obviously, **this is an approximation**. This is not an exact exchange rate. We say a Reading question is worth 6 points, but you can't get a score of 506. Section scores only go up in increments of 10. In reality, getting one specific Reading question right might move your score up 10 points or zero points. But we're looking at the test as a whole here. Getting 5 Reading questions right will *on average* increase your score 30 points.

- Remember also that all SAT scores should be considered **ranges**. There are all sorts of factors that contribute to your test score besides the scoring table. Not every change in your scores constitutes an actual increase or decrease. Even if you do no

---

* It's important to note: we're not talking about *every* question you missed, just the ones that you *should've gotten right*. Some questions are legitimately hard. Some may involve weird concepts, or concepts that you haven't gotten to yet. Here we're just talking about the questions that involve concepts you've studied and that you are fully capable of getting.

† Don't worry if you don't know what these terms mean. We'll explain them soon enough in the Math Techniques chapter.

‡ We call this the "Shoulda Score", because it's what you shoulda scored.

work, you're not going to get exactly the same score every time out. You could score 30 points higher or lower just by pure chance. According to the College Board, total scores must differ by 60 points to be considered a "true change". And you know what? Colleges know that too. Your school probably isn't going to reject you just because of 10 points. So don't sweat the small points.

> ✐ On the other hand, *do* sweat the big points. Doing a lot of little things better can quickly add up to big score increases. Substantial increases are well within your reach.

The Guessing Rule

As we already mentioned, **the SAT does not take off points for wrong answers.** A wrong answer will simply get you zero points, the same as a blank. Therefore, **you should always fill in an answer for every question.** If you are about to run out of time and there are questions you haven't done yet, guess something. We can't say this enough times:

NEVER LEAVE ANY BLANKS FOR ANY REASON!

Why, you ask? Well, why not? If wrongs are treated the same as blanks, then even if you guess wrong on every question, it won't hurt your score. But even when you guess totally randomly, you'll guess correctly a few times by accident. That means you'll pick up a couple of extra points for those guesses.

There's no secret method for guessing. If you want to always guess C or always B, whatever. Some people like to pick choices they've chosen the least in that section so far. Some people have a set letter combination they always guess. There's no real pattern here, no secret code of answer choices. **Don't spend time thinking about it.** Just guess something.

When we say you should guess, it's important to note that that we *don't* mean to say you should haphazardly guess on *every* question. Don't be afraid to take your time and be sure of your answers on all the questions you get to. Our point is that *if you do* run out of time, or if you are unsure of an answer, just pick something. No blanks.

The Target Number Rule

In the Math chapter, we're going to talk about a strategy we call Target Numbers. The basic idea is that unless you're trying to get an 800, you don't need to get every question right in order to get the score that you want. So rather than doing a lot of questions and making a lot of careless mistakes, you should do fewer questions more accurately. This general principle holds over the entire test:

ACCURACY IS MORE IMPORTANT THAN BULK

It's more important for you to be accurate on the questions you do than for you to do all the questions. That means that it's okay if you don't finish a section. It's okay to move slowly: if it you can cut down on carelessness, you can get a better score by doing fewer questions.

Of course, don't forget the guessing rule. Even if you don't *attempt* a question, you should still put an answer down. Never leave anything blank.

III. THE TESTS

Here is a quick overview of each Test in the SAT. For more information (probably more than you really need), skip ahead to the relevant chapters in this book.

Reading

You will be given 5 passages, each of which has 10-11 questions that ask about the content of the passages, inferences or conclusions that can be drawn from the passages, or the author's rhetorical strategies.

The five passages will be taken from three topics: Fiction, History/Social Studies, or Science.

You will not get any subscores for the Reading Test alone. However, some questions from the Reading Test will contribute to subscores that include material from other tests.

The nice thing about Reading questions is that they are grounded in the passages. You don't need outside information and you won't have to do too much complex interpretation. It's mostly about understanding what the passage says. The bad thing is that questions don't always tell you where to find the information you need in the passage, and some passages can use complex language that is tough to understand.

Writing

You will be given 4 short passages, each of which has 11 questions that ask about the grammar, usage, style, and rhetoric of the passage.

You will get two subscores (1–15) in these areas:

- **Standard English Conventions** (20 Questions): These questions ask you to correct errors in grammar, usage, and punctuation. For most questions, there will be a word or phrase underlined, and you will be given four options to either rewrite the word or phrase to correct an error, or to make no change.

- **Expression of Ideas** (24 Questions): These questions ask about the development, organization, or style of the passage. Questions may ask you what the author should do to improve the passage.

Math

You will be given two sections, each made up of multiple-choice questions and grid-ins. The questions are ordered by difficulty, so the first ones should be easy and the last ones should be hard. Math is the only section where this is true.

You will get three subscores (1–15) in these areas:

- **Heart of Algebra** (19 questions): These questions deal with basic algebraic manipulation of linear equations and expressions, along with graphing in the coordinate plane.

- **Passport to Advanced Math** (16 questions): These questions deal with more advanced algebraic manipulation, including quadratic and exponential equations, along with graphing in the coordinate plane.

- **Problem Solving and Data Analysis** (17 questions): These questions deal with statistics, data interpretation, and numerical relationships such as ratios, units, or percentages.

Additionally, there is a fourth content category for which you will not receive a subscore:

- **Additional Topics in Math** (6 questions): These questions deal with geometry, trigonometry, and complex numbers.

Calculators are permitted on section 4 of the Math Test but not on section 3. While they are allowed on section 4, calculators are not required. Every question can be done by hand if necessary, but sometimes you don't really want to do that. Get a calculator.

Essay

The SAT offers a 50-minute essay, always the last section of the test. It is optional, so you do not have to take it if you don't want to. But be advised that some colleges may require it.

The essay will always take the same form. You will be given a passage (roughly the length of a passage from the Reading Test) in the form of a persuasive essay on a particular topic. You will be asked to write an essay analyzing how the author makes his or her argument, paying attention to the passage's use of **evidence**, **reasoning**, and **stylistic or persuasive elements**.

The essay will be read by two readers. Each will giving the essay a score from 1 to 4 in three categories, for a total score of 2 to 8 in each category. Those categories are:

- **Reading:** How well did you understand the passage? Was your portrayal of the passage accurate?

- **Analysis:** How well did you analyze the evidence, reasoning, or stylistic elements of the passage? How well did you support your claims?

- **Writing:** How well did you write? Was your essay organized and coherent? How was your language?

Your essay score is entirely separate and will not be factored into any of your other scores.

IV. THE PSAT

What is it?

The PSAT is practice for the SAT. It's basically a shorter version of the SAT. Students have three opportunities to take the PSAT:

1. **In 8th or 9th grade**, students may take the **PSAT 8/9**, which is an abbreviated version of the PSAT.

2. **In 10th grade**, students may take the **PSAT 10**. This is identical to the PSAT given to juniors.

3. **In 11th grade**, students may take the **PSAT/NMSQT.*** Almost all juniors will take the PSAT.

Why do I have to take it?

You don't, actually. Some schools may require their students to take the PSAT in their junior year. But for most of you it's optional. It is *not* a factor in college admissions. Your colleges will not see your PSAT scores. It is purely practice.

It does count for one thing, though: the National Merit Scholarship program. Students scoring around the top 4% of PSAT scores in their state will get a National Merit Letter of Commendation. Students scoring around the top 1% of PSAT scores in their state will qualify as National Merit Semifinalists. These are good things. They will look very good on your college applications and may help you get scholarships. The qualifying scores are different every year and differ from state to state but if you think you're scoring at high levels, you definitely want to do as well as you can on the PSAT.†

Of course, even if you're not scoring in the top 4%, it's still a good idea to take the PSAT. It's good practice in a real-test situation. It gives you an accurate sense of where your score is. It gives you feedback on your strengths and weaknesses. And it's low pressure: if you do poorly, it doesn't matter—colleges never see these scores.

Note that only your junior-year PSAT/NMSQT score will be eligible for National Merit Scholarship consideration. Your PSAT 10 and PSAT 8/9 scores are good for nothing but your own self-assessment.

---

*   "NMSQT" stands for *National Merit Scholarship Qualifying Test*. "PSAT" stands for *Preliminary SAT*. "SAT" used to stand for *Scholastic Aptitude Test*, then *Scholastic Assessment Test*, and now it stands for nothing.

†   For example, in New York State, the qualifying score in the past for the old pre-2016 PSAT was generally been around 660 per section for a Letter of Commendation and around 700 per section to be a Semifinalist. But again, these numbers will vary from year to year and state to state.

How is it different from the SAT?

It's shorter
But not by much.

Portion	SAT		PSAT	
	Number of Questions	**Time**	**Number of Questions**	**Time**
Reading Test	52 questions 5 passages, 10–11 Q each	65 min	47 questions 5 passages, 9–10 Q each	60 min
Writing & Language Test	44 questions 4 passages, 11 Q each	35 min	44 questions 4 passages, 11 Q each	35 min
EBRAW Total	**96 questions**	**100 min**	**91 questions**	**95 min**
Math: No Calculator	20 questions 15 MC, 5 GI	25 min	17 questions 13 MC, 4 GI	25 min
Math: Calculator OK	38 questions 30 MC, 8 GI	55 min	31 questions 27 MC, 4 GI	45 min
Math Total	**58 questions**	**80 min**	**48 questions**	**70 min**
Essay	1 essay Optional. One 1–4 page essay.	50 min	None	None
Total	**154 questions**	**180 min** **(3 hrs)**	**139 questions**	**165 min** **(2h 45m)**
with essay	*154 questions* *+ 1 essay*	*3 hours* *50 min*		

Each section is slightly shorter on the PSAT (except the Writing, which is exactly the same length). And the Essay is not offered at all on the PSAT. But we're only talking about a difference of 15 total minutes between the tests, so they're basically the same experience.

Scoring

SAT and PSAT scores are calibrated to each other. That means you can expect that your PSAT score is roughly the same as what you'd get on the SAT *if you took it the same day*. So if you got a 510 on the PSAT Math, you would have gotten around a 510 on an SAT Math if you took it that day.*

The only difference in the scores is that the endpoints are different: instead of going from 200 to 800 like the SAT, PSAT section scores range from **160 to 760**. Therefore, the total score ranges from **320 to 1520**. Similarly, test scores and cross-test scores range from **8 to 38** instead of 10 to 40 on the SAT. Subscores are still 1 to 15.

The difference in the scale arises because PSAT test-takers are expected to score lower than older, more experienced students. But again, the point values are *directly comparable*. A 510 on the PSAT is worth the same as a 510 on the SAT.

Many students naturally will do better on the SAT than the PSAT, both because they've learned more by the time they take the SAT, and because they've had more practice.[†] Historically, the average junior-year PSAT score has been around 950 total, while the average SAT score is around 1000. Since average SAT scores are higher than average PSAT scores, the same *percentile* on the two tests will correspond to a higher SAT score and a lower PSAT score. And the same score will have a higher percentile on the PSAT.

---

* *Around* a 510, that is. As we've said, scores can fluctuate up or down 20-30 points just from sheer chance. You might get a 490 or a 530. You probably wouldn't get a 650 or a 400 (barring some sort of catastrophe).

† Of course, this does **NOT** mean that you will automatically improve from your PSAT score without doing any work. There is a lot of variation between individuals. Only around 55% of students improve their scores on both individual sections from the PSAT to the SAT.

PSAT 8/9

The PSAT 8/9 is slightly different. It's shorter than the other PSATs:

Portion	Number of Questions	Time
Reading Test	42 questions	55 min
Writing & Language Test	40 questions	30 min
EBRAW Total	82 questions	85 min
No Calculator	13 questions (10 MC, 3 GI)	20 min
Calculator OK	25 questions (21 MC, 4 GI)	40 min
Math Total	38 questions (31 MC, 7 GI)	60 min
Total	120 questions	145 min (2 hrs 25 min)

Additionally, the scoring is once again slightly different. The section scores come in a range of **120 to 720** instead of 200 to 800, thus the total score ranges from **240 to 1440** instead of 400 to 1600. The test scores range from **6 to 36** instead of 10 to 40. However, the scores are meant to be *directly comparable.* Thus a student who gets a 400 on the PSAT 8/9 would expect to get a 400 on the PSAT 10 *if taken the same day.*

EVIDENCE-BASED READING AND WRITING

Introduction to Evidence-Based Reading and Writing   23

Reading   29

Writing   109

Introduction to Evidence-Based Reading & Writing

The Evidence-Based Reading and Writing section is a bit of an oddity. As we saw in the overall introduction, your final SAT score has two parts: the Math score and the Evidence-Based Reading and Writing score, each on a 200-800 point scale.

The math on the SAT is pretty self-explanatory; there are two sections that combine to a single score, but they don't differ too much. Math is math. The so-called Evidence-Based Reading and Writing section also has two sections, but those two sections contain entirely different kinds of questions. The Reading Test is a reading comprehension test, where you'll be asked if you've understood the form and content of a passage you've just read. The Writing and Language Test is an editing test, where you'll be asked to make changes or corrections to a flawed piece of writing. In addition to your overall score, you'll also get separate Test scores for Reading, Writing and Language, and Math on a 10-40 point scale.

On one hand it's natural for these two Tests to be scored together since they're both things that you predominantly do in your English class at school. On the other hand, it's weird because they are testing very different things. Some students will find that they are good at one of these tests but bad at the other. That's why, outside of this introductory chapter, we'll be mostly treating them entirely separately in this book. Once we're done here, hopefully I'll never have to type out "Evidence-Based Reading and Writing" again.*

The optional essay is NOT a part of the Evidence-Based Reading and Writing section. Should you choose to take the essay, your score will be reported separately from the other sections.

---

* Ugh, these names. Why did they make that name so long? Am I going to have to type out that whole thing every time? All these names are terrible. And why is it "Evidence-Based Reading and Writing", but the subsection is "Writing and Language", not "Writing"? If you're going to be long-winded, why not go all out and call it the "Evidence-Based Reading and Writing and Language" section?

Well, luckily, once we start looking at questions, we'll usually only be talking about either the Reading Test or the Writing and Language Test at any given moment. We'll rarely have to refer to the entire section. And I'm also going to call the Writing and Language Test just the Writing Test whenever possible.

We shouldn't complain, though. These are far less stupid than the names they use for Math topics.

Format

Let's look at how these two sections overlap before looking at their individual characteristics. Since both these sections have similar passage-based formats, let's look at them side-by-side.

	Reading	Writing and Language
Time	65 min	35 min
Passages	5 passages	4 passages
Avg time per passage	13 min/passage	9 min/passage
Questions	52 questions	44 questions
Questions per passage	10–11 questions per passage	11 questions per passage
Passage content areas	Fiction/Literature (1 passage) History/Social Science (2 passages) Science (2 passages)	Careers (1 passage) Humanities (1 passage) History/Social Science (1 passage) Science (1 passage)
Graphics	On 2 passages, 1–2 figures each 2 questions per passage	On 1 or more passages, 1–2 figures each 2 questions per passage
Test-specific Subscores	None	Expression of Ideas (24 questions) Standard English Conventions (20 questions)
Multi-test Subscores	Words in Context (10 questions) Command of Evidence (10 questions)	Words in Context (8 questions) Command of Evidence (8 questions)
Cross-Test scores	Analysis in History/Social Studies (21 questions) Analysis in Science (21 questions)	Analysis in History/Social Studies (6 questions) Analysis in Science (6 questions)

Scoring

There will be four levels of scores you'll receive on these sections

- A single Evidence-Based Reading and Writing Section score on a 200–800 point scale calculated from your performance on all questions on both tests.

- Separate test scores on a 10–40 point scale for each of the tests, one for Reading and one for Writing and Language. You can calculate your section score by adding your two test scores and multiplying by 10.

- Two subscores on a 1–15 point scale for the Writing and Language Test based only on Writing questions. The Reading Test has no such subscores. You will get two 1–15 point subscores covering questions from both tests in the EBRAW section.

- Two cross-test scores also on a 10–40 point scale using some questions from each of the tests. These cross-test scores will also include some Math questions.

Subscores and Cross-Test scores

As we've seen, you will get two subscores and two cross-test scores that are computed using questions from different tests. Note that these numbers may vary from test to test, but not by more than 1 question.

Score	Reading		Writing	
	Number	Type	Number	Type
Words in Context	10 questions, 2 per passage	All Vocab-in-context questions	8 questions 2 per passage	All Effective Language Use questions
Command of Evidence	10 questions 2 per passage	All Evidence questions	8 questions 2 per passage	All Development questions
Analysis in History/ Social Studies*	21 questions across 2 passages	All questions on the two History/Social Studies passages	6 questions in 1 passage	All Expression of Ideas questions on the History/Social Studies passage
Analysis in Science*	21 questions across 2 passages	All questions on the two Science passages	6 questions in 1 passage	All Expression of Ideas questions on the Science passage

* These scores also include questions from the Math Test.

Should I care about these?

Probably not. You only need to care about scores that are relevant to college admissions, and most colleges will only care about your Test and Section scores. The subscores may be more interesting to you when you're reviewing your results to see which areas you're doing well or poorly on. But you shouldn't spend too much time sweating all these numbers.

Content

As we mentioned, there is little overlap in the actual content of the two Tests. They are very much testing different skills and will be treated separately. That said, there are a few areas where they are similar to each other.

Passage contents

As we saw in the first chart, passages in each Test will have topics taken from a specific list of possible content areas. These content areas are similar to each other, but not identical. For example, both tests will have science and history passages. However, the Reading Test will contain a fiction passage, while the Writing Test will not.

One of the passages on the Reading Test will always be a primary source of historical importance, such as a presidential speech or noteworthy political writing. But you still won't need any prior knowledge of the topic.

How important are these content areas? It depends on the student, of course, but they're generally more significant on the Reading Test than on the Writing Test. Some students' Reading performance can vary noticeably on passages of different topics. They may excel at Fiction passages but struggle on Science passages, or vice versa. On the Writing Test, however, it rarely makes a difference what the passage contents are. Verbs are verbs, regardless of content.

It's important to emphasize that **students will not be required to know anything about the topic ahead of time.** This goes for both the Reading and Writing Tests; if a passage is about science, students will not be expected to know anything at all about that science topic. For the Reading Test, all required information is written on the page. For the Writing Test, students will be expected to bring specific knowledge to the test, but only knowledge of English grammar and usage, which will be the same regardless of the passage's topic. Verbs are verbs.

Data elements

Each of the two tests will contain some passages that have a figure, graph, or other graphic that displays data relevant to the topic of the passage. For any such passage, there will be two questions that directly ask you about the figure. *These figures do not just appear on science passages.* They may also appear on passages in other content areas as well. For the Reading Test, there will be one graphic on a science passage and one on a history/social studies passage. For the Writing Test, any passage may contain a graphic.

Questions about these figures will be a little different for the two tests because of the difference in format. But both tests will ask you to be able to read the graph and understand the data within it, *no more, no less*. On the Reading Test, that means you'll be asked what the graph explicitly says and how it implicitly relates to the passage. On the Writing Test, you may be asked to rewrite sentences in the passage to make sure the passage agrees with the data in the figure.

The level of understanding you need will be fairly basic. You do not need any outside knowledge of the topic. You will not need to do any computation that would require a calculator. I repeat: **you will not need to do math.** You may be asked to find values on the graph, or to evaluate the relative values of different fields, but you won't have to do a bunch of adding or multiplying.

Questions about these figures will be a little different for the two tests because of the difference in format. But both tests will ask you to be able to read the graph and understand the data within a minute or less. On the Reading Test, that means you'll be asked what the graph explicitly says and how it implicitly relates to the passage. On the Writing Test, you may be asked to rewrite sentences in the passage to make sure the passage agrees with the data in the figure.

The level of understanding you need will be fairly basic. You do not need any outside knowledge of the topic. You will not need to do any computation that would require a calculator. I repeat: you will not need to do math. You may be asked to find values on the graph or to evaluate the relative values of different fields, but you won't have to do a lot of adding or multiplying.

READING

Introduction to Reading   31

Reading Techniques   37

Reading Question Types   65

Introduction to Reading

Welcome to Reading! The Reading section is everyone's least favorite section on the SAT.* It's tedious because there's a lot of, you know, *reading* on it. Ugh. Reading. So much reading. But that's okay! There's *so* much you can do to improve your score, by getting better at reading and getting better at answering the questions.

Reading passages are one of the most hated parts of the SAT because nobody likes to read. Ugh... so many words... it's not fair. Well, suck it up. We're going to have to do some reading. If the hardest thing you do on this test is read, you'll do fine.

Overview

We already discussed the format of the test in the Introduction to Evidence-Based Reading and Writing chapter, but let's have a quick reminder:

- You'll have 5 passages, 10–11 questions each, for a total of 52 questions.

- The passages will be from one of three content areas: **Fiction** (1 passage), **History/Social Studies** (2 passages), and **Science** (2 passages).

- One of the History passages on the Reading Test will always be a **primary source** of historical importance, such as a presidential speech or noteworthy political writing. But don't worry: just like the other passages, *you still won't need any prior knowledge of the topic.*

- Each test will contain one **double passage**. Here, you'll see two passages on a similar topic followed by questions on both of them. Note that the double passage is not twice as long; the two parts together will be about the same length as a single passage. The double passage may be in any topic.

- Two passages will have one or two **figures**, graphs, or other data element: 1 Science passage and 1 History/Social Studies passage. Each passage that contains a figure

Passages topics are usually presented in this order:

1. Fiction
2. History/Social Studies
3. Science
4. History/Social Studies
5. Science

---

* Except for Writing and Math.

will have 2–4 questions specifically addressing it. There will be about 6 total data questions on the test. We'll talk more about dealing with these kinds of questions in the Question Type chapter.

Timing

So you've got **5 passages** to do in **65 minutes**. If you remember your math,* you can see that's **13 minutes per passage**. With that in mind, here are three guidelines to timing on an SAT Reading section.

1. Take 13 minutes total per passage.

2. Take 4 minutes to read each passage. <u>Do not spend more than 4 minutes.</u> After 4 minutes, STOP and go to the questions.

3. Take the remaining 9–11 minutes on the questions. That's about 1 minute per question.

Remember: **these are guidelines not rules**. You don't have to spend exactly 13 minutes per passage. But don't deviate from this plan *too* much. If you spend 15 minutes per passage you'll only have 5 minutes left for the last one. If you spend 8 minutes reading a passage before answering any questions, you need to move along more quickly.

Time yourself.

Literally. As you practice—either in full-length proctored practice tests or sections you do at home by yourself—get a stopwatch and time yourself. Jot down your start and end time for reading the passage and for doing each question. See how long it's taking you to do a full passage and try to make adjustments.

You may find your ideal ratio of reading to question-answering is slightly different. Maybe you'd prefer to read for 5 minutes but you can zip through the questions in 7 minutes. That's fine, as long as you're getting the level of accuracy you want. The point is to find an equilibrium. Spend too much time on the passage and you won't have enough time for the questions. Spend too little time on the passage, and you won't understand it well enough to do the questions effectively.

Don't leave blanks.

Just like all the other sections, there's no penalty for wrong answers on the Reading Test. **Don't ever leave anything blank. Guess randomly** on the questions you didn't answer.

---

* *Do* you remember your math?

You don't even have to read the questions—just fill in bubbles at random. Since there are four choices per question, on average you'll get about one fourth of those guesses right, so you'll pick up a few extra points. The ones you guess wrong are scored the same as a blank, so there's no harm done.

I can't do it that fast. What should I do?

It may be worth your time to actually **skip a full passage.** You may actually find that you can get the score you want by doing fewer questions. This is the Target Number Rule. The target scores shown are the scores you can get **if you get *all or most* of the questions you do** and you pick up a few extra points from guessing randomly.*

Skip how many passages?	Do how many questions?	Time per passage	Target Test score[†] (no guessing)	Target Test score[†] (with guessing)
Skip 1 passage	41–42 questions	16 min	32	34
Skip 2 passages	30–32 questions	21 min	27	30

The key here is finding an equilibrium between speed and accuracy. You want to do as many questions as you can without being so rushed that you work carelessly. When you first start taking practice tests, don't worry about timing; just try to get through as much as you can. Then, take a look at how well you did and use the results to determine a speed you're comfortable with. It might take a couple of practice tests before you find the right pace.

Do your strongest passage type first.

You don't have to do the passages in the order they're presented. Use your knowledge of passage types to your advantage. Try to figure out if you have a particular strength or weakness on a particular type of passage—not everyone does, but a lot of people do. Say you take a few practice tests and find that you tend to do well on the Science passages and tend to do poorly on Fiction passages. You'll want to make sure that you do the Science passages *first* and save the Fiction for last—otherwise you might run out of time before you get to the

---

* The scores listed here are *approximations*. These are not guarantees; they're goals—the high end of what you *can* achieve if you do the specified number of questions effectively. But remember that every test has a different scoring table, you won't always get 100% of the questions you try, and your success at randomly guessing is pure luck.

† The target scores shown here are the Reading Test scores. Your EBRAW score, of course, will be dependent on how well you do on the Writing Test. Remember that you can find your EBRAW score by adding the two Test scores and multiplying by 10.

problems you're best at.*

This is particularly important if you're planning to skip a passage. You don't have to skip the last passage. If you're bad at Fiction, which is the first passage, then skip the Fiction passage.

Running out of time?

Say you've got two minutes left and there's a whole passage you haven't even started yet. That's not enough time to read a full passage and do all the questions. Oh no! What should you do?

- Don't panic.
- **Don't read the passage**. If you spend all your remaining time reading, you won't have time to answer questions. Then you'll get no points and all that time you spend reading will be for nothing. That's bad.
- Seriously, stop panicking. It'll be okay.
- Jump to **questions with specific line references.** A question that asks about a very specific word or line can often be done just by reading that particular word or line, even if you don't understand the larger context.
- Two good types of questions to try are **Vocab-in-context questions** (which just ask about the meaning of a word in a sentence) and **Data questions** (which ask about a figure or graph that accompanies the passage). Both these types can usually be done independently of the rest of the passage. We'll talk more about question types in the next chapter.
- For all other questions you haven't done, **guess randomly**. There's no penalty for wrong answers. **Don't ever leave questions blank.**

Skip "Black Hole" questions.

Sometimes you'll encounter a question where you just can't figure out what's going on. The question asks about cats, and you remember it said something about cats, but you look and you look and you just can't find it. Or, even worse, it asks about a detail that you don't remember seeing at all, and you have no idea where to look for it. And it's driving you crazy and freaking you out.

We call these **Black Hole questions**, because they suck up all your time and you cannot escape their pull. Don't get trapped. Don't spend 5 minutes on single question: **skip it**. That

---

* Don't just rely on your gut when figuring out what topics you're best at—look at actual results, too. It's easy to say "oh, I'm bad at science," but that doesn't mean you should skip the Science passages. Just because you don't *like* a topic doesn't mean you're *bad* at it (and you won't have to actually do science here). That's not to say you should ignore your gut. Use a combination of your personal preference and the results of your practice tests to determine the order you do the passages.

one question can mess up your timing for the entire section. You might run out of time before getting to questions you'd otherwise be able to do.

When you skip it, you have a few options. Maybe as you do the other questions in the passage you'll stumble across the detail you're looking for. If you don't, and you have time at the end of the test, you can come back to it and try again to look for the detail. Or you can just give up on it and guess randomly. (Don't ever, *ever* leave a question blank.) The important thing is to not let one question ruin the whole test.

Techniques

Here's a preview of our two fundamental Reading techniques:

1. Anticipation

As we said, all the information you need to answer the question is given to you on the page. The question will often give you a line reference and tell you exactly which part of the passage contains the answer. That means you can read the sentence or go back to the passage and **anticipate** what the answer will be.

An important part of anticipation is to **ignore the answer choices**. Wrong answers are full of distractions and misleading information that can affect the way you read the passage or sentence. We want to base our anticipation *only* on the material on the page, not the choices.

You won't be able to predict *exactly* what the answer choice will be. Instead, you're determining what the *meaning* of the answer choice will be. Follow the line reference back into the passage, and see what those lines say about the question. Try to *paraphrase* the lines in your own words. The right answer will rarely be an *exact* match for the anticipation. The anticipation gives you the *meaning* you're looking for. The right answer will have the same meaning as the anticipation, but will be worded differently.

2. Elimination

Once you have an anticipation, go to the choices and look for one that has the same meaning. Sometimes, you can spot it right away. Great, you're done!

But it often doesn't work out so easily. You may not be able to find a choice that matches your anticipation perfectly. But that's okay! You can still **eliminate** choices that are obviously wrong. Remember that three out of four choices are wrong—that's 75% of all the choices. It's easier to find a wrong choice than a right choice. There's often at least one choice that you can tell is obviously wrong, even on the hardest questions.

You may have difficulty eliminating some choices. But there is usually at least one choice that is obviously wrong. Some choices are totally *random*—the choice talks about things the passage doesn't mention. Others are clearly *false*—they're explicitly contradicted by the passage. Even on the hardest questions, there's usually something you know. Seeing that a wrong choice is wrong is often simpler that understanding the nuances of the correct answer. It's easier to spot a wrong choice than a right choice—after all, 75% of the choices are wrong.

The most important part of elimination is to **write stuff down**. Don't do this in your head. Mark up the choices. Cross out the words in a passage choice that make the choice wrong. **Don't rely on your memory. YOUR MEMORY IS FALLIBLE. WRITE THINGS DOWN.**

Reading Techniques

Okay, enough introduction. Let's get to some questions already.

General Strategies

One of the most important thing to keep in mind about the Reading section is this:

> **You do not need outside knowledge to do the questions.**

Other than knowledge of the English language, that is. It may seem like you need more knowledge than you actually do. You'll see fiction passages from Great Literature. You'll see passages by or about Famous Historical Figures. You'll see charts and graphs about Fancy Science. But you will not be tested on specific content of literary history, nor of any historical events or scientific principles. You do not need to be a historian or a scientist.

The natural consequence of this is:

> **All the information you need is given to you on the test.**

Either in the sentence, in the passage, or in the figures, everything you need is on the page. You just need to be able to read and understand what you've read. When we say this is a test of reading, we mean exactly that: *can you read?* Nothing more. All of our strategies flow from this fact.

The point of this section is to understand something you just read. Sometimes this is *really easy* and *really dumb*. It's literally a question of whether you read the passage. Not whether you understand it, not whether you know where to find a thesis, not whether you know what a thesis is, not whether you caught the nuances of the author's biting satire on the bourgeoisie—no: *can you read English?* That is all.

Here's your passage:	And here's your question:

Passage 1

I like cats.

1. Which of the following statements would the author most likely agree with?

   A) The U. S. government must dedicate more time and resources to preserving its native wildlife.
   B) Pet ownership has therapeutic effects on people recovering from traumatic events.
   C) I like cats.
   D) Cats are dangerous creatures that are a threat to modern society.

It's a tough one, I know. Do you need extra time?

Obviously this is a joke, but it's not *that* much of a joke. You'd be astounded by how much of this section can be done with little more than knowing *what* the passage says. Not any fancy interpretations: literally "what does it say?"

Before we get into specifics, here are three "don'ts" to remember for the reading passages:

1. Don't enjoy yourself.

None of the passages will be fun. You will not like them. They will be on subjects you don't care about. They will not be things you will want to read on the beach in your leisure time. Get used to it.

2. Don't know anything.

Just because the passage is about particle physics doesn't mean you have to know anything about particle physics. This is a *reading* test. You're being tested on *what you just read*. Everything you need to answer the questions is *in the passage*, written on the page itself. In fact, it's actually counterproductive to know anything about the topic, because you may be tempted to use your existing knowledge or beliefs to help you answer the question. Don't do that. No one cares what *you* think about the topic. We only care what the *author* thinks about the topic.

3. Don't remember everything.

You don't have to memorize the passage. It's all on the page and it's going to stay on the page. If you can't remember what the author said in line 35, *go back to line 35 and check*! It's right there! Don't waste a lot of time trying to memorize all the details of the passage; just get a sense of what it's about and move on to the questions. This brings us to our first strategy: *main ideas.*

I. READING THE PASSAGE: MAIN IDEAS

One of the biggest problems kids have with the passages is that reading them takes a loooong time. Kids try to memorize every point and understand every subtle detail and convoluted sentence in the passage. That's bad. It's a waste of time—it takes forever and it doesn't actually help you.

Instead, read the passage quickly and just get the **MAIN IDEAS**. Every paragraph is nothing more than a collection of sentences that have some common theme. That common theme is the main idea of the paragraph. It's the answer to this question:

What's it about?

That's it. For each paragraph, just get a sense of the topic of that paragraph. Paraphrase the idea into a short phrase. It doesn't have to be a quote from the passage or even a complete sentence. It's a note to yourself about what the paragraph is about.

Here are a few tips on finding main ideas:

Skim the details

Don't worry about all the piddly little details. We don't care about *every* idea, just the *main* idea. All those details are confusing and unnecessary.

The goal here is to **spend less time reading the passage** so you can spend more time on the questions, since the questions are the things that actually matter. Therefore, when you read the passage, you just want to get a sense of what it's about. We'll worry about the details later.

You may be asking yourself, "But wait, don't I need those details?" Surprisingly, no. For two reasons:

1. **The questions might never ask you about those details.**
   Why would you spend five minutes trying to understand a sentence *that they never ask you about!* That's five minutes you wasted and won't get back. Yes, you'll need *some* of the details to answer the questions. But *every* passage has *huge* chunks of information that never show up in the questions. And when you're reading the passage, you don't know which details are important and which ones aren't.

2. **If a question *does* ask you about details, you can go back and check.**
   If they do ask you about line 35, well, *go back to line 35 and see what it says!* Questions

about specific details usually come with specific line references, so you know exactly where to go to find the answer. So even if a detail *is* important to a question, you don't have to worry about it while you're reading the passage. Worry about it when they ask you about it, not before.

Not all questions are about specific lines; some are about entire paragraphs or the passage as a whole. But if that's the case, *you can use your main idea to answer the question.*

Skip hard sentences

Passages will *often* contain difficult writing. Sentences can be long, intricate, or convoluted. They may use subtle or confusing metaphors. The vocabulary can be difficult. With main ideas, if you encounter a sentence you don't immediately understand, **skip it**. You don't need to understand every single sentence to understand the paragraph. If the details of that sentence are important, you can deal with them if and when the question asks you about them.

Skip the figures and graphs

Two of the five passages will come with some sort of figure—a graph or table or other diagram that's relevant to the passage somehow. But these figures are *supplementary:* you will not need them to understand the main idea of the passage. Don't get me wrong, you *will* be asked about those figures. But don't worry about them *until a question asks about them.*

Check the first and last sentence

The difficulty of finding the main idea for a paragraph can vary depending on the particular passage. Sometimes it's really obvious, sometimes not so much. If you're having trouble, **check the first and last sentence of the paragraph.** That's often the introduction to the topic and the conclusion to the topic, so that will help you find the theme of the paragraph.

<u>This is a guideline, not a rule.</u> The main idea is often in the first and last sentence, but not always. If the main idea *isn't* there, but that's all you've read, you'll be confused, you'll have to backtrack, and it'll be a mess. So you should read the whole paragraph. But if you're having trouble finding the main idea, the first and last sentences are a good place to look.

Look for transitional language

By "transitional language" we mean all the words that connect clauses and sentences to each other, words like *but, however, furthermore,* etc. Words like this can signal a shift in the topic, which often affects the overall point of the sentence or paragraph.

For example, here is the first beginning of a paragraph:

> ✏ **David, you have been a wonderful boyfriend for several years now. You have been kind and caring towards me, and you're always a lot of fun to be with.**

Aww, thanks honey! I love you, too. It's nice to know I'm apprecia—oh, I'm sorry, you weren't finished?

> ✏ **David, you have been a wonderful boyfriend for several years now. You have been kind and caring towards me, and you're always a lot of fun to be with. However,**

Uh oh…

> ✏ **David, you have been a wonderful boyfriend for several years now. You have been kind and caring towards me, and you're always a lot of fun to be with. However, I've met someone else and I'm going to have to break up with you.**

Now, if you were to ask David what the main idea of this paragraph was, which part of it do you think he's going to focus on? Would he say "this is my girlfriend talking about how great I am"? *No!* He'd say "this is what she said *when she dumped me*." That "however" was a big warning sign that the paragraph was about to be transformed into a whole new set of ideas.

So if you see transitional words like this, **circle them**. They can be important clues about the author's ultimate point.

Write your main ideas down

Once you find a main idea, **write it down in the margin**. You'll need it later. If you do this for every paragraph, you'll wind up with a nice little outline of the passage. This way, when you get a question that *doesn't* have a line reference, the main ideas will be in the margin, like the table of contents for a book, telling you exactly where to go.

Writing out all your main ideas does take up time, but it's especially important when you first start trying the strategy. You might struggle with it. It takes some practice before you get good at it, and writing everything down helps. The more practice tests you do, the easier it will become.

Don't spend too much time on this

Remember that the point of this is to *spend less time reading the passage*. Don't spend a lot of time trying to get your main idea absolutely perfect. Don't struggle with the precise wording or try to capture all the nuances of the paragraph. This is supposed to be quick and dirty.

- Your main ideas should be short—don't even use complete sentences. Something like *"author likes cats"* or *"cats are cute and smart"* or *"dogs = not as good"*.

- If a paragraph is so dense and confusing that you can't figure out the main idea at all, just skip it. Move on. Maybe make your main idea some sort of vague placeholder (*"something about cats"*).

- If single paragraph has several different ideas in it, you can split up the paragraph and give two main ideas. Maybe the first half of the paragraph is about one thing and the second half is about something else. That's fine.

- If a fiction passage has long stretches of dialogue, each line of speech will be its own paragraph. Here, you can group the paragraphs to assign main ideas based on the topic of the dialogue. In the first 10 lines they're arguing about where to eat; in the second 10 lines they're trying to find the restaurant; etc.

- If you're having trouble finding main ideas, **move on to the questions.** You can actually learn a lot about the passage as you do the questions. And you can always go back to the passage to fill in the gaps as necessary.

MAIN IDEA DRILL

Read the following passage and write the main idea for each paragraph in the space on the right.

One of the most important discoveries in the history of astronomy was made by a computer in 1908. This may sound like an anachronism; computing machines of the early twentieth century, predecessors of our modern PC's, were nowhere near advanced enough to be making discoveries. However, this "computer" was not a machine at all, but a woman named Henrietta Swan Leavitt.

Line 5

MAIN IDEA:

Throughout the nineteenth century, as optic technology burgeoned, academic institutions built larger and larger telescopes that could peer farther and farther into the night sky. With the invention of photography, observatories could now produce records of the images their telescopes captured. This meant the astronomers could leave the tedious work of data collection to low-paid workers without wasting valuable telescope time. These workers were called "computers", women who would compute the data in the photographs for 25 cents an hour.

10

15

MAIN IDEA:

Henrietta Leavitt was one such computer. Having graduated from Radcliffe College in 1892, she developed an interest in astronomy. The opportunities open to women in the scientific world being few and far between, she joined the photographic photometry department at the Harvard College Observatory as a computer. Her particular task was to search for "variables", stars whose brightness would vary over regular intervals, like a flashing street light. This sort of work resonated with her meticulous disposition, and she catalogued thousands of variables at an incredible rate.

20

25

MAIN IDEA:

While examining a group of variables within one of the Magellanic Clouds*, she noticed that the magnitude of the variables was directly proportional to the period of their pulsation. The brighter the star, the slower it flashed. This discovery was groundbreaking. For centuries, one of the chief mysteries of the universe was its size. Astronomers had no way of determining the distance to the stars. Brightness could be used as a guide, since objects are brighter when they are close and dimmer when they are far away. Brightness alone, however, can be deceptive without a frame of reference. To the casual observer, Venus seems about as bright as the North Star. But Venus is a planet, and is therefore much dimmer than any star. It only seems brighter because it is much, much closer to us. With Leavitt's discovery of the period-luminosity relationship, there was now a way to determine the *true* brightness of stars, not just the apparent brightness. While there were still a number of

30

35

40

45

MAIN IDEA:

CONTINUE

---

* The Magellanic Clouds are two galaxies visible from Earth.

Main Idea Drill

These are just suggestions for the Main Ideas. Your answers will vary. But they shouldn't be much more detailed than this. The point is to paint with *broad strokes* here. Worry about the details when you're asked for them.

Introduction or, computer made a discovery or "computer" = not a computer
"computers" = data entry women
HSL [Henrietta Swan Leavitt] background, early life
Details of her discovery ("period-luminosity relationship")

discovery = important
or HSL = never did anything else

questions to be answered before actual distances could be determined, Leavitt's discovery was fundamental to the
50 eventual calculation of the size of the universe.

Leavitt never produced any other important work. She only worked sporadically, since she was plagued by poor health for most of her life. The most obvious factors working against her were her position and her sex. As a
55 computer, she had no autonomy and could only work on what she was assigned, and as a woman, she had no chance for advancement. The tide of women's rights had begun to turn—Harvard would award a PhD in astronomy to a woman for the first time in 1925—but these changes
60 came too late for Leavitt, who died of cancer in 1921. However, the importance of her discovery did not go unnoticed by the scientific community. Later astronomers such as Hubble and Hertzsprung acknowledged how indebted their work was to her discovery, and she was
65 even nominated for a Nobel Prize five years after her death. Yet outside of academia, she remains little more than a footnote of history.

MAIN IDEA:

Spoiler alert: We're going to look at some questions about this passage over the next few pages. But this passage also appears in full with questions attached as a drill at the end of this chapter. Skip ahead to the end drill if you want to try them yourself first.

END TIME:

© A-List Education

SAT Reading | Reading Techniques   45

II. ANSWERING THE QUESTIONS

There's often more than one way to do a Reading question. Sometimes it's easier to get the answer directly from the passage, sometimes it's easier to eliminate from the answer choices, and sometimes you'll want to do both. Here we'll outline a number of different strategies for tackling all types of Reading questions.

1. Go Back to the @#&*%$! Passage!!

We told you not to worry about the details when reading the passage. Now that you're actually asked about the details, you can worry about them. Luckily, you don't have to rely on what you remember about the passage. *This is an open-book test. You can look it up.*

Many questions will give specific line references in the question itself. Once you read the question, before you do anything else, **go back to the passage and check the line reference**. If they ask you a question about line 35, go back to line 35 and see what it says, *before you even look at the choices.*

Don't just read the literal line mentioned in the question: **read the whole sentence that includes that line.** Most sentences stretch over a couple of lines, and you'll need the full sentence to understand the context.

The effectiveness of this technique is a testament to how little they're asking of you on this test. Most questions will give you specific line references. Not only are all the answers literally written on the page, but *they even tell you where the answers are!*

Okay, we've gone back to the passage and read the sentence. Now what?

2. Anticipate

The key to anticipation is that **all the information you need to answer the question is in the passage**. That's why we look in the passage, not in the choices, for our answers.

Read the question, follow the line reference back into the passage, and see what those lines say about the question. That's your anticipation. Then look at the choices and see which one matches your anticipation.

When you go back to the paragraph, think about what the lines say and what they mean. Try to **paraphrase** the lines in your own words. The right answer will rarely be an *exact* match for your anticipation. Your anticipation gives you the *meaning* you're looking for. The right answer will have the same meaning as your anticipation, but will be worded differently.

Reading questions are ordered roughly "chronologically", with questions asking about details in the order they appear in the passage (e.g. questions about paragraph 1, then questions about paragraph 2, etc.)

Keep in mind that the line reference might not tell you exactly where the answer is; it might just point you to the ballpark. If you don't find the answer in the line you're given, **check one sentence before or after the line reference** to get a fuller context.

Let's look at a sample question from the Henrietta Leavitt passage:

> **9.** **The author mentions Hubble and Hertzsprung (line 63) in order to emphasize**
> **A)** the recognition she got from the general public.
> **B)** the extent to which astronomy was dominated by men.
> **C)** her dependence on the work of earlier scientists.
> **D)** the esteem other scientists had for her work.

First, we'll ignore the answer choices and just focus on the question:

> **9.** **The author mentions Hubble and Hertzsprung (line 63) in order to emphasize**

The question asks about line 63, so let's see what that line says. Remember to read the whole sentence, not just the lines mentioned, so let's start at line 62. We'll reproduce that sentence here:

> *Later astronomers such as Hubble and Hertzsprung acknowledged how indebted their work was to her discovery, and she was even nominated for a Nobel Prize five years after her death.*

What does this sentence say about Hubble and Hertzsprung? You don't have to use the exact words in the sentence—just paraphrase. It says that **they thought her work was important**.

Great. Now let's go to the choices and see which one sounds closest to our anticipation. Remember: the choice won't *exactly* match our anticipation. We just want a choice that has the same *meaning* as our anticipation.

A) ✕ the recognition she got from ~~the general public.~~
Hubble and Hertzsprung are astronomers, not "the general public".

B) ✕ the extent to which astronomy was ~~dominated by men.~~
This has nothing to do with our sentence.*

---

* We don't even know whether Hubble and Hertzsprung were men. (They were, but the passage doesn't say that.)

The sample questions about this passage are all taken from the drill at the end of the chapter. They are numbered out of order here because we retain the question numbers from that drill.

C) ✗ her dependence on the work of ~~earlier scientists.~~

Hubble and Hertzsprung were *later* scientists, not earlier.

D) ✓ the esteem other scientists had for her work.

Perfect! Hubble and Hertzsprung were "astronomers", so they were "other scientists". And they thought her work was important, so they had "esteem for her work."

Notice that we can pinpoint very specific reasons why each of the wrong answers is wrong. When you find something in an answer choice that makes the choice obviously wrong, you should **literally cross those words out**. This may seem silly, but the act of writing on a choice can help you focus your thoughts and be more certain of your elimination.

Let's try another one:

---

3.   The "invention of photography" (line 11) was important to astronomers because it
    A) allowed them to see farther into the night sky.
    B) made data collection easier.
    C) gave them more leisure time.
    D) provided opportunities for women.

Let's go back to line 11 and see what that sentence says:

> With the invention of photography, observatories could now produce records of the images their telescopes captured.

Okay. Astronomers could produce records of the images. But that doesn't match *any* of the choices; none of them talk about producing records. Let's keep reading to the **sentence after** the line reference:

> This meant the astronomers could leave the tedious work of data collection to low-paid workers without wasting valuable telescope time.

So having records meant **they could hire other people to do data collection**. That's our anticipation.

Now we see which choice best matches it. Again, the right answer won't be *exactly* what we anticipated. Let's see which ones come close:

A) ✗ allowed them ~~to see farther~~ into the night sky.

There's nothing about how far they can see.

B) ✓ **made data collection easier.**

Okay, it did mention data collection.

C) ✓ **gave them more leisure time.**

Okay, it did mention freeing up time.

D) ✗ **provided opportunities ~~for women~~.**

Women are not mentioned here.

This time, we had two choices that sound good, B) and C). What should we do?

First of all, **eliminate the choices that are definitely wrong**. We're down to two choices, so even if we have no idea what else to do, we could guess one. There's no way we're leaving this blank now.

So which is better? What's the difference between these two choices? Are there any words here that don't fit what the sentence says?

Let's focus on choice C): it "gave them more leisure time". That sounds plausible. If the scientists have other people to do the work, won't they have more time to themselves?

Well, maybe, but what is *leisure* time? "Leisure time" means free time, time to relax, vacation time. Are the astronomers going to the beach? Playing a few holes at the golf course? Do they have an all-astronomer softball league? All the passage says is that *they don't have to collect data anymore*; it doesn't say what they do with their extra time. That one word, "leisure", makes the whole choice wrong. That leaves us with **choice B): it made data collection easier**. That's it!

The key is to eliminate choices **quickly**. If you're not sure whether a choice works, just skip it and check the next one. If you're having trouble, just try to get it down to two choices and see which one is better. Go through the choices in several waves: first get rid of the choices that are obviously wrong, then go back to what's left and look for nuances.

Use your Main Ideas

The questions we've seen so far have all been about single lines or sentences. But sometimes a question will ask you about a whole paragraph, or a large chunk of text that includes several sentences. In that case, we can use the main ideas to answer the question.

For example:

4. The third paragraph (lines 19-29) chiefly serves to
   A)   discuss opportunities available to women in astronomy.
   B)   describe the daily activities of a typical computer.
   C)   provide biographical background on the subject.
   D)   examine the role of technology in the observatory.

Here, the question is asking about the entire third paragraph. That's 11 lines, which are made up of 5 sentences. Ugh. We still want to anticipate, but that's a lot of text to go back, read, and paraphrase. If only we had a summary of this paragraph…

Wait, we do! We already got the **main idea** of each paragraph. We can just use our main idea as our anticipation.

Your main idea for paragraph 3 may have differed from ours, but it should be something like "**How Leavitt became a computer**" or "**background about Leavitt**". Let's look at our choices:

   A)   ✕ discuss opportunities ~~available to women~~ in astronomy
            Too broad. The paragraph is about Leavitt, not women in general.

   B)   ✕ describe the daily activities of ~~a typical computer~~
            It's about Leavitt specifically, not the "typical" computer.

   C)   ✓ provide biographical background on the subject
            Perfect! She went to Radcliffe, she got a job at Harvard, and she became a computer.

   D)   ✕ examine the role of ~~technology~~ in the observatory
            No technology is mentioned in this paragraph. That was in paragraph 2.

Choice C) is our answer.

Of course, you also may need the main idea for the whole passage. Let's try another one:

1. The primary purpose of the passage is to
   A)   show how technology contributed to Leavitt's work.
   B)   detail how astronomers calculated the size of the universe.
   C)   discuss women's rights in the early twentieth century.
   D)   describe a scientist who made an important discovery.

This question asks about the purpose of the whole passage, so let's find the main idea of the whole passage:

✍ **What's the passage about?**

It's about this woman, Leavitt.

✍ **What does it say about her?**

She's a scientist and she figured out some important stuff.

✍ **What stuff?**

I dunno. Uhh... something about stars?

Good enough! We don't care about the specifics of the discovery unless they ask us about it. So we'll just say the main idea is

> **Henrietta Leavitt figured out some important stuff about stars.**

Perfect. Let's look at our choices:

A) ✗ show ~~how technology contributed~~ to Leavitt's work

It mentions how photography (i.e. technology) contributed to astronomy in paragraph 2, but is that the purpose *of the passage*? No, that's just one bit in one paragraph. Yes, Leavitt used technology, but this is too specific. The passage is about a lot more than just the technology she used.

B) ✗ detail how astronomers ~~calculated the size of the universe~~

No, no, no. Again, the passage does mention that Leavitt's discovery was "fundamental to the eventual calculation of the size of the universe" (lines 49-50), but that's the only mention of it. It doesn't say how it was calculated, or even who did it. It certainly doesn't provide any "details" about it.

C) ✗ discuss ~~women's rights~~ in the early twentieth century

No. True, the last paragraph does say that Leavitt had fewer opportunities because she was a woman. But the passage isn't about women's rights throughout the twentieth century. It's about this one woman and how she was a good scientist. The passage isn't about women's rights in general—it's about Leavitt in particular.

D) ✓ describe a scientist who made an important discovery

Does it describe a scientist? Yes! Henrietta Leavitt! Did she make a discovery? Yes! That thing about the stars, variables or whatever they're called. Perfect. **Choice D)** is our answer.

> **PLEASE NOTE:** The right answer here doesn't mention Leavitt herself by name; it just mentions a vague "scientist" and a vague "discovery". This is a common trick the test likes to pull. Students generally prefer to pick a choice that mentions something specific they saw in the passage, like choice B). Don't be fooled. The fact that a choice was mentioned in the passage isn't necessarily enough to make it right. It also has to answer the question.

No matter what, once we read the question we'll go back to the passage to see what it says. But what we do when we get there depends on the question.

- If the question asks about a **single line or sentence**, we'll read the line and get an **anticipation**.

- If the question asks about a **paragraph or chunk of text**, we'll use our **main idea** as our anticipation.

But sometimes passages are hard to understand. What if we can't figure out what the passage says? That's were the third strategy comes in...

3. Eliminate Nonsense

When you anticipate successfully, you can often jump right to the correct answer. But it's not always that easy. Sometimes when you go back to the passage, you can't get an anticipation. Maybe you don't understand what the line says. Maybe you understand the line, but you don't understand what it has to do with the question.

That's okay. There's still *a lot* we can do even if we don't understand what the passage says. All reading passages are loaded with nonsense choices—choices that are obviously wrong. If we can **eliminate the nonsense** and guess from what's left, we can greatly increase our odds of getting the question. If we can get each tough question down to two choices, we'll get half of them right.

There are three main ways that a choice can be wrong:

1. Random   The choice talks about things that the passage doesn't even mention. You'd be *astounded* to learn how often this happens. (See the question about cats on the first page for an example. All three wrong choices were random.)

2. False   The choice is explicitly contradicted by the passage.

3. Irrelevant   The choice is something the author *says*, but it doesn't actually *answer the question.*

Here are some tips to keep in mind:

- As before, you should **literally cross out** the words that make a choice wrong. This will greatly help you keep track of what you're doing.

- We're not looking for the right choice, **we're looking for wrong choices**. If you're not sure whether a choice fits, just leave it in. Just ask whether the choice is Random, False, or Irrelevant. If you can't find a specific reason to eliminate it, leave it in for now. On every question, three out of four choices are wrong. So if we think a choice is wrong, there's a 75% chance we're right.

- Again, the key here is to **work quickly**. Don't spend too much time agonizing over every choice. Go through the choices, get rid of the ones that are *obviously* wrong, and see what you have left.

- Once you get down to two choices, you can go back to the passage again to see which is better. If you really can't decide which is better, **guess one**.

Let's look at an example:

5.   Lines 21-24 ("The opportunities...computer") suggest that
   A)   women had fewer opportunities in astronomy than in other sciences.
   B)   only men were allowed to work at Harvard College Observatory.
   C)   being a computer was one of the only positions available to Leavitt.
   D)   Leavitt was particularly skilled at searching for variables.

It asks about 21-24, so let's go back:

The opportunities open to women in the scientific world being few and far between, she joined the photographic photometry department at the Harvard College Observatory as a computer.

That's a bit of a complicated sentence, and it may be tough to come up with an anticipation here. Let's do this one by *Eliminating Nonsense* instead.

A)   × women had fewer opportunities in astronomy ~~than in other sciences.~~
   Random! Nowhere does the passage compare astronomy to other sciences. If anything, the first part of this line implies that the situation was *the same* across "the scientific world". A lot people pick this choice because it looks pretty good at first, until you get to the last four words. Please: don't be one of those people too lazy to be bothered to read the last four words of a choice.

B)   × ~~only men were allowed to work~~ at Harvard College Observatory.
   False! Henrietta Leavitt *did* get a job at the Observatory! In the photographic

photometry department! So women *could* work there.

C) ✓ **being a computer was one of the only positions available to Leavitt.**
Bingo. "Opportunities" were "few", so she became a computer. That means that being a computer was an opportunity that was available to her.

D) ✗ **Leavitt was particularly skilled at** ~~searching for variables.~~
Irrelevant. This choice is true—the passage says so explicitly. But it doesn't say that until lines 27-29! This question specifically asks what lines 21-24 suggest, and these lines say nothing about Leavitt's skill at finding variables.

Note here that you don't have to understand why C) is right because it's easy to see why all the other three choices are wrong.

Let's look at a harder example:

> **2.** **It can be inferred that the "anachronism" mentioned in line 3 results from the fact that**
> **A)** a common word is being used in a different sense.
> **B)** predecessors of modern PC's were unavailable in 1908.
> **C)** Harvard had access to more advanced technology than other institutions.
> **D)** computer science advanced at a greater rate than astronomy.

A demonstrative pronoun like *this* or *these* can be a big clue. If you see one, check the previous sentence to find what it refers to.

As always, let's start by going back to the passage. The sentence starts at line 2:

> *This may sound like an **anachronism**;*

We can already see we'll have to go one sentence earlier to see what "this" refers to. Let's start with line 1:

> *One of the most important discoveries in the history of astronomy was made by a computer in 1908. This may sound like an **anachronism**; computing machines of the early twentieth century, predecessors of our modern PC's, were nowhere near advanced enough to be making discoveries.*

Hmm. I still don't know what that means. Let's do it by *Eliminating Nonsense*. We'll look through the choices and eliminate anything that's *Random, False,* or *Irrelevant.*

A) **a common word is being used in a different sense.**
Not sure what this means. We'll leave it in.

B) **predecessors of modern PC's were unavailable in 1908.**

Not sure what this means either. We'll leave this in, too.

C) × ~~Harvard~~ had access to more advanced technology than ~~other institutions.~~

Random! The passage doesn't mention Harvard until line 24, and it doesn't compare it to any other institutions.

D) × computer science advanced at a ~~greater rate than astronomy.~~

False! The passage doesn't actually say anything about the rate of advancement for either computer science or astronomy. But it strongly implies that this is *backwards*: in 1908 astronomy was pretty advanced and computing machines "were nowhere near advanced".

Great! We're down to two choices now, A) and B). If we can't figure anything else out, we can guess.

Let's take a closer look at our two remaining choices. Choice A) is totally confusing, so let's pick apart choice B). It says "*predecessors* of modern PC's were unavailable." "Predecessor" means "precursor" or "ancestor". So "predecessors of modern PC's" are the devices that came before our modern PC's. But the computing machines available in 1908 *were* the predecessors of modern PC's. It says so right in line 4. *Modern* PC's were unavailable, not their predecessors. So choice B) is *false*. **Choice A) is our answer**.

Even though we still don't understand what choice A), the correct answer, means, we can still get the question right.

Let's go back to what we know. The question asks how to explain the anachronism in line 3.* Lines 1-6 say that a computer made a discovery in 1908, but computers as we know them weren't around in 1908. That *is* the anachronism, but it doesn't *explain* the anachronism. If computers weren't around, how is it possible that one made a discovery? Let's keep reading one more line:

> *However, this "computer" was not a machine at all, but a woman named Henrietta Swan Leavitt.*

Aha! It seemed like an anachronism because we thought the word "computer" meant a machine like a laptop. But it really means a *person*. So in this sentence the word "computer"

---

* It helps to know what "anachronism" means: "something in the wrong time period". Of course, you may be able to see that from the context as well.

doesn't mean what it usually means. That's **choice A) a common word is being used in a different sense**.

This was a tough question, and you may have some trouble understanding why A) is right. But that's not the point. The point here is that *even on hard questions*, there are *a lot* of choices that you can easily eliminate. If you narrow every hard question down to two choices, the odds are in your favor—you can get half of them right just by guessing.

Whether you do a question by anticipating or eliminating nonsense is entirely up to you. If you understand the lines in the passage perfectly, then you'll be able to jump to the correct answer. But if you didn't understand the lines, or if there isn't a choice that matches you first anticipation, *you can still get the question right*. Just eliminate aggressively and you'll make progress.

And remember: if you can't eliminate *all* the wrong choices, **guess from what's left.** The key is to **eliminate choices quickly.** If you're not sure whether a choice works, just skip it and check the next one. If you're having trouble, try to get it down to two choices and see which one is better. Go through the choices in several waves: first get rid of the choices that are obviously wrong, then go back to what's left and look for nuances.

Working together

Almost every question on the Reading section can be done with some combination of anticipation and elimination, but the exact ratio is flexible. You'll often do both. You'll anticipate easily, no choices perfectly match your anticipation, so you'll eliminate the ones that are obviously wrong.

The point is that both these strategies are working together for you. On any given question, the more you use one, the less you'll use the other. If one fails, look to the other. They complement each other into a harmonious unity of test-taking peace and perfection.

READING TECHNIQUE SUMMARY

1. The Passage

- Read quickly and get the **main ideas** of the passage, paragraph by paragraph.
- To find the main idea, just ask yourself: **what's it about?**
- If you can't find the main idea, read the **first and last sentences** of the paragraph.
- Don't spend too much time. Don't overanalyze. If you're not sure, **move on**.

2. The Question

- Read the question, **ignore the choices**.
- When there's a line reference, **go back to the passage** and read the line.
- **Read the whole sentence**, not just the line referred to.
- If that line is unclear, read **the sentence before or the sentence after**.
- Try to answer the question with what you just learned. That's your **anticipation**.
- If you can't anticipate, go to the choices to **eliminate**.

3. The Choices

- If you find a choice that matches your anticipation, pick it.
- If you don't find a match or if you don't have an anticipation, don't look for right choice, **look for wrong choices**. 75% of the choices are wrong. You can eliminate wildly wrong choices even if you don't understand the passage or question.
- **Work quickly**. If you're not sure about a choice, skip it and come back later.
- Eliminate choices that are **random**, **false**, or **irrelevant**.
- As you eliminate, **cross out** words that make a choice wrong.
- If you get down to two or three choices and can't decide, **guess one**.

ANTICIPATION DRILL

Read the passage and anticipate for the questions. You get no answer choices. Deal with it. Just look up the line references, see what the passage says, and try to answer the question in your own words.

"Form ever follows function," the American architect Louis Sullivan decreed in 1896. Sullivan's motto offered a new way of approaching design problems, becoming the guiding principle for modernist movement in
Line
5   architecture for nearly a century. Up until this point, architecture throughout Europe and the United States had been dominated by Neoclassicism, a revival of Greek and Roman architectural styles. But as the twentieth century ushered in industrial innovations, designers
10 sought to shake off conventions of the past and embrace a new aesthetic. In this era of growing cities and new production methods, buildings with fluted columns and gilded angels suddenly seemed old fashioned and out of touch. Modernists rejected these established styles,
15 believing that the shape and substance of buildings should be dictated only by their purpose, not unnecessary adornment. The results of this philosophy were radical: details were pared down, and buildings took on a sleek, simple, almost naked quality. The ornate stone buildings
20 of the past were replaced with minimalist structures made from plate glass and steel.

One noteworthy example of modernist architecture is the Guggenheim Museum, designed by Frank Lloyd Wright. The Guggenheim derives its visual appeal from
25 its unusual shape, a simple spiral that gradually widens as it rises, standing in stark contrast to its rectilinear neighbors. This shape was inspired by the building's primary purpose of exhibiting artworks. Visitors enter the gallery at the ground level and slowly ascend the
30 ramp, viewing pieces that are displayed on the periphery of the spiral, as light floods the center through a glass ceiling. In this way, visitors enjoy a traffic-free, continuous experience through the exhibition. By addressing function first, Wright was able to create a
35 visually striking design that is also a work of art in its own right.

The modernist viewpoint was not confined to architecture, but was also adopted in the larger world of industrial and graphic design. Furniture designers, for
40 example, rejected the traditional idea of a piece's value being defined by the quality of workmanship. Modernist furniture like the Eames lounge chair emphasized simplicity and accessibility. Designed by Charles and Ray Eames, the chair was made of three shell-shaped
45 pieces fitted with leather cushions that could be easily disassembled for shipping. By separating the pieces of the chair, the design offered greater flexibility in reclining, but remained uncluttered and sophisticated. Likewise, poster designers in Switzerland developed
50 Helvetica, a new typeface that epitomized the minimalism of modernist design by presenting stark,

unadorned letters. Since the purpose of any text should be to convey information, Helvetica's simple letter shapes offered no curlicues or flourishes that might
55 distract from the content of printed words.

Although modernism gave way to some of the most iconic designs of the twentieth century, other designers argued that whimsical elements can also contribute to an object's appeal. These dissenters felt that too strict an
60 adherence to the "form follows function" mentality results in stifling uniformity and aesthetic boredom. After decades of impassive simplicity, they rediscovered the expressive power of decorative elements: architectural details, vibrant upholstery, or quirky fonts.

1

As used in line 7, the word "dominated" most nearly means

_____

_____

_____

2

The reference to "fluted columns and gilded angels" in line 12-13 is given in order to

_____

_____

_____

3

Lines 14-17 ("Modernists... adornment") suggest that modernist buildings

_____

_____

_____

CONTINUE

Anticipation Drill

MAIN IDEAS: (Yours may vary)
    Par. 1:   Modernism = form follows function, no decorations
    Par. 2:   Gug. Museum's shape follows function
    Par. 3:   Modernism in other fields, furniture and typography
    Par. 4:   Other people like decorations

You're trying to answer the questions on your own by looking in the passage. You don't have to use complete sentences, but you can't just underline the information in the passage. You have to actually write down the answer. It's okay to directly quote the passage in your anticipation as long as you understand what it means. Your wording can differ. That's okay. As long as you understand the meaning of the text. Remember also that your anticipation won't exactly match the correct answer choice. That's okay. Don't worry about the choices yet. Just try to see and understand what the passage says.

1.   Go back to line 7. The sentence starts in line 5:
        Up until this point, architecture throughout Europe and the
        United States had been dominated by Neoclassicism, a
        revival of Greek and Roman architectural styles.

     It can be tough to come up with a precise anticipation here, but
     let's try.

     The sentence is talking about a particular style of architecture
     called "Neoclassicism". What does this sentence say about
     Neoclassicism? That it was **really popular**. Because of parts of
     speech confusion, "was really popular" doesn't fit in our sentence
     as an anticipation (you couldn't *replace* "dominated" with "really
     popular"; the sentence wouldn't make sense.)

     But what we're trying to do here is capture the meaning of the
     word as best we can. What the sentence means is that **everyone
     used Neoclassical architecture.**

2.   The sentence containing the quote starts in line 11:
        In this era of growing cities and new production methods,
        buildings with fluted columns and gilded angels suddenly
        seemed old fashioned and out of touch.

     So the columns and angels are **examples of things that seemed
     old-fashioned.** If you want to know *who* thinks they're old
     fashioned, just keep reading to the beginning of the next sentence:
        Modernists rejected these established styles…

     fluted = *having grooves*
     gilded = *covered in gold*

3.   Go back to line 14:
        Modernists rejected these established styles, believing that
        the shape and substance of buildings should be dictated only
        by their purpose, not unnecessary adornment.

     The phrase "these established styles" refers to the sentence
     before—the columns and angels mentioned in question #2. So
     what do modernists think about buildings?
     •   Their shape should be **dictated by purpose**
     •   They should have **no unnecessary adornment**.

     adornment = *decoration, ornamentation*

4. The sentence containing the quote starts in line 24:

   The Guggenheim derives its visual appeal from its <u>unusual shape</u>, a simple spiral that gradually widens as it rises, standing in stark contrast to its rectilinear neighbors.

   Hmm. That doesn't tell us anything about the purpose. Let's keep reading to the next sentence, starting in line 27:

   This shape was inspired by the building's primary purpose of exhibiting artworks.

   Aha! So purpose of the unusual shape is **to reflect the purpose of the building**, which is exhibiting artworks. The rest of that paragraph gets into the specific ways it does that—how the ramps aid the flow of traffic, etc—but that's not important to us now.

5. This question is about the same sentence we just saw, line 24:

   The Guggenheim derives its visual appeal from its unusual shape, a simple spiral that gradually widens as it rises, <u>standing in stark contrast to its rectilinear neighbors</u>.

   [Please note that the "neighbors" here are neighboring *buildings*, not people.]

   What do we know?
   - The Guggenheim's spiral shape was *unusual*
   - The shape was *in contrast to* the shape of its neighbors.
   - Those neighbors were *rectilinear*.

   All we know about the neighbors is that **they are shaped differently from the Guggenheim**. The Gug is a spiral, the other buildings are rectangular.

   rectilinear = *made up of straight lines*

6. Go back, starting in line 34:

   Wright was able to create a visually <u>striking</u> design that is also a work of art in its own right.

   It's *visually* striking, so we know we're talking about the *appearance* of the building. We know the building is "a work of art" and the author likes it, so it should be a *positive* word. So our anticipation should be something like **beautiful**, but even something more neutral like **noticeable** or **interesting** would get us on the right track.

   And it helps if you know that "striking" means *"attractive in an interesting way"*

7. It's asking about the whole third paragraph. What was our main idea for that paragraph? I had:

   Par. 3: **Modernism in other fields, furniture and typography**

   That'll do nicely as our anticipation.

8. Go back to lines 43-48:

   Designed by Charles and Ray Eames, the chair was made of three shell-shaped pieces fitted with leather cushions that could be easily disassembled for shipping. By separating the pieces of the chair, the design offered greater flexibility in reclining, but remained uncluttered and sophisticated.

   What are these lines describing? Check the previous sentence, lines 41-43:

   Modernist furniture like the Eames lounge chair emphasized simplicity and accessibility.

   So lines 43-46 are a **description of the Eames lounge chair**, a chair which was **simple and accessible.** These lines explain how it was so simple and accessible.

9. The sentence containing the quote begins in line 56:

   Although modernism gave way to some of the most iconic designs of the twentieth century, other <u>designers</u> argued that whimsical elements can also contribute to an object's appeal.

   "Although" is a contrast word, a big clue that we're now talking about people who **disagree with modernism**. Even if you don't understand what the second half of this sentence means, you should be able to see that contrast.

   To get more specific, look at the next sentence, starting in line 59:

   These dissenters felt that too strict an adherence to the "form follows function" mentality results in stifling uniformity and aesthetic boredom.

   The word "dissenters" again tells us they disagree with modernism. More specifically, it says "form follows function" (a modernist idea) **leads to uniformity and boredom**.

   whimsical = *fanciful, impulsive*
   dissenter *one who disagrees*
   uniformity = *sameness*

10. Let's look at the larger context of the sentence, starting in line 62:

    After decades of impassive simplicity, they rediscovered the expressive power of decorative elements: architectural details, vibrant upholstery, or quirky fonts.

    The list at the end is a list of the "decorative elements" that "they" thought were powerful. Who is "they"? The group mentioned in the previous sentence: the "dissenters" from question #9.
    So the list in line 64 is a list of **things people who disagree with modernism enjoy**.

4

The passage states that the purpose of the "unusual shape" (line 25) of the Guggenheim is to

_____

_____

_____

5

The passage suggests that, compared to the Guggenheim, the "neighbors" mentioned in line 27

_____

_____

_____

6

As used in line 35, the word "striking" most nearly means

_____

_____

_____

7

The primary purpose of the third paragraph (lines 37-55) is to

_____

_____

_____

8

Lines 43-48 ("Designed ... sophisticated") serve primarily to

_____

_____

_____

9

Which of the following most closely describes the views of the "designers" mentioned in line 57?

_____

_____

_____

10

The list in line 64 ("architectural... fonts") is intended to give examples of

_____

_____

_____

CONTINUE

ELIMINATION DRILL

Here are the same passage and questions, but with answer choices. **Use your anticipations from the last drill** *and match them to the choices.* **Explain your reasoning** *by writing in the line below the choice, or by crossing out words that make the choice wrong.*

"Form ever follows function," the American architect Louis Sullivan decreed in 1896. Sullivan's motto offered a new way of approaching design problems, becoming
Line the guiding principle for modernist movement in
5 architecture for nearly a century. Up until this point, architecture throughout Europe and the United States had been dominated by Neoclassicism, a revival of Greek and Roman architectural styles. But as the twentieth century ushered in industrial innovations, designers
10 sought to shake off conventions of the past and embrace a new aesthetic. In this era of growing cities and new production methods, buildings with fluted columns and gilded angels suddenly seemed old fashioned and out of touch. Modernists rejected these established styles,
15 believing that the shape and substance of buildings should be dictated only by their purpose, not unnecessary adornment. The results of this philosophy were radical: details were pared down, and buildings took on a sleek, simple, almost naked quality. The ornate stone buildings
20 of the past were replaced with minimalist structures made from plate glass and steel.

One noteworthy example of modernist architecture is the Guggenheim Museum, designed by Frank Lloyd Wright. The Guggenheim derives its visual appeal from
25 its unusual shape, a simple spiral that gradually widens as it rises, standing in stark contrast to its rectilinear neighbors. This shape was inspired by the building's primary purpose of exhibiting artworks. Visitors enter the gallery at the ground level and slowly ascend the
30 ramp, viewing pieces that are displayed on the periphery of the spiral, as light floods the center through a glass ceiling. In this way, visitors enjoy a traffic-free, continuous experience through the exhibition. By addressing function first, Wright was able to create a
35 visually striking design that is also a work of art in its own right.

The modernist viewpoint was not confined to architecture, but was also adopted in the larger world of industrial and graphic design. Furniture designers, for
40 example, rejected the traditional idea of a piece's value being defined by the quality of workmanship. Modernist furniture like the Eames lounge chair emphasized simplicity and accessibility. Designed by Charles and Ray Eames, the chair was made of three shell-shaped
45 pieces fitted with leather cushions that could be easily disassembled for shipping. By separating the pieces of the chair, the design offered greater flexibility in reclining, but remained uncluttered and sophisticated. Likewise, poster designers in Switzerland developed
50 Helvetica, a new typeface that epitomized the minimalism of modernist design by presenting stark,

unadorned letters. Since the purpose of any text should be to convey information, Helvetica's simple letter shapes offered no curlicues or flourishes that might
55 distract from the content of printed words.

Although modernism gave way to some of the most iconic designs of the twentieth century, other designers argued that whimsical elements can also contribute to an object's appeal. These dissenters felt that too strict an
60 adherence to the "form follows function" mentality results in stifling uniformity and aesthetic boredom. After decades of impassive simplicity, they rediscovered the expressive power of decorative elements: architectural details, vibrant upholstery, or quirky fonts.

1

As used in line 7, the word "dominated" most nearly means

A) subdued.

B) intimidated.

C) characterized.

D) overshadowed.

2

The reference to "fluted columns and gilded angels" in line 12-13 is given in order to

A) describe some typical elements of modernist architecture.

B) bemoan the decline of artistic quality due to industrial growth.

C) give examples of stylistic elements that came to be seen as antiquated.

D) advocate for the renovation of dilapidated old structures.

CONTINUE →

Preliminary Note

Many of the explanations here are given in two ways. First, we'll go back to the passage, anticipate, and see which answer matches our anticipation. Second, we'll go through all the other choices and see what's wrong with them.

However, students don't necessarily have to do *both* these things on every question. Sometimes, once kids anticipate, they can jump directly to the right answer. Other times, the anticipation will be tricky or doesn't quite match any choice, but they can still get the question by eliminating the obviously wrong choices. Students can differ in which method is easier for them, so we give both methods when possible.

Elimination Drill

Use the anticipations we just wrote. Find a choice that matches the *meaning* of your anticipation. You may not find a choice that perfectly matches your anticipation. That's why you should **eliminate** as you go. Eliminate choices that are **random, false,** or **irrelevant** to the question.

1. **Answer: C.**

   Anticipation: Neoclassicism was **popular.**

   None of our choices here exactly match "popular", but A), B,) and D) are both negative, so they're out.

   C), characterized, means "being a typical feature of something". That means the style was common, widespread, and popular.

   This is a good question to show off how anticipation often won't get you the *precise* answer to a question, but will get you to the *ballpark*.

   In choice A), subdued in this context a passive verb construction ("was subdued by") means "apprehended", like a policeman catching a criminal. Uhh, no.

2. **Answer: C.**

   Anticipation: These are **examples of things that seemed old-fashioned.**

   A) False. These are elements of the "established styles" that the "modernists rejected" (line 14).
   B) Random. The passage says nothing about the quality of the art produced and does not say it was declining.
   C) **Correct.** Exactly matches our anticipation. Antiquated = *old, out of date*
   D) Random. No mention of any renovation. Advocate = *to promote or speak in favor of.* Dilapidated = *run-down.*

3. Answer: A.

Anticipation: The buildings should be **dictated by purpose** and have **no unnecessary adornment**.

A) **Correct.** Adornment = *ornamentation*.
B) False. Greek and Roman styles were dominant *before* modernism (lines 5-8). Modernists rejected the established styles (line 14). Aesthetic = *concerning art or beauty*.
C) Random. These lines say nothing about the way in which buildings are constructed. Note that lines 19-21 do talk about the materials buildings are made of, but that's not the same thing. (Also, the question is about lines 14-17, not 19-21). Innovative (**2**) = *new and creative*
D) Random. No critics are mentioned here.

4. Answer: D.

Anticipation: The purpose of the unusual shape is **to reflect the purpose of the building, exhibiting artwork.**

A) Random. The passage says nothing about what the Guggenheim is made of.
B) Random. The passage does not mention any other museums.
C) Irrelevant. The passage does mention that Wright designed the building, and it does say that the building is "a work of art". But the purpose of the shape isn't to show off how great Wright is.
D) **Correct.** The spiral makes it easier for people to walk around and "enjoy a traffic-free, continuous experience through the exhibition" (lines 32-33).

Choice C) is a great example of the importance of anticipation. If you just look at choice C), you can come up with all sorts of reasons why it might sound good. But if you anticipate *before* looking at the choices, you won't come up with anything like C). It's just another choice that doesn't match your anticipation.

5. Answer: A.

Anticipation: The neighbors **are shaped differently from the Guggenheim**.

A) **Correct.** The neighboring buildings look different.
B) Random. It doesn't say whether the neighbors communicate their function.
C) Random. Are the neighbors museums? Do they contain art? We don't know! It doesn't say.
D) Random. Just because the Guggenheim is pretty and the neighbors are different does not mean the neighbors aren't pretty. They might be pretty in different ways.

6. Answer: B.

Anticipation: **beautiful, noticeable, interesting..**

A) shocking. This does mean *interesting*, but in a negative way, as in *offensive*. There's nothing in the passage that suggests the building was offensive. The author *likes* it.
B) remarkable = *noteworthy*. **Perfect.**
C) functional = *practical, working properly*. The building is functional, but that has nothing to do with this sentence.
D) forceful = *with force*. Totally random.

7. Answer: A.

Anticipation: **Modernism in other fields, furniture and typography..**

A) **Correct.** The "other fields" are furniture and typography.
B) Irrelevant. The passage does praise the Eames chair, but that's not the point of the paragraph. The only reason we brought it up was as another example of modernism.
C) False. This can seem a bit tempting if you interpret the "changes" as the birth of modernism. But "repercussions" is the wrong word here. It means "something *bad* that happens as a consequence of something else." But the author *likes* the Eames chair.
D) Random. There's no critical response here.

8. Answer: D.

Anticipation: These lines are a **description of the Eames lounge chair**, which was **simple and accessible.**

A) Random. The passage does not say how difficult it is to produce the chair. It praises the chair's flexibility, saying that it's *easy* to disassemble and ship the chair.
B) Random. It does not say how difficult it is to apply these principles to other fields. (If anything, the passage implies it's easy, since so many other fields used it.)
C) Irrelevant. One might infer that this choice is true based on the passage. Architecture and furniture design both used modernist principles, and modernists believed the fields *used to* rely on outdated ideas. But none of that is in *these lines*. These lines are about what the chair looks like.
D) **Correct.** The chair was "uncluttered and sophisticated."

3

Lines 14-17 ("Modernists… adornment") suggest that modernist buildings

A) intentionally lacked excessive ornamentation.

B) used aesthetics based on Greek and Roman styles.

C) were constructed using innovative technology.

D) were harshly received by older critics.

4

The passage states that the purpose of the "unusual shape" (line 25) of the Guggenheim is to

A) exploit new construction materials.

B) distinguish it from older museums.

C) demonstrate Wright's artistic virtuosity.

D) enhance the building's intended use.

5

The passage suggests that, compared to the Guggenheim, the "neighbors" mentioned in line 27

A) are significantly different in appearance.

B) do not properly communicate their function.

C) display their artworks less effectively.

D) are not as visually appealing.

6

As used in line 35, the word "striking" most nearly means

A) shocking.

B) remarkable.

C) functional.

D) forceful.

7

The primary purpose of the third paragraph (lines 37-55) is to

A) extend the discussion of the previous paragraphs into other fields.

B) praise the simplicity and ingenuity of the Eames chair's design.

C) assess the repercussions of the changes previously mentioned.

D) analyze the critical response to the modernist aesthetic.

8

Lines 43-48 ("Designed … sophisticated") serve primarily to

A) demonstrate the expense and effort required to produce a high-quality chair.

B) show the difficulties of applying modernist principles to furniture design.

C) argue that architecture and furniture design both rely on outdated ideas.

D) elaborate on the convenience and innovation of a particular design.

CONTINUE

Which of the following most closely describes the views of the "designers" mentioned in line 57?

A) A building's shape should be dictated by its function.

B) Excessive focus on an object's purpose can lead to monotonous designs.

C) Modernism allows museums to be works of art in their own right.

D) Industrial materials like plate-glass and steel provide sleek, elegant construction.

The list in line 64 ("architectural…fonts") is intended to give examples of

A) embellishments that modernists valued for their expressive power.

B) features whose presence helps designers emphasize an object's function.

C) architectural elements that Sullivan sought to eliminate.

D) details that critics of modernism have come to appreciate.

STOP

9. **Answer: B.**
Anticipation: They **disagree with modernism**, saying it **leads to uniformity and boredom**.

A) False. This is what *modernists* believe. The designers in question are *dissenters*, who disagree with modernism.
B) **Correct.** "Excessive focus on an object's purpose" means "too strict an adherence to the 'form follow function' mentality" (lines 59-60). Monotonous = *boring, unvarying*.
C) Random. Museums aren't mentioned in this paragraph. Also, this is a modernist idea, and these dissenters don't like modernism. Also irrelevant: This idea is mentioned at the end of paragraph 2, but that has nothing to do with these lines.
D) Random. There's nothing about industrial materials here. Also, this is a modernist idea, and these dissenters don't like modernism.

Just seeing that these designers *disagree with modernists* might be enough to get this question.

10. **Answer: D.**
Anticipation: It's a list of **things people who disagree with modernism enjoy**.

A) False. Modernists *don't like embellishment*. This is a list of what the dissenters like. Embellish *= to decorate*.
B) False. The dissenters thought too much function is boring. These details are the antidote to function.
C) Random. This paragraph does not mention Sullivan.
D) **Correct.** Modernists don't like these things, but critics of modernism do.

Choice C) may be tempting if you create a chain of reasoning like this:

- Sullivan believed form followed function.
- Modernists believed form followed function.
- Modernists sought to eliminate details.
- Therefore, Sullivan sought to eliminate details.

But the passage doesn't actually say anything about Sullivan. All we know about him is that he said that quote. We don't know he sought to eliminate details. We don't even know that he himself was a modernist, only that he inspired modernists.

Also, the question is very specific: what is the *purpose of this list*? This list is clearly meant to tell us something about the dissenters, not about Sullivan.

Reading Exercise 1

Some of these questions were discussed at length in the chapter already. Those that weren't will be discussed here

Here's a reminder of our main ideas for this passage:

Par. 1: Introduction or, computer made a discovery
   or "computer" = not a computer
Par. 2: "computers" = data entry women
Par. 3: HSL [Henrietta Swan Leavitt] background, early life
Par. 4: Details of her discovery ("period-luminosity relationship")
Par. 5: discovery = important
   or HSL = never did anything else

1. **Answer: D.**
   This question was discussed in the text of this chapter.

2. **Answer: A.**
   This question was discussed in the text of this chapter.

3. **Answer: B.**
   This question was discussed in the text of this chapter.

4. **Answer: C.**
   This question was discussed in the text of this chapter.

5. **Answer: C.**
   This question was discussed in the text of this chapter.

READING EXERCISE 1

One of the most important discoveries in the history of astronomy was made by a computer in 1908. This may sound like an anachronism; computing machines of the early twentieth century, predecessors of our modern PC's, were nowhere near advanced enough to be making discoveries. However, this "computer" was not a machine at all, but a woman named Henrietta Swan Leavitt.

Throughout the nineteenth century, as optic technology burgeoned, academic institutions built larger and larger telescopes that could peer farther and farther into the night sky. With the invention of photography, observatories could now produce records of the images their telescopes captured. This meant the astronomers could leave the tedious work of data collection to low-paid workers without wasting valuable telescope time. These workers were called "computers", women who would compute the data in the photographs for 25 cents an hour.

Henrietta Leavitt was one such computer. Having graduated from Radcliffe College in 1892, she developed an interest in astronomy. The opportunities open to women in the scientific world being few and far between, she joined the photographic photometry department at the Harvard College Observatory as a computer. Her particular task was to search for "variables", stars whose brightness would vary over regular intervals, like a flashing street light. This sort of work resonated with her meticulous disposition, and she catalogued thousands of variables at an incredible rate.

While examining a group of variables within one of the Magellanic Clouds*, she noticed that the magnitude of the variables was directly proportional to the period of their pulsation. The brighter the star, the slower it flashed. This discovery was groundbreaking. For centuries, one of the chief mysteries of the universe was its size. Astronomers had no way of determining the distance to the stars. Brightness could be used as a guide, since objects are brighter when they are close and dimmer when they are far away. Brightness alone, however, can be deceptive without a frame of reference. To the casual ob-server, Venus seems about as bright as the North Star. But Venus is a planet, and is therefore much dimmer than any star. It only seems brighter because it is much, much closer to us. With Leavitt's discovery of the period-luminosity relationship, there was now a way to determine the *true* brightness of stars, not just the apparent brightness. While there were still a number of questions to be answered before actual distances could be determined, Leavitt's discovery was fundamental to the eventual calculation of the size of the universe.

Leavitt never produced any other important work. She only worked sporadically, since she was plagued by poor health for most of her life. The most obvious factors working against her were her position and her sex. As a computer, she had no autonomy and could only work on what she was assigned, and as a woman, she had no chance for advancement. The tide of women's rights had begun to turn—Harvard would award a PhD in astronomy to a woman for the first time in 1925—but these changes came too late for Leavitt, who died of cancer in 1921. However, the importance of her discovery did not go unnoticed by the scientific community. Later astronomers such as Hubble and Hertzsprung acknowledged how indebted their work was to her discovery, and she was even nominated for a Nobel Prize five years after her death. Yet outside of academia, she remains little more than a footnote of history.

1

The primary purpose of the passage is to

A) show how technology contributed to Leavitt's work.

B) detail how astronomers calculated the size of the universe.

C) discuss women's rights in the early twentieth century.

D) describe a scientist who made an important discovery.

2

It can be inferred that the "anachronism" mentioned in line 3 results from the fact that

A) a common word is being used in a different sense.

B) predecessors of modern PC's were unavailable in 1908.

C) Harvard had access to more advanced technology than other institutions.

D) computer science advanced at a greater rate than astronomy.

---

* The Magellanic Clouds are two galaxies visible from Earth.

CONTINUE

3

The "invention of photography" (line 11) was important to astronomers because it

A) allowed them to see farther into the night sky.

B) made data collection easier.

C) gave them more leisure time.

D) provided opportunities for women.

4

The third paragraph (lines 19-29) chiefly serves to

A) discuss opportunities available to women in astronomy.

B) describe the daily activities of a typical computer.

C) provide biographical background on the subject.

D) examine the role of technology in the observatory.

5

Lines 21-24 ("The opportunities…computer") suggest that

A) women had fewer opportunities in astronomy than in other sciences.

B) only men were allowed to work at Harvard College Observatory.

C) being a computer was one of the only positions available to Leavitt.

D) Leavitt was particularly skilled at searching for variables.

6

As used in line 27, the word "resonated" most nearly means

A) vibrated.

B) agreed.

C) sympathized.

D) rejoiced.

7

The discussion of Venus in lines 40-44 is intended as

A) a counterexample that disproves Leavitt's theory.

B) an example of the period-luminosity relationship.

C) an analogy that illustrates an astronomical phenomenon.

D) a question that astronomers could not answer.

8

In lines 51-60 ("Leavitt never…in 1921"), all of the following are given as reasons that Leavitt did not produce more work EXCEPT

A) her deteriorating health kept her from her work.

B) she did not have the same opportunities for advancement that men had.

C) the academic community did not realize the importance of her achievements.

D) she died before she could achieve greater power.

9

The author mentions Hubble and Hertzsprung (line 63) in order to emphasize

A) the recognition she got from the general public.

B) the extent to which astronomy was dominated by men.

C) her dependence on the work of earlier scientists.

D) the esteem other scientists had for her work.

10

The author refers to Leavitt as "a footnote of history" (line 67) because

A) despite early promise, she never made any important scientific contributions.

B) she made an important step in the advancement of women's rights.

C) she is still unknown to those outside her field.

D) her work was not as important as that of Hubble.

11

The author's tone throughout the passage can best be described as

A) scholarly appreciation.

B) objective criticism.

C) scornful ridicule.

D) celebratory adoration.

STOP

6. **Answer: B.**
Don't just try to define "resonate"; we have to look at its meaning *in the context of the sentence.* So let's go back to line 27. (We'll start with the sentence before to remind you of the context.)

> *Her particular task was to search for "variables", stars whose brightness would vary over regular intervals, like a flashing street light. This sort of work* **resonated** *with her meticulous disposition, and she catalogued thousands of variables at an incredible rate.*

The second part of the second sentence says that she was good at her job. So by nature she was well suited to this kind of work. So the work **suited** or **fit** or **worked well with** her disposition. We're just trying to figure out the *meaning* of the word in the blank, so any of these is a fine anticipation.

Now we'll go back the choices. Do any of our choices mean something like *suited, fit,* or *worked well with?* **Choice B), agreed,** works nicely.

Note that choice A), vibrated, is what "resonated" literally means most of the time. However, that's not how the word is being used *in this context.*

7. **Answer: C.**
This question is asking what the *role* of the discussion of Venus is. Why does he talk about Venus? We'll start by going back to the passage. Lines 40-44:

> *To the casual observer, Venus seems about as bright as the North Star. But Venus is a planet, and is therefore much dimmer than any star. It only seems brighter because it is much, much closer to us.*

It's tough to anticipate based purely on that quote. So let's just go through the choices and see which choices *could describe* that quote.

A) False. Leavitt's theory was about how stars flash (line 33). The brightness of Venus does not disprove that. The author believes Leavitt's theory is true.
B) Hmm. This seems plausible. The paragraph is about that luminosity thingy. We'll leave it in.
C) This s kind of vague, but it might work. It's certainly about astronomical stuff. We'll leave it in.
D) Random. What question? How bright Venus is? Is that a question astronomers couldn't answer?

Great! We're down to two choices, B) and C). Worst-case scenario, we'll guess one. Let's take a closer look at these guys. Choice B) mentions the "period-luminosity relationship"—that's the fancy name for Leavitt's discovery. *What was* her discovery? Line 33: "The brighter the star, the slower it flashed." Is Venus an example of a flashing star? **No!** It doesn't flash, and it's not a star—it's a planet! It says so in line 42. So the Venus discussion *can't possibly* be an example of this relationship. **Our answer must be choice C).**

It's easy to be afraid of a choice like C) because it sounds so *broad.* "An astronomical phenomenon." What is that? Choice B) is more tempting because it's *specific.* It mentions that "period" thingy, and we know the paragraph is about that period thingy. *But that's backwards.* Like we saw with the Main Idea question above, the *correct* answer is the broad and vague, while a *wrong* choice specifically mentions something in the passage. In fact, when a choice does have specific details, it's easier to show that choice to be wrong.

So why is C) right? Lines 41-44 say that Venus looks as bright as the North Star, not because it *is* as bright, but because it's closer to us. Go a few lines earlier:

> *Astronomers had no way of determining the distance to the stars. Brightness could be used as a guide, since objects are brighter when they are close and dimmer when they are far away.* **Brightness alone, however, can be deceptive without a frame of reference.**

So the Venus discussion is intended to explain *why* brightness alone is not a reliable way to determine the distance to the stars. That's the "astronomical phenomenon" that Venus illustrates. This is the same thing as the difference between "true brightness" and "apparent brightness" mentioned in lines 46-47.

8. **Answer: C.**
The question tells us that three choices are *given* in the passage, and one isn't. So let's go back and read lines 51-60. As we see the answer choices in the text, we'll eliminate them:

> *Leavitt never produced any other important work. She only worked sporadically, since* **she was plagued by poor health [eliminate A)]** *for most of her life. The most obvious factors working against her were her position and her sex. As a computer, she had no autonomy and could only work on what she was assigned and* **as a woman, she had no chance for advancement [eliminate B)].** *The tide of women's rights had begun to turn—Harvard would award a PhD in astronomy to a woman for the first time in 1925—but* **these changes came too late for Leavitt, who died of cancer in 1921 [eliminate D)].**

Choice C) is the only one not mentioned in these lines.

9. **Answer: D.**
This question was discussed in the text of this chapter.

10. **Answer: C.**
Go Back. We just established in the previous sentence that her colleagues had esteem for her work. Next sentence: "**yet** [contrast!] outside of academia, she remains little more than a footnote of history."

So **non-astronomers (the general public) don't know about her.** That's **choice C).**

A) True, but irrelevant. That's not what *this* line means.
B) Random. Women's rights not mentioned here.
C) **Correct.**
D) Random. What did Hubble do? We don't know.

11. **Answer: A**
This is a tone question. We'll talk more about these next chapter. The main question to ask is: *is the narrator happy, unhappy, or neutral?*

Where does the author of the Leavitt passage fall in this spectrum? Generally, he's a *historian.* Most of the passage simply *gives the facts* of her life and discovery. She grew up here, worked there, discovered this, and died.

At the same time, he seems to *like* Henrietta Leavitt. He thinks she's a good scientist. He does say that she made "One of the most important discoveries in the history of astronomy" (lines 1–2). So that's good. We can certainly agree that he doesn't say *bad* things about her.

The tone should be somewhere between ☺ and ☺. Each choice has two words, so we'll rate both of them:

A) scholarly appreciation ☺/☺   ✓ That looks perfect.
B) objective criticism   ☺/☹   ✗ Tthere's no "criticism".
C) scornful derision   ☹/☹   ✗ Too angry.
D) celebratory exaltation ☺/☺   ✗ Way too happy.

THIS PAGE INTENTIONALLY LEFT BLANK

Reading Question Types

Let's take a closer look at the different types of questions you'll see with the passages. In the following sections we're going to provide some short passages to give examples of different kinds of questions.

PLEASE NOTE: these categories may overlap, and there may be situations in which you're not sure which category a question belongs to. Don't worry about it. These are just suggestions to help you make sense of these questions; it doesn't really matter whether a particular question is "inferential" or "strategy" or whatever. Don't ever spend any time trying to 'categorize' a question.

1. Explicit Questions

These are the questions that ask you **what the passage literally says**. We've already established that most Reading questions give you specific line references, so all you have to do is go back, anticipate the answer, then match your anticipation to the choices.

It's important to see that every answer you put to explicit questions must be grounded in the passage. Don't pick a choice unless you can show us *exactly* where in the passage it says that. Don't just say, "Well, somewhere in the middle the author kinda says something about how cats are good." Say, "*Look*: in line 23 he says QUOTE 'I like cats.'"

Most explicit questions can be done by anticipating, and we've already seen tons of examples in the last chapter. These questions may vary in difficulty. "Explicit" doesn't necessarily mean *easy*; it just means that the answer is written in the text of the passage.

Take a look at these:

These passages are only intended as demonstrations of the types. Real passages will never be this short and will always have more than 2 questions about them.

Questions 1 and 2 are based on the following passage.

The German filmmaker F.W. Murnau's silent film *The Last Laugh* may be less widely known today than his darkly expressionist *Nosferatu*, but it is arguably the
Line more important film because of its technical accomplish-
5 ments. It was in this film that Murnau first experimented with the "unchained camera technique", in which the camera moved around during filming, mounted on a trolley, a crane, and even the cameraman's stomach. This allowed Murnau not only to tell the story from the literal
10 perspective of the protagonist but also to reflect his shifting mental state in the camera angles. This kind of camerawork was unheard of at a time when cameras were very bulky and very heavy. Despite the film's lackluster box-office performance, this innovation was
15 hugely influential with other directors at the time.

MAIN IDEA:

_____

1. According to the passage, one reason *The Last Laugh* was "arguably the more important film" (lines 3-4) was because of its
   ANTICIPATION: _____
   A)   method of filming.
   B)   dark lighting.
   C)   complex protagonist.
   D)   innovative script.

2. The passage states that the "unchained camera technique" (line 6)
   ANTICIPATION: _____
   A)   was the primary explanation for the box-office success of *The Last Laugh*
   B)   provided the director with new methods of expression
   C)   contributed to the uniquely dark mood of *Nosferatu*
   D)   was dismissed by other directors as too impractical

Explicit Questions

1. **Answer: A.**
This question was discussed in the text of this chapter.

2. **Answer: B.**
More about "the unchained camera technique". Again: what is it? It's when you move the camera around during filming.

Hmm. No choices say that. Let's keep reading. Why was this technique important? Line 8-11:

> *This allowed Murnau not only to tell the story from the literal perspective of the protagonist but also to reflect his shifting mental state in the camera angles.*

Okay! It affected the way that Murnau told his story. Let's see which choices look good.

A) False. The film did not have box-office success. Lines 13-14: "Despite the film's *lackluster* box-office performance". Lackluster = *sluggish, slow*.

B) **Correct.** Murnau was the director and lines 8-11 detail new methods of expression (e.g. reflecting a character's mental state via camera angles).

C) False. This technique was used in *The Last Laugh*, not *Nosferatu*. The passage does not say outright whether *Nosferatu* used it, but lines 1-5 imply that it did not.

D) False. Lines 14-15: the technique "was hugely influential with other directors at the time." Dismiss = *to reject*

THIS PAGE INTENTIONALLY LEFT BLANK

THIS PAGE INTENTIONALLY LEFT BLANK

Let's take a look at **question 1** together.

> **1.** **According to the passage, one reason The Last Laugh was "arguably the more important film" (lines 3-4) was because of its**

This question is asking about a detail that was explicitly stated in the passage. So let's go back! What makes *The Last Laugh* important? Line 3:

> *It is arguably the more important film because of its technical accomplishments.*

Okay, so it's <u>something technical</u>. That eliminates C) and D)—those have to do with the story, not with technology.*

Choice B), lighting, is a technical aspect, but the passage doesn't say anything about the lighting for *The Last Laugh* anywhere.†

It must be **choice A)**, the method of filming.

Clearly, most of the passage was about "the unchained camera technique". What's that? That's when you move the camera around. That's a method of filming.

Try question 2 on your own!

---

* A "protagonist" is the main character of a story.

† It does use the word "darkly" in line 3, which might sound like it's about lighting. But: a) the context seems to imply it means 'dark' as in *sinister* or *macabre*, not literally dark, and b) *that word is referring to a different movie!* The darkly expressionistic *Nosferatu*.

2. Vocab-in-context Questions

There will usually be two Vocab-in-context questions per passage, 10 in all in the Reading section.

Sometimes a question will ask you the meaning of a specific use of a specific word in the passage. Just like explicit questions, these questions can be done by going back to the passage to see how the word is used.

On these questions, it's *doubly* important to go back and anticipate. Usually, the word they're asking you about has more than one possible meaning—*any* of the chocies *could* be the word's meaning, depending on the context of the sentence. So look up the context! Don't just go by what you think the word means; go back and look at what it means in the sentence.

Let's try some:

Questions 3 and 4 are based on the following passage.

Allegiances during the Civil War were far more complex than a simple dichotomy of North versus South. Some people from Northern states were sympathetic to
Line and fought for the South, and vice versa. Letters from
5 soldiers in battle primarily reveal concerns not of loyalty to country or political ideals but of returning to their homes and providing for their families. Personal conflicts of duty and conscience were not unique to low-level soldiers. President Lincoln himself openly mourned
10 the death of Confederate brigadier general Benjamin Helm, his own brother-in-law.

MAIN IDEA:

_____

3. As used in line 3, "sympathetic to" most nearly means

   ANTICIPATION: _____

   A) supportive of.
   B) affectionate with.
   C) cordial with.
   D) consolatory for.

4. As used in line 8, "unique" most nearly means

   ANTICIPATION: _____

   A) eccentric.
   B) bizarre.
   C) inexplicable.
   D) exclusive.

Vocab-in-Context Questions

3. **Answer: A.**
This question was discussed in the text of this chapter.

4. **Answer: D.**
Let's look at the word in context:

> *Personal conflicts of duty and conscience were not* **unique** *to low-level soldiers.*

Previously, the passage gives soldiers in battle as examples of the complexity of the North/South relationship. Following this sentence, it gives General Lee and President Lincoln as examples of such complexities.
What could we replace the word with? What's our anticipation?

These conflicts were not **only** felt by soldiers: others felt them too.
Which choice means something like "only"? **Choice D), exclusive**.

A)	eccentric	= *strange, unconventional*
B)	bizarre	= *strange, unconventional*
C)	inexplicable	= *cannot be explained, strange*
D)	**exclusive**	= *limited to one party.*

THIS PAGE INTENTIONALLY LEFT BLANK

THIS PAGE INTENTIONALLY LEFT BLANK

Let's try **question 3** together.

3. As used in line 3, "sympathetic to" most nearly means

It asks about a word in line 3, so let's look at those words in the context of the sentence:

> *Some people from Northern states were **sympathetic to** and fought for the South, and vice versa.*

The previous sentence said that the sides were "more complex" than simply "North versus South". So what could we replace this word with? What's our anticipation here?

Look at the other words in the sentence for clues. Besides being sympathetic, they also "fought for" the South. "Fought" is probably too strong for this word, but we clearly want something like **on the same side as**. Maybe **loyal to**. Let's look at our choices:

A)   **supportive of**   ✓ = tending to support
B)   **affectionate with**   ✗ = in love with
C)   **cordial with**   ✗ = polite to
D)   **consolatory for**   ✗ = giving comfort to in a time of grief

Don't be fooled by your existing knowledge of the word "sympathetic". Our sentence has nothing to do with *emotions*. We're talking about fighting in a war here.

Note that Vocab-in-context questions are much more interested in testing the *context* than the *vocab*. Usually, these aren't actually difficult words—they're just words that have more than one meaning. The difficult part is picking which meaning is intended for the sentence.*

Try question 4 on your own!

---

* Your Words in Context subscore is composed almost entirely of Vocab-in-context questions. But these two groups are not always identical. Questions of other types might contribute to your Words in Context score, and some Vocab-in-context questions might not count toward that score.

3. Evidence Questions

Let's look at another passage:

Questions 5 and 6 are based on the following passage.

It is difficult for modern eyes to see why Manet's *Olympia* was so scandalous in 1863. It simply depicts a reclining nude. Hadn't artists been painting nudes for centuries? A museumgoer today might walk past it
Line
5   without looking twice. Two factors contributed to the outrage. The nude, traditionally an ideal of perfect beauty, was here a woman of ill repute, staring at the viewer with cold, accusatory eyes. Furthermore, it was painted in a deliberately flat style that flouted the conventions of
10   artistic representation. These elements seem tame by today's standards, in which provocation is ubiquitous in art, and conventions of representation have been all but flouted out of existence. It was *Olympia*, however, that opened the modernist floodgates for taboo.

MAIN IDEA:

_____

5.   The author suggests that, compared to people in Manet's time, people today
      ANTICIPATION: _____
      A)   prefer art that is more conventional.
      B)   are less concerned with moral values.
      C)   have a different idea of what is offensive.
      D)   are less offended by nudity in art.

6.   Which choice provides the best evidence for the answer to the previous question?
      ANTICIPATION: _____
      A)   Lines 2-4 ("It ... centuries")
      B)   Lines 6-8 ("The nude ... eyes")
      C)   Lines 8-10 ("Furthermore ... representation")
      D)   Lines 10-13 ("These elements ... existence")

Now things are getting weird. Evidence questions are the only ones that will specifically refer to other questions on the test. They usually take the same form, asking you where in the passage you can find evidence for your answer to the previous question.

There will usually be 2 Evidence questions per passage, 10 in all in the Reading section.

This shouldn't really be a problem for us, since our main strategy so far has already been to find actual text in the passage supporting our answers. So in a lot of cases, these questions simply allow us to get two questions at the same time.

Let's start by looking at **question 5**:

5. **The author suggests that, compared to people in Manet's time, people today**

This seems like an explicit question with one problem: there's no line reference. So we're going to have to go find the answer ourselves. Ugh. Fine. This particular passage is only 15 lines long, so it shouldn't be too hard to rummage around for the answer. For longer passages, we'll have our main ideas written in the margins, so we should be able to at least narrow our answer down to a particular. But still, sometimes it's really tough to find the spot in the passage that tells us the answer.

HOWEVER, if we peek ahead to **question 6**, we see an Evidence question:

6. **Which choice provides the best evidence for the answer to the previous question?**

This question is basically asking: *where in the passage can we find the right answer for question 5?* Well, if we didn't know where to find the answer before, now we have four possible candidates!

Our main strategy here is **Backsolve**:

1. Go to the choices and read the lines referred to in each one.
2. Ask yourself, *does this choice answer the previous question?*
3. Once you find a choice that matches, pick it.
4. Then, go back to the previous question and make sure your answer there matches the line reference you chose in the Evidence question.

Let's try it here. Remember, question 5 asked for a choice describing **people today** compared with people in Manet's time. We'll treat that like an anticipation: our choice should have something to do with *people today*.

Now let's go to the choices and find the lines:

A) ✗ **Lines 2-4:** *It simply depicts a reclining nude. Hadn't artists been painting nudes for centuries?*
The first part here describes the painting. The second part notes that nudes should be unremarkable. Neither makes reference to people today.

B) ✗ **Lines 6-8:** *The nude, traditionally an ideal of perfect beauty, was here a woman of ill repute, staring at the viewer with cold, accusatory eyes.*
This still describes the painting. Now it talks about why it looked offensive to people in Manet's time, but still doesn't refer to people today.

C) ✗ **Lines 8-10:** *Furthermore, it was painted in a deliberately flat style that flouted the conventions of artistic representation.*
No different from B). We're talking about the painting and about Manet's time, not our time.

D) ✓ **Lines 10-13:** *These elements seem tame by today's standards, in which provocation is ubiquitous in art, and conventions of representation have been all but flouted out of existence.*
Bingo! Now we're talking about **today's standards.** This sentence says people today think that the things Manet's people found offensive "seem tame".

Now that we've answered question 6, let's go back to question 5 and see which choice matches our line. We can use that line as our anticipation: **people today aren't offended by the same things.**

A) ✗ prefer art that is ~~more conventional~~
False. Today's art is even crazier. Provocation is ubiquitous now.

B) ✗ are less concerned with ~~moral values~~
Random. It doesn't say people today don't have moral values, just that their standards are *different.*

C) ✓ have a different idea of what is offensive
Correct! They aren't offended by the things Manet's people were offended by.

D) ✗ are less ~~offended by nudity~~ in art
Tempting, but too specific. The passage does imply that people today aren't offended by nudity. But there's a subtle problem with this choice. The choice says that *compared to people in Manet's time,* people today "are less offended

by nudity in art." But people in Manet's time *weren't* offended by nudity. The nudity wasn't what shocked people. Line 3-4: artists had been painting nudes for centuries!

Now, it's quite possible that you were able to get question 5 on your own before you even looked at question 6. Perhaps you remembered where to find the line, or you just understood the passage well enough that it was obvious. If so, good for you. That should make the Evidence question easier for you. As you go through the line references, you can use your answer to the previous question as your anticipation.

But when you go through the choices, **make sure your answer to the Evidence question matches your answer to the previous question.** If they don't match, you might have gotten the previous question wrong. If you chose A) for question 5 and D) for question 6, that doesn't match. The line reference in D) in question 6 *specifically contradicts* choice A) in question 5.

Here are a few more thoughts about Evidence questions:*

- Evidence questions do not have to refer to any particular question type. The previous question may be Explicit, Inferential, Strategy, basically anything.

- Evidence questions do not even have to refer to another question at all. Some Evidence questions will ask for evidence of a statement given in the question itself.

- The sentence in the correct answer of an Evidence question *might not be the only evidence* that supports the previous answer. It's very possible that more than one sentence can help you answer the previous question.[†]

For example, on question 5, lines 4-5 say "A museumgoer today might walk past [*Olympia*] without looking twice." That implies that today's viewer *isn't* offended by it; but we know from lines 1-2 that it was "scandalous" in Manet's time. Taken together, that should lead us to C) for question 5.

---

* Your Command of Evidence subscore is composed almost entirely of Evidence questions. But these two groups are not always identical. Questions of other types might contribute to your Command of Evidence score, and some Evidence questions might not count toward that score.

† As we've seen, questions on the Reading test generally appear in order of the lines in the passage they refer to. However, answers to Evidence questions might deviate from that order. So just because question #6 refers to line 50, that doesn't mean Evidence question #8 has to refer to a line after line 50. The answer could be in line 3 for all you know.

4. Main Idea Questions

Often, questions will literally just be looking for the main ideas. We've already seen some examples of that in the last chapter. You of course should be figuring out the main ideas of the paragraphs and the passages *anyway*, so if a question asks about an entire paragraph or the whole passage, you can often use your main ideas as your anticipation.

Questions 7 and 8 are based on the following passage.

> Given the multitude of wastes and toxins that
> permeate modern life, it is a moral imperative for all of
> us to live environmentally friendly lives. If we are not
> attentive to the way we consume, we are in real danger
> *Line*
> 5 of using up precious resources, poisoning our air and
> water, and putting future generations at risk.
> But what exactly does it mean to be environmentally
> friendly? Is it better to use paper towels that kill trees, or
> electric hand dryers that use electricity (which, in most
> 10 areas, means burning coal)? Is it worse to use light bulbs
> that draw a lot of power and must be replaced frequently,
> or long-lasting bulbs that contain deadly mercury?

MAIN IDEA:

_____

7.   The primary purpose of the first paragraph is to

      ANTICIPATION: _____

      A)   detail the damage that toxins can inflict on natural habitats.
      B)   explain how best to live an environmentally friendly life.
      C)   convey the significance of the impact modern life has on environmental concerns.
      D)   foretell the inescapable hazards that modernity will cause for future generations.

8.   The main idea of the second paragraph is

      ANTICIPATION: _____

      A)   daily household decisions have a negligible impact on the environment.
      B)   consuming excess energy is ultimately more detrimental than creating excess waste.
      C)   determining the most environmentally ethical choice can be difficult.
      D)   earlier warnings about the dangers of wastefulness were exaggerated.

Main Idea Questions

7. **Answer: C.**
This question was discussed in the text of this chapter.

8. **Answer: C.**
What's the Main Idea of the second paragraph?
The whole paragraph is just a string of questions. These questions ask which of two options is environmentally better (two options that both seem bad).

Something like: **questions about what's better** would work.
Or even just the first question in line 7: **what does it mean to be environmentally friendly**.

A) False. The first paragraph clearly states that these dangers are a part of our daily lives. The second paragraph gives examples of environmental hazards connected to these decisions.
Negligible = *insignificant*.

B) Random. The example in lines 10-12 compares light bulbs that use excess energy with those that contain hazardous waste. But the passage only raises the question. It does not actually say which is better.

C) **Correct.** This matches our Main Ideas nicely. It's not obvious "what it means to be environmentally friendly". There are questions about it.

D) Random. Nothing in paragraph 2 implies that these concerns aren't important or that dangers don't really exist.

THIS PAGE INTENTIONALLY LEFT BLANK

THIS PAGE INTENTIONALLY LEFT BLANK

Let's look at **question 7** together:

> 7.   **The primary purpose of the first paragraph is to**

This is basically another way of asking: *What's the main idea of the first paragraph?* Your main ideas may vary, but it should be something like what it says in lines 2-3:

> [I]t is a moral imperative for all of us to live environmentally friendly lives.

(Of course, your main idea needn't be that wordy. A simple **environment = important** would suffice.)

Let's look at the choices and see which comes closest:

A)   ✕ ~~detail~~ the damage that toxins can inflict on natural habitats.
      There are no *details* in paragraph 1. It doesn't mention any *specific* toxins, nor the *specific* damage those toxins can harm. It just says some bad things can happen.

B)   ✕ explain ~~how best to live~~ an environmentally friendly life.
      The paragraph does not specify *how* to live environmentally friendly life. (In fact, that's what paragraph 2 is about.)

C)   ✓ convey the significance of the impact modern life has on environmental concerns.
      Correct. "Modern life" is mentioned in line 2. Lines 3-6 talk about its impact on the environment.

D)   ✕ foretell the ~~inescapable~~ hazards that modernity will cause for future generations.
      Too strong. It does say we are "endangering future generations", but it doesn't say that's *inescapable*. Lines 3-6 imply that if we *are* attentive to our consumption, we can *prevent* these hazards.

Try question 8 on your own!

5. Inferential Questions

Sometimes, the answer isn't literally said in the passage, but the answer is a *conclusion* that we can reasonably draw from what is stated in the passage.

Questions 9 and 10 are based on the following passage.

> The so-called "Spanish" flu of 1918 claimed more victims in a single year than the Black Death claimed in a century. However, as the disease raged, most were *Line* unaware of the extent of the destruction. Countries
> 5 fighting in World War I suppressed news of the flu's devastation in order to protect morale. Spain, neutral during the war, was the lone country in Europe producing accurate coverage of the disease's toll, so it got the blame for the outbreak. In reality, scientists now
> 10 believe that the disease likely emerged near Fort Riley, Kansas, where it spread from U.S. military encampments to battlefields worldwide.

MAIN IDEA:

_____

9. The author would most likely agree with which of the following statements?
   ANTICIPATION: _____

   A)   Spain was the only nation to accurately report its war deaths.
   B)   During the Black Death most countries were not significantly affected by war.
   C)   The name of a disease does not necessarily reflect its actual origin.
   D)   The unsanitary conditions of the war allowed the flu to spread more rapidly.

10. It can be inferred from line 4-9 ("Countries... outbreak.") that some people
    ANTICIPATION: _____

    A)   were unhappy with Spain's neutrality during the war.
    B)   tried to prevent Spain from accurately reporting its death toll.
    C)   lacked technology necessary to calculate the death toll of the disease.
    D)   erroneously believed that Spain had higher flu casualties than the rest of Europe.

Inferential Questions

9. **Answer: C.**
    This question was discussed in the text of this chapter.

10. **Answer: D.**
    We have a line reference, so let's go back to lines 4-9:

    > *Countries fighting in World War I suppressed news of the*
    > *flu's devastation in order to protect morale. Spain, neutral*
    > *during the war, was the lone country in Europe producing*
    > *accurate coverage of the disease's toll, so it got the blame for*
    > *the outbreak.*

    Again, tough to anticipate, so let's go right to the choices.

A) Random. Nothing here implies that other countries wanted Spain to join the war.
B) Random. Nothing here implies other countries were actively doing anything at all to Spain.
C) Random. Technology is not mentioned anywhere in the passage.
D) **Correct**. Spain was reporting flu deaths and other countries were not. So it looked like Spain had a much higher death toll. So Spain was blamed for the disease—by having it named "the Spanish flu".

    Even if you don't understand why D) is right, there's *lots* of nonsense in the wrong answers here, so you should be able to eliminate very effectively.

THIS PAGE INTENTIONALLY LEFT BLANK

Let's look at **question 9** together:

> **9.** **The author would most likely agree with which of the following statements?**

Tough one. There's no line reference here, so we can't go back to a specific part of the passage. Let's just go to the choices and see what we can eliminate.

A) ✗ **Spain was the only nation to accurately report ~~its war deaths~~.**

False! This looks good at first, but one word makes it wrong: "*war* deaths". Line 6-7: Spain wasn't fighting in the war! It was neutral. Spain was the only nation to accurately report its *flu* deaths, but that's not what this choice says.

B) ✗ ~~During the Black Death~~ **most countries were not significantly affected by war.**

Random. The Black Death was only mentioned in passing in order to convey the magnitude of the casualty rate for the flu. The passage says nothing about politics during that time.

C) ✓ **The name of a disease does not necessarily reflect its actual origin.**
Correct. This may seem weird at first, but let's break down the choice. Does it talk about a disease? Yes: the Spanish flu. Does the name of that disease reflect its origin? Was the flu from Spain? No, it started in Kansas. That's exactly what the main idea of this paragraph is.

D) ✗ **The ~~unsanitary conditions~~ of the war allowed the flu to spread more rapidly.**

Random. Lines 11-12 do imply that the war helped the disease spread, but the passage does not mention anything about "unsanitary conditions".

With a question like this, it's okay if you don't anticipate perfectly. Some of you might be able to anticipate choice C) based the main idea, but many will not. **That's okay.** Everyone will face multiple situations where you have no idea what the answer to a question is. But even in those situations, **you can do productive work.** Read the choices and eliminate the ones that are obviously false. If you're not sure about one, leave it and come back. But if you can eliminate 1 or 2 choices, you can guess from what's left, and the odds are in your favor.

Try question 10 on your own!

6. Strategy Questions

The trend towards multiculturalism in the academy has been a positive one. Multiculturalism is clearly beneficial to fostering understanding and tolerance. But
Line   multiculturalism is utterly irrelevant to scientific
5   inquiry. There's no such thing as "Western medicine" and "alternative medicine"; there is medicine and there is nonsense. It is important for me to respect your culture's traditions and customs, but not if you're making claims about medicine. When your culture
10   claims that a certain herb relieves headaches, that's an empirical question: either it works or it doesn't. If it doesn't, then I'm not taking the herb. If it works, then you should be able to rigorously prove it. That's science: a formalized way to distinguish truth from
15   rubbish.

MAIN IDEA:

_____

11.   The author uses quotation marks in lines 5-6 in order to

ANTICIPATION: _____

     A)   quote an authority on the topic.
     B)   characterize terms as illegitimate.
     C)   emphasize an important distinction.
     D)   identify expressions that are defined later.

12.   With respect to the rest of the passage, the first two sentences (The trend... tolerance.") serve as a

ANTICIPATION: _____

     A)   clarification of the scope of the author's argument.
     B)   thesis statement for which evidence is later given.
     C)   counterpoint that is refuted by the rest of the passage.
     D)   personal anecdote that demonstrates the author's point.

Strategy Questions

11. Answer: B.
This question was discussed in the text of this chapter.

12. Answer: A.
Let's look at the first two sentences:

> *The trend towards multiculturalism in the academy has been a positive one. Multiculturalism is clearly beneficial to fostering understanding and tolerance.*

These are saying that *multiculturalism is good.*

What about the rest of the passage? Let's look at the next sentence in lines 3-5:

> *But multiculturalism is utterly irrelevant to scientific inquiry.*

That's the main idea of the passage as a whole, that science only cares about what's true, and it doesn't need to respect other cultures if their beliefs are not provably true.

So clearly the first two sentences show **contrast** with the rest of the passage: one says multiculturalism is good, the other that it's bad. Just seeing that is enough to go to the choices and start eliminating.

To go further, what is the difference? **The context.** Multiculturalism is valuable *in general*, but it's irrelevant to the specific context of scientific inquiry.

Let's look at our choices. Remember that our choice should describe the first two sentences.

A) **Correct.** The author's main argument is that multiculturalism is irrelevant to science. But he starts by clarifying that this doesn't mean multiculturalism has *no* value. In certain contexts, it's a very good thing.

B) The opening sentences show contrast with his main thesis and no evidence is given to support them.

C) Tempting, because this choice does show contrast. But the rest of the passage isn't saying that the first two sentences are *false*. It says that *sometimes* multiculturalism is good and other times it isn't. Refute = *to disprove.*

D) This is not a personal anecdote. Anecdote = *a short account of an interesting incident.*

THIS PAGE INTENTIONALLY LEFT BLANK

Most questions ask about the *content* of the passage: what happened, who did what, what does the author say? Some questions, however, ask about the *form* of the passage, about the author's *rhetorical strategies*. That is, why does the author or narrator write what he or she writes?

Let's look at **question 11** together:

11.	The author uses quotation marks in lines 5-6 in order to

So go back to lines 5-6:

> *There's no such thing as "Western medicine" and "alternative medicine"; there is medicine and there is nonsense.*

Here the question is asking about the author's strategy: why he or she made the choices that were made. In this case, the question is why the author put the words "Western medicine" and "alternative medicine" in quotation marks.

It might be tough to understand questions like this. We know the answer will have something to do with those two terms, but it might not be obvious exactly what they mean. So let's just dive into the choices and see what we have.

A) ✗ **quote an authority on the topic.**
What authority? Who? There's no authority mentioned. There's no other person mentioned at all. The passage isn't actually quoting someone.

B) ✓ **characterize terms as illegitimate.**
Correct. The author thinks author thinks *there is no such thing* as Western or alternative medicine. These concepts do not exist.

C) ✗ **emphasize an important distinction.**
Tempting, because this sentence does talk about distinctions, and the author is clearly passionate about the topic. But the quotes are around the terms that the author thinks *don't exist*. The quotes are highlighting a distinction, but they're highlighting the *wrong* distinction. The important distinction is "medicine" versus "nonsense".

D) ✗ **identify expressions that are defined later.**
The author never explicitly defines either one of these terms.

Try question 12 on your own!

7. Tone Questions

Questions 13 and 14 are based on the following passage.

One consequence of the sudden outpouring of precious minerals in the West was an unusual confluence of wealth and wildness. Take, for example,
Line the city of Leadville, Colorado, founded in 1877 after
5 the discovery of huge silver deposits nearby. It was the second most populous city in Colorado and had a renowned opera house that often hosted celebrities, including the writer Oscar Wilde. Yet it was still very much a city of the West. Wilde, who called Leadville
10 "the richest city in the world", spent one evening in a saloon where he reported seeing "the only rational method of art criticism I have ever come across. Over the piano was printed a notice: 'Please do not shoot the pianist. He is doing his best.'"

MAIN IDEA:

_____

13. The tone of the passage as a whole is
ANTICIPATION: _____
A) hostile.
B) nostalgic.
C) objective.
D) reverent.

14. Wilde's statement "the only ... across" (lines 11-12) can best be described as
ANTICIPATION: _____
A) earnest.
B) disrespectful.
C) ironic.
D) analytical.

Tone Questions

13. Answer: C.

This question was discussed in the text of this chapter.

14. Answer: C.

This one is a little more subtle than just happy-face/sad-face. Let's look at the line reference. Wilde saw:

> *"the only rational method of art criticism I have ever come across. Over the piano was printed a notice: 'Please do not shoot the pianist. He is doing his best.'"*

What is the tone of his statement? Is he serious? **No. He's making a joke**. He doesn't *literally* think that it's rational to shoot the pianist. So we want a choice that expresses the jokey-ness.

A)	earnest	= *sincere, serious*
B)	contemptuous	= *disrespectful*
C)	**ironic**	= *intending the opposite of the literal meaning of one's words.*
D)	analytical	= *logical, tending to analyze*

(I'd like to imagine that some students pick choice A) because it's about Oscar Wilde, but somehow I doubt that happens often.)

THIS PAGE INTENTIONALLY LEFT BLANK

We saw with Strategy questions that you may be asked about the form of the passage instead of the content. Similarly, Tone questions ask you about the emotional character of the text. How does the author or narrator *feel* about a particular subject, and what feeling is conveyed in the language? It's the difference between saying "Cats are popular" and "I adore cats!" Tone questions are somewhat infrequent, but they can often throw you for a loop. Let's look at some:

Let's look at **question 13** together:

---

13. The tone of the passage as a whole is

To help you determine the tone of a passage, we here at A-List have spent millions of dollars in research using the most advanced computer analytic technology to develop the **A-List Tone Scale™**:

Let's take a minute to explain this complicated terminology:

 means the author **likes** the subject. This could mean he's arguing *in favor of* something, that he's saying someone is a good person, or just telling a happy anecdote.

 means the author **does not like** the subject. This could mean he's arguing *against* something, that he's giving a warning about something, or that he's telling a sad or angry anecdote.

 means the author **does not have an opinion** about the subject. This means the author is *just presenting the facts* without saying if they're good or bad. Think of this author as a *historian* or a *scientist*. Imagine that he has little glasses and a pipe.*

Where on the A-List Tone Scale™ does the author rank? Does he *like* Leadville? Does he not like Leadville? Most of the passage simply *gives the facts* about Leadville: it was founded in 1877, silver was found nearby, etc. He strays a little bit away from purely factual reporting when he characterizes it as 'wild', but still there's no sense of whether he means that to be good or bad. He has **no opinion** about Leadville. He is the pipe-smoking historian who simply tells us the facts. He is neutral-faced: ☺

Passages can be informative, giving you facts of a situation, persuasive, arguing for a particular position, or narrative, telling a story.

---

* Despite our vast technology budget, it's very difficult to draw a little pipe. You'll have to use your imagination.

A) ☹ **hostile**

✗ Definitely bad.

B) ☹☺ **nostalgic**

✗ That means "bittersweet longing for the past". That's kinda happy, kinda sad. But that's *not* the same as neutral. This means the author feels both happy and sad. That's no good.

C) ☺ **objective**

✓ That means "unbiased". Perfect!

D) ☺ **reverent**

✗ That means "showing a lot of respect". That's too positive. If it was just "respectful", that might be okay, but this word is too strong.

Of course, tone questions can also be more complicated than this. A passage certainly may have a nuanced tone that doesn't fit well into this scale. Or there may be more than one choice that matches the smiley faces you want. But at the very least this is a good place to start. Use it to eliminate some choices and see what's left.

Try question 14 on your own!

8. Data Questions

There's more to passages than just the passage. Every test will have two passages—one science passage and one history/social studies passage—that contain some kind of figure or graph at the end. These figures will show data that is somehow relevant to or strengthens the author's argument.

Graphs can be scary, especially if you're not particularly strong in math or science. But being able to read a chart or graph is not just a skill for scientists. Read any newspaper and you're bound to see some articles that have accompanying graphics. These graphics often color a reader's perception of a story, so being able to understand them is an important element of being a good reader.

The relationship between the figure and the passage can vary:

- The figure may or may not be explicitly mentioned in the passage itself.
- Sometimes the information in the figure is also explicitly stated in the passage, so you don't need to read the figure to answer the question about it.
- Sometimes the figure may be read and interpreted separately from the passage. That means that if you're running out of time you can often jump to figure questions before reading the passage.

But because the focus here is on reading, **you won't need to do actual math on these questions.** You won't have to do any computation, the kind of stuff you might need a calculator for.

There will be numbers, but you'll just be asked to read the numbers and see how they relate to each other. Most of the questions you'll see boil down to two things:

- Understanding what the parts of the graph mean. What are the units, what is being measured, etc.
- Reading the literal or relative values shown. Literal values are just a question of "this bar stops at the number 25." Relative values are a question of "The first bar is bigger than the second bar."

Let's look at an example. A real figure would accompany a full passage. But as we said, Data questions can often be done totally separately from the passage. So let's just look at the figure itself.

There will be 2–4 Data questions for each passage that has a figure, and about 6 total Data questions on each test.

Questions 15 and 16 are based on the following passage and supplementary material

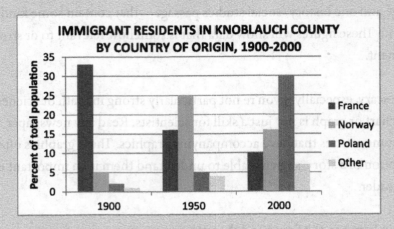

IMMIGRANT RESIDENTS IN KNOBLAUCH COUNTY
BY COUNTRY OF ORIGIN, 1900-2000

15. Which of the following statements is true for the information depicted in the graph?

   A) The percentage of French residents was lowest in 1900.
   B) The percentage of Norwegian residents peaked in 1950.
   C) The percentage of Norwegian residents grew steadily over the years shown.
   D) The percentage of Polish residents grew at a constant rate over the years shown.

16. Which of the following statements about the population of Knoblauch County in 2000 is supported by the graph?

   A) The number of residents from Norway was lower than in 1950.
   B) The residents from France made up 10% of the immigrant population.
   C) The number of residents from Poland increased by 30% since 1950.
   D) There were almost twice as many immigrants from Poland as from Norway.

Let's look at **question 15** together:

15.   Which of the following statements is true for the information depicted in the graph?

This is the most common type of Data question. It just asks you to go through the choices and see which one is true.

First, let's look at the figure. The title tells us we're talking about immigrants who live in Knoblauch County. The vertical axis tells us each bar represents the percentage of total residents from each country in each year. It shows three different years' worth of data: 1900, 1950, and 2000. For each of these years, it has data for four different groups of people: from France, from Norway, from Poland, and from all other countries.

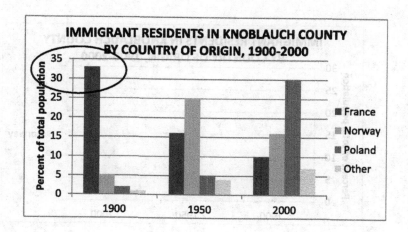

So, for example, the first bar shows the percent of the population in 1900 who were from France. The bar stops between 30 and 35, so call it 33. Therefore, that bar tells us that in 1900, 33% of the total population of Knoblauch County immigrated from France.

OK, let's look at the choices. As we discuss each choice we'll reproduce the graph but only highlight the relevant bars.

A)   ✗ **The percentage of French residents was lowest in 1900.**

        False! This is backwards. 1900 clearly has the highest bar for France, around 33% versus 15% for 1950 and 10% for 2000. Of course, we don't need the actual values here—we can clearly see that it's much higher in 1900.

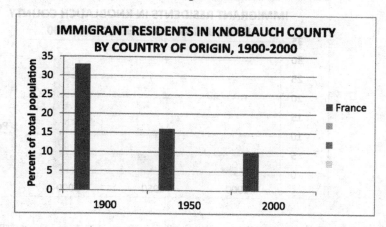

B)   ✓ **The percentage of Norwegian residents peaked in 1950.**

        Correct! The Norway bar was clearly highest in 1950, around 25%, compared with 5% in 1900 and 16% in 2000.

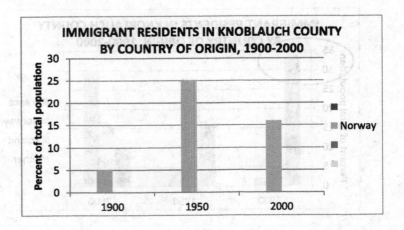

IMMIGRANT RESIDENTS IN KNOBLAUCH COUNTY
BY COUNTRY OF ORIGIN, 1900-2000

C)   × **The percentage of Norwegian residents grew steadily over the years shown.**

False! As we just saw in choice B), from 1900 to 1950 the percentage shot up from 5% to 25%. But from 1950 to 2000, it went back down from 25% to 16%. Again, you don't need the actual values here. You can see how the bars go up and down.

D)   × **The percentage of Polish residents grew at a constant rate over the years shown.**

False! The percentage of residents from Poland did rise over the years, but not at a constant rate. From 1900 to 1950 it barely blipped up, from 2% to 5%. Then from 1950 to 2000 it skyrocketed up to 30%.

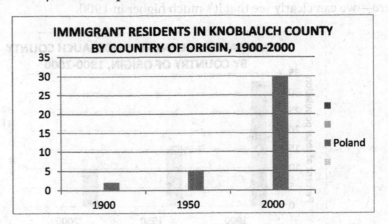

IMMIGRANT RESIDENTS IN KNOBLAUCH COUNTY
BY COUNTRY OF ORIGIN, 1900-2000

Try question 16 on your own!

You know what, I'm feeling lucky. Let's look at **question 16** together, too:

> **16.   Which of the following statements about the population of Knoblauch County in 2000 is supported by the graph?**

We already talked about the graph, so let's dive into the choices. This question is a bit trickier, so let's tread carefully:

A)   ✗ ~~The number of residents~~ from Norway was lower than in 1950.

>   Tempting! As we saw in question 15, the bar for Norway was lower in 2000 (16%) than in 1950 (25%). Great, let's pick it?

>   NO. What do the bars represent here? What does the label on the vertical axis say? It *doesn't* say "number of residents"—it says **percent of total residents**. All we know is that the percentage is lower in 2000; we don't know if the actual number of residents was lower.

>   But wait—doesn't having a lower percentage mean there were also fewer people? Not necessarily! It might be true, it might not. The missing question here is: *how many people live in Knoblauch County?* What if the population of Knoblauch county *doubled* between 1950 and 2000? What if it *skyrocketed:*

	1950	2000
Population of Knoblauch County	100,000	1,000,000
Percentage born in Norway	25%	16%
Number of Norwegian residents	25,000	160,000

>   The point is not that you have to come up with these numbers. The point is that *we don't know*. The question asks for a choice that is "supported by the graph," and the graph *does not say anything* about the actual number of residents. And we know that by just reading the vertical axis.

B)   ✗ The residents from France made up 10% ~~of the immigrant population.~~

>   False! Again, this may be tempting because the France bar in 2000 says "10". And it is a percent. Great, let's pick it?

>   NO. Again, read the axis: it says percent of **total residents**, not percent of

the immigrant population. So 10% out of all the people in Knoblauch county were born in France, not just out of those people who were immigrants.*

C) ✗ ~~The number of residents from Poland increased by~~ 30% since 1950.

False! Once again, we do see the bar from Poland does equal 30%. But the bar does not show percent increase. It just shows the percent of total residents.

D) ✓ **There were almost twice as many immigrants from Poland as from Norway.**
Correct. You can tell this by just looking at the bars. The Poland bar looks about twice as tall as the Norway bar. You can also tell by the values: Norway is around 16% and Poland is 30%, which is "almost twice as many." Not exactly, but almost. **Let's pick it.**

"But wait," you say. "You said we don't know anything about the number of immigrants, so how can we know there are twice as many?"

Ah, good question. It's true we don't know how many actual residents there are. But this choice is asking us to compare two groups *from the same year.* No matter how many total residents there are in the year 2000—be it 100,000, 1 million, or whatever—30% of a number will always be twice as big as 15% of that same number.

	1950	2000
Population of Knoblauch County	100,000	1,000,000
Percentage born in Norway	25%	16%
Number of Norwegian residents	25,000	160,000

the point is not that you have to come up with these numbers. The point is that we don't know. The question asks for a choice that is "supported by the graph," and the graph does *not* say anything about the actual number of residents. And we know that by just reading the vertical axis.

---

* We can actually tell what percent of the immigrants the French make up. If we add all the bars together, we get 10 + 16 + 30 + 7 = 63. That means 63% of the residents were immigrants from somewhere. France made up 10 out of 63, which is about 16% of the immigrants. We don't need to actually do this, though. Do not do this.

9. Double Passages

Each test will contain one double passage. Here, you'll see two passages on a similar topic followed by questions on both of them. Note that the double passage is not twice as long; the two parts of the double together will be about the same length as a single passage.

For the most part, questions on double passages are just like questions on single passages. There will usually be line references, you'll need main ideas, etc. The main difference is that you'll see some **questions on both passages**—questions that ask you to directly compare or contrast the two.

Because they give you both passages upfront, you may be tempted to read both passages before you start the questions. Do NOT do that.

The questions about the double passage are roughly ordered like this:

1. Questions about Passage 1
2. Questions about Passage 2
3. Questions about Both Passages

If you read both passages upfront, you'll read Passage 1, then read Passage 2, then try to answer questions on 1—but you just read 2, so you get them mixed up in your head. And we promise you: the wrong answers on these questions are banking on that. There'll be questions about Passage 1 that have choices describing Passage 2.

Instead, do this:

1. **Read Passage 1.** Just like you would with any other passage.
2. **Answer the questions about Passage 1.** Usually the first few questions will be *only* about Passage 1. That way, when you're doing the questions about Passage 1, it's still fresh in your mind. Plus, you haven't even *looked* at 2 yet, so you're not confused about which is which. As soon as you get to a question about something you haven't read yet…
3. **Go back and read Passage 2.** Just like you would with any other passage.
4. **Answer the rest of the questions.** There will be some *only* about 2, then some about *both* of them together.

Here are a few tips to keep in mind:

- Questions about Passage 1 are *usually* first, but there may be some questions on both passages first. It's easy to tell which passage a question is asking about—just look at the line references in the question. If you see a question about both, skip it and come

> The questions are usually fairly evenly distributed, so you will have 3-4 questions in each of these three categories.

back to it after you read Passage 2. Questions about only Passage 1 will always come before questions about only Passage 2.

- When you do read Passage 2, think about what you read in Passage 1. Think about how they agree and how they disagree. You *know* you'll be asked questions that directly compare and contrast the passages, so you might as well start thinking about it now. Questions that ask about both passages often rely on the main ideas of the passages, so make sure to look for them.

- Often, it's pretty easy to see that difference between the passages. It can sometimes be boiled down to a simple disagreement: Passage 1 thinks X is good, Passage 2 thinks X is bad. But don't assume it will be that easy. The connection between them can sometimes be more subtle.

Let's look at a sample double passage so we can see some examples of **Questions about Both Passages:**

THIS PAGE INTENTIONALLY LEFT BLANK

Questions 17-20 are based on the following passages.

Passage 1

There is unquestionably a great deal of stupidity, incoherence, and bile on the Internet, feelings that can be deleterious to actual constructive communication.

Line Granted, this is not a new phenomenon—people have
5 been angry and inarticulate since the dawn of civilization. But the anonymity of the Internet makes it easier for that unpleasant side to be unleashed. In the real world, social interactions are governed by rules that prevent people from acting inappropriately, for fear of
10 embarrassment or opprobrium. But people can wander online freely without anyone knowing anything about them. This gives them a total freedom of expression that allows them to write whatever is on their minds, no matter how ugly, without fear of repercussion.

Passage 2

15 Some people list the growth of the online news as a contributing cause of the current wave of sensationalism in journalism, in which objective reporting and civil debate have been replaced by shouting, name-calling, and irresponsible rumor-mongering. But while the
20 Internet certainly does its share of those things, it also has become an important antidote to 24-hour news stations. Despite the vast number of available channels, television news is still controlled by a small number of corporations. But because anyone with a computer can
25 start a web page, the Internet encourages "citizen journalism". Whereas in the past the public was forced to blindly accept media accounts of news stories, now anyone can start a website to fact-check, challenge, and expose fraudulent politicians or lazy journalism.

MAIN IDEAS FOR PASSAGES:

Passage 1: _____

Passage 2: _____

THIS PAGE INTENTIONALLY LEFT BLANK

Double Passages

17. Answer: A.
Explanation given in the text of the student edition.

18. Answer: B.
We want something that Passage 2 talks about and Passage 1 does not talk about.

A) *Both* passages discuss people's behavior. Passage 1, line 13: they "write whatever is on their minds". Passage 2, line 25-26, the Internet "encourages 'citizen journalism'".

B) Correct. Passage 2 talks about how the Internet be an antidote to television news (line 21). Television is another medium. Passage 1 does not mention any other media.

C) Random. Passage 2 does say that "anyone can start a website" (line 24-25), but it does not mention the technology that allows that to happen.

D) Random. This is just a mishmash of buzzwords from both passages. Passage 1 mentions social rules in lines 8-10, and Passage 2 mentions objective journalism in line 17. But put together, this choice is random nonsense.

19. Answer: C.
We want something that *both* passages say.

A) Only Passage 1. Passage 1 implies this in lines 7-10 (if the Internet is more free, behavior in the real world is more restricted). But Passage 2 doesn't mention anything like this.

B) Only Passage 2. Passage 1 doesn't mention news sites.

C) Correct. Passage 1, lines 1-3 "stupidity, incoherence, and bile". Passage 2 has an overall positive attitude toward the Internet, but it does admit that the Internet "does its share" of "shouting, name-calling, and irresponsible rumor-mongering" (lines 18-19)

D) Only Passage 1. Passage 2 admits there is unpleasantness on the Internet, but it does not say that the Internet *caused* that unpleasantness. In fact, it does say that there are positive things on the Internet, so certainly not everyone online is "incoherent and belligerent"

It may be tough for some kids to distinguish between C) and D) here. That's okay. As long as they get it down to two choices, they should guess from what's left.

20. Answer: C.
Go back to Passage 1, lines 12-14:
> *This gives them a total freedom of expression that allows them to write whatever is on their minds, no matter how ugly, without fear of repercussion.*

So the freedom of expression allows anyone to say whatever they want. Does Passage 2 talk about anyone saying anything whatever they want? How about starting at line 24:
> *But because* **anyone** *with a computer can start a web page, the Internet encourages "citizen journalism". Whereas in the past the public was forced to blindly accept media accounts of news stories, now* **anyone** *can start a website to fact-check, challenge, and expose fraudulent politicians or lazy journalism*

So this same freedom allows people to say constructive things, not just ugly things.

It may be tough to anticipate this, so let's look at our choices. Remember: our choice will say what *Passage 2* thinks about "freedom of expression".

A) False. Citizen journalism is *an example of* the freedom to say what you want. Undermine = *to weaken*.

B) Random. Passage 2 doesn't say anything about people revealing their identities.

C) Correct. Because people can write what they want, they are free to criticize "lazy journalism".

D) False. Passage 2 thinks the Internet is good. Belligerent = *eager to fight*.

17. Which of the following best describes the relationship between the two passages?

A) Passage 1 discusses a negative aspect of the Internet, while Passage 2 focuses on a positive effect.

B) Passage 1 praises television news channels, while Passage 2 denounces them.

C) Passage 1 argues that the public is objective and civil, while Passage 2 says they are irresponsible.

D) Passage 1 condemns the Internet as a whole, while Passage 2 claims that only online news is irresponsible.

18. Unlike Passage 1, Passage 2 is primarily concerned with

A) the effect of the Internet on people's behavior.

B) the relationship between the Internet and other media.

C) the technology that allows anyone to start a website.

D) social rules that govern objective journalism.

19. The authors of both passages agree that

A) social interactions in the real world are more repressive than social interactions online.

B) online news sites can make constructive contributions to society.

C) some websites contain material that is excessively unpleasant or hostile.

D) the Internet makes people incoherent and belligerent.

20. The author of Passage 2 would likely argue that the "freedom of expression" mentioned in line 12 of Passage 1 is

A) undermined by people who practice citizen journalism.

B) nonexistent when Internet users reveal their identities.

C) the phenomenon that allows the public to challenge claims by the media.

D) the main reason people become more irrational and belligerent.

First let's get the main ideas of the two passages. Yours may vary, but remember to *keep them short*:

> Passage 1: Internet is ugly (because of anonymity).
> Passage 2: Internet can be good (by encouraging citizen journalism).

Now let's take a look at **question 17** together:

17. **Which of the following best describes the relationship between the two passages?**

Notice that each choice here contains two statements—the first about Passage 1 and the second about Passage 2. We can eliminate choices one passage at a time. Let's go through and *only read the first half of each choice*. If the first half doesn't accurately describe Passage 1, we'll eliminate it.

A) ✓ **Passage 1 discusses a negative aspect of the Internet,**
Sure. Passage 1 definitely discusses "stupidity, incoherence, and bile on the Internet" (lines 1-2).

B) ✗ **Passage 1 praises ~~television news channels~~,**
Random. Passage 1 doesn't mention television news channels at all.

C) ✗ **Passage 1 argues that the public is ~~objective and civil~~,**
False. It says "people have been angry and inarticulate since the dawn of civilization" (lines 4-6).

D) ✓ **Passage 1 condemns the Internet as a whole,**
Sure. Lines 1-3 list "stupidity" and other "deleterious" things, and the passage only refers to "the Internet", not to any specific parts of the Internet.

Great! Right away, we eliminated two choices without even looking at Passage 2!

Now we'll just read the second half of each choice and see which accurately describe Passage 2. Remember: we already eliminated two choices, so we'll only check the remaining ones, A) and D):

A) ✓ **... while Passage 2 focuses on a positive effect.**
Sure. Passage 2 says websites can "expose fraudulent politicians or lazy journalism" (line 29).

D) ✗ ... while Passage 2 claims only online news is ~~irresponsible~~.

> *False*. Passage 2 *likes* online news. It's "an important antidote to the 24-hour cable news stations" (lines 21-22).

So **choice A)** is our answer.

As we've seen before on many different types of questions, if we eliminate *systematically*, we can do the question *quickly*. And even if we aren't sure of the right answer, we can easily eliminate some wrong answers.

Try questions 18-20 on your own!

READING FLOW CHART

Here's a quick outline of what you should be doing on pretty much every Reading question.

The Passage
- Read quickly and get the **main ideas** of the passage, paragraph by paragraph.
- To find the main idea, just ask yourself: **what's it about?**
- If you're not sure what the main idea is, check the **first and last sentences** of the paragraph.
- Don't spend too much time. Don't overanalyze. If you're not sure, move on.

The Question
- Read the question, **ignore the choices**.
- *Is the question about a large chunk of text or a specific line or sentence?*
  - <u>Chunk</u>: get the **main idea** of the chunk.
  - <u>Line</u>: go back to the line reference and read **the whole sentence**.
- *Can you answer the question with what you just learned?*
  - <u>Yes</u>: that's your **anticipation**. Go to the choices.
  - <u>No</u>: read the **sentence before** and/or the **sentence after** to understand the context.
- *Now can you answer the question?*
  - <u>Yes</u>: that's your **anticipation**. Go to the choices.
  - <u>No</u>: go to **elimination**.

The Choices

Anticipation

- How many choices match your anticipation?
  - <u>None</u>: Your anticipation wasn't good enough. Go back to the passage and try again, or go to elimination.
  - <u>One</u>: **That's your answer! Pick it!**
  - <u>Two</u>:
    - **Eliminate** the ones that fail.
    - Ask yourself: what's the difference between the choices?
    - Go back and check the line again to see which is better.
    - If you can't decide, **guess one**.
  - <u>Three or four</u>: Go to Elimination.

Elimination

- Go through the choices looking for wrong answers.
  - Don't look for the right answer, **look for the wrong answers**.
  - **Work quickly**. If you can't eliminate a choice, skip it and come back to it later.
  - As you eliminate, **cross out** the words that make a choice wrong.
- Eliminate for three reasons:
  - Is the choice *mentioned* in the passage? If not, it's **random**.
  - Is the choice *true* according to the passage? If not, it's **false**.
  - Does the choice *answer the question*? If not, it's **irrelevant**.
- After you eliminate, *how many choices do you have left?*
  - <u>None</u>: You eliminated all of them! Try again. Don't eliminate choices you don't understand.
  - <u>One</u>: **That's your answer! Pick it!**
  - <u>Two</u>:
    - **Eliminate** the ones that fail.
    - Ask yourself: what's the difference between the choices?
    - Go back and check the line again to see which is better.
    - If you can't decide, **guess one**.
  - <u>Three or four</u>:
    - You didn't eliminate enough. Run through them again and look more closely.
    - If you really can't eliminate anything else, **guess one** and move on.

READING QUESTION TYPE SUMMARY
Here are some question types you will encounter on the Reading test

1. Explicit Questions

- These questions ask what the passage literally said. If there's a line reference, go back to the passage and anticipate. If not, use your main ideas to help you find it.

2. Vocab-in-context Questions

- Don't just define the word. Anticipate for these just like for Explicit questions.
- Use the context of the sentence to anticipate the meaning of the word.

3. Evidence Questions

- These questions ask you to find a line reference to justify your answer to the previous question.
- It's often helpful to do Evidence questions together with the questions they refer to questions they refer to (**Backsolve**):
  - Go back to the passage and check the line references.
  - See if the lines answer the previous question.

4. Main Idea Questions

- If a question asks about a full paragraph or the entire passage, use your main ideas as your anticipation.

5. Inferential Questions

- These questions ask about things that the passage doesn't literally say, but that must be true based on what the passage does say.
- While sometimes they are easy to anticipate for, Inferential questions are often more likely to be solved by elimination than by anticipation because the answer isn't literally stated in the passage.

6. Strategy Questions

- These questions ask why the author wrote the passage the way that he or she did. They often discuss the author's rhetorical strategies

7. Tone Questions

- These questions often come down to whether the author has a positive, negative, or neutral attitude towards the subject.

8. Data Questions

- Some Data questions will ask you to lookup values that appear on the figure.
- Some Data questions will ask you to understand the meaning of the values in the figure.

9. Double Passages

- Do the passages separately.
  - Read the passage 1 and do the questions about passage 2.
  - Then read passage 2 and do the questions about passage 2 and then questions about both passages.

READING EXERCISE 2

Now you're ready to do the following passages. For each passage, **write the main ideas** *for the passage and/or for individual paragraphs within the passage. For each question, anticipate whenever possible, and* **write your anticipation** *in the space provided.*

Questions 1-10 are based on the following passage.

This passage is adapted from Natsume Soseki, *Botchan*, originally published in 1906. The narrator has left Tokyo to become a math teacher in a small town.

I had been to the school the previous day, so I had a good idea of how to get there, and after turning a few corners I came to the front gate. On my way to the
Line school, I met a number of the students in cotton drill
5 uniforms coming through this gate. Some of them were taller than I and looked much stronger. When I thought of teaching these people, I suddenly felt an odd sort of uneasiness. When I arrived, my card was taken to the principal, and I was quickly ushered to his room. With a
10 scant mustache, dark skin, and big eyes, the principal looked a bit like a badger. He studiously assumed an air of superiority, and, saying he would like me to do my best, handed me a certificate of appointment stamped with a big, official seal. He said he would introduce me
15 to all my fellow teachers, and I was to present the certificate to each one of them. What a bother! It would be far better to post it up in the teachers' room instead of going through such a monkey process.
  The other teachers would not arrive until the first
20 bugle was sounded, and there was still plenty of time. The principal looked at his watch and said that he would acquaint me with the school soon enough, but now he would discuss general matters with me. With that, he started a long lecture on the spirit of education. For a
25 while I listened to him with my mind half somewhere else, but about halfway through his lecture, I began to realize that I would soon be in a bad fix. I could not do, by any means, all he expected of me. He expected that besides teaching technical knowledge, I had to make
30 myself an example to the students, to become an object of admiration for the whole school and to exert my moral influence in order to become a real educator, or something ridiculously high-sounding. No man with such admirable qualities would come to this faraway place for
35 only 40 yen* a month! Like most people, if I get angry, I'm likely to get into a fight. According to what the principal said, however, I could hardly open my mouth or even take a stroll around the place. If they wanted me to fill such an onerous post, they should have told me all
40 that before. I hate lying, so I would have to face up to the fact that I had been cheated and get out of this mess like a man, there and then.
  "I cannot do everything you want me to," I told the principal. "I therefore return this appointment."

45 I shoved back the certificate. The principal blinked his badger-like eyes and stared at me. Then he said, "I am only talking about my ideal for you. I know well that you cannot do it all, so don't worry," and he laughed. If he knew it so well already, why on earth did he scare me
50 with that big speech?
  Meanwhile, the bugle sounded. The teachers would be ready now, the principal said, and I followed him to the teachers' room. In a spacious rectangular room, they sat each before a table lined along the walls. When I
55 entered the room, they all turned and stared at me in unison, as if my face were a show. Then, as per instructions, I introduced myself and showed the certificate to each one of them. Most of them stood and made a slight bow of acknowledgment. But some of the
60 more painfully polite ones actually took the certificate, read it, and respectfully returned it to me. It was all like a cheap performance at a play! When I came to the fifteenth, the gym teacher, I got impatient at repeating the same old thing over and over. They each had to do it
65 only once, but I had to do it fifteen times. They ought to have some sympathy.

* the currency of Japan.

MAIN IDEAS:

Paragraph 1: _____

Paragraph 2: _____

Paragraph 3-4: _____

Paragraph 5: _____

1

The narrator indicates he is concerned that the students are

ANTICIPATION: _____

A) morally irresponsible.
B) academically advanced.
C) overly traditional.
D) physically imposing.

CONTINUE ▶

Passage I: Fiction

[This passage was taken from the novel *Botchan* by Natsume Soseki. A very funny book, highly recommended.]

MAIN IDEAS: (Yours may vary)

Par. 1: New teacher, first day of school
Par. 2: meeting w/ principal. Narr. upset: principal asking too much.
Par. 3-4: Principal not really asking too much.
Par. 5: Stupid ceremony with teachers.

Main ideas can be tricky for fiction passages like this one, particularly for sections that have dialogue. Don't be too picky. You don't have to literally do every single paragraph. The goal is to just get a sense of what the passage is about; in the case of fiction passages, that just means what literally happens in the story. Don't dawdle, and don't get caught up on interpretation. If you're not sure what's going on, just move on.

Don't forget to read the italicized intro, too. It gives important background info, especially for fiction passages.

1. Answer: D.

Confused? **Peek ahead at question 2** to get some potential sources of evidence.

The only time he interacts with students in this passage is at the beginning of the first paragraph. Starting at line 5:

> *Some of them were taller than I and looked much stronger. When I thought of teaching these people, I suddenly felt an odd sort of uneasiness.*

That's clearly **D): physically imposing**. All other choices are random.

2. Answer: C.

Let's Backsolve! Check these line references and see which one has to do with question 1. We're looking for the narrator's *concern* about the *students*.

A) Lines 1-3: No! He's just giving directions. No mention of students. Possibly the most boring sentence in the passage.

B) Lines 3-5: Okay, now we meet the students. But so what? They're just walking to school. Is the narrator concerned about their cotton uniforms?

C) **Lines 5-6: Correct.** *Some of them were **taller** than I and looked much **stronger**.* They're big. That's why he's worried.

D) Lines 11-14: This is the principal looking at the narrator's card. There are no students here.

Note that lines 5-6 don't actually say that the author is concerned. That comes next in lines 6-8 ("an odd sort of uneasiness"). But question 1 asks *why* the author is concerned, and lines 5-6 tell us the source of his unease.

3. Answer: A.

Let's go back to line 11:

> *He studiously **assumed** an air of superiority, and, saying he would like me to do my best, handed me a certificate of appointment stamped with a big, official seal.*

So he assumed "an air of superiority". This means that he changed his appearance to look superior. Our anticipation could be something like **took on** or **gained**. Let's look at the choices.

A) **acquired   Correct.** He took on that look of superiority.
B) inferred   = *to make a conclusion*. Makes no sense in the context
C) seized   = *grab violently*. There's no violence here.
D) imitated   This might be tempting because of the narrator's disdain towards the situation, particularly in the context of the last paragraph where he calls the ceremony a "cheap performance". But it's not quite right here. Imitate means more literally copying someone or something. Even if his air of superiority is unjustified, there's no indication that he's *copying* anyone.

Vocab-in-context questions often take into account *nuance*. You may have two choices that mean very similar things, but one of them just… isn't quite right for this sentence. There may be other words similar to imitate that would work better here ("feign" might be good), but imitate just isn't the right word.

4. Answer: D.

Confused? Peek ahead at question 5 to get some potential sources of evidence.

This issue comes up in the whole second paragraph, but let's just start with a few lines following line 27:

> *…I would soon be in a bad fix. **I could not do, by any means, all he expected of me.** He expected that besides teaching technical knowledge, I had to make myself an example to the students, to become an object of admiration for the whole school and to exert my moral influence in order to become a real educator, or something ridiculously high-sounding.*

He's worried **he can't satisfy the moral requirements of the job**.

The paragraph is a bit dense, so it can be tough to see. You can also simply use your Main Idea for this paragraph as your anticipation. But because it's so dense, kids might have trouble getting the Main Idea in the first place.

However, we can still get this by eliminating. Let's look at the choices:

A) This is tempting, but it's *too strong*. The narrator doesn't say that he doesn't possess *any* moral qualities; only that the principal is demanding *too much*. (In fact, later in the paragraph he says he "hates lying", which certainly could be considered a moral quality.)

B) False. That's not what he's got a problem with. It's the stuff *besides* the technical knowledge.

C) Random. He thinks the principal misrepresented the qualifications. He himself hates lying. (line 40)

D) **Correct**. This may sound weird or random, but this is exactly what we're looking for. See lines 35-36 for more on how his actual lifestyle doesn't meet these moral requirements.

5. Answer: C.

Let's Backsolve! Check these line references and see which one has to do with question 4. We're looking for a reason that the author cannot perform the tasks.

A) Lines 16-18: Here he's just complaining about having to present his certificate. He *can* do that—he just doesn't want to.

B) Lines 28-33: Getting close. This is a list of *what* the principal is asking him to do, that he expects the narrator to be a good moral person. But nothing here tells us why the narrator can't do them

C) Lines 35-38: Correct. He says he tends to fight when he's angry, but the principal's rules wouldn't allow it. He can't perform the tasks because he fights a lot.

D) Lines 38-40: This is just him complaining more, saying they should have told him about the requirements ear

6. Answer: B.

Go back. Lines 33-35:

> *No man with such admirable qualities would come to this faraway place for only 40 yen a month!*

So if the narrator *had* the admirable qualities, he wouldn't have taken such a low-paying job. The word "only" is our clue that 40 yen a month is not a lot of money.

A) Random. It doesn't mention how much the principal is paid.

B) Correct. If the principal wants someone with admirable qualities, he needs to pay more.

C) Random. You might be tempted by this because of the mention of "this faraway place". But that's an unjustified jump to conclusions: he doesn't mention of the cost of the trip at all. (It's more likely that he mentions the distance simply because he's far from home.)

D) Tempting, perhaps. But it doesn't say that *no one* possesses these qualities; just that if you did, you wouldn't take such a low-paying job.

7. Answer: D.

Let's go back:

> *"I cannot do everything you want me to," I told the principal. "I therefore return this appointment."*

He's saying that he can't take **the job.**

A) promotion:
This is sort of like a job. But a promotion is when you get a better job within the same company. This is the narrator's first time at this school, so it is not a promotion.

B) equipment:
The only object in this scene is the certificate, and that is not equipment. Equipment is a *tool,* something you use to do your job. You don't do anything with a certificate.

C) interview:
He's returning the interview? What does that mean? Also, he's not being interviewed here; he already has the job.

D) assignment:
Correct. An assignment is a kind of job, and it has the same connotation as "appointment", of being given the job by someone else.

There's a sense here that by "appointment" he might be referring to the literal certificate, mostly because the very next line says "I shoved back the certificate." That's certainly plausible, but then none of the choices would fit. And of course, "appointment" does not literally mean "certificate".

8. Answer: D.

Let's see what the principal does:

> *The principal blinked his badger-like eyes and **stared at me**. Then he said, "I am only talking about my ideal for you. I know well that you cannot do it all, so don't worry," and **he laughed**.*

First he stared silently, then he laughed. Our two-word answer choice should correspond to these two reactions.

It may not be clear what the staring means, but laughing is easy. The second word must have something to do with *laughing*. Only C) "mirth" and D) "amusement" could work. Eliminate A) and B): they have no laughing words.

The first word in the choice should correspond to the staring. Let's see what's left:

C) "elation" is related to *elated*, meaning "filled with delight". This could cause laughing, but not staring and blinking.

D) "perplexity" means "confusion". That could certainly be staring and blinking. **Choice D)** is our answer.

There might be some mystery words here, so you may not be able to eliminate as quickly as we did. But everyone should at least be able to eliminate A) and B) and guess from what's left.

9. Answer: B.

The narrator's problem in this scene is that this is a stupid pointless ceremony that nobody really cares about.

Look back, for example, at lines 16-18, when he's first told about the ceremony:

> *What a bother! It would be far better to post [the certificate] up in the teachers' room instead of going through such a monkey process.*

So who are the "polite ones"? Line 58+:

> *Most of [the teachers] stood and made a slight bow of acknowledgment. But some of the more painfully polite ones actually took the certificate, read it, and respectfully returned it to me. It was all like a cheap performance at a play!*

Most teachers moved the ceremony along quickly. But some tried to be polite by really putting their heart into it and actually *reading* the certificate. But it's all just a "cheap performance". This is more detail than you might need. Let's just dive into the choices.

A) *No.* The problem is that they *don't* really care. It's all just a performance.

B) Correct. They were irritating because they read the certificate *as if* they really cared what it said. But it was just a performance.

C) Random. It's not *literally* a play. They're just reading his certificate.

E) He doesn't just think they're *polite*; he thinks they're *painfully* polite. That's bad.

10. Answer: A.

This is basically the same question as number 9! This happens all the time—there will be multiple questions about the same lines. Use the things we learned in doing previous questions to answer this question.

The narrator is complaining that it's a **fake** ceremony that no one really cares about. That's choice A).

2

Which choice provides the best evidence for the answer to the previous question?

ANTICIPATION: _____

A) Lines 1-3 ("I had . . . gate.")
B) Lines 3-5 ("On my . . . gate.")
C) Lines 5-6 ("Some . . . stronger.")
D) Lines 11-14 ("He studiously . . . seal.")

3

As used in line 11, the word "assumed" most nearly means

ANTICIPATION: _____

A) acquired.
B) inferred.
C) seized.
D) imitated.

4

The narrator believes he cannot perform the tasks required because he

ANTICIPATION: _____

A) does not possess any admirable moral qualities.
B) is unqualified to teach the technical knowledge required for his class.
C) has lied about his qualifications for the position.
D) thinks the demands of his position are incompatible with his lifestyle.

5

Which choice provides the best evidence for the answer to the previous question?

A) Lines 16-18 ("It would . . . process.")
B) Lines 28-33 ("He expected . . . high-sounding.")
C) Lines 35-38 ("Like . . . place.")
D) Lines 38-40 ("If they . . . before.")

6

It can be inferred from lines 33-35 ("No man...month") that the narrator believes

ANTICIPATION: _____

A) the principal is paid more than the other teachers at the school.
B) his compensation is not appropriate for the principal's expectations.
C) most admirable people cannot afford the cost of the trip to this school.
D) it is impossible for anyone to meet the principal's moral expectations.

7

As used in line 44, the word "appointment" most nearly means

ANTICIPATION: _____

A) promotion.
B) equipment.
C) interview.
D) assignment.

8

In the fourth paragraph (lines 45-50), the principal reacts to the narrator with

ANTICIPATION: _____

A) disappointment and shame.
B) anger and resentment.
C) elation and mirth.
D) perplexity and amusement.

9

The narrator apparently believes that the "polite ones" (line 60) are

ANTICIPATION: _____

A) overly concerned about the narrator's qualifications.
B) not actually interested in what the certificate says.
C) not adequately prepared for the performance.
D) courteous in accepting the new teacher.

10

The reference to "a cheap performance at a play" (line 61-62) serves to emphasize the

ANTICIPATION: _____

A) artificiality of the situation.
B) narrator's lack of moral qualities.
C) importance of ceremony in Japanese culture.
D) teachers' need for better theatrical training.

CONTINUE

Questions 11-21 are based on the following passages

The following passages discuss the decrease in the number of different languages spoken around the world. Passage 1 is from an article about language death. Passage 2 is from a book about linguistic fieldwork written by a British linguist.

Passage 1

On October 7, 1992, Tevfik Esenc died peacefully in his sleep at the age of 88, and with him died an entire language. His gravestone memorializes him as "the last person able to speak the language they called Ubykh".

Line 5 Imagine if this were to happen to your language, if all the vocabulary, the sounds and poetry, the intricate grammars of English simply died quietly overnight. The phenomenon is called language death and unfortunately it is all too common. Some sociolinguists estimate that a

10 language dies every two weeks. This means that, of the 6,000 languages that are currently spoken throughout the world, half will be extinct within a century.

How does this happen? When people hear the term "language death", they often think of "dead languages",

15 imagining lost civilizations, and ruins filled with broken stone pillars. True, there are thousands of ancient languages no longer in use, but most didn't simply vanish—they evolved into other languages over the course of hundreds of years. Latin didn't "die"; it turned

20 into French, Italian, and other Romance languages. Language death, however, is a different phenomenon. It's happening now and it happens suddenly, sometimes over the course of just a few generations. Furthermore, the death of a language does not even require the death

25 of the culture that speaks it. A language dies from disuse, when another language becomes dominant in the area, and the speakers of the indigenous language shift to the dominant one. The Ubykh language may be dead, but the Ubykh people live on, their native language having been

30 supplanted by Turkish.

One way to preserve a dying language is through documentation. At a minimum, it ensures that future generations can continue to study its sounds and structures. Occasionally, documentation can even allow a

35 dead language to be resurrected. Hebrew had fallen out of everyday use around the time of the late Roman Empire, kept alive only by religious scholars. A revival in the nineteenth century brought it back, and it is now spoken by 15 million people worldwide, over 1500 years

40 after its original displacement. Several studies of Ubykh were published before the death of poor Tevfik. Perhaps it too will be revived in a few hundred years.

Passage 2

Language death, more often than not, is more like language suicide: when parents stop teaching their native

45 tongue to their children in infancy, children will not be fluent speakers. They will identify with the language they learned, which they will in turn pass on to their children. While many people bemoan this loss of the diversity of speech, it is important to note that only the

50 speakers can decide what they pass to the next generation; we cannot force other cultures to save their own languages.

When a community abandons its language, there is often good reason to do so—sometimes it even can mean

55 the difference between life and death. In areas of extreme poverty, speaking the dominant language can mean better economic opportunities, a greater income, or a better life. In imperialist colonies or war-torn regions, a group in power will sometimes prohibit the use of in-

60 digenous languages, sometimes even under penalty of death. It is easy for cozy scholars to lament the loss of curious phonetic systems, but if faced with the choice between your language and your life, you will not take long to deliberate.

65 Even when members of a community aren't in actual physical danger, field linguists working to save dying languages often have encountered resistance, even animosity from the indigenous people. Some cultures have strong feelings of ownership towards their

70 languages and are unwilling to share them with outsiders. Some feel that the act of documenting or recording a language deprives it of its spirit. Some communities are interested in saving their languages, but distrust European linguists, who resemble speakers of the

75 dominant language more closely than they do members of the community.

Efforts to revive dying languages can be successful, but the spark for revitalization must originate internally. Welsh* was once on the verge of vanishing, but a

80 resurgence of interest in the late twentieth century helped revive it, and it now enjoys equal footing with English in the Welsh government. The key to its success was the support and enthusiasm of *the people*, who see their language as the heart of their culture. It is vital for lin-

85 guists to approach a dying language not like a physicist, but like a physician. A language is not a cold object of study but an element of a culture made up of living people. It is their interests and their safety that must be taken into account before we worry about their tenses

90 and conjugations.

* Welsh is the language of Wales, a nation in the United Kingdom.

CONTINUE

Passage II: History/Social Studies

MAIN IDEAS: (Yours may vary.)

PASSAGE 1: LANGUAGE DEATH (LD) IS BAD
     Par. 1: Ubykh language died; LD is big problem
     Par. 2: Why does LD happen?
     Par. 3: Prevent LD through documentation

Stop. Go do questions 11-13.

PASSAGE 2: PREVENTING LD IS TOUGH
     Par. 1: Cultures kill their own languages
     Par. 2: LD happens from necessity
     Par. 3: Some don't want outsider help
     Par. 4: How to prevent LD

11. Answer: A.
Confused? **Peek ahead to question 12.** That's an evidence question referring to this one.

Question (spoiler alert) will point us towards lines 25-28:
A language dies from disuse, when another language becomes dominant in the area, and the speakers of the indigenous language shift to the dominant language.

So for a language to die, another language must **become dominant in the area**.

A) **Correct.** To say a language is "dominant in an area" means that it is *widely spoken*.
B) Random. Nothing in passage 1 implies that languages die by force. Passage 2 will mention that in lines 53-64, but not Passage 1.
C) Random. Nothing in the passage mentions historical connections between languages. We don't know whether Ubykh is related to Turkish.
D) Random. Nothing the passage mentions the structure of any languages.

12. Answer: D.
Question 11 asks what conditions must be present for a language to die, specifically with regard to a different language. Let's look at these choices and see what we have.

A) Lines 5-7
This just describes what happens when a language dies.
B) Lines 10-12
This gives statistics about how many languages are dying.
C) Lines 16-19
Getting closer now. This talks about the mechanism for how languages change. But these lines describe a different phenomenon. This is just language evolution. The author specifically says Latin *didn't die*. So this is not language death.
D) **Lines 25-28**
Correct. This line describes how a language dies "when another language becomes dominant in the area."

13. Answer: C.
Go back to line 13:
*When people hear the term "language death", they often think of "dead languages", imagining lost civilizations, and ruins filled with **broken stone pillars**.*

"Lost civilizations" implies we're talking about **old** civilizations. Line 16-17, too, says that we're talking about "ancient languages." That's **choice C): evoke something archaic and inactive.**

B) and D) are random.
A) is false: this *isn't* what language death is. And language death doesn't actually cause devastation; it doesn't break stone pillars.

That's it for Passage 1 questions. Go read Passage 2 and do questions 14-21.

14. Answer: C.
Go back:
Language death, more often than not, is more like language suicide: when parents stop teaching their native tongue to their children in infancy, children will not be fluent speakers.

And later in the same paragraph:
only the speakers can decide what they pass to the next generation;

So a language's speakers are (at least partly) responsible for the language's death. They kill themselves.

That's **Choice C): language death is often self-inflicted.** All other choices are random and miss the point of the paragraph.

Note that this was also our Main Idea for the paragraph: "**cultures kill their own languages**". Also, it's pretty easy to see, just by the meaning of the word "suicide".

15. Answer: C.
Let's look at the context:
*It is easy for **cozy** scholars to lament the loss of curious phonetic systems, but if faced with the choice between your language and your life, you will not take long to deliberate.*

It says that these scholars don't appreciate the difficult situations these people are in, where lives are at risk.
The choice of the word "cozy" emphasizes that the scholars live comfortably, in contrast with the people whose lives are at risk.

A) We're saying something *bad* about the scholars: that they don't understand the difficult situations of these people.
B) Random, random, random. We're saying something *bad* about the scholars. No mention of "satisfaction".
C) **Correct**. The scholars are far from the languages, so they don't appreciate the difficult situations.
D) Random. We're not talking about ancient languages.

16. Answer: D.
Vocab-in-context. Let's go back :
*Welsh was once on the verge of vanishing, but a resurgence of interest in the late twentieth century helped revive it, and it now **enjoys** equal footing with English in the Welsh government.*

Anticipation: something like **possesses**, perhaps.

A) ?✗ apprehends   = to understand; to arrest; to fear
B) ✗ tolerates
C) ✗ desires
D) ✓ **retains**   = to keep or hold.

17. Answer: C.
Let's start at line 84:
It is vital for linguists to approach a dying language not like a physicist, but like a physician.

Great. That wasn't helpful. Let's check out the next sentence:
A language is not a cold object of study but an element of a culture made up of living people.

Okay. So a "physicist" **studies cold things**, while a "physician" **cares about people**. That's C).

There's some hard vocab here. Let's take a look:

A) ✗ precision   approximation
Doctors are approximate? Clearly wrong.
B) ✗ professional   dilettante
"expert" vs. "amateur, dabbler, hobbyist". No.
C) ✓ **objectivity**   **compassion**
"unprejudiced, unemotional" vs. "emotional". **Yes.**
D) ✗ dominance   subservience
"master" vs. "slave". No.

MAIN IDEAS FOR FULL PASSAGES:

Passage 1: _____

Passage 2: _____

MAIN IDEAS, Passage 1:

Paragraph 1: _____

Paragraph 2: _____

Paragraph 3: _____

MAIN IDEAS, Passage 2:

Paragraph 1: _____

Paragraph 2: _____

Paragraph 3: _____

Paragraph 4: _____

11

Passage 1 states that in order for a language to die, another language must

ANTICIPATION: _____

A) be widely spoken nearby the dying language.
B) be forcibly imposed upon speakers of the dying language.
C) be historically related to the dying language.
D) have a similar structure to the dying language.

12

Which choice provides the best evidence for the answer to the previous question?

ANTICIPATION: _____

A) Lines 5-7 ("Imagine . . . overnight.")
B) Lines 10-12 ("This means . . . century.")
C) Lines 16-19 ("True . . . years.")
D) Lines 25-28 ("A language . . . one.")

13

The author of Passage 1 mentions "stone pillars" (line 16) primarily in order to

ANTICIPATION: _____

A) describe the devastation language death causes.
B) demonstrate the rapidity of language death.
C) evoke something archaic and inactive.
D) connect language to a cultural past.

14

The author of Passage 2 uses the term "language suicide" (lines 44) primarily to emphasize

ANTICIPATION: _____

A) the suddenness with which language death occurs.
B) the hopelessness of trying to save a dying language.
C) that language death is often self-inflicted.
D) the tragic nature of language death.

15

In line 61, the word "cozy" serves to

ANTICIPATION: _____

A) praise the warm and caring attitude of linguists.
B) affirm the satisfaction of helping a dying language.
C) highlight scholars' distance from the reality of the communities.
D) encourage interest in preserving ancient languages.

16

As used in line 81 "enjoys" most nearly means

ANTICIPATION: _____

A) apprehends.
B) tolerates.
C) desires.
D) retains.

17

The difference between being a "physicist" and being a "physician" (lines 85-86) is best described as the distinction between

ANTICIPATION: _____

A) precision and approximation.
B) a professional and a dilettante.
C) objectivity and compassion.
D) dominance and subservience.

CONTINUE ➤

18

The author of Passage 2 would most likely respond to lines 31-35 of Passage 1 ("One way ... resurrected") by

ANTICIPATION: _____

A) mocking the futility of trying to save endangered languages.
B) illustrating the difficulty of accurately transcribing a dead language.
C) arguing that the community's consent is crucial to saving a dying language.
D) restating the benefits of children being fluent in the dominant language.

19

Which choice provides the best evidence for the answer to the previous question?

ANTICIPATION: _____

A) Lines 43-46 ("Language . . . speakers.")
B) Lines 53-55 ("When . . . death.")
C) Lines 58-61 ("In imperialist. . . death.")
D) Lines 82-84 ("The key . . . culture.")

20

Unlike the author of Passage 2, the author of Passage 1 supports his argument by

ANTICIPATION: _____

A) recounting personal experiences.
B) providing statistics to substantiate a claim.
C) refuting statements posed by opponents.
D) citing specific cases as models of success.

21

Which of the following best describes the relationship between the two passages?

ANTICIPATION: _____

A) Passage 1 identifies the benefits of a situation while Passage 2 identifies its drawbacks.
B) Passage 1 outlines a problem while Passage 2 describes obstacles to its resolution.
C) Passage 1 argues against the policies recommended by Passage 2.
D) Passage 1 catalogs ancient phenomena that Passage 2 applies to the modern day.

CONTINUE

18. Answer: D.
Confused? **Peek ahead to question 19**. That's an evidence question referring to this one.

How would Passage 2 respond to Passage 1's comment? Let's start by looking at 1's comment:
> *One way to preserve a dying language is through documentation. At a minimum, it ensures that future generations can continue to study its sounds and structures.*

Does Passage 2 mention documentation? Sure! Line 71:
> *Some [communities] feel that the act of documenting or recording a language deprives it of its spirit.*

Question 19 also points us in the direction of lines 82-84:
> *The key to [Welsh's] success was the support and enthusiasm of the people, who see their language as the heart of their culture.*

This paragraph talks about resistance to efforts to save the language from the indigenous people. In short, some communities don't want outsiders documenting their languages. **That's D)**.

A) Too strong. Passage 2 *does* want to save languages. See paragraph 4.
B) Random. We're not talking about *dead* languages, we're talking about *dying* languages.
C) Correct. See line 78, too: *the spark for revitalization must originate nternally*.
D) Random. Passage 2 does not advocate having children speak the dominant language, though he does say that's what's killing the dying languages.

19. Answer: D.
Question 18 asks how Passage 2 would respond to Passage 1's statement about resurrecting dead languages. Let's look at these choices and see what we have.

A) Lines 43-46
This says that speakers themselves cause a language to die. This has nothing to do with resurrecting dead languages.
B) Lines 53-55
This discusses the reasons why a language might die. We want one about bringing them back.
C) Lines 58-61
More about the harsh conditions that might cause language death. Still nothing about resurrection.
D) Lines 82-84
Correct. This sentence is referring to the example of a successful revival of a dying language, Welsh. This is the only choice that deals with the question of reviving dying languages.

20. Answer: B.
We want something that Passage 1 *does* and Passage 2 *doesn't do*. Let's go through the list:

A) Neither gives personal examples. (1 gives the example of Tevfik, but that's not personal *to the author*).
B) Correct. Passage 1 gives stats about the rate of language death in lines 9-12. Passage 2 gives no stats.
C) Passage 1 does not do this.
D) Both do this: Hebrew in 1, Welsh in 2.

21. Answer: B.
Questions like this are *very* common on the double passage. That's why, for the double passage, it's a good idea to do Main Ideas for each entire passage as well as individual paragraphs. We did that above:
> *Passage 1: Language Death is bad.*
> *Passage 2: Preventing LD is tough.*

That looks like **Choice B)**.

We could also do this simply by elimination. When going through the choices, you want to eliminate quickly. If a choice says something false about Passage 1, immediately eliminate it; don't even read what the choice says about Passage 2.

A) False. Passage 1 thinks language death is bad.
B) True! Exactly what our main ideas say.
C) Random. Passage 1 doesn't argue against any policies.
D) False. Passage 1 is about modern times. The opening words are "On October 7, *1992*"!!

We could actually get this question without having read Passage 2 at all; we eliminated everything because of Passage 1.

Passage III: Science

MAIN IDEAS: (Yours may vary)

Par. 1:   Geologists tell stories from rocks.
Par. 2:   Formation of continents
Par. 3:   Learned about it from types of rocks
Par. 4:   Pillow basalts = rocks formed from underwater lava
Par. 5:   Pillows have bubbles
Par. 6   Vesicularity = bubble. Deeper water = fewer, smaller bubbles
Par. 7   Counting bubbles tell us depth of rock's formation.

Questions 22-31 are based on the following passage and supplementary material.

The following passage is adapted from Lisa Smith, "How Geology Explains the World."

Geologists look at old rocks and the clues they left behind to figure out the stories behind them. To look at a rock and be able to read the clues it gives you is to read an epic poem on a larger and more beautiful scale than *The Iliad*. Every rock has a story. Every mountain, every ocean, every river has a story.

For example, the convergent event that created the supercontinent Pangea took deep ocean beds and coastal plains and shoved them into the jumbled mass that is the Appalachian mountain range. This range also used to connect with and extend through into the Little Atlas mountain range in what is currently Morocco, before the formation of the Atlantic Ocean pushed apart the supercontinent Pangea into its current continental formation.

We know this grand story of the formation and subsequent destruction of the supercontinent Pangea because geologists have learned to read rocks. Many rocks currently on the tops of mountains are types that can only have been formed underwater, such as limestones, deep-water shales, pillow basalts, or their metamorphosed equivalents. And since these mountains are not currently underwater, we must infer that the rocks once were and have since been moved, by some exciting processes, to the tops of mountains.

There are many types of rocks that can imply an aqueous formation, but one of the most informative is pillow basalt. Pillows can often be found off the coasts of volcanic islands, deep under the ocean along mid-ocean ridges, or in meltwater from glacier-covered fissures. The evocative name comes from the rounded, bulbous shapes that are created as lava oozes into water. The extreme shock of hot lava erupting into cold water causes the lava to form an almost instantaneous crust around its outside layer. The force of the lava continually pushes on that bubble-like pillow until a crack forms in its crust and a new pillow extrudes from the original one, and so on.

More interesting, however, are the bubbles trapped inside these pillows. Most liquids have some bubbles in them. Lavas are no exception. Looking at the distributions and sizes of these bubbles—known as *vesicles*—allow one to infer other, even more interesting information about what an eruptive event was like than simply that it occurred underwater. After all, knowing that a rock was formed underwater does not give us all the information we could possibly want. Was this rock formed on a continental shelf, above an active subduction zone? Was it formed at a mid-ocean ridge on one side of a divergent boundary or above a hot spot? These questions are vital pieces of the overall storyline of these rocks.

One of the clues that can answer such questions is vesicularity—the percentage of total pillow volume that is represented by open porosity. There is a direct relationship between an increase in depth under water and an increase in pressure. And with any lava, a greater pressure will result in fewer and smaller vesicles. If an outcrop of pillows has smaller vesicles, showing a greater depth of formation, we can tell that they were likely formed at a mid-ocean ridge. If they have larger vesicles, they were likely formed close to the surface, near a coastline.

Studying the vesicularity of basalts found within rock outcrops—on the tops of mountains, within the ocean's depths, or anywhere in between—allows us to infer the general depth at which those pillows were originally formed. It is one more piece of the puzzle that is the earth's storyline.

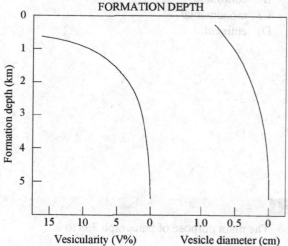

ESTIMATED RELATIONSHIPS BETWEEN PILLOW BASALT CHARACTERISTICS AND PILLOW FORMATION DEPTH

MAIN IDEAS:

Paragraph 1: _____

Paragraph 2: _____

Paragraph 3: _____

Paragraph 4: _____

Paragraph 5: _____

Paragraph 6: _____

Paragraph 7: _____

CONTINUE

22

As used in line 11, "extend" most nearly means

ANTICIPATION: _____

A) prolong.
B) enlarge.
C) amplify.
D) stretch.

23

As used in line 16, "grand" most nearly means

ANTICIPATION: _____

A) opulent.
B) admirable.
C) monumental.
D) eminent.

24

The main purpose of paragraph 3 is to

ANTICIPATION: _____

A) describe one way scientists formed the theory discussed the previous paragraph.
B) criticize the conventional theory about the formation of Pangea.
C) show how pillow basalts can teach us about natural history.
D) demonstrate how the presence of vesicles given information about formation depth.

25

Based on the passage, pillows quickly form crusts during their formation due to

ANTICIPATION: _____

A) greater vesicularity.
B) an increase in pressure.
C) a sudden change in temperature.
D) the force of the lava pushing.

26

The passage indicates that pillow basalts are only formed

ANTICIPATION: _____

A) inside a volcano.
B) underwater.
C) on tops of mountains.
D) on a continental shelf.

27

Which choice provides the best evidence for the answer to the previous question?

ANTICIPATION: _____

A) Lines 10-15 ("This . . . .formation")
B) Lines 18-22 ("Many . . . equivalents")
C) Lines 22-25 ("And. . . mountains")
D) Lines 48-51 ("Was . . . spot")

CONTINUE →

22. Answer: D.

Let's go back to line 11.

> [The Appalachian mountain] range also used to connect with and **extend** through into the Little Atlas mountain range in what is currently Morocco, before the formation of the Atlantic Ocean pushed apart the supercontinent Pangea into its current continental formation

The sentence is just describing *where* the mountain range used to be, how it lay **across a large area**.

A) prolong = *to lengthen a duration of time*. We're talking about space, not time here.

B) enlarge = *get bigger*. The mountains are not getting bigger here. True, the paragraph does say that the mountains have changed over time, that the mountains formed out of the sea, presumably getting bigger in the process. But *this word* in *this sentence* is only talking about their *location*.

C) amplify = *make more intense*. How would a mountain get intense?

D) stretch. **Correct.** Stretch can sometimes mean *become longer*, like when you stretch out your arms. But it can also just mean to *be* long, as in "This road stretches all the way to Delaware." That is exactly the sense we want for "extend" here.

23. Answer: C.

Another vocab-in context! Let's go back again! Line 16:

> We know this **grand** story of the formation and subsequent destruction of the supercontinent Pangea because geologists have learned to read rocks.

It's certainly a **big** story. **Really big.** It's about the formation of mountains and continents. Let's see our options.

A) opulent = *rich, wealthy*. Definitely not.

B) admirable. This has a *moral* component to it, that it's a *good* story. That seems inappropriate here. There's nothing morally right or wrong about the formation of continents. It's just rocks.

C) monumental. **Correct.** *Massive, extreme, very great.* What could be more "like a monument" than a bunch of big rocks?

D) eminent = *well-known and respected; prominent*. The "respected" sense doesn't fit here, but that sense is usually reserved for describing people. The "prominent" sense can describe rocks in a physical way, as in *noticeable*. That may be true, but we're talking about the *story* of the rocks here.

The anticipation is pretty straightforward here but some of the words in the choices can be tough.

24. Answer: A.

What was our main idea for paragraph 3? I had: **Learned about it from types of rocks.** The "it" referred to the formation of continents in paragraph 2.

Let's check our choices:

A) **Correct.** The second paragraph was about what we know about Pangea. The third discusses how details about rocks helped scientist figure it out, "because geologists have learned to read rocks." (line 18)

B) Random. There is no criticism of any theories.

C) Close. The paragraph does mention pillow basalts, but pillow basalts are not the main idea of the paragraph. They're only mentioned once in line 21, and that's in the middle of a list of a number of different rock types. We don't get deep into the world of pillows until later.

D) Irrelevant. It doesn't talk about vesicles until paragraph 6.

25. Answer: C.

There's no line reference here, and no Evidence Question to give us hints, so we're on our own. However, we can use our Main Ideas to see where it talked about pillow formation.

How about Paragraph 4? Yours may differ, but my Main Idea was "**Pillow basalts = rocks formed from underwater lava.**" So that's a good spot to find info about their formation. Does it mention "crusts" anywhere in there?

Sure! Line 35! Starting in line 33:

> The extreme shock of hot lava erupting into cold water causes the lava to form an almost instantaneous **crust** around its outside layer.

So it's the *hot* lava touching *cold* water that forms the crust. That's **choice C), a sudden change in temperature.**

A) Vesicularity isn't mentioned until paragraph 6. That refers to the bubbles inside the rock; it's not relevant to the formation of crusts.

B) Pressure is related to the vesicularity, as described in paragraph 6, but it is not mentioned in the discussion of pillow formation.

C) **Correct.** Hot lava to cold water.

D) The force of the lava is mentioned in line 35, but that's not how the *crusts* form. The force pushes "until a crack forms in its crust.," which contributes to its pillow-like shape.

26. Answer: B.

There's no line reference here, but this time there's an Evidence Question to help. **Peek ahead to question 27** to check the references. If we did that question properly, it led us to lines 18-22 in the third paragraph:

> Many rocks currently on the tops of mountains are types **that can only have been formed underwater**, such as limestones, deep-water shales, **pillow basalts**, or their metamorphosed equivalents.

So pillow basalts are among the rocks that can only be formed underwater. All signs point to **choice B).**

We might also remember that already talked about this in question 25. It's paragraph 4: "**Pillow basalts = rocks formed from underwater lava.**" What did we say in question 25 about the formation of crusts? That the crust forms when the lava touches cold *water*. Line 31-33:

> The evocative name comes from the rounded, bulbous shapes that are created as lava oozes into **water**.

A) This is tempting because they're made of lava. But they clearly do not form *inside* a volcano. Near volcanoes, sure, but on the outside, where the water is.

B) **Correct.** And in line 27, it says they have "an aqueous formation." Aqueous means having to do with water..

C) Line 19 does say that pillow basalts can be found on the tops of mountains. But that's the point of the geologists' theory: the mountains contain rocks that couldn't have been formed in the mountains. They must have been formed underwater, so the mountains must have been underwater.

D) Continental shelf was mentioned in line 48 as *one* possible source of a rock. Not the *only* place of formation.

27. Answer: B.

Question 26 asks about *where* pillow basalts are *formed*. Which of these references talk about that?

A) Lines 10-15
Random. This is just describing where the Appalachian Mountains used to be. Nothing to do with what we're talking about.

B) **Lines 18-22**
Correct. Let's look at it:

> *Many rocks currently on the tops of mountains are types that can only have been formed underwater, such as limestones, deep-water shales, pillow basalts, or their metamorphosed equivalents.*

So it looks like pillow basalts can only be formed underwater.

C) Lines 22-25
This mentions the fact that the rocks must have moved from underwater to the tops of mountains. All that occurs after they were formed. We're asking about their original formation.

D) Lines 48-51
Okay, these questions ask about where pillow are formed, good. But it gives several possible places within the water where they might be formed. We're looking for the place where they can "only" be formed. This choice gives questions, not answers.

28. Answer: B.

Confused? **Peek ahead to question 29.** It's an Evidence Question referring to this one.

There are two curves in the figure. The one on the left is about vesicularity, and the one on the right is about vesicle diameter. The question asks about vesicularity, so we want the curve on the left.

Depth is on the vertical axis. Note that here the numbers go up as the line goes down, so higher numbers are at the bottom and lower numbers are at the top, which is the opposite of what we usually see from graphs, but it does that because we're talking about *depth*. With depth, a bigger number means *further down*, below the sea.

To look at how ocean depth *increases*, we'll go from the top of the curve *down* to the bottom. As the line goes down, the vesicularity **decreases**, from 15 to 0.

29. Answer: C.

We did question 28 by looking at the graph, but also could have figured it out from the text of the passage. Remember, the question is asking about the relationship between *ocean depth* and *vesicularity*. Let's look at our options:

A) Lines 35-38 ("The force... so on")
This is about the formation of pillow basalts. There's no mention of vesicularity here.

B) Lines 41-45 ("Looking ... underwater")
This defines vesicles and tells us they're going to be important. But we don't know why yet. It doesn't mention depth at all.

C) Lines 57-59 ("And with... vesicles")
Correct. This line doesn't mention depth directly, but it does say that greater pressure means fewer vesicles. And lines 55-57 just told us that an increase in depth means an increase in pressure. Therefore, an increase in depth means a decrease in vesiculariy.

D) Lines 59-61 ("If an outcrop ... ridge")
This is tempting because it does specifically say that "smaller vesicles, [show] a greater depth of formation." However, the question asks about *vesicularity*, which is the percentage of volume made up of bubbles. This line is about the diameter (that's the right side of the graph).

30. Answer: A.

Let's look through the choices and see which one is supported by the graph:

A) **Correct.** Start at the 5 on the depth axis on the left and draw a straight line across till you hit the vesicularity curve. You'll see the point where it intersects is almost at zero.

B) False. A linear relationship means the graph forms a straight line. This is a curved line.

C) False. This asks us to compare the two curves. They both are mapped against depth, so we can infer a relationship between them. We already said in question 28 that vesicularity decreases as depth increases. On the right side we see that diameter also decreases as depth increases. So when diameter decreases, depth increases, therefore vesicularity also decreases.

D) Random. The graph doesn't say anything about coastal areas.

31. Answer: D.

Just look up the values on the graph. This can be tricky because
   a) there are no gridlines
   b) the vesicularity graph on the left is in the way.

Before you do anything: look at the numbers on the graph. The values for diameter go from 1.0 to 0. So choices A) 15 and B) 10 are *definitely out!* Those are values from the vesicularity graph. RTFQ!

Regardless, find the 1 km point on the left axis and draw a straight line across until you hit the diameter curve. Draw a straight line from that intersection point straight down to the diameter axis. You should be right around **0.5, choice D)**.

Based on the figure and the passage, as ocean depth increases, a pillow basalt's vesicularity

ANTICIPATION: _____

A) Increases only.
B) Decreases only.
C) Increases then decreases.
D) Decreases then increases.

Which of the following statements is best supported by the figure?

ANTICIPATION: _____

A) Pillow basalts formed 5 km below the ocean surface have virtually no vesicles.
B) There is a linear relationship between formation depth and vesicularity
C) As vesicle diameter of pillow basalts decreases, vesicularity increases.
D) Pillow basalts found near coastal areas will have smaller values for vesicularity.

Which statement made by the author gives information that best explains the answer to the previous question?

ANTICIPATION: _____

A) Lines 35-38 ("The force… so on")
B) Lines 41-45 ("Looking … underwater")
C) Lines 57-59 ("And with… vesicles")
D) Lines 59-61 ("If an outcrop … ridge")

According to the figure, at a depth of 1 km, a pillow basalt will likely have a diameter of approximately

ANTICIPATION: _____

A) 15 cm
B) 10 cm
C) 1.0 cm
D) 0.5 cm

STOP

WRITING AND LANGUAGE

Introduction to Writing and Language   111

Standard English Conventions: Conventions of Usage   121

Standard English Conventions: Sentence Structure   163

Standard English Conventions: Conventions of Punctuation   189

Expression of Ideas   211

■ Introduction to Writing and Language

Welcome to SAT Writing! The Writing section is everyone's least favorite section on the SAT.* The SAT Writing and Language Test will test you on effective writing strategies and the rules of Standard Written English. The task is intended to mimic the process you would go through in your own writing: review a draft of an essay you've written and make changes, both to correct outright errors and to strengthen weak writing.

OVERVIEW

Passages

The test is composed of 4 short essays, each with 11 questions. Questions may ask you to correct grammatical errors, re-phrase awkward sentences, add or delete phrases, or understand the purpose of a paragraph, among other things.

Passages will be drawn from each of these four content areas: **Careers**, **History/Social Studies**, **Humanities**, and **Science**. These are similar to the content areas that we saw on the Reading Test, though not exactly the same. The main differences are that Fiction/Literature does not appear on the Writing Test, while Careers and Humanities do.[†]

Don't worry too much about these passage types. Your strategies and techniques will be the same regardless of the topic of the passage, so the content shouldn't affect your performance much.

---

* Except for Reading and Math.

† Careers? What kind of topic is that? It means the passage will be about an interesting field of work.

Effectively, that means it will be a nonfiction piece that doesn't quite count as Social Studies. But really, these content areas don't matter.

Timing

You have 35 minutes to do 44 questions: that's about 48 seconds per question. That sounds fast, but it's actually not bad—it's much better than the ACT, which uses a similar format but only allows 36 seconds per question. Generally speaking, timing on the SAT Writing doesn't tend to be as much of an issue with students as it is on the Reading or Math Tests.

On one hand, 48 seconds per question is the fastest of any section on the SAT. But on the other hand, students complain about timing problems far less on the Writing than on the other tests. Individual SAT Writing questions tend to be pretty direct, so even the hardest problems don't take much time to do. And they test the same mistakes over and over again.

If you do find yourself having timing problems, remember our two rules of timing:

1. **The Target Number Rule:** *accuracy is more important than bulk.* It's better to be accurate on fewer questions than to carelessly do a lot of questions. So don't worry if you don't finish the test, as long as you're careful on the questions you do.

2. **The Guessing Rule:** *never leave anything blank for any reason.* You do not lose points for a wrong answer. There's never any reason to leave a blank. If you can't finish all the questions, *guess randomly on the ones you don't get to.*

Subscores

The questions fall into two large categories—**Standard English Conventions** and **Expression of Ideas**—each of which has three subtypes. Your Writing Score will include two subscores, each out of 15 points, showing your performance in the two main categories.

CATEGORY	NUMBER OF QUESTIONS	SUBTYPES
Standard English Conventions	20 questions (5 per passage)	Conventions of Usage
		Sentence Structure
		Conventions of Punctuation
Expression of Ideas	24 questions (6 per passage)	Effective Language Use
		Organization
		Development

The test doesn't specify how many questions of each subtype will occur, but they're generally evenly distributed. That means each passage of 11 questions will have 1–2 questions of each subtype, with about 6–8 questions of each subtype across the whole test.

Don't worry too much about these categories. Questions on the test won't say if they're

Standard English Conventions or Expression of Ideas.* But this is a convenient way to organize the material. The more tests you take, the more you'll start to notice patterns in the types of things they ask you about. Once you start to notice the patterns, you'll be able to answer the questions much more quickly.

The test-makers lay out definitions of what sort of concepts belong to which category, but questions don't always fit into these categories neatly.[†] There will often be overlap. For example, a question may have three choices dealing with a verb issue and one with a comma issue; is that a Usage question or a Punctuation question? Even the concepts themselves are often closely related—run-on sentences are a Sentence Structure issue, but you can't talk about run-ons without talking about punctuation.

You will also get two subscores in categories that stretch across both the Reading and the Writing tests. We discussed these in the Introduction to Evidence-Based Reading and Writing chapter, but here's a quick reminder:

CATEGORY	NUMBER OF QUESTIONS ON WRITING TEST	WHICH QUESTIONS
Words in Context	8 questions (2 per passage)	All Effective Langauge Use questions
Command of Evidence	8 questions (2 per passage)	All Development questions

Cross-test scores

Besides the subscores, the Writing test will also contribute to two cross-test scores. We discussed these in the Introduction to Evidence-Based Reading and Writing chapter, but here's a quick reminder:

---

*   When you get your results, questions will be labeled as Standard English Conventions or Expression of Ideas, but the subcategories will not be labeled.

†   All these categories come straight from the SAT makers. The coming chapters are roughly organized according to the types listed here, but we've switched some of them around in order to make the material easier to follow. For example, the SAT considers Verb Tense to be a Sentence Structure issue, but we discuss it with Conventions of Usage so that we can discuss all verb issues in one section.

CROSS-TEST SCORE	NUMBER OF QUESTIONS ON WRITING TEST	WHICH QUESTIONS
Analysis in History/ Social Studies	6 questions from 1 passage	All Expression of Ideas questions in the History/ Social Studies passage
Analysis in Science	6 questions from 1 passage	All Expression of Ideas questions in the Science passage

Including these scores for the Writing is a little odd to say the least. It's not like Reading where you're trying to understand the author's main ideas. The actual content of the passage is irrelevant to the task of most of these questions. Even Expressions of Ideas questions, which can sometimes deal with content, still include a lot of questions on things such as choosing transition words between paragraphs or eliminating redundant words. Please ignore the cross-test scores.

CONTENT

Standard English Conventions

Standard English Conventions questions ask you to identify **errors in a sentence**. Generally, a word or part of a sentence will be underlined and you will be asked to choose how to rewrite the phrase according to rules of grammar, usage, and punctuation. Choice A) will usually be "NO CHANGE", meaning you can leave the phrase as it was originally written.

There are three types of Standard English Conventions questions:

- **Conventions of Usage**: These questions test relationships between single words and phrases within a sentence, relationships such as subject and verb, or pronoun and antecedent.

- **Sentence Structure**: These questions deal with the way larger parts of sentences are connected, such as the way to properly connect clauses and where to place long phrases.

- **Conventions of Punctuation**: These questions will usually present four choices that differ *only* in their punctuation. You will be tested on when to use (and when *not* to use) commas, apostrophes, and other common punctuation marks.

Expression of Ideas

Expression of Ideas questions focus less on writing *grammatically* and more on writing *effectively*. They test you on how to choose the best way to word a sentence, the best way to structure a paragraph, or the best way to accomplish your goal as a writer. Unlike Standard English Conventions questions, Expression of Ideas questions may ask you about the essay as a whole, not just single words or phrases.

There are three types of Expression of Ideas questions:

- **Effective Language Use**: These questions ask about the choice of language in the essay, as well as errors that are stylistic instead of grammatical or structural. You will be asked to trim wordy sentences, make phrases more specific, or ensure the language accurately reflects the essay's tone.

- **Organization**: These questions ask about the logic and organization of the essay. You will be asked about the location and ordering of sentences and the transitions between sentences or paragraphs.

- **Development**: These questions ask about what the author should do to the essay to improve it. In fact, Development questions will often explicitly phrase the question that way, asking what action the author should take. Common questions include whether the author should add or delete a sentence and whether the essay fulfills a certain goal. All questions dealing with figures and data are Development questions.

GENERAL STRATEGIES

In the coming chapters, we'll talk more about the specific rules you'll encounter, but here are a few general strategies that can be applied to the test as a whole.

1. Read the whole sentence.
One of the most common reasons students don't notice grammatical errors is that they miss the big picture. Students often focus too much on just the words that are underlined. But there are often key words at the *beginning* of a sentence that tell you there's an error at the *end* of the sentence.

2. Read the whole paragraph.
Even though these questions usually ask about a single sentence, these sentences aren't islands—they're part of a larger passage. The sentences before it can be important to understanding the meaning of this sentence. If you're not sure which form of a word to use—which pronoun to use, say, or what tense the verb should have—the answer may be somewhere else in the paragraph.

3. Read the whole passage.

Most questions will deal either with parts of a single sentence or the relationship between two sentences. But there will also be questions that deal with the passage as a whole. You will have to know what the passage was about. You don't have to worry about it as much as you would on a Reading passage, but it will matter.

That said, *don't read the whole passage before starting the questions.* You'll encounter questions as you read; you should do them as you reach them, even if you haven't read the whole passage yet. You'll quickly run out of time if you read the whole passage, and then go back to the questions.

4. Read all the choices.

The following chapters are going to present a lot of material. Learning all these new rules can often seem overwhelming—how are you supposed to know which rules to check on which questions? You're in luck! Often, the question will tell you *exactly* what to look for.

Grammatical questions usually have short choices, each having only a few words. That means it's relatively easy to see the **differences between the choices**. The differences between the choices will give you clues about what grammatical errors you should be looking for in the sentence.

Let's say that a question gave you these four choices:

A)   hope to
B)   hope for
C)   hopes to
D)   hopes for

There are two differences between these choices—"hope" versus "hopes" and "to" versus "for"—so we know right away that those are the two things to check. In this example it's pretty clear what to look for, but sometimes it can be more subtle. Make sure to scan all the choices when you first read a question; it will be easier to home in on the important words in the sentence.

5. Eliminate and Guess.

As we've mentioned, there's no penalty for wrong answers on the SAT, so *you should never leave a question blank for any reason.* But you are on a tight time limit, and of course there will be some tricky questions. This makes it all the more important to **eliminate quickly**.

Look for differences in forms of words in the choices. Once you spot a rule violation in an answer choice, eliminate **all** choices that make that mistake. There may be more than one reason why a choice is wrong, but you don't have to understand all of them. Once you find one thing wrong with a choice, it's *out*.

If you're down to two choices but you can't figure out which one is better, don't dawdle: **just pick one.** Again, there's no penalty for wrong answers on the SAT, so there's no harm in guessing. You've got a lot of questions to do. If you're stuck, just pick a choice and move on quickly.

PARTS OF SPEECH

Before we begin, it's useful to take a minute to familiarize ourselves with a few basic parts of speech. This is not an exhaustive list. There are other parts of speech we'll talk about later,* but these are the basics that will give us the foundation we need get us started.

Nouns

Nouns include words that refer to a person, place or thing, though there are abstract nouns, too. Frankly, you may see more abstract nouns than any of the other categories.

- **Person:** *girl, chef, researcher, Doug, Phil Collins*
- **Place:** *house, hospital, dining room, Belgium, Cleveland*
- **Thing:** *stapler, horseshoe, broccoli, foot, water, fire*
- **Abstract:** *odor, justice, love, manslaughter, emancipation, action, indecision, illusion, despair*

They can be the subject or object of a verb, as well as the object of a preposition:

- **The <u>dog</u> ate a <u>donut</u> with <u>sprinkles</u>.**

- "dog" is the subject of the verb "ate" (the dog performed the eating).
- "donut" is the object of the verb "ate" (the donut was the thing that was eaten).
- "sprinkles" is the object of the preposition "with".

Verbs

Verbs include words that refer to concrete actions, but some are also more abstract. Anything that something can *do* is a verb.

---

* And some we won't talk about at all. There's no reason to talk about "determinatives" on the SAT.

- **Concrete actions:** *jump, play, kick, move, speak, poke, smolder*
- **Abstract actions and states:** *stand, live, believe, assume, develop, hire, fire, despair*

Some words can be either nouns or verbs depending on the context—notice that "fire" and "despair" appeared in our lists for both.

There are a number of "auxiliary" (or "helping") verbs. These usually appear along with other verbs in order to change their tense.

- **Auxiliary verbs:** *is/are/was/were, have/has/had, will/would, can/could*

Verbs show **tense** that indicate the time the action occurred. Some tenses require auxiliary verbs.

- **Yesterday the dog <u>ate</u> a donut.**
- **The dog <u>is eating</u> a donut right now.**
- **The dog <u>will eat</u> a donut tomorrow.**

The **main verb** in a clause is directly tied to its subject.* The main verb must have a subject associated with it. But there may be other verbs in a sentence as well.†

- **After <u>leaving</u> home, Bob <u>went</u> to the store <u>to buy</u> a kite.**

- "went" is the main verb, with subject "Bob"
- "leaving" and "to buy" are also verbs. They do describe actions Bob did, but they are not the main verb in the sentence.

Prepositions

A preposition is a small word that often shows direction or location (like "in" or "out"). Some prepositions can also be more abstract (like "of").

- **Prepositions:** *of, in, on, to, at, with, from, towards, upon*

Prepositions usually take a noun as an object. Together they form a prepositional phrase. That prepositional phrase in turn often describes another noun.

- **The dog [<u>in</u> the yard] ate a donut [<u>with</u> sprinkles]**

---

* Note that some auxiliary verbs can also appear alone as the main verb in a sentence, like *John <u>is</u> fat* or *John <u>has</u> a gut*, whereas other auxiliary verbs, like *will/would* or *can/could* cannot be main verbs.

† Verb forms that are not a main verb are called "nonfinite verbs".

- "in" is a preposition whose object is the noun "the yard"
- "in the yard" is a prepositional phrase describing the noun "dog"
- "with" is a preposition whose object is the noun "sprinkles"
- "with sprinkles" is a prepositional phrase describing the noun "donut"

There are other parts of speech, too, you know. This is but a small taste of what you'll see on the SAT. Shall we begin?

■ Standard English Conventions: Conventions of Usage

Conventions of Usage questions on the SAT generally ask about the relationship between individual words in a sentence. Does this verb agree with its subject? Does this pronoun agree with this antecedent? Does this adjective properly modify a noun? Is this the right preposition to use with this verb? All of these questions will be discussed here.

If you don't have a lot of experience with English grammar—*that's okay.* A lot of students have very little exposure to grammar in high school. We're not going to discuss everything there is to know about English grammar—there's a lot to know, way more than we need for the SAT.* Nor will we cover every single rule that has ever shown up on an SAT. If a rule shows up on one question for every 20 tests, we're not going to talk about it. You probably won't see it when you take the test, and even if you do, it would only be one question and won't significantly affect your score.

Instead, we're going to focus on the big picture. We're going to discuss **the rules that appear most frequently on the SAT**. We've done all the legwork for you—we've pored over real tests to find out which rules matter and which ones don't.

I. VERBS

A verb is traditionally defined as an **action word,** like *jump, go,* or *bake.* That's not entirely accurate; not every verb is an "action". These underlined words are verbs—*I like cats; the book sat on the table; Pittsburgh is in Pennsylvania*—even though none describes an "action". But a lot of verbs do describe actions, so this definition will help you develop a sense of which words are verbs.

---

* One of the most definitive books about English is *The Cambridge Grammar of the English Language.* It's over 1,800 pages long. We will not be discussing all of it.

Before we begin, here's an outline of the basic forms all verbs take, demonstrated with three different verbs. All the verb constructions we'll see use some combination of these forms.

Form	"Bake" (Regular)	"Eat" (Irregular)	"Be" (Irregular)
Simple Present	He <u>bakes</u> cookies. They <u>bake</u> cookies.	He <u>eats</u> chicken. They <u>eat</u> chicken.	I <u>am</u> rude. He <u>is</u> rude. They <u>are</u> rude
Simple Past	He <u>baked</u> cookies. They <u>baked</u> cookies.	He <u>ate</u> chicken. They <u>ate</u> chicken.	He <u>was</u> rude. They <u>were</u> rude.
Past Participle	He has <u>baked</u> cookies. The cookies were <u>baked</u>.	He has <u>eaten</u> chicken. The chicken was <u>eaten</u>.	He has <u>been</u> rude.
Present Participle	He is <u>baking</u> cookies. <u>Baking</u> cookies is fun.	He is <u>eating</u> chicken. <u>Eating</u> chicken is fun.	He is <u>being</u> rude. <u>Being</u> rude is fun.
Infinitive	He should <u>bake</u> cookies. He likes <u>to bake</u> cookies.	He should <u>eat</u> chicken. He likes <u>to eat</u> chicken.	He will <u>be</u> rude. He likes <u>to be</u> rude.

Any time a verb is underlined, check the following things:

1. Agreement

Every sentence contains at least one main verb, and that verb will have a **subject**. The subject is a noun that identifies who performs the action of the verb.*

In present tense verbs, the verb will be in a different form depending on whether the subject is singular or plural. That is, the subject and verb must **agree in number:**†

> ✓ *THE DOG* <u>eats</u> meat.   ✗ *THE DOG* <u>eat</u> meat.
> ✓ *THE DOGS* <u>eat</u> meat.   ✗ *THE DOGS* <u>eats</u> meat.

If a verb is a multi-word phrase, only the first word (called an "auxiliary verb") agrees with the subject, so we can ignore the second word (for now).

---

*   Unless it's a passive verb. More on those in a second.

†   Confusingly, nouns and verbs have the opposite rules of formation: *plural nouns* take an "s" at the end ("dogs"), but *singular verbs* take an "s" ("eats"). Once you find the subject and verb, you can use your ear to tell if they match: "The dogs eats meat" just sounds wrong.

✓ *THE DOG* <u>is</u> barking.	✗ *THE DOG* <u>are</u> barking.
✓ *THE DOGS* <u>are</u> barking.	✗ *THE DOGS* <u>is</u> barking.
✓ *THE DOG* <u>has</u> barked.	✗ *THE DOG* <u>have</u> barked.
✓ *THE DOGS* <u>have</u> barked.	✗ *THE DOGS* <u>has</u> barked.

If a verb underlined, find the subject and see that it agrees with the verb. To find the subject, ask yourself:

> ## Who is performing the action?

Sound easy? Well, it's not. Sentences often describe abstract concepts where it's hard to identify actors and actions. Furthermore, there are a number of ways the subject can be *hidden* so that the subject isn't what you think it is. So how can you tell which word is the subject?

The core sentence

On the SAT, the subject may not be the word immediately in front of the verb. In fact, it probably isn't. In real life, sentences are rarely simple statements like "The dog is barking." There are usually a lot of extra words that modify, describe, or elaborate on the words and concepts.

> ✓ <u>**The dog**</u> *in the yard* <u>**is barking**</u>.
> ✓ <u>**The dog**</u> *that I got from the pound last week* <u>**is barking**</u>.
> ✓ <u>**The dog**</u>, *which I bought for my ex-girlfriend Jessica in a pathetic attempt to win her affection back after she dumped me—right in front of everyone in the hallway outside math class—a little over three months ago,* <u>**is barking**</u>.

Note that the verb here is "is barking", not just "barking". An "-ing" verb alone cannot be the main verb of a sentence.

But in every sentence, you can strip away all the extra stuff and find a **core sentence**, a simple statement composed of just the subject and verb: **the dog… is barking**. Once you pull out the subject put it next to the verb, you can easily tell by ear whether the verb agrees with the subject.

Interrupting phrases

If you see a phrase **surrounded by commas,** the subject won't be in there. Take a look at this sentence:

> ✐ **The Queen, who has absolute power over her subjects as well as all the dukes and other aristocrats,** <u>**are**</u> **rich.**

All that stuff between the commas isn't part of the core sentence. It's like a parenthetical phrase or a footnote, an extra chunk of information thrown in the middle of the sentence. But it doesn't affect the core sentence. So let's get rid of it.

> ✗ THE QUEEN, ~~who has absolute power over all her subjects as well as all the dukes and other aristocrats,~~ <u>are</u> rich.

We can see the core sentence is "The Queen are rich." Does that sound right? Of course not. It should be:

> ✓ THE QUEEN, … , <u>is</u> rich.

In the original sentence, the verb might have sounded okay to you because there are a lot of plural nouns in between the subject and the verb—"subjects", "dukes", and "aristocrats". Those words trick your ear into thinking we need a plural verb. If you **literally cross out** comma phrases like this until all you have left is the subject, it's much easier to hear whether the verb is correct.*

Phrases surrounded by **dashes** work the same way:

> ✎ The sequel's budget—estimated to be over 100 million dollars—<u>is</u> more than double that of the original movie.
> ✓ The sequel's BUDGET—~~estimated to be over 100 million dollars~~—<u>is</u> more than double that of the original movie.

The punctuation marks make these interrupting phrases easy to spot. However, a sentence might also have long interrupting clauses like this without any punctuation at all:

> ✓ THE DOG that I got from the pound last week <u>is</u> barking.

Prepositional phrases

Prepositions are small words like *of, in,* or *on* that show a relationship between two words (usually two nouns). In the phrase **"the dog in the yard"**:

- The word "in" is a *preposition* and "the yard" is its *object*.
- The phrase "in the yard" is a *prepositional phrase*. It describes (or *modifies*) "the dog".

---

* The grand majority of SAT verb agreement questions require you to change the verb. But occasionally you might have to change the subject instead. In the sentence "*The work* of Monet are beautiful," the subject "the work" doesn't agree with the verb "are". But we can't change the verb because it isn't underlined. Instead, we'll make the subject plural to match the verb: "*The works* of Monet are beautiful."

The subject cannot be the **object of a preposition.** For example:

> ✓ **THE QUEEN** of England <u>is</u> rich.

The phrase "of England" is a prepositional phrase: "of" is a preposition and "England" is its *object*. The phrase "of England" describes the Queen—it tells us *which* Queen we're talking about. *The Queen* is the subject of the verb "is", not *England*. She's the one who's rich.*

This holds true for *all* prepositional phrases—they are not part of the core sentence. So if you see a prepositional phrase, **cross it out.** The subject *cannot* be in there:

> ✓ **THE DOGS** ~~in the yard~~ <u>are</u> barking.
> ✓ **THE MAN** ~~with three children~~ <u>is</u> married.
> ✓ **ALL FLIGHTS** ~~to Denver~~ <u>have</u> been delayed.
> ✓ **THE MOVIE** ~~about vampires~~ <u>is</u> scary

Of course, there may not be just one prepositional phrase. There could be a whole string of them.

> ☞ The construction of several groups of townhouses across the street from the complex of office buildings <u>have improved</u> the neighborhood.

What improved the neighborhood? The groups? The townhouses? Let's cross out the prepositional phrases:

> ✗ **THE CONSTRUCTION** ~~(of several groups) (of townhouses) (across the street) (from the complex) (of office buildings)~~ <u>have improved</u> the neighborhood.

The core sentence is "the *construction* have improved the neighborhood". That doesn't match.

> ✓ **THE CONSTRUCTION** ... <u>has improved</u> the neighborhood.

You can see how the sentence tried to fool you: the actual subject is singular, but there are several plural words after it, so the verb sounded okay. Don't be fooled. The subject will **not** be in a prepositional phrase.

---

* Strictly speaking, the *entire* phrase "The Queen of England" is the subject of "is". But the verb only has to agree with the head of the phrase—the core noun that everything else in the phrase is describing. Since "Queen" is the word that agrees with the verb, that's all we care about, so we'll call it the subject as a shorthand description.

Multiple subjects and multiple verbs

It's easy to see that the subject is plural when it's a plural noun:

> ✓ *THE DOGS* <u>are</u> barking.

But sometimes the subject is a compound of two *singular nouns* joined by "and". Even though each of these words is singular, the two of them together make a plural subject:

> ✗ *THE BULLDOG AND THE BEAGLE* <u>is</u> barking.
> ✓ *THE BULLDOG AND THE BEAGLE* <u>are</u> barking.

Similarly, a single subject can have two verbs joined by "and":

> ✓ *THE DOG* <u>eats</u> meat and <u>loves</u> bones.

Here, *each* verb, "eats" and "loves", agrees with the same subject "the dog". We could write the same sentence as two separate clauses (though it would sound a bit repetitive):

> ✓ *THE DOG* <u>eats</u> meat, and *THE DOG* <u>loves</u> bones.

The subject might come after the verb

Take a look at this sentence:

> ✎ At the front of the building <u>stands</u> two bronze statues.

What is the subject of the verb "stands"? What is doing the standing? The building? The front? No: the *statues* <u>stand</u>. Here, the subject comes *after* the verb, so it's easy to miss the fact that they don't agree. But look: "at the front" and "of the building" are prepositional phrases. The subject *can't* be in there. Sometimes you can see the verb agreement error more easily if you play with the order of words in the sentence. What the sentence really *means* is

> ✓ *Two bronze statues* <u>stand</u> at the front of the building.

It's perfectly alright to put the subject after the verb. You probably do it all the time. Look:

> ✎ There <u>is</u> two people from Portugal in my math class.

Does the verb agree? Hmm. "There is" sounds okay, doesn't it? Ah, but "there" isn't the subject. "Two people" is the subject. The sentence should read:

> ✓ There <u>are</u> *two people* from Portugal in my math class.

THIS PAGE INTENTIONALLY LEFT BLANK

Verb Agreement

ANSWERS:

- The *TEMPERATURE AND HUMIDITY* [has / **have**] been rising for the past week.

- The *CHEF* ~~who started all three of these restaurants~~ [**was** / were] trained at a school in France.

- Dave's new *INVENTION*, ~~a set of rocket-powered rollerblades that can propel you 100 yards in just three seconds~~, [are / **is**] both pointless and unsafe.

- The veterinarian said that the *PROBLEMS* ~~with my dog's skin~~ [**come** / comes] from a genetic condition rather than an infection.

- Mayor Black's *ANNOUNCEMENT* ~~of the addition of four new bridges to the city's redevelopment designs~~ [**was** / were] met with mixed reactions from the public.

Any time you see the phrase "there is" underlined, alarms should go off.* Look *after* "there is" to find the subject. It should come right after the verb.

TRY SOME:

In each of the following sentences, circle the appropriate verb form.

- 🖋 The temperature and humidity [**has** / **have**] been rising for the past week.

- 🖋 The chef who started all three of these restaurants [**was** / **were**] trained at a school in France.

- 🖋 Dave's new invention, a set of rocket-powered rollerblades that can propel you 100 yards in just three seconds, [**are** / **is**] both pointless and unsafe.

- 🖋 The veterinarian said that the problems with my dog's skin [**come** / **comes**] from a genetic condition rather than an infection.

- 🖋 Mayor Black's announcement of the addition of four new bridges to the city's redevelopment designs [**was** / **were**] met with mixed reactions from the public.

---

2. Tense

A verb's *tense* tells us when the action takes place. Tense can be scary; if you've ever taken a foreign language, you've probably been through some of the misery of studying tenses. However, tense questions on the SAT are usually fairly straightforward. The main goal is **consistency.** When events happen in the past, present, or future, the verbs should reflect that. If events happen at the same time, the verbs should be in the same tense. So how can you tell what tense the verb should be in?

The easiest way is to look for words that **literally refer to time.** If you see any such words, the tense of the verb should match the time they refer to.

- ✗ *IN 1776*, America <u>is declaring</u> independence.
- ✓ *IN 1776*, America <u>declared</u> independence.

- ✗ *NEXT YEAR*, our team <u>has won</u> 30 games.
- ✓ *NEXT YEAR*, our team <u>will win</u> 30 games.

Other times, you can look at the tense of **other verbs in the sentence.** Verbs should be

---

* In your head.

consistent within the sentence; if events happen at the same time, the verbs should be in the same tense.

> ✗ Dave <u>sees</u> several museums when he *WENT* to Belgium.
> ✗ Mrs. Jones <u>made</u> us sit in the corner whenever we *ARE* bad.

In the first sentence, the verb "went" is in the past, so we know his trip to Belgium happened in the past. Since the museum trips occurred *while* he was in Belgium, "sees" must also be put into the past. Similarly, in the second sentence, "are" is in the present. The word "whenever" tells us that the act of sitting in the corner happens *at the same time* as being bad, so "made" should be put into the present.*

> ✓ Dave <u>saw</u> several museums when he *WENT* to Belgium.
> ✓ Mrs. Jones <u>makes</u> us sit in the corner whenever we *ARE* bad.

Similarly, you can look at the tense of verbs **in other sentences nearby.** Most of the time, the passage as a whole will be set in a particular tense, so you can check the larger context to see which tense is appropriate. For example, by itself this sentence seems fine just the way it is:

> ☛ The waiter <u>took</u> their orders.

But put into a larger context, that tense may not be appropriate:

> ✗ The restaurant workers always *FOLLOW* the same routine. First, the hostess *SHOWS* the guests to their table. Then, the chef *COMES* out and *TELLS* them about the specials. Finally, the waiter <u>took</u> their orders.

Here, "took" is in the past, but all of the other verbs in this paragraph are in the present tense.[†] That doesn't match. The last sentence should also be in the present: **the waiter <u>takes</u> their orders.**

Perfect verbs

The majority of SAT tense questions just test whether the verb should be *present* or *past*. There are lots of other verb categories in English that won't be tested on the SAT. However,

---

* This does NOT mean that *all* verbs in a sentence must be in the same tense—only verbs that refer to the same time. Sentences often have multiple verbs in different tenses: "Bob *went* to the zoo yesterday, and Scott *will go* tomorrow."

† Note that just because a verb is present tense doesn't mean it's referring to an action that's occurring right now. In this paragraph, all the present tense verbs refer to repeated actions that occur *generally*. But don't worry about this; you don't have to understand the finer points to see that "took" doesn't match the other verbs here.

you still might see these forms used, so it's helpful to know a little about them. Look at this:

> ✓ Bob <u>was</u> class president *IN 2016*.

This sentence is the **simple past**. It refers to a specific time in the past and only the past. Compare it to this:

> ✓ Bob <u>has been</u> class president *SINCE 2016*.

This sentence is in the **present perfect**. Not only was Bob president in the past, but he's *still* president now. The present perfect is used for time periods that extend *from the past up to the present.*

> The present perfect is formed with the present tense of the verb "to have", plus the past participle of the main verb.

Additionally, you may see verbs in the **past perfect**. This structure is used for *the past of the past,* when an event happened before another past event:

> ✓ Lucas <u>had read</u> the book *BEFORE HE SAW* the film adaptation.

Both the reading of the book and the watching of the movie are past events, but the reading was *further* in the past, so "had read" is in the past perfect.

> The past perfect is formed with past tense of the verb "to have", plus the past participle of the main verb.

The past perfect is often interchangeable with the simple past, however, so we could also say:

> ✓ Lucas <u>read</u> the book before he saw the film adaptation.

Would

Would is a special kind of verb that has several different uses.* It isn't tested on the SAT very frequently, but it does show up every once in a while, so it's good to know a little about it.

First of all, *would* is simply the past form of *will*. It can be used to describe events occurring in the future *from a point in the past.*

> ✓ Dave *TOLD* Jennifer that he <u>would go</u> to the store.

From Dave and Jennifer's perspective, his trip to the store will occur in the future. But the act of telling Jennifer occurred in the past. So his trip to the store is set in the future from that moment.

---

* If you're interested, the fancy name for this kind of verb is "modal auxiliary verb". *Will, can, could, should,* and *must* are other examples of modal auxiliaries.

Second, *would* can be used to describe *habitual* actions in the past.

> ✓ **WHEN HE WAS** a child, Dave <u>would go</u> to the park every Saturday.

This sentence is set in the past, when Dave was a child. But it doesn't refer to any specific event in the past—it refers to events in the past that would happen *repeatedly*.

Finally, *would* can occur in *conditional* sentences—sentences containing an "if" clause. Conditional sentences can use several different tenses. The tense of the verb in the second clause is determined by the tense of the first.*

> ✓ If you **ASK** me to the dance, I <u>will go</u> with you.
> ✓ If you **ASKED** me to the dance, I <u>would go</u> with you.
> ✓ If you **HAD ASKED** me to the dance, I <u>would have gone</u> with you.

(Note that the verb in the last sentence is "would have gone", not "would of gone". "Would of" is never right in any context. We'll talk more about this in the "Commonly Confused Words" section.)

TRY SOME:

In each of the following sentences, circle the appropriate verb form.

- ✐ My dog [**sleeps / slept**] on my bed every night when he was a puppy.

- ✐ The war is finally over, but its effects [**were felt / will be felt**] for many years to come.

- ✐ Larry [**brings / brought**] some nuts and a loaf of bread when he goes to the park so he can feed the ducks and the squirrels.

- ✐ We worked together to speed up the preparations for the party: I [**cooked / will cook**] dinner while Naomi cleaned the dining room.

- ✐ Whenever I went fishing with my mother we [**buy / would buy**] bait from the same shop about a mile from the lake.

---

* Conditional statements don't occur often on the SAT, so don't worry too much about the difference between these sentences.

Verb Tense

> **ANSWERS:**
>
> - My dog [sleeps / **slept**] on my bed every night *WHEN HE WAS* a puppy.
>
> - The war *IS* finally over, but its effects [were felt / **will be felt**] *FOR MANY YEARS TO COME*.
>
> - Larry [**brings** / brought] some nuts and a loaf of bread *WHEN HE GOES* to the park so he can feed the ducks and the squirrels.
>
> - We *WORKED* together to speed up the preparations for the party: I [**cooked** / will cook] dinner while Naomi *CLEANED* the dining room.
>
> - *WHENEVER I WENT* fishing with my mother we [buy / **would buy**] bait from the same shop about a mile from the lake.

THIS PAGE INTENTIONALLY LEFT BLANK

3. Irregular verbs and past participles

Most verbs form the past tense simply by adding "-ed". Some verbs, however, have special forms for the past. Others even use the same form for past and present. We call these verbs **irregular verbs:**

REGULAR:

    ✓ I <u>walk</u> the dog.   ✓ I <u>walked</u> the dog.

IRREGULAR:

    ✓ I <u>catch</u> the fish.   ✓ I <u>caught</u> the fish.   ✗ I <u>catched</u> the fish.

IRREGULAR:

    ✓ I <u>hit</u> the ball today.   ✓ I <u>hit</u> the ball yesterday.   ✗ I <u>hitted</u> the ball.

The "perfect" forms mentioned above were compound tenses that require more than one verb: a form of the verb "to have" plus the **past participle** of the verb. For regular verbs—and even some irregular verbs—the past participle looks exactly the same as the simple past:

   ✓ I <u>walk</u> the dog.   ✓ I <u>walked</u> the dog.   ✓ I <u>have walked</u> the dog.
   ✓ I <u>catch</u> the fish.   ✓ I <u>caught</u> the fish.   ✓ I <u>have caught</u> the fish.
   ✓ I <u>hit</u> the ball today.   ✓ I <u>hit</u> the ball yesterday.   ✓ I <u>have hit</u> the ball.

However, some irregular verbs have distinct past participles—they use different words in the simple past and perfect tenses. Here are a few examples:

Present	Simple Past	Past Participle
begin	*began*	had/have *begun*
choose	*chose*	had/have *chosen*
freeze	*froze*	had/have *frozen*
grow	*grew*	had/have *grown*
give	*gave*	had/have *given*
take	*took*	had/have *taken*

When a verb has different forms like this, don't confuse the two. The past participle must be used only in compound forms, not by itself.*

---

*   That is, the past participle can't be used by itself as a *main verb*. But it can appear by itself in a modifier:

     <u>Begun</u> *in 1887, the Eiffel Tower was completed in 1889.* We'll talk about modifiers in the Sentence Structure chapter.

| ✓ I <u>chose</u> an outfit for the dance. | ✗ I <u>chosen</u> an outfit for the dance. |
| ✓ I <u>have chosen</u> an outfit for the dance. | ✗ I <u>have chose</u> an outfit for the dance. |

4. Active vs. Passive

There's one more distinction we can make among verb forms: *active voice* and *passive voice*.

An **active** verb is one in which the subject of the verb is the person or thing *doing* the action. A **passive** verb is one in which the subject is the person or thing *receiving* the action.

The passive is usually formed with a form of the verb "to be", plus the past participle of the verb.

ACTIVE: A car <u>hit</u> Chapman.   **PASSIVE: Chapman <u>was hit</u> by a car.**

See the difference? Both these sentences mean the same thing: the car *did* the hitting, and Chapman *received* the hitting. But in the first sentence, the "car" is the subject of the verb "hit", and in the second, "Chapman" is the subject of the verb "was hit".

How can you tell whether the verb should be active or passive? First, look at the **context**:

✗ **Because Roger sold the most toasters, he <u>gave</u> a prize.**

The underlined verb is *active* here: it tells us that Roger was the one who did the giving. But the first part tells us that Roger did something special,* so it's more likely that he *received* a prize. Therefore, we should use the passive:

✓ **Because Roger sold the most toasters, he <u>was given</u> a prize.**

Some people will tell you that the passive is always wrong, but that's a myth. Passive verbs are *not wrong*; they're just another way to say something. Just like every other verb form, sometimes it's right, and sometimes it's wrong. The important thing is to understand the context.

Passive verbs can be handy if the order of the words matters to us. For example, if we want the receiver of the action to come at the beginning of the sentence:

✓ ***WHILE CROSSING THE STREET*, <u>Chapman was hit by a car.</u>**

Here, we need "Chapman" to be the subject of the sentence so we can connect him directly to the phrase "while crossing the street".[†]

---

* It's hard to sell toasters. He deserves that prize.

† If we didn't, we'd have a *dangling modifier*. More on that in the Sentence Structure chapter.

Passives are also useful if we don't know who performed the action:

✓ **Scott <u>was fired</u> yesterday.**

We don't know who actually performed the firing here. But we don't really *care* who did the firing. So the passive voice works perfectly.[*]

However, the passive can become a problem when we do know who performed the action.

× **After Paolo read the menu, <u>a sandwich was picked.</u>**

The second clause is passive: the noun "sandwich" is the subject of "was picked", but the sandwich didn't *do* the picking. The second clause doesn't tell us who did the picking. But wait! We know who did the picking—Paolo did. So why don't we say that?

✓ **After Paolo read the menu, <u>he picked a sandwich.</u>**

We could leave the clause in the passive and add a prepositional phrase to tell us who the performer is, but sentences like that often sound ugly and weird:

× **After Paolo read the menu, <u>a sandwich was picked by him.</u>**

---

[*] Don't confuse "passive" with "past"—*any* tense can be put into the passive voice by adding a form of "to be" and the past participle: "Scott <u>will be fired</u> tomorrow." "These toys <u>are made</u> out of wood." "The neighborhood <u>has been improved</u> by the construction of townhouses."

VERB SUMMARY
When a verb is underlined, check the following:

1. Agreement
- Subject and verb must agree in **number**, singular or plural.
- To find the **subject**, ask: Who is **performing** the action of verb?
- Ignore **interrupting phrases** and **prepositional phrases**.
- One verb can have **multiple subjects;** one subject can have **multiple verbs.**
- The subject might come **after the verb;** watch out for **there is.**

2. Tense
- Look for **time words.** Verbs must refer to the right time.
- Look at **other verbs** in the sentence. Verbs that occur at the same time must be in the same tense.
- Look at verbs in **nearby sentences.**
- Watch out for special tenses: **present perfect, past perfect, would.**

3. Irregular forms
- Some verbs need **irregular** past tense forms.
- Some irregular verbs' **past participles** are different from their **simple past** forms.

4. Active vs. Passive
- In a passive verb, the **subject does not perform the action.**
- In general, if we **know** who the actor is, **don't** use the passive.

THIS PAGE INTENTIONALLY LEFT BLANK

Verb Drill

Gerald *WENT* to three different grocery stores *BEFORE* he finally <u>finds</u> the brand of cereal he *WAS* looking for.	**1.** A) NO CHANGE **B) found** C) will find D) has found	*Tense* **Correct** *Tense* *Tense*
The room *IS* a mess: the desk *IS* covered with papers, and *A PILE* ~~of dirty clothes~~ <u>are lying</u> on the floor.	**2.** A) NO CHANGE **B) is lying** C) had been lying D) have been laid	*Agreement* **Correct** *Tense* *Agreement*
Although the overall crime rate is much lower this year, *THE NUMBER* ~~of car thefts in suburban areas~~ <u>are</u> rising.	**3.** A) NO CHANGE B) were **C) is** D) have been	*Agreement* *Agreement* **Correct** *Agreement*
BEFORE HE BECAME a children's book author, Dr. Seuss <u>is making</u> training films for the U.S. Army *DURING WORLD WAR II*.	**4.** A) NO CHANGE B) makes C) has made **D) made**	*Tense* *Tense* *Tense* **Correct**
THE POSSIBILITY ~~of the existence of black holes~~ <u>were proposed</u> by the geologist John Michell in 1784 in a letter to Henry Cavendish.	**5.** A) NO CHANGE B) have been proposed **C) was proposed** D) proposes	*Agreement* *Agreement* **Correct** *Tense, Active/Passive*
ONE ~~of the biggest surprises in the former governor's memoirs~~ <u>was</u> the news that he did not seek reelection because he had fallen ill.	**6.** **A) NO CHANGE** B) were C) are D) have been	**Correct** *Agreement* *Agreement* *Agreement*
A joint *ORGANIZATION* ~~of teachers and library workers~~ <u>have agreed to</u> sponsor a fundraiser to raise money for the museum.	**7.** A) NO CHANGE **B) has agreed to** C) are agreed on D) are in agreement about	*Agreement* **Correct** *Agreement* *Agreement*

VERB DRILL

All the questions in this exercise deal with verbs. Unlike the real SAT, the sentences in this exercise do not make up a full passage—each question refers to a single stand-alone sentence.

Gerald went to three different grocery stores before he finally <u>finds</u> the brand of cereal he was looking for.

1. A) NO CHANGE
    B) found
    C) will find
    D) has found

The room is a mess: the desk is covered with papers, and a pile of dirty clothes <u>are lying</u> on the floor.

2. A) NO CHANGE
    B) is lying
    C) had been lying
    D) have been laid

Although the overall crime rate is much lower this year, the number of car thefts in suburban areas <u>are rising</u>.

3. A) NO CHANGE
    B) were
    C) is
    D) have been

Before he became a children's book author, Dr. Seuss <u>is making</u> training films for the U.S. Army during World War II.

4. A) NO CHANGE
    B) makes
    C) has made
    D) made

The possibility of the existence of black holes <u>were proposed</u> by the geologist John Michell in 1784 in a letter to Henry Cavendish.

5. A) NO CHANGE
    B) have been proposed
    C) was proposed
    D) proposes

One of the biggest surprises in the former governor's memoirs <u>was</u> the news that he did not seek reelection because he had fallen ill.

6. A) NO CHANGE
    B) were
    C) are
    D) have been

A joint organization of teachers and library workers <u>have agreed to</u> sponsor a fundraiser to raise money for the museum.

7. A) NO CHANGE
    B) has agreed to
    C) are agreed on
    D) are in agreement about

The increasing use of smart phones has made it much easier for companies to do business on the road.

8.
A) NO CHANGE
B) make
C) have made
D) are making

Whenever my family and I go to the movies, my father gets an extra-large popcorn and will refuse to share it with any of us.

9.
A) NO CHANGE
B) would refuse
C) refuses
D) refused

The orangelo—a hybrid fruit resulting from a cross between an orange and a grapefruit—have grown naturally in Puerto Rico.

10.
A) NO CHANGE
B) has grew
C) grow
D) grows

Measuring over ten feet long, the Mekong giant catfish seems frightening, but it actually has no teeth and has ate only algae and small plants.

11.
A) NO CHANGE
B) eats
C) ate
D) would eat

Once a reliable method for measuring degrees of longitude were discovered, cartographers were able to draw accurate maps of the oceans.

12.
A) NO CHANGE
B) discovers
C) was discovered
D) would have discovered

My fascination with science begins on my eighth birthday when I received a simple toy microscope as a present from my grandmother.

13.
A) NO CHANGE
B) had began
C) begun
D) began

When we started this company, we believed that it takes at least five years of growth for it to become profitable, but it only took two.

14.
A) NO CHANGE
B) would take
C) will take
D) took

Both the wildlife in the area and the population of a nearby village was seriously damaged after a factory spilled toxic chemicals into the river.

15.
A) NO CHANGE
B) have
C) has been
D) were

The increasing *USE* of smart phones has made it much easier for companies to do business on the road.

8. **A) NO CHANGE** — **Correct**
    B) make — *Agreement*
    C) have made — *Agreement*
    D) are making — *Agreement*

WHENEVER my family and I *GO* to the movies, my father *GETS* an extra-large popcorn and will refuse to share it with any of us.

9. A) NO CHANGE — *Tense*
    B) would refuse — *Tense*
    C) refuses — **Correct**
    D) refused — *Tense*

The *ORANGELO* — a hybrid fruit resulting from a cross between an orange and a grapefruit — have grown naturally in Puerto Rico.

10. A) NO CHANGE — *Agreement*
    B) has grew — *Irregular verb*
    C) grow — *Agreement*
    D) grows — **Correct**

Measuring over ten feet long, the Mekong giant catfish *SEEMS* frightening, but it actually *HAS* no teeth and has ate only algae and small plants.

11. A) NO CHANGE — *Irregular verb*
    B) eats — **Correct**
    C) ate — *Tense*
    D) would eat — *Tense*

Once a reliable *METHOD* for measuring degrees of longitude were discovered, cartographers *WERE* able to draw accurate maps of the oceans.

12. A) NO CHANGE — *Agreement*
    B) discovers — *Active/Passive*
    C) was discovered — **Correct**
    D) would have discovered — *Tense, Active/Passive*

My fascination with science begins on my eighth birthday *WHEN I RECEIVED* a simple toy microscope as a present from my grandmother.

13. A) NO CHANGE — *Tense*
    B) had began — *Irregular verb*
    C) begun — *Irregular verb*
    D) began — **Correct**

When we *STARTED* this company, we *BELIEVED* that it takes at least *FIVE YEARS* of growth for it to become profitable, but it only took two.

14. A) NO CHANGE — *Tense*
    B) would take — **Correct**
    C) will take — *Tense*
    D) took — *Tense*

Both the *WILDLIFE* in the area *AND* the *POPULATION* of a nearby village was seriously *DAMAGED* after a factory spilled toxic chemicals into the river.

15. A) NO CHANGE — *Agreement*
    B) have — *Active/Passive*
    C) has been — *Agreement*
    D) were — **Correct**

THIS PAGE INTENTIONALLY LEFT BLANK

II. PRONOUNS

Pronouns are words like *they, it,* or *her* that take the place of nouns. They work like abbreviations; they refer to some other noun in the sentence so you don't have to repeat that noun. The noun a pronoun refers to is called the **antecedent**.

> ✓ *THE SNAKE* swallows <u>its</u> prey whole.

"Its" is a pronoun and "the snake" is its antecedent; "its" refers to "the snake".

> ✓ *THE SNAKE* swallows <u>[the snake's]</u> prey whole.

Just like with verbs, there are several different ways pronouns can change their form, so there are a few things you'll want to check whenever a pronoun is underlined on the SAT.

> **Any time a pronoun is underlined, check the following things:**

1. Agreement

Just like verbs, pronouns must **agree in number** with their antecedents: match singular to singular and plural to plural.

> ✓ *THE SNAKE* swallows <u>its</u> prey whole.
> ✗ *THE SNAKE* swallows <u>their</u> prey whole.
>
> ✓ *SNAKES* swallow <u>their</u> prey whole.
> ✗ *SNAKES* swallow <u>its</u> prey whole.

Any time you see a pronoun underlined, find its antecedent and make sure they agree in number. The best way to find the antecedent is to ask:

> **Who or what does the pronoun refer to?**

That is, if you replaced the pronoun with another word in the sentence, which would you use?

> ✗ This new mobile phone looks great, but <u>they</u> can break very easily.

"They" is a pronoun, so let's find the antecedent. What does "they" refer to? What can break? The *phone* can break easily. "Phone" is singular, so we must say "it".

> ✓ This new mobile *PHONE* looks great, but <u>it</u> can break very easily.

A chart outlining all the different pronoun forms can be found at the end of this section.

Sometimes there may be more than one noun the pronoun could refer to, so you'll have to use the context to figure out which one the pronoun is supposed to refer to.

> ✓ The *AGE* of some *TREES* <u>is</u> determined by counting <u>their</u> rings.

Note that the subject of the verb may or may not be the same word as the antecedent of a pronoun. Here, the subject of the verb "is" is "age", but the antecedent of the pronoun "their" is "trees". Unlike the subject, the antecedent *can be* inside a prepositional phrase. The antecedent can be anywhere in the sentence, or even in a previous sentence. Take it slow. What is *determined*? The *age* is determined. But what has *rings*? *Trees* have rings.

Vague pronouns

> ✗ Scott and Bob were partners until <u>he</u> quit.

Here we have two options for who quit: Scott or Bob. How can you tell which it is? You can't; that's the problem. In this case, we can't use a pronoun at all. We have to specify who quit.

> ✓ Scott and Bob were partners until <u>Bob</u> quit.

Of course, if they *both* quit, then we'd have to say "they".

Mystery pronouns

> ✗ In gymnastics, <u>they</u> take off points for bad dismounts.

Sounds fine? Well, it's not. Who's "they"? *Gymnastics*? Gymnastics take off points? Are you kidding me? The problem here is that there isn't any word in the sentence that could possibly be the antecedent of the pronoun.* "They" is a *mystery pronoun*—we have no idea what it refers to. The only way to correct it is to not use a pronoun at all: we must specify who we're talking about.

> ✓ In gymnastics, <u>judges</u> take off points for bad dismounts.

Generic pronoun shift

It's okay for a pronoun to lack a specific antecedent when we're not talking about any specific people. "One", for example, is a pronoun that basically means "anyone" or "someone". "You"

---

* It's okay for a pronoun to refer to a word in a previous sentence. So before you declare a pronoun to be a mystery pronoun, check the previous sentence for any words that might be the antecedent.

works the same way:

> ✓ If *ONE* is sick, <u>one</u> should go to the hospital.
> ✓ If *YOU* are sick, <u>you</u> should go to the hospital.

These sentences mean the same thing (the only difference is that "one" is more formal). Neither "one" nor "you" has an actual antecedent—you can't point to anything in the sentence that they refer to. That's okay because they refer to people in general—they're *generic pronouns*. In these cases, either "one" or "you" would be fine. But you can't use both of them:

> ✕ If *ONE* is sick, <u>you</u> should go to the hospital.

If "one" and "you" show up in the same sentence, one of them is probably wrong. Furthermore, any time you see a generic pronoun, **check the other sentences in the passage.** If a generic pronoun was used earlier in the paragraph, you must keep using that pronoun throughout the passage.

This rule doesn't just apply to "one" and "you". You must be consistent with *all* generic pronouns:

> ✕ If *WE* examine this painting closely, <u>one</u> can tell that the artist was left-handed.
> ✓ If *WE* examine this painting closely, <u>we</u> can tell that the artist was left-handed.
>
> ✕ When *PEOPLE* spend all day typing, <u>your</u> hands get tired quickly.
> ✓ When *PEOPLE* spend all day typing, <u>their</u> hands get tired quickly.

Noun agreement

Just as pronouns must agree with antecedents, sometimes nouns have to agree with the words they refer to.

> ✕ Scott and Bob want to be <u>an astronaut.</u>

Here, the subject "Scott and Bob" is plural, but "astronaut" is singular. They don't match. Scott and Bob don't want to be one astronaut. They're two people! What we really mean is:

> ✓ *SCOTT AND BOB* want to be <u>astronauts</u>.

- Cucumbers are generally considered to be vegetables, but [**its** / **their**] structure more closely fits the botanical definition of fruit.

- Despite our growing interest in the processes of the brain, there is still much that [**they** / **we**] don't understand about the way we think.

- The construction of the towers had to be delayed because the architect decided to alter the materials with which [**it** / **they**] would be built.

- The naked mole rat is unique among mammals in that, due to the lack of a chemical called "Substance P", [**it** / **they**] cannot feel pain.

- A well-written magazine article should be easily accessible for all readers, regardless of [**its** / **their**] knowledge of the subject.

2. Case

Pronouns also take different forms depending on what they do in the sentence. We call that the pronoun's **case**.

Subject and object

> ✓ <u>I</u> love Derek Jeter.
> ✓ Derek Jeter loves <u>me</u>.

In these two sentences, "I" and "me" refer to the same person, but in different roles. Therefore, we put the pronouns in different *cases*: we use "I" when the person is *the subject* (performing the action) and "me" when the person is the *object* (receiving the action). So when you see a pronoun underlined, ask yourself: is the person *performing* the action (subject) or *receiving* the action (object).

The object case is also used if the pronoun is the object of a preposition:

> ✓ *I* am talking <u>to him.</u>
> ✓ *HE* is talking <u>to me.</u>

Pronoun Agreement

> **ANSWERS:**
>
> ➢ *CUCUMBERS* are generally considered to be vegetables, but [its / **their**] structure more closely fits the botanical definition of fruit.
>
> ➢ Despite *OUR* growing interest in the processes of the brain, there is still much that [they / **we**] don't understand about the way *WE* think.
>
> ➢ The construction of the *TOWERS* had to be delayed because the architect decided to alter the materials with which [it / **they**] would be built.
>
> ➢ *THE NAKED MOLE RAT* is unique among mammals in that, due to the lack of a chemical called "Substance P", [**it** / they] cannot feel pain.
>
> ➢ A well-written magazine article should be easily accessible for all *READERS*, regardless of [its / **their**] knowledge of the subject.

THIS PAGE INTENTIONALLY LEFT BLANK

If the pronoun is next to another person, it can be hard to tell whether the pronoun is in the right form:

> ✒ The studio loved the screenplay <u>Roger and him</u> wrote.

In cases like this, if you delete the other person, it's much easier to see whether the pronoun is correct.

> ✗ The studio loved the screenplay ~~Roger and~~ <u>him</u> wrote.

That sounds wrong. "Him" is the subject of the verb "wrote", so we need the subject pronoun, "he":[*]

> ✓ The studio loved the screenplay <u>he</u> wrote.

Reflexive pronouns

As we saw, pronouns have different forms depending on whether they are the subject or object:

> ✓ <u>I</u> love Derek Jeter.   ✓ Derek Jeter loves <u>me</u>.

But when the subject and object refer to the same person, the object pronoun needs the **reflexive** form:[†]

> ✓ *I* love <u>myself.</u>   ✓ *YOU* love <u>yourself.</u>
> ✓ *DEREK JETER* loves <u>himself.</u>   ✓ *THE YANKEES* love <u>themselves.</u>

These forms can be confusing since some of them are formed from the possessive pronoun (<u>my</u>self, <u>your</u>self, <u>our</u>selves) but others are formed from the object pronoun (<u>him</u>self, <u>them</u>selves). Don't mix them up: *hisself* and *theirselves* are not words.

Contractions and possessive pronouns

All nouns have **possessive** forms, usually formed by adding an **apostrophe** and an -*s*:

> ✓ *BOB* has a *CAT*. This is <u>Bob's</u> cat. The <u>cat's</u> name is Gretchen.

---

[*] This is why those grammar jerks are always telling you to say "I" instead of "me". In casual speech, it's exceedingly common for people to prefer "me" to "I" whenever there are two people like this, regardless of the pronoun's role in the sentence.

[†] Reflexive pronouns are also sometimes used for emphasis, as in "I *myself* have never been a gardener, but I hear it's quite relaxing." Or "Ulysses S. Grant *himself* couldn't grow a beard that big."

We'll talk more
about apostrophes
and possessive
forms in the
Punctuation
chapter.

But pronouns do not take *'s*. They have special possessive pronoun forms:

> ✓ *BOB* has a *CAT*. This is <u>his</u> cat. <u>Her</u> name is Gretchen.

HOWEVER, pronouns *do* use apostrophes for **contractions**. Contractions are when two words are stuck together into a single word. An apostrophe takes the place of the missing letters.

✓ <u>I'm</u> Swedish.	=	<u>I am</u> Swedish.
✓ <u>We're</u> Swedish.	=	<u>We are</u> Swedish.
✓ <u>He's</u> Swedish.	=	<u>He is</u> Swedish.
✓ <u>She's</u> Swedish.	=	<u>She is</u> Swedish.

Several pronouns have possessive and contraction forms that sound the same, so it can be **very** confusing to tell them apart. Just remember this simple rule:

Pronouns use CONTRACTION apostrophes, but NOT POSSESSIVE apostrophes.

It's vs. Its vs. Its'	*It's* means *it is*.	<u>It's</u> a beautiful day!	<u>It is</u> a beautiful day!
	Its shows **possession**.	The dog wagged <u>its</u> tail.	The tail <u>belongs to</u> the dog.
	Its' is <u>never</u> correct.	**NEVER USE <u>ITS'</u> FOR ANY REASON.**	
You're vs. Your	*You're* means *you are*.	<u>You're</u> a jerk.	<u>You are</u> a jerk.
	Your shows **possession**.	<u>Your</u> fly is open.	The fly <u>belongs to</u> you.
They're vs. Their vs. There	*They're* means *they are*.	<u>They're</u> going to win.	<u>They are</u> going to win.
	Their shows **possession**.	I like <u>their</u> uniforms.	The uniforms <u>belong to</u> them.
	There shows **location**.	Put it over <u>there</u>.	I'm telling you <u>where</u> to put it.

"There" isn't a pronoun at all, but it sounds the same as the other two, so it's easy to confuse all three. You can remember that *there* is the direction word because it looks like other direction words, *here* and *where*.

If you're not sure whether to use an apostrophe, try **switching it with a different pronoun:**

> ✐ The snake swallows <u>it's</u> prey whole.

Not sure if that's right? What if it was a girl snake? Would we use an apostrophe? No, we'd say *her*.

> ✗ The snake swallows <u>she's</u> prey whole.
> ✓ The snake swallows <u>her</u> prey whole.

Since we don't use the apostrophe with *her*, we shouldn't use an apostrophe with *its*.

> ✗ The snake swallows <u>it's</u> prey whole.
> ✓ The snake swallows <u>its</u> prey whole.

Try this one:

> ✐ <u>Your</u> going to the zoo today.

If we change the sentence from *you* to *me*, we can easily see the pronoun should be *I'm*, not *my*.

> ✗ <u>My</u> going to the zoo today.
> ✓ <u>I'm</u> going to the zoo today.

Since we do use the apostrophe with *I'm*, we should also use an apostrophe with *you*.

> ✗ <u>Your</u> going to the zoo today.
> ✓ <u>You're</u> going to the zoo today.

- ✒ A pronoun must always agree in number with [**its** / **it's**] antecedent.

- ✒ [**You're** / **Your**] lucky that you weren't in school today: you missed a pop quiz in math class.

- ✒ Mr. and Mrs. Walsh are a little dim-witted, but [**their** / **they're**] children are actually quite bright.

- ✒ I hope Professor Rodchenko will give Sherwyn and [**I** / **me**] a good grade on our art project even though we turned it in late.

- ✒ Located above the 23rd parallel, the Florida Keys are technically in a subtropical zone, but [**their** / **there**] climate is nonetheless considered tropical.

3. Relative pronouns

There is a special class of pronouns called **relative pronouns:** words like *who, which,* or *that.* Relative pronouns act like regular pronouns in that they refer to nouns in the sentence, but they also can connect different clauses together.

Verb agreement

Relative pronouns **use the same form for singular and plural.** That means they don't have to agree with their antecedents like regular pronouns. But we do still care about their antecedents. Take a look at this:

> ✒ **Bob is talking to a man <u>who is</u> from Cincinnati.**

The subject of the verb "is" is the pronoun "who". Is that right? Do we say "who is" or "who are"?

The antecedent of a relative pronoun is usually the word directly before it.

It depends. When a relative pronoun is the subject of a verb, the **verb must agree with the antecedent** of the pronoun. In this sentence the antecedent of "who" is "a man", which is singular. "A *man* <u>is</u> from Cincinnati" sounds fine, so "a *man* <u>who is</u> from Cincinnati" is fine, too.

If the antecedent is plural, we use a plural verb:

Pronoun Case

ANSWERS:

- A pronoun must always agree in number with [**its** / it's] *ANTECEDENT*.

  The antecedent belongs to *the pronoun.*

- [**You're** / Your] *LUCKY* that you weren't in school today: you missed a pop quiz in math class.

  You are *lucky.*

- Mr. and Mrs. Walsh are a little dim-witted, but [**their** / they're] *CHILDREN* are actually quite bright.

  The children belong to *Mr. and Mrs. Walsh.*

- I hope Professor Rodchenko *WILL GIVE* ~~Sherwyn and~~ [I / **me**] a good grade on our art project even though we turned it in late.

  "Me" is the object *of "give".*

- Located above the 23rd parallel, the Florida Keys are technically in a subtropical zone, but [**their** / there] *CLIMATE* is nonetheless considered tropical.

  The climate belongs to *the Keys.*

THIS PAGE INTENTIONALLY LEFT BLANK

✓ Bob is talking to some *PEOPLE* <u>who are</u> from Cincinnati.

Who vs. Whom

Just like other pronouns, *who* has a special form when it's an object: *whom*.

✓ I met a man <u>who</u> likes French people.
✓ I met a man <u>whom</u> French people like.

In the first sentence, "who" is the *subject* of the verb "likes": this man likes French people. But in the second sentence, "whom" is the *object* of "like" and "French people" is the subject: French people like this man.

This is exactly like the case issues we saw with other pronouns:

✓ <u>He</u> likes French people.
✓ French people like <u>him</u>.

Similarly, "whom" is used as the object of a preposition:*

✓ The judges will give a prize <u>*TO* the best *SINGER*</u>.
✓ Roger is the *SINGER* <u>*TO* whom</u> the judges gave the prize.

Who's vs. Whose

Just like other pronouns, relative pronouns have confusingly similar possessive and contraction forms. And just like other pronouns, relative pronouns take apostrophes with *contractions*, but *not* with possessives:

Who's	*Who's* means **who is**	the man <u>who's</u> buying my car	the man <u>who is</u> buying my car
Whose	*Whose* shows **possession**	the man <u>whose</u> car I'm buying	the car <u>belongs to</u> the man

Relative pronouns do not have reflexive forms. There's no such word as *whoseself*.

---

* "Whom" is a bit of an odd word. In real life, people *often* say "who" in places where they're "supposed" to say "whom". Not just in lazy, slang-filled teenager speech—in political speeches, in college lectures, and in heavily edited books and newspapers. Many people still cling to "whom", and knowing how to use it properly is still a sign of a careful writer. But frankly, "whom" is dying out.

Who vs. Which

Besides "who", the other common relative pronoun is "which". The difference is that "who" can only refer to **people,** and "which" can only refer to **non-people.**

> ✓ Audrey is the girl <u>who</u> ate all the cookies.
> ✗ Audrey is the girl <u>which</u> ate all the cookies.
>
> ✓ Audrey ate the one <u>which</u> had chocolate chips.
> ✗ Audrey ate the one <u>who</u> had chocolate chips.

Note that "which" can be used as the subject or object. But it does not have any possessive form: **"whose" is the only possessive relative pronoun.**

That

"Which" is often interchangeable with *that:**

> ✓ Audrey ate the one <u>which</u> had chocolate chips.
> ✓ Audrey ate the one <u>that</u> had chocolate chips.
>
> ✓ This is the cookie <u>which</u> Audrey ate.
> ✓ This is the cookie <u>that</u> Audrey ate.

"That" can be used as a subject ("that had chocolate chips") or object ("that Audrey ate").[†] But "that" cannot be the object of a preposition. You must use "which" instead:

> ✓ This exhibit contains the pen <u>with which</u> George Washington signed the Constitution.
> ✗ This exhibit contains the pen <u>with that</u> George Washington signed the Constitution.

"That" is a confusing word because it has two other uses besides the relative pronoun. First, it can be used as a "pointing" word, similar in meaning to "this" or the plural "those":

> ✓ I want <u>that</u> car.   ✓ <u>That</u> guy is a jerk.
> ✓ I want <u>this</u> car.   ✓ <u>This</u> guy is a jerk.
> ✓ I want <u>those</u> cars.   ✓ <u>Those</u> guys are jerks.

---

*   In fact, some people will tell you "that" is *required* in these sentences because they're *restrictive* clauses. These people are wrong: "which" can be used in restrictive clauses. More on restrictive clauses in the Punctuation chapter.

†   When used as an object, you can even omit the relative pronoun entirely: "This is the cookie Audrey ate."

THIS PAGE INTENTIONALLY LEFT BLANK

Relative Pronouns

ANSWERS:

- The factory employs over thirty *WORKERS* [**who are** / who is] well trained in woodworking.

  The workers are well trained.

- The guy [**who's** / whose] *RENTING* my apartment for the summer is a visiting student from France.

  The guy who is renting.

- Yesterday I got a chance to meet the district's *SUPERINTENDENT OF SCHOOLS*, [which / **who**] was a very friendly and charming person.

  The superintendent is a person.

- After living in a dump for three years, I'd be happy to find an apartment [that's / **whose**] *WALLS* are perpendicular to the floor.

  The walls belong to the apartment. "That's" is a contraction, not a possessive.

- Once a bill is approved by both houses of Congress, it is passed along to the President, [**who** / whom] *CAN VETO* it or sign it into law.

  "Who" is the subject of "can veto".

Note that these words are *not* relative pronouns and cannot be used to link clauses together:

| ✗ | She ate the cookie <u>this</u> had chocolate chips. |
| ✗ | She ate the cookies <u>those</u> had chocolate chips. |

Second, "that" can connect certain kinds of verbs with full clauses:

| ✓ | I said <u>that</u> I want the red car. |
| ✓ | I think <u>that</u> you are a jerk. |

TRY SOME:

In each of the following sentences, circle the appropriate pronoun form.

- The factory employs over thirty workers [**who are / who is**] well trained in woodworking.

- The guy [**who's / whose**] renting my apartment for the summer is a visiting student from France.

- Yesterday I got a chance to meet the district's superintendent of schools, [**which / who**] was a very friendly and charming person.

- After living in a dump for three years, I'd be happy to find an apartment [**that's / whose**] walls are perpendicular to the floor.

- Once a bill is approved by both houses of Congress, it is passed along to the President, [**who / whom**] can veto it or sign it into law.

Pronoun Chart

Here's an outline of all the different pronoun forms we discussed in this section:*

	Subject	Object	Possessive	Contraction	Reflexive
Singular	I	me	my	I'm (I am)	myself
	you	you	your	you're (you are)	yourself
	he	him	his	he's (he is)	himself
	she	her	her	she's (she is)	herself
	it	it	its	it's (it is)	itself
Plural	we	us	our	we're (we are)	ourselves
	you	you	your	you're (you are)	yourselves
	they	them	their	they're (they are)	themselves
Relative	who	whom	whose	who's (who is)*	---
	which	which	whose	---	---
	that	that/which	whose	that's (that is)	---

---

* We mentioned that relative pronouns can be singular or plural. When "who" and "that" are plural, they take the verb "are" instead of "is". But the contractions "who're" or "that're" are very rare and would never show up on the SAT. (Perhaps partly because, without its apostrophe, the former resembles an unfortunate word.)

PRONOUN SUMMARY
When a pronoun is underlined, check the following:

1. Agreement
- Pronouns and antecedents must agree in **number**, singular or plural.
- To find the **antecedent**, ask: Who or what does the pronoun **refer to**?
- Watch for **vague pronouns**, when the antecedent is unclear.
- Watch for **mystery pronouns**, when there is no antecedent.
- Be consistent with **generic pronouns.**
- Sometimes **nouns must agree** with each other, too.

2. Case
- Pronouns have different forms depending on their **role** in the sentence.
- **Subjects and objects** use different forms.
- Use **reflexive** pronouns when subject and object refer to the same thing.
- **Contractions** use apostrophes, **possessive** pronouns do not.

3. Relative pronouns
- Relative pronouns are words like *who, which,* or *that.*
- **Verbs** agree with the **antecedent** of the relative.
- Relatives have **cases** just like regular pronouns.
- **Who** is for people, **which** is for non-people.
- **That** is generally interchangeable with *which.*

PRONOUN DRILL

All the questions in this exercise deal with **pronouns**. Unlike the real SAT, the sentences in this exercise do not make up a full passage—each question refers to a single stand-alone sentence.

When you listen to the music of early rock bands, one can hear the influence of the blues in their guitar melodies.	1.	A) NO CHANGE B) you C) we D) they
Public safety groups are concerned about the injuries an airbag can cause from the force with which they are deployed.	2.	A) NO CHANGE B) they were C) those are D) it is
Many of the people who went to our annual holiday party last year have decided not to go this year.	3.	A) NO CHANGE B) whom C) whose D) which
Some paleontologists believe the *Tyrannosaurus* was a scavenger, eating animals that were already dead rather than hunting it's own prey.	4.	A) NO CHANGE B) its C) its' D) their
Although their still experiencing financial difficulties, the investment firm has shown significant growth in the past year.	5.	A) NO CHANGE B) there C) its D) it's
The proposed new contract provides higher wages for employees which have worked at the company for over three years.	6.	A) NO CHANGE B) whom has worked C) who has worked D) who have worked
Because of their magnificent plumage and exotic origins, peacocks were often kept in European gardens to flaunt the wealth of the king.	7.	A) NO CHANGE B) they're C) it's D) its

Pronoun Drill

When *YOU* listen to the music of early rock bands, <u>one</u> can hear the influence of the blues in their guitar melodies.	1. A) NO CHANGE **B) you** C) we D) they	*Pronoun shift* **Correct** *Pronoun shift* *Pronoun shift*
Public safety groups are concerned about the injuries *AN AIRBAG* can cause from the force with which <u>they are</u> deployed.	2. A) NO CHANGE B) they were C) those are **D) it is**	*Agreement* *Agreement* *Agreement* **Correct**
Many of the *PEOPLE* <u>who</u> *WENT* to our annual holiday party last year have decided not to go this year.	3. **A) NO CHANGE** B) whom C) whose D) which *"Who" is the <u>subject</u> of "went".*	**Correct** *Case* *Case* *"People"*
Some paleontologists believe the *TYRANNOSAURUS* was a scavenger, eating animals that were already dead rather than hunting <u>it's</u> *OWN PREY*.	4. A) NO CHANGE **B) its** C) its' D) their *The prey <u>belongs to</u> the Tyrannosaurus.*	*Case* **Correct** *Case* *Agreement*
Although <u>their</u> still *EXPERIENCING* financial difficulties, *THE INVESTMENT FIRM* has shown significant growth in the past year.	5. A) NO CHANGE B) there C) its **D) it's** *The firm <u>is</u> experiencing difficulties.*	*Agreement, Case* *Agreement, Case* *Case* **Correct**
The proposed new contract provides higher wages for *EMPLOYEES* <u>which have worked</u> at the company for over three years.	6. A) NO CHANGE B) whom has worked C) who has worked **D) who have worked** *Employees are <u>people</u>. "Who" is the <u>subject</u> of "have worked".*	*People* *Case* *Agreement* **Correct**
Because of <u>their</u> *MAGNIFICENT PLUMAGE* and exotic origins, *PEACOCKS* were often kept in the European gardens to flaunt the wealth of the king.	7. **A) NO CHANGE** B) they're C) it's D) its	**Correct** *Case* *Agreement* *Agreement*

Lindsay got an extension on the report that <u>her and her lab partner</u> should have finished by today.	**8.** A) NO CHANGE **B) she and her lab partner** C) her lab partner and herself D) her lab partner and her	*Case* **Correct** *Case* *Case*
	"She" is the <u>subject</u> of "should have finished".	
An architect has designed a new skyscraper <u>who's</u> top floors house giant wind turbines that generate much of the building's power.	**9.** A) NO CHANGE B) thats **C) whose** D) which	*Case* *Not a word* **Correct** *Case*
In the event of a fire drill, *EMPLOYEES* must immediately evacuate the building and should not return to <u>his or her desk</u> until the alarm stops.	**10.** A) NO CHANGE **B) their desks** C) they're desks D) it's desk	*Agreement* **Correct** *Case* *Agreement*
	The desks <u>belong</u> to the employees.	
Marie Curie performed many experiments on *RADIOACTIVE ELEMENTS* without realizing that <u>one's exposure to it</u> was slowly killing *HER*.	**11.** A) NO CHANGE **B) her exposure to them** C) a person exposed to them D) their exposure to it	*Agreement* **Correct** *Agreement* *Agreement*
	This is not generic: the elements were killing <u>her</u>.	
Before my trip to Europe, I asked for travel advice from my friend Paul, <u>whom</u> *GREW UP* in Austria and frequently flies internationally.	**12.** A) NO CHANGE B) whose C) who's **D) who**	*Case* *Case* *Case* **Correct**
	"Who" is the <u>subject</u> of "grew up".	
When the *MOVIE* first opened, critics loved <u>its'</u> stunning and innovative visual *EFFECTS*, but they were turned off by its formulaic plot.	**13.** A) NO CHANGE B) their C) it's **D) its**	*Case* *Agreement* *Case* **Correct**
	The effects <u>belong</u> to the movie.	
The *FIELD OF VISION* produced by *OUR* eyes is actually curved, but <u>we experience it</u> as being straight because our brains reinterpret the images.	**14. A) NO CHANGE** B) we experience them C) they experience it D) one experiences them	**Correct** *Agreement* *Pronoun shift* *Pronoun shift*
<u>Its</u> difficult *TO PREDICT* exactly where hurricanes will hit, but forecasters can give the probabilities of various scenarios.	**15.** A) NO CHANGE B) They're **C) It's** D) Ones	*Case* *Agreement* **Correct** *Case*
	It <u>is</u> difficult. "It" has no antecedent. It's a dummy pronoun referring to "to predict". "It is difficult to predict hurricanes." means "To predict hurricanes is difficult." The antecedent is <u>not</u> "hurricanes".	

Lindsay got an extension on the report that her and her lab partner should have finished by today.

8.
A) NO CHANGE
B) she and her lab partner
C) her lab partner and herself
D) her lab partner and her

An architect has designed a new skyscraper who's top floors house giant wind turbines that generate much of the building's power.

9.
A) NO CHANGE
B) thats
C) whose
D) which

In the event of a fire drill, employees must immediately evacuate the building and should not return to his or her desk until the alarm stops.

10.
A) NO CHANGE
B) their desks
C) they're desks
D) it's desk

Marie Curie performed many experiments on radioactive elements without realizing that one's exposure to it was slowly killing her.

11.
A) NO CHANGE
B) her exposure to them
C) a person exposed to them
D) their exposure to it

Before my trip to Europe, I asked for travel advice from my friend Paul, whom grew up in Austria and frequently flies internationally.

12.
A) NO CHANGE
B) whose
C) who's
D) who

When the movie first opened, critics loved its' stunning and innovative visual effects, but they were turned off by its formulaic plot.

13.
A) NO CHANGE
B) their
C) it's
D) its

The field of vision produced by our eyes is actually curved, but we experience it as being straight because our brains reinterpret the images.

14.
A) NO CHANGE
B) we experience them
C) they experience it
D) one experiences them

Its difficult to predict exactly where hurricanes will hit, but forecasters can give the probabilities of various scenarios.

15.
A) NO CHANGE
B) They're
C) It's
D) Ones

III. OTHER TOPICS

Verbs and pronouns make up the bulk of the grammatical errors you'll see on the SAT. But of course, there are other parts of speech in English. Here are a few more rules that you may encounter on the test.

Adjectives and Adverbs

An adjective describes a noun. An adverb describes a verb, adjective, or other adverb.

> **ADJECTIVE: This is an <u>easy</u> TEST.** ("Easy" describes "test")
> **ADVERB: I <u>easily</u> PASSED the test.** ("Easily" describes "passed")

It's easy to tell when this concept is being tested. Just scan the choices: if some choices contain adjectives and others contain adverbs, you know it's an issue. To figure out which one you want, ask yourself:

What is the word describing?

If it's describing a *noun*, it should be an **adjective**.* If it's describing *anything else*, it should be an **adverb**.

> ✗ He died of a <u>previous</u> unknown disease.

What is "previous" here? The disease? It's a previous disease? No, the disease was previously *unknown*. "Unknown" is an adjective, not a noun, so we need an adverb to describe it:

> ✓ He died of a <u>previously</u> UNKNOWN disease.

Look at this one:

> ✗ He had an <u>extraordinarily</u> method for preparing pork chops.

What is "extraordinarily" supposed to describe here? It's not "preparing"—it's his **method** for preparing. "Method" is a noun, so we need an adjective to describe it:

> ✓ He had an <u>extraordinary</u> METHOD for preparing pork chops.

---

* Adjectives almost always describe nouns with one exception: adjectives can also act like the object of certain verbs like *is, feel,* or *seem*: "I am <u>sad</u>," "I feel <u>happy</u>," or "She seems <u>nice</u>." You wouldn't say: "I am <u>sadly</u>," "I feel <u>happily</u>," or "She seems <u>nicely</u>."

Comparatives and Superlatives

Adjectives can have different forms when they're used for comparisons. When you compare **two** people or things, use the **comparative**—either an "-er" word or the word "more".

> ✓ Alaska is <u>larger</u> than Texas.
> ✓ Of the *TWO* candidates, Julio is <u>more qualified</u> for the position.

When you compare **three or more** things, use the **superlative**—either an "-est" word or the word "most".

> ✓ Alaska is <u>the largest</u> of the *FIFTY* states.
> ✓ Of the *THREE* candidates, Julio is <u>the most qualified</u> for the position.

Don't mix up these forms. If a sentence uses a comparative or superlative form, check how many people or things it's talking about.

> ✗ Alaska is <u>the larger</u> of the *FIFTY* states.
> ✗ Of the *TWO* candidates, Julio is <u>the most qualified</u> for the position.

And don't mix up the different ways of forming them: use either "more/most" or "-er/-est", not both.*

> ✗ Alaska is <u>more larger</u> than Texas.
> ✗ Alaska is <u>the most largest</u> of the fifty states.

Adverbs can also be modified this way, but they can only take "more" and "most":

> ✓ Bob *CHOPPED* wood <u>more quickly</u> than Dave did.
> ✓ Out of everyone in the class, Bob *CHOPPED* the wood <u>most quickly</u>.

Comparisons

As we just saw, comparisons always require two or more things that are being compared. But we have to make sure that we compare *the same type of thing*. You can't compare apples and orangutans. Observe:

> ✗ Scott's apples taste better than Bob.

These words usually indicate there's a comparison in the sentence:

- ➤ Than
- ➤ As
- ➤ Like/unlike
- ➤ Differs from
- ➤ Similar to

---

* Most adjectives require one particular form: either *more/most* or *-er/-est*. You usually can't mix and match. In general, shorter words take -er/-est (larger/largest) and longer words take more/most (more qualified/most qualified).

This sentence says that Scott's apples taste better than *Bob himself*. That's no good. I mean, you *could* say that. I should hope they do taste better than Bob. But that's not what we meant to say. What we mean is:

> ✓ *Scott's apples* taste better than <u>Bob's apples</u>.

As always, when the sentences get more abstract, it becomes more difficult to spot.

> ✗ **Professor Starsky's *explanation* of Feynman's principles of subatomic particles was much more lucid than <u>his colleague</u>.**

In this sentence, we're comparing the "explanation" to the "colleague". That doesn't match. There are three main ways to correct this type of error.

> ✓ **...than <u>his colleague's explanation</u>.** (Repeat the thing you're comparing.)
> ✓ **...than <u>his colleague's</u>.** (Use a *possessive*; the object of comparison is implied.)
> ✓ **...than <u>that of his colleague</u>.** ("that" is a pronoun referring to "explanation".)

Please note that in the last correction, the word "that" is a kind of *pronoun*. That means it must *agree with its antecedent*. In this sentence, the antecedent of "that" is *explanation*, which is singular. However, if the object of comparison was plural, we'd use "those":

> ✓ *Scott's apples* taste better than <u>those of Bob</u>.

In this sentence, the object of comparison is "apples". That's plural, so we need a plural pronoun, "those".

Prepositions

We've already mentioned prepositions in the discussion of Verb Agreement. They're small words that connect words with regard to direction, location, or some other relationship. We saw some examples of prepositional phrases that describe nouns:

> ✓ *THE QUEEN* <u>of England</u> is rich.
> ✓ *THE DOGS* <u>in the yard</u> are barking.
> ✓ *THE MAN* <u>with three children</u> is married.
> ✓ *THE MOVIE* <u>about vampires</u> is scary.

Prepositional phrases don't have to modify nouns. They can also refer to verbs:

- ✓ I am *GOING* <u>to Kansas City</u>.
- ✓ I *LOOKED* <u>at the baby</u>.
- ✓ I am *TRAVELING* <u>with three children</u>.
- ✓ I was *BITTEN* <u>by a vampire</u>.

Here are some examples of prepositions:

To	With
Of	As
In	At
For	By
On	From

While it's sometimes difficult to define a preposition—how do you explain what "to" means?—it's usually clear from the context which preposition you should use:

- ✓ **Dave complained (<u>*TO* his mother</u>) (<u>*ABOUT* his sister</u>).**

This sentence has two prepositional phrases performing two jobs: "to my mother" tells us who Dave was talking to, and "about his sister" tells us the topic of the complaint. If we use the wrong prepositions, the sentence won't make any sense:

- ✕ **Dave complained (<u>*ON* his mother</u>) (<u>*BY* his sister</u>).**

Sometimes a word can take multiple prepositions, but our choice of preposition changes the meaning of the sentence. Compare:

- ✓ **I have <u>heard</u> the song.**   = I actually listened to the song.
- ✓ **I have <u>heard of</u> the song.**   = I know that the song exists.
- ✓ **I have <u>heard about</u> the song.**   = Someone talked to me about the song.

Other times, certain words will even *require* certain prepositions to follow them:

- ✕ **Dave is <u>listening at</u> the radio.**
- ✓ **Dave is <u>listening to</u> the radio.**

The prepositions "at" and "to" are very similar in meaning. But the word "listen" must be followed by the preposition "to". Why? That's just the way it is. We call this kind of rule an **idiomatic** rule: you can't figure out by knowing the meanings of the individual words—you just have to know the rule.

Sometimes, your choice of preposition will affect the verb that follows it. For example:

- ✕ **In times of danger, an ordinary person is *CAPABLE* <u>to perform</u> extraordinary acts.**
- ✓ **In times of danger, an ordinary person is *CAPABLE* <u>of performing</u> extraordinary acts.**

In this sentence, the word "capable" must be followed by the preposition "of" and the "-ing" form of the verb (the present participle); you *cannot* use the "to" form of the verb (the infinitive). The key to determining which verb form to use here has nothing to do with the word "perform"; it depends on the word that comes before it, "capable".

Of course, some words work the other way; they have to take the infinitive, not the participle:

> ✗ **An ordinary person is** *ABLE* <u>of performing</u> **extraordinary acts.**
> ✓ **An ordinary person is** *ABLE* <u>to perform</u> **extraordinary acts.**

This is an idiomatic rule: "capable" and "able" mean *exactly the same thing*, but one takes the "to" form and one takes the "-ing" form. Why? That's just the way it is.

Often you'll be able to "hear" idiomatic errors—a preposition will sound weird in a certain sentence. But they can sometimes be hard to spot. If you're not sure which preposition to use in a sentence, first eliminate any choices that make *other* errors that are easier to spot (verb tense, pronoun agreement, etc.) Then make sure you understand the intended meaning of the sentence. And if all else fails, *guess*.

Commonly Confused Words

English has a lot of words that sound very similar to each other but are spelled differently and mean different things. These words are easy to mix up, and the SAT frequently tests your knowledge of the differences between them.

Pronouns

We've already seen an example of spelling confusion: the difference between contraction and possessive pronoun forms. Here's a summary of the forms we discussed:

It's means *it is.* *Its* shows **possession.** *Its'* is **never correct.**	It's a beautiful day! The dog wagged <u>its</u> tail. Never use <u>its'</u> for any reason.	[= <u>It is</u> a beautiful day!] [= The tail <u>belongs to</u> the dog.]
You're means *you are.* *Your* shows **possession.**	<u>You're</u> a jerk. <u>Your</u> fly is open.	[= <u>You are</u> a jerk.] [= The fly <u>belongs to</u> you.]
They're means *they are.* *Their* shows **possession.** *There* shows **location.**	<u>They're</u> going to win. I like <u>their</u> uniforms. Put it over <u>there.</u>	[= <u>They are</u> going to win.] [= The uniforms <u>belong to</u> them.] [= I'm telling you <u>where to</u> put it.]
Who's means **who is.** *Whose* shows **possession.**	the man <u>who's</u> buying my car the man <u>whose</u> car I'm buying	[= the man <u>who is</u> buying my car] [= the car <u>belongs to</u> the man]

Would *have* vs. Would *of*

We've already seen some verb forms that use "have".

> ✓ **If you had asked me to the dance, I <u>would have gone</u> with you.**

Verb forms using "would have" can be contracted to "would've".

> ✓ **If you had asked me to the dance, I <u>would've gone</u> with you.**

The contraction *sounds* a lot like "would of". But don't be fooled: **"would of" is never correct.**

> ✗ **If you had asked me to the dance, I <u>would of gone</u> with you.**

The same is true for any other verbs that use "have".

> ✓ **I <u>might have gone</u> with you.**
> ✗ **I <u>might of</u> gone with you.**
>
> ✓ **I <u>could have gone</u> with you.**
> ✗ **I <u>could of</u> gone with you.**
>
> ✓ **I <u>will have gone</u> with you.**
> ✗ **I <u>will of</u> gone with you**

It may not always be clear which tense or verb form you need in any given sentence. **But you should NEVER say "would of".** There is no legitimate English sentence in which "would" is followed by "of". *

Than vs. Then

Than is used for comparisons. Don't confuse it with *then*, which means "next" or "following".

> ✓ **I am better <u>than</u> you.**
> ✗ **I am better <u>then</u> you.**
>
> ✓ **I went to the store, and <u>then</u> got a snack.**
> ✗ **I went to the store and <u>than</u> got a snack.**

---

*   Except for the sentence, "You should never say 'would of'".

Other Commonly Confused Words

Here are a few examples of commonly confused words. None of these will show up very frequently on the SAT, but you may see one every once in a while.

To is a preposition used with infinitive verbs. **Too** means "more than necessary".	I am <u>too</u> tired <u>to</u> go out. I tried <u>to</u> solve the problem, but it was <u>too</u> hard.
Affect is a *verb* meaning "produce a change". **Effect** is a *noun* meaning "a change".	The accident <u>affected</u> me deeply. I still feel those <u>effects</u> today.
Accept means to receive. **Except** is a preposition meaning "but not".	I will <u>accept</u> any currency… … <u>except</u> Canadian Dollars.
Principal means "main or primary". **Principle** means "guiding rule".	I am the <u>principal</u> officer in the company. I live by one <u>principle</u>: always be polite.

CONVENTIONS OF USAGE SUMMARY
Here are the key rules to look out for on SAT Usage questions

1. Verbs
- The verb must **agree** in number with the subject.
- The verb must be in the appropriate **tense**.
- **Irregular** verbs may have special forms.
- Don't confuse active and **passive** voice.

2. Pronouns
- A pronoun must **agree** in number with its antecedent.
- A pronoun's **case** is determined by its role in the sentence.
- Don't confuse **contractions** and **possessive** pronouns.
- **Relative** pronouns behave similarly to regular pronouns.

3. Other issues
- **Adjectives** describe nouns. **Adverbs** describe all other words.
- **Comparatives** compare two things, **superlatives** compare three or more.
- Make sure to use the correct **prepositions**.
- Your choice of preposition may affect the form of the **verb** that follows.
- Beware of **commonly confused words:**
  - Use "would **have**", not "would of".
  - Use "**than**" for comparisons, not "then".

CONVENTIONS OF USAGE EXERCISE

*This exercise contains a full passage with 11 questions, just like an SAT passage. Unlike a real SAT passage, it only features **Conventions of Usage** questions. Look out for all the rules discussed above.*

PASSAGE I

Bicycling the Copenhagen Way

Last summer, while my parents and I spent a few weeks in Copenhagen, I **1** developed a new fascination with bicycles. We noticed that bicycle culture there was far different from what we were used to in America. The number of bicycles on the city streets **2** were astounding. Almost every block in the center of town had a bike rack filled with them, sometimes overflowing onto the street. The city even had a free bicycle sharing program. **3** You could pick up a bike from an outpost in one part of the city and drop it off at our destination.

Americans don't use bicycles this way. Back home, people usually cycle for recreation or fitness. People associate bikes with memories of Dad running alongside them the first time they **4** had took off their training wheels, or teenagers riding mountain bikes down homemade ramps. Others think of triathlons or cardio machines at the gym. But places like Copenhagen engage in "utility cycling": locals use bikes simply as a way to get around town. About 500,000 residents of the city—over a third of **5** its population— **6** commutes by bicycle every day.

1
A) NO CHANGE
B) develop
C) am developing
D) would of developed

2
A) NO CHANGE
B) was
C) is
D) are

3
A) NO CHANGE
B) People
C) We
D) One

4
A) NO CHANGE
B) had took in
C) took off
D) take to

5
A) NO CHANGE
B) it's
C) they're
D) there

6
A) NO CHANGE
B) commuted
C) will commute
D) commute

CONTINUE →

Conventions of Usage Exercise

PASSAGE I

Bicycling the Copenhagen Way

Last summer, while my parents and I *SPENT* a few weeks in Copenhagen, I **1** developed a new fascination with bicycles. We noticed that bicycle culture there *WAS* far different from what we were used to in America. The *NUMBER* ~~of bicycles on the city streets~~ **2** were astounding. Almost every block in the center of town *HAD* a bike rack filled with them, sometimes overflowing onto the street. The city even had a free bicycle sharing program. **3** You could pick up a bike from an outpost in one part of the city and drop it off at *OUR* destination.

Americans don't use bicycles this way. Back home, people usually cycle for recreation or fitness. People associate bikes with memories of Dad running alongside them the first time they **4** had took off their training wheels, or teenagers riding mountain bikes down homemade ramps. Others think of triathlons or cardio machines at the gym. But places like Copenhagen engage in "utility cycling": locals use bikes simply as a way to get around town. About 500,000 *RESIDENTS* of the *CITY*—over a third of **5** its population— **6** commutes by bicycle every day.

1

A)	**NO CHANGE**	**Correct**
B)	develop	*Tense*
C)	am developing	*Tense*
D)	would of developed	*Tense/Spelling*

2

A)	NO CHANGE	*Verb Agreement*
B)	**was**	**Correct**
C)	is	*Tense*
D)	are	*Tense, Verb Agreement*

3

A)	NO CHANGE	*Pronoun Shift*
B)	People	*Pronoun Shift*
C)	**We**	**Correct** "our destination"
D)	One	*Pronoun Shift*

4

A)	NO CHANGE	*Irregular verb*
B)	had took in	*Idiomatic preposition*
C)	**took off**	**Correct**
D)	take to	*Tense, Idiomatic preposition*

Take in = receive; take to = become accustomed to.

5

A)	**NO CHANGE**	**Correct**
B)	it's	*Case*
C)	they're	*Pronoun Agreement, Case*
D)	there	*Pronoun Agreement, Case*

Antecedent is "city"; the population belongs to it.

6

A)	NO CHANGE	*Verb Agreement*
B)	commuted	*Tense*
C)	will commute	*Tense*
D)	**commute**	**Correct**

Subject is "residents". Previous sentence is <u>present</u>.

Utility cycling has many advantages over commuting by car, both for individuals and for the community as a whole. *CYCLING* is a cleaner form of transportation because it produces no emissions. *CYCLING* is safer than driving, both for passengers and for pedestrians. [7] It's also more economical than driving—*BICYCLES ARE* cheap to own and only [8] requires the fuel you need to run your body. On top of all that, it's great exercise and promotes a healthy lifestyle.

If utility cycling is so great, why don't more Americans do it? One problem is that American cities are not well equipped for bike travel. Most American cities are dominated by suburban *AREAS* [9] which *NEIGHBORHOODS* are far from each other, making commutes too long and often too dangerous for bike travel. European cities have smaller, interconnected streets that are more bicycle-friendly.

While *UTILITY CYCLING* in the United States [10] are still far less common than in Europe, more and more people *HAVE* [11] started using bicycles for transportation. Cities from New York to Seattle have launched initiatives to encourage utility cycling. They have even contemplated bike sharing programs like the one in Copenhagen. "All big cities should promote bicycle use," one transit official said. "Bicycles take cars off the road, which is a big win for everyone."

7

A)	**NO CHANGE**	Correct
B)	Its	*Case*
C)	Its'	*Case*
D)	Their	*Case, Pronoun Agreement*

Antecedent is "Cycling" in previous sentence.

8

A)	NO CHANGE	*Verb Agreement*
B)	required	*Tense*
C)	were required by	*Tense, Active/Passive*
D)	**require**	Correct

9

A)	NO CHANGE	*Case*
B)	whom	*Case*
C)	**whose**	Correct
D)	who's	*Case*

The neighborhoods belong to the suburban areas.

10

A)	NO CHANGE	*Verb Agreement*
B)	were	*Verb Agreement*
C)	**is**	Correct
D)	was	*Tense*

11

Which of the following alternatives to the underlined portion would NOT be acceptable?

A)	begun to use	*Idiomatic*
B)	**started with using**	Correct
C)	started to use	*Idiomatic*
D)	begun using	*Idiomatic*

Both "begin" and "start" can be followed by either the infinitive or the "ing" form.

Utility cycling has many advantages over commuting by car, both for individuals and for the community as a whole. Cycling is a cleaner form of transportation because it produces no emissions. Cycling is safer than driving, both for passengers and for pedestrians. [7] It's also more economical than driving—bicycles are cheap to own and only [8] requires the fuel you need to run your body. On top of all that, it's great exercise and promotes a healthy lifestyle.

If utility cycling is so great, why don't more Americans do it? One problem is that American cities are not well equipped for bike travel. Most American cities are dominated by suburban areas [9] which neighborhoods are far from each other, making commutes too long and often too dangerous for bike travel. European cities have smaller, interconnected streets that are more bicycle-friendly.

While utility cycling in the United States [10] are still far less common than in Europe, more and more people have [11] started using bicycles for transportation. Cities from New York to Seattle have launched initiatives to encourage utility cycling. They have even contemplated bike-sharing programs like the one in Copenhagen. "All big cities should promote bicycle use," one transit official said. "Bicycles take cars off the road, which is a big win for everyone."

7

A) NO CHANGE
B) Its
C) Its'
D) Their

8

A) NO CHANGE
B) required
C) were required by
D) require

9

A) NO CHANGE
B) whom
C) whose
D) who's

10

A) NO CHANGE
B) were
C) is
D) was

11

Which of the following alternatives to the underlined portion would NOT be acceptable?

A) begun to use
B) started with using
C) started to use
D) begun using

■ Standard English Conventions: Sentence Structure

The Conventions of Usage rules we already saw dealt with the relationship between individual words, while Sentence Structure questions deal with the relationships between larger parts of a sentence—how to join clauses, where to place modifiers, etc. Since the rules we discuss in this chapter deal with larger parts of a sentence, it's important to remember to **read the entire sentence**, not just the underlined portion, before picking an answer choice.

There's a lot of overlap between these categories, and the rules discussed in this chapter are still "rules of grammar and usage". On the real test, you may see a question that has a Fragment in one choice and a Verb Agreement error in another. *Everything is important, and everything is connected.*

I. WHAT'S A CLAUSE

We'll start by defining a few basic parts of a sentence. Several of the common errors on Sentence Structure questions deal with the same concepts, so everything will be clearer if we lay some groundwork first.

Sentences are made up of **clauses**. A clause is any phrase that contains a subject and a verb. There are two main types of clauses that we're concerned with here.

Independent clauses

An **independent clause** is a clause that can stand alone as a complete sentence:

> ✓ **Chapman is a doctor.**

The subject is "Chapman" and the verb is "is". It's "independent" because it doesn't *need* anything else; it sounds fine as it is. However, we could add another clause if we wanted:

> ✓ **Chapman is a doctor, and he cured my acne.**

This sentence has two independent clauses, linked together with the word "and". We happened to put them together in the same sentence, but either of the underlined phrases would sound fine all by itself, with or without the "and".

✓ **Chapman is a doctor**	✓ **He cured my acne**
✓ **Chapman is a doctor**	✓ **And he cured my acne.***

Dependent clauses

A **dependent clause** is a clause that *cannot* stand alone as a complete sentence.

> ✓ <u>**After he cured my acne**</u>**, I felt much better.**
> ✓ <u>**When I go out**</u>**, I am no longer embarrassed by my skin.**

Each of these sentences contains one dependent clause followed by an independent clause. In each case, the dependent clause cannot stand by itself as a sentence. They *describe* the main clauses, *dependent* on them.[†]

✗ **After he cured my acne.**	✓ **I felt much better.**
✗ **When I go out.**	✓ **I am no longer embarrassed by my skin.**

The second clauses here sound fine as sentences, but the first ones do not. "After he cured my acne" is not a complete sentence: what happened after he cured my acne? It *depends* on the main clause to tell us what it's talking about.

---

* Some people may have told you it's wrong to start a sentence with "and" or "but". That is a lie. When teachers tell you not to do this, they really mean that you shouldn't do it a lot because it makes you sound like a five year old ("I went to the zoo. And then I went to the park. And then I went to lunch. And then I got a sandwich.") But don't worry about this rule—it won't be tested on the SAT.

† Dependent clauses are also called *subordinate* clauses. "Subordinate" means *submissive, subservient,* or *less important.* These clauses are *servants* to the main clauses.

Relative clauses

Relative clauses are special kinds of dependent clauses that use **relative pronouns**. We talked about relative pronouns in the Conventions of Usage chapter, remember?* They're words that can connect clauses, but they're also pronouns that have specific antecedents.

✓ **Chapman is the doctor who cured my acne.**

In this sentence, "who cured my acne" is a relative clause: its subject is "who" and its verb is "cured". "Who" is a relative pronoun whose antecedent is "the doctor", so the whole clause "who cured my acne" describes "the doctor". The antecedent of a relative pronoun is almost always the word directly before it.

Relative clauses are different from other dependent clauses because *they are directly connected to a word in the main clause*. In the earlier example, the dependent clause "after he cured my acne" didn't refer to any one word in the main clause—it referred to the whole situation. But here, the clause is specifically linked to "the doctor."

But the relative clause is still dependent because "who cured my acne" cannot stand alone as a sentence.[†]

✓ **Chapman is the doctor.**   ✗ **Who cured my acne.**

It's not a complete thought; it's a description of someone. Thus it *depends* on the independent clause "Chapman is the doctor" to tell us what it's talking about.

Here are some more examples of dependent and independent clauses. The first three sentences contain relative clauses, the last two do not. In each of these examples, the independent clause would sound fine as a sentence all by itself, but the dependent clause would not—it needs the independent clause to tell us what it's talking about.

> Relative clauses begin with relative pronouns— words like *who*, *which*, or *that*.

---

* Do you remember? Do you?

† Unless it's a question: "Who cured my acne?" But that's a whole different issue. Don't worry about questions.

Sentence	Independent Clause	Dependent Clause
I want to meet a woman <u>who loves fishing</u>.	I want to meet a woman	who loves fishing
Harold got a new bike, <u>which he really liked</u>.	Harold got a new bike	which he really liked
The team <u>that scores the most points</u> will win.	The team will win	that scores the most points
You have been a real jerk <u>since you got your promotion</u>.	You have been a real jerk	since you got your promotion
<u>Once you finish your broccoli</u> you can have dessert.	you can have dessert	Once you finish your broccoli

Modifiers

Both clause types we've seen have a subject and verb. But what about phrases that don't have a subject and verb? Take a look at this:

> ✓ <u>**Hoping to cure my acne**</u>, **Chapman gave me a special herb.**

This sentence contains an independent clause, "Chapman gave me a special herb," and a separate opening phrase, "Hoping to cure my acne." The opening phrase is clearly not an independent clause, since it clearly can't stand by itself as a sentence. But it's not a dependent clause either, since it doesn't have a subject-verb pair. Nor does it have any kind of connecting word to link it to the main clause.

We'll call this kind of phrase a **modifier**, because it modifies the main clause. "Modifies" is just a fancy word for "describes". So any bunch of words that isn't a clause we'll call a modifier. There are lots of different types of modifiers. Often, they start with a verb without a subject: *

---

* Notice that the verbs here—"hoping", "known", and "to perform"—are the present participle, past participle, and infinitive forms (the last three rows of the verb chart at the beginning of the Conventions of Usage chapter). These forms (called "non-finite verbs" by fancy people) cannot be the main verb of an independent clause, but they can occur in modifiers like this.

> ✓ <u>**Hoping to cure my acne**</u>, Chapman gave me a special herb.
> ✓ <u>**Known only to a few specialists**</u>, this herb grows naturally in Asia.
> ✓ <u>**To obtain it**</u>, you need to know the right people.

Or they could just be long noun phrases without a verb:

> ✓ <u>**A brilliant doctor**</u>, Chapman cured my acne.

And they don't have to come at the beginning of a sentence:

> ✓ Chapman gave me a special herb, <u>**hoping to cure my acne**</u>.
> ✓ Chapman, <u>**hoping to cure my acne**</u>, gave me a special herb.

So there are three things of interest to us: independent clauses, dependent clauses, and modifiers.

II. FRAGMENTS

As we mentioned earlier when we were talking about verb agreement, every sentence must have a **subject** and a **verb**. If it *doesn't*, it's not a sentence—it's a **sentence fragment**. That is:

> ## Every sentence must have at least one independent clause.

Back in the Conventions of Usage chapter, we talked about the idea of a *core sentence*—the main subject and verb of a sentence stripped of all the extra descriptive stuff. We found the core sentence by deleting prepositional phrases and phrases set off by commas.*

We can do exactly the same thing to find an independent clause. Sentences can often have very complicated structures, jumbles of commas and modifiers and clauses. But no matter how long and complicated a sentence is, if you can't find a core sentence with a subject and a verb buried in there, it's a fragment.

> ## There are three main ways to fix a fragment:

1. Change the verb

Here's an example of a fragment:

> ✗ **Riding the bus.**

See that? That's not a sentence. First of all, it has no subject. Who's riding the bus? We don't know. Okay, so let's **add a subject**:

> ✗ <u>**Bob**</u> **riding the bus.**

Hmm. That's better, but it's still not a sentence. It sounds like something a caveman would say. This is a fragment because it has **no main verb**. That's bad.

Wait, isn't "riding" a verb? Yes, but it's only **part of a verb**. A word like "riding" is a *participle* and *cannot stand by itself as a main verb*. It can be in a modifier, and it can be part of a multi-word verb phrase (like "is riding"). But it can't be the main verb by itself in an independent clause.

We can fix it by changing the verb to a form that can be a main verb:

---

* We talked about this in the Conventions of Usage chapter. Don't you remember? Of course you don't. Look it up.

✓ Bob <u>is riding</u> the bus.   ✓ Bob <u>rides</u> the bus.

Much better.

2. Remove a connector

Take a look at this sentence:

> ✏ Dr. Steve, who studies cell biology and is trying to develop new cancer drugs.

Hmmm. It *kinda* sounds like a sentence. We have a subject, "Dr. Steve". And we actually have two verbs: "studies" and "is trying". So what's wrong here?

The problem is that the verbs are stuck behind "who". *Everything* after the comma is a *dependent clause*:

> ✏ who studies cell biology and is trying to develop new cancer drugs.

See that? It can't stand alone as a sentence. That means it's a dependent clause (more specifically, a relative clause). **Dependent clauses and modifiers are not part of the core sentence.** So let's ignore it and see what we're left with.

> ✕ Dr. Steve, ~~who studies cell biology and is trying to develop new cancer drugs.~~

"Dr. Steve" is definitely not a sentence. This is a fragment.

The problem is that the word "who" *starts* a relative clause, but there's nothing to *stop* it until the end of the sentence. "Who" is the subject of both verbs, so there's no verb to go with "Dr. Steve".

There are two ways we could fix it. First, we could *delete the relative pronoun*:

> ✓ Dr. <u>Steve studies</u> cell biology and is trying to develop new cancer drugs.

Now, there's no dependent clause at all. We just have one subject with two verbs: *Dr. Steve studies… and is trying*. That's an independent clause.

Second, we could *end the relative clause* with a comma and *remove the conjunction* "and":

> ✓ Dr. Steve, who studies cell <u>biology, is</u> trying to develop new cancer drugs.

Now the relative clause is just "who studies cell biology". If we ignore that clause, we're left with an independent clause:

> ✓ Dr. Steve, ~~who studies cell biology,~~ *IS TRYING* to develop new cancer drugs.

Our main clause is *Dr. Steve... is trying*. That's a complete sentence. Excellent.

3. Join another sentence

Of course, the easiest way to fix a fragment is to link it to the sentence next door:

> ✗ While riding the bus. My father lost his wallet.

The second sentence is fine, but the first one is a fragment. It's just a modifier; it can't stand by itself. But it *can* be linked to the second sentence:

> ✓ While riding the bus, my father lost his wallet.

In the above example, we replaced the period with a comma. But sometimes we might not need a comma to connect them:

> ✗ Dave got a tutor. To help him with his math homework.
> ✓ Dave got a tutor to help him with his math homework.

We'll talk more about how to use commas in the Punctuation chapter.

THIS PAGE INTENTIONALLY LEFT BLANK

Fragment Drill

Core sentences of independent clauses are highlighted for complete sentences and for the corrections of fragments. Possible corrections are given for each fragment, but there are often several different ways to turn a fragment into a sentence, and there may be other legitimate corrections.
In corrected sentences, deletions are crossed out; additions are underlined.

1. **Complete Sentence.**
   I AM GOING to the library to study, and *I WILL COME* back at six.

2. **Fragment.**
   Delete "which" and the comma before it, or delete "but" and add a comma:
   Possible correction:
   a) *SACRAMENTO, which IS* the capital of California *BUT IS* only its seventh largest city.

   b) *SACRAMENTO*, which is the capital of California, but *IS* only its seventh largest city.

3. **Complete Sentence.**
   THE MOTORCYCLE, [weaving from lane to lane and quickly darting between cars,] *WAS BEING FOLLOWED* by a pack of police cruisers.

4. **Fragment.**
   The first sentence has no subject. Join it to the second with a comma:
   Possible correction:
   Produced thirty years after the original film, *THE SEQUEL WAS MADE* with sophisticated computer technology that has only recently been developed.

5. **Fragment.**
   Delete "who" and the comma before it:
   Possible correction:
   MOE BERG, who HELD degrees from two Ivy League schools, an education that was, to say the least, unusual for a baseball player of his era.

6. **Fragment.**
   Turn the –ing verb into a main verb:
   Possible corrections:
   THE DOUBLE AGENT running *RAN* up and down the labyrinthine hallways of the National Security Agency, keeping a tight grip on the flash memory card that held the schematics of the doomsday machine.

7. **Fragment.**
   "Because" makes the first sentence a dependent clause. Join it to the second with a comma:
   Possible correction:
   Because Gary was worried about losing everything he owns, *HE DECIDED* that getting fire insurance would best protect his assets.

8. **Complete Sentence.**
   THOMAS PAINE WAS an outspoken supporter of American Independence. *HIS PAMPHLET*, Common Sense, *WAS* a harsh denouncement of British rule over the colonies.

FRAGMENT DRILL

Take a look at these examples and see if they are complete sentences or sentence fragments. If it is a complete sentence, **circle the subject and verb** *of each independent clause. If it is a fragment, write a corrected sentence below it. If there are two sentences, make sure both are complete and circle the subject and verb of each of them.*

1. I am going to the library to study, and I will come back at six.

2. Sacramento, which is the capital of California but is only its seventh largest city.

3. The motorcycle, weaving from lane to lane and quickly darting between cars, was being followed by a pack of police cruisers.

4. Produced thirty years after the original film. The sequel was made with sophisticated computer technology that has only recently been developed.

5. Moe Berg, who held degrees from two Ivy League schools, an education that was, to say the least, unusual for a baseball player of his era.

6. The double agent running up and down the labyrinthine hallways of the National Security Agency, keeping a tight grip on the flash memory card that held the schematics of the doomsday machine.

7. Because Gary was worried about losing everything he owns. He decided that getting fire insurance would best protect his assets.

8. Thomas Paine was an outspoken supporter of American Independence. His pamphlet, *Common Sense*, was a harsh denouncement of British rule over the colonies.

9. Eddy Merckx, who is perhaps the greatest cyclist of all time and is one of the most famous people in Belgium.

10. Plato and Aristotle are still the most widely read ancient Greek philosophers on college campuses today. Despite the recent surge in interest in earlier thinkers such as Heraclitus and Empedocles.

11. The nineteenth-century French writer Gustave Flaubert spending almost six years writing the novel *Madame Bovary* because of his meticulous method of composition.

12. Every year, countries around the globe sponsor ultra-marathons, races that can last over 24 hours and stretch across a track 60 miles or longer—more than twice as long as a traditional marathon.

13. Having already revolutionized the scientific world with his theory of relativity, Albert Einstein spent the remainder of his life searching for a unified field theory. Which he ultimately was unable to discover.

14. The founder of Lego, Ole Kirk Christiansen, first making toys in the early 1930s. It was not until 1949, however, that he started producing the famous plastic bricks that bear the name today.

15. Upset by the barrage of news stories about recent scandals at Harvard, Mr. Bennett, who has been one of the most generous donors to the University since he graduated from its undergraduate engineering school in 1982, began to have doubts about the amount of his annual donation.

9. **Fragment.**

Delete "who" and the comma before it, or delete "and" and add a comma:
Possible corrections:

a) *EDDY MERCKX, who IS* perhaps the greatest cyclist of all time *AND IS* one of the most famous people in Belgium.

b) *EDDY MERCKX,* who is perhaps the greatest cyclist of all ~~time, and~~ *IS* one of the most famous people in Belgium.

His name is pronounced <Merx>.

10. **Fragment.**

The second sentence lacks a subject or verb. Join it to the first with a comma:
Possible correction:

PLATO AND ARISTOTLE ARE still the most widely read ancient Greek philosophers on college campuses today, despite the recent surge in interest in earlier thinkers such as Heraclitus and Empedocles.

11. **Fragment.**

Turn the –ing verb into a main verb:
Possible correction:

The nineteenth-century French writer *GUSTAVE FLAUBERT* ~~spending~~ *SPENT* almost six years writing the novel *Madame Bovary* because of his meticulous method of composition.

12. **Complete Sentence.**

Every year, *COUNTRIES* around the globe *SPONSOR* ultra-marathons, races that can last over 24 hours and stretch across a track 60 miles or longer—more than twice as long as a traditional marathon.

13. **Fragment.**

The second sentence is a relative clause. Join it to the first with a comma:
Possible correction:

Having already revolutionized the scientific world with his theory of relativity, *ALBERT EINSTEIN SPENT* the remainder of his life searching for a unified field theory, which he ultimately was unable to discover.

14. **Fragment.**

The first sentence lacks a main verb. Turn its –ing verb into a main verb.
Possible correction:

THE FOUNDER OF LEGO, Ole Kirk Christiansen, first ~~making~~ *MADE* toys in the early 1930s. *IT WAS* not until 1949, however, that he started producing the famous plastic bricks that bear the name today.

15. **Complete Sentence.**

[Upset by the barrage of news stories about recent scandals at Harvard,] *MR. BENNETT,* [who has been one of the most generous donors to the University since he graduated from its undergraduate engineering school in 1982,] *BEGAN* to have doubts about the amount of his annual donation.

THIS PAGE INTENTIONALLY LEFT BLANK

III. RUN-ON SENTENCES

We said that every sentence must have *at least one* independent clause. But what if we have two independent clauses in the same sentence? Take a look at these sentences:

> ✓ *I AM GOING* to the game. *SCOTT WILL MEET* me there.

These two sentences are fine; each is an independent clause with a subject and verb. However, there are rules about how you can combine them into *one* sentence. If you don't follow the rules, you get a **run-on sentence**.

First, you can't just shove one clause next to the other **without any connection at all**. This is sometimes called a *fused sentence*:

> ✗ *I AM GOING* to the <u>game</u> <u>*SCOTT*</u> *WILL MEET* me there.

Second, you cannot combine independent clauses **with a comma alone**. This is sometimes called a *comma splice* or *comma fault*.

> ✗ *I AM GOING* to the <u>game,</u> <u>*SCOTT*</u> *WILL MEET* me there.

The key to spotting run-on sentences is to ***look for subject-verb pairs***. As we saw with Fragments, the subject-verb pair makes up the core of an independent clause. If you see two subject-verb pairs with no connection between them, or with only a comma between them, then it's a run-on.*

There are three main ways to fix a run-on:

1. Use a period

Since independent clauses, by definition, can stand alone as sentences, the easiest way to fix a run-on is to simply make two separate sentences:

> ✓ *I AM GOING* to the <u>game.</u> *SCOTT WILL MEET* me there.

---

* There is one case in which you can join subject-verb pairs directly. A relative pronoun is often optional: instead of "Dave watched the movie <u>that I made</u>" you can say "Dave watched the movie <u>I made</u>." Here we have two subject-verb pairs with nothing connecting them, but it's implied that the second pair "I made" directly modifies "the movie". You may see sentences like this on the SAT, but they're usually pretty easy to distinguish from fused sentences.

Nice. Just make sure that both your clauses are independent clauses before you separate them with a period.

Other punctuation

Some punctuation marks can directly connect independent clauses without making separate sentences.*

Dash	✓ I am going to the game—Scott will meet me there.
Colon	✓ I am going to the game: Scott will meet me there.
Semicolon	✓ I am going to the game; Scott will meet me there.

Every semicolon *must* have an independent clause before and after it.

However, unlike a colon or a dash, *a **semicolon** must separate independent clauses.*

✓ I am going to one game this <u>year—the Super Bowl</u>.
✓ I am going to one game this <u>year: the Super Bowl</u>.
✗ I am going to one game this <u>year; the Super Bowl</u>.

"The Super Bowl" is not an independent clause (it has no verb), so we *cannot* connect it to the main clause with a semicolon. But we can use a dash or a colon (or even a comma).

2. Add a conjunction

You could also use a **comma with a conjunction**.†

✓ *I AM GOING* to the game, <u>and</u> *SCOTT WILL MEET* me there.

Here are some examples of conjunctions:

and	although
but	because
or	while

Conjunctions are words like "and", "but", or "or" that can be used to directly join independent clauses.‡ We saw this construction earlier when we were talking about independent clauses, remember?

---

* The different punctuation marks do create slightly different meanings in these sentences, but don't worry about that right now. We'll talk more about these marks in the Punctuation chapter.

† Can I use a conjunction *without* a comma? Well, sometimes. It's usually not against the rules (especially if the clauses are short). But on the SAT, a choice like that is usually wrong (albeit for other reasons). If you see independent clauses joined with a conjunction and no comma, there's probably a better choice somewhere else.

‡ There are actually two different kinds of conjunctions. Words like "and", "but", and "or" are *coordinating* conjunctions, while "although", "because", or "while" are *subordinating* conjunctions. You can use either kind to join independent clauses. But technically, if you put a subordinating conjunction before a clause, it becomes a dependent clause. Either one will fix the run-on problem, so it doesn't matter.

✓ CHAPMAN IS a doctor, <u>and</u> HE CURED my acne.

Conjunctions usually come between clauses, but they don't have to:

✓ CHOCOLATE IS my favorite, <u>but</u> I'M GOING to get vanilla.
✓ <u>Although</u> CHOCOLATE IS my favorite, I'M GOING to get vanilla.

The second sentence means (roughly) the same thing as the first, but it puts its conjunction at the beginning of the sentence instead of between the clauses. That's totally fine.

Remember to use only *one* conjunction at a time:

✗ <u>Although</u> CHOCOLATE IS my favorite, <u>but</u> I'M GOING to get vanilla.

Furthermore, each conjunction can *only* link two clauses. What if the sentence has more than two clauses?

✗ I WILL ARRIVE at the game at three o'clock, although SCOTT WILL MEET me there, HE WON'T ARRIVE until four.

We've got three clauses here, but only one conjunction: "although". The conjunction can connect the first and the second, or it can connect the second and the third, but it can't do both. Either way, there is one clause that isn't properly connected. This is a run-on. Sentences this long are usually best corrected by splitting them up with a period:

✓ I WILL ARRIVE at the game at three o'clock. Although SCOTT WILL MEET me there, HE WON'T ARRIVE until four.

3. Change one clause

The run-on rule deals with the connection between *two or more* independent clauses. Therefore, we could fix a run-on by **getting rid of one of the independent clauses**.

✗ I WENT to a game at Wrigley Field, IT IS one of the oldest stadiums in America.

This is a run-on because it has two independent clauses linked with a comma alone. We could fix it with a semicolon or a conjunction. But instead, let's change the second clause so it's no longer independent:

> ✓ I went to a game at Wrigley Field, <u>one of the oldest stadiums in America</u>.
> ✓ I went to a game at Wrigley Field, <u>which is one of the oldest stadiums in America</u>.

Relative clauses behave a lot like modifiers: a relative clause must describe the noun that comes before it.

In the first sentence, the second half is a modifier describing "Wrigley Field". In the second, it's a relative clause. In both cases, we avoid the run-on because there simply aren't two independent clauses anymore.

You can even sometimes combine the two clauses into a *single* clause with two verbs:

> ✗ *DR. STEVE HAS BEEN DEVELOPING* new cancer <u>drugs, *HE HAS MADE*</u> a breakthrough.

This is a run-on. It has two subject-verb pairs, "Dr. Steve *has been trying*" and "he *has made*", with only a comma between them. But the subject of the second clause, "he", is the same person as the subject of the first clause, "Dr. Steve". So let's combine them into one clause with two verbs:

> ✓ Dr. Steve *HAS BEEN DEVELOPING* new cancer <u>drugs and *HAS MADE*</u> a breakthrough.

THIS PAGE INTENTIONALLY LEFT BLANK

Run-on Drill

NOTE: "Run-on (CS)" is a Comma Splice. "Run-on (FS)" is a Fused Sentence.

I TRIED to go to the <u>library, it was</u> closed.	1. A) NO CHANGE B) library it was <u>**C) library, but it was**</u> D) library but was	*Run-on (CS)* *Run-on (FS)* Correct *Compound verb*

Choice D makes a compound verb with a single subject, "I"
That makes no sense here: I tried ... but [I] was closed.

TRAVIS IS very excited about the science fair next <u>week; hoping</u> that his experiment about crickets will win the top prize.	2. A) NO CHANGE <u>**B) week, hoping**</u> C) week, he hopes D) week. Hoping	*Semicolon fragment* **Correct** *Run-on (CS)* *Fragment*

THE BOARD of directors *WILL NAME* a wing of the hospital after Dr. <u>Robinson, since it</u> *WAS* his donation that made the new construction possible.	3. Which of the following alternatives to the underlined portion would NOT be acceptable? A) Robinson. It B) Robinson; it <u>**C) Robinson, it**</u> D) Robinson—it	 *Period* *Semicolon* **Correct.** *Run-on (CS)* *Dash*

PROFESSOR FULLINGTON TEACHES the introductory course on <u>thermodynamics, it is</u> one of the hardest classes in the department.	4. A) NO CHANGE B) thermodynamics it is C) thermodynamics. Which is <u>**D) thermodynamics,**</u>	*Run-on (CS)* *Run-on (FS)* *Fragment* **Correct**

Choice D turns the second independent clause into a modifier.

While hiking on a mountain trail through the state park, *FRANK NOTICED* a strange type of large, blue <u>flower he had never seen anything like it</u> before.	5. A) NO CHANGE B) flower. Never having seen anything like it C) flower, they were unlike anything he had seen <u>**D) flower that was unlike anything he had seen**</u>	*Run-on (FS)* *Fragment* *Run-on (FS)* **Correct**

This turns the second independent clause into a relative.

Although *THE BICYCLE WAS* not the color she wanted, *LAUREN* *BOUGHT IT* <u>anyway it was</u> the last one in stock, **and** *THE NEXT* *SHIPMENT WOULDN'T ARRIVE* for six months.	6. A) NO CHANGE <u>**B) anyway. It was**</u> C) anyway, it was D) anyway. Because it was	*Run-on (FS)* **Correct** *Run-on (CS)* *Fragment*

There are four clauses here: the first two are joined by "although", and the second two are joined by "and". Choice D) can't use "because" in the second sentence because it already joins its clauses with "and".

In the fifteenth century, Johannes *GUTENBERG INVENTED* the mechanical printing <u>press, a device that</u> would vastly change the course of history.	7. <u>**A) NO CHANGE**</u> B) press, it was a device that C) press, this device D) press, it	**Correct** *Run-on (CS)* *Run-on (CS)* *Run-on (CS)*

Choice A) makes the second clause a modifier.

RUN-ON DRILL

*All the questions in this exercise deal with **run-on sentences**. Unlike the real SAT, the sentences in this exercise do not make up a full passage—each question refers to a single stand-alone sentence.*

I tried to go to the <u>library, it was</u> closed.

1. A) NO CHANGE
   B) library it was
   C) library, but it was
   D) library but was

Travis is very excited about the science fair next <u>week; hoping</u> that his experiment about crickets will win the top prize.

2. A) NO CHANGE
   B) week, hoping
   C) week, he hopes
   D) week. Hoping

The board of directors will name a wing of the hospital after Dr. <u>Robinson, since it</u> was his donation that made the new construction possible.

3. Which of the following alternatives to the underlined portion would NOT be acceptable?
   A) Robinson. It
   B) Robinson; it
   C) Robinson, it
   D) Robinson—it

Professor Fullington teaches the introductory course on <u>thermodynamics, it is</u> one of the hardest classes in the department.

4. A) NO CHANGE
   B) thermodynamics it is
   C) thermodynamics. Which is
   D) thermodynamics,

While hiking on a mountain trail through the state park, Frank noticed a strange type of large, blue <u>flower he had never seen anything like it</u> before.

5. A) NO CHANGE
   B) flower. Never having seen anything like it
   C) flower, they were unlike anything he had seen
   D) flower that was unlike anything he had seen

Although the bicycle was not the color she wanted, Lauren bought it <u>anyway it was</u> the last one in stock, and the next shipment wouldn't arrive for six months.

6. A) NO CHANGE
   B) anyway. It was
   C) anyway, it was
   D) anyway. Because it was

In the fifteenth century, Johannes Gutenberg invented the mechanical printing <u>press, a device that</u> would vastly change the course of history.

7. A) NO CHANGE
   B) press, it was a device that
   C) press, this device
   D) press, it

The football team and the soccer team both want to use the main field this <u>Saturday the</u> director of athletics can't decide what to do about it.

8. A) NO CHANGE
   B) Saturday, the
   C) Saturday, and the
   D) Saturday, it is a problem that the

Karl has been the leading advocate for animal cruelty cases in the <u>district; he</u> has helped rescue hundreds of abused animals.

9. Which of the following alternatives to the underlined portion would NOT be acceptable?
   A) district, and he
   B) district and
   C) district he
   D) district. He

Douglas hates using his debit card, believing that someone could easily steal it and gain access to his <u>account, he prefers</u> using cash whenever he can.

10. A) NO CHANGE
    B) account. He prefers
    C) account he prefers
    D) account. Preferring

<u>Harold returns from the store, then</u> we can begin to prepare all the food for the dinner party.

11. A) NO CHANGE
    B) When Harold returns from the store,
    C) As soon as Harold returns from the store;
    D) Harold returns from the store then

New research has confirmed that the medication is <u>effective, according</u> to the scientists who conducted the study, proper dosages of the serum can both relieve symptoms and treat the underlying cause of the disease.

12. A) NO CHANGE
    B) effective according,
    C) effective according
    D) effective. According

All the woodworking skills that Brian has today were gained in his <u>childhood his</u> father was a carpenter and taught him everything he knows.

13. A) NO CHANGE
    B) childhood, his
    C) childhood, which his
    D) childhood: his

The state government is horrendously over <u>budget; this is a problem that</u> will only get worse over the next four years.

14. Which of the following alternatives to the underlined portion would NOT be acceptable?
    A) budget, this problem
    B) budget; this problem
    C) budget, a problem that
    D) budget, which is a problem that

The new director of marketing, who previously ran a major advertising campaign for one of our competitors, had some radical ideas about how to promote our main product <u>line, as a result,</u> our sales in the first year of implementation almost doubled.

15. A) NO CHANGE
    B) line. As a result,
    C) line, as a result
    D) line, the result was that

The *FOOTBALL TEAM* and *THE SOCCER TEAM* both *WANT* to use the main field this <u>Saturday the</u> director of athletics can't decide what to do about it.

8. A) NO CHANGE — *Run-on (FS)*
   B) Saturday, the — *Run-on (CS)*
   C) Saturday, and the — Correct
   D) Saturday, it is a problem that the — *Run-on (CS)*

KARL HAS BEEN the leading advocate for animal cruelty cases in the <u>district; he</u> *HAS HELPED* rescue hundreds of abused animals.

9. Which of the following alternatives to the underlined portion would NOT be acceptable?
   A) district, and he — *Comma plus conjunction*
   B) district and — *Compound verb*
   C) district he — Correct. Run-on (FS)
   D) district. He — *Separate sentence*

DOUGLAS HATES using his debit card, believing that someone could easily steal it and gain access to his <u>account, he prefers</u> using cash whenever he can.

10. A) NO CHANGE — *Run-on (CS)*
    B) account. He prefers — Correct
    C) account he prefers — *Run-on (FS)*
    D) account. Preferring — *Fragment*

<u>Harold returns from the store, then</u> *WE CAN BEGIN* to prepare all the food for the dinner party.

11. A) NO CHANGE — *Run-on (CS)*
    "Then" is not a conjunction.
    B) When Harold returns from the store, — Correct
    C) As soon as Harold returns from the store; — *Fragment before a semicolon*
    D) Harold returns from the store then — *Run-on (FS)*

NEW RESEARCH HAS CONFIRMED that the medication is <u>effective, according</u> to the scientists who conducted the study, *PROPER DOSAGES* of the serum *CAN BOTH RELIEVE* symptoms *AND TREAT* the underlying cause of the disease.

12. A) NO CHANGE — *Run-on (CS)*
    B) effective according, — *Run-on (CS)*
    C) effective according — *Run-on (CS)*
    D) effective. According — Correct

    Ignore the prepositional phrase "according to the scientists who conducted the study", and you'll see there's no conjunction to connect the two independent clauses.

All the woodworking *SKILLS* ~~that Brian has today~~ *WERE GAINED* in his <u>childhood his</u>father was a carpenter and taught him everything he knows.

13. A) NO CHANGE — *Run-on (FS)*
    B) childhood, his — *Run-on (CS)*
    C) childhood, which his — *Pronoun Agreement*
    D) childhood: his — Correct
    In choice C), the relative pronoun "which" seems to refer to the word "childhood", but the clause does not describe Brian's childhood. "During which" would work.

THE STATE GOVERNMENT IS horrendously over <u>budget; this is a problem that</u> *WILL ONLY* get worse over the next four years.

14. Which of the following alternatives to the underlined portion would NOT be acceptable?
    A) budget, this problem — Correct. Run-on (CS)
    B) budget; this problem — *Semicolon*
    C) budget, a problem that — *Modifier*
    D) budget, which is a problem that — *Relative clause*

The new *DIRECTOR* of marketing, ~~who previously ran a major advertising campaign for one of our competitors~~, *HAD* some radical ideas about how to promote our main product <u>line, as a result,</u> *OUR SALES* in the first year of implementation almost *DOUBLED*.

15. A) NO CHANGE — *Run-on (CS)*
    B) line. As a result, — Correct
    C) line, as a result — *Run-on (CS)*
    D) line, the result was that — *Run-on (CS)*

    "As a result" is not a conjunction.

THIS PAGE INTENTIONALLY LEFT BLANK

IV. MODIFIERS

Dangling Modifiers

Remember: modifiers are phrases that aren't clauses, but describe something else in the sentence. When a sentence *begins* with a modifier, the thing that phrase describes must come *immediately after the comma*, as the *subject* of the main clause. Otherwise, it's a *dangling modifier*. Observe:

> ✗ **Sitting close to the field, *A FOUL BALL* hit Bob.**

Who is sitting close to the field? *Bob*. The opening phrase is supposed to describe "Bob". But here, "a foul ball" comes after the comma. We call this a **dangling modifier**. That's bad. We need "Bob" to be the subject of the main clause:

> ✓ **Sitting close to the field, *BOB* was hit by a foul ball.**

Finding a dangling modifier error is essentially the same process as checking pronoun agreement. The opening phrase refers to something, so we'll figure out what it refers to and put it after the comma. Ask yourself:

> ## Who or what does the modifier refer to?

> ✗ **An excellent salesman, Ms. LEVINSON gave Roger a raise.**

Who is an excellent salesman? *Roger* is—that's why he got the raise. This sentence makes it sound like *Ms. Levinson* is the salesman. That's a dangling modifier. Here, we can't re-write the main clause because it isn't underlined, so we have to change the modifier. If we make the first part a *clause*, then there won't be any modifiers at all, thus there'll be no danger of a dangling modifier:

> ✓ **Because he is an excellent salesman, Ms. Levinson gave Roger a raise.**

¡Perfecto!

Modifiers at the end of a sentence

Modifiers that open a sentence describe the subject of the sentence, which is usually the noun right next to it. But if a modifier comes at the *end* of a sentence, the noun right next to it isn't the subject. What should we do?

Sometimes, an ending modifier will describe the word right before it:

> ✗ **A cake was made by *THE CHEF* <u>covered in chocolate</u>.**

This sentence suggests that the chef was covered with chocolate. That's probably not what we meant to say.* Let's rewrite the main clause to fix it:

> ✓ <u>**The chef made *A CAKE* covered in chocolate.**</u>

But other times, modifiers describe the **subject** of the main clause. When this is true, the modifier is separated by a *comma*:

> ✓ ***CHAPMAN* sat in the park, <u>eating an apple</u>.**

Here, it's clear that it was Chapman who was eating the apple, not the park. There's none of the weird confusion that the chocolate sentence had. If the modifier describes the **subject** of the sentence, not the word next to it, then it is separated by a comma. It's just like adding a second verb to the subject:

> ✓ ***CHAPMAN SAT* in the park <u>and *ATE* an apple</u>.**

If you don't use a comma, a modifier can describe the word directly before it:[†]

> ✓ **Chapman walked through *A CLOUD OF STEAM* <u>spewing from the subway grate</u>.**

Here, it's clear that the cloud of steam was spewing from the grate, not Chapman. This is just like using a relative clause.

> ✓ **Chapman walked through a cloud of steam *THAT WAS* <u>spewing from the subway grate</u>.**

And as we saw before, modifiers don't need verbs at all; they can be simple noun phrases, too. **Noun phrases are always separated with a comma**, and they must always be right next to the words they describe, no matter where that noun is in the main clause:

> ✓ <u>**A brilliant doctor**</u>**, Chapman cured my acne.**
> ✓ **My acne was cured by Chapman, <u>a brilliant doctor</u>.**

---

* To say nothing of the fact that this clause is *passive* and sounds awkward. The active version is more direct and concise. Remember when we talked about active and passive verbs? All this stuff is connected!

† This is an oversimplification: in real life modifiers are quite a bit more complicated. But this rule generally holds for sentence-final modifiers *on SAT questions*, which is all we're concerned with right now.

Prepositional phrase placement

Modifier questions are all about making sure a phrase is in the right place so it describes the right word. But that's also true of *prepositional phrases*.

We mentioned prepositional phrases several times in the Conventions of Usage chapter. Remember that prepositional phrases are made up of a preposition and its object. Prepositional phrases act very much the same way as modifiers in that they describe other words in a sentence.

Prepositional phrases often have very strong connections with words they describe. You must be careful to put the prepositional phrase **directly after** the word it's supposed to describe:

> ✓ *THE BOY* in short pants likes dogs.
> ✗ The boy likes *DOGS* in short pants.

In the first sentence, the prepositional phrase "in short pants" describes the boy. In the second sentence, it describes the dogs.*

Some prepositional phrases have stronger connections than others. Take a look at this sentence:

> ✓ The Queen of England drinks tea in the afternoon.

There are two prepositional phrases in this sentence, "of England" and "in the afternoon". The phrase "of England" directly describes "the Queen", so it must be placed directly after "the Queen". But the phrase "in the afternoon" doesn't have that strong a connection to any particular word in the sentence. So we can move it around if we want:[†]

> ✓ In the afternoon, the Queen of England drinks tea.
> ✓ The Queen of England in the afternoon drinks tea.

But we can't put it between "the Queen" and "of England":

> ✗ *THE QUEEN* in the afternoon *OF ENGLAND* drinks tea.

Now it sounds like "of England" describes "afternoon". Notice that the reason this is wrong has nothing to do with the underlined phrase itself—it's just that we can't separate "the Queen" from "of England" with *any* phrase.

---

* To be fair, the second sentence isn't wrong, per se. Who *doesn't* like dogs that wear short pants?

† Not all of these options are equally good. Putting the prepositional phrase in the middle sounds a bit weird in this case. The point is that there are places where it *can* go and places where it *can never* go.

So how can you tell whether a prepositional phrase is allowed to move around? Ask yourself:

> # Does the prepositional phrase directly
> # describe a word in the sentence?

If it does, put it directly after that word. If it doesn't, you can put it almost anywhere as long as you don't split up other prepositional phrases that have strong connections.

V. PARALLELISM

Parallelism applies to several different concepts, but the overall point is *matching*. When you have two or more elements in a sentence that are similar to each other in certain ways, their forms must match.

It's easy to see this when you have a **list** of three items.

> ✓ I like jogging, fishing, and hiking.
> ✓ I like to jog, to fish, and to hike.*
> ✗ I like *JOGGING, FISHING*, and <u>to hike</u>.

Either the "to" form or the "-ing" form can be okay here. What's not okay is mixing them up: if we start a list using one form, we must *repeat* that form for every element of the list.

Similarly, don't repeat the subject if you don't have to:

> ✗ Fred Astaire could *SING, DANCE*, and <u>he could act</u>.
> ✓ Fred Astaire could *SING, DANCE*, and <u>act</u>.

We started with simple verbs, so we should end it with simple verbs. We don't have to repeat the subject.

When we make a list, we use commas alone between all the first terms and the word "and" between the last two. So as soon as we see those two verbs connected with a comma alone ("...sing, dance...") we know that we're starting a list.

This doesn't apply just to verbs, but to any type of list:

> ✗ This book is about *PATIENCE, HARD WORK*, and <u>how to be a leader</u>.
> ✓ This book is about *PATIENCE, HARD WORK*, and <u>leadership</u>.

Here, we started a list of nouns, "... patience, hard work, ..." so we should end it with another noun, "leadership".

Why do we have to do this? Because when things aren't parallel, they sound nasty. Parallelism makes your sentences beautiful and catchy. I mean, which of these sounds better?

The key word for parallelism is the word "AND". Any words joined by "and" should be in parallel forms.

---

* We repeated the "to" here to make the parallelism more obvious, but when all items of a list take the same preposition, you don't have to repeat it. We could also say "I like to jog, fish, and hike."

> ✗ A government *OF THE PEOPLE, BY THE PEOPLE,* and <u>it is meant for those</u> <u>people, too...</u>
> ✓ A government *OF THE PEOPLE, BY THE PEOPLE,* and <u>for the people...</u>

See? We didn't make this up. Parallelism has been around for a while.

But besides just sounding pretty, parallelism falls under the larger concept of **coordination**. Coordination is a fancy word for joining words or phrases using a conjunction like *and, or,* or *but.** Of those three, "and" is by far the most common one on the SAT.

Any words or phrases joined with the word "and" must be in parallel forms.

This doesn't just apply to lists of three terms. If a sentence has *two* elements linked with "and" they must be in parallel forms:

> ✓ I have <u>cleaned the windows</u> AND <u>scrubbed the tiles</u>.
> ✓ I take this woman to be my wife <u>in sickness</u> AND <u>in health</u>.
> ✓ I use <u>my debit card</u> <u>for personal expenses</u> AND <u>my credit card</u> <u>for business</u> <u>expenses</u>.
> ✓ I think <u>that you're wrong</u> AND <u>that you're acting like a jerk</u>.

Of course, the converse is also true: if you *don't* have parallel forms, don't use "and":

> ✗ Chapman *SAT* in the park, <u>and</u> *EATING* an apple.

Here, the word "and" connects "*sat* in the park" with "*eating* an apple". That's no good, because "sat" is not the same form as "eating". We could fix it by matching the verb forms (*sat... and ate*), but in this question the verbs aren't underlined, so we can't change them. So instead, we have to change the connection. We can just omit the underlined portion entirely, making "eating an apple" a modifier:

> ✓ Chapman sat in the park, eating an apple.

Much better.

---

* The key to coordination is that the elements being coordinated are *of the same importance.* That's obvious in a list of three things—there's nothing to indicate whether any one of "jogging, fishing, and hiking" is any more important than the other two. This is different from *subordination.* When one clause is subordinate, it is less important than the main clause. This is the difference between using "but" and using "although".

1. Definitions

- An **independent clause** *can stand by itself* as a sentence.
- A **dependent clause** *cannot stand by itself* as a sentence.
- A **relative clause** is a dependent clause with a *relative pronoun* that *describes a single word* in the sentence.
- A **modifier** is a phrase with *no main verb* that modifies something in the sentence.

2. Fragments

- Every sentence *must have at least one independent clause*, or else it's a **fragment.**
- Fix a fragment by:
  - Turning a *partial verb* into a **main verb.**
  - **Removing unnecessary connectors** or relative pronouns.
  - **Joining it to another sentence** by *removing the period.*

3. Run-on sentences

- **Don't** connect independent clauses with a **comma alone**, or with **no connection** at all.
- Fix a run-on by:
  - Separating the clauses with a **period.**
  - Using a **comma with a conjunction.**
  - Making one of the independent clauses a **dependent clause or modifier.**

4. Modifiers

- A modifier at the *beginning of a sentence* must describe the *subject of the main clause* (the word right after the comma) or else it's a **dangling modifier.**
- A modifier at *the end of a sentence* may describe:
  - the **subject**, if there's a *comma.*
  - the **word next to it,** if there's *no comma.*
- Prepositional phrases must be **placed right after** the words they describe.

5. Parallelism

- Use **parallel forms** for **parallel ideas.** Any words or phrases joined with the word "and" must be in parallel forms.
- **Don't use "and"** if the forms **aren't parallel.**

SENTENCE STRUCTURE EXERCISE

This exercise contains a full passage with 11 questions, just like an SAT passage. Unlike a real SAT passage, it only features **Sentence Structure** *questions. Look out for all the rules discussed above. Enjoy!*

PASSAGE II

Scraping the Sky

As long as people have known how to build, people have tried to build tall structures. Skyscrapers as we know them are a modern **1** invention, but we can find examples of very tall buildings throughout ancient history. The Romans lived in *insulae*, high-rise apartment buildings that could rise to heights over 10 stories. Some medieval Italian cities featured stone towers over 200 feet **2** tall. Such as the Towers of Bologna or the Tower of Pisa. In Yemen, the walled city of **3** Shibam, which was built in the sixteenth century and consists entirely of buildings with five to eleven stories.

Buildings that tall, however, were rare until the nineteenth century. Because older buildings were made of materials like stone and brick, the outer walls bore the brunt of the building's **4** weight, this limited the maximum height that a tower could safely be built. However, **5** once engineer Henry Bessemer discovered a process for cheap steel production, buildings could be made with skeletal steel construction. A network of steel beams would distribute the weight of the building away from the outer walls, allowing taller construction on relatively small plots of land.

1
A) NO CHANGE
B) invention, we can find
C) invention. But finding
D) invention we can find

2
A) NO CHANGE
B) tall, some examples are
C) tall; such as
D) tall, such as

3
A) NO CHANGE
B) Shibam, built in the sixteenth century,
C) Shibam was built in the sixteenth century, it
D) Shibam, a sixteenth century building that

4
A) NO CHANGE
B) weight. Limiting
C) weight. This design limited
D) weight. Thus limiting

5
A) NO CHANGE
B) a process for cheap steel production, engineer Henry Bessemer discovered that
C) engineer Henry Bessemer, a process for cheap steel production, discovered
D) the discovery by engineer Henry Bessemer of a process for cheap steel production,

CONTINUE →

Sentence Structure Exercise

PASSAGE II

Scraping the Sky

As long as people have known how to build, people have tried to build tall structures. *SKYSCRAPERS* as we know them *ARE* a modern [1] invention, but we can find examples of very tall buildings throughout ancient history. The Romans lived in *insulae*, high-rise apartment buildings that could rise to heights over 10 stories. Some medieval Italian cities featured stone towers over 200 feet [2] tall. Such as the Towers of Bologna or the Tower of Pisa. In Yemen, *THE WALLED CITY* of [3] Shibam, which was built in the sixteenth century and *CONSISTS* entirely of buildings with five to eleven stories.

Buildings that tall, however, were rare until the nineteenth century. Because older buildings were made of materials like stone and brick, the outer *WALLS BORE* the brunt of the building's [4] weight, this limited the maximum height that a tower could safely be built. However, [5] once engineer Henry Bessemer discovered a process for cheap steel production, *BUILDINGS* could be made with skeletal steel construction. A network of steel beams would distribute the weight of the building away from the outer walls, allowing taller construction on relatively small plots of land.

1

A)	**NO CHANGE**	**Correct**
B)	invention, we can find	*Run-on (CS)*
C)	invention. But finding	*Fragment*
D)	invention we can find	*Run-on (FS)*

2

A)	NO CHANGE	*Fragment*
B)	tall, some examples are	*Run-on (CS)*
C)	tall; such as	*Semicolon fragment*
D)	**tall, such as**	**Correct**

3

A)	NO CHANGE	*Fragment*

Everything after the comma is a dependent clause.

B)	**Shibam, built in the sixteenth century,**
	Correct.

The main clause is "the city... consists".

C)	Shibam was built in the sixteenth century, it	
		Run-on (CS)

"The city was built..., it consists"

D)	Shibam, a sixteenth century building that	
		Fragment

There's no verb to go with the subject, "the walled city".

4

A)	NO CHANGE	*Run-on (CS)*
B)	weight. Limiting	*Fragment*
C)	**weight. This design limited**	**Correct**
D)	weight. Thus limiting	*Fragment*

5

A)	**NO CHANGE**	**Correct**
B)	a process for cheap steel production, engineer Henry Bessemer discovered that	
		Dangling Modifier
C)	engineer Henry Bessemer, a process for cheap steel production, discovered	
		Dangling Modifier
D)	the discovery by engineer Henry Bessemer of a process for cheap steel production,	
		Dangling Modifier

Choice D entirely modifies "buildings".

Choice A is a clause, not a modifier, so it can't dangle.

ANOTHER PROBLEM WAS that tall buildings were

[6] inconvenient; no one likes climbing ten flights of stairs

every day. Elevators had existed in primitive form since

the time of the Greek mathematician Archimedes, but

they were cumbersome and dangerous. In 1852, Elisha

OTIS CREATED the first safety elevator it was equipped

with a braking system to stop the car if the cables

snapped. Furthermore, innovations in hydraulic and

electric power made these new elevators practical *TO*

INSTALL AND

[7] they were maintained in urban environments.

These advancements, along with a few others like

central heating and electric water pumps, made modern

skyscrapers possible. *INSPIRED* by these developments,

[8] a construction boom was started by engineers at the

turn of the century. Soon, taller and taller *SKYSCRAPERS*

[9] popped up in cities like Chicago and New York at an

incredible rate. From 1890 to 1913, the record for the

world's tallest skyscraper was broken eight times.

NEW DESIGNS in engineering *CONTINUE* to push the

limits of human [10] achievement, this *RACE* to be the

tallest *HAS NOT STOPPED.* In 2010, *THE CITY* of Dubai

celebrated the opening of the Burj [11] Khalifa. A huge

tower that stands at 2,717 feet tall—over twice as tall as

the Empire State Building. As we continue to create new

technologies and building techniques, we will keep rising

to new heights.

6

Which of the following alternatives to the underlined portion would NOT be acceptable?

A)   inconvenient: no one   *Colon*
B)   inconvenient. No one   *Period*
C)   **inconvenient, no one**   **Correct** *Run-on (CS)*
D)   inconvenient—no one   *Dash*

7

A)   NO CHANGE   *Parallelism*
B)   for maintenance   *Parallelism*
C)   maintaining   *Parallelism*
D)   **to maintain**   **Correct**
To install and *to maintain*

8

A)   NO CHANGE   *Dangling Modifier*
B)   **engineers started a construction boom at the turn of the century.**   **Correct**
C)   *A BOOM* in construction at the turn of the century was started by engineers.   *Dangling Modifier*
D)   *THE TURN OF THE CENTURY* saw a construction boom started by engineers.
Dangling Modifier
Who was inspired? The engineers. So they must be the subject of the main clause, right after the comma.

9

A)   **NO CHANGE**   **Correct**
B)   that popped   *Fragment*
C)   popping   *Fragment*
D)   to pop   *Fragment*
The subject "skyscrapers" needs a main verb.

10

A)   NO CHANGE   *Run-on (CS)*
B)   **achievement, and this** **Correct**
C)   achievement the   *Run-on (FS)*
D)   achievement, the   *Run-on (CS)*
There are two independent clauses: "New designs… continue" and "this race… has not stopped."

11

A)   NO CHANGE   *Fragment.*
There's no main verb to go with "tower".
B)   Khalifa and is a huge tower standing
Compound verb. The subject of "is" is "the city"
C)   Khalifa, a huge tower stands
Run-on (CS). "A huge tower stands" is an independent clause
D)   **Khalifa, a huge tower that stands**
"A huge tower that…" is a modifier describing "Burj Khalifa"

Another problem was that tall buildings were [6] inconvenient; no one likes climbing ten flights of stairs every day. Elevators had existed in primitive form since the time of the Greek mathematician Archimedes, but they were cumbersome and dangerous. In 1852, Elisha Otis created the first safety elevator, which was equipped with a braking system to stop the car if the cables snapped. Furthermore, innovations in hydraulic and electric power made these new elevators practical to install and [7] they were maintained in urban environments.

These advancements, along with a few others like central heating and electric water pumps, made modern skyscrapers possible. Inspired by these developments, [8] a construction boom was started by engineers at the turn of the century. Soon, taller and taller skyscrapers [9] popped up in cities like Chicago and New York at an incredible rate. From 1890 to 1913, the record for the world's tallest skyscraper was broken eight times.

New designs in engineering continue to push the limits of human [10] achievement, this race to be the tallest has not stopped. In 2010, the city of Dubai celebrated the opening of the Burj [11] Khalifa. A huge tower that stands at 2,717 feet tall—over twice as tall as the Empire State Building. As we continue to create new technologies and building techniques, we will keep rising to new heights.

6

Which of the following alternatives to the underlined portion would NOT be acceptable?

A) inconvenient: no one
B) inconvenient. No one
C) inconvenient, no one
D) inconvenient—no one

7

A) NO CHANGE
B) for maintenance
C) maintaining
D) to maintain

8

A) NO CHANGE
B) engineers started a construction boom at the turn of the century.
C) a boom in construction at the turn of the century was started by engineers.
D) the turn of the century saw a construction boom started by engineers.

9

A) NO CHANGE
B) that popped
C) popping
D) to pop

10

A) NO CHANGE
B) achievement, and this
C) achievement the
D) achievement, the

11

A) NO CHANGE
B) Khalifa and is a huge tower standing
C) Khalifa, a huge tower stands
D) Khalifa, a huge tower that stands

STOP

A Note about Punctuation

You may have noticed that this book treats quotation marks a little bit differently than how you're accustomed to seeing them. If you're interested, allow us to explain.

There are two schools of thought about how to use quotation marks when they fall next to periods and commas.

One group will always put commas and periods inside quotation marks:

- Carl said, "I like that shirt."
- The word written on the desk was "plump."

The other group will only put commas and periods inside the quotation marks if they're actually part of the quoted material:

- Carl said, "I like that shirt."
- The word written on the desk was "plump".

In the first sentence, Carl said an entire sentence, so the period is part of the quoted material. In the second sentence, only one word was written, so the period ends the sentence but is not part of the quoted material.

Almost all American publishers follow the first method, while the second is mostly followed by British publishers.

The American system was originally adopted for aesthetic reasons and has been the dominant system for years. However, a number of Americans do prefer the British version. They argue that is more logical than the American system: placing something inside the quotation marks necessarily implies that it being quoted. For this reason, the outside-the-quotes system is often called "logical" punctuation. The American system agrees that other sentence-final marks such as question marks or exclamation points belong outside the quotation marks. Logical punctuation simply extends that thinking to all marks.

A-List uses the logical system in *The Book of Knowledge*. The book frequently uses quotation marks, but almost exclusively to quote single words from an example sentence. Thus, commas and periods are almost never part of the quoted material. With so many instances of single words quoted at the end of a sentence, both logic and aesthetics compelled us to place commas and periods outside the quotation marks. We feel that despite being in the minority, there is certainly precedent for use of this system. For example, *Language*, the journal of the Linguistics Society of America, uses logical punctuation. Furthermore, the SAT itself used to use this system on certain questions in their previous format, likely for the same reason we do. Generally, SAT questions generally italicize single words in lieu of using quotation marks, thus avoiding the issue entirely.

By no means do we want to imply that our method is the "correct" method. We recognize that most American publishers disagree and we welcome that disagreement. Punctuation is not grammar and different publishers should have the freedom to punctuate in the way they see fit. We like it when publishers have their own styles, such as *The New Yorker*'s bizarre insistence on spelling words like "coöperation" with a dieresis.

It is important to remember, though, that **rules about quotation marks are utterly irrelevant to the SAT**. While the SAT does test punctuation, it does not test these matters of quotation marks, so you need not mention this to your students at all. But if you'd like to talk about it with your students, feel free! In your classroom, you may adopt whatever house rules you wish. We only ask that you recognize that our decisions are not made hastily and we have reasons for what we do.

■ Standard English Conventions: Conventions of Punctuation

Punctuation questions on the SAT are easy to spot: their choices will all be worded identically and differ only in their punctuation. Of course, as we've already seen, Conventions of Usage or Sentence Structure questions may also involve issues of punctuation—fixing run-on sentences, for example, requires you to look at commas and periods. But correcting these errors often requires changes in the wording of the sentence, too. Punctuation questions will *only* test you on punctuation marks.

In some ways, punctuation is one of the trickier concepts on the SAT because punctuation isn't *pronounced*. Grammatical errors will often "sound" wrong to you. You can tell that the sentence "The dog have being barking" *sounds really messed up*, even if you don't understand exactly why. But you can't really *hear* whether a comma is in the right place.

Thankfully, there are only a few rules of punctuation that you'll need to know for the SAT. Once you learn to recognize the basic rules, you'll speed through these questions.

I. COMMAS

There are a lot of different rules for comma use. It can be overwhelming to try to remember all these rules. To help guide you, keep two simple rules in mind. First, many of the comma rules have the same motivation at heart:

> **DO use commas between words with WEAK connections.**
> **DON'T use commas between words with STRONG connections.**

For example, there's a strong connection between a subject and verb, so you should not separate them with a comma. But there's a weak connection between a parenthetical phrase and the rest of a sentence, so you should separate it with commas:

> **STRONG:** <u>Dave likes</u> cats. (No comma between the subject and verb.)
> **WEAK:**   Dave, <u>who is from Ottawa</u>, likes cats. (Commas around the parenthetical phrase.)

This is more of a guideline than a rule—it won't apply to every single situation. But it does connect a lot of situations that might otherwise seem unrelated to each other.

Second, people **usually use too many commas, not too few.** So in general, a comma is more likely to be wrong than right. If you're really not sure whether a certain spot needs a comma, better to guess that it doesn't. Remember, a comma literally divides a sentence into parts. Don't split up the sentence unless you've got a good reason for doing so.

Draw a line

Commas have a wide variety of different uses, but one thing all commas have in common is that they separate parts of sentences. Whenever you're judging whether a particular comma is acceptable, you must ask yourself: what parts of the sentence does this comma separate?

One way to help you figure that out is to **draw a line through the comma**, a big vertical line the whole height of the sentence. So these sentences…

> ×   I am going to the game, Scott will meet me there.
>
> ✓   Dave, who is from Canada, likes cats.

…become these:

> ×   I am going to the game | Scott will meet me there.
>
> ✓   Dave | who is from Canada | likes cats.

Drawing in these lines will serve several purposes. First of all, it will simply help you keep track of all the commas in a sentence. Sometimes the four choices will put commas in a lot of different places, and you might overlook one. Second, it will clearly delineate what the different parts of the sentence are, which will make it easier to see if the comma is acceptable. In the first sentence, each side of the line has an independent clause, and the comma alone produces a run-on. In the second, the commas surround a relative clause in the middle of the sentence, "who is from Canada," with an independent clause wrapped around the edges.

There are many more types of phrases that can or cannot use commas, of course. But no matter what the context, always draw lines through the commas first to help you see the structure.

So when should we use commas? More importantly, when should we *not* use them?

When *can* I use a comma?

1. Between independent clauses joined with a conjunction

We already discussed this at length in the Sentence Structure chapter. You can use a comma and a conjunction to separate independent clauses.* But don't use a use a comma between independent clauses without a conjunction—that's a run-on.

> ✓ I am going to the <u>game, and</u> Scott will meet me there.
> ✓ I wanted to go to the <u>movies, but</u> the show was sold out.
> ✗ I am going to the <u>game, Scott</u> will meet me there.

Run-on issues appear on Sentence Strategy questions more frequently than on Punctuation questions, because fixing them often involves changing the wording of the sentences. So we won't discuss them at length here.

2. Around parenthetical phrases

We mentioned earlier that dependent clauses and modifiers are not part of the "core sentence". If the sentence **would still make sense without the phrase**, you can put commas on *both sides* of the phrase. This relates directly to our first rule: phrases with *weak connections* take commas. These phrases can take many different forms:

> ✓ Ottawa, <u>the capital of Canada</u>, is very beautiful in the wintertime.
> ✓ Ottawa, <u>established in 1850</u>, is very beautiful in the wintertime.
> ✓ Ottawa, <u>if you ask me</u>, is very beautiful in the wintertime.
> ✓ Ottawa, <u>which is known for its 5-mile skating rink on the Rideau Canal</u>, is very beautiful in the wintertime.

In each of these sentences, the underlined phrase gives extra information that doesn't affect the main clause. We could delete each phrase and still be left with a complete sentence.

> ✓ Ottawa, <u>...</u> , is very beautiful in the wintertime.

---

* A comma is not always *required* before the conjunction here. Commas are used here more often than not, but they are sometimes optional if the clauses are short. So "She thinks you're ugly and I agree" would be acceptable.

There are several things to keep in mind when dealing with parenthetical phrases. First, if you start a parenthetical, make sure to end it. The phrase needs commas **on both sides**:

> ✕ Ottawa, the capital of <u>Canada is</u> very beautiful in the wintertime.

Second, when you do end it, make sure you end it in the right place.

> ✕ Ottawa, the <u>capital, of</u> Canada is very beautiful in the wintertime.

If you're not sure whether a parenthetical has its commas in the right place, try ignoring the words between the commas to see if the sentence still makes sense.

> ✕ Ottawa, ... , of Canada is very beautiful in the wintertime.

Of course, phrases like this can also appear at the beginning or end of a sentence. Then they just need one comma to separate them from the main clause. We've already seen tons of examples like this in the Sentence Structure chapter.

> ✓ <u>The capital of Canada</u>, Ottawa is very beautiful in the wintertime.
> ✓ Ottawa is very beautiful in the wintertime, <u>if you ask me</u>.

Parenthetical phrases can be particularly tricky when dealing with people's names and titles:

> ✕ <u>Former Minnesota governor, Jesse Ventura,</u> has appeared in ten films.

This kinds sounds okay. But since "Jesse Ventura" is surrounded by commas, it's a parenthetical phrase. So we should be able to delete it. Let's try:

> ✕ Former Minnesota governor, ... , has appeared in ten films.

"Former Minnesota governor has appeared" sounds weird. So "Jesse Ventura" is *not* a parenthetical phrase—it's the core subject of the verb "has appeared", and no comma should separate the subject and verb. "Former Minnesota governor" is Ventura's *title*, sort of like a long adjective.

> ✓ <u>Former Minnesota governor Jesse Ventura</u> has appeared in ten films.

Of course, we could also phrase the sentence differently so that there *is* a parenthetical:

- ✓ The former governor of Minnesota, <u>Jesse Ventura</u>, has appeared in ten films.
- ✓ The former governor of Minnesota, ... , has appeared in ten films.
- ✓ Jesse Ventura, <u>former governor of Minnesota</u>, has appeared in ten films.
- ✓ Jesse Ventura, ... , has appeared in ten films.

3. Between items of a list with three or more items

Any list of three or more should have commas alone separating the first items and the word "and" separating the last item.*

- ✓ <u>Dave, Ted and Roger</u> all like cats
- ✓ <u>Dave, Ted, and Roger</u> all like cats.
- ✗ <u>Dave Ted and Roger</u> all like cats.

This applies to *any* list of three: nouns, verbs, prepositional phrases, or even clauses. This is the only time you can legally combine independent clauses with a comma but no conjunction—when they're the first two in a list of three.

- ✓ Dave went to market, Ted stayed home, and Roger ate roast beef.

4. Between coordinate adjectives

If a noun has two adjectives that are of *equal importance* and each adjective directly describes the noun *in the same way*, use a comma to separate the adjectives:

- ✓ Cindy just got a <u>happy, healthy</u> cat.

Here are two quick tests: if you can **switch the order** of the adjectives, or if you can **insert "and"** between the adjectives without changing the meaning of the sentence, use a comma:

- ✓ Cindy just got a <u>healthy, happy</u> cat.
- ✓ Cindy just got a <u>happy and healthy</u> cat.

Compare to this sentence:

- ✓ Cindy just got a <u>healthy Siamese</u> cat.
- ✗ Cindy just got a <u>healthy, Siamese</u> cat.

---

* The comma before the "and" at the end of a list is *optional*. Some people love it, some hate it. This kind of comma is sometimes known as a "serial comma" or an "Oxford comma". This will not be tested on the SAT.

The adjectives "healthy" and "Siamese" are not coordinate. "Siamese" is more closely tied to "cat" than "healthy" is. So we should **not** use a comma. If we switch the adjectives or insert "and", the sentence is clearly nonsense:

> ✗ Cindy just got a <u>Siamese, healthy</u> cat.
> ✗ Cindy just got a <u>healthy and Siamese</u> cat.

5. Before a direct quote

Use a comma before a **direct quote**.

> ✓ Darth Vader <u>said, "Luke</u>, I am your father."*

But **DO NOT** use a comma before a **description** of a quote.†

> ✓ Darth Vader <u>said he</u> was Luke's father.
> ✗ Darth Vader <u>said, he</u> was Luke's father.

6. Around sentence adverbs

These are adverbs that modify the *entire* sentence, sometimes connecting it to the previous sentence:

> ✓ <u>Luckily,</u> Dave decided not to sue.
> ✓ I like cats. I do not, <u>however,</u> like dogs.

But **DO NOT** use a comma after **conjunctions**, like *and, or,* or *but.*

> ✓ I like cats, <u>but I</u> do not like dogs.
> ✗ I like cats, <u>but, I</u> do not like dogs.

When should I *not* use a comma?
1. Between the subject and verb or between the verb and object

---

* Yes, yes, yes, I'm well aware that Vader doesn't actually say this quote in the movie. I wanted to include Luke's name in order to show the comparative structures of the different example sentences here. I'm quoting a *different* instance of Vader saying this. It was off-camera, you didn't see it. Please stop sending angry emails.

† This is actually just a "that" clause with a missing "that": *Darth Vader said <u>that</u> he was Luke's father.*

✓ **Dave likes cats.**

✗ **Dave, likes cats.**

✗ **Dave likes, cats.**

This rule ties back to our first rule: *Don't use commas for strong connections.* There are no stronger connections in a sentence than those between subject, verb, and object. Don't interrupt them with commas.

Unless of course *something else* comes between them:

✓ **Dave, who is from Ottawa, likes cats.**

Here, there's a *parenthetical phrase* stuck between the subject, "Dave", and the verb, "likes". So we need the commas for the parenthetical phrase, even though they come between the subject and verb.

Similarly, we can separate the verb and the object if there's a *list*:

✓ **Dave bought a cat, a dog, and a monkey.**

In this sentence, we have three objects of the verb *bought*: "a cat, a dog, and a monkey". Since that's a list of three, we need commas between the list items. But **don't** use a comma to **introduce the list**:

✗ **Dave bought, a cat, a dog, and a monkey.**

Now there's a comma separating the verb from its three objects. That's no good.

So if you see any comma between a verb and its subject, or between a verb and its object, check to see if it's used for a parenthetical phrase or a list. If it's not, then the comma probably shouldn't be there.

2. Before infinitives

Remember that infinitives are the form of a verb that begin with "to". Infinitives behave sort of like the objects of verbs. They have strong connections to the verbs, so they should not be separated by commas:

✓ **I want to go home**

✗ **I want, to go home**

UNLESS the infinitive phrase comes **at the beginning** of a sentence.

> ✓ <u>To get home</u>, walk ten blocks south on Broadway and turn right.

3. Around prepositional phrases

We've mentioned prepositional phrases several times, so you should be able to identify them by now. In general, you should not separate them with commas:

> ✓ Many people <u>in Ottawa</u> speak French.
> ✗ Many people, <u>in Ottawa</u>, speak French.

> ✓ Many people speak French <u>in Ottawa</u>.
> ✗ Many people speak French, <u>in Ottawa</u>.

UNLESS the phrase comes **at the beginning** of the sentence.*

> ✓ <u>In Ottawa</u>, many people speak French.

Additionally, do not use a comma **between a preposition and its object**.

> ✓ Many people <u>in Ottawa</u> speak French.
> ✗ Many people <u>in, Ottawa</u> speak French

4. In a two-part list (a compound with a conjunction)

We mentioned that you should use commas to separate items in a list of three or more. But if you're only listing *two* things, just use a conjunction with no comma.

> ✓ <u>Dogs and cats</u> are prohibited.
> ✗ <u>Dogs, and cats</u> are prohibited.

> ✓ Gretchen is a <u>small but fierce</u> kitten.
> ✗ Gretchen is a <u>small, but fierce</u> kitten.

Unless, of course, you're combining two independent clauses with a conjunction. Then you need a comma:

> ✓ I am going to the <u>game, and</u> Scott will meet me there.

---

* These rules are a bit fluid. It is sometimes okay to separate a prepositional phrase with commas if you intend it to be a parenthetical statement. And sometimes it's okay to not use a comma with a prepositional phrase at the beginning of the sentence. But on the SAT you'll rarely see either of those situations.

But if you're linking anything else, don't use a comma. Similarly, don't use a comma to separate **two verbs with a single subject**.

> ✓ The dog *EATS* meat and *LOVES* bones
> ✗ The dog *EATS* meat, and *LOVES* bones

And as we mentioned earlier, you should never use a comma *after* a conjunction.

> ✗ I like cats, but, I do not like dogs.
> ✗ The dog eats meat and, loves bones

5. With a "that" clause

In general, you should not use a comma before or after "that":*

> ✓ I think that the Rockets will win it all this year.
> ✗ I think, that the Rockets will win it all this year.
> ✗ I think that, the Rockets will win it all this year.

6. With restrictive clauses or modifiers

We mentioned before that parenthetical phrases and modifiers can be separated by commas. But not *every* dependent clause or modifier is a parenthetical.

A **restrictive** (or *integrated*) clause is one that identifies or defines what we're talking about.

A **nonrestrictive** (or *supplementary*) clause is one that gives additional information about the topic. This is what we mean by "parenthetical phrases".

> ✐ **RESTRICTIVE:**   Our professor told us to buy the book that he wrote.
> ✐ **NONRESTRICTIVE:**   Our professor told us to buy his book, which was expensive.

In these sentences we know two things about the book: the professor wrote it, and it was expensive. The clause "that he wrote" identifies exactly which book we should buy. The clause "which was expensive" gives an additional characteristic about the book but doesn't *define* the book. The professor didn't tell us to buy the expensive book. He told us to buy *his* book. It just happened to be expensive.

---

* As we mentioned in the Conventions of Usage chapter, "that" has several very different uses. So it is *possible* to have a sentence that needs a comma before or after "that". But you probably won't see any on the SAT.

This ties back to our first guideline: restrictive clauses are *strongly* connected to the main clause (so we *don't* use a comma), while nonrestrictive clauses are *weakly* connected (so we *do* use a comma). If the clause is *necessary information* that identifies the noun, don't use a comma. If it is *additional information* describing the noun, use a comma.

RESTRICTIVE	NONRESTRICTIVE
There was a big fire in the town <u>where I was born.</u>	There was a big fire in Cleveland, <u>where I was born.</u>
The man <u>running down the street</u> is my father.	<u>Running down the street</u>, my father tried to catch the bus.
The one <u>who gets the most votes</u> wins the election.	The president, <u>who was just re-elected</u>, is still a jerk.

THIS PAGE INTENTIONALLY LEFT BLANK

Comma Drill

*For each question, the corrected sentence is given, followed by an explanation of where commas should and shouldn't be placed. After each explanation, the choices that break the given rule—that is, **those you can eliminate**— are listed in parentheses.*

1. **Answer: D.**
   Correct: *the English language has a* **series of specific, complex rules** *about proper use of punctuation marks.*

   - Prepositional phrases: **DON'T** put a comma before "of" (A, B, C) or before "about" (C).

   - Coordinate adjectives: **DO** put a comma between "specific" and "complex" (A, C).

2. **Answer: A.**
   Correct: *Today's* **rules, however,** *have not existed…*

   - Sentence adverbs: **DO** put commas around both sides of "however" (B, C, D).

3. **Answer: C.**
   Correct: **Ancient Greek playwrights** *began using simple punctuation marks…*

   - Non-coordinate adjectives: **DON'T** put a comma between "ancient" and "Greek" (A, B).

   - Subject-verb: **DON'T** put a comma between the subject "playwrights" and the verb "began" (A, D).

4. **Answer: C.**
   Correct: *Books gradually started to become more* **widespread, and punctuation began** *to apply…*

   - Independent clauses: **DO** put a comma before "and", separating the independent clauses "Books … started" and "punctuation began" with a comma followed by a conjunction (B).

   - Conjunctions: **DON'T** put a comma after the conjunction "and" (A).

   - Infinitives: **DON'T** put a comma before the infinitive "to apply" (B, D).

5. **Answer: A.**
   Correct: *… the shapes and meanings of these* **symbols still varied, often** *drastically, from book to book.*

   - Subject-verb: **DON'T** put a comma before "still", separating the subject "the shapes and meanings" its verb "varied" (B, C).

   - Parenthetical phrases: **DO** put a comma before "often", separating both sides of the parenthetical phrase "often drastically" (B, D).

6. **Answer: D.**
   Correct: *The shapes of punctuation marks became* **standardized with the invention of** *the printing press.*

   - Prepositional phrases: **DON'T** put a comma before the preposition "with" (A, B) or the preposition "of" (A).

   - Prepositional phrases: **DON'T** put a comma between the preposition "of" and its object "the printing press" (C).

COMMA DRILL

*All of these questions deal with **commas** and only commas. Have fun!*

PASSAGE III

The Rise of Punctuation

Every student of grammar knows that the English language has a **1** series, of specific complex rules about proper use of punctuation marks. Today's **2** rules, however, have not existed since the birth of writing. Punctuation has radically evolved over the centuries.

The earliest writing had no punctuation whatsoever. Even worse, there weren't even any spaces between words. Texts were dense blocks of uninterrupted letters. **3** Ancient, Greek playwrights, began using simple punctuation marks in their texts so that actors reciting their lines would know when to pause. Even through the start of the Middle Ages, books were meant to be tools for reading aloud, and punctuation continued to be used primarily to regulate the rhythm of speech.

Books gradually started to become more **4** widespread, and, punctuation began to apply to grammatical structures not just to spoken units. But because books were copied and produced by hand, the shapes and meanings of these **5** symbols still varied, often drastically, from book to book. The shapes of punctuation marks became **6** standardized, with the invention, of the printing press. Printers could now mechanically reproduce the same punctuation marks over and over again.

1
A) NO CHANGE
B) series, of specific, complex rules
C) series, of specific complex rules,
D) series of specific, complex rules

2
A) NO CHANGE
B) rules however
C) rules, however
D) rules however,

3
A) NO CHANGE
B) Ancient, Greek playwrights
C) Ancient Greek playwrights
D) Ancient Greek playwrights,

4
A) NO CHANGE
B) widespread and punctuation began,
C) widespread, and punctuation began
D) widespread, and punctuation began,

5
A) NO CHANGE
B) symbols, still varied often
C) symbols, still varied, often
D) symbols still varied often

6
A) NO CHANGE
B) standardized, with the invention of
C) standardized with the invention of,
D) standardized with the invention of

CONTINUE

The Italian publisher and printer Aldus Manutius was the source of several important innovations. In a manuscript printed in 1494, Manutius took an earlier mark called the *virgula* [7] *suspensiva* a mark that resembled a forward slash, curved it and lowered it to produce the mark we know today as the comma. Manutius was also one of the first printers to [8] use semicolons round parentheses and, italic type.

Even after the shapes of punctuation marks became uniform, it still took [9] several, hundred years for their uses to become fixed. [10] Commas for example, were far more widespread in the seventeenth and eighteenth centuries than they are today. Try reading the U.S. Constitution as it was originally written and you'll be overwhelmed by seemingly unnecessary commas. Today, while there is some variation between British and American [11] usage, English punctuation marks have been standardized into well-defined roles. But who knows? Maybe in another two hundred years, a different set of new, barely recognizable marks will be standard.

7
A) NO CHANGE
B) *suspensiva* a mark that,
C) *suspensiva*, a mark, that
D) *suspensiva*, a mark that

8
A) NO CHANGE
B) use, semicolons, round parentheses, and
C) use semicolons, round parentheses, and
D) use, semicolons, round parentheses, and,

9
A) NO CHANGE
B) several hundred years
C) several hundred years,
D) several, hundred years,

10
A) NO CHANGE
B) Commas, for example, were
C) Commas, for example were,
D) Commas for example were,

11
A) NO CHANGE
B) usage, English punctuation marks,
C) usage English, punctuation marks
D) usage English punctuation marks,

STOP

7. Answer: D.

Correct: ... *Manutius took an earlier mark called the* virgula <u>*suspensiva, a mark that*</u> *resembled a forward slash, curved it and lowered it to produce....*

- Parenthetical phrases: **DO** put a comma before "a mark" to separate both sides of the parenthetical phrase "a mark that resembled a forward slash" (A, B).

- "That": **DON'T** put a comma before or after the word "that" (B, C).

8. Answer: C.

Correct: *Manutius was also one of the first printers to* <u>**use semicolons, round parentheses, and**</u> *italic type.*

- Three-part lists: **DO** put a comma between items in a three-part list: before "round" (and before "and") (A).

- Conjunctions: **DON'T** put a comma after the conjunction "and" (A, D).

- Verb-object: **DON'T** put a comma between the verb "use" and object "semicolons... type" (B, D).

9. Answer: B.

Correct: *...it still took* <u>**several hundred years**</u> *for their uses to become fixed.*

- Non-coordinate adjectives: **DON'T** put a comma between "several" and "hundred" (A, D).*

- Prepositional phrases: **DON'T** put a comma before the prepositional phrase "for their uses" (C, D).

10. Answer: B.

Correct: <u>**Commas, for example, were**</u> *far more widespread in the seventeenth and eighteenth centuries...*

- Parenthetical phrases: **DO** put commas on *both* sides of the parenthetical phrase "for example" (A, C, D).

- Verb-object: **DON'T** put commas between the verb "were" and object "far more widespread" (C, D).

11. Answer: A.

Correct: *Today, while there is some variation between British and American* <u>**usage, English punctuation marks**</u> *have been standardized into well-defined roles.*

- Parenthetical phrases: **DO** put a comma at the end of the parenthetical phrase "while there is... usage" (D).

- Non-coordinate adjectives: **DON'T** put a comma between "English" and "punctuation" (C).†

- Subject-verb: **DON'T** put a comma between the subject "marks" and its verb "have been standardized" (B, D).

---

* FYI: While "several" and "hundred" have traditionally been called adjectives, today they are generally classified as *determiners*, more similar to articles like "the" than to adjectives like "happy". It doesn't matter though; you shouldn't use a comma between determiners, either.

† "Punctuation" isn't actually an adjective; it's a noun. Nouns can be used to modify nouns, just like adjectives do, as in "dog collar" or "phone bill" or "lunch buffet". But the comma rule still applies. In fact, you should *never* use commas with noun compounds like this.

THIS PAGE INTENTIONALLY LEFT BLANK

II. APOSTROPHES

Possession

Use *s* for **plurals**:

> ✓ One <u>dog</u>
> ✓ Two <u>dogs</u>

Use *'s* for **possessives**:*

> ✓ This is my <u>dog</u>.
> ✓ This is my <u>dog's</u> bed.

Use *s'* for **plural possessives**:

> ✓ I have two <u>dogs</u>.
> ✓ This is my <u>dogs'</u> room.
> ✓ These are my <u>dogs'</u> beds.

Note that we are adding an apostrophe to an already-plural noun, so we should keep any spelling changes that occur in the plural form:

> ✓ Dave has one <u>puppy</u>.
> ✓ This is his <u>puppy's</u> bed.
>
> ✓ Linda has two <u>puppies</u>.
> ✓ These are her <u>puppies'</u> toys.
> ✗ These are her <u>puppys'</u> toys.

Plurals that don't end in *s* take *'s* for plural possessives:

> ✓ Dave has one <u>child</u>.
> ✓ This is his <u>child's</u> bed.
>
> ✓ Linda has two <u>children</u>.
> ✓ These are her <u>children's</u> toys.

---

* This form has sometimes been called *the Saxon genitive*, presumably because derives from a case ending from Old English. However, some linguists now consider *'s* to be a *clitic*, not a true inflectional ending. None of this matters to you, but "Saxon genitive" and "clitic" are both really awesome terms.

Not sure if you need a possessive form? Try rewriting it as an **"of" phrase**. Possessives can usually be rewritten as a prepositional phrase starting with "of":

> ✓ This is <u>my father's</u> boyhood home.
> ✓ This is the boyhood home <u>of my father</u>.
>
> ✓ I am moving into <u>my parents'</u> basement.
> ✓ I am moving into the basement <u>of my parents</u>.

Notice also that possessive nouns should have something to possess: my father's *home*, my parents' *basement*.

Contractions

Apostrophes can also be used in **contractions**. When two words are stuck together, an apostrophe takes the place of the missing letters.

> ✓ <u>That's</u> my dog.
> ✓ <u>That is</u> my dog.
>
> ✓ <u>He's</u> a jerk.
> ✓ <u>He is</u> a jerk.
>
> ✓ <u>They're</u> great!
> ✓ <u>They are</u> great!
>
> ✓ <u>Dave's</u> going to win.
> ✓ <u>Dave is</u> going to win.
>
> ✓ <u>My dog's</u> cute.*
> ✓ <u>My dog is</u> cute.

Contractions aren't just for forms of "to be". They can also be used for forms of "to have":

> ✓ <u>He's</u> been to Paris.
> ✓ <u>He has</u> been to Paris.
>
> ✓ <u>I've</u> never heard of it.
> ✓ <u>I have</u> never heard of it.

Or negation:

> ✓ He <u>isn't</u> Swedish.
> ✓ He <u>is not</u> Swedish.
>
> ✓ They <u>aren't</u> Japanese.
> ✓ They <u>are not</u> Japanese.

---

* Contractions like this, with regular nouns instead of pronouns, are often considered colloquial, informal, or nonstandard.

Or any time a word has omitted letters:

✓ **y'all** = you all	✓ **'bout** = about
✓ **'tis** = it is	✓ **fo'c's'le*** = forecastle

Pronouns

We already discussed pronoun forms in the Conventions of Usage chapter. To review:

Pronouns DO NOT use possessive apostrophes.

Pronouns have special forms for possessives:

My feet	**His** feet	**Its** feet	**Our** feet
Your feet	**Her** feet	**Their** feet	**Whose** feet?

Pronouns DO use contraction apostrophes:

✓ **I'm** French. = **I am** French.	✓ **It's** French. = **It is** French.
✓ **You're** French. = **You are** French.	✓ **We're** French. = **We are** French.
✓ **He's** French. = **He is** French.	✓ **They're** French. = **They are** French
✓ **She's** French. = **She is** French.	✓ **Who's** French? = **Who is** French?.

**Remember: pronouns use CONTRACTION apostrophes
but *NOT* POSSESSIVE apostrophes.**

---

* Yes, *fo'c's'le* is a real word. It's pronounced <FOX-ll>, as in "the fox'll eat the chicken". It's a nautical term.

It's vs. Its vs. Its'	*It's* means *it is*.	<u>It's</u> a beautiful day!	[= <u>It is</u> a beautiful day!]
	Its shows **possession**.	The dog wagged <u>its</u> tail.	[= The tail <u>belongs to</u> the dog.]
	Its' is <u>never</u> correct.	<div align="center">**NEVER USE <u>ITS'</u> FOR ANY REASON.**</div>	
You're vs. Your	*You're* means *you are*.	<u>You're</u> a jerk.	[= <u>You are</u> a jerk.]
	Your shows **possession**.	<u>Your</u> fly is open.	[= The fly <u>belongs to</u> you.]
They're vs. Their vs. There	*They're* means *they are*.	<u>They're</u> going to win.	[= <u>They are</u> going to win.]
	Their shows **possession**.	I like <u>their</u> uniforms.	[= The uniforms <u>belong to</u> them.]
	There shows **location**.	Put it over <u>there</u>.	[= I'm telling you <u>where</u> to put it.]
Who's vs. Whose	*Who's* means **who is**.	the man <u>who's</u> buying my car	[= the man <u>who is</u> buying my car]
	Whose shows **possession**.	the man <u>whose</u> car I'm buying	[= the car <u>belongs to</u> the man]

III. OTHER PUNCTUATION MARKS

Semicolon (;)

A semicolon is basically the same thing as a period. They follow the same rules. Why bother with the semicolon, then? Because it puts the two clauses into *the same sentence*. Therefore, it connects the ideas more strongly than if they were separate sentences with a period.

In fact, a semicolon is exactly what it looks like—a combination of a period and a comma. It separates independent clauses as a period does, but it separates parts of a single sentence as a comma does.

Because a semicolon works just like a period, a semicolon **must** be used to separate **independent clauses**. If you're not sure whether you can put a semicolon somewhere, try replacing it with a period. A semicolon should always be **interchangeable with a period** without making any other changes to the sentence (except capitalization). If you can't replace it with a period without changing the words, you can't use a semicolon.

> ✓ Dave has been studying more; his grades have improved as a result.
> ✓ Dave has been studying more. His grades have improved as a result.
> ✗ <u>While riding the bus</u>; my father lost his wallet.
> ✗ <u>While riding the bus</u>. My father lost his wallet.

Every semicolon must have an independent clause before and after it.

The semicolon can be a nice tool, and using it properly can help you improve your writing. However, for some reason, **on the SAT semicolons are wrong far more often than they are right.** So if you're not sure whether a semicolon is correct, it probably isn't.

Occasionally, semicolons can be used instead of commas to separate items in a list when those items contain commas. But this does not occur often.

> ✓ I've met three people at the conference: Dave, who likes cats; Roger, the man from Portland, Oregon; and a third man whose name, I think, was Jesse.

Colon (:)

A colon **strongly connects** two clauses. Use a colon when what follows is a quotation, an elaboration on, or a direct example of what precedes it.

> ✓ Steve is a bibliophile: he spends all his time reading.

In this example, the colon separates independent clauses. But unlike semicolons, colons don't *have to* separate independent clauses:

> ✓ **I am going to one game this year: the Super Bowl.**

Here, "the Super Bowl" is not an independent clause, but the colon is just fine.

A colon may be used to introduce a list, especially a list of long, wordy items:

> ✓ **He had several tasks ahead of him: hiking the trail from the campsite down the side of the mountain, collecting enough firewood to last the evening, then hiking back up the mountain while carrying the wood.**

But you can't use a colon between the verb and its object, even if it's a list:

> ✗ **Dave bought: a cat, a dog, and a monkey.**

Dash (—)

Dashes may be used to surround a parenthetical remark or aside, just like commas.* They often give greater emphasis than commas would:

> ✓ **The sequel's budget—estimated to be over 100 million dollars—is more than double that of the original movie.**
> ✓ **This dress—if you ask me—is not the right color for your skin tone.**
> ✓ **He accidentally revealed his home address—a mistake that would cost him his life!**

Dash phrases at the end of a sentence only need one dash, but phrases in the middle need dashes on both sides. If you open a phrase with a dash, don't forget to close it with another dash.

> ✗ **This dress—if you ask <u>me is</u> not the right color for your skin tone.**

And like colons, dashes can be used to join independent clauses:

> ✓ **Steve is a bibliophile—he spends all his time reading.**

_____

* There are several kinds of dashes, and usage among them can vary. This one is called an *em-dash*. An *en-dash* is shorter than an em-dash and is used for ranges of values, as in "1910–1918" or "pages 22–35". A *hyphen* is even shorter than an en-dash and is used to connect words and parts of words, as in "en-dash". You will not be tested on hyphens or en-dashes on the SAT.

Sentence-final marks

Period (.)

A period is used to separate **complete sentences**. We discussed this in the section on sentence fragments. A complete sentence must have at least one independent clause with a subject and verb.

> ✓ Since Dave has been studying more, his grades have improved as a result.
> ✗ <u>Since Dave has been studying more.</u> His grades have improved as a result.
> ✓ My father was running down the street, trying to catch the bus.
> ✗ My father was running down the street. <u>Trying to catch the bus.</u>

Besides periods, there are several other marks we can use to end a sentence.

Question mark (?)

A question mark indicates that a sentence is a question. It *cannot* be used for non-questions.*

> ✓ What did you have for dinner?

Exclamation point (!)

An exclamation point works like a period that shows excitement or surprise.

> ✓ I got a four-pound hamburger and ate the whole thing!

Interrobang (‽)

An interrobang is a combination of an exclamation point and a question mark. It's used for questions that show excitement or surprise.

> ✓ You ate a what‽

Okay, that last one probably won't show up on the SAT.† But the other three might.

---

* Fun fact: in Greek a semicolon is used for questions instead of our question mark. Why would they do that;

† Maybe it won't be on the SAT, but the interrobang is all too real. It was invented in 1962 by advertising agent Martin Speckter to replace the clumsy practice of alternating question marks and exclamation points ("You ate a what?!?!") Sadly, the interrobang never quite caught on.

CONVENTIONS OF PUNCTUATION SUMMARY
Here are the key rules to look out for on SAT Punctuation questions

1. DO use commas:
- between **independent clauses** with a **conjunction**.
- around **parenthetical phrases**.
- in a list of **three or more**.
- with **coordinate adjectives**.
- before a **direct quote**.
- around **sentence adverbs**.

2. DON'T use commas:
- between **subject and verb** or **verb and object**.
- before **infinitives**.
- before or in the middle of **prepositional phrases**.
- with a **two part list** (two nouns or verbs with a conjunction).
- with a **"that" clause**.
- before **restrictive** clauses.

3. Apostrophes
- **Plurals** take -s, **possessives** take -'s, **plural possessives** take -s'.
- **Contractions** use apostrophes for missing letters.
- **Pronouns** take **contraction** apostrophes but **not possessive** apostrophes.

4. Other marks
- A **semicolon** separates *independent clauses* (interchangeable with a period).
- A **colon** *strongly* connects phrases.
- A **dash** connects *independent clauses* or *parenthetical phrases*.
- Don't mix up **sentence-final marks**: *periods, question marks,* and *exclamation points*.

THIS PAGE INTENTIONALLY LEFT BLANK

Conventions of Punctuation Exercise

*For each question, the corrected sentence is given, followed by an explanation of where punctuation marks should and shouldn't be placed. After each explanation, the choices that break the given rule—that is, **those you can eliminate**—are listed in parentheses.*

1. **Answer: C.**
    Correct: *It's* **tiny, it's inconveniently located, and** *it's too expensive.*

    - Use "**IT'S**", not "its". <u>It is</u> inconveniently located. Look at the other two clauses: both use "it's" (A).

    - Three-part list: **DO** put commas between items in the list: after "tiny" (B), and after "located" (D).

      Note: In choice D) the semicolon after "located" turns the first two clauses into a run-on: "It's tiny, it's inconveniently located."

    - Conjunctions: **DON'T** put a comma after "and" (A).

2. **Answer: C.**
    Correct: *But the best thing about my apartment* **is the fact that it sits above** *a wonderful place called Emily's Bakery.*

    - Verb-object: **DON'T** put a comma between the verb "is" and the object "the fact" (A).

    - "That": **DON'T** put a comma before the word "that" (B).

    - Prepositional phrases: **DON'T** put a comma before the preposition "above" (D).

3. **Answer: A.**
    Correct: *All independent* **bakeries** *have a certain small-town charm to them…*

    - The word should be **PLURAL**. The word "all" is a big clue, as well as the verb "have" instead of "has" (C, D).

    - The word is **NOT POSSESSIVE**. "Bakeries" alone is the subject of the sentence: Bakeries have a charm (B, C, D).

    - Choice B), *bakeries'*, is plural possessive. Choice C), *bakery's*, is singular possessive. Choice D), *bakerys'*, is not a word.

4. **Answer: D.**
    Correct: *…than having a walk-in closet or* **beautiful wood floors.**

    - Non-coordinate adjectives: **DON'T** put a comma between "beautiful" and "wood" (B, C).

    These adjectives fail both tests for coordination: you *cannot* add "and" ("beautiful and wood floors") or switch their order ("wood beautiful floors").

    - **DON'T** put a comma between the adjective "wood" and the noun "floors" (A).

    - "Floors" is **PLURAL**, but **NOT POSSESSIVE**. (C).

5. **Answer: D.**
    Correct: *There's one thing that makes life above Emily's so* **great: the** *smell.*

    - Fragment: the last phrase, "the smell", is not an independent clause. It's just a noun. A semicolon must separate two independent clauses (A).

    - Ending the first clause with a question mark (B) or exclamation point (C) would leave "the smell" hanging as a fragment.

    - But a **COLON** does not have to separate two independent clauses. A colon also captures the meaning of the sentence. There's a *strong* connection between the two parts, "the smell" *is* the "one thing" mentioned in the first part.

6. **Answer: B.**
    Correct: *… I don't even need an alarm* **clock—the aroma** *of warm rolls nudges me awake and eases me into the day.*

    - Independent clauses: **DON'T** put a comma between the independent clauses "I don't even need an alarm clock" and "the aroma of warm rolls nudges me…" (A, C).

    - But you can use a **DASH** to separate the clauses, as choice B does.

    - Prepositional phrases: **DON'T** put a comma (or a semicolon) before the prepositional phrase "of warm rolls" (C, D)

    - Choice D uses a semicolon. That's a fine way to separate independent clauses. But it puts the semicolon between "aroma" and "of". "The aroma" is part of the second clause: it's the subject of "nudges" and it's being described by "of warm rolls".

CONVENTIONS OF PUNCTUATION EXERCISE

Here it is! Another passage! **Punctuation** *only! Wheeee!*

PASSAGE IV

My Dream Home

I recently moved into the apartment of my dreams. It's **1** tiny, its inconveniently located, and, it's too expensive. But the best thing about my apartment **2** is, the fact that it sits above a wonderful place called Emily's Bakery.

All independent **3** bakeries have a certain small-town charm to them, and this one is no different. The store, actually owned by a woman named Emily, is a very cute place, but proximity to a bakery is not the sort of thing one usually makes living decisions around. Living above a bakery, though, is more important to me than having walk-in closets or **4** beautiful wood, floors.

There's one thing that makes life above Emily's so **5** great; the smell. Nothing in the world is better than the smell of fresh bread coming into your apartment first thing in the morning. Because the store starts baking when I get up in the morning, I don't even need an alarm **6** clock, the aroma of warm rolls nudges me awake and eases me into the day. I can't imagine a more pleasant way to get up.

1
A) NO CHANGE
B) tiny it's inconveniently located, and
C) tiny, it's inconveniently located, and
D) tiny, it's inconveniently located; and

2
A) NO CHANGE
B) is the fact, that it sits above
C) is the fact that it sits above
D) is the fact that it sits, above

3
A) NO CHANGE
B) bakeries'
C) bakery's
D) bakerys'

4
A) NO CHANGE
B) beautiful, wood floors.
C) beautiful, wood floor's.
D) beautiful wood floors.

5
A) NO CHANGE
B) great? The
C) great! The
D) great: the

6
A) NO CHANGE
B) clock—the aroma
C) clock, the aroma,
D) clock the aroma;

CONTINUE

By now I can even distinguish all the different
7 rolls scents. I can tell what's coming out of the oven
without leaving my bedroom. Baguettes have a rich,
dense aroma. Surprisingly, the sourdough loaves smell
more sweet than sour, almost like maple syrup. My
favorites are the croissants. They're nice and buttery, and
it's easy to detect the chocolate ones.

People are amazed to learn that, despite my
obsession, I rarely keep any bread in the apartment. Why
would I? If I want bread, I can just go downstairs and
pick up something fresh. When I first moved in, this
convenience made me a bit concerned about my weight.
Fresh **8** cupcakes and doughnuts, sit literally steps
away from my bedroom all day and much of the night!
I've done a good job of staying in shape—I've actually
lost **9** weight since moving here but, I have to be
careful not to indulge myself too often.

I was also **10** worried that, constant exposure to the
bakery's smell might desensitize me until I no longer
noticed it. Even worse, I might start to resent the smell or
even hate it. My friend Paul used to love Indian food
before he moved next to an Indian restaurant. After three
months there, the smell drove him so crazy that he had to
move. But I've been here over a year now. The smell is
still as wonderful as it was on the first **11** day and, I
have no intention of ever leaving.

7
A) NO CHANGE
B) rolls' scent's.
C) roll's scents'.
D) rolls' scents.

8
A) NO CHANGE
B) cupcakes, and doughnuts sit
C) cupcakes and doughnuts sit
D) cupcakes and, doughnuts, sit

9
A) NO CHANGE
B) weight, since moving here but
C) weight since moving here—but
D) weight—since moving here but,

10
A) NO CHANGE
B) worried, that
C) worried, that,
D) worried that

11
A) NO CHANGE
B) day, and I have
C) day, and I have,
D) day and I have,

STOP

7. **Answer: D.**

Correct: *By now I can even distinguish all the different* **rolls' scents**.

- The first word, *rolls'*, is **PLURAL POSSESSIVE**. The phrase "all the different" tells us it should be plural (C). It should be possessive because the scents *belong to* the rolls; they are the "scents *of the rolls*" (A).

- The second word, *scents*, is **PLURAL NON-POSSESSIVE**. It's plural because we know that the rolls are plural; if there are many rolls, there should be many scents (B). It's non-possessive because the scents don't possess anything— they're *being possessed* by the rolls. The rolls are possessive so the scents should not be (C).

A: ✗ plural non-possessive   ✓ plural non-possessive
B: ✓ plural possessive   ✗ singular possessive
C: ✗ singular possessive   ✗ plural possessive
D: ✓ plural possessive   ✓ plural non-possessive

8. **Answer: C.**

Correct: *Fresh* **cupcakes and doughnuts sit** *literally steps away from my bedroom* ...

- Two-part list: **DON'T** put a comma before or after "and" in the two-part list "cupcakes and doughnuts" (B, D).

- Subject-verb: **DON'T** put a comma between the subject "cupcakes and doughnuts" and the verb "sit" (A, D).

9. **Answer: C.**

Correct: *I've done a good job of staying in shape—I've actually lost* **weight since moving here—but** *I have to be careful not to indulge myself too often.*

- Conjunctions: **DON'T** put a comma after the conjunction "but" (A).

- Dashes: put **DASHES** on *both* sides of the parenthetical phrase "I've actually lost weight since moving here" (A, B, D).

Note: Choice D) uses a second dash but puts it in the wrong place. The phrase "since moving here" tells us when the author lost weight. The conjunction "but" signals the beginning of a new clause.

10. **Answer: D.**

Correct: *I was also* **worried that** *constant exposure to the bakery's smell might desensitize me* ...

- "That": **DON'T** put a comma before or after "that" (A, B, C).

11. **Answer: B.**

Correct: *The smell is still as wonderful as it was on the first* **day, and I have** *no intention of ever leaving.*

- Independent clauses: **DO** put a comma before the conjunction before the independent clause "and I have no intention..." (A, D).

- Conjunction: **DON'T** put a comma after the conjunction "and" (A).

- Verb-object: **DON'T** put a comma between the verb "have" and the object "no intention" (C, D).

THIS PAGE INTENTIONALLY LEFT BLANK

■ EXPRESSION OF IDEAS

So far we've spent just about all our time talking about the rules of *grammar*. These are the rules that an English sentence must follow in order to be considered English. If you've mastered these by now, congratulations! You no longer sound like a poorly dubbed kung fu movie.

But wait! It turns out that following all the rules of grammar isn't enough to actually make you a *good writer*. So your sentence has the right verb, and the clauses are properly connected, and the commas are all in the right places. Your sentence is *acceptable*. But maybe we could make a *better* sentence.

Furthermore, we've only been discussing individual words and sentences. What about the paragraph? What about the whole essay? Are the sentences in the right order? Does it make the point it was trying to make?

These are all questions about *Expression of Ideas*. In this chapter we will go beyond grammar and look at rules for composing the most *effective* essay. Thankfully, Expression of Ideas questions fall into a few easily identifiable categories, so it won't be too hard to figure out what we want.

Expression of Ideas questions fall into three subcategories: ***Effective Language Use, Organization,*** and ***Development.***

I. EFFECTIVE LANGUAGE USE

Effective Language questions deal with saying things the right way. In order for a sentence to be most effective, we want it to convey exactly the right information—enough that we know what it's talking about, but not so much that the sentence weighs us down.

The Effective Language Use questions contribute to your Words in Context subscore.

> ## These three guidelines will help you with
> ## most Effective Language Use questions:

1. Be concise

Redundancy

Take a look at this sentence:

> ✕ Picking the right equipment is an <u>essential and important</u> step before you climb a mountain.

Why does the sentence say "essential" *and* "important"? Those words mean the same thing! This phrase is **redundant**—that's a fancy word for *saying the same thing twice*. Using both words doesn't add any new information; it just makes the sentence unnecessarily longer. So let's get rid of one of them:

> ✓ Picking the right equipment is an <u>important</u> step before you climb a mountain.

Much simpler; much better. Sometimes you can even DELETE the underlined phrase entirely.

> ✕ Greek geometry was more advanced than *earlier* forms of mathematics <u>that came before it</u>.

We already said we're talking about "earlier" forms of math. That *means* they "came before". The last phrase doesn't add any information to the sentence. So let's get rid of it.*

> ✓ Greek geometry was more advanced than earlier forms of mathematics.

This is another reason why it's important to **read the whole sentence**. The redundancy may not be apparent from the underlined portion alone—the phrase "that came before it" seems perfectly reasonable if you didn't see the word "earlier". If a choice is redundant, there are words *somewhere in the sentence* that mean exactly the same thing as the words in the underlined portion. Those other words might be earlier or later in the sentence, but you have to read the whole sentence to find them.

Most of the time, the key words will be fairly close to the underlined portion. But they might not even be in the same sentence:

> ✕ Samantha was pleased with her decision. <u>Her choice made her happy.</u>

---

* "OMIT the underlined portion" doesn't show up as a choice too often. When it's right, it's usually because of redundancy. When it's wrong, it's usually for a grammatical reason. Like, you can't just omit the verb from the sentence.

The second sentence here means *exactly the same thing as the first sentence!* The second sentence literally adds no new information. So why say it twice?

> ✓ **Samantha was pleased with her decision.**

If you don't notice a redundant phrase right away, the answer choices can tip you off: if, say, three choices are all roughly the same length, but one is significantly shorter. Or if all the choices contain words that mean the same thing, but one doesn't. For example:

> **The first crafts sent into space were unmanned [1] rockets without any people in them.**
>
> 1. A) NO CHANGE
>   B) rockets that did not carry astronauts.
>   C) rockets lacking human passengers of any kind.
>   D) rockets.

Notice that the first three choices all contain long phrases that refer to people, but the last choice does not. Perhaps, then, we don't *need* to refer to people here. Sure enough, the word just before the underlined portion, *unmanned*, means "without people".

Wordiness

There are other ways that a sentence can have too many words. Look at this one:

> ✗ **Steven helped <u>in the establishment of</u> the organization.**

There's nothing *redundant* about this phrase—it doesn't *repeat* anything. But it's still longer than it needs to be. Instead of using those four words, we can get the same meaning from just one word:

> ✓ **Steven helped <u>establish</u> the organization.**

That's more concise and more direct. Much better.

Many students think that it's better to use more words because it makes your writing sound fancier or more adult. **That's backwards.** It's *much* better to use *fewer* words. Using too many words makes it harder to pick apart what you're trying to say.*

I mean, which of the following do *you* prefer?

---

* It is true that a lot of adults write long, wordy, and complicated sentences. But a lot of adults are *terrible* writers.

✗	**The bake sale was organized by Steve, <u>the person who, at the time of the</u> <u>event, was leading</u> the club.**
✓	**The bake sale was organized by Steve, <u>the leader of</u> the club.**

Redundancy and wordiness are the most common kinds of error among Effective Language Use questions. Since conciseness is so important, when in doubt, **check the shortest choice**. A shorter sentence is almost always preferable to a longer sentence, as long as it doesn't violate any rules.

2. Be specific

Word count alone does not make a good sentence. Sometimes a sentence won't give *enough* information. The sentence may not contain any errors, but it doesn't give us enough detail.

> ✐ **My cat left <u>something</u> on my doorstep.**

This sentence is **too vague.** I can think of any number of things that a cat could leave on my doorstep. Can we be more specific?

> ✐ **My cat left <u>something awful</u> on my doorstep.**

Hmm. That doesn't help. Now I'm kind of scared.

> ✐ **My cat left <u>an object—something so disgusting it made me sick—</u>on my doorstep.**

Oh no! What is it‽ This is longer, but it's not actually more specific. It's more *vivid*. That's good: vivid sentences can be effective. But it's not *detailed*. It doesn't give us any more *information*. We still don't know what it was, only that it was something awful.

> ✐ **My cat left <u>a large, sticky hairball</u> on my doorstep.**

Now we know exactly what it was. Much better. Gross, but better.

How will you know when a choice is too vague? Often a question will *explicitly* ask you for a more specific choice:

> When a tornado hit my town, it **2** <u>significantly damaged everything</u> on my street.

2. Which choice provides the most specific and detailed information?
   A) NO CHANGE
   B) caused a lot of destruction
   C) knocked down many trees and houses
   D) left everything in great disarray

We can see here that three choices are vague, talking about "damage", "destruction", or "disarray" without actually saying *what happened*. Only choice C) gives a specific example of what the damage was.

Vague pronouns

This idea of vagueness relates back to something we said about pronouns in the Conventions of Usage chapter. Remember that a pronoun is a word that refers back to another word in the sentence. You have to make sure that it's clear which word the pronoun refers to.

> ✗ Scott and Bob were partners <u>until he quit</u>.

Here we have two options for who quit: Scott or Bob. How can you tell which it is? You *can't*—that's the problem. In this case, we can't use a pronoun at all. We have to specify who quit.

> ✓ Scott and Bob were partners <u>until Bob quit</u>.

Of course, if they *both* quit, then we'd have to say "they".

3. Choose the right word

Often there are many different ways of saying the same thing. But words that seem to have the same meaning may have slight differences. We must use the word that *precisely* gives the meaning we intend.

> The candidate gave a **3** <u>forceful</u> speech thanking his supporters for helping him win the election.

3. A) NO CHANGE
   B) harsh
   C) passionate
   D) violent

All of the choices here have similar meanings: all imply that the speech was given with a lot of energy. But what kind of energy do we want here? What kind of speech is it? He's *thanking his supporters*. So it should be a *positive* speech. He's saying nice things. "Forceful", "harsh", and "violent" are all *negative* words. Only "passionate" could be used to describe positive energy.

Obviously, context is important here. Don't just read the words in the choices, and don't just rely on which one "sounds" best. Look at the whole sentence, the whole paragraph, or even the rest of the essay to find clues about what sort of word you want.*

Tone

Sometimes words will mean the same thing but differ in *tone*. There's a difference between *formal* and *informal* speech, for example. Many of the things you say to your friends you would never write in a school essay.[†] But sometimes the line between formal and informal speech is hard to judge. Take a look at this:

This chimpanzee has been observed engaging in behavior that is **4** <u>atypical</u> for its species.	4.	A)	NO CHANGE
		B)	messed up
		C)	way out there
		D)	totally freaky

All choices here mean the same thing, but choices B), C), and D) are all informal phrases. The sentence, however, is very formal, so only choice A) has the appropriate tone for the sentence.

That's not to say that informal language is *never* allowed. In fact, some SAT passages are personal narratives that have a slightly relaxed tone. You don't want the language to be *too* formal:

✗ I was at the mall when all of a sudden my girlfriend <u>terminated our romantic affiliation.</u>
✓ I was at the mall when all of a sudden my girlfriend <u>broke up with me.</u>

The important thing is for the language to be **appropriate**, for it to match the tone of the rest of the essay.

---

* Even in this example, we'd want to take a look at the rest of the paragraph, just to be safe. Maybe he *did* give a violent speech thanking people. Maybe he's a werewolf. Maybe he's just kind of a jerk. But the rest of the paragraph should give us all the clues we need.

† We're not talking about *vulgarity* here. I'm sure there are some terrible, *terrible* things you say to your friends that you wouldn't even say to your parents, let alone use on a school essay. You won't see any cursing on the SAT.

II. ORGANIZATION

Organization is all about the flow of information in the essay. Sentences and paragraphs should be put into a logical order and the transitions between them should be appropriate.

Transition words

About half of all Organization questions deal with *transitions* between sentences. Transition words are words that connect parts of sentences or that connect different sentences. The key to picking the right transition word is to understand the **relationship** between the sentences.

Let's look at a few examples:

When sentences have **contrasting** meanings, the connecting word should reflect that contrast.

> ✗ Johnny has never been a very good athlete. <u>Additionally,</u> he has won his last five races.
> ✓ Johnny has never been a very good athlete. <u>However,</u> he has won his last five races.

Obviously, these two sentences are different: if Johnny's not a good athlete, we wouldn't expect him to win any races. So we want to connect the sentences with a contrast word like "however", not a similarity word like "additionally".

Other sentences may show **similarity**, or they may be a **continuation** of an idea in the previous sentence.

> ✗ Sergio has never liked cats. <u>On the other hand</u>, he refuses to be in the same room as one.
> ✓ Sergio has never liked cats. <u>In fact</u>, he refuses to be in the same room as one.

"On the other hand" shows contrast, but both sentences have similar meanings—Sergio hates cats. The second sentence is an *elaboration* on the first one. It gives an example of the *great extent* of Sergio's hatred.

A special kind of similarity is a **cause-and-effect** relationship:

> ✗ **Kristen needed a lot of different colors for her project. <u>Nevertheless,</u> she bought the large box of crayons.**
> ✓ **Kristen needed a lot of different colors for her project. <u>Therefore,</u> she bought the large box of crayons.**

The first sentence gives a reason for the second sentence. Kristen's need for a lot of colors *explains why* she bought the large box.

Of course, you don't need transition words between *every* two sentences. Sometimes the best transition is **no transition**. Observe:

> ✗ **Robinson completed his study on cat ownership. <u>However, it</u> found that cat owners were more likely to be happy than those without cats.**
> ✗ **Robinson completed his study on cat ownership. <u>Additionally, it</u> found that cat owners were more likely to be happy than those without cats.**

Neither of these transitions makes much sense here. "However" doesn't make sense since there's no contrast. But "additionally" doesn't make sense either: the second sentence isn't making a *new* point. It's giving details about the study mentioned in the first sentence.

We might be able to come up with a transition word that would work. But we don't really need a transition word here at all.

> ✓ **Robinson completed his study on cat ownership. <u>It</u> found that cat owners were more likely to be happy than those without cats.**

Here are some examples of transition words that show different relationships:

Contrast	*although, in contrast, instead, nevertheless, on the other hand, while, yet*
Cause and effect	*as a result, because, consequently, since, so, therefore, thus*
Similarity or continuation	*additionally, finally, for example, furthermore, indeed, in fact, that is*

These words don't all have exactly the same meaning. And these lists are not exhaustive— you'll almost certainly encounter other transition words that aren't listed here. But don't worry about the nuances; for most SAT questions, all you have to know is the *general* kind of word you need. If there's no contrast, don't use a contrast word. If there is contrast, don't use a similarity word.

Transition sentences

Transitions don't have to be simple words. Sometimes a clause or a full sentence can provide a transition:

> Joy used to think sudoku puzzles were impossible. **5** She can now solve the hardest puzzles in just a few minutes.

5. Given that all the choices are true, which provides the most effective transition from the preceding sentence to the next one:

A) Once she learned a few tricks, though, they became easy for her.

B) Sudoku puzzles were invented in Japan.

C) The newspaper prints a new sudoku puzzle every day.

D) She loves crossword puzzles, but these things confused her.

What's the relationship between these sentences? The first sentence says that Joy has trouble with the puzzles. The next one says she can solve the hardest ones. What are we missing? She must have *learned how to solve them*. We need a choice that teaches Joy how to solve the puzzles. Only **choice A)** fits.

Let's try another:

> Firefighter training prepares you for any danger you may face. **6** <u>The program can be expensive, and</u> you will immediately know how to safely and effectively react to it.

6. Assuming that all the choices are accurate, which provides the most effective transition from the preceding sentence to this one:

A) NO CHANGE

B) When you're in a life-threatening situation,

C) While it's exciting to be a firefighter,

D) You get to ride the truck, where

What's the relationship between these sentences? The first has to do with firefighter training. Well, *all* the choices are about being a firefighter. But what does it say *about* firefighter training? It prepares you for *danger*. The second sentence is about how you "safely and effectively react to it." What's "*it*"? A *danger!* So we want a choice that says something about *dangers.* Only **choice B)** works.

The key to both these examples is that the transition phrase is **relevant to both sentences**, the one before it and the one after it.* That's the point of a transition—to connect the things on either side. Sentences that are *next to* each other should *refer to* each other in some way.

Introductions and conclusions

Similarly, a question might ask you to provide an **introductory sentence** to a paragraph. An introductory sentence often serves as a transition between the previous paragraph and the new one. But sometimes an introductory sentence simply gives you the *topic* of the paragraph. So you need to know what the paragraph is *about*—the **main idea** of the paragraph.[†]

---

7 <u>While not as diverse as dogs, cats come in many different breeds.</u> Having a sleepy cat purring on your lap can relax you and relieve stress. Cats can be playful and fun, making adventures using normal household objects. In addition, cats can catch mice and other household pests.

7. Given that all the choices are true, which one most effectively introduces the subject of this paragraph?

A) NO CHANGE
B) Cats were first domesticated thousands of years ago.
C) Owning a cat has both personal and practical benefits.
D) Some cats can live to be over 15 years old.

In order to answer the question, we need to figure out the main idea of the paragraph. It's obviously about cats, but all the choices are about cats. We need to be more specific. What does it say *about* cats? It tells us why it's *good* to have cats—they're relaxing, they're fun, and they catch pests. That's **choice C)**.

If you have trouble finding the main idea of the paragraph, try **eliminating irrelevant choices**. Our introductory sentence should be about the same thing as the rest of the paragraph. Let's check the choices:

---

* Notice that all the wrong choices are *irrelevant* to the other two sentences. We'll talk more about this in a minute.

† Similarly, a question may ask you to provide a **concluding sentence**. Conclusions usually work just like introductions: they summarize the main idea of the paragraph.

A) Is the paragraph about different breeds of cats? No, it doesn't mention any different breeds.

B) Is the paragraph about the history of cats' domestication? No, it doesn't mention any history or the process of domestication.

C) Is the paragraph about benefits of owning a cat? **Yes!** They're relaxing, fun, and they catch pests.

D) Is the paragraph about how long cats live? No, it doesn't mention cats' life spans at all.

Sentence order

Sometimes a paragraph will have all the right sentences, but they'll be in the wrong order.

Observe:

[1] Having diverse plant life can be good for an ecosystem. [2] However, sometimes exotic species can cause unexpected destruction. [3] Originally from Asia, it rapidly spread across the American South with devastating results. [4] One such example is the vine-like plant called kudzu. **8**

8. For the sake of the logic and coherence of this paragraph, Sentence 4 should be placed

A) where it is now.
B) before Sentence 1.
C) before Sentence 2.
D) before Sentence 3.

We want to find the best place to put Sentence 4. One thing we **don't** recommend is putting Sentence 4 in each of the four spots in the choices and reading the paragraph four times to see which *sounds best*. That will take forever and won't help you a get an answer.

Instead, look for clues in Sentence 4 itself. It starts with the phrase "one such example": one example of *what*? What is kudzu an example of? It's an example of an exotic species that caused destruction—that's what Sentence 2 mentioned. Since Sentence 4 refers to something mentioned in Sentence 2, we should put Sentence 4 right after Sentence 2.

Furthermore, Sentence 3 says "*it* rapidly spread". What does it refer to? *Kudzu!* Thus the mention of kudzu in Sentence 4 should come *before* Sentence 3 so we can tell what "it" is supposed to mean. That's **choice D)**.

The key to sentence order questions is to look for references between sentences. Pronouns like "it" or words like "such" or "this" refer to concepts that came *before* them. Sentences that *refer to* each other should be *next to* each other.

III. DEVELOPMENT

Development questions often overlap with the concepts we saw in Effective Lanuage Use and Organization questions. They primarily differ in that they *explicitly* ask you what you as the writer should do. Should you add this sentence? Should you delete it? What is the intended purpose of this sentence? Does it achieve that purpose? If you want to achieve a certain goal, what should you do?

Development questions commonly ask three questions:

---

1. Does it fulfill the writer's goals?

Some questions will tell you exactly what the writer wants to do and ask you the best way to accomplish that goal. Look at this:

> Cameron lay in his sleeping bag, staring up at the stars, **9** shivering in the cold wind.

9. The writer wants to suggest the feeling that Cameron is far from civilization. Which choice best fulfills the writer's goal?

A) NO CHANGE
B) which twinkled in the sky above him.
C) alone with the chirping crickets.
D) worried about scorpions.

Any of these choices would make a fine sentence, depending on the context. The sentence we pick will depend on what the writer wants to say. Ah, but we *know* what the writer wants to say—the question tells us "the writer wants to suggest the feeling that Cameron is far from civilization." We need the choice that comes closest to *that goal*. **Choice C)** fits nicely: Cameron is "*alone*", with only "*crickets*" around him.

These questions are pretty easy to spot. If you encounter one, don't pick the choice that sounds best *to you*; pick the choice that **fulfills the stated goal.**

2. Should you add it?

Take a look at this paragraph:

> Heather has come to a crossroads: she has been accepted into four colleges and must choose which one she wants to attend. **10** She has to decide what's most important to her: the school's location, its academic standing, or the size of the scholarship it offers.

10. At this point, the writer is considering adding the following true sentence:

> Heather had the highest grades in her high school graduating class.

Should the writer make this addition here?

A) Yes, because it provides background on Heather that may influence her decision.

B) Yes, because Heather's grades were a factor in her acceptance to these colleges.

C) No, because the sentence does not tell us what colleges the rest of her class got into.

D) No, because it is not relevant to Heather's decision about which college to attend.

There are two parts to this question. First we have to determine whether to add the sentence, then we have to provide a reason for our decision. To do that, we need to understand the **main idea** of the paragraph to determine if the sentence belongs here.

What's going on in this paragraph? Heather is deciding which college to go to. Would it help to know how good her high school grades were? No! Her high school grades don't matter anymore—she's already been accepted into college. **Choice D)** is our answer: the sentence is **irrelevant** to the rest of the essay.

Irrelevant details

Irrelevant details pop up in wrong answers all over the SAT. We've already seen several examples of them (such as questions 6 and 7 above).

Take a look at this question:

Cameron had just woken up in his tent when he noticed a scorpion sitting in his boot. **11** <u>Scorpions are actually arachnids, like spiders.</u> He froze, paralyzed with fear.

11. A) NO CHANGE
    B) Scorpions' bodies are segmented into three parts.
    C) Scorpions can be found on every continent except Antarctica.
    D) DELETE the underlined portion.

This looks similar to some of the questions we've already seen, like the questions about redundancy or wordiness. But these choices are slightly different. Choices A), B), and C) give specific, detailed information. Yet *none* of those details are relevant to the rest of the paragraph. Do you think that Cameron cares how many segments scorpions' bodies have? No! *There's a freaking scorpion in his boot!* Since all these choices are irrelevant, our best bet is to DELETE the phrase entirely.

3. What would the essay lose?

We've seen questions about eliminating sentences that don't contribute anything to the passage. But some questions will *assume* that the sentence contributes something, and you have to figure out what that is.

Hank found an old figurine while hiking in the mountains of Mexico. He noticed a strange inscription on the artifact, so he showed it to his friend Larissa, a linguist who specializes in ancient languages. **12** At first, she thought the inscription looked like a very common form of hieroglyphics. But try as she might, Larissa couldn't decipher its meaning.

12. The writer is considering deleting the phrase "a linguist who specializes in ancient languages." If the writer were to make this deletion, the paragraph would primarily lose:
    A) information suggesting that Larissa will not be able to read the inscription.
    B) details that explain Hank's motivation for showing Larissa the figurine.
    C) evidence supporting Hank's idea about the artifact.
    D) a description of the writing on the figurine.

This question tells us that deleting that part of the sentence would make the essay lose something. That's good: that means we know that it contributes something. But what does it add? Basically, the question is asking the **purpose** of the phrase.

Let's look at the *literal meaning* of the phrase in question. That phrase gives us background information about Larissa. Larissa is an expert on ancient languages, so Hank thinks she'll be able to read the inscription on the figurine. Therefore, the fact that she's an expert tells us *why* Hank showed her the figurine. That's **choice B)**.

Let's look at another example in the same paragraph:

Hank found an old figurine while hiking in the mountains of Mexico. He noticed a strange inscription on the artifact, so he showed it to his friend Larissa, a linguist who specializes in ancient languages. At first, she thought the inscription looked like a very common form of hieroglyphics. But try as she might, Larissa couldn't decipher its meaning. **13**

13. If the writer were to delete the phrase "try as she might" (and the comma), the paragraph would primarily lose:

A) a sense of how difficult the task was for Larissa.

B) a humorous comment that lightens the mood.

C) an explanation of how to understand hieroglyphics.

D) nothing, since this information was given earlier in the paragraph.

Here, the phrase in question doesn't give *information* the way that the phrase in the last question did. Instead, it modifies the description in the last sentence. In that sentence, the main clause tells us that Larissa couldn't figure out what the inscription said, and this phrase tells us she was *trying hard* to figure it out. Which choice talks about trying hard? Only **choice A)**.

The key to answering questions like this is figuring out the *meaning* of the phrase in question, and seeing how it *relates to* the rest of the paragraph.

4. Data Analysis

Aha, I said three questions, but there's one bonus category. One additional subtype of Development questions are those that deal with interpreting figures and graphs. These are similar to the Data questions we've seen in the Reading section: you'll be asked either to identify values on the figure or to understand the meaning of the figure.

For more on Data analysis, refer to the Data questions section of the Reading Question Type chapter.

The main difference between these questions and those from the Reading is the form. On the Writing section, Data questions will offer four different ways of phrasing part of a sentence, much like many other question types we've seen. But only one choice will be *accurate* with respect to the figure. So while other Writing questions ask about the *grammar* or *style* of a sentence, these are concerned with the *content* of the sentence.

Data analysis will make up a much smaller percentage of questions on the Writing than it does on the Reading. Only one passage will contain a figure, and only 1 or 2 questions on the entire section will ask about it.

1. Effective Language Use

- Be **concise**. Avoid redundant or wordy choices.
- Be **specific**. Avoid vague choices and vague pronouns.
- Choose **the right word**. Make sure it has the right meaning and tone.

2. Organization

- Choose the right **transition word** to connect similar or contrasting sentences.
- Choose the right **transition phrase** to connect the topics of adjacent sentences.
- An **introductory or concluding sentence** should state the main idea of the paragraph.
- Find the right **sentence order** by looking at references within the sentences.

3. Development

- Does a choice **fulfill the writer's goal**? Focus on the *stated goal*, not your opinion.
- Should the writer **add** or **delete** a sentence? Look out for irrelevant choices.
- If the writer deleted a phrase, **what would the essay lose**? Find the meaning of the phrase and how it relates to the paragraph.
- Is the sentence true according to a **data figure**?

EXPRESSION OF IDEAS EXERCISE

This exercise contains a full passage with 11 questions, just like an SAT passage. Unlike a real SAT passage, it only features **Expression of Ideas** *questions. Look out for all the rules discussed above. Enjoy!*

Margaret Mitchell's First Novel

[1] It was clear from a young age that Margaret Mitchell had a knack for storytelling. [2] As a child growing up in Atlanta, she would make up tales by the hundreds, writing them in homemade **1** books, which she made herself. [3] After spending one year at Smith College, she eventually got a job as a columnist for the *Atlanta Journal*. [4] As she got older, she would write plays that she would act out with her friends. [5] Later, she was a literary editor of her high school yearbook and founded a drama society. [6] She became one of the first women to write for a major newspaper in the South. **2**

While working at the newspaper, **3** an accidental injury launched her literary career. In 1926, she broke her ankle and was forced to stay home while it healed. Bored with her bed rest, she began to occupy herself by writing chapters for a novel. **4** She kept writing after her ankle healed, and the manuscript soon evolved into her masterpiece, the Civil War epic *Gone with the Wind*.

1

A) NO CHANGE
B) books by herself in her youth.
C) books she assembled by herself.
D) books.

2

For the sake of the logic and coherence of the paragraph, Sentence 3 should be placed:

A) where it is now.
B) after Sentence 1.
C) after Sentence 4.
D) after Sentence 5.

3

Which choice provides the most specific and detailed information?

A) NO CHANGE
B) a freak occurrence
C) a life-changing episode
D) the occasion of an unexpected event

4

The writer wishes to indicate that writing the manuscript took a great deal of work. Which of the choices provides a vivid and specific detail that accomplishes that goal?

A) NO CHANGE
B) Three years and one thousand pages later,
C) Written with exquisite prose,
D) A story about the daughter of a Georgia plantation owner,

CONTINUE

Expression of Ideas Exercise

1. **Answer: D.**
   REDUNDANT. We already know the books are "homemade" and that she made them "as a child". Choices A, B, C all repeat that information.

2. **Answer: D.**
   SENTENCE ORDER. Focus on the chronological order of events. Sentence 3 tells us she got a job at the newspaper after college. It fits perfectly between sentences 5 and 6: sentence 5 is about her high school, and sentence 6 is about her job at the newspaper. High school leads to college, which leads to the newspaper job.

3. **Answer: A.**
   SPECIFIC DETAILS. Choices B, C, and D tell us the event was important and unexpected, but none tells us what the event was. Only choice A tells us it was an *injury*.

4. **Answer: B.**
   SENTENCE GOAL. The question tells us we want the phrase to emphasize "*a great deal of work*".

   A: tells us she "kept writing after her ankle healed" but doesn't say how long it took her ankle to heal or how much beyond that she kept writing. Maybe it was finished in six weeks.

   B: **Correct.** This choice gives a specific length of time she worked and a specific length for the manuscript. Both are huge.

   C: tells us about the quality of the writing. This is irrelevant.

   D: tells us about the story itself. This is irrelevant.

5. **Answer: C.**

INTRODUCTION/TRANSITION SENTENCE. We want a transition between paragraphs, so let's get the main ideas for both of them. The previous paragraph was about how she came to write the manuscript. This paragraph is about how it came to be published. Our choice should also be relevant to the second sentence in this paragraph, which tells us she was too shy to show anyone her manuscript.

A) is about where she got the ideas for the story. Neither paragraph is about the story itself.

B) is about the order in which she wrote the chapters. That might be a relevant detail for the previous paragraph, but it has nothing to do with this paragraph.

C) **Correct.** The previous paragraph told us that she started writing in 1926 and finished three years later (in 1929). This sentence tells us it wasn't actually published until 1936—that's ten years after she started. The next sentence explains the delay: she was too shy to tell anyone about it.

D) is about the title of the book. This may seem relevant to the previous sentence, which mentions the title by name, but this detail is irrelevant to the rest of this paragraph.

6. **Answer: A.**

TRANSITION SENTENCE. We want a transition sentence, so let's look at the sentences before and after this spot. The sentence before tells us she met an editor but didn't show him the manuscript. The sentence after tells us it was published the following year. What's missing? At some point, *she must have shown him the manuscript.* That's choice A. Choices B, C, and D are all irrelevant to both sentences.

7. **Answer: D.**

WOULD LOSE. What does the fact that the book won the Pulitzer Prize have to do with the rest of the paragraph?

A) It does not explain why she wrote the book. Because she really wanted a Pulitzer? The essay doesn't say that.

B) It's not a contrast, it's a similarity. The high sales and the Pulitzer Prize both support the idea that the book "received near universal praise".

C) The film has not been mentioned yet.

D) **Correct.** The high sales and the Pulitzer Prize both support the idea that the book "received near universal praise". The beginning of the sentence says the book was well received "both from the general public and from critics". The high sales show popularity with the public, and the Pulitzer Prize shows praise from critics.

8. **Answer: D.**

DATA. This question asks which choice accurately describes the information on the graph.

Let's go through the choices and check them out.

A) *Gone with the Wind* did take in more money than any other film, but not *twice* as much money. Is the *Gone with the Wind* bar twice as long as any of the other bars?

B) This is probably true; the graph clearly shows that *Gone with the Wind* grossed the most money of *all* films, so it probably also grossed the most money of 1939 films. But *this graph doesn't say that.* This graph doesn't mention any other 1939 films. So this is not an accurate representation of the graph.

C) Random. The graph doesn't mention costs at all.

D) **Correct.** The title of the graph is "Inflation-adjusted revenue for all-time highest-grossing films" and *Gone with the Wind* is number 1. Choice D) doesn't say anything about inflation, but the rest of the sentence after the underline does. So we're good.

[5] She got some of the ideas for the book from her grandfather, a Civil War veteran. She was too humble and too bashful to show it to anyone or even to acknowledge that she had written anything. One day, when an editor from New York came to Atlanta looking for talented new authors, she graciously showed him around town without even mentioning her own book. [6] It was quickly accepted and finally published the following year.

Gone with the Wind received near universal praise both from the general public and from critics: the book sold millions of copies and won the Pulitzer Prize. [7] The film adaptation, premiering in Atlanta three years later, was just as popular as the book. It won ten Academy Awards, and [8] took in more than twice as much money as any other film in history when prices are adjusted for inflation.

INFLATION-ADJUSTED REVENUE FOR ALL-TIME HIGHEST-GROSSING FILMS

Gone with the Wind (1939), $3.44
Avatar (2009), $3.02
Star Wars (1977), $2.83
Titanic (1997), $2.52
The Sound of Music (1965), $2.37

$0 $1 $2 $3

Gross Revenue in 2014 dollars (in billions)

5

Given that all the choices are true, which choice would provide the most effective transition from the previous paragraph while introducing the topic of this one?

A) NO CHANGE
B) She wrote the last chapter first and filled in earlier chapters in a random order.
C) It wasn't until 1936, however, that the book was actually published.
D) While most of the book was finished, she had not yet given the book a title.

6

Assuming that all the choices are accurate, which provides the most effective transition from the preceding sentence to this one?

A) Later that night, she changed her mind and decided to show him the manuscript.
B) Most publishing houses were based in the northeast.
C) Besides, at the time it was difficult for a woman to get a novel published.
D) Her job at the newspaper made her rather well known around town.

7

If the writer were to delete the phrase "and won the Pulitzer Prize" from the preceding sentence, the paragraph would primarily lose:

A) a detail that explains why Mitchell decided to write the book.
B) a contrast to the phrase "sold millions of copies" in the same sentence.
C) a statement that reveals how the book was made into a film.
D) a detail supporting the idea that the book was well received.

8

Which of the following most accurately and effectively represents the information on the graph?

A) NO CHANGE
B) took in more money in 1939 than any other film
C) cost more to make than any other movie in history
D) still holds the record as the highest-grossing movie of all time

CONTINUE →

Despite the success of *Gone with the Wind*, Mitchell never published another novel. **9** In fact, the success of her first book may have prevented her from writing another. She had immediately become an international **10** celebrity almost overnight, but the constant demands of fame were overwhelming for her. **11** When a reporter once asked her whether she had been writing anything, she said she was too busy responding to mail about her last book to work on anything new. But even without writing any other books, she had secured literary immortality. Upon her death in 1949, her obituary described *Gone with the Wind* as "the most phenomenal best seller ever written by an unknown author of a first novel."

9
A) NO CHANGE
B) Consequently,
C) Therefore,
D) On the other hand,

10
A) NO CHANGE
B) celebrity incredibly quickly,
C) celebrity at once,
D) celebrity,

11
At this point, the writer is considering adding the following true statement:

> A steadfast humanitarian, she dedicated herself to volunteering with the American Red Cross upon the start of World War II.

Should the writer make this addition here?

A) Yes, because it provides evidence of Mitchell's international fame.
B) Yes, because it helps clarify Mitchell's reasons for writing the book.
C) No, because it repeats information given earlier in the essay.
D) No, because it is irrelevant to the focus of the paragraph.

STOP

9   Answer: A.
TRANSITION WORD. The second sentence continues
the idea of the first sentence, explaining why the first
sentence is true. The first sentence says she never
published another book. The second tells us why she
never wrote another book.

A) **Correct.** "In fact" shows a continuation of or
elaboration on the previous sentence. That's exactly
what we want.

B) "Consequently" does show causation, but in the
wrong direction. "Consequently" would mean that
the first sentence explains why the second sentence is
true.

C) "Therefore" does show causation, but in the wrong
direction. "Therefore" would mean that the first
sentence explains why the second sentence is true.

D) "On the other hand" shows *contrast*. Our two
sentences are *similar*.

10. Answer: D.
REDUNDANT. The sentence already said that she
became a celebrity "*immediately*". Choices A, B, and
C all mean the same thing as "immediately", so they
don't add any new information.

11. Answer: D.
ADDITION. First, find the main idea of this
paragraph: it's about Mitchell's fame and the fact that
she never wrote another book. The sentence gives us
a detail about her humanitarian work. That's totally
irrelevant to the rest of the paragraph. So we **should
not** add the sentence (eliminate A and B) because it's
irrelevant to the paragraph (eliminate C).

THIS PAGE INTENTIONALLY LEFT BLANK

MATHEMATICS

Introduction to Math	233
Math Techniques	257
Math Fundamentals	279
Heart of Algebra	309
Passport to Advanced Math	333
Graphing	357
Problem Solving and Data Analysis	379
Additional Topics in Math	407

Introduction To Math

Welcome to SAT Math! I think you'll like it here. Let's take a look around.

SAT math is not exactly the same as the math you do in school. Yes, a lot of your old favorites will show up here (ratios, two-variable equations, the Pythagorean Theorem, and many more!) but the questions are a little bit different. In school, you learn *content*. They teach you something and then test you on it. The SAT is a *reasoning* test. That means it's less about specific rules and methods than about problem solving. For example, in school, they teach you *algebra* and then test you on *how well you use algebra*. On the SAT, they give you a *problem* and ask you to solve it *any way you can*. That could mean algebra or it could mean arithmetic or geometry. On any given problem, there's no one way that's "the right way" to do it. Almost every problem on the SAT can be done several different ways. Now, some ways are faster or safer than others, so our job is to show you *the best way* to do a given problem.

Throughout the next few chapters, we'll be talking about two types of things: content and techniques. *Content* is the literal stuff you need to know (like the Pythagorean Theorem*). *Techniques* are methods for doing lots of different kinds of problems (like Plug In). Both are equally important. However, a lot of the content you'll already be familiar with from your adventures in school; it's the techniques that will be new for you, so that's where we should concentrate.

---

* Actually, you don't even need to know that either.

I. FORMAT

You will see two math sections on the SAT:

Section	Time	Questions
Section 3: No calculator	25 minutes	20 questions: 15 multiple-choice questions 5 student-produced response questions (grid-ins)
Section 4: Calculator OK	55 minutes	38 questions: 30 multiple-choice questions 8 student-produced response questions (grid-ins)
	80 minutes	**58 Questions**

Some general comments about the format:

- **Calculators are allowed only on section 4.** Section 3 is a NO CALCULATOR section. You may not use a calculator on any other part of the test (including the Reading and Writing sections).

- For section 4, you may use most four-function, scientific or graphing calculators. You won't have to clear the memory from your calculator.

- According to College Board guidelines, you may <u>not</u> use:
  - cell phone, smart phone, or laptop calculators;
  - calculators that can access the Internet, have wireless, Bluetooth, cellular, audio/video recording and playing, camera, or any other smart phone type feature;
  - models that have typewriter-like keypad, pen-input, or stylus;
  - models that use electrical outlets, make noise, or have a paper tape;
  - calculator function on a mobile phone (Yes I know we already said that. Stop asking to use your phone.);
  - calculators that are too big to fit on your desk, in the testing room, or in the testing center;
  - calculators that possess empathy or can feel pain;
  - calculators that are armed with any sort of weapon;
  - calculators that are actually another student hiding in a box labeled "calculator";
  - everything else is fine, though.

- **Questions within each section are ordered by difficulty.** The first questions are easy, the last questions are hard.

- Each section begins with multiple-choice questions and ends with grid-ins.

- All figures are drawn to scale unless otherwise indicated.

Grid-ins

The Student-Produced Response Questions (called "grid-ins" for short) are the only questions on the SAT that are not multiple-choice (except the Essay, of course). Here, you will be expected to come up with your own answer and fill it into the grid provided (thus the term "grid-in"). At right, you'll see an example of the space in which you must put your answer.

We don't have any specific techniques or strategies for the grid-ins other than those we have for all the other math questions. The content and style of these questions will be just like the rest of the section; the math itself is no different. However, they may seem a bit weird to those of you who are unfamiliar with the test. Here are some miscellaneous notes about the grid-ins:

- As mentioned above, math sections are ordered by difficulty. However, **grid-ins are ordered by difficulty** *separately*. So on section 3, question #15 (the last multiple-choice question) will be hard, while question #16 (the first grid-in) will be easy.

- Notice that the grid has two elements to it: spaces at the top to write in your answer, and bubbles at the bottom to fill in (just like when you fill out your name at the beginning). **You must fill in the bubbles.** The spaces at the top *are not scored by the machine.* They are only there for your benefit so you can easily read your answer and can fill in the bubbles more easily. If you write in the boxes but don't fill in the bubbles, the machine will read it as a blank.*

- You can put your answer in any column. It doesn't matter how you position it (to the right or left).

- Notice that there is **no negative symbol** in the grid—there will never be a negative answer on the grid-ins. If you get a negative answer, you messed up. Try again.

- If your answer is a decimal, you must be as accurate as possible when gridding in your answer. For example, if the right answer is 2/3 (which, as a decimal, is .66666 repeating), .666 would be okay, and .667 would be okay, but .6 and .66 are not okay.

---

* Conversely, that means that you don't *have* to write anything in the boxes at all. You could draw little pictures of ducks in there or write messages to the College Board and no one will ever know.

Take the decimal as far as space allows. (Of course, you could also just enter 2/3 and avoid the whole issue).

> You do *not* have to reduce to the lowest possible fraction. If the right answer is 2/3, an answer of 4/6 will still give you credit. Of course, if you get a fraction that doesn't fit into four spaces, like 10/15, then you will have to reduce (or convert to a decimal).

Calculator vs. No-calculator

One of the changes to the SAT in 2016 was that to limit the use of calculators. Math section 3 will not permit calculators, while math section 4 will. Previously, the test permitted calculators on all sections. (Of course, some of us remember a time when calculators weren't allowed at all.)*

What does this really mean, though? What's the difference between the calculator questions and the non-calculator questions?

Honestly, it means **very little**. Most questions between the two sections are incredibly similar. True, there are some questions on the no-calculator section that you'd probably prefer to have a calculator for. But you're not going to have to do any crazy computation by hand, like long division or multiply five-digit numbers. Similarly, you will probably see a few questions on the calculator section that do involve tough computations that you don't want to do by hand. But most of the questions can be easily done without one. *Calculator allowed* does not mean *calculator required*.

You will want to have a calculator. But you don't have to go out and buy a fancy calculator just for the SAT. A simple scientific will do. Frankly, most of your calculator use will be simple adding and multiplying, so a cheap-o four-function drug-store calculator that's missing the 7-key will be fine.[†]

Now, if you already have a fancy graphing calculator, you *may* see some questions on which a graphing calculator can help you. Being able to graph equations or look up values in a table can save you some time—if you know how to use it. But if you don't have one, or if you have one but barely know how to turn it on, don't sweat it. You'll be fine.

Using your calculator

Sometimes a question will ask you to understand some deep math concept, but a calculator can allow you to do it by brute force. Let's look at a particular situation:

There will often be situations where you get an answer that isn't one of the choices. Usually,

---

* Some of us are very old.

† Well, okay, you probably need the 7-key.

that will be because you did something wrong (it happens). But sometimes your answer is right, but the correct choice expresses that answer in a different form.

One of the great benefits of having a calculator is the ability to manipulate Ugly Numbers. For example, say you did a question and got $\sqrt{20}$ as your answer. But here are your choices:

A. $2\sqrt{5}$

B. $4\sqrt{5}$

C. $5\sqrt{2}$

D. $10\sqrt{2}$

Agh, you know there's some way to simplify $\sqrt{20}$ into one of these terms, but you forgot exactly how. Don't worry about it! Just punch $\sqrt{20}$ into your calculator to get about 4.47. Now punch out all the choices and see which one comes out to the same thing. It's choice A!

There are a lot of different scenarios when you might want to do something like this—when you get radicals in the denominator, for example. Don't be afraid to use the calculator to your benefit.

II. CONTENT

Math questions on the SAT are sorted into four content categories. You will get subscores for three of these categories but not the fourth.

WARNING: these categories have the dumbest names used on the SAT.

Content Category	Section 3 No Calc	Section 4 Calc OK	Total	Percent of test
Heart of Algebra	8	11	19	33%
Passport to Advanced Math	9	7	16	28%
Problem Solving and Data Analysis	0	17	17	29%
Additional Topics in Math (*no subscore*)	3	3	6	10%

Heart of Algebra

These questions are the most common type (thought the main three types are fairly evenly distributed), and have the second dumbest name. The main theme of these questions is **algebra of linear equations.*** These are simple expressions that have no exponents and can be represented as a straight line in a graph.

- Writing, solving, and understanding linear equations
- Writing, solving, and understanding linear inequalities
- Graphing lines
- Solving systems of 2 linear equations

Passport to Advanced Math

These questions involve **higher-order algebra** and have the dumbest name.

- Writing, solving, and understanding quadratic equations
- Writing, solving, and understanding exponential functions
- Manipulating polynomials
- Rational functions and long division
- Graphing parabolas
- Function notation

---

* This is not to be confused with "linear algebra" which is something else entirely. Linear algebra is what you take in college after you're done with calculus. It involves vector spaces and hyperplanes. Let us never speak of it again.

Problem Solving and Data Analysis

Note that these questions *only* appear on section 4, the calculator section. These questions fall into two general content areas:

- Proportions: fractions, ratios, unit conversions, percentages
- Statistics: data visualization, tables, scatterplots, probability, averages

Additional Topics in Math

This is the only category that doesn't give you a subscore, and it's by far the smallest, with only 6 total questions on the test. These questions fall into three general content areas:

- Geometry: angles, triangles, circles, area, volume
- Trigonometry
- Imaginary and complex numbers

III. GENERAL STRATEGIES

We'll start with two quick and easy things you can do to help organize your time, be more efficient, and cut down on careless mistakes:

> ## 1. Circle the Question
> ## 2. Show Your Work

Circle the Question

This takes all of two seconds to do but can significantly help you.

- ✐ It can help reduce the number of careless mistakes you make (more about this in the next section).
- ✐ It will help you understand how to do the problem. By focusing on the thing you're trying to find rather than the things they give you, it's easier to think about what you need in order to find it.

Do this on every problem. No exceptions.

Show Your Work

You're probably tired of hearing math teachers to tell you to "Show your work!" Well, too bad.

> ## SHOW YOUR WORK!

We can already hear you complaining:

"Why bother? It's not like you get partial credit for doing it correctly."

True, you don't get partial credit, and there is no single "correct method". But that's not the point at all.

The point is that not writing down your steps is *the single greatest reason* for students' careless mistakes. We are astounded by how often we see students do an entire test worth of math problems without writing a thing on any page. These students are not getting the scores they want.

This is not a memory test. You can't possibly keep track of everything in your head, and you should never have more than one step in your head at any moment. By just writing down what you're doing as you do it, you can turn a complex problem into a series of small, basic steps. And you can significantly reduce your odds of making a careless mistake, like adding instead of subtracting, or solving for the wrong variable.

Furthermore, showing your work gives you a record of what you've done. This makes it easier to find mistakes when you're checking your work during a test. And it makes it easier to look over your performance when you're reviewing a practice test you just finished. This way, when you want to know why you got #10 wrong, you'll see what you did to get your answer.

"But I don't need to write stuff down. I'm good at math and can do it all in my head."

No, you can't.

"No, really, I can."

No, really, you can't. SAT problems are <u>complicated</u>. You can't hold every step in your head at once. And you know what? You don't have to! If you write stuff down, you don't have to remember everything.

And these questions <u>are designed to fool you</u>. Many students' biggest problem isn't that they don't know enough math—it's that they're missing questions *that they already know how to do*, because they make careless, stupid mistakes.

"That just slows me down. I don't have time to show my work."

You don't have time to write down numbers? That's ridiculous. What, are you writing with a calligraphy pen? We're not asking you to write out every single step in complete sentences and perfect penmanship. Don't write out annotated Euclidean proofs; just keep track of which variable is which.

Seriously, we're not kidding around. Just write stuff down.

Let's look at a sample problem to see how this works:

> 6. Points *A, B, C,* and *D* lie on a line in that order. The length of $\overline{AB}$ is 8, and the length of $\overline{CD}$ is 7. Point *C* is the midpoint of segment $\overline{BD}$. What is the length of segment $\overline{AD}$?
>
> A) 7
> B) 14
> C) 15
> D) 22

SAT math questions are numbered by difficulty. Accordingly, all sample questions throughout this book are numbered as if they were part of a 30-question miltiple choice section. A question #6 for example should be relatively simple.

First thing to do: **circle the question**. Not the whole problem, smart guy; just circle the thing that they're asking you to find.

WRONG

> Points *A*, *B*, *C*, and *D* lie on a line in that order. The length of $\overline{AB}$ is 8, and the length of $\overline{CD}$ is 7. Point *C* is the midpoint of segment $\overline{BD}$. What is the length of segment $\overline{AD}$?

RIGHT

Points *A*, *B*, *C*, and *D* lie on a line in that order. The length of $\overline{AB}$ is 8, and the length of $\overline{CD}$ is 7. Point *C* is the midpoint of segment $\overline{BD}$. What is the length of segment $\overline{AD}$?

Okay, now what?

SAT questions are complicated. There's often a lot going on within a question, and it's easy to take your eye off the ball. There might be so much information that you're not sure what to do with it. If you're not sure how to get started, **ask yourself two questions:**

1. **What do I *want*?** That is, what is the question asking me for?
2. **What do I *know*?** That is, what information does the problem give me?

Then your goal is to **connect these questions.** Look at what you want and work backwards to see what you need in order to get it. Or use what you already know and see what else that tells you.

What you want: The length of $\overline{AD}$.
That's why we circled the question—to find out what we want.

What you know: $AB = 8$, $CD = 7$, *C* is midpoint of $\overline{BD}$.
Write down what you know. This question is about a line, but no figure is given. So draw the figure.

First draw the points in order:

A   B   C   D

Then label the lengths you're given:

8 · · · · · 7
A   B   C   D

And since C is the midpoint of $\overline{BD}$, $BC = CD$:

$\overline{AD}$ is the whole length, so we have everything we need: $AD = 8 + 7 + 7 = \mathbf{22}$.

Our answer is **choice D).**

This is an addition to our rule about showing your work: if a geometry problem doesn't already have a picture, **DRAW A PICTURE!** It doesn't have to be perfect; even a rough sketch can help you understand the problem and catch careless mistakes.

Notice that we didn't know where we were going when we started. We just played with the stuff we knew until we got what we needed. The point here is to not be scared. There's always *something* that you know, and something that you can figure out. If you work forward from what you know or backwards from what you want, chances are you can connect them in the middle. Even if you're not sure where you're going, the more you write down, the easier it will be to make a connection.

GUESSTIMATE

As a rule of the SAT, **all figures are drawn to scale unless otherwise indicated.** So if the problem doesn't say "not drawn to scale", you can assume that it is drawn to scale. If it's drawn to scale, you can use the picture to guess the values you need.

Take a look at this problem:

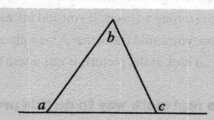

29.   In the figure above, *c* is equal to 5 less than twice
        b. What is the value of *a + b*?

        A)   60
        B)   100
        C)   135
        D)   185

They're asking us for $a + b$. So let's take a look at those angles.

✒ Angle *a* is pretty big. Let's say… 120? 130? Let's say **130**.

- Angle *b* is smaller, maybe 50 or 60. Let's say **60**.

- So *a* + *b* must be about 130 + 60 or about **190**. So our answer should be pretty close to 190.

- Hmm, 190 isn't a choice, but 185 is! That's pretty darn close. We'll take it. The answer is D).

Look how easy that was! We didn't do a darn thing other than just looking at the picture. I got #29 in all of 10 seconds and all I did was add two numbers.

Frequently Asked Questions about Guesstimate

1. That's all well and good, but how do I know that's right? I just made up those numbers. I could have been wrong.

That's true, but you didn't *randomly* make up those numbers; you measured the angles in the problem, the angles they give you.

Seriously, just look at the other choices they give you. A)? 60? Could *a* + *b* be 60? Angle *a* is **obtuse**! Angle *a* <u>alone</u> has to be bigger than 90! So A) is out right away. B) is still too small—angle *a* is still probably bigger than 100, and when you add *b* to the mix, there's no way the two of them come out that small. C) still looks too small.

And here's the thing: if you do this problem algebraically, there are ways you can mess it up that will make you pick one of those wrong answers. If you add instead of subtract or forget to distribute across parentheses, you could think that A) is a plausible answer because of your flawed algebra. But if you look at the picture, it just doesn't make sense.

2. Okay, I see that. But what's the real math way to do this problem?

Are you kidding? *This is real math.* There's nothing mathematically illegitimate about doing this. In math, as in all the sciences, there are two ways of solving any problem: *analytically*, by using pure logic and deducing (that's algebra), or *empirically*, by gathering evidence and measuring (that's Guesstimate).

Say you have a dining-room table and you want to figure out how tall it is. Well, one way I could figure out the height of the table is to construct a line from my eye to the top of the table and a line from my eye to the bottom of the table, measure the angle of declination, and use the law of cosines to find the third side of the triangle. ***OR I COULD GET A @#%$!*& RULER AND MEASURE IT!***

Here are your choices for how tall the table is:

A) 2.5 inches
B) 3 feet
C) 60 yards
D) 7.8 miles

But how do I *know* the table isn't 7.8 miles tall? Because it's in my living room.

This concept, by the way, is **the entire point of the xy-coordinate plane**. Graphing is a way to visualize the relationship between variables. Questions involving the coordinate plane often *require* you to make conclusions based on pictures. So get used to it.

3. Does this only work with angles?

Of course not! You can use this on just about any problem that has a picture, as long as it's drawn to scale. Take a look at this one:

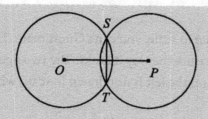

27.   In the figure above, $\overline{ST}$ is a chord and
        $\overline{OP}$ connects the centers of the two circles
        with equal radii. If $ST = 4$ and $OP = 4\sqrt{3}$,
        what is the radius of circle O?

        A) 2
        B) $2\sqrt{3}$
        C) 4
        D) $4\sqrt{3}$

What do we want? The radius of O. Hmm, we don't have a radius there. So let's draw one in. Just draw a line from the center to anywhere on the side.

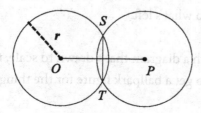

So that r is the length we're looking for. Let's compare that to the lines we know. Well, it definitely looks smaller than OP, which we know is $4\sqrt{3}$ (or about 6.92). So D) is out. Good so far.

We also know that ST is 4, so let's compare r to ST. Hey, they look the same. Maybe $r = 4$. Wait a minute—they're *exactly* the same! How do I know? **Measure them**. Take a piece of paper (try your answer sheet) and lay the side of the paper against r and mark off its length. Then lay that paper you marked off against ST. What do you find? ***They're the same!*** We're done! So the radius is 4. So the answer is C).

At the very least, if we go purely by our eyes, we know right away that the radius should be *close* to 4, so only B) and C) make sense ($2\sqrt{3}$ is about 3.46, which is close). If we actually measure it out, we can see that the radius is *exactly* 4. Perfect.

4. Does Guesstimate always work?

Unfortunately, Guesstimate isn't always going to work as beautifully as it did on these questions.

> ✏ If the figure says it's not drawn to scale, you can't Guesstimate. Then the picture does not have to actually measure the way it looks. The two figures below depict the same shape, but the one on the left is not drawn to scale, while the one on the right is.

Note: Figure not drawn to scale.

> ✏ If the choices are too close together there's nothing I can do. If, in #29 above, my choices were 175, 180, 185, 190, I can't eliminate anything. I'm not that good of a guesser.

You're also not always going to be able to zero in on the right answer like this. However, you can often eliminate *something*, even if it's only one choice. And once you eliminate something, your odds of getting the problem increase. Even if you can't figure out any other solution, you can guess from what's left.

So *any time* you see a problem with a diagram that's drawn to scale, ***try Guesstimate first***. Before you do <u>anything</u> else, try to get a ballpark figure for the thing they're asking for.

Guesstimate won't work on drawings of 3-D figures because they're drawn with perspective. You may be able to visualize them but you can't measure them.

IV. COMMON MISTAKES

The people who make the SAT aren't chumps. They know how high school kids think. More importantly, they know how high school kids mess up. Therefore, when they write the test they intentionally include wrong answer choices that kids who make certain common mistakes will choose. However, once you know what these mistakes are and how to avoid them, you will be much less likely to make them.

RTFQ

Take a look at this question:

> 8. A certain bookstore gets a shipment of 24 copies of a new book and sells 18 of them. What percentage of the books was NOT sold?
>
>   A) 75%
>   B) 67%
>   C) 33%
>   D) 25%

Okay, so 18 over 24 is 0.75, which is 75%. That's choice A), right?

WRONG! That's the number of books that were *sold*; the question is asking for those that were *not sold.* They even put it in CAPITAL LETTERS! Pay attention!

We call choice A the **RTFQ** choice. "RTFQ" stands for "Read the full question." It's what happens when all of your math was correct, but you didn't solve for the thing they were asking for.

RTFQ choices show up *all over* the test. They could show up on question #60 or on question #1. It is a very easy mistake to make. But it's also a very easy mistake to avoid: *just read the question.* Take an extra two seconds to make sure that the number you're choosing is the number they want.

In fact, we've already given you two ways to help cut down on RTFQ mistakes: **Circle the Question** and **Show Your Work.** Both of these things will significantly help you keep track of what you're doing.

A lot of people don't put enough weight on these mistakes on practice tests. "Oh, I *knew* how to do that one," they say. "I just wrote down the wrong answer." What? That's *so much worse!* If you don't know how to do the math, fine. We'll teach you how to do math. But you don't know how to write down what they're asking for? <u>You are throwing away points</u> by missing questions *that you already know how to do*. Remember: each math question is worth 10 points. If you make just three RTFQ mistakes, that's 30 points you've tossed out the window. These things add up.

Here's a harder one. Give it a shot, and make sure you *read every word of the question*.

$$A = \{1, 2, 3\}$$
$$B = \{3, 5, 7\}$$

23. If *a* is a number selected from the set *A* and *b* is a number selected from set *B*, how many different values for *a* + *b* are possible?

A) 6

B) 7

C) 8

D) 9

Fool's Gold

Take a look at this problem:

30. Scott drives to Bob's house at a speed of 30 miles per hour and drives back at a speed of 50 miles per hour. If he takes the same route both ways, what was his average speed, in miles per hour, for the whole trip?

A) 37.5

B) 40

C) 42.5

D) It cannot be determined from the information given.

We want the average speed for the trip. His two speeds are 30 and 50. So the average is 30 + 50 divided by two. That's 40. Choice B).

Wow, that was easy. Hmm. A little *too* easy.

Wait a minute. This is question number 30 out of 30. Questions are ordered by difficulty. That means this is the *hardest* question on the test. There's *no way* that the hardest question on the test can be done by just taking the average of two numbers *that they give me!* That can't possibly be right.

RTFQ

ANSWER:

23. Answer: B

The RTFQ choice is D). It's true, there are 9 different *pairings* of a and b, but the questions asks how many **different values for $a + b$**. So let's write out all possible sums:

$1 + 3 = 4$	$2 + 3 = 5$	$\cancel{3 + 3 = 6}$
$1 + 5 = 6$	$2 + 5 = 7$	$\cancel{3 + 5 = 8}$
$1 + 7 = 8$	$2 + 7 = 9$	$3 + 7 = 10$

6 and 8 each appear twice. So there are only **7 different values** for the sum.

THIS PAGE INTENTIONALLY LEFT BLANK

Look at it this way:

1. We know for a fact that SAT Math Test questions are ordered by difficulty.
2. A question's difficulty is determined by looking at the percentage of students who get it right.
3. Most kids probably had the same instinct I did: take the average of the speeds.
4. But I <u>know</u> that most kids get it wrong. *That's why it's number 30.*
5. Therefore, taking the average of 30 and 50 is wrong. If it were right, most kids would get it right. *So it wouldn't be number 30.*
6. Therefore, I can eliminate it.

We call this a ***Fool's Gold*** choice. It's when a hard question has a choice that's so easy and so obvious that it can't possibly be right. We *know* the question must be harder than this. It must be a trap.

So if you see an easy choice on a hard question—***eliminate it.*** You know most people get it wrong. So the obvious answer *can't* be right.* Sometimes we see students who even recognize a choice as a Fool's Gold choice, and then pick it anyway because they can't think of any other way of doing the problem. They wind up choosing the <u>one</u> choice that they *know* is wrong. That's madness. Utter, utter madness.

Let's go back and take another look at that #30 above. We eliminated B) as Fool's Gold. Hmm. But if that's not right, how else would you do the problem? All it tells us is the two speeds; we don't know the distance traveled or the time it took. So maybe there isn't enough information. That's Choice D). Right?

Wrong! "Cannot be determined" is a *classic* Fool's Gold choice. Number 30 is not going to be as easy as, "Well, uhh, they don't tell me anything, so I guess I dunno." Don't be a quitter.

So we've eliminated B) and D). Worst-case scenario, we can guess from the two remaining choices. Remember, no matter what, we must pick something. We must never leave anything blank.

So how do we do actually do this? The reason you can't just take the average of 30 and 50 is because those are already rates. In order to find the average speed for a trip, you have to take the rate of the *total* distance over the *total* time. Hmm. If we knew the distance traveled, we could find the time it took, but we don't know either. But the answer can't be D)—that's too easy. So it probably *doesn't matter* what the distance is. You probably get the same answer no matter what.

---

*   Obviously, Fool's Gold choices only occur on the hardest questions—about the last third of the test. If there's a choice on question #3 that looks really easy, it probably really is that easy.

So let's **make up a value for the distance.** Let's say it's **150 miles** from Scott's house to Bob's house. Since $d = rt$, we can use the distance to find the time each leg of Scott's trip took:

To Bob's: $150 = 30t_1$ From Bob's: $150 = 50t_2$

$\qquad\qquad$ 5 hours = t_1 $\qquad\qquad\qquad\qquad$ 3 hours = t_2

So Scott's trip took 5 hours one way and 3 hours back for a total of **8 hours.** His total distance traveled is **300 miles** (*two* trips, 150 each). So:

$$\text{Average Speed} = \frac{\text{Total Distance}}{\text{Total Time}} = \frac{300}{8} = \boxed{37.5 \text{ mph}}$$

That's **Choice A)!** We're done! Wait, but we only got A) after using a number we made up. How do we know we won't get a different answer if we chose another number? Well, try it. Make the distance 300 miles and see what you get.*

---

* You've just seen a sneak preview of Plug In, one of our fundamental Math Techniques. We'll see a lot more of this very soon...

V. TARGET NUMBERS

This is one of the most powerful strategies that we have, so much so that it gets its own section. If you ignore everything else we say, at least pay attention to this.

One of the biggest problems that students have on the test is *timing*. You've got a finite amount of time to do a lot of questions. As a result, most students feel rushed trying to finish the test. Remember that the questions are arranged in order of difficulty—number 1 is easy, number 30 is hard. So kids rush through the early questions and make a lot of careless mistakes: they add instead of subtract, they solve for *x* instead of *y*, they misread the question, etc. Then they spend a lot of time on the hard ones and get those wrong too—because they're really hard. So you're getting nailed on both ends of the test. You're missing hard questions because they're hard and easy questions because you're trying to get to the hard ones.

But here's the thing: *the easy questions are worth the same number of points as the hard ones.* The solution is incredibly simple: **DON'T DO THE WHOLE TEST.** You don't have to get *every* question in order to get the score that you want. The biggest problem most kids have isn't that they don't know enough math; it's that they're missing questions *that they already know how to do.*

Here are some charts to figure out your target numbers:

| Start Score | DO THIS MANY QUESTIONS | | Total | Target Score | Target Score including guessing |
	Sec 3 (No Calc) 15 MC, 5 GI	Sec 4 (Calc OK) 30 MC, 8 GI			
650 & up	20 (15 MC, 5 GI)	38 (30 MC, 8 GI)	58	800	800
600	18 (14 MC, 4 GI)	35 (27 MC, 8 GI)	53	750	760
550	16 (12 MC, 4 GI)	32 (24 MC, 8 GI)	48	690	720
500	14 (11 MC, 3 GI)	29 (23 MC, 6 GI)	43	650	680
450	13 (10 MC, 3 GI)	25 (20 MC, 5 GI)	38	600	650
400	11 (8 MC, 3 GI)	22 (17 MC, 5 GI)	33	560	610
350 & below	9 (7 MC, 2 GI)	19 (15 MC, 4 GI)	28	520	590

Or, to look at it from another perspective:

| Start Score | SKIP THIS MANY QUESTIONS | | Total | Target Score | Target Score including guessing |
	Sec 3 (No Calc) 15 MC, 5 GI	Sec 4 (Calc OK) 30 MC, 8 GI			
650 & up	None	None	None	800	800
600	2 (1 MC, 1 GI)	3 (3 MC, 0 GI)	5	750	760
550	4 (3 MC, 1 GI)	6 (6 MC, 0 GI)	10	690	720
500	6 (4 MC, 2 GI)	9 (7 MC, 2 GI)	15	650	680
450	7 (5 MC, 2 GI)	13 (10 MC, 3 GI)	20	600	650
400	9 (7 MC, 2 GI)	16 (13 MC, 3 GI)	25	560	610
350 & below	11 (8 MC, 3 GI)	19 (15 MC, 4 GI)	30	520	590

Use the charts above to find your target score and the number of questions you have to do to get that score. Do those questions, and those questions only. For example, let's say you're scoring around a 500 right now. According to the chart above, you'll do 14 of the 20 questions in section 3, and you'll do 29 of the 38 questions in section 4. You will do all of these questions and you will do *only* these questions. If you do them successfully, you will score a 650. If you pick up some points from randomly guessing, you will score a 680. That's your target score.* *That's a 180-point increase! On just the math section! Wow!* And you get it by doing *less* work.

For those last questions you didn't do, **guess something**. Don't leave them blank. It doesn't matter what you pick, just pick something. You don't lose points for wrong answers, so you'll pick up a few points by chance. **The points you pick up by random guessing are factored into the score in the last column.**

Okay, so you're doing fewer problems, but how do you know you'll do any better on those

---

* The target scores listed in the chart above are approximate. Each test has its own scoring table, so if you get the exact same number of questions right on two different tests, you may get different scores. In this table, we list the average score you would receive if you get all your target questions right. In the example above, you'd probably get around a 650, but you might score anywhere from 620 to 680, depending on the scoring table.

problems than you were doing before? Because now you've got *fewer questions in the same amount of time*, so you can spend more time on each question. The more time you spend on a question, the more confident you can be of your answer. Those careless errors you fix will translate into a higher score.

People tend to think about SAT scores in the wrong context. People tend to think of them like figure skating scores—there's a perfect ten and then points deducted for your flaws.* Instead, think of them like basketball scores—you're just trying to get as many points as possible. As such, your *shooting percentage* is much more important than the number of shots you take.

This strategy is amazing. You can get a score increase by literally doing *less* work. You can get a higher score not by learning new things but by nailing all the things you already know how to do. It's miraculous.

Frequently Asked Questions about Target Numbers

1. Why are you making me do this? What, you think I'm too *dumb* to get #30? Jerk.

Let's say this right upfront: *we're not saying you're too dumb to get #30*. We firmly believe that *anyone* could get #30 if given enough time for it. **This isn't about skipping questions that are too hard for you.** The goal here is simply to **do fewer questions.** That's it. So if we're doing fewer questions, we're not going to skip the easy ones; we're going to skip the hard ones. That's just common sense.

Yes, if you did the whole test, you *might* get number #28. But why worry about #28 when you're still missing #3? We *know* you can get #3. That's the goal here—to nail *all* the easy questions. Why worry about the hard stuff when you're still missing points on the easy stuff? Let's get those down pat before we do anything else.

2. I finished my target numbers, but I've still got some time left. Should I move on to more questions?

NO! If you finish your target numbers and still have time, *go back and check your work*. Again, the point here is to make sure that you're as sharp as can be on the easy questions. If you have time left over, don't keep going, and don't stare blankly at the wall for five minutes. Go back and check your work.

---

* Wait, is that how figure skating is scored? I have no idea.

3. I stuck to my target questions, but there were still some hard ones in there, so I left them blank too. Is that okay?

NO! Never leave anything blank! First of all, there's no penalty for guessing. Secondly, the goal here isn't to "skip hard questions". We're telling you exactly how many questions you need to do to get a good score increase. That means you have to do *all* the questions within your target numbers.

Yes, there will still be some hard ones in there. They aren't all as easy as #2. *But that's why we have seven more chapters about Math!* You didn't think we'd just stop here, did you? There's a lot more we have to go through, and we're going to show you some great techniques that will help you with those hard questions that are within your target numbers.

4. I'm supposed to stop at #24, but I don't know how to do it. But I think I can do #26. Can I skip #24 and do #26 instead?

The very fact that you're asking this question means you've thought about two questions. **That takes time**, time you could've spent checking your work on the easy questions. Again, the point here is timing—we want you to spend time making sure you get the easy questions. We do NOT want you to spend time on trying to figure out which questions to do. We want your game plan to be set before you go to the test.

Now, we do realize that there is a wide variety of question types on the test, and some people really are better at some types than others. Maybe #24 is a weird trigonometry question, but #26 is a graphing question and you're really good at graphing. Or it's a question that can be really easy with a technique like Plug In. That seems okay. But be careful: it may only *look* like you can do #26. It might be more complicated than it seems. Maybe there's a trick you didn't see. Maybe there's a Fool's Gold choice. Who knows?

But you know what we do know? **That you know how to do #2.** If you've done everything you can on #24 and still can't even eliminate one choice, *GO BACK AND CHECK NUMBER TWO!!!* Do not move on. Yes, there may be questions beyond your target numbers that you are capable of doing. But the goal of this technique is to **make sure you get the easy questions.** The questions past your target numbers are not there. They do not exist. We would tell you to rip those pages out of the test book if you were allowed to do that.*

---

* You're not. Please do not rip pages out of your test book.

5. **So those questions I skip, I should just leave them blank?**

NO. FILL IN RANDOM ANSWERS. NEVER LEAVE ANYTHING BLANK. You don't lose points for wrong answers, so there's nothing to lose by guessing randomly. You should not *attempt* those questions, but you should fill in random bubbles for those you skip, just in case you pick up some points by chance.

6. **I nailed my target numbers on this practice test. Can I do more on the next one?**

First of all, if you nailed all your target numbers, congratulations. You probably have a 100-point increase in your math score. Fantastic. But for the next practice test, keep the same numbers. We want to see you do it again. Once might have been a fluke—maybe you were in the zone that day or just happened to get a lot of question types that you're really good at. If you nail all your target numbers *twice in a row*, then we can start to talk about raising them.

But then again, you might not want to raise them. If you really do nail your target numbers, I think you'll be pleasantly surprised by what that does for your score. You might be happy where you are.

7. **I work really slowly and I never finish the test. What should I do?**

We were going to tell you not to finish the test anyway. Congratulations! You're one step ahead of us. Are you psychic?

Again, the goal here is to be *accurate* on the questions that you *do*. If you're not quite making it through all of your target numbers, that's okay—as long as you've got a high shooting percentage on the ones you *do* get to. Plus, once we get to work on the nuts and bolts of the math, you should be able to get through those easy problems much faster.

8. **How do I split up my time between multiple-choice questions and grid-ins?**

Remember that each section contains multiple-choice questions first and grid-ins at the end. Remember also that these parts are organized separately by difficulty—in section 3, number 15 (the last multiple-choice) will be a hard question, while 16 (the first grid-in) will be easy. It's probably a good idea to skip a few questions from each part. If you're supposed to skip 5 questions in section 3, don't just skip all 5 grid ins, because there are probably some easy ones in there.

On the table we included suggestions for how to split your time between the multiple-choice and grid-in questions. For example, if you're starting with a 500 and going for a 670, you'd skip 6 questions in section 3. You can split that up as skipping 4 multiple-choice and 2 grid-ins, thus you'd do questions 1–11 and 16–18.

But this is just a suggestion. The total number of questions answered and skipped is more important than how you divide that total over the question types.

9. Do these pants make me look fat?

Of course not. You look great. Now stop thinking about your outfit and pay attention.

10. I have extended/unlimited time for the SAT. Do I still have to do this?

Hmm… are you still making careless mistakes, even with extra time? Then yes. Yes you do.

11. Do I have to do this on the real test too?

What? Of course you do! Is that a serious question? Why would we tell you to do this only on practice tests? For fun? You think we're just messing with you? Everything we tell you to do in this book is something you should do on the real test.

12. Should I do this on the Reading and Writing as well?

Not exactly. The reason we do this for the math is **questions are numbered by difficulty**, so we know the first questions are the easy questions. Students make careless errors on early questions, questions they know how to do. Questions on the Reading and Writing tests, however, are not ordered by difficulty, so there's no guarantee that skipping the last questions means skipping the hard questions.

On the other hand, timing certainly can be an issue on the other tests. Remember that the same principle applies everywhere: **it's more important to be accurate on the questions you do than to do a lot of questions**. So if you are having trouble finishing the other tests, take heart. You can still get a good score there without answering all the questions, as long as you're accurate on the questions you do.

Math Techniques

The techniques are *ways of doing problems*. They can be used on just about any type of problem: on hard problems or easy problems, arithmetic or algebra, with triangles or circles, <u>anywhere</u>. They are powerful, versatile, and very, very easy.

We're going to show you two techniques for SAT Math problems: Plug In and Backsolve. Together they can be used on about 40% of the math problems on the SAT. That's a lot. While each has its quirks and relative strengths, they all have the same fundamental principle—they turn **abstract** problems into **concrete** problems. The goal is to turn everything into arithmetic, to get rid of vague unknowns, intangible ideas, and long equations and make every problem into simple stuff you can punch into your calculator.

I. PLUG IN

Let's take a look at this problem:

9. Bob has 4 dollars more than Lisa does. If Lisa has
    x dollars, how much would Bob have if he doubled
    his money?

    A) $x + 4$
    B) $2x$
    C) $2x + 4$
    D) $2x + 8$

Notice that this question is a number 9—not too hard, but not too easy, just in the middle of the pack. We can see what they want us to do here. They give us a word problem and expect us to translate from sentences into mathematical expressions. I don't want to do that.

Take a look at the answer choices here. They all have x's in them, and x is a variable. That means it can stand for any number. Let's say the answer turned out to be choice A). Well, if the answer is A), then that's the answer. That's how much money Bob has: $x + 4$ dollars. So it will *always* be $x + 4$, *no matter what x is*. If x is 5, if x is 10, if x is 953,234,124.5255, the answer would always be A).

So let's pick an *x*. If the answer comes out the same no matter what number *x* is, we can choose any value for *x* that we like and we'll always get the same thing.

This is *Plug In*. It has three steps.

1. Pick a number.

What should we choose? Something small, something manageable, preferably something that isn't already in the problem (to avoid confusion). Try to avoid weird numbers that have special properties like 0, 1, negatives, or fractions. Just a nice easy counting number. I like 3. Let's say *x* is 3.

Once you choose a number, make sure you *write it down and put a box around it*, so you remember that's the number you made up.

$$\boxed{x = 3}$$

2. Do the problem with your number.

Read the problem again, but instead of *x*, use 3.

> 9.   Bob has 4 dollars more than Lisa does. If Lisa has
>   3 dollars, how much would Bob have if he doubled
>   his money?

Lisa has *x* dollars, so now we'll say Lisa has 3 dollars. Bob has 4 more, so Bob has 7 dollars. So if Bob doubled his money, he'd have **14 dollars**. That's our answer: 14. Once you have an answer, circle it.

Wait, but 14 isn't an answer choice. Ah, one more step:

3. Put the numbers into the choices.

Our answer isn't a choice, but all the choices have *x*'s. Aha! We have an *x* now. Let's put 3 in for *x* in the choices and see which one comes out to 14.

A)	$x + 4$	$3 + 4 = 7$ ✗
B)	$2x$	$2(3) = 6$ ✗
C)	$2x + 4$	$2(3) + 4 = 6 + 4 = 10$ ✗
D)	$2x + 8$	$2(3) + 8 = 6 + 8 = 14$ ✓

Only D) works. That's our answer. We got the problem by adding one-digit numbers.

Think of the problem as a little function, a series of steps. If I put in this number, I get out that number. When I put in 3, I got 14. The right answer choice should give me the same function. When I put in 3, I should get out 14.

Don't believe me? Try a different number for *x*. You should still get D) as your answer.

Frequently Asked Questions about Plug In

1. Do I have to test every choice?

Yes, just to be safe. It is possible that two answer choices both give you the answer you're looking for. This could happen if you choose a number with special properties (like 1) or a number that was already in the problem. Or it could happen purely by chance. So you should check all the choices to make sure there aren't two choices that work.

2. So what do I do if I get two choices that work out?

First of all, eliminate everything else. You know it's going to be one of those two. Worst-case scenario, guess one; you've got a 50-50 chance.

But before you guess, why not try a different number? If two choices work, it's probably because you happened to pick a weird number. Pick a different one and test the choices that are left. Try different kind of number. If you picked a small one before, try a big one now, and vice versa.

If you keep getting the same two answers, try a weird number, like 0, 1, a fraction, or a negative.* These numbers have special properties, so they can help you notice scenarios that you might miss otherwise.

3. Why do I have to do this? That seemed like a lot of work for a #9.

First of all, we're demonstrating the technique on an easier problem so you can see how it works. The problems only get harder from here, yet Plug In is still little more than adding one-digit numbers. Heck, we already saw a Plug-In question—the Fool's Gold example about Scott driving to Bob's house. Try doing *that* sucker with algebra. It ain't pretty.

Second, Plug In may seem weird because *it's new for you*. The more you do it, the more you'll get the hang of it. Pretty soon, you'll be able to churn out problems in a fraction of the time.

If a question asks what "MUST" be true that's a sign you might want to try several different numbers.

---

* Conveniently, <u>F</u>ration, <u>O</u>ne, <u>N</u>egative, and <u>Z</u>ero spell *FONZ*.

Third, algebraic methods are fraught with possible careless mistakes—even on #9.

Let's try some algebra on that #9 just for kicks. Bob has 4 more than Lisa, so Bob has $x + 4$. Multiply it by two, you get $2x + 4$, right? That's C), right? Of course not. It's not $2x + 4$; it's $2(x + 4)$. That comes out to $2x + 8$, which is D), just like we got with Plug In. As brilliant as we all are with algebra, it's *really* easy to make a small stupid mistake like forgetting the parentheses. But with Plug In, you're *much* less likely to make that mistake because you're working with concrete numbers. You understand what all these terms represent; they're not just abstract letters on the page. C) is no more tempting than any other wrong choice; it's just another choice that doesn't come out to 14.

There are other ways you can mess this up, too. If you forget to double Bob's money, you get A). If you double Lisa's money instead of Bob's, you get B). None of these mistakes are likely with Plug In because all you're doing is simple arithmetic.

So it's not just that Plug In is faster or easier than algebra; it's also <u>safer</u> than algebra. You're much less likely to make an RTFQ or Fool's Gold mistake with Plug In.

Types of Plug In Problems

1. Explicit Variables

As we've already seen, having a *variable in the answer choices* is the first sign of a Plug In problem. But it also works when there is *more than one variable*.

Sometimes you can Plug In for each variable **independently**:

15.	How many hours are there in d days and h hours?
	A) $\quad 24h + d$
	B) $\quad h + 24d$
	C) $\quad 24(h + d)$
	D) $\quad h + \dfrac{d}{24}$

Because there's no relationship between h and d here, we can come up with totally different numbers for each of them. To make things easy, let's use $d = 1$ and $h = 3$.* One day has 24 hours, plus 3 gives a total of **27 hours**. Which choice matches 27?

---

* Picking 1 makes things nice and quick on a problem like this. But because multiplying and dividing by 1 each give you the same answer, picking 1 can sometimes give you two choices that work. Therefore, if your question has a lot of division in the choices, particularly if you see the variable on the bottom of the fraction, you probably shouldn't pick 1. And any time you get more than one choice that works, just eliminate and pick a different number.

A) $24h + d$ $24(3) + 1 = 73$ ✗

B)   **$h + 24d$** $3 + 24(1) = 27$ ✓

C) $24(h + d)$ $24(3 + 1) = 96$ ✗

D) $h + \dfrac{d}{24}$ $3 + \dfrac{1}{24}$ ✗

On the other hand, sometimes the problem will give you some **restrictions** on the variables. In these cases, you can Plug In for one variable, and then use that value to figure out the other variable:

---

14.   **If $x + 5$ is 3 less than y, then $x - 2$ is how much less than y?**

       A)   **6**

       B)   **7**

       C)   **8**

       D)   **10**

Here we have two variables, but this time, if we pick an x, we can use that number to find y. Let's say $x = 4$. Read the beginning of the problem with our number for x: "If $4 + 5$ is 3 less than y". $4 + 5 = 9$. That means "9 is 3 less than y," so y is 3 more than 9. So $y = 12$. Picking an x allowed us to find y.

We're not done yet. The question asks "$x - 2$ is how much less than y?" $4 - 2 = 2$. So 2 is how much less than 12? 2 is **10** less than 12. That's **choice D)**.

Notice also that we could still use Plug In even though there weren't any variables in the answer choices.

2. Implicit Variables

Take a look at this problem. It's a *grid-in* question, so there are no answer choices:*

> 33. Larry cuts a piece of paper into two equal pieces.
> He takes one of those pieces and cuts it into three
> equal pieces. The area of one of the smallest pieces
> is what fraction of the area of the original piece
> of paper?

There's no variable anywhere in the problem or the answer choices, so we can't use Plug In, right?

Wrong! Even though no variable was explicitly mentioned, there is an **implicit** variable—the area. There's no way for us to find the area of the original piece of paper, right? It doesn't tell us the length or width or any numbers at all (we don't even know whether it's a rectangle!), but we're still expected to get an answer. So *it must not matter* what the starting area is—we'll get the same answer no matter where we start. There's no actual letter, but we *could* assign it a variable if we wanted.

Let's not. Let's say the original piece has an area of **12**.

- ✐ He cuts it into *two* pieces, so each has an area of 6. ($12 \div 6 = 2$)

- ✐ He cuts one of those into *three* pieces, so each of the smaller pieces has an area of **2**. ($6 \div 3 = 2$)

- ✐ So each smaller piece is $\dfrac{2}{12}$ or $\dfrac{1}{6}$ of the original.

We already saw a problem with implicit variables in the Fool's Gold section. Remember this?

> 30. Scott drives to Bob's house at a speed of 30 miles
> per hour and drives back at a speed of 50 miles
> per hour. If he takes the same route both ways,
> what was his average speed, in miles per hour, for
> the whole trip?
>
> A) 37.5
> B) 40
> C) 42.5
> D) It cannot be determined from the
>   information given

---

* This is question #33, so it might appear that it should be hard, but remember that question difficulty numbering resets with the grid-ins. So #31 is the first grid-in and should be easy. #33 is the third out of 8.

© A-List Education

Even though there are no variables at all, the distance is an implicit variable. We can make up a value for the distance and do the problem with that number. That's Plug In.

3. Geometry

Take a look at this problem:

Note: Figure not drawn to scale.

15. In the figure above, if $y = 90 - x$, what is z in terms of x?

A) $90 + x$
B) $90 - x$
C) $180 + x$
D) $180 - x$

> Whenever a question contains the words **"in terms of"** as in "what is z in terms of x", you can almost always use Plug In.

Geometry can be scary for a lot of kids, and we'll talk a lot more about it in a later chapter. But look: we've got variables in the answer choices! That means we can Plug In for x, just like any other normal problem.

Let's say $x = 30$. We know $y = 90 - x$, so $y = 60$.

We can tell from the picture that z and y make a straight line; that means $z + y = 180$. Since $y = 60$, we know $z = 120$. So when $x = 30$, $z = 120$. Put 30 in for x in the answer choices and see which gives you 120:

A) $90 + x$ $90 + 30 = 120$ ✓
B) $90 - x$ $90 - 30 = 60$ ✗
C) $180 + x$ $180 + 30 = 210$ ✗
D) $180 - x$ $180 - 30 = 150$ ✗

Don't be scared off by figures. If you're confused, don't worry: we'll talk about geometry rules soon enough. But at its heart, this problem is no different than any other Plug In. As soon as you see all those variables in the choices, you know you can Plug In.

And keep in mind that Geometry Plug Ins come in all the same flavors that we've already seen: there may be explicit variables or implicit variables; sometimes you plug in for different variables separately, sometimes you plug in for one and figure out the others (as we just did in #10).

PLUG IN DRILL

8

If p, q, r, and s are consecutive even integers such that $p < q < r < s$, then how much greater is $s - p$ than $r - q$?

A) 1
B) 2
C) 3
D) 4

12

Garth has x books, which is 20 more books than Henrietta has. If Garth gives Henrietta 7 books, how many books does Henrietta now have?

A) $x - 27$
B) $x - 20$
C) $x - 13$
D) $x - 7$

14

If $a^2b = c$ and $b \neq 0$, then $\dfrac{1}{b} =$

A) a^2c

B) $\dfrac{a^2}{c}$

C) $\dfrac{c}{a^2}$

D) $\dfrac{1}{a^2c}$

17

A number p is divided by 3 and the result is increased by 3. This result is then multiplied by 3. Finally, that result is decreased by 3. In terms of p, what is the final result?

A) p
B) $p + 6$
C) $p - 6$
D) $3p + 6$

18

Lisa uses 2 pieces of copper wire, each 9 feet long, for each robot she builds. If she started with a 500-yard roll of copper wire, which of the following represents the number of <u>yards</u> of wire left on the roll after Lisa built r robots? (3 feet = 1 yard)

A) $500 - 2r$
B) $500 - 6r$
C) $500 - 9r$
D) $500 - 18r$

CONTINUE

Plug In Drill

8. Answer: D.

Plug in four consecutive even integers (make sure you label the variables)

$$p = 2 \qquad q = 4 \qquad r = 6 \qquad s = 8$$

$$s - p = 8 - 2 = 6$$
$$r - q = 6 - 4 = 2$$

6 is 4 more than 2. That's choice D).

Note that in this question we used Plug In even though there are no variables in the answer choices. A bit atypical, certainly, but kids shouldn't have any trouble spotting the Plug In opportunity here.

12. Answer: C.

Plug in a regular number, like $x = 3$, and you'll quickly see it doesn't work:

"Garth has 3 books, which is 20 more books than Henrietta has". Clearly, that's nonsense. So pick an x bigger than 20. Say, $x = 30$. Now just read the question again, but replace "x" with "30":

"Garth has **30** books, which is 20 more books than Henrietta has."
So Henrietta has 10 books.

"Garth gives Henrietta 7 books"
So now Henrietta has **17** books.

"how many books does Henrietta now have?"
She has 17.

When $x = 30$, the answer is 17:

A) $30 - 27 = 3$ ✗
B) $30 - 20 = 10$ ✗ That's how many Henrietta *used to* have.
C) $30 - 13 = 17$ ✓
D) $30 - 7 = 23$ ✗ That's how many *Garth* has now.

14. Answer: B.

Let's say $a = 3$. What can we do?

$$(3)^2 b = c \qquad\qquad 9b = c$$

That's not enough to figure out the other two. Let's say $b = 2$, too.

$$(3)^2 2 = c \qquad\qquad 18 = c$$

So in this case, we had to plug in for *two* of the variables to give us the third.

The question asks for $\frac{1}{b}$, which is $\frac{1}{2}$.

Let's put $a = 3$ and $c = 18$ into the choices and see which works:

A) $(3)^2 18 = 162$ ✗

B) $\dfrac{(3)^2}{18} = \dfrac{9}{18} = \dfrac{1}{2}$ ✓

C) $\dfrac{18}{(3)^2} = \dfrac{18}{9} = 2$ ✗ That's b! We want $\frac{1}{b}$. RTFQ!

D) $\dfrac{1}{(3)^2 18} = \dfrac{1}{162}$ ✗

17. Answer: B.

Pick a multiple of 3. Let's say $p = 6$.
(Plug In will *work* with any number, but the math is simpler and decimal-free if we start with a multiple of 3. And that's easy to see since the first step in the instructions is to divide by 3).
Now just follow instructions:

$$6 \div 3 = 2$$
$$2 + 3 = 5$$
$$5 \times 3 = 15$$
$$15 - 3 = \mathbf{12}$$

Put $p = 6$ into the choices and see which comes out to 12.

A) 6 ✗
B) $6 + 6 = \mathbf{12}$ ✓
C) $6 - 6 = 0$ ✗
D) $3(6) + 6 = 24$ ✗

Choice A) is a popular wrong answer for kids who think all the various operations cancel each other out. Careless parentheses in your algebra can lead to any number of wrong answers. But with Plug In, you're doing ridiculously easy math.

18. Answer: B.

Let's say $r = 10$ robots.
She needs 2 pieces of wire per robot, that's 20 pieces.
Each piece is 9 feet, that's $9 \times 20 = 180$ feet.
180 feet is $180 \div 3 = 60$ yards of wire.
The wire roll is 500, so $500 - 60 = \mathbf{440\ yards}$ left on the roll.

A) $500 - 2(10) = 500 - 20 = 480$ ✗
B) $500 - 6(10) = 500 - 60 = \mathbf{440}$ ✓
C) $500 - 9(10) = 500 - 90 = 410$ ✗
D) $500 - 18(10) = 500 - 180 = 320$ ✗

21. Answer: D.

Let's say $h = 3$ and $p = 5$. Let's just read the question again with our numbers:

"Hot dogs cost 3 dollars each and pretzels cost 5 dollars each. How much would it cost, in dollars, to buy 4 hot dogs and 4 pretzels?"

Hot dogs: $4 \times 3 = \$12$
Pretzels: $4 \times 5 = \$20$.
For a total of **$32**

A) $h + p$ $3 + 5 = 8$ ✗

B) $hp - h + p - 1$ $3(5) - 3 + 5 - 1 = 15 - 3 + 4 = 16$ ✗

C) $h^2 + p^2$ $3^2 + 5^2 = 9 + 25 = 34$ ✗

D) $h^2 + h + p^2 - p$ $3^2 + 3 + 5^2 - 5 = 9 + 3 + 25 - 5 = $ **32** ✓

23. Answer: C.

Instead of plugging in for s, plug in the three consecutive numbers. Say my numbers are **2, 3, 4**. Their sum is $9 = s$.
The question asks for the greatest number—that's **4**. Put $s = 9$ into the choices and see which gives you 4:

A) $\dfrac{9}{3} - 1 = 3 - 1 = 2$ ✗ That's the smallest. RTFQ!

B) $\dfrac{9}{3} = 3$ ✗ That's the average, or the middle number.

C) $\dfrac{9}{3} + 1 = 3 + 1 = $ **4** ✓

D) $\dfrac{9}{3} + 2 = 3 + 2 = 5$ ✗

24. Answer: D.

It's easier to pick a t than an s. Let's say $t = 2$. So $s = \dfrac{1}{2}$. Let's go the choices and see which are true:

A) **0.5 < 2**   ✓ Don't stop! Check all the choices!
B) $0.5 > 2$ ✗
C) $(0.5)2 > 1,\ 1 > 1$ ✗
D) $(0.5)2 > 0,\ 1 > 0$ ✓

Hmm. We get two answers that both are true. The first lesson here is to **always check all choices** when doing Plug In. You might get two choices that work.

Now what? Well, you can certainly eliminate B), C), and D). Worst case scenario: guess. You're down to two choices, so you've got a 50-50 chance, and The Guessing Rule tells us that if you eliminate, you *must* put an answer down.

Even better, we can plug in again, but this time just try A) and D) But if you try another normal number, like 4 or 7, you'll get the same results. So we'll have to be a bit more careful about what numbers we pick. Let's pick a *weird number*, one that has special properties, such as **Fractions, One, Negatives, or Zero (FONZ!)**.

The question says $t \neq 0$, so let's try $t = 1$. Therefore, $s = \mathbf{1}$ too.

A) $1 < 1$ ✗
D) $(1)\ 1 > 0,\ \mathbf{1 > 0}$ ✓

Picking a negative for t would also eliminate A):

$$t = -2,\ s = -\dfrac{1}{2}$$

A) $-0.5 < -2$ ✗ False! $-0.5 > -2$
D) $(-0.5)\ -2 > 0,\ \mathbf{1 > 0}$ ✓

Or picking a fraction for t:

$$t = \dfrac{1}{2},\ s = 2$$

A) $2 < 0.5$ ✗
D) $2(0.5) > 0,\ \mathbf{1 > 0}$ ✓

Since s is the reciprocal of t, the product st must equal 1, (which is greater than 0.) You can see that by cross multiplying the original equation. And we can see that in both examples above, sure enough, $st = 1$.

29. Answer: C.

This problem is crazy hard with algebra, but careful Plug In can make it a snap. The key is to pick $n = 2$: that will make the fraction *much* easier to deal with. You can pick whatever you want for k. Say $k = 10$. Let's read the problem again with our numbers:

"If Leslie gives away 10 celery sticks, she will have $\dfrac{1}{2}$ as many as she had originally."

So originally, she had **20**. Which choice comes out to 20?

A) $10 + \dfrac{1}{2}$ $= 10.5$ ✗

B) $10(2) + 10$ $= 30$ ✗

C) $\dfrac{10(2)}{2-1} = \dfrac{20}{1}$ $= 20$ ✓ *SO EASY!!*

D) $\dfrac{10}{2+1}$ $= \dfrac{10}{3}$ ✗

30. Answer: B.

Any time you see percents on a Plug In, **pick 100**. The numbers will come out much more beautifully.
Start with $w = 100$.

100 decreased by 40% of 100 yields $x = \mathbf{60}$
60 increased by 50% of 60 yields $y = \mathbf{90}$
90 decreased by 10% of 90 yields $z = \mathbf{81}$

So: 81 is what percent of 100? **81%.**

21

Hot dogs cost h dollars each and pretzels cost p dollars each. How much would it cost, in dollars, to buy $h + 1$ hot dogs and $p - 1$ pretzels?

A) $h + p$

B) $hp - h + p - 1$

C) $h^2 + p^2$

D) $h^2 + h + p^2 - p$

23

The sum of 3 consecutive integers is s. What is the greatest of these integers, in terms of s?

A) $\dfrac{s}{3} - 1$

B) $\dfrac{s}{3}$

C) $\dfrac{s}{3} + 1$

D) $\dfrac{s}{3} + 2$

24

If $t \neq 0$ and $s = \dfrac{1}{t}$, which of the following must be true?

A) $s < t$

B) $s > t$

C) $st > 1$

D) $st > 0$

29

If Leslie gives away k celery sticks, she will have $\dfrac{1}{n}$ times as many as she had originally. In terms of k and n, how many celery sticks did Leslie have originally?

A) $k + \dfrac{1}{n}$

B) $kn + k$

C) $\dfrac{kn}{n-1}$

D) $\dfrac{k}{n+1}$

30

w decreased by 40% of w yields x
x increased by 50% of x yields y
y decreased by 10% of y yields z

According to the information above, z is what percent of w?

A) 27%

B) 81%

C) 90%

D) 100%

II. BACKSOLVE

Take a look at this one.

> **17.** Gerry's age is 5 more than three times Carol's age. If the sum of their ages is 45, how old is Carol?
>
> A) 10
> B) 12
> C) 14
> D) 16

Here, we can't just make up a number for Carol's age because that's the whole point of the question. The value *does* matter—there's only one number that works for Carol's age. So Plug In is out.

However, like we did with Plug In, we can still turn this into a simple arithmetic problem. But instead of picking *random* numbers, let's use the numbers *in the answer choices*. We know one of these 4 numbers is Carol's age, so let's try them until we find one that works.

That's **Backsolve**. It also has three steps.

1. Pick a choice and make it the answer.

It's often best to pick either B) or C). When there are numbers in the answers like this, they always put the choices in order. So if we try choice C) and it doesn't work, we can figure out if it was too small or too big and eliminate two answer choices in one fell swoop.

Okay. So let's say that **C)** is the answer. C) is **14**. So what does that mean? What's 14? Well, 14 is the answer to the question. In this case, the question is "how old is Carol?" That means if C) is right, then Carol is 14.

2. Do the problem and see if it fits.

What else do we know? We know that Gerry's age is 5 more than three times Carol's age. Again, we're saying Carol is 14, so:

C) **Carol = 14.**

$3 \times 14 = 42$ "Gerry's age is 5 more than 3 times 14."

$42 + 5 = \mathbf{47} = \mathbf{Gerry}.$ So if Carol is 14, then Gerry is **47**.

How do I know if C) is the right answer, then? Well, what *else* does the problem tell us? Their ages should add up to 45. Do they? Of course not. Gerry's age *alone* is bigger than 45. So C) is too big.

3. If it fails, figure out if you need a bigger or smaller number and repeat.

Well, C) was definitely too big, so we'll need a smaller number. So we'll move on to B):

B) Carol = 12.

$12 \times 3 + 5 = 41 = $ **Gerry**.

$12 + 41 = 53$ ✗

Still too big. Their ages should add up to 45. Let's move on to A):

A) Carol = 10.

$10 \times 3 + 5 = 35 = $ **Gerry**.

$10 + 35 = 45$ ✓

Bingo! A) is our answer.

That was a word problem. Just like we saw before when we were discussing Plug In, this problem didn't have any explicit variables mentioned, but it did have **implicit** variables. There were no actual letters assigned to Carol or Gerry's age, but we could still put numbers in for them all the same. That's one of the strengths of these techniques. We don't need to worry about variables; we can work directly with the underlying concepts in the problem. But Backsolve works just as well when there are **explicit** variables. Observe:

21.	**If *j* + *k* = 9 and *j*^{2} + *jk* = 36 then *k* =**
	A) 3
	B) 4
	C) 5
	D) 6

Any time a problem asks for the value of a variable, we can Backsolve. Just put the numbers in the choices in for the variable and see if it works.

We'll start with C), that's 5. They're asking for *k*, so we'll say **k = 5**. Okay, fine. We know that $j + k = 9$. Since $k = 5$, **j = 4**. So far, so good. Now let's put *j* and *k* into that giant equation and see if it comes out to 36.

$$j^2 + jk = 4^2 + 4(5) = 16 + 20 = 36 \checkmark$$

It works! Since C) worked, I don't even have to look at anything else. The answer is C). I'm done!

Let's take a minute to think about how to do this problem with algebra. First of all, you could solve one equation for *j*, and then substitute that into the other equation. Ugh. I guess we could do that, but it's a lot of work and easy to mess up. Backsolve is much quicker and easier. Now, if you've got a really good eye, you might notice this:

$j + k = 9$ and $j^2 + jk = 36$ We're given two equations.

$j(j + k) = j^2 + jk$ The second equation is just the first equation times *a*.

$j(9) = 36$ So we can just substitute the values we know,

$\boldsymbol{j = 4}$ And our answer is 4. That's B).

Wait a minute: 4? B)? Didn't we get C)? Isn't C) 5? Aha! $j = 4$; they're asking us for **k**. RTFQ! So even if we're really clever with our algebra, the algebra easily leads to an RTFQ. You're much less likely to make an RTFQ mistake with Backsolve because you're working *directly* from the question. You pick C), and then make C) *the answer to the question.*

So there are basically two algebraic ways of doing this problem. One is slow and painful. The other almost inevitably leads you to an RTFQ mistake. Like Plug In, Backsolve is faster, easier, and *safer* than algebra.

Frequently Asked Questions about Backsolve

1. **If the first choice I try works, should I try the other choices to be safe?**

   No. Unlike Plug In, with Backsolve there's no way that more than one choice will work out. Once you find a choice that works, stop. That's your answer.

2. **What if I'm not sure whether I want a higher or lower number?**

   Then just pick one! Don't go crazy trying to deduce which way to go. Part of the point of Backsolve is to work quickly and methodically. If C) fails and you're not sure whether you should go to B) or D), just pick one. You're just doing simple math here. The worst-case scenario is that you go the wrong way and wind up having to test all four choices. But really, that's not very much work. And you know that eventually you'll find the answer.

THIS PAGE INTENTIONALLY LEFT BLANK

Backsolve Drill

Since there's no single choice in the middle, we'll switch around, sometimes starting with B), sometimes with C).

5. Answer: A.
Put the choices into the left side of the equation and see which comes out to $\frac{8}{3}$ or **2.666**.

B) $x = 54$. $\frac{54+10}{12} = \frac{64}{12} = \frac{16}{3} = 5.333$ ✗

The decimal makes it easier to see this choice is too big.

A) $x = 22$. $\frac{22+10}{12} = \frac{32}{12} = \frac{8}{3} = 2.666$ ✓

The algebra here isn't too hard, but this is a nice easy introduction to how Backsolve works. Any time the question asks for the value of a variable ("$x = ?$") you can try the numbers in the choices.

8. Answer: D.
Set choice C) equal to p, find the two averages and see if they match each other.

B) $p = 6$. $\quad \frac{2+6}{2} = 4$ ✗ $\quad \frac{1+6+6}{3} = \frac{13}{3} = 4.333$ ✗

No match. It's hard to tell which direction to go. Pick one.

C) $p = 7$. $\quad \frac{2+7}{2} = \frac{9}{2} = 4.5$ ✗ $\quad \frac{1+6+7}{3} = \frac{14}{3} = 4.667$ ✗

Still no match, but they're closer together...

D) $p = 8$. $\quad \frac{2+8}{2} = \frac{10}{2} = 5$ ✓ $\quad \frac{1+6+8}{3} = \frac{15}{3} = 5$ ✓ Huzzah!

11. Answer: A.
Man, this is a really cheap spa!

B) $9 = Back rub. Stick this into the three things we know and see if everything matches.
Manicure + 9 = 18 → Manicure = $9
9 + Facial = 19 → Facial = $10
Manicure + Facial = $19 ✗ No match.
Should be $21. Looks like we should go *up*.

C) $10 = Back rub.
Manicure + 10 = 18 → Manicure = $8
10 + Facial = 19 → Facial = $9
Manicure + Facial = $17 ✗ No match.
Hey, we're going *down*. Wrong direction!

A) $8 = Back rub.
Manicure + 8 = 18 → Manicure = $10
8 + Facial = 19 → Facial = $11
Manicure + Facial = **$21** ✓ Bingo!

If you prefer, you can arrange this information in a table:

Back Rub		Manicure (18 − BR)	Facial (19 − BR)	Manicure + Facial
B)	$9	18 − 9 = $9	19 − 9 = $10	9 + 10 = $19 ✗
C)	$10	18 − 10 = $8	19 − 10 = $9	8 + 9 = $17 ✗
A)	**$8**	18 − 8 = $10	19 − 8 = $11	10 + 11 = **$21** ✓

This is a classic Backsolve: do the problem with one piece of information, and check if it matches the other.

Don't worry about going the wrong direction in checking the choices. Just pick one! Because each step is just addition and subtraction, going the wrong way will cost you just a few extra seconds. Once you've tested one choice, you develop a rhythm so that subsequent choices go more quickly. Plus there are only five choices—you know you'll get the right one eventually.

Some kids may groan at having to do so many choices. But what's the hardest thing we did here? 19 minus 8? Each step is easy enough for a fifth grader to do, whereas the algebra is fraught with potential for missteps and careless errors. It may be *physically* more work, but the actual steps are *easier* and *safer*.

14. Answer: B.
They want x, so set choice B) equal to x.

B) $x = -11$. $(-11 + 4)^2 = (-7)^2 = \mathbf{49}$. It worked! We're done!

It's sooo nice when our first choice comes out to be the right answer. The time we saved here makes up for the extra few seconds we spent going the wrong direction on #7.

Kids who don't use Backsolve will often pick choice D) here because they don't consider negative numbers. But look: the question tells us that $x < 0$. RTFQ!

With Backsolve, we don't even *look* at choice D). Once B) works, we stop and move on. We don't even know that choice D) is there. Again, Backsolve is a *safer* method because it eliminates the possibility of choosing the RTFQ choice.

15. Answer: A.
Just dive into choice C) and start eliminating. Each choice will be the smallest of four consecutive odd integers.

C) $3 \times 5 \times 7 \times 9 = 945$ ✗ Way too big.
You don't even really have to do it out: One of the numbers *is* 9, no way does this come out to nine.

B) $1 \times 3 \times 5 \times 7 = 105$ ✗ Still too big.

A) $\mathbf{-3} \times -1 \times 1 \times 3 = \mathbf{9}$ ✓

This is a great demonstration of Backsolve. Students who just look at the question can get easily baffled because they never consider the possibility that the first number could be negative. But you don't have to figure that out on your own—just check all the choices until you found one that works. There's no reasoning involved; it's pure calculation.

17. Answer: D.
C) 570 logs on Monday.
On Tuesday, half were burned.
So 285 were burned, and 285 remain.
On Wednesday, 110 more logs were burned.
285 − 110 = 175. ✗ No Match.
Answer should be a third of the original. 175 is not 1/3 of 570.
(570 ÷ 3 = 190; or 175 × 3 = 525)
(Some kids may now realize that our answer should be divisible by three. But if they don't, that's okay.)

D) **660 logs on Monday.**
On Tuesday, half were burned.
So 330 were burned, and 330 remain.
On Wednesday, 110 more logs were burned.
330 − 110 = 220. ✓ **Match!** 220 is 1/3 of 660.
(660 ÷ 3 = 220; or 220 × 3 = 660)

BACKSOLVE DRILL

5

If $\dfrac{x+10}{12} = \dfrac{8}{3}$, then $x =$

A) 22
B) 54
C) 66
D) 96

14

If $(x + 4)^2 = 49$ and $x < 0$, what is the value of x?
A) −45
B) −11
C) −3
D) 3

8

If the average of 2 and p is equal to the average of 1, 6, and p, what is the value of p?

A) 5
B) 6
C) 7
D) 8

15

The product of four consecutive odd integers is 9. What is the least of these integers?

A) −3
B) 1
C) 3
D) 5

11

Allen is reviewing his receipts from three different visits to a spa, trying to determine the individual costs of his favorite spa treatments. From his receipts he knows:

> A manicure and a back rub together cost $18.
> A back rub and a facial together cost $19.
> A manicure and a facial together cost $21.

What is the cost of a back rub?

A) $8
B) $9
C) $10
D) $11

17

Erica had a stack of firewood on Monday. On Tuesday she used $\dfrac{1}{2}$ of the logs, and on Wednesday she used 110 logs, leaving Erica with $\dfrac{1}{3}$ of her original supply.

How many logs of firewood did Erica originally have on Monday?

A) 220
B) 500
C) 570
D) 660

CONTINUE

Vladimir sold 18 books on Monday. He sold paperback books for $7.50 each and hardcover books for $15 each. If he made a total of $210, how many paperback books did he sell?

A) 11
B) 10
C) 9
D) 8

Marion brought some biscuits to a tea party. If everyone at the party takes 5 biscuits, there will be 10 remaining. If 4 people do not take any and everyone else takes 8, there will be none remaining. How many biscuits did Marion bring to the party?

A) 56
B) 70
C) 80
D) 95

The sum of five consecutive integers a, b, c, d, and e is 55. What is the median of the set $\{a, b, c, d, e\}$?

A) 9
B) 10
C) 11
D) 12

It took Adam 6 hours to canoe upstream from his campsite to the lake and back again. While paddling upstream, he averaged 2 miles per hour; while paddling back, he averaged 4 miles per hour. How many miles was it from his campsite to the lake?

A) 4
B) 8
C) 10
D) 12

STOP

20. Answer: D.

B) 10 paperback books.
There are 18 total books, so there are 8 hardcover books. Let's see how much this costs.

Paperback: 10 ×	$7.50	= $75
Hardcover: 8 ×	$15	= $120
		= $195 ✗

Too small. Should be $210. It seems like we want a bigger number. Let's try A).

A) 11 paperback books.

Paperback: 11 ×	$7.50	= $82.50
Hardcover: 7 ×	$15	= $105
		= $187.50 ✗

That's smaller than the last one! We're going the wrong way.

C) 9 paperback books.

Paperback: 9 ×	$7.50	= $67.50
Hardcover: 9 ×	$15	= $135
		= $202.50 ✗

Getting close… (Some students might notice that we need an *even* number so we're not left with an extra $0.50.)

D) **8 paperback books.**

Paperback: 8 ×	$7.50	= $60
Hardcover: 10 ×	$15	= $150
		= **$210** ✓ It worked!

The reason we had to go to a smaller number to get a bigger total is that the answer represents the *cheaper* books. If we have less of the cheap stuff, we'll have more of the expensive stuff, and the total price goes up. But look, the whole point to Backsolve is to not think like that—just test the choices till you find one that works. If you can't tell which choice to go to: pick one! If you're wrong, all it cost you was an extra 15 seconds. You know you'll get to the answer eventually.

Notice choice B) is an RTFQ: 10 is the number of *hardcover* books.

23. Answer: C.

C) **11** is the median.   So the integers are 9, 10, 11, 12, 13.
$9 + 10 + 11 + 12 + 13 = $ **55** ✓ It worked!

Note that algebraic methods of solving this will almost invariably lead to an RTFQ. Kids will call the numbers x, $x + 1$, $x + 2$, etc, and then solve for x. But here, x is the *smallest* number, not the median. Again, Backsolve avoids the RTFQ mistake.

26. Answer: C.

This can be confusing. We're Backsolving, so just start with C) and take your time.

C) **80.** Marion brought 80 biscuits to the party.
"If everyone takes 5, there will be 10 remaining."
80 – 10 = 70 biscuits are taken.
70 ÷ 5 = **14 people** at the party

"If 4 people do not take any,
14 – 4 = 10
and everyone else takes 8,
10 × 8 = **80**
there will be none remaining"
80 matches what we started with! **C) is my answer**.

There are often alternate ways to go about Backsolve. What matters is that there are multiple pieces of information, and you must make sure that one piece matches up with the other. Here, we also could have run 80 through the second sentence to see if it also gives us 14 people:
80 ÷ 8 = 10 people take some.
10 + 4 take none = **14 total people**. ✓ It matches.

This is a great example of Backsolve as a way to understand a problem. Most kids will look at this problem and have no idea what's going on or how to get started. But Backsolve gives you a way in. Make C) the answer to the question. Then just read the question again, using the number in choice C), and see what the consequences are. If you get to a contradiction, the choice is wrong. If everything matches, the choice is correct.

27. Answer: B.

C) 10 miles from camp to lake.

Upstream:	10 miles ÷ 2 mph =	5 hours
Downstream:	10 miles ÷ 4 mph =	2.5 hours
		7.5 hrs total. ✗

Too big. Should be 6 hrs.

B) **8 miles** from camp to lake.

Upstream:	8 miles ÷ 2 mph =	4 hours
Downstream:	8 miles ÷ 4 mph =	2 hours
		6 hrs total. ✓

That was ridiculously easy with Backsolve.

THIS PAGE INTENTIONALLY LEFT BLANK

III. USING THE TECHNIQUES

It's one thing to understand how these techniques work. It's another to be able to use them and use them effectively in a real-test situation. It's incredibly difficult to change your habits. These techniques are a fundamentally different approach than what you're used to doing in school. Therefore, you have to make a *conscious* effort to use them on your practice tests. *Every* time you do a problem, your *first* thought should be "Can I use a technique here?" Even if you see another way of doing the problem. Even if you think that other way is better than the technique. **You must try to use the techniques every chance you get**.

We can already hear you complaining, but trust us: it's for your own good. Clearly, your old ways of doing problems aren't working for you—if they were, you wouldn't be reading this now. Your old methods have gotten you the score you have now. If you want a different score, you have to try different things.

Of course, you can't use the techniques on every single problem you see. And sometimes, there will be problems where the algebra isn't so bad and you can get the problem without the techniques. But here's the thing: *you're not qualified to make that call yet*. The techniques are still new for you, so you don't know whether or not they're the best method on this or that problem. The only way you can *become* qualified is to try to use the techniques every time you possibly can.

This is no different from any time you learn something new. In sports or in music, the only way to get good at something is to do it a thousand times in a row. The more you practice, the better you become.

Techniques and Target Numbers

As we've seen already, the techniques can turn a really hard problem into a really easy problem. But techniques can't be used on every question. There will be some legitimately tough questions that can't be done with Plug In or Backsolve. Luckily, a lot of those tough questions will be past your target numbers, so you'll never see them. But it's not unusual for the last question in your target numbers to be a legitimately tough non-technique question. Therefore, if the last question in your assigned set is *not* a technique question, and you see a question past your target numbers that's *obviously* a technique question, you may do the technique question instead of one of your target questions.

This exception is *only* for technique questions. If you see a non-technique problem—even if you think you can do it—it's not worth your time. Remember that one of the dangers of the harder questions is the possibility of a Fool's Gold choice, a wrong choice that looks like an easy answer. But we've already seen that using the techniques actually *reduces* your chances of making those mistakes.

And this doesn't mean you can do *all* technique questions past your target numbers. Remember: the goal of target numbers is *do fewer questions*. Your first goal should still be to do your target questions and *only* your target questions. But at the end of the section, if you notice a Plug In past your assignment, it's okay to swap it with one of your assigned questions.

So how can you tell if you can use a technique on a problem? Glad you asked.

Identifying Techniques

Circle the Question

This bears repeating. It's quite remarkable, but a simple act like circling the question—that is, the thing they're actually asking you to solve for—can do wonders for your performance.

We already saw how it can help you avoid RTFQ mistakes. Circling the question helps you remember what the point of the problem is, and will clear your mind on everything you do. But more importantly, it can help you decide *which* technique, if any, is applicable on a question.

Here's a general rule of thumb:

> ### If the question asks for a VALUE, try Backsolve.
> ### If the question asks for a RELATIONSHIP, try Plug In.

While it may seem like they ask you about a million different things on the test, they actually repeat the same kinds of question over and over again. The more questions you do, the easier it is to spot the techniques.

Let's recap some common characteristics of the Three Fundamental Techniques:

Plug In

Make up numbers for the variables. Do the problem with your numbers until you get a number for an answer. Then see which choice gives you that same number.

Here are some common characteristics of Plug-In problems, with examples from problems we've seen:

- ✎ Any time you see a problem that has *variables in the answer choices*, you can definitely use Plug In. Because if the answer is $x + 4$, it will always be $x + 4$, no matter what x is.

- ✎ In particular, look out for questions that ask for "*x* in terms of *y*". That's a big sign that Plug In is possible.

- ✎ Sometimes you can also use Plug In when there are variables in the question but not in the choices. Sometimes if you plug in for one variable you can figure out the other variables.

- ✎ You can use Plug In on problems with *implicit* variables. You can use Plug In any time there's some concept in the problem and:

    1. You don't know its value
    2. There's no way to figure out its value
    3. They still expect you to get an answer
    4. So it doesn't matter what that value is; you'll get the same answer no matter what.

9. Bob has 4 dollars more than Lisa does. If Lisa has x dollars, how much would Bob have if he doubled his money?

   A) $x + 4$
   B) $2x$
   C) $2x + 4$
   D) $2x + 8$

14. If $x + 5$ is 3 less than y, then $x - 2$ is how much less than y?

   A) 6
   B) 7
   C) 8
   D) 10

30. Scott drives to Bob's house at a speed of 30 miles per hour and drives back at a speed of 50 miles per hour. If he takes the same route both ways, what was his average speed, in miles per hour, for the whole trip?

   A) 37.5
   B) 40
   C) 42.5
   D) It cannot be determined from the information given.

Backsolve

Test the numbers in the answer choices. Start with the middle number. Put it through the problem, and see if it matches what you know. If it doesn't, pick a bigger or smaller choice until you find one that works.

Some common characteristics of Backsolve problems:

- If there are whole numbers in the answer choices you can usually use Backsolve. Any time you need to find some kind of single value or quantity, you've got four options for that value right here. Three of them are wrong, one of them is right. Test them.

17. Gerry's age is 5 more than three times Carol's age. If the sum of their ages is 45, how old is Carol?

    A) 10
    B) 12
    C) 14
    D) 16

- If they're asking you for the *value of a variable* (i.e., what number does x equal), you can usually use Backsolve. They want to know x? Well, here are four options. Try 'em until you find one that works.

21. If $j + k = 9$ and $j^2 + jk = 36$ then $k =$

    A) 3
    B) 4
    C) 5
    D) 6

Often, Backsolve questions have *two pieces of information*. When you test an answer choice, you run the choice through one piece of information and see if it matches the other. In #17 above, we started with "5 more than three times" and checked that the resulting sums were 45. In #21, we started with the first equation and checked that the second came out to 36.

THIS PAGE INTENTIONALLY LEFT BLANK

Big Technique Exercise

Note about techniques:

The purpose of this chapter is to teach kids the main math techniques. We do that by showing them how to apply those techniques on SAT-style questions over and over again.

The purpose of this drill is *not* to get these questions right. The questions themselves don't matter; they're just a device to practice the techniques. So if a kid gets the right answer without using the techniques, that's a failure. Our purpose here is to practice the techniques.

Later, we'll care about getting questions right, but not now. This is a scrimmage; this game does not count in the standings. Here, the answers don't matter. You could even give the kids all the answers at the beginning. All that matters is whether they can identify when and how to use each technique. So make sure every kid applies a technique on every single question in this chapter.

Remember: all we care about here is practicing techniques. If a student doesn't use a technique on a question, that counts as wrong.

1. **Answer: A. Plug In.**
   Say $a = 3$.
   So $12(3) = 36$.
   25% of 36 is **9**.

   Put 3 into the answers and see which gives you 9.

   A) $3(3) = 9$ ✓
   B) $4(3) = 12$ ✗
   C) $8(3) = 24$ ✗
   D) $9(3) = 18$ ✗

   The algebra here is so easy that Plug In may seem unnecessary. But remember: our goal on this drill is not to get the question right; it's simply to *practice the techniques*, to drill them to death until they're tattooed onto our brains.

2. **Answer: A. Plug In.**
   Plug In for Sal: $S = 3$. Now re-read the question:

   "Rita has 5 fewer than 4 times **3**."
   So Rita has 5 fewer than 12. Rita has 7. $R = 7$.

   Put those numbers into the choices and see which equation is true:

   A) $7 = 4(3) - 5 = 12 - 5 = 7$ ✓
   B) $7 = 4(3 - 5) = 4(-1) = -4$ ✗
   C) $7 = 5(3) - 4 = 15 - 4 = 11$ ✗
   D) $7 = 5(3) + 4 = 15 + 4 = 19$ ✗

3. **Answer: D. Backsolve.**
   Pick choice C) and make it the greatest of four consecutive integers:

   C) $7 + 6 + 5 + 4 = 22$ ✗ Too small.
   D) $8 + 7 + 6 + 5 = 26$ ✓ Perfect.

   If you were to do this with algebra, you'd probably set it up like this:
   $$x + (x + 1) + (x + 2) + (x + 3) = 26$$
   $$4x + 6 = 26$$
   $$4x = 20$$
   $$x = 5$$
   Ah, but 5 is choice A). That's the *smallest* number. **RTFQ!** Now, obviously, you *could* do this problem algebraically and still get it right, but you're *much more likely* to make the RTFQ mistake with algebra than you are with Backsolve, where the first step is to find out what the question is asking you for. The technique is *safer* than algebra.

4. **Answer: D. Backsolve.**
   Put the choice in for x on the left side of the equation, and see if it comes out to 1/4 (or 0.25).

   C) $x = 4.$ $\dfrac{4+3}{2^4} = \dfrac{7}{16}$ ✗ $(= 0.4375)$

   D) $x = 5.$ $\dfrac{5+3}{2^5} = \dfrac{8}{32} = \dfrac{1}{4}$ ✓

   The algebra here is ridiculously hard.

BIG TECHNIQUE EXERCISE

Please enjoy this Big Technique Exercise! **You must use one of the Techniques—Plug In or Backsolve—on every problem on this exercise.** *If you get a question right, but did not use a technique, you will get no credit.*

1

If $a \neq 0$, then 25% of $12a$ equals

A) $3a$
B) $4a$
C) $8a$
D) $9a$

3

What is the <u>greatest</u> of four consecutive integers whose sum is 26?

A) 5
B) 6
C) 7
D) 8

2

Rita has 5 fewer than 4 times the number of peaches that Sal has. If R represents the number of Rita's peaches and S represents the number of Sal's peaches, which of the following expressions correctly relates R and S?

A) $R = 4S - 5$
B) $R = 4(S - 5)$
C) $R = 5S - 4$
D) $R = 5S + 4$

4

If x is a positive integer and $\dfrac{x+3}{2^x} = \dfrac{1}{4}$, then $x =$

A) 2
B) 3
C) 4
D) 5

CONTINUE

5

Last month Company A sold 200 more copy machines than Company B. This month, Company A sold 75 fewer than Company B. Which of the following must be true about Company A's total sales for the two months compared to Company B's?

A) Company A sold 275 fewer machines than Company B.

B) Company A sold 125 fewer machines than Company B.

C) Company A sold 125 more machines than Company B.

D) Company A sold 275 more machines than Company B.

To steam rice, Paul uses m cups of water for every p cups of rice. In terms of m and p, how many cups of water are needed to steam $p + 2$ cups of rice?

A) $m(p + 2)$

B) $\dfrac{m}{p + 2}$

C) $\dfrac{m(p + 2)}{p}$

D) $\dfrac{p}{m(p + 2)}$

The width of a rectangular rug is one-sixth of the length. If the perimeter is 56, what is the rug's width?

A) 4
B) 7
C) 12
D) 24

The combined price of a pair of pants and a shirt is 100 dollars. If the pants cost 14 dollars less than 2 times the shirt, what is the price, in dollars, of the shirt?

A) 28
B) 38
C) 46
D) 62

CONTINUE

5. Answer: C. Plug In.
While there are no explicit variables here, we can still Plug In for the unknown values here. (We called these *implicit variables*—quantities that could be given as variables but aren't actually labeled in the problem.)

Let's say that Company B sold the same each month. We could pick different numbers for each month, but if we make it the same we'll have fewer numbers to deal with. So let's say that **Company B sold 100 machines each month:**

	Company B		Company A
Month 1	100	+ 200	300
Month 2	100	− 75	25
Totals	**200**		**325**

Theoretically, we could put these numbers into every answer choice, but it's easy enough to just calculate the difference: 325 − 200 = **125.**

So **Company A sold 125 more machines than Company B.** That's **choice C).**

RTFQ: choice B) means they did the math right but mixed up Company A and Company B.

6. Answer: C. Plug In.
Plug in both variables separately. Say $m = 2$ and $p = 4$. So
Paul uses **2** cups of water for every **4** cups of rice.
How many cups of water are needed to steam $4 + 2 = 6$ cups of rice?
He uses twice as much rice as water, so 6 cups of rice need **3 cups of water.**
Put $m = 2$ and $p = 4$ into the choices and see which gives us 3.

A) $2(4 + 2) = 12$ ✗

B) $\dfrac{2}{4+2} = \dfrac{2}{6} = \dfrac{1}{3}$ ✗

C) $\dfrac{2(4+2)}{4} = \dfrac{12}{4} = 3$ ✓

D) $\dfrac{4}{2(4+2)} = \dfrac{4}{12} = \dfrac{1}{3}$ ✗

Kids have *a lot* of trouble with ratios like this—even just seeing that it *is* a ratio question can be difficult. So take your time with it.

This is just a ratio: $\dfrac{2}{4} = \dfrac{x}{6}$, so $x = 3$. But to do that we had to introduce a new variable, x. It's incredibly easy to lose track of which entity has which variable. Avoid using variables and keep things *concrete*.

If kids are struggling with this, you could try plugging in for the proportion directly. That is, start by assuming there's **twice as much rice as water**. Then come up with an m and p that fit—say, $m = 2$, and $p = 4$, as above. It might be easier for some kids to follow along if they focus on the relationship itself.

7. Answer: A. Backsolve.
Since we don't have a picture, start by drawing a rectangle:

This may seem unnecessary, but it's important to help keep track of which one's the length and which is the width. How can you tell which is which? Let's do some Backsolve to find out.

C) 12. That'll be the width of the rug. Let's re-read the problem carefully:
12 is *one-sixth* of the length. So that means the width is the *shorter* side. So the length is $12 \times 6 = \textbf{72}$ ✗
The length alone is bigger than the perimeter is supposed to be. Way too big.

B) 7 is the width. $7 \times 6 = 42$ is the length.
Perimeter $= \ell + \ell + w + w = 42 + 42 + 7 + 7 = 98$ ✗ Still too big.

A) $4 = w$. $4 \times 6 = 24 = \ell$
Perimeter $= \ell + \ell + w + w$
$= 24 + 24 + 4 + 4 = \textbf{56}$ ✓

It's *very* easy to mix up the length and width and get D) 24, particularly because it's easy to confuse the "one-sixth of the length" with "six times the length". That's why it's important to draw a figure. With Backsolve, you should literally re-read the question with your number so you can prevent this type of confusion.

8. Answer: B. Backsolve.
C) 46 = shirt. Re-read the second sentence with our choice:
"The pants cost 14 dollars less than 2 times 46"
$2 \times 46 = 92.$
"The pants cost 14 dollars less than 92"
14 less than 92 is $92 − 14 = 78.$
The pants are $78.

$46 + 78 = 124$ ✗ Too big. The total should be 100.

B) **38 = shirt.**
$2 \times 38 = 76.$
14 less than 76 is $76 − 14 = 62 =$ pants.
$38 + 62 = \textbf{100}$ ✓

RFTQ: D). That's the price of the pants.

9. **Answer: C. Plug In.**
    Pick a *small a*. Say $a = 2$. (If you pick $a = 1$ here, more than one choice will work.)

    $4^2 = b = 16$.

    $16b^2 = 16(16)^2 = \mathbf{4096}$.

    Now put 2 into the choices and see which gives you 4096.

    A) $4^{4(2)} = 4^8 = 65{,}536$ ✗

    B) $4^{2^4} = 4^{16} = 4{,}294{,}967{,}296$ ✗ Yikes!

    C) $4^{2(2)+2} = 4^6 = 4096$ ✓

    D) $4^{2(2)^2} = 4^{2(4)} = 4^8 = 65{,}536$ ✗

    Notice that it's perfectly possible to mess up the exponent rules and get, say, choice B) as your answer. But with Plug In, we can see that choice B) is *nowhere near* what we're looking for.

10. **Answer: B. Backsolve.**
    This time, we'll Backsolve slightly differently: we'll start with D) instead of C). They want the greatest possible value of *j*, so we'll start with the greatest choice. If we start with C) and it works, we still wouldn't know for sure that it's the *greatest* possible choice. So we'll start with the biggest and work our way down the list. The first one that works will be our answer.

    D) $60 = j$ $60 \times k \times m = 120$ $km = 2$. ✗
        The only integers that work are 2×1. But *k* and *m* both must be greater than 1. Keep going.

    C) $30 = j$ $30 \times k \times m = 120$ $km = 4$.
        Two options here: $k = 4, m = 1$ ✗   *m* must be > 1
                           $k = 2, m = 2$ ✗   *k* must be > *m*

    B) $\mathbf{20 = j}$ $20 \times k \times m = 120$ $km = 6$.
        Two options here: $k = 6, m = 1$ ✗   *m* must be > 1
                           $\mathbf{k = 3, m = 2}$ ✓   This would work!
        B) is our answer.

11. **Answer: A. Plug In.**
    Here, the problem has no variable. But there's still an unknown quantity here. It's confusing because not only do they not give you a variable, but they don't even mention this unknown quantity at all. But trust me, it's there.

    Pick any number. **Let's pick 5.** So the question now becomes:

    "Which of the following would yield the same result as multiplying **5** by $\frac{6}{7}$ and then dividing by $\frac{2}{7}$?"

    Now just punch it out on your calculator (carefully!):

    $$5 \times \frac{6}{7} = \frac{30}{7} = 4.2857\ldots$$

    $$(4.2857\ldots) \div \left(\frac{2}{7}\right) = \mathbf{15}$$

    We started with 5, did some fraction stuff, and got out 15. That's the same thing as *multiplying 5 by 3*.

    So doing all those fraction operations was the same thing as **multiplying by 3**. That's **Choice A)**.

    It might be easier to *convert the fractions to decimals first*. But realize that this is an approximation, so the result won't be *exactly* correct.

$\frac{6}{7} = 0.857$ $\frac{2}{7} = 0.286$

$5 \times 0.857 = 4.285$ $4.285 \div 0.286 = \mathbf{14.983}$

Obviously, the math would be easier if you picked a multiple of 7. Of course, if you have enough foresight to do that, you probably don't need Plug In. It's important to tell your kids that, while sometimes certain numbers can make their lives easier, you don't *have* to pick the good numbers. **Any number will work.**

If you're good at the fraction rules, you can see why this is true:

$$5 \times \frac{6}{7} \div \frac{2}{7} =$$

$$5 \times \frac{6}{\cancel{7}} \times \frac{\cancel{7}}{2} = 5 \times \frac{6}{2} = 5 \times 3 = 15$$

Of course, you don't have to understand the fraction rules here; you can just punch it out on your calculator and see that it comes out to 15. But even if you prefer dealing with fractions, plug in helps you see what's going on in the problem.

12. **Answer: C. Guesstimate *or* Plug In.**
    The picture's drawn to scale, so let's start with some **Guesstimate**. Each of the six angles is definitely bigger than 90°. $6 \times 90 = 540$, so our answer should be bigger than 540.
    That kills A) and B) right away!

    Let's be more specific. The angles are all about the same. Say they're each 130°. $130 \times 6 = 780°$. **Choice C) is closest.**

    Notice, though, that there is no way to determine the actual value of any one of those angles. But they still expect us to get a value for the sum. So it probably doesn't matter what the angles are *individually*, the sum will always be the same.

    So let's Plug In for the middle triangle. Say that middle triangle was equilateral, so all angles are 60°. Each of the marked angles would be 120°. $\mathbf{120 \times 6 = 720}$**. That's C).**

    Don't believe me? Try a different triangle. Say the middle triangle was 45-45-90. So two of the marked angles would be 90° and four would be 135°.

    $$\begin{array}{r} 2 \times 90 = 180 \\ 4 \times 135 = 540 \\ \hline = 720 \end{array}$$ ✓ **It still works.**

    Either Plug In or Guesstimate will work here, but there is a subtle difference between them. Plug In says that we'll always get the same answer no matter how we draw it. Guesstimate says that one way we can draw it is the way that it's drawn right now.

    Curious about the algebra? Here goes:
    Let's label the angles inside the triangle *a*, *b*, and *c*. Each large marked angle is supplementary to one of the triangle angles, so they would be $180 - a$, $180 - b$, and $180 - c$, respectively. There are two of each of these angles, so the total sum would be

    $$2(180 - a) + 2(180 - b) + 2(180 - c)$$
    $$= 360 - 2a + 360 - 2b + 360 - 2c$$
    $$= 1080 - 2a - 2b - 2c$$
    $$= 1080 - 2(a + b + c) \qquad \text{Ah, } (a + b + c) \text{ is the sum of the triangle, so it's 180.}$$

    $$= 1080 - 2(180)$$
    $$= 1080 - 360 = \mathbf{720}.$$

9

If $4^a = b$, which of the following equals $16b^2$?

A) 4^{4a}

B) 4^{a^4}

C) 4^{2a+2}

D) 4^{2a^2}

10

Let j, k, and m be integers, where $j > k > m > 1$.
If $j \times k \times m = 120$, what is the greatest possible
value of j?

A) 15
B) 20
C) 30
D) 60

11

Which of the following would yield the same result as

multiplying by $\dfrac{6}{7}$ and then dividing by $\dfrac{2}{7}$?

A) Multiplying by 3

B) Multiplying by $\dfrac{1}{3}$

C) Dividing by 2

D) Dividing by $\dfrac{1}{2}$

12

In the figure above, what is the sum of the measures of
the marked angles?

A) 360
B) 540
C) 720
D) 900

CONTINUE

If $x \neq 0$, what is the value, in terms of x, of

$$\frac{\dfrac{3}{2}}{x} + \frac{\dfrac{1}{4}}{10x} ?$$

A) $\dfrac{1}{4x}$

B) $\dfrac{4}{x}$

C) $\dfrac{x}{4}$

D) $4x$

At a certain gym, 18 people take an aerobics class and 24 people take a karate class. If 32 people take only one of the two classes, how many people take both classes?

A)   5
B)   10
C)   13
D)   15

The length and width of a rectangle are both reduced by 60%. Its length and width are then both increased by 50%. The area of the rectangle is what percent of its original area?

A)   10%
B)   36%
C)   81%
D)   90%

STOP

Or: each of the three intersection points is composed of 4 angles that make a circle. So all the angles in the figure—marked and unmarked—together are $360 \times 3 = 1080$. We're removing the inner triangle, which is 180. We're also removing the three other unmarked angles, each of which is a vertical angle with one of the triangle angles. So the three unmarked angles outside the triangle will equal the three unmarked angles inside the triangle, so they will also be 180.

$1080 - 180 - 180 = \textbf{720}$.

So you could do that. Or you could just do $120 \times 6 = 720$. You know where we stand.

13. Answer: D. Plug In.
$x = 2$ works very nicely.

$$\frac{3}{\frac{2}{2}} + \frac{1}{\frac{4}{10(2)}} = \frac{3}{1} + \frac{1}{\left(\frac{1}{5}\right)} = 3 + 5 = \textbf{8}.$$

If you don't like dealing with fractions, you can use your calculator. Just be careful about the parentheses:
$4/20 = 0.2 \quad 1/0.2 = 5$

A) $\dfrac{1}{4(2)} = \dfrac{1}{8}$ ✗

B) $\dfrac{4}{2} = 2$ ✗

C) $\dfrac{2}{4} = \dfrac{1}{2}$ ✗

D) $4(2) = 8$ ✓

14. Answer: A. Backsolve.
This is a confusing problem. The beauty of Backsolve is that you can dive into it before you know what you're doing. Just pick C), declare that to be the answer to the question, then re-read the question and see what follows.

C) 13. That means 13 people took *both* classes.
18 total people took aerobics, 13 of them were also in karate, so $18 - 13 = \textbf{5}$ people took aerobics only.

24 total people took karate, 13 of them were also in aerobics, so $24 - 13 = \textbf{11}$ people took aerobics only.

Does that work? What else do we know?
We know **32 people** took only one class. Is that true here? **NO.**
$5 + 11 = \textbf{16 people}$ took only one class. ✗   That doesn't work!

Once C) fails, it's tough to tell whether to go to B) or D). Don't waste time thinking about it: just pick one.

B) 10 took both classes.
18 aerobics – 10 both =   8   aerobics only
24 karate – 10 both =   14   karate only
= 22 only one class. ✗ No match.
But we went from 16 to 22, so we're getting closer.

A) **5 took both**

18 aerobics – 5 both =   13   aerobics only
24 karate – 5 both =   19   karate only
= **32 only one class.** ✓

---

* Fun fact: The Venn Diagram was invented by the British logician John Venn in the 1880s. To honor his achievement, there is a stained glass window in Cambridge depicting a Venn Diagram.

Choice B) is a big Fool's Gold here. Students will add $18 + 24$ to get 42 total students, then subtract the 32 in only one class to get $42 - 32 = 10$ students in both.

The problem here is that you can't add $18 + 24$ to get the total, because some people are in both. You're counting the overlap *twice*. So the correct answer is $10 \div 2 = 5$.

Backsolve is easier because you don't have to think about it abstractly; you start with the number for the overlap and proceed using real numbers.

This Venn Diagram might help you understand.*

15. Answer: B. Plug In.
We don't know the length or width, so let's say *each* is 10. It's perfectly alright to make them the same number. It doesn't say they *have* to be different, and a square is a type of rectangle.

1. Our first square is **10 by 10**, so it has an **area of 100**.
2. We'll reduce each side by 60 %, so we take away 6. Now it's **4 by 4**.
3. Now we'll increase *those* sides by 50%. That makes it **6 by 6** with an **area of 36**.

The question asks: the area of the rectangle now is what percent of its original area. 36 is what percent of 100? **36%**. That's B).

As we saw earlier, any time you see percents on a Plug In, *pick 100*. Here we picked 10 for the side so the *area* came out to 100. You could also pick 100 for the side. That makes the calculations for the side reductions a little easier. But then the areas come out much bigger. You could even do both and make it a 10×100 rectangle. Any of these is fine.

C) is an RTFQ. This means in step 2, you just *found* 60% of the original, instead of *reducing* by 60%.

D) is a Fool's Gold choice. It's tempting to do:
$100 - 60 + 50 = 90$.

But that's taking 50 % of the *original* rectangle, not 50% of the *intermediate* rectangle. That's hard to see in the abstract, but easy to see when you've got real numbers in there. That's the beauty of Plug In.

THIS PAGE INTENTIONALLY LEFT BLANK

Math Fundamentals

The math techniques—Plug In and Backsolve—can be applied to a lot of different problems. However, the techniques won't work on every problem. We need to talk about *content*—the actual rules of math you have to know on the SAT.

Let's begin at the beginning, as one should. This chapter deals with the nuts and bolts that make up the basic rules of math. Much of the content in this chapter isn't directly tested so much as it underlies many of the harder concepts we'll see down the road. You can't solve equations dealing with complicated multi-variable rational functions unless you know a little something about fractions.

Since we're talking about the basics here, much of this will probably not be new to you. Therefore, you may be tempted to skip over this part. "This is so boring! Why do we have to talk about fractions? We did this in, like, seventh grade! I hate you!"

Ah, but it's because this is stuff we've seen before that we must make sure we know it well. Remember: most students' problem *isn't* that they don't know enough math; it's that they're missing questions that they already know how to do. Therefore, we've got to make sure we know all this stuff backwards and forwards.

I. NUMBER CONCEPTS AND DEFINITIONS

Let's get some terminology out of the way to avoid confusion down the line.

Integer: Any number that does not have a fraction or decimal part: … −3, −2, −1, 0, 1, 2, 3…

Factor: An integer that can be divided into another integer without a remainder. For example, 3 is a factor of 12 because 12 ÷ 3 = 4. We say the larger number "*is divisible by*" the

Concepts in this chapter that deal with **proportions** (like ratios, rates, and percentages), are generally used on **Problem Solving and Data Analysis** questions. Therefore, they appear only on the Calculator OK section, not on the No Calculator section.

Note that zero is an even integer but it is neither positive nor negative.

smaller number, so here 12 is divisible by 3.*

Multiple: An integer that has another integer as a factor. For example, 12 is a multiple of 3 because $3 \times 4 = 12$.

Prime Number: A number that is divisible only by 1 and itself. 1 is not a prime number. The only even prime number is 2. Examples of prime numbers include 2, 3, 5, 7, 11, and 13.

Remainder: The integer left over when an integer is divided by an integer that is not its factor. For example: $13 \div 5 = 2$ with a *remainder of 3*. That means you can fit two fives in 13, but there will be 3 left over: $5 \times 2 = 10$, and $10 + 3 = 13$. Remainders are whole numbers, **NOT** decimals. If you punch "$13 \div 5$" on your calculator you'll get 2.6. The remainder is NOT 6.

Properties of Positive and Negative numbers: Bigger digits give smaller negative numbers. That is, –10 is *smaller* than –2.

$$(\text{Pos}) \times (\text{Pos}) = \text{Pos} \qquad (\text{Neg}) \times (\text{Pos}) = \text{Neg} \qquad (\text{Neg}) \times (\text{Neg}) = \text{Pos}$$

Properties of Odd and Even Integers:

$(\text{Even}) \times (\text{Even}) = \text{Even}$	$\text{Even} + \text{Even} = \text{Even}$
$(\text{Even}) \times (\text{Odd}) = \text{Even}$	$\text{Even} + \text{Odd} = \text{Odd}$
$(\text{Odd}) \times (\text{Odd}) = \text{Odd}$	$\text{Odd} + \text{Odd} = \text{Even}$

Decimal places: In the number **25.97**
- 2 is the "tens digit" and is in the "tens place"
- 5 is the "units digit" and is in the "units place"
- 9 is the "tenths digit" and is in the "tenths place"
- 7 is the "hundredths digit" and is in the "hundredths place"

Scientific Notation: Because decimal numbers are based on powers of ten (hundreds, tens, tenths, hundredths, etc), you can express *any* number as a decimal multiplied by a power of ten. So the number 43,500 becomes 4.35×10^4, and 0.00524 becomes 5.24×10^{-3}. This is just a way to make it easier to write really big or really small numbers. Instead of 8,000,000,000 we write 8.0×10^9.

You don't have to know much about this notation. SAT questions may ask you to manipulate

---

* Here's a trick to help you find factors: if the sum of the number's digits is divisible by 3, then the number is divisible by 3. 12 is divisible by 3 because $1 + 2 = 3$. And 945 is divisible by 3 because $9 + 4 + 5 = 18$, and 18 is divisible by 3. The rule is true for 9, too: if the sum of the digits is divisible by 9, the number is divisible by 9.

numbers in this form, but usually that's easy to do on your calculator.* Just remember that the exponent next to the "10" has the biggest effect on the value of the number: 2×10^9 is much, much bigger than 9×10^2.

Prime Factors

As we said above, integers can be broken down into *factors*, and a *prime number* is one that can't be broken down into factors. Therefore, a *prime factor* is a factor that can't be broken down into smaller factors. Any number that isn't prime can be reduced to a unique set of prime factors. And *all* that number's factors are just different combinations of its prime factors.

☛ **What are the prime factors of 12?**

All we have to do is break 12 up into any factors, then keep splitting up the factors until we can't anymore.

- ☛ We know $3 \times 4 = 12$, so 3 and 4 are factors of 12.

- ☛ 3 is prime, so it can't go any further.

- ☛ 4 is not prime, so we can break it up into 2 and 2.

- ☛ 2 is prime, so it can't go any further.

- ☛ So the prime factors of 12 are **3, 2, and 2**. (Because we found two 2's, we list both of them in our list of prime factors.)

If we had started with a different pair of factors—say, 2 and 6—we'd still get the same set of prime factors. All the factors of 12 can be produced by multiplying the prime factors together:

Factor	2	3	4	6	12
Prime factors	2	3	2×2	2×3	$2 \times 2 \times 3$

The branching diagram shown here makes it easy to find the prime factors of any integer. Split up the number into any factors. If one of the factors is prime, circle it. Otherwise, keep factoring. It helps to start with a small prime numbers on the left, so you only have to expand the tree on the right branch. The diagram to the right shows that the prime factors of 180 are 2, 2, 5, 3, and 3.

---

* On some calculators, the "EE" button is shorthand for this notation. Typing "4.24 EE 4" gives you 4.24×10^4 (though it's often displayed with one "E" as "4.24 E4").

© A-List Education

SAT Math | Math Fundamentals   281

✍ In the number 379.045, what digit is in the units place?

✍ If x is an odd positive integer, which of the following expressions must be *even*?

      I. $2x$

      II. $x + 2$

      III. $3x + 1$

✍ If x has a remainder of 5 when divided by 6 and $x > 10$, what is the smallest possible value of x?

✍ If j is the largest prime factor of 42, and k is the largest prime factor of 36, what is the value of $j + k$?

✍ If x and y are integers such that $xy = -12$ and $x > 0$, what is the greatest possible value of y?

1. Number Concepts and Definitions

ANSWERS:

✎ In the number 379.045, what digit is in the units place?

Answer: 9.

✎ If x is an odd positive integer, which of the following expressions must be *even*?

Answer: I and III.

I. $2x$ **Must be even.** 2 is even, x is odd. Even × odd = even

II. $x + 2$ **Must be odd.** Odd + 1 = even, even + 1 = odd. So odd + 2 = odd

III. $3x + 1$ **Must be even.** 3 is odd, x is odd. Odd × odd = odd, so $3x$ is odd. Odd + 1 = even, so $3x + 1$ is even.

Plug in works great here. Pick an odd x, say $x = 3$.

I. $2(3) = $ **6** ✓
II. $3 + 2 = 5$ ✗
III. $3(3) + 1 = $ **10** ✓

✎ If x has a remainder of 5 when divided by 6 and $x > 10$, what is the smallest possible value of x?

Answer: 11.

The smallest multiple of 6 is 6. Just add $6 + 5 = $ **11**.

✎ If j is the largest prime factor of 42, and k is the largest prime factor of 36, what is the value of $j + k$?

Answer: 10.

The prime factors of 42 are 7, 3, and 2, so $j = 7$.
The prime factors of 36 are 3, 3, 2, and 2, so $k = 3$.
$j + k = 7 + 3 = $ **10**.

✎ If x and y are integers such that $xy = -12$ and $x > 0$, what is the greatest possible value of y?

Answer: –1.

Their product is negative and x is positive, so y must be negative.

Both x and y are integers, so all possible values are:

x	1	2	3	4	6	12
y	−12	−6	−4	−3	−2	−1

Of those options for y, **−1 is the greatest** (*NOT* −12).

THIS PAGE INTENTIONALLY LEFT BLANK

II. FRACTIONS

A fraction is nothing more than one number divided by another. As such, to convert a fraction to a decimal, just divide the numbers. The top number is called the *numerator*; the bottom number is called the *denominator*.

$$\frac{3}{4} = 3 \div 4 = 0.75$$

You must know how to add, subtract, multiply and divide fractions.

To **add or subtract** fractions, you must find a *common denominator*. This just means that you can't add or subtract fractions that have different numbers on the bottom.

$$\frac{3}{4} - \frac{2}{3} = \frac{3 \times 3}{3 \times 4} - \frac{4 \times 2}{4 \times 3} = \frac{9}{12} - \frac{8}{12} = \frac{1}{12}$$

To **multiply** fractions, you don't have to do any preparation. Just multiply *straight across*: top × top; bottom × bottom.

$$\frac{2}{9} \times \frac{3}{4} = \frac{(2 \times 3)}{(9 \times 4)} = \frac{6}{36} = \frac{1}{6}$$

Notice that our answer could be **reduced** because the top and bottom had a **common factor**. We also could have taken out the common factors before we multiplied:

$$\frac{\overset{1}{\cancel{2}}}{9} \times \frac{3}{\underset{2}{\cancel{4}}} = \frac{1}{\underset{3}{\cancel{9}}} \times \frac{\overset{1}{\cancel{3}}}{2} = \frac{1}{3} \times \frac{1}{2} = \frac{1}{(3 \times 2)} = \frac{1}{6}$$

To **divide** fractions, you must take the *reciprocal* of the second fraction, and then multiply. "Reciprocal" just means to flip the fraction over.

$$\frac{3}{10} \div \frac{2}{5} = \frac{3}{\underset{2}{\cancel{10}}} \times \frac{\overset{1}{\cancel{5}}}{2} = \frac{3}{2} \times \frac{1}{2} = \frac{3}{4}$$

A *compound fraction* is one in which the numerator and/or denominator contain fractions. This is equivalent to dividing fractions. Remember: fractions just mean "divide".

$$\frac{\frac{1}{3}}{\frac{1}{2}} = \frac{1}{3} \div \frac{1}{2} = \frac{1}{3} \times \frac{2}{1} = \frac{2}{3}$$

If you ever want to combine a fraction with a whole number, remember that any whole number can be written as a fraction with a numerator of 1:

$$3 = \frac{3}{1} \qquad 12 = \frac{12}{1} \qquad -10 = \frac{-10}{1} \qquad x = \frac{x}{1}$$

When multiplying a whole number by a fraction, this means that the whole number can multiply straight across to the numerator and can cancel out directly with the denominator of the fraction:

✎ $7\left(\dfrac{3}{5}\right) = \dfrac{7 \times 3}{5} = \dfrac{21}{5}$

✎ $9\left(\dfrac{5}{6}\right) = \dfrac{9 \times 5}{6} = \dfrac{3 \times 5}{2} = \dfrac{15}{2}$

When adding or subtracting, it's best to write in the denominator of 1 under the whole number to help find the lowest common denominator.

✎ $3 + \dfrac{1}{4} = \dfrac{3}{1} + \dfrac{1}{4} = \dfrac{3 \times 4}{4} + \dfrac{1}{4} = \dfrac{12}{4} + \dfrac{1}{4} = \dfrac{13}{4}$

When the numerator is larger than the denominator like this, we call that an *improper fraction*. A *mixed number* contains a whole number and a fraction.

$$3\frac{1}{4} \text{ (Mixed number)} \qquad\qquad \frac{13}{4} \text{ (Improper fraction)}$$

Manipulating fractions is a lost art. With the advent of calculators, a lot of problems that used to require knowledge of fractions can now be done quickly with decimals, since fractions can be easily converted to decimals on your calculator.

That's fine. We're all for doing problems quickly. But don't forget about fractions. Often, using fractions effectively can actually make a problem *faster* than typing the problem out on your calculator.

- First of all, sometimes you're not allowed to use a calculator, remember?
- Secondly, some fractions become repeating decimals, so the calculator will give *approximate* answers—this can be deadly if you have a long computation.
- Third, you must be careful of parentheses. If you try to do $(1/3) \div (1/2)$ by typing in "$1 \div 3 \div 1 \div 2$", you'll get it wrong. You must type "$(1 \div 3) \div (1 \div 2)$". *
- Fourth, using fractions is often easier than it seems because you can often cancel out common factors, thus turning hard math into easy math.

_____

* Fun fact: the technical name for a division symbol (÷) is an *obelus*.

THIS PAGE INTENTIONALLY LEFT BLANK

2. Fractions

ANSWERS:

$\dfrac{5}{4} + \dfrac{10}{3} = ?$

Answer: $\dfrac{55}{12}$ or $4\dfrac{7}{12}$

$$\frac{5}{4} + \frac{10}{3} = \frac{15}{12} + \frac{40}{12} = \frac{55}{12} = 4\frac{7}{12}$$

$\dfrac{1}{3} + \dfrac{5}{6} = ?$

Answer: $\dfrac{7}{6}$ or $1\dfrac{1}{6}$

$$\frac{1}{3} + \frac{5}{6} = \frac{2}{6} + \frac{5}{6} = \frac{7}{6} = 1\frac{1}{6}$$

$2\dfrac{2}{5} - \dfrac{1}{2} = ?$

Answer: $\dfrac{19}{10}$ or $1\dfrac{9}{10}$

$$2\frac{2}{5} - \frac{1}{2} = \frac{12}{5} - \frac{1}{2} = \frac{24}{10} - \frac{5}{10} = \frac{19}{10} = 1\frac{9}{10}$$

$\left(\dfrac{28}{15}\right)\left(\dfrac{3}{7}\right) = ?$

Answer: $\dfrac{4}{5}$

$$\left(\frac{28}{15}\right)\left(\frac{3}{7}\right) = \left(\frac{4}{15}\right)\left(\frac{3}{1}\right) = \left(\frac{4}{5}\right)\left(\frac{1}{1}\right) = \frac{4}{5}$$

$\dfrac{\frac{9}{4}}{\frac{3}{10}} = ?$

Answer: $\dfrac{15}{2}$ or $7\dfrac{1}{2}$

$$\frac{\frac{9}{4}}{\frac{3}{10}} = \left(\frac{9}{4}\right) \div \left(\frac{3}{10}\right) = \left(\frac{9}{4}\right) \times \left(\frac{10}{3}\right) = \left(\frac{3}{2}\right) \times \left(\frac{5}{1}\right)$$

$$= \frac{15}{2} = 7\frac{1}{2}$$

📎 Most importantly, fractions are the basis of a *lot* of different concepts on the SAT. Ratios, rates, and percentages all rely on fractions. You'll even see some algebra problems with fractions composed of variables. You won't be able to do those on your calculator, so you'd better know how to deal with fractions.

TRY SOME:

📎 $\dfrac{5}{4} + \dfrac{10}{3} = ?$

📎 $\dfrac{1}{3} + \dfrac{5}{6} = ?$

📎 $2\dfrac{2}{5} - \dfrac{1}{2} = ?$

📎 $\left(\dfrac{28}{15}\right)\left(\dfrac{3}{7}\right) = ?$

📎 $\dfrac{\dfrac{9}{4}}{\dfrac{3}{10}} = ?$

III. RATIOS

A ratio is just a relationship between two or more quantities. Ratios are usually expressed as fractions, but there are many ways of describing them. All of the following mean the same thing:

The ratio of boys to girls is 2:3.   The ratio of boys to girls is 2 to 3.

The ratio of boys to girls is $\frac{2}{3}$.   There are two boys for every three girls.

Take a look at this problem:

> ✎ A recipe calls for 3 cups of sugar for every 7 cups of flour. If Bill uses 28 cups of flour, how many cups of sugar should he use?

You can set this up as two fractions equal to each other, then solve the equation by cross-multiplying the terms across the equals sign.*

$$\frac{x \text{ sugar}}{28 \text{ flour}} = \frac{3 \text{ sugar}}{7 \text{ flour}}$$

$$\frac{x \text{ sugar}}{28 \text{ flour}} = \frac{3 \text{ sugar}}{7 \text{ flour}}$$

$$7x = 28 \times 3$$
$$7x = 84$$
$$\mathbf{x = 12}$$

The only tricky thing about ratios is that you must make sure your *units match*.

> ✎ A certain park contains only maple and elm trees in a ratio of 2 to 3, respectively. If there are a total of 40 trees, how many maple trees are there in the park?

You may be tempted to set up the ratio like this:

$$\times \quad \frac{x \text{ maple}}{40 \text{ total trees}} = \frac{2 \text{ maple}}{3 \text{ elm}}$$

But look: the units in the denominators don't match. The left ratio is "maple" to "total trees",

---

* Another way to solve equations like this is to look across the equals sign. Notice that 28 is *four times* 7, therefore x will be *four times* 3. Which is 12. It doesn't always work this easily, but when it does it can save you some time.

but the right ratio is "maple" to "elm". That's bad.

Luckily, we can fix the right ratio rather easily—just add. If there are 2 maple trees and 3 elm trees, then there are 5 total trees. So there are 2 maple trees for every 5 total trees.

$$\checkmark \quad \frac{x \text{ maple}}{40 \text{ total trees}} = \frac{2 \text{ maple}}{5 \text{ total trees}}$$

Now we can cross-multiply:

$$5x = 2 \times 40$$
$$5x = 80$$
$$\mathbf{x = 16}$$

Once again, circling the question will help you on ratio problems. Here, the question is "If there are a *total* of 40 trees, how many *maple* trees are there in the park?" That tells us the ratio we're looking for is "maple" to "total trees", so we should set up our fractions using those units.

To avoid mismatching units, always **write the fraction with the quantity you're looking for FIRST.** Then set up a second fraction with matching units.

Direct and Inverse Proportions

Ratios like the ones above are also called **direct proportions**. It just means that one quantity **divided** by the other always comes out to the same number, so we can set two fractions equal to each other. Saying one quantity "**varies directly**" with the other means the same thing.

Direct Proportion $\qquad x = cy \qquad\qquad \dfrac{x}{y} = c \qquad\qquad \dfrac{x_1}{y_1} = \dfrac{x_2}{y_2}$

In a direct proportion, the variables go in the **same direction**: as the value of x goes up, the value of y also goes up.* For example, consider the direct proportion $\dfrac{x}{y} = \dfrac{1}{2}$:

x	y	$x/y = 0.5$
1	2	$1 \div 2 = 0.5$
2	4	$2 \div 4 = 0.5$
3	6	$3 \div 6 = 0.5$

As x increases (1, 2, 3, …),
y also increases (2, 4, 6, …)

On the other hand, you may also encounter "inverse proportions". That means that one quantity **multiplied** by the other always comes out to the same number, so we can set two *products* equal to each other.

Inverse Proportion $\qquad xy = c \qquad\qquad x_1 y_1 = x_2 y_2$

---

* Legal disclaimer: it's actually the *absolute value* of the variables that go in the same direction. If the fraction equals to a negative constant, the values go in opposite directions. But you'll never see that on the SAT, so don't worry.

In an inverse proportion, the variables go in **opposite directions**: as the value of x goes up, the value of y goes *down*. For example, consider the inverse proportion $xy = 12$.

x	y	$xy = 12$
1	12	$1 \times 12 = 12$
2	6	$2 \times 6 = 12$
3	4	$3 \times 4 = 12$

As x increases (1, 2, 3, …),
y decreases (12, 6, 4, …)

THIS PAGE INTENTIONALLY LEFT BLANK

3. Ratios

ANSWERS:

⚓ Bob makes some fruit punch that contains apple juice and mango juice in a 1:5 ratio. If he uses 15 pints of the mango juice, how many pints of apple juice will he need?

Answer: 3

$$\frac{1 \, \text{apple}}{5 \, \text{mango}} = \frac{x \, \text{apple}}{15 \, \text{mango}}$$

$15 = 5x$
$x = 3$

⚓ An animal shelter has 2 cats for every 3 dogs. If there are 45 animals in the shelter, how many dogs are there?

Answer: 27

$$\frac{2 \, \text{cats}}{3 \, \text{dogs}} \rightarrow \frac{3 \, \text{dogs}}{5 \, \text{animals}} = \frac{x \, \text{dogs}}{45 \, \text{animals}}$$

$135 = 5x$
$x = 27$

⚓ Asif's library has 3 hardcover books for every 8 paperback books. If he has 121 books in his library, how many of them are paperbacks?

Answer: 88

$$\frac{3 \, \text{hardcover}}{8 \, \text{paperback}} \rightarrow \frac{8 \, \text{paperback}}{11 \, \text{books}} = \frac{x \, \text{paperback}}{121 \, \text{books}}$$

Cross multiply:
to keep 8/11
$968 = 11x$
over 121, so
$x = 88$

Note: It might be easier here as a fraction and multiply you can cancel out 11:

$$121 \times \left(\frac{8}{11} \right) = x$$

$11 \times 8 = x$
$88 = x$

⚓ At a certain school, the ratio of boys to girls in the seventh grade is 3 to 5. If there are 56 total seventh-graders, how many of them are girls?

Answer: 35

$$\frac{3 \, \text{boys}}{5 \, \text{girls}} \rightarrow \frac{5 \, \text{girls}}{8 \, \text{students}} = \frac{x \, \text{girls}}{56 \, \text{students}}$$

$280 = 8x$
$x = 35$

⚓ Two numbers x and y are in a direct proportion such that when $x = 2$, $y = 9$. What is the value of y when $x = 7$?

Answer: 31.5

$$\frac{x}{y} = \frac{2}{9} = \frac{7}{y}$$

$2y = 63$

$y = 31.5$

✏ **Bob makes some fruit punch that contains apple juice and mango juice in a 1:5 ratio. If he uses 15 pints of the mango juice, how many pints of apple juice will he need?**

✏ **An animal shelter has 2 cats for every 3 dogs. If there are 45 animals in the shelter, how many dogs are there?**

✏ **Asif's library has 3 hardcover books for every 8 paperback books. If he has 121 books in his library, how many of them are paperbacks?**

✏ **At a certain school, the ratio of boys to girls in the seventh grade is 3 to 5. If there are 56 total seventh-graders, how many of them are girls?**

✏ **Two numbers x and y are in a direct proportion such that when $x = 2$, $y = 9$. What is the value of y when $x = 7$?**

IV. RATES AND UNITS

One of the more common question types on the SAT involve **conversion of units**. For example:

> ✒ **How many inches are in 3 feet? (1 foot = 12 inches)**

This one is pretty easy. Most of you can probably intuitively see we just multiply 3 by 12 to get **36**.

But we could also write this as *multiplication of fractions*:

$$3 \text{ feet} \times \left(\frac{12 \text{ inches}}{1 \text{ foot}} \right) = 36 \text{ inches}$$

That may seem like unnecessary setup here, but it shows us why we multiply by 12 instead of dividing by 12. When we talked about multiplying fractions, we saw that we can cancel out common factors across the top and bottom of a fraction:

$$\frac{2}{9} \times \frac{3}{4} = \frac{\overset{1}{\cancel{2}}}{9} \times \frac{3}{\underset{2}{\cancel{4}}} = \frac{1}{\underset{3}{\cancel{9}}} \times \frac{\overset{1}{\cancel{3}}}{2} = \frac{1}{3} \times \frac{1}{2} = \frac{1}{(3 \times 2)} = \frac{1}{6}$$

Units can be cancelled out just like numbers can. The "feet" in the first number cancels out the "feet" in the denominator of the second: *

$$3 \cancel{\text{ feet}} \times \left(\frac{12 \text{ inches}}{1 \cancel{\text{ foot}}} \right) = 3 \times 12 \text{ inches} = 36 \text{ inches}$$

This becomes important when we want to do more complicated conversions:

> ✒ **How many seconds are there in 2 days?**

$$2 \text{ days} \times \left(\frac{24 \text{ hours}}{1 \text{ day}} \right) \times \left(\frac{60 \text{ minutes}}{1 \text{ hour}} \right) \times \left(\frac{60 \text{ seconds}}{1 \text{ minute}} \right) = 2 \times 24 \times 60 \times 60 \text{ seconds} = 172{,}800 \text{ seconds}$$

Set up the fractions so that the units you *don't* want get cancelled out. Do that by making sure those units appear both in the top of one fraction *and* in the bottom of another.

The same principle applies to questions about **rates**:

---

*   Remember: if a number doesn't look like a fraction, it counts as a numerator (a fraction top) because there's
an implied "÷ 1" under it. So "3 feet" in our equation here is a numerator, which cancels out with the
"1 foot" in the denominator of the fraction.

> **If Molly can bake 3 pies in 2 hours, how many pies can she make in 10 hours?**

This kind of question can be set up like a ratio, as we saw earlier:

$$\frac{3 \text{ pies}}{2 \text{ hours}} = \frac{x \text{ pies}}{10 \text{ hours}}$$

But if we take this equation and multiply both sides by 10 hours, we'll see it's the same sort of problem as a unit conversion:

$$10 \text{ hours} \times \left(\frac{3 \text{ pies}}{2 \text{ hours}}\right) = x \text{ pies} = 5 \times 3 \text{ pies} = 15 \text{ pies}$$

It's easy enough to solve this particular question by cross-multiplying the ratio. But rate questions can get more complicated:

> **Janelle is using a copy machine to make books for her class. Each book contains 120 pages, and the machine can copy 100 pages per minute. How many hours will it take her to make 300 books?**

That's a lot of rates. Here are all the rates we know:

$$\frac{1 \text{ book}}{120 \text{ pages}} \qquad \frac{100 \text{ pages}}{1 \text{ minute}} \qquad \frac{1 \text{ hour}}{60 \text{ minutes}}$$

Let's focus on the question itself:

> **How many hours will it take her to make 300 books?**

Basically we want to convert 300 books into hours. So we'll start with 300 books and we'll add on rates until we get to hours.

Do we know any rates that use "books"? Yes, 1 book has 120 pages:

$$300 \text{ books} \times \frac{120 \text{ pages}}{1 \text{ book}}$$

Don't do it out yet. Let's find all the rates first. Now the books cancel out and we're left with pages. Do we have any rates that use "pages"? Yes, 100 pages in 1 minute.

$$300 \text{ books} \times \frac{120 \text{ pages}}{1 \text{ book}} \times \frac{1 \text{ minute}}{100 \text{ pages}}$$

The pages cancel out and we're left with minutes. Now we just have to convert minutes to hours:

$$300 \; \cancel{books} \times \frac{120 \; \cancel{pages}}{1 \; \cancel{book}} \times \frac{1 \; \cancel{minute}}{100 \; \cancel{pages}} \times \frac{1 \; hour}{60 \; \cancel{minutes}}$$

We're left with hours. That's what we want! Great! Now that the units are straight, let's ignore the units and try to cancel out some common factors in the numbers:

$$300 \times \frac{120}{1} \times \frac{1}{100} \times \frac{1}{60}$$

$$3 \times \frac{120}{1} \times \frac{1}{1} \times \frac{1}{60}$$

$$3 \times \frac{2}{1} \times \frac{1}{1} \times \frac{1}{1} = 6 \; hours$$

It may tough to see how to set up that one big expression at the beginning. But we don't have to be able to see the end; we can just add on rates and keep converting until we get to the units we want.

THIS PAGE INTENTIONALLY LEFT BLANK

4. Rates and Units

ANSWERS:

✐ Mark can eat 20 hot dogs in 4 minutes. How many hot dogs can he eat in 5 hours?

Answer: 1,500

$$\left(\frac{20\text{ hot dogs}}{4\text{ minues}}\right) \times \left(\frac{60\text{ minutes}}{1\text{ hour}}\right)$$

$$= \frac{5}{1} \times \frac{60}{1} = \frac{300\text{ hot dogs}}{1\text{ hour}}$$

$$\frac{300\text{ hot dogs}}{1\text{ hour}} = \frac{x\text{ hot dogs}}{5\text{ hour}}$$

$$300 \times 5 = \mathbf{1,500}\text{ hot dogs in 5 hours}$$

✐ Elizabeth jogs for 2 hours each day. Her average jogging speed is 4 miles per hour. If she jogs 5 days a week, how far will she jog over 3 weeks?

Answer: 120

$$\left(\frac{4\text{ miles}}{1\text{ hour}}\right) \times \left(\frac{2\text{ hours}}{1\text{ day}}\right) \times \left(\frac{5\text{ days}}{1\text{ week}}\right) = \frac{40\text{ miles}}{1\text{ week}}$$

$$\frac{40\text{ miles}}{1\text{ week}} = \frac{x\text{ miles}}{3\text{ weeks}}$$

$$40 \times 3\text{ weeks} = \mathbf{120}\text{ miles in 3 weeks}$$

✐ If a car is travelling at a speed of 90 kilometers per hour, how fast is it travelling in meters per second? (1 kilometer = 1,000 meters)

Answer: 25

$$\left(\frac{90\text{ km}}{1\text{ hour}}\right) \times \left(\frac{1\text{ hour}}{60\text{ min}}\right) \times \left(\frac{1\text{ min}}{60\text{ sec}}\right) \times \left(\frac{1,000\text{ m}}{1\text{ km}}\right)$$

$$= \left(\frac{9}{1}\right) \times \left(\frac{1}{6}\right) \times \left(\frac{1}{6}\right) \times \left(\frac{100}{1}\right) = \left(\frac{3}{1}\right) \times \left(\frac{1}{2}\right) \times \left(\frac{1}{3}\right) \times \left(\frac{50}{1}\right)$$

$$= \left(\frac{1}{1}\right) \times \left(\frac{1}{2}\right) \times \left(\frac{1}{1}\right) \times \left(\frac{50}{1}\right) = \left(\frac{1}{1}\right) \times \left(\frac{1}{1}\right) \times \left(\frac{1}{1}\right) \times \left(\frac{25}{1}\right)$$

$$= \mathbf{25\text{ meters per second}}$$

✐ A town is painting parking spots along the curbs of its streets. Each spot must be 20 feet long, and each block is 300 feet long. What is the maximum number of parking spots that can fit on one side of a street that is 4 blocks long?

Answer: 60

$$\left(\frac{1\text{ spot}}{20\text{ feet}}\right) \times \left(\frac{300\text{ feet}}{1\text{ block}}\right) = \frac{15\text{ spots}}{1\text{ block}}$$

$$\frac{15\text{ spots}}{1\text{ block}} = \frac{x\text{ spots}}{4\text{ blocks}}$$

$$15 \times 4 = \mathbf{60\text{ spots}}\text{ in 4 blocks}$$

✐ Mark can eat 20 hot dogs in 4 minutes. Hot dogs are sold in packages containing 12 hot dogs, and packages cost $6 each. How much money will it cost if Mark buys enough hot dogs to eat for 3 hours continuously?

Answer: 450

$$\left(\frac{20\text{ hot dogs}}{4\text{ minues}}\right) \times \left(\frac{60\text{ minutes}}{1\text{ hour}}\right) = \frac{300\text{ hot dogs}}{1\text{ hour}}$$

$$\left(\frac{300\text{ hot dogs}}{1\text{ hour}}\right) \times \left(\frac{1\text{ package}}{12\text{ hot dogs}}\right) \times \left(\frac{\$6}{1\text{ package}}\right)$$

$$= \frac{300}{1} \times \frac{1}{12} \times \frac{6}{1} = \frac{300}{1} \times \frac{1}{2} \times \frac{1}{1} = \frac{\$150}{1\text{ hour}}$$

$$\frac{\$150}{1\text{ hour}} = \frac{x}{3\text{ hours}}$$

$$3 \times 150 = \mathbf{\$450}\text{ for 3 hours.}$$

✎ Mark can eat 20 hot dogs in 4 minutes. How many hot dogs can he eat in 5 hours?

✎ Elizabeth jogs for 2 hours each day. Her average jogging speed is 4 miles per hour. If she jogs 5 days a week, how far will she jog over 3 weeks?

✎ If a car is travelling at a speed of 90 kilometers per hour, how fast is it travelling in meters per second? (1 kilometer = 1,000 meters)

✎ A town is painting parking spots along the curbs of its streets. Each spot must be 20 feet long, and each block is 300 feet long. What is the maximum number of parking spots that can fit on one side of a street that is 4 blocks long?

✎ Mark can eat 20 hot dogs in 4 minutes. Hot dogs are sold in packages containing 12 hot dogs, and packages cost $6 each. How much money will it cost if Mark buys enough hot dogs to eat for 3 hours continuously?

V. PERCENTS

By now, we should all at least be familiar with percents. The simplest way to do percents is by pure division.

> 🖊 **8 is what percent of 32?**

All you do is divide, then multiply by 100:

$$\frac{8}{32} = 0.25 \qquad 0.25 \times 100 = 25\%$$

Do you want to know a secret? Percents are really nothing more than glorified ratios. Percent literally means "out of one hundred". So you're just converting a ratio into another ratio out of 100. This problem is the same thing as cross-multiplying:

$$\frac{8}{32} = \frac{x}{100}$$

"8 out of 32" is the same thing as "25 out of 100", or 25 "percent".

Of course, percent problems on the SAT can get more complicated than that. We've devised the following table for percent problems:

Read	Write
what	n
is	$=$
percent	$\overline{100}$
of	$\times$ (multiply)

Whenever you see one of the words in the left column, write the corresponding symbol in the right column. If you see a number, just write the number. For example:

> 🖊 **12 is 40% of what number?**

becomes $12 = \dfrac{40}{100} \times n$

You know, a lot of students freak out about word problems. But really, the language we use to describe problems is exactly the same stuff as all the signs and symbols we use in equations. So as long as you can speak English, you can write equations; the words mean exactly what you think they mean.

The advantage of using the table is that it makes percent problems automatic and robotic. You can go directly from words to an equation without thinking about anything.

There are other similar ways of doing percent problems (some of you may know the "is-over-of" method), but this table is particularly effective on harder SAT problems. Take a look at this problem:

> **If 25 percent of 12 percent of _s_ is 18, _s_ = ?**

This can be really nasty with other ways of doing percents. But with the table, we don't care. Do it robotically; when you see a word, write its symbol. So this question becomes:

$$\frac{25}{100} \times \frac{12}{100} \times s = 18$$

Now we have a one-variable equation and we can solve for _s_. We didn't have to think about a thing. The equation came almost instantly.

Here's another toughie:

> **If _x_ is $\frac{1}{2}$ percent of 600, _x_ = ?**

Oh, well half of 600 is 300. Right?

WRONG! It doesn't say _x_ is <u>half</u> of 600; it says _x_ is <u>one-half percent</u> of 600. That is, half of one percent. RTFQ!

With the table, we don't make this mistake because we just write what we see:

$$x = \frac{\frac{1}{2}}{100} \times 600$$

Because we aren't *thinking* about the problem—we're just automatically writing down what we read—we're much less likely to make the RTFQ.

Percent Increase and Decrease

A percent increase or decrease just means:

> ### The amount of the *change* is what percent of the original amount?

Or:

$$\text{Percent Change} = \frac{\text{Change}}{\text{Original}} \times 100$$

> ✒ Joe made 150 dollars last week and 180 dollars this week. What was the percent increase in his pay?

In this problem, the amount of the change is **30** (that's 180 – 150) and the original amount is **150**. So the question is "30 is what percent of 150?" Now we can just use the table to set up an equation:

$$30 = \frac{n}{100} \times 150$$

You can also think of percent change as just the *change* divided by the *original*.

$$\frac{30}{150} = \frac{1}{5} = 0.2 = \frac{20}{100} = 20\%$$

There are several different ways of expressing a percent increase. In this problem, we're saying Joe received 20% *more than* the past week. But for some problems, it may be useful to write a percent increase in a decimal expression in terms of the original.

Here, there's a 20% increase over the original, which we see can also be written as the decimal 0.2. That 20% was added to the original amount, so the new price is 120% *of* the original, or 1.2 times the original. In this form, instead of using the change, we're saying:

> ### The *new amount* is what percent of the original amount.

$$180 = \frac{n}{100} \times 150 \qquad \text{or} \qquad \frac{180}{150} = \frac{6}{5} = 1.2 = \frac{120}{100} \qquad \text{or} \qquad \textbf{120\%}$$

THIS PAGE INTENTIONALLY LEFT BLANK

5. Percentages

ANSWERS:

✐ What is 42% of 50?

Answer: 21.

$$n = \frac{42}{100} \times 50$$

$$n = \frac{42}{2}$$

$$n = 21$$

✐ 5 is what percent of 4?

Answer: 125.

$$5 = \frac{n}{100} \times 4$$

$$5 = \frac{n}{25}$$

$$125 = n$$

✐ 21 is 35% of what number?

Answer: 60.

$$21 = \frac{35}{100} \times n$$

$$\left(\frac{100}{35}\right) 21 = n$$

$$60 = n$$

✐ What is 15% of 75% of 80?

Answer: 9.

$$n = \frac{15}{100} \times \frac{75}{100} \times 80$$

$$n = \frac{3}{20} \times \frac{3}{4} \times 80$$

$$n = \frac{3}{1} \times \frac{3}{4} \times 4$$

$$n = 3 \times 3 = 9$$

✐ A school had 30 reported absences one week and 27 reported absences the following week. What was the percent decrease in the number of absences between the two weeks?

Answer: 10.

Change = 3. Original = 30.

$$3 = \frac{n}{100} \times 30$$

$$n = 10$$

✒ **What is 42% of 50?**

✒ **5 is what percent of 4?**

✒ **21 is 35% of what number?**

✒ **What is 15% of 75% of 80?**

✒ **A school had 30 reported absences one week
and 27 reported absences the following
week. What was the percent decrease in the
number of absences between the two weeks?**

VI. EXPONENTS

1. Properties

Exponents tell you how many times to multiply a number or term by itself. The number that is being multiplied is called the "base". Giving a number an exponent is also called taking it to that "power".

$$base \rightarrow 4^2 \leftarrow exponent$$

Here are a few definitions and properties of exponents to remember:

- An exponent tells you how many times to multiply a number by itself.

$$5^2 = 5 \times 5 \qquad\qquad h^4 = h \times h \times h \times h$$

- A **negative base** taken to an *even* exponent will become *positive*.
  A negative base taken to an *odd* exponent will stay *negative*.

$$(-2)^2 = (-2) \times (-2) = 4 \qquad\qquad (-2)^3 = (-2) \times (-2) \times (-2) = -8$$

- When taking a positive **fraction** to a power, the result is *smaller* than the original number.

$$\left(\frac{1}{2}\right)^2 = \frac{1}{4} \qquad\qquad \frac{1}{2} > \frac{1}{4}$$

- A **negative exponent** is the same as the reciprocal of the base with a positive exponent (that is, 1 divided by the number with a positive exponent).

$$x^{-3} = \frac{1}{x^3} \qquad\qquad \frac{1}{x^{-3}} = x^3$$

- Any number to the **zero power** equals one.

$$x^0 = 1$$

- A **root** is the inverse (the opposite) of its corresponding power. A square root is the inverse of a square, a cube root is the inverse of a cube, the fourth root is the inverse of the fourth power, etc. That means that doing both at the same time will cancel them out.

$$\sqrt{x} \times \sqrt{x} = x \qquad \sqrt{x^2} = x \qquad \sqrt[3]{x^3} = x \qquad \sqrt[4]{x^4} = x$$

- A **fractional exponent** is the same as a root.

$$x^{\frac{1}{2}} = \sqrt{x} \qquad x^{\frac{1}{3}} = \sqrt[3]{x} \qquad x^{\frac{1}{n}} = \sqrt[n]{x} \qquad x^{\frac{2}{3}} = \sqrt[3]{x^2}$$

A word about parentheses

On exponent problems, it's especially important to pay attention to what's inside and outside the parentheses.

> **If an exponent is next to parentheses, it applies to the *entire* expression *inside* the parentheses.**
>
> **If there are no parentheses, the exponent applies *only* to the number or variable *right next to it*.**

ab^2: Only b is squared, not a. $\qquad$ $-2x^2$: Only x is squared.

$(ab)^2$: Both a and b are squared. $\qquad$ $-(2x)^2$: $2x$ is squared. This equals $-4x^2$.

$\qquad\qquad\qquad\qquad\qquad\qquad\qquad$ $(-2x)^2$: -2 and x are both squared. This equals $4x^2$.

2. Combining exponents

There are a few rules for dealing with exponential numbers that you should know:

1. **To multiply exponential numbers with the same base, add the exponents.**

$$2^5 \times 2^3 = 2^{5+3} = 2^8$$

2. **To divide exponential numbers with the same base, subtract the exponents.**

$$\frac{2^5}{2^3} = 2^{5-3} = 2^2$$

3. **To raise an exponential number to another exponent, multiply the exponents.**

$$(2^5)^3 = 2^{5 \times 3} = 2^{15}$$

Note that for these rules, the base does not change.

WARNING: You can add variables with the same exponent, but you **cannot** add bases with different exponents:

$\qquad$ OK: $2x^2 + 7x^2 = 9x^2$ $\qquad\qquad$ NOT OK: $2^5 + 2^3 \neq 2^8$

WARNING: All these rules only apply to exponential numbers *with the same base*. If you're given exponential numbers in different bases, try to get them in the same base.

Variables in exponents, Different bases

If an equation has variables in its exponents, you can usually set the exponents equal to each other.

> ✏ If $2^{a+10} = 2^{3a}$, then $a = ?$

Both sides of the equation have the same base, so we can just set the exponents equal to each other:

$$a + 10 = 3a \qquad\qquad 10 = 2a \qquad\qquad \mathbf{5 = a}$$

If we're given numbers that don't have the same base, we should try to put them in the same base:

> ✏ If $3^x = 9^5$, then $x = ?$

We can't just set x equal to 5 because one base is 3 and the other is 9. But look: 9 is a power of 3. If we rewrite 9 as 3^2, we'll have the same base on both sides.

$$3^x = \left(3^2\right)^5 = 3^{10} \qquad\qquad \mathbf{x = 10}$$

THIS PAGE INTENTIONALLY LEFT BLANK

6. Exponents

ANSWERS:

🖋 $a^5\left(a^3\right)^2 = ?$

Answer: a^{11}.

$$a^5\left(a^{3\times2}\right) = a^5\left(a^6\right) = a^{5+6} = \boldsymbol{a^{11}}$$

🖋 $\left(3^2\right)^{\frac{1}{2}} = ?$

Answer: 3

$= \sqrt{3^2} = \sqrt{9} = \boldsymbol{3}$.

Remember: a fractional exponent is the same as a root.

🖋 $\dfrac{x^4x^3}{x^5} = ?$

Answer: x^2

$= \dfrac{x^{4+3}}{x^5} \quad = \dfrac{x^7}{x^5} \quad = x^{7-5} \quad = \boldsymbol{x^2}$

🖋 $2x^2 - (3x)^2 = ?$

Answer: $-7x^2$

$= 2x^2 - (3)^2x^2$
$= 2x^2 - 9\,x^2$
$= \boldsymbol{-7x^2}$

🖋 $9^{-\left(\frac{1}{2}\right)} = ?$

Answer: $\dfrac{1}{3}$

$$\dfrac{1}{9^{\frac{1}{2}}} = \dfrac{1}{\sqrt{9}} = \boldsymbol{\dfrac{1}{3}}$$

🖋 $\left(-2x^2\right)^3 = ?$

Answer: $-8x^6$:

$= (-2)^3\left(x^2\right)^3 = \boldsymbol{-8x^6}$

🖋 If $8^{13} = 2^x$, then $x = ?$

Answer: 39

Put both sides in the same base: $8 = 2^3$

$8^{13} = 2^x$

$\left(2^3\right)^{13} = 2^x$

$2^{39} = 2^x$

$\boldsymbol{39 = x}$

🖋 $5y^2 \times 2x^4y \times 3x^3y^2 = ?$

Answer: $30x^7y^5$

Let's re-order it to put similar terms next to each other.

$= \left(5 \times 2 \times 3\right)\left(x^4 \times x^3\right)\left(y^2 \times y \times y^2\right)$ Add exponents as necessary

$= \boldsymbol{30x^7y^5}$

🖋 $\left(a^3b^4c^{10}\right)\left(a^8b^{-1}c^2\right)^3 = ?$

Answer: $a^{27}bc^{16}$

First, multiply exponents inside the parentheses by "3".

$= \left(a^3b^4c^{10}\right)\left(a^{8\cdot3}b^{-1\cdot3}c^{2\cdot3}\right)$

$= \left(a^3b^4c^{10}\right)\left(a^{24}b^{-3}c^6\right)$

Now, combine numbers with the same base by *adding* exponents.

$= a^{3+24}b^{4-3}c^{10+6}$

$= \boldsymbol{a^{27}bc^{16}}$

🖋 For all nonzero x and y, $\dfrac{\left(5xy^3\right)\left(-2x^3y\right)}{x^2y^{-2}} = ?$

Answer: $-10x^2y^6$

$$\dfrac{\left(5xy^3\right)\left(-2x^3y\right)}{x^2y^{-2}}$$

$= \dfrac{5(-2)x^{1+3}y^{3+1}}{x^2y^{-2}} = \dfrac{-10x^4y^4}{x^2y^{-2}}$

$= -10x^{4-2}y^{4-(-2)} = \boldsymbol{-10x^2y^6}$

TRY SOME:

☛ $a^5\left(a^3\right)^2 = ?$

☛ $\left(3^2\right)^{\frac{1}{2}} = ?$

☛ $\dfrac{x^4 x^3}{x^5} = ?$

☛ $2x^2 - (3x)^2 = ?$

☛ $9^{-\left(\frac{1}{2}\right)} = ?$

☛ $\left(-2x^2\right)^3 = ?$

☛ If $8^{13} = 2^x$, then $x = ?$

☛ $5y^2 \times 2x^4y \times 3x^2y^2 = ?$

☛ $\left(a^3 b^4 c^{10}\right)\left(a^8 b^{-1} c^2\right)^3 = ?$

☛ For all nonzero x and y, $\dfrac{\left(5xy^3\right)\left(-2x^3 y\right)}{x^2 y^{-2}} = ?$

© A-List Education

SAT Math | Math Fundamentals 301

VII. ABSOLUTE VALUE

The **absolute value** of a number is its numerical value without its sign. That means that *negative numbers become positive and positive numbers stay positive.*

$$|5| = 5 \qquad |-5| = 5$$

When you want to compute expressions with absolute value, do whatever is inside the lines first, then strip away any negatives between the lines: Let's look at an example:

> ✐ $|10 - 8| - |5 - 11|$

$|10 - 8| - |5 - 11|$	First, do the stuff inside the lines.
$= |2| - |-6|$	Now, strip away the negatives inside the lines, so -6 becomes 6.
$= 2 - 6 \quad \boxed{= -4}$	

Solving for a variable

Take a look at this:

> ✐ $|x| = 7$

The variable x is inside the absolute value lines, and its absolute value is 7. There are two possible solutions:

- ✐ Ether $x = 7$ and the absolute value keeps it positive 7,
- ✐ or $x = -7$ and the absolute value strips its negative to make it positive 7.

The key to absolute value problems is: ***DON'T FORGET ABOUT THE NEGATIVES.***

> ✐ If $|n - 12| = 7$, what is one possible value of n?

If $|n - 12| = 7$, then we have two options:

$$n - 12 = 7 \qquad \text{or} \qquad n - 12 = -7$$
$$\boxed{n = 19} \qquad\qquad\qquad \boxed{n = 5}$$

It's sometimes helpful to think of absolute value as **distance**: *The absolute value of a difference* *gives the distance between the two points.* That is:

$$|\text{Point A} - \text{Point B}| = \text{distance between points}$$

A simple subtraction will always tell us the distance. If we want to find the distance between 19 and 12, we'd subtract $19 - 12$. But if we want the distance between 5 and 12, subtracting $5 - 12$ gives us -7, and we generally don't like to use negative distances. The nice thing about the absolute value is that it gives us the distance *in either direction*.

In the problem above, the expression "$|n - 12| = 7$" means "point n is a distance of 7 away from 12". That is, n is either 7 more than 12 or 7 less than 12.

So any time you have a problem that asks you for a range like this, just remember this expression:

$$|\text{variable} - \text{midpoint}| < \text{half the total range}$$

TRY SOME:

✏ $|8 - 2| = ?$

✏ $|2 - 8| = ?$

✏ $|6 - 15| - |5(-4)| = ?$

✏ If $|x - 2| = 6$, what are all possible values of x?

✏ If $|x + 11| = 23$, what are all possible values of x?

7. Absolute Value

ANSWERS:

$|8 - 2| = ?$

Answer: 6

$$|8 - 2|$$
$$= |6| = 6$$

$|2 - 8| = ?$

Answer: 6

$$|2 - 8|$$
$$= |-6| = 6$$

$|6 - 15| - |5(-4)| = ?$

Answer: −11

$$|-9| - |-20|$$
$$= 9 - 20$$
$$= -11$$

If $|x - 2| = 6$, what are all possible values of x?

Answer: 8 or −4

$x - 2 = 6$	or	$x - 2 = -6$
$x = 8$	or	$x = -4$

If $|x + 11| = 23$, what are all possible values of x?

Answer: 12 or −34

$x + 11 = 23$	or	$x + 11 = -23$
$x = 12$	or	$x = -34$

Math Fundamentals Exercise

1. **Answer: A.**
Don't multiply it out. Cross out everything!

2. **Answer: D.**

$$\frac{3\,\text{defective}}{200\,\text{phones}} = \frac{x\,\text{defective}}{50{,}000\,\text{phones}}$$

$$3 \times 50{,}000 = 200x$$
$$150{,}000 = 200x$$
$$\mathbf{750 = x}$$

Backsolve works too, if you're using a calculator.
Punch out $3 \div 200 = 0.015$. That's the defective rate.
Take the answer choices and divide by 50,000 to see which also comes out to 0.015.

C) $500 \div 50{,}000 = 0.01$ ✗
D) $750 \div 50{,}000 = 0.015$ ✓ **Choice D) works.**

3. **Answer: D.**
Tricky for a #3, but let's try some *Plug In*.
This will be a bit of a *Plug-In/Backsolve combo*.
We'll go through the choices and try variables that satisfy each rule to see which ones work and which don't. We want a choice that <u>must</u> be true, so if we find a case where a choice isn't true, we can eliminate it.

A) $a \le -1$. So say $a = -2$.
$|-2 - 1| + 1 = |-3| + 1 = 3 + 1 = 4 = b$. That worked.

What does that mean? Now we know that a is allowed to be less than -1. That means it doesn't have to be bigger than 1, so we can eliminate B).
We also saw that b could be 4, so b doesn't have to be less than -1. So we can eliminate C). We're down to A) or D).

Well, we said a didn't *have* to be greater than 1. But *could* it be? Let's try it! Say $a = 2$.
$|2 - 1| + 1 = |1| + 1 = 1 + 1 = 2 = b$. That worked, too.

That means a could be greater than 1. That means a doesn't have to be less than -1. So we can eliminate A). **Choice D) must be our answer.**
Indeed, we saw that again we got a b that was greater than 1.

Why? It has to do with absolute value. We know that the absolute value expression $|a - 1|$ *must* come out to a positive number or zero. That means b will be a positive number plus 1, or zero plus 1. The lowest possible value of b would be if the absolute value came out to zero, then $b = 1$.

Algebraically:
$|a - 1| \ge 0$	Because it's an absolute value.
	Let's solve the equation for this expression.
$|a - 1| = b - 1$	Now substitute $b - 1$ into the inequality. .
$b - 1 \ge 0$	Just add 1 to both sides.
$b \ge 1$	

That was a little rough. Maybe we should just plug in.

4. **Answer: C.**
4 feet = 48 inches. $48 \div 5 = 9$ Remainder 3.
That means that we can get *nine* 5-inch strips from a 48-inch ribbon, with **3 inches left over**.

If you're not comfortable with remainders, Backsolve works too:

C) **3 inches remainder.** $48 - 3 = 45$ inches are used for strips. ✓
45 is divisible by 5, so this choice works.

5. **Answer: A.**
When you have variables in an exponent, get both sides of the equation in the same base.
$$5^{2x+1} = 125$$
$$5^{2x+1} = 5^3$$
$$2x + 1 = 3 \quad x = 1$$

6. **Answer: C.**

$$5\,\text{km} \times \left(\frac{1{,}000\,\text{m}}{1\,\text{km}}\right) \times \left(\frac{1{,}000\,\text{mm}}{1\,\text{m}}\right) = 5{,}000{,}000\,\text{mm}.$$

But which answer choice means 5 million?

The simplest way to convert to scientific notation is to count the decimal places. With our number, that's easy, because we can just count the zeroes.

There are 6 zeroes in 5,000,000. So we want 10 to the *sixth* power. Our number is equal to $\mathbf{5 \times 10^6}$

MATH FUNDAMENTALS EXERCISE

1

What is the value of $\dfrac{1}{2} \times \dfrac{2}{3} \times \dfrac{3}{4} \times \dfrac{4}{5}$?

A) $\dfrac{1}{5}$

B) $\dfrac{5}{6}$

C) $\dfrac{4}{5}$

D) 1

2

A technology company determined that an average of 3 phones were defective for every 200 phones it produced. At this rate, about how many phones were defective if the company produced 50,000 phones?

A) 250
B) 300
C) 500
D) 750

3

If $|a-1| + 1 = b$, which of the following must be true?

A) $a \leq -1$
B) $a \geq 1$
C) $b \leq -1$
D) $b \geq 1$

4

If as many 5-inch strips of ribbon as possible are cut from a ribbon that is 4 feet long, what is the total length of the ribbon that is left over? (12 inches = 1 foot)

A) 1 inch
B) 2 inches
C) 3 inches
D) 4 inches

5

If $5^{2x+1} = 125$, what is the value of x?

A) 1
B) 2
C) 3
D) 4

6

There are 1,000 meters in a kilometer and 1,000 millimeters in a meter. How many millimeters are there in 5 kilometers?

A) 5×10^3
B) 5×10^4
C) 5×10^6
D) 5×10^8

CONTINUE

7

If a is directly proportional to b and if $a = 30$ when $b = 21$, what is the value of a when $b = 10\frac{1}{2}$?

A) $\dfrac{20}{3}$

B) 10

C) 15

D) 30

8

Larissa takes a dose of 4 drops of medicine every day, three times a day. One milliliter (mL) of the medicine contains about 20 drops. If the medicine comes in a 12 mL bottle, approximately how many days will the bottle last?

A) 1
B) 5
C) 12
D) 20

9

What number is 175 percent of 16?

A) 12
B) 24
C) 28
D) 32

10

An arrow shot from a bow travels at an average speed of 180 miles per hour. Of the following, which is the closest to its average speed in feet per second? (1 mile = 5,280 feet).

A) 125
B) 250
C) 2,500
D) 15,000

11

$\left(\sqrt[3]{2x}\right)^6$ is equivalent to:

A) $2x^2$
B) $4x^2$
C) $6x^6$
D) $8x^3$

12

Loretta had 60 roses and 80 daffodils. If she sold 40% of her roses and 75% of her daffodils, what percent of her flowers remain?

A) 40%
B) 56%
C) 60%
D) 80%

CONTINUE

7. Answer: C.

"Direct proportion" just means ratio:

$$\frac{a}{10.5} = \frac{30}{21}$$

$$21a = 315$$

$$\boldsymbol{a = 15}$$

Notice also that 10.5 is half of 21, so a will be half of 30. That's 15.

8. Answer: D.

There's a lot going on here, so let's think a bit about how we want to set this up before we start.

Wait, no. Let's not do that. Let's just **Backsolve.** We'll figure it out as we go.

C) 12 days.

Okay. What do we know about days?

She takes the medicine 3 times a day. So how many doses in 12 days?

$12 \times 3 = 36$ doses.

Each dose is 4 drops. So how many drops in 36 doses?

$36 \times 4 = 144$ drops.

There are 20 drops in 1 mL. So how many mL are 144 drops?

$144 \div 20 = 7.2$ mL ✗ That doesn't work.

The question asks how many drops are in a 12 mL bottle. 12 days only uses up 7.2 mL. That's too small.

D) 20 days.

3 doses a day $20 \times 3 = 60$ doses.

4 drops per dose $60 \times 4 = 240$ drops

20 drops in 1 mL $240 \div 20 = 12$ ✓ It worked!

Here's the unit conversion:

$$\left(\frac{1\,\text{day}}{3\,\text{doses}}\right) \times \left(\frac{1\,\text{dose}}{4\,\text{drops}}\right) \times \left(\frac{20\,\text{drops}}{1\,\text{mL}}\right) \times \left(\frac{12\,\text{mL}}{1\,\text{bottle}}\right)$$

$$= \left(\frac{1}{3}\right) \times \left(\frac{1}{4}\right) \times \left(\frac{20}{1}\right) \times \left(\frac{12\,\text{mL}}{1}\right)$$

Once you get here, you can see that the 12 on top will cancel out with the 3 and 4 on the bottom, so we'll just be left with **20 days per bottle**

9. Answer: C.

$$n = \frac{175}{100} \times 16$$

$$n = \frac{7}{4} \times 16$$

$$n = 7 \times 4$$

$$\boldsymbol{n = 28}$$

10. Answer: B.

Aha, my favorite word: "closest"! That means we can *approximate*.

First, we'll set it up:

$$\left(\frac{180\,\text{mi}}{1\,\text{hour}}\right) \times \left(\frac{1\,\text{hour}}{60\,\text{min}}\right) \times \left(\frac{1\,\text{min}}{60\,\text{sec}}\right) \times \left(\frac{5,280\,\text{ft}}{1\,\text{mi}}\right)$$

But instead of that big number, let's just use 5,000.

$$\left(\frac{180\,\text{mi}}{1\,\text{hour}}\right) \times \left(\frac{1\,\text{hour}}{60\,\text{min}}\right) \times \left(\frac{1\,\text{min}}{60\,\text{sec}}\right) \times \left(\frac{5,000\,\text{ft}}{1\,\text{mi}}\right)$$

$$= \left(\frac{3}{1}\right) \times \left(\frac{1}{1}\right) \times \left(\frac{1}{60\,\text{sec}}\right) \times \left(\frac{5,000\,\text{ft}}{1}\right)$$

$$= \left(\frac{1}{1}\right) \times \left(\frac{1}{1}\right) \times \left(\frac{1}{20\,\text{sec}}\right) \times \left(\frac{5,000\,\text{ft}}{1}\right)$$

$$= \left(\frac{1}{1}\right) \times \left(\frac{1}{1}\right) \times \left(\frac{1}{2\,\text{sec}}\right) \times \left(\frac{500\,\text{ft}}{1}\right)$$

$$= \left(\frac{1}{1}\right) \times \left(\frac{1}{1}\right) \times \left(\frac{1}{1\,\text{sec}}\right) \times \left(\frac{250\,\text{ft}}{1}\right)$$ So it's going **about 250 ft/sec.**

11. Answer: B.

Remember that a root is the same thing as a fractional exponent. The third root is the one-third power:

$$\left(\sqrt[3]{2x}\right)^6 = \left((2x)^{\frac{1}{3}}\right)^6$$ Now multiply the exponents.

$$= (2x)^{\frac{1}{3} \times 6} = (2x)^2 = \boldsymbol{4x^2}$$

Or, use **Plug In.** Choose $x = 4$.

$$\left(\sqrt[3]{2(4)}\right)^6 = \left(\sqrt[3]{8}\right)^6 = 2^6 = \boldsymbol{64}$$

A)	$2(4)^2$	$= 2(16)$	$= 32$ ✗
B)	$4(4)^2$	$= 4(16)$	$= \boldsymbol{64}$ ✓
C)	$6(4)^6$	$= 6(4096)$	$= 24{,}576$ ✗
D)	$8(4)^3$	$= 8(64)$	$= 512$ ✗

Now, we cheated a little by choosing $x = 4$, because that gave us a perfect cube under the radical. But what if we didn't have that foresight? If you have a calculator that has a cube root function, Plug In will still work with *any number*. You'll just have to deal with some ugly decimals.

For example, try $\boldsymbol{x = 3}$.

$$\left(\sqrt[3]{2(3)}\right)^6 = \left(\sqrt[3]{6}\right)^6 = (1.817\ldots)^6 = \boldsymbol{36}.$$

(As always, you may have to approximate when using decimals.)

B) $4(3)^2 = \boldsymbol{36}.$

12. Answer: A.

$60 + 80 = 140$ total flowers

$60 \times (0.40) = 24$ Roses sold
$80 \times (0.75) = \underline{60}$ Daffodils sold
                              84 flowers sold

$60 - 24\quad = \boldsymbol{36}$ Roses unsold
$80 - 60\quad = \underline{\boldsymbol{20}}$ Daffodils unsold
                       $= \boldsymbol{56}$ flowers unsold

$$\frac{56}{140} \times 100 = \boldsymbol{40\ \%}$$

B) is RTFQ: That's the *number* of flowers left; we want the *percentage*.

C) is RTFQ: That's the percentage *sold*. Subtract from 100 to get the percentage unsold.

13. Answer: A.
Backsolve!

B) 30 new red hats.

He's getting 100 total new hats, so he's getting 70 new blue hats. Lets' add those hats to the current ratio and see if it comes out to 1:2.

$$\frac{80 \text{ red}}{120 \text{ blue}} \rightarrow \frac{80+30}{120+70} = \frac{110}{190} = \frac{11}{19} \text{ ✗ That doesn't match.}$$

It may not be obvious wheter we want a bigger or smaller number, so just pick one.

A) **20 new red hats.**

$100 - 20 = 80$ new blue hats.

$$\frac{80+20}{120+80} = \frac{100}{200} = \frac{1}{2} \checkmark \text{ It works!}$$

Algebra:
Let r = his *new* red hats and b = his *new* blue hats.
$r + b = 100$ therefore $b = 100 - r$

After he buys hats, his total red will be $80 + r$ and his total blue will be $120 + b$.

$$\frac{80+r}{120+b} = \frac{1}{2} \qquad \text{Substitute } b = 100 - r$$

$$\frac{80+r}{120+(100-r)} = \frac{1}{2}$$

$$\frac{80+r}{220-r} = \frac{1}{2}$$

$2(80 + r) = 220 - r$
$160 + 2r = 220 - r$
$160 + 3r = 220$
$3r = 60$
$r = 20$

14. Answer: C.

Three-part ratios can be confusing, but they work exactly the same way as the two-part ratios we're used to. Focus on what they're *asking* for. The question asks:

"How many pounds of <u>red candy</u> will be found in a <u>4-pound bag</u>?"

So the ratio we want is **red: total**.

We're told the bag is 7:3:2 ratio of blue:red:brown.
$7 + 3 + 2 = 12$ total pounds, 3 of which are red. So:

$$\frac{x \text{ red}}{4 \text{ total}} = \frac{3 \text{ red}}{12 \text{ total}}$$

$12x = 12$
$x = 1$

15. Answer: C.
Plug In.

As we've done before, let's plug in $c = 100$. That'll be August's price.

August:	100	Decrease 100 by 20%
September:	80	Increase 80 by 40%
		$0.40 \times 80 = 32$
		$80 + 32 = 112$
October:	112	

112 is what percent of 100? **112%.**

Note that "increasing by 40%" is the same thing as taking 140% of 80. So $1.40 \times 80 = 112$.

Alan has 80 red hats and 120 blue hats. If he plans to buy 100 more hats, how many of these must be red hats so that the ratio of red hats to blue hats is 1 to 2?

A) 20
B) 30
C) 70
D) 80

A certain car cost c dollars in August. In September, the price was cut by 20 percent. In October, the price increased by 40 percent of the previous month's price. The price of the car at the end of October was what percent of the price in August?

A) 48%
B) 80%
C) 112%
D) 120%

A multi-colored candy is sold in a ratio of 7:3:2 of blue, red, and brown candies, respectively. How many pounds of red candies will be found in a 4-pound bag of this multi-colored candy?

A) $\dfrac{1}{2}$

B) $\dfrac{2}{3}$

C) 1

D) 2

STOP

■ Heart of Algebra

This chapter discusses the basics of what we generally call *algebra*: solving equations, substituting values, and all sorts of other fun stuff like that. Of course, in the real world there's a lot more to algebra than what's in this chapter. We'll see some more complicated problems in the next chapter. But a good grounding in the basics of algebra is necessary to move on to the nimbler bits.

I. TECHNIQUES!

While this chapter will show you how to solve various types of algebra problems, don't forget the Math Techniques! Plug In and Backsolve were created to help you *avoid* algebra. **Over half of the Heart of Algebra problems can be done with techniques**, more than any other question type. So they should always be in your mind, and your heart.

Obviously, problems that are swimming in variables are good candidates for both techniques. If a question has variables in the choices, it doesn't matter what their values are, so we can use Plug In. If a question asks you for the value of a variable, you can use Backsolve and test the choices for that variable.

You will still need to learn some algebra; the techniques won't work on every question, and on some problems techniques are possible but algebra is faster. In this chapter we're going to emphasize algebraic solutions over technique solutions. But don't forget that the techniques are here to help you.

II. EVALUATING AN EXPRESSION

When we talk about "algebra", we generally mean problems that involve *variables*—letters that can stand for an unknown value.* The simplest algebra problems on the SAT will give you an expression containing a variable and ask you to evaluate the expression when the variable has a certain value. Observe:

> ✒ **What is the value of the expression $\dfrac{10x - 4}{x - 1}$ when $x = 7$?**

We know that the value of x is 7, so we can replace every x in the expression with a 7 and solve:

$$\frac{10(7) - 4}{7 - 1} \qquad = \frac{70 - 4}{6} \qquad = \frac{66}{6} \qquad \boxed{=11}$$

Problems like this may involve more than one variable:

> ✒ **If $a = 3$, $b = -4$, and $c = 8$, what is the value of $ac - ab$?**

Substitute the values for the corresponding letters. Just be careful to put the numbers in the right spots:

$$ac - ab = \ (3)(8) - (3)(-4) \qquad = 24 - (-12) \qquad = 24 + 12 \qquad = \mathbf{36}$$

Sometime these questions may seem complicated:

> ✒ **What is the volume of a right circular cone whose base has a radius of 3 and whose height is 10?**

Wait a minute—why are we looking at a geometry problem in the algebra chapter? Because all the problem asks you to do is substitute values into a given expression. Don't worry about what a cone is; just stick the numbers in for the letters in the formula:

$$V = \frac{1}{3}\pi r^2 h \qquad V = \frac{1}{3}\pi(3)^2(10) \quad = \quad \frac{1}{3}\pi(9)(10) \quad = \quad \frac{1}{3}\pi(90) \quad \boxed{= 30\pi}$$

---

* It is sometimes said that algebra was invented by Arabic mathematicians, but that's not true. The *word* "algebra" does come from the Arabic word *al-jabr*, meaning "the completion" or "bone-setting" (yes, bone-setting). But algebraic problems date as far back as ancient Babylonia, over 3,500 years ago, and algebra involving symbols and letters began in 17th century Europe.

THIS PAGE INTENTIONALLY LEFT BLANK

Evaluating an expression

ANSWERS:

🖎 If $x = 5$ and $y = 4$, what is the value of $3x - 4y$?

Answer: –1.

$3(5) - 4(4) = 15 - 16 = -1$

🖎 If $x = 3$ and $k = 12$, what is the value of $x^2 + kx + 6$?

Answer: 51.

$3^2 + 12 \times 3 + 6 = 9 + 36 + 6 = \mathbf{51}$

🖎 If $a = \dfrac{3b + 4c}{2}$ what is the value of a when $b = 6$ and $c = 10$?

Answer: 29.

$a = \dfrac{3(6) + 4(10)}{2} = \dfrac{18 + 40}{2} = \dfrac{58}{2}$

$a = \mathbf{29}$

🖎 If $j = 6km - n$, what is the value of j when $k = 100$, $m = 2$ and $n = -10$

Answer: 1,210.

$j = 6(100)(2) - (-10)$
$j = 1200 + 10$
$j = \mathbf{1210}$

🖎 What is the value of $\dfrac{8x - 9}{x}$ when $x = \dfrac{1}{2}$?

Answer: –10.

$\dfrac{8\left(\frac{1}{2}\right) - 9}{\frac{1}{2}} = (4 - 9) \div \left(\dfrac{1}{2}\right) = (-5) \times 2 = \mathbf{-10}$

If you're not comfortable manipulating fractions, you can use 0.5 instead and use your calculator:

$\dfrac{8(0.5) - 9}{0.5} = \dfrac{-5}{0.5} = \mathbf{-10}$

✏ If $x = 5$ and $y = 4$, what is the value of $3x - 4y$?

✏ If $x = 3$ and $k = 12$, what is the value of $x^2 + kx + 6$?

✏ If $a = \dfrac{3b + 4c}{2}$, what is the value of a when $b = 6$ and $c = 10$?

✏ If $j = 6km - n$, what is the value of j when $k = 100$, $m = 2$ and $n = -10$?

✏ What is the value of $\dfrac{8x - 9}{x}$ when $x = \dfrac{1}{2}$?

III. SOLVING AN EQUATION

Most of the examples above were *expressions,* not *equations.* That just means that they have no equals sign. But a lot of algebra involves equations. When an equation has one variable in it, there will usually be only one value for the variable that makes the equation true.*

> ✐ If $3x + 5 = 23$, $x = $?

You can solve an equation by **getting the variable by itself on one side of the equation**. That means we have to move all the stuff next the x to the other side of the equals sign. You can do this by **doing the opposite** of anything you see to **both sides of the equation**:

$$3x + 5 = 23$$ To move "+ 5", subtract 5 from both sides.
$$3x + 5 - 5 = 23 - 5$$
$$3x = 18$$ To move "× 3", divide both sides by 3.
$$\frac{3x}{3} = \frac{18}{3}$$
$$\boxed{x = 6}$$

This, my friend, is the heart of algebra: to get x by itself, do the opposite of anything you see to both sides. We'll see more complicated concepts, of course, but this is pretty much it. Sometimes an equation may seem more complicated, but just remember to do the opposite to get rid of something:

> ✐ If $\dfrac{\sqrt{x-3}}{2} = 4$, $x = $?

$$\frac{\sqrt{x-3}}{2} = 4$$ To remove "÷ 2", multiply both sides by 2.

$$\sqrt{x-3} = 8$$ To remove the square root, square both sides.

$$x - 3 = 64$$ To remove "−3", add 3 to both sides.

$$\boxed{x = 67}$$

---

* Why is x always the first variable we use? There are several theories, but this is my favorite. This notation started in 1637 with the French mathematician and philosopher René Descartes in his book *La Géométrie*. Originally, he wanted to use z as the first variable, y as the second, x as the third, etc. But when the book went to be published, the publisher didn't have enough z's (back then, books were printed using individual blocks of metal for each letter). He had plenty of x's though—very few French words use x. So we use x as our variables because the French language uses too many z's.

How do you know which operations to do first? Think of an equation as a package with many layers of ribbons, wrapping paper, and boxes, and the variable is your birthday present inside the package.* To unwrap the package, you've got to start with the outermost ribbon, then the wrapping paper, then the box underneath. Each layer you remove is covering all the layers below it.

When solving an equation, **start with the operations that apply to *everything* else on that side of the equation.** In the first equation above, $3x + 5$, the "$\times 3$" only applies to the x, not the 5. But the "$+ 5$" applies to everything before it, so we start there. In the second equation above, the square root only applies to the "$x - 3$", not to the 2. The "$\div 2$" applies to everything else on that side, so we start there.

x in terms of y

Not every algebra problem will just deal with numbers. Observe:

> ✎ **If $y = 5x + 3$, what is x in terms of y?**

Right now, the equation gives "y in terms of x". That means the equation defines y and uses x's in its definition: y is by itself on one side of the equation, and its value is $5x + 3$. But we want "x in terms of y". That means that we want to get x by itself on one side of the equation and nothing but y's and numbers on the other side. We do this **exactly the same way** we solved for x above. But now instead of a number, our answer will have a bunch of y's.

Many questions that ask for "x in terms of y" can be done with Plug In.

$$y = 5x + 3 \qquad \text{Subtract 3 from both sides.}$$
$$y - 3 = 5x + 3 - 3$$
$$y - 3 = 5x \qquad \text{Divide both sides by 5.}$$
$$\frac{y-3}{5} = \frac{5x}{5}$$
$$\boxed{\frac{y-3}{5} = x}$$

Fractions

Students often get confused about how to deal with fractions in algebra problems. Even if you have no trouble dealing with fractions that have numbers, they can suddenly become difficult when they have letters instead. So let's take a minute to talk about the different ways they can show up.

---

* Surprise! It's just what you wanted!

1. Fraction times a variable

First, a fraction may show up as the coefficient of a variable. For example:

☞ $\dfrac{2}{3}x = 10$

When a variable is multiplied by a fraction like this, you can think of the variable as being **in the numerator of the fraction**. That way, you can see how to break down the steps to solve it.

$$\frac{2}{3}x = 10 \qquad \frac{2x}{3} = 10 \qquad 2x = 10 \times 3 \qquad 2x = 30 \qquad x = 15$$

A faster way to do it is to see that it simply means x *times* 2/3. To solve for x, we can do the opposite and *divide* by 2/3. Dividing by a fraction is the same thing as multiplying by the reciprocal. So:

$$\frac{2}{3}x = 10 \qquad \left(\frac{3}{2}\right) \times \left(\frac{2}{3}x\right) = 10 \times \left(\frac{3}{2}\right) \qquad x = 10\left(\frac{3}{2}\right) \qquad x = 5 \times 3 \qquad x = 15$$

The same principles hold true whether the fraction contains variables or numbers:

$$\left(\frac{a}{c}\right)b = d \qquad \frac{ab}{c} = d \qquad ab = dc \qquad b = \frac{dc}{a}$$

Or:

$$\left(\frac{a}{c}\right)b = d \qquad b = d\left(\frac{c}{a}\right) \qquad b = \frac{dc}{a}$$

2. Variable in denominator

Okay, so what do you do if the variable is in the denominator instead of the numerator?

☞ $\dfrac{18}{x} = 6$, $x = ?$

We want to get the variable into the numerator to solve it. How do we do that? Let's do the same thing! If something is on the bottom, multiply to get it to the top.

$$\frac{18}{x} = 6 \qquad x\left(\frac{18}{x}\right) = 6x \qquad 18 = 6x \qquad 3 = x$$

This process has a lot in common with **cross-multiplying**, a method we saw when we were solving ratio questions in the Fundamentals chapter. If we imagine that 6 is actually 6/1, we can see this is just two fractions multiplied together:

$$\frac{18}{x} = \frac{6}{1}$$

When two fractions are set equal, we can cross multiply to solve. In fact, we can even take a shortcut. The top of one side and the bottom of the other can **switch places:**

$$\frac{18}{x} = \frac{6}{1} \qquad \rightarrow \qquad \frac{18}{6} = \frac{x}{1} \qquad 3 = x$$

3. Adding and subtracting with variables

All these situations so far have involved *only multiplying and dividing*. Things can get trickier when **addition and subtraction** are involved.

The first thing to keep in mind is to be careful when simplifying fractions. Remember that we can cross out common factors from the top and bottom of a fraction:

$$\frac{3 \times 10}{2} = \frac{3 \times 5}{1}$$

But you can only do this with multiplication. Take a look at this expression:

$$\frac{2x + 6}{6}$$

It is *very tempting* to try to cancel out the 6 in the denominator with the 6 on the numerator, leaving us with $2x$. **That is not allowed.** Why not? Because the 6 on the bottom is being divided into the six on the top *and* the $2x$. If you cancel it out, the $2x$ doesn't get that sweet division.

You *can* split it up into two fractions, each divided by 6. Then you can simplify each fraction:

$$\frac{2x + 6}{6} \qquad = \frac{2x}{6} + \frac{6}{6} \qquad = \frac{x}{3} + 1$$

Splitting this fraction into two fractions is simply the opposite of what we normally do when we add fractions:

$$1 + \frac{1}{3} \qquad = \frac{3}{3} + \frac{1}{3} \qquad = \frac{3+1}{3} \qquad = \frac{4}{3}$$

Notice that in the algebra problem above, we divided each of the terms in $2x + 6$ by 2. We could also pull out that 2 first by **factoring** the numerator. Then the numerator will be the product of two things: 2 and $(x + 3)$. So you can divide the 2 out of the top and the bottom:

$$\frac{2x + 6}{6} \qquad \frac{(2 \times x) + (2 \times 3)}{6} = \frac{2(x + 3)}{6} \qquad = \frac{x + 3}{3} \qquad = \frac{x}{3} + 1$$

Note that you can *only* split up numerators this way, not denominators. So $\dfrac{3}{x+3}$ CANNOT be split into $\dfrac{3}{x}+\dfrac{3}{3}$. Denominators must remain together. There's no way you can simplify $\dfrac{3}{x+3}$.*

Okay, so what do you do if you have variables in the denominator and you want to add fractions?

$$\dfrac{3}{x}+\dfrac{4}{y}=?$$

Remember when we added fractions before? We just have to find a **common denominator**. As before, the easiest way to find one is to multiply the two denominators together. In this case, that's xy. So we'll change each fraction to have a xy on the bottom:

$$\dfrac{3}{x}+\dfrac{4}{y} = \left(\dfrac{y}{y}\right)\left(\dfrac{3}{x}\right)+\left(\dfrac{x}{x}\right)\left(\dfrac{4}{y}\right) = \dfrac{3y}{xy}+\dfrac{4x}{xy} = \dfrac{3y+4x}{xy}$$

4. A single unit

Finally, remember that you can treat an entire numerator or denominator as a single unit. Observe:

$$\text{If } \dfrac{y}{x}=5, \text{ what is } y \text{ in terms of } x?$$

To get y in terms of x, we need to get y by itself. To do that, we simply multiply both sides by x to get $y = 5x$. Fine. But what about this:

$$\text{If } \dfrac{y}{3x+20}=5, \text{ what is } y \text{ in terms of } x?$$

As we saw, we cannot split the denominator to make two fractions. But we can treat that whole denominator, "$3x+20$", as one entity and cross multiply it just like we did before.

$$y = 5(3x+20)$$
$$y = 15x + 100$$

---

* Why not? Plug In to think about it in terms of numbers. Say $x = 2$, so our original expression is 3/5 or 0.6. But $3/2 + 3/3 = 1.5 + 1 = 2.5$. Clearly not the same as 0.6.

THIS PAGE INTENTIONALLY LEFT BLANK

Solving an equation

ANSWERS:

✐ If $4 + (a - 4) = 9$, $a = ?$

Answer: 9.
The 4's cancel out, leaving $a = 9$.

✐ If $\dfrac{5x+6}{6} = 11$, $x = ?$

Answer: 12.
$5x + 6 = 66 \qquad 5x = 60 \qquad x = 12$

✐ If $4u + 11 = 3$, $u = ?$

Answer: −2

$4u + 11 = 3$	Subtract 11
$4u = -8$	Divide by 4
$u = -2$	

✐ If $\dfrac{12x+4}{4} = 12$, $x = ?$

Answer: 11/3

$12x + 4 = 48 \qquad\qquad 12x = 44 \qquad\qquad x = \dfrac{44}{12} = \dfrac{11}{3}$

✐ If $13 - 3z = 15z + 4$, $z = ?$

Answer: 1/2

$13 - 3z = 15z + 4$	Add 3z
$13 = 18z + 4$	Subtract 4
$9 = 18z$	Divide by 18

$\dfrac{9}{18} = z = \dfrac{1}{2}$

✐ If $\dfrac{3x}{x+5} = 4$, $x = ?$

Answer: −20
$3x = 4(x + 5)$
$3x = 4x + 20$
$-x = 20 \qquad\qquad x = -20$

✐ If $\dfrac{8}{x} + \dfrac{2}{3} = 5$, $x = ?$

Answer: 24/13

$\dfrac{3(8)}{3x} + \dfrac{2x}{3x} = 5 \qquad or \qquad \dfrac{8}{x} = 5 - \dfrac{2}{3}$

$\dfrac{24 + 2x}{3x} = 5 \qquad\qquad\qquad \dfrac{8}{x} = \dfrac{13}{3}$

$24 + 2x = 15x \qquad\qquad 24 = 13x \qquad\qquad x = \dfrac{24}{13}$

$24 = 13x$

✐ If $P = 5(a + 8)$, what is a in terms of P?

Answer: $a = \dfrac{P}{5} - 8$

$P = 5(a + 8) \qquad\qquad \dfrac{P}{5} = a + 8 \qquad\qquad \dfrac{P}{5} - 8 = a$

✐ If $\dfrac{2}{3}x - 6 = y$, what is x in terms of y?

Answer: $x = \dfrac{3}{2}y + 9$

$\dfrac{2}{3}x - 6 = y$	Add 6
$\dfrac{2}{3}x = y + 6$	Multiply by $\dfrac{3}{2}$
$x = \dfrac{3}{2}(y + 6) \qquad or \qquad x = \dfrac{3}{2}y + 9$	

✐ If $\dfrac{ab}{cd} = e$, what is b in terms of a, c, d, and e?

Answer: $b = \dfrac{cde}{a}$

$\dfrac{ab}{cd} = e \qquad\qquad ab = cde \qquad\qquad b = \dfrac{cde}{a}$

✒ If $4 + (a - 4) = 9$, $a = ?$

✒ If $\dfrac{5x + 6}{6} = 11$, $x = ?$

✒ If $4u + 11 = 3$, $u = ?$

✒ If $\dfrac{12x + 4}{4} = 12$, $x = ?$

✒ If $13 - 3z = 15z + 4$, $z = ?$

✒ If $\dfrac{3x}{x + 5} = 4$, $x = ?$

✒ If $\dfrac{8}{x} + \dfrac{2}{3} = 5$, $x = ?$

✒ If $P = 5(a + 8)$, what is a in terms of P?

✒ If $\dfrac{2}{3}x - 6 = y$, what is x in terms of y?

✒ If $\dfrac{ab}{cd} = e$, what is b in terms of a, c, d, and e?

IV. WRITING EQUATIONS

Often questions will ask you to write your own equations or expressions. You may not even have to solve them; they're just testing you if you know how to set them up.

> ✏ **If x is 3 less than twice y, what is x in terms of y?**

Here we just have to read the question and **translate** the English words into mathematical expression or algebraic equations. Let's try it:

Words	Meaning	Symbol
"x is"	x equals	$x =$
"three less"	minus 3	-3
"twice y"	two times y	$2y$

Note that you must switch the order of terms for "less than". It's $2y - 3$ not $3 - 2y$.

Therefore: "x is three less than twice y" means $x = 2y - 3$.

Translation problems can often be done with **techniques**. In problems like this, it's often much easier to use real numbers and bypass the equations altogether. We saw a ton of questions like this in the Math Techniques chapter, remember?

> 9. **Bob has 4 dollars more than Lisa does. If Lisa has x dollars, how much would Bob have if he doubled his money?**
>
> 14. **If $x + 5$ is 3 less than y, then $x - 2$ is how much less than y?**

Linear translation

An *expression* is like one side of an equation with no equals sign. It's just a group of variables and numbers connected to each other.

There's a special subset of translation questions involving **linear equations**. A linear equation is an equation that can be drawn as a line on the xy-coordinate plane. In algebraic terms that means:

- It has two variables, usually x and y. (If it's an expression instead of an equation, it will often have just one variable.)
- Neither variable is taken to any power other than 1. That is, they do not have any exponents, nor are either one in a denominator of a fraction.

We see that this type of function show up a *ton* on the SAT; that's what the Heart of Algebra category is all about. But it's not enough just to be able to evaluate or solve them. We have to *understand* how they work. For example:

> **There are too many goats in the basement. Dad pays you a flat fee of $200 (for being brave enough to go down there at all) plus $50 for every goat you catch. Write an expression for the total amount of money you'll get if you catch _x_ goats.**

A payment situation is a classic context for a linear function. There's a **flat fee** that you get no matter what you do, and a **rate** that's dependent on how well you do (how many hours you work, how many things you sell, how many goats you catch, etc.)

Let's Plug In to see how this works. Say $x = 3$, so you catch 3 goats. You'll get $200 plus 3 times $50.

$$200 + 50 \times 3 = 200 + 150 = 350.$$

Now let's say $x = 10$, so you catch 10 goats. You'll get that $200 plus 10 times $50.

$$200 + 50 \times 10 = 200 + 500 = 700.$$

Following that pattern, for every _x_ goats you catch, you get

$$200 + 50x$$

That's an expression, not an equation. If we want an equation, we'll just set it equal to something:

$$y = 200 + 50x$$

The _y_ represents the total money you get for every _x_ goats you catch.

This is basically how all linear functions work. There's a number you multiply by a variable—that's the **rate**—and a number you add to or subtract from it—that's the **starting point**.

> **The equation _g_ = 350 – 6_h_ shows how many goats are remaining in the basement after you work for _h_ hours. How many goats do you catch each hour?**

What do you think these numbers represent? Like before, there's a number by itself and a number with a variable. Like before, they represent a starting point and a rate. The starting point is the number by itself. The rate is the number multiplied by the variable—in this case, how long you work. The final answer, _g_, is in terms of goats. Therefore,

- 350 must be the initial number of goats, and
- 6 must be the number of goats per hour you catch.

The key to this sort of question is that you must understand the **meaning** of the equation, and what each term represents. But because these equations so often take the same linear form, the more you see them the easier it'll be to pick up.

THIS PAGE INTENTIONALLY LEFT BLANK

Writing equations

ANSWERS:

✎ Freddie bought a flower for his garden. The equation $h = 2.5d + 12$ models the height, h, in inches of the flower d days after he purchased it. How much does the plant grow, in inches, every day?

Answer: 2.5

The rate is 2.5 inches per day.
The starting value was 12 inches. The flower was 12 inches tall when he got it.

✎ Sophie runs a lemonade stand and puts the money she makes in her piggy bank. This is modeled by the equation $P = 2l + 14$, where P is the amount of money in dollars in her bank and l is the number of cups of lemonade she has sold. How much money in dollars does Sophie get for each cup of lemonade?

Answer: 2

The rate is 2 dollars per cup.
The starting amount is $14. She had $14 in her bank before she started to sell lemonade.

✎ Lana got a box of donuts. The equation $d = 120 - 5h$ shows the total number of donuts, d, remaining in the box after h hours. How many donuts were originally in the box?

Answer: 120

The starting value is 120 donuts.
She eats 5 donuts per hour. That amount is then subtracted from 120 to give the remaining donuts.

✎ The equation $c = 0.1m + 0.15t + 50$ shows the total cost, c, in dollars, of Glenda's mobile phone service each month, where m is the number of minutes of phone calls and t is the number of text messages she sent. How much is Glenda charged each month, in dollars, for each text message?

Answer: 0.15

Tricky because we have multiple variables.
The starting value is 50. That's a $50 flat fee each month.
The rate for phone calls is $0.10 per minute.
The rate for text messages is $0.15 per message.

✎ Andrew spent one day building a wall in his backyard and has added to it every week since. The equation $b = 25(w + 10)$ models the total number of bricks in the wall w weeks after he started. How many bricks did he put in the wall on the first day?

Answer: 250

Distribute the 25 first.
$b = 25w + 250.$ *That's* our equation.

The rate is 25 bricks per week.
The starting value is 250 bricks.

The Fool's Gold answer is 10 because there's a "+ 10" hanging out at the end in the original equation. But that 10 is not alone. It's inside the parentheses, meaning it's being multiplied by 25. $25 \times 10 = 250$.

✒ Freddie bought a flower for his garden. The equation $h = 2.5d + 12$ models the height, h, in inches of the flower d days after he purchased it. How much does the plant grow, in inches, every day?

✒ Sophie runs a lemonade stand and puts the money she makes in her piggy bank. This is modeled by the equation $P = 2l + 14$, where P is the amount of money in dollars in her bank and l is the number of cups of lemonade she has sold. How much money in dollars does Sophie get for each cup of lemonade?

✒ Lana got a box of donuts. The equation $d = 120 - 5h$ shows the total number of donuts, d, remaining in the box after h hours. How many donuts were originally in the box?

✒ The equation $c = 0.1m + 0.15t + 50$ shows the total cost, c, in dollars, of Glenda's mobile phone service each month, where m is the number of minutes of phone calls and t is the number of text messages she sent. How much is Glenda charged each month, in dollars, for each text message?

✒ Andrew spent one day building a wall in his backyard and has added to it every week since. The equation $b = 25(w + 10)$ models the total number of bricks in the wall w weeks after he started. How many bricks did he put in the wall on the first day?

V. MULTIPLE EQUATIONS

So far we've been dealing with a single equation at a time, but some problems may give you multiple equations with multiple variables. There are several ways to deal with them:

Substitution

Often the most straightforward way to solve these problems is **substitution**. For example:

> If $a = 3x - 6$, and $5x + a = 10$, then $x = ?$

We're given two equations with two variables, x and a. Notice that the first equation has a on one side of the equation by itself. Since "a" is equivalent to "$3x - 6$", we can **substitute** "$3x - 6$" into the second equation wherever we see an "a".

$$5x + a = 10$$
$$5x + (3x - 6) = 10$$
$$8x - 6 = 10$$
$$8x = 16$$
$$x = 2$$

Try another:

> When $x + y = 4$, what is the value of $5(x + y) - 6$?

It might seem like we have to solve for x or y individually, but we don't. The first equation gives a value for "$x + y$", and the second equation also contains "$x + y$". So we can substitute 4 for that whole expression:

$$5(x + y) - 6 \quad = 5(4) - 6 \quad = 20 - 6 \quad = \mathbf{14}$$

If a problem has two or more variables in it, **don't forget the techniques**. Being able to solve intricate algebra problems is a good skill to have, but Plug In and Backsolve can help turn complicated problems into simple ones.

Systems

Other times, it may be easier to add or subtract the equations directly. Observe:

$$5x + 2y = 10$$
$$6x - 2y = 23$$

34. According to the system of equations above, what is the value of x?

Here it's not easy to substitute because we'd have to do a little bit of maneuvering the get either question in terms of a single variable. Ugh. But look! Notice that they wrote the two equations so that the x's and y's line up. That's not an accident. They did that to help you. And *look*: one equation has a $2y$ and the other has a $-2y$. *If we add the equations the $2y$'s will cancel out.*

$$
\begin{array}{r}
5x + 2y = 10 \\
+\quad 6x - 2y = 23 \\
\hline
11x \qquad = 33 \\
x = 3
\end{array}
$$

Systems don't always work out so beautifully. Sometimes you have to work for it:

$$2x - 7y = 15$$
$$4x - 2y = 18$$

35.   According to the system of equations above, what is the value of x?

Now we can't just add or subtract the equations because neither variable will cancel out. However, we can change one of the equations so that they will. Let's multiply the first equation by 2:

$$2(2x - 7y) = 2(15)$$
$$4x - 14y = 30$$

Now both equations start with $4x$. Last time, one term was positive and the other negative, so adding them made them cancel out. This time, since both terms are positive, let's *subtract* them.

$$
\begin{array}{r}
4x - 14y = 30 \\
-\quad [4x - 2y = 18] \\
\hline
-12y = 12 \\
y = -1
\end{array}
$$

But wait! Don't stop! We're not done yet. That's y. We want x. RTFQ. But getting x is easy now. Just put $y = -1$ into either equation and solve for x.

$$
\begin{aligned}
2x - 7(-1) &= 15 & \qquad 4x - 2(-1) &= 18 \\
2x + 7 &= 15 & 4x + 2 &= 18 \\
2x &= 8 & 4x &= 16 \\
x &= 4 & x &= 4
\end{aligned}
$$

When solving a system, we often give values of both variables together as an **ordered pair** (x, y). So the solution to this problem is $(4, -1)$. If a system contains two linear equations, there will be one pair of values—and only one pair—that solve the system: one value for *x* and one for *y* that together work in both equations. You can think of the two equations as straight lines in the *xy*-coordinate plane. They will cross at one point, and that point (x, y) will be the solution to the system. (We'll talk more about the coordinate plane soon enough…)

However, not all lines cross. Look at this system:

$$2x - 3y = 16$$
$$4x - 6y = 32$$

Okay, let's just multiply the first equation by 2, and we get:

$$4x - 6y = 32$$
$$4x - 6y = 32$$

Hey, wait a minute. The second equation *is* the first equation multiplied by two. *These are the same equation.* It's not two lines; it's the same line, written twice. So *any* pair of values that work for the second equation will also work for the first equation. So there are **infinitely many solutions**.

Similarly, look at this system:

$$3x + y = 10$$
$$6x + 2y = 14$$

Let's multiply the first equation by two so the *y*'s cancel out:

$$
\begin{aligned}
6x + 2y &= 20 \\
- \quad 6x + 2y &= 14 \\
\hline
0 &= 6
\end{aligned}
$$

Huh? That's weird. If I try to cancel out the *y*'s I also wind up cancelling out the *x*'s. Here, the left halves of the equations are identical but the right halves are not. So this system has **no solution**. Think about it: both equations have "$6x + 2y$" on the left, but they're supposed to equal 2 different numbers: 20 or 14. Can't equal 20 and 14 at the same time, so there's no set of numbers that will solve both equations. If we were to graph these two lines, they would appear as *parallel lines*, which never intersect.

Solving Directly for Expressions

Take a look at this problem:

> ✐ **If $4x - 3y = 13$ and $x + 2y = 3$, then $5x - y = ?$**

There are some *very painful* ways to do this with normal algebra. You could try to solve one equation for x, then substitute your answer in for x in the other equation, solve for y, then put y back into the first equation and solve for x, then stick x and y into the expression they're asking for and you're done:

$$\boxed{y = -\frac{1}{11}} \qquad \boxed{x = \frac{35}{11}} \qquad 5\left(\frac{35}{11}\right) - \left(-\frac{1}{11}\right) = \frac{175}{11} + \frac{1}{11} = \frac{176}{11} = 16$$

Ugh. I mean, we could do it, but it isn't fun. No one wants that.

Wait a minute—take another look at this question.

> ✐ **If $4x - 3y = 13$ and $x + 2y = 3$, then $5x - y = ?$**

They're <u>not</u> asking you for x or y individually; they're asking for an *expression*: $5x - y$. Instead of solving for x or y, let's try to solve directly for $5x - y$.

To make it easier, let's write the equations on top of each other so the x and y values line up:

$$
\begin{array}{r}
4x - 3y = 13 \\
+ \quad x + 2y = 3 \\
\hline
5x - y = 16
\end{array}
$$

Aha! If we **add** the equations, we get $5x - y$! That's what we're looking for. It's just $13 + 3$! It's 16!

Wait, what about x? How do we find x? Forget x! They're not asking me for it, so I don't care. Any time they ask you for an *expression*, don't solve for individual variables; try to solve directly for the expression. Try adding equations, multiplying by two, whatever it takes. Try to play with what they give you until it looks like what they're asking for. Why do you think they're asking for *that* expression, anyway? Why specifically $5x - y$? They didn't come up with that randomly; they're asking you for that *because* that's what you get when you add the equations.

Once again, this is another reason circling the question will help you. If you see they're asking you for an *expression*, don't worry about the individual variables; try to solve directly for the expression.

🖎 If $j = 3x - 5$ and $k = 6x + 1$, then $2j + 3k = ?$

🖎 If $\dfrac{a}{b} = 5$ and $4a + 7b = 9$, what is the value of b?

🖎 If $x - y = 10$ and $z = 3x - 3y - 8$, then $z = ?$

$$3x + y = 12$$
$$7x - y = 18$$

🖎 What is the solution (x, y) to the system of equations above?

$$4x - 3y = 34$$
$$2x + 5y = 4$$

🖎 What is the solution (x, y) to the system of equations above?

$$6x - 7y = 36$$
$$2y - 3x = -27$$

🖎 What is the solution (x, y) to the system of equations above?

🖎 If $5x + 2y = 41$ and $3x + 2y = 27$, then $x = ?$

🖎 If $3x + 8y = 58$ and $x + 2y = 12$, then $y = ?$

🖎 If $3p + 2q = 8$ and $4p + 3q = 11$, then $7p + 5q = ?$

🖎 If $2x + y = 23$ and $x + 2y = 17$, then $3x - 3y = ?$

Multiple equations

ANSWERS:

✍ If $j = 3x - 5$ and $k = 6x + 1$, then $2j + 3k = $?

Answer: $24x - 7$

Substitute the first two equations in for j and k into the expression
$$
\begin{aligned}
2j + 3k &= 2(3x - 5) + 3(6x + 1) \\
&= 6x - 10 + 18x + 3 \\
&= 24x - 7
\end{aligned}
$$

✍ If $\dfrac{a}{b} = 5$ and $4a + 7b = 9$, what is the value of b?

Answer: $\dfrac{1}{3}$

$\dfrac{a}{b} = 5$ Solve for a by multiplying both sides by b

$a = 5b$ Now substitute this into the second equation:
$$
\begin{aligned}
4(5b) + 7b &= 9 \\
20b + 7b &= 9 \\
27b &= 9 \qquad b = \frac{9}{27} = \frac{1}{3}
\end{aligned}
$$

✍ If $x - y = 10$ and $z = 3x - 3y - 8$, then $z = $?

Answer: 22

Two options here:
1.) Solve the first equation for x and substitute into the second:
$$
\begin{aligned}
x &= 10 + y \\
z &= 3(10 + y) - 3y - 8 \\
z &= 30 + 3y - 3y - 8 \\
z &= 30 - 8 = 22
\end{aligned}
$$
2.) Multiply the first equation by 3 to get
$3x - 3y = 30$.   Now substitute:
$$
\begin{aligned}
z &= (3x - 3y) - 8 \\
z &= 30 - 8 = 22.
\end{aligned}
$$

$3x + y = 12$
$7x - y = 18$

✍ What is the solution (x, y) to the system of equations above?

Answer: (3,3)

$3x + y = 12$ $3(3) + y = 12$
$\underline{7x - y = 18}$ $9 + y = 12$
$10x = 30$ $y = 3$
$x = 3$

Now put this into one of the equations above.

$4x - 3y = 34$
$2x + 5y = 4$

✍ What is the solution (x, y) to the system of equations above?

Answer: (7,−2)

Multiply the second equation by -2 and add the equations.
$4x - 3y = 34$
$\underline{-4x - 10y = -8}$ $4x - 3(-2) = 34$
$-13y = 26$ $4x + 6 = 34$
$y = -2$ $4x = 28$
                            $x = 7$

$6x - 7y = 36$
$2y - 3x = -27$

✍ What is the solution (x, y) to the system of equations above?

Answer: (13,6)

BE CAREFUL! The x's and y's are not lined up! Rearrange them.
Multiply the second equation by 2 and add the equations to solve for y.
$6x - 7y = 36$ $2(6) - 3x = -27$
$\underline{+-6x + 4y = -54}$ $12 - 3x = -27$
$-3y = -18$ $-3x = -39$
$y = 6$ $x = 13$

✍ If $5x + 2y = 41$ and $3x + 2y = 27$, then $x = $?

Answer: 7

Subtract the equations to make y cancel out:
$5x + 2y = 41$
$\underline{-3x + 2y = 27}$
$2x = 14$ y will equal 3, but we don't care
$x = 7$ this time.

✍ If $3x + 8y = 58$ and $x + 2y = 12$, then $y = $?

Answer: 11

Multiply the second equation by -3 and add to make x cancel out:
$3x + 8y = 58$
$\underline{-3x - 6y = -36}$
$2y = 22$ x will equal -10, but we don't care
$y = 11$ this time.

[CONTINUED ON NEXT PAGE]

☛ If $3p + 2q = 8$ and $4p + 3q = 11$, then $7p + 5q = ?$

Answer: 19.
$$\begin{array}{r} 3p + 2q = 8 \\ + \quad 4p + 3q = 11 \\ \hline 7p + 5q = \mathbf{19} \end{array}$$

☛ If $2x + y = 23$ and $x + 2y = 17$, then $3x - 3y = ?$

Answer: 18.
$$\begin{array}{r} 2x + y = 23 \\ - \quad x + 2y = 17 \\ \hline x - y = 6 \\ 3x - 3y = \mathbf{18} \end{array}$$

Inequalities

ANSWERS:

☛ $3(x + 2) < 12$

Answer: $x < 2$
Two ways to start here: divide by 3 or distribute the 3 into the parentheses:

$$\begin{array}{ll} x + 2 < 4 & 3x + 6 < 12 \\ x < 4 - 2 & 3x < 6 \\ x < 2 & x < 2 \end{array}$$

☛ $17 - x > 23$

Answer: $x < -6$
$$\begin{array}{ll} -x > 23 - 17 & \text{Subtract 17} \\ -x > 6 & \text{Divide by } -1 \textbf{ and flip the sign.} \\ x < -6 \end{array}$$

You can avoid the negative sign-flipping issue by moving x to the other side first:

$$\begin{array}{ll} 17 > 23 + x & \text{Subtract 23} \\ -6 > x \end{array}$$

☛ $5x + 6 < -3x - 10$

Answer: $x < -2$
$$\begin{array}{ll} 5x + 3x + 6 > -10 & \text{Add } 3x \\ 8x + 6 > -10 & \text{Subtract 6} \\ 8x > -16 & \text{Divide by 8} \\ x < -2 \end{array}$$

☛ $\dfrac{x + 4}{3} > \dfrac{x}{5}$

Answer: $x > -10$
Start by cross multiplying. **NOTE**: *keep the numerators where they are with respect to the inequality sign*:

$$\begin{array}{ll} 5(x + 4) > 3x & \text{Distribute the 5 into the parentheses.} \\ 5x + 20 > 3x & \text{Subtract 20.} \\ 5x > 3x - 20 & \text{Subtract } x \\ 2x > -20 & \text{Divide by 2.} \\ x > -10 \end{array}$$

☛ $7 - 4x \le 35$

Answer: $x \ge -7$
$$\begin{array}{ll} 7 - 4x \le 35 & \text{Subtract 7} \\ -4x \le 28 & \text{Divide by } -4 \textbf{ and flip the sign.} \\ x \ge -7 \end{array}$$

VI. INEQUALITIES

Inequalities work just like equations for the most part. You can solve for variables just like you do with equations. The only difference is that **if you multiply or divide by a negative number, you have to flip the inequality.**

Permit us to demonstrate:

$$7 - 3x > 16$$
$$7 - 3x - 7 > 16 - 7$$
$$-3x > 9$$
$$\frac{-3x}{-3} < \frac{9}{-3} \qquad \leftarrow\text{Watch out here. This is where the sign flips.}$$
$$x < -3$$

More complicated inequality questions—particularly those involving multiple variables—are often difficult to solve with algebraic manipulation. Don't forget: techniques like Plug In and Backsolve are here to help!

TRY SOME:

Solve these inequalities for x:

✎ $3(x + 2) < 12$

✎ $17 - x > 23$

✎ $5x + 6 < -3x - 10$

✎ $\dfrac{x + 4}{3} > \dfrac{x}{5}$

✎ $7 - 4x \leq 35$

HEART OF ALGEBRA EXERCISE

1

If $3x - 5 = 5x + 3$, then $x = ?$

A)   4
B)   1
C)   −1
D)   −4

2

If $9(x - 8) = -12$, $x = ?$

A) $-\dfrac{4}{3}$

B) $-\dfrac{3}{2}$

C) $\dfrac{20}{3}$

D) $\dfrac{69}{9}$

3

Weng is cataloguing all the books in the library. Each day he must enter one bookcase's books into a database. The number of books remaining to be catalogued at any point during the day can be modeled with the equation $B = 200 - 30h$, where B is the number of books remaining and h is the number of hours he has worked that day. What is the meaning of the number 30 in this equation?

A)   There are 30 books in each bookcase.
B)   It takes Weng 30 hours to catalogue all the books in one bookcase.
C)   Weng catalogues books at a rate of 30 books per hour.
D)   Weng catalogues books at a rate of 30 books per day.

4

The number of games that the baseball team won in 2010 is twice the number of games that it won in 2012. If the team won 42 games in 2010 and x games in 2012, which of the following equations is true?

A) $\dfrac{x}{2} = 42$

B) $x + 2 = 42$

C) $2x = 42$

D) $42x = 2$

CONTINUE

Heart of Algebra Exercise

1. Answer: D.

$$3x - 5 = 5x + 3 \qquad \text{Subtract 3 from both sides.}$$
$$3x - 8 = 5x \qquad \text{Subtract } 3x.$$
$$-8 = 2x \qquad \text{Divide by 2.}$$
$$-4 = x$$

Alternatively, use *Backsolve*. Put the choices in for x and see if you get the same thing on both sides.

C) $x = -1$:
$$3(-1) - 5 = 5(-1) + 3$$
$$-3 - 5 = -5 + 3$$
$$-8 = -2 \text{ ✗}$$

D) $x = -4$:
$$3(-4) - 5 = 5(-4) + 3$$
$$-12 - 5 = -20 + 3$$
$$-17 = -17 \text{ ✓}$$

2. Answer: C.

$$9(x - 8) = -12 \qquad \text{Distribute the 9.}$$
$$9x - 72 = -12$$
$$9x = -12 + 72$$
$$9x = 60$$
$$x = \frac{60}{9} = \frac{20}{3} \approx \mathbf{6.67}$$

Instead of distributing the 9 in the first step, you could also divide by 9 first, but then you'd have to deal with some fractions. (Eww.)

You could also use *Backsolve*. Put the choices in for x on the left side of the equation and see which one comes out to −12:

B) $x = -\dfrac{3}{2} = -1.5 \qquad 9(-1.5 - 8) = 9(-9.5) = -85.5$ ✗ Too small.

Let's go bigger.

C) $x = \dfrac{20}{3} \qquad 9\left(\dfrac{20}{3} - 8\right) = 9\left(\dfrac{20}{3} - \dfrac{24}{3}\right) = 9\left(-\dfrac{4}{3}\right) = \mathbf{-12}$ ✓

You can use decimals and use your calculator if you prefer:

$x = 6.666\ldots$
$9(6.666\ldots - 8) = 9(-1.333\ldots) = \mathbf{-12}$

Beware that there's a danger with repeating decimals. If you use, say 6.66 as an approximation, your answer won't *quite* come out equal to 12, though it'll be close enough (12.06) that C is your best choice. But you actually don't have to approximate. Type $20 \div 3$ and enter. Then type -8, enter. Then $\times 9$, enter. And you're done.

3. Answer: C.

The equation $B = 200 - 30h$ is a linear equation like we've seen before. It has a starting point and a rate.

30 is the number next to the variable. That will be the rate, in this case, Weng's rate for cataloging books. Eliminate A) and B). It must be either C) or D).

The question now is: what rate is it? The books per hour or the books per day? The variable next to the rate, h, is defined as the number of *hours* he worked. Since the 30 is multiplied by hours, it must be the rate per hour.

(Think about it: the left side of the equation , B, is in terms of *books*, so 30h has to come out to a number of books. That means we'll take (books/hour) and multiply by hours. The hours cancel out and we're left with books.)

The starting point in the equation is 200. That's the number of books he starts with at the beginning of the day, or, the number of books in one bookcase. That's Choice A).

Choice B) is the number of hours it takes him to finish an entire bookcase. We could determine that by setting $B = 0$ and solving for h. That will give us the number of hours after which there are no books remaining.

4. Answer: C.

We know this:
The number of wins in 2010 is twice the number of wins in 2012.

We know there are 42 wins in 2010 and x wins in 2012. So we know:
42 is twice x.

That's $\mathbf{42 = 2x}$

It seems like you can plug in here, but it's a bit weird because you can't just pick any x. There's only one value of x that will be the true number of wins in 2012.

Backsolve is a little better. Solve the equations in the choices and see if the x you get matches what we know.

A) $\dfrac{x}{2} = 42 \qquad x = (42)2 = 84$ ✗ 42 is not twice 84

B) $x + 2 = 42 \qquad x = 40$ ✗ 42 is not twice 40

C) $2x = 42 \qquad x = 21$ ✓ 42 **is** twice 21

D) $42x = 2 \qquad x = 0.0476$ 42 is not twice that ugly decimal.

5. Answer: D.

Solve the inequality directly for x.

$$3(3x - 5) + 1 < 2x + 7 \qquad \text{Distribute the 3.}$$
$$9x - 15 + 1 < 2x + 7$$
$$9x - 14 < 2x + 7 \qquad \text{Add 14 to both sides.}$$
$$9x < 2x + 21 \qquad \text{Subtract } 2x \text{ from both sides.}$$
$$9x - 2x < 21$$
$$7x < 21 \qquad \text{Divide both sides by 7.}$$
$$x < 3$$

Or, use *Plug In*. First, try $x = 2$. Plug it into the inequality and see if the inequality is true.

$$3(3(2) - 5) + 1 < 2(2) + 7$$
$$3(6 - 5) + 1 < 4 + 7$$
$$3(1) + 1 < 11$$
$$4 < 11 \checkmark \qquad \textbf{It works!}$$

That means $x = 2$ is in the solution set, so we can eliminate any choices that *don't* allow x to be 2.
Eliminate A and C. We're down to B or D.

Next, choose $x = 4$:

$$3(3(4) - 5) + 1 < 2(4) + 7$$
$$3(12 - 5) + 1 < 8 + 7$$
$$3(7) + 1 < 15$$
$$22 < 15 \; \textbf{x} \qquad \textbf{It fails!}$$

Since $22 > 15$, $x = 4$ is not in the solution set, so we can eliminate any choices that *do* allow $x = 4$.
Eliminate b. We're left with d. In summary:

		$x = 2 \checkmark$	$x = 4 \; \textbf{x}$
A)	$x < -1$	$2 < -1$ **x**	
B)	$x > -1$	$2 > -1$ $\checkmark$	$4 > -1$ **x** We want false.
C)	$x > 3$	$2 > 3$ **x**	
D)	$x < 3$	$2 < 3$ $\checkmark$	$4 < 3$ $\checkmark$ That's false!

6. Answer: B.

Solve the equation for x by getting x by itself on one side:

$$mx + n = p \qquad \text{Subtract } n \text{ from both sides}$$
$$mx = p - n \qquad \text{Divide both sides by } m$$
$$x = \frac{p - n}{m}$$

Or, *Plug In*. Pick values for m, x and n to find p. Say $m = 2$, $x = 3$, and $n = 4$. $2(3) + 4 = 10 = p$
The question asks for x, so plug these values for m, n and p into the answers to find one that equals 3:

A) $\dfrac{10 + 4}{2} = \dfrac{14}{2} = 7$ **x**

B) $\dfrac{10 - 4}{2} = \dfrac{6}{2} = 3$ $\checkmark$

C) $\dfrac{4 - 10}{2} = \dfrac{6}{2} = -3$ **x**

D) $\dfrac{10}{2} - 4 = 5 - 4 = 1$ **x**

7. Answer: D.

1.) Backsolve

C) $-7 = x$
Put $x = -7$ into both equations and see if you get the same y in both of them.
$$-7 + 2y = -13 \qquad 2y = -6 \qquad y = -3 \; \textbf{x}$$
$$-7 + 3y = -22 \qquad 3y = -15 \qquad y = -5 \; \textbf{x} \text{ No match.}$$

D) $5 = x$
$$5 + 2y = -13 \qquad 2y = -18 \qquad y = -9 \checkmark$$
$$5 + 3y = -22 \qquad 3y = -27 \qquad y = -9 \checkmark \textbf{ It's a match!}$$

2.) Substitution. Solve one equation for x and substitute into the other.

$$x + 2y = -13 \qquad\qquad x = -13 - 2y$$

$$x + 3y = -22$$
$$(-13 - 2y) + 3y = -22$$
$$-13 + y = -22$$
$$y = -9. \qquad \text{But don't stop!}$$
Now we have to put $y = -9$ back into one of the equations to solve for x.
$$x + 2y = -13$$
$$x + 2(-9) = -13$$
$$x - 18 = -13$$
$$x = 5$$

3.) Subtract the equations
$$x + 2y = -13.$$
$$\underline{- \; (x + 3y = -22)}$$
$$-y = 9$$
$$y = -9$$
Now put this into one of the equations just like we did in 2 above.

8. Answer: C.

Plug In
Let's say $T = 10$
Isn't that kind of cold to be selling ice cream?
Sure is! But it doesn't matter. That equation should work with any number.
Let's find C when $T = 10$:
$$C = 8(10) + 36$$
$$C = 80 + 36$$
$$C = 116 \qquad \text{Okay, remember that number.}$$

The question asks what happens to C when T increases by 4. So let's try $T = 14$ and find C:
$$C = 8(14) + 36$$
$$C = 8112 + 36$$
$$C = 140$$

The number of cones sold went from 116 to 140.
$$140 - 116 = \textbf{32.}$$

So when the temperature increased by 4°F, the number of cones sold increases by 32.

Because our equation was linear, this increase is entirely the result of the *rate*. That's the number next to the variable, which is 8. (That's the slope of our line.) So when T goes up by 4, C will go up by $8 \times 4 = 32$.

If $3(3x - 5) + 1 < 2x + 7$, which of the following expressions gives the solution set for x?

A) $x < -1$
B) $x > -1$
C) $x > 3$
D) $x < 3$

$$x + 2y = -13$$
$$x + 3y = -22$$

According to the system of equations above, what is the value of x?

A) -35
B) -9
C) -7
D) 5

For all nonzero values of m, n and p, which of the following expressions gives the solution set for x of the equation $mx + n = p$?

A) $\dfrac{p + n}{m}$

B) $\dfrac{p - n}{m}$

C) $\dfrac{n - p}{m}$

D) $\dfrac{p}{m} - n$

$$C = 8T + 36$$

Amir has determined that the number of ice cream cones he will sell on a given day is related to the temperature. The equation above estimates the relationship where T is the day's high temperature in °F and C is the number of ice cream cones he sells that day. How will the number of ice cream cones he sells change if the temperature increases by 4°F?

A) Amir will sell 4 more ice cream cones.
B) Amir will sell 8 more ice cream cones.
C) Amir will sell 32 more ice cream cones.
D) Amir will sell 40 more ice cream cones.

CONTINUE

$$4x + 5y = 2$$
$$3y - 2x = 10$$

What is the solution (x, y) to the system of equations above?

A) $(-7, 6)$
B) $(-2, 2)$
C) $(1, 4)$
D) $(4, 6)$

Raoul opens a bank account with simple interest, which can be calculated using $I = Prt$, where I is the interest, P is the initial amount of money invested, r is annual interest rate expressed as a decimal, and t is the time, in years. If Raoul invests \$1,000 with a 4% interest rate, how much interest will he earn after 5 years?

A) \$200
B) \$400
C) \$4,000
D) \$20,000

If $5x - 3 \leq 2$, what is the greatest possible value of $5x + 3$?

A) 1
B) 3
C) 5
D) 8

$$ax + 3y = -2$$
$$5x + 8y = -9$$

In the system of equations above, a is a constant and x and y are variables. For what value of a will the system of equations have no solution?

A) $-\dfrac{10}{9}$

B) $\dfrac{3}{8}$

C) $\dfrac{10}{9}$

D) $\dfrac{15}{8}$

CONTINUE

9. Answer: B.

Start by rearranging the second equation so the x's and y's line up:

$$4x + 5y = 2$$
$$-2x + 3y = 10$$

Now multiply the second equation by 2 and add:

$$\begin{array}{r} 4x + 5y = 2 \\ -4x + 6y = 20 \\ \hline 11y = 22 \\ y = 2 \end{array}$$

Great, so now we can plug $y = 2$ back into one of the—hey, wait a minute. There's only one choice that has $y = 2$ as a solution! **Choice B)!** That must be our answer.

Alternatively, might I suggest *Backsolve*?
Pick a choice and put those values in for x and y into the left sides of both equations. Then see if you get the right numbers on the right side.

C)   (1, 4) $x = 1, y = 4$

$4(1) + 5(4) = 4 + 20 = 24$ ✘ Should be 2.
Once the first equation fails, I don't have to check the other one.

B)   (−2, 2) $x = -2, y = 2$

$4(-2) + 5(2) = -8 + 10 = 2$ ✓
$3(2) - 2(-2) = 6 - (-4) = 10$ ✓ It works!

10. Answer: D.

Solve directly for the expression

$$5x - 3 \leq 2$$
$$5x \leq 5 \qquad \text{Stop! We want "5x + 3" so just add 3 to both sides.}$$
$$5x + 3 \leq 8$$

So the greatest possible value of $5x + 3$ is **8**.

RTFQ: choice A). That's the value of x. That RTFQ choice is one of the only reasons why anyone gets this wrong.

11. Answer: A.

Just substitute the values we're given!
Plug in $P = 1{,}000$, $r = 0.04$, and $t = 5$.
$I = (1000)(0.04)(5) = $ **200**

RTFQ: D). Students who get D) used $r = 4$. The rate is 4%, but the question says "r is the annual interest rate **expressed as a decimal**." So $r = 0.04$.

12. Answer: D.

Weird question. Let's get through it together.

Remember in the chapter we said that if a system of equations had the same stuff on the right, but different numbers on the left, there would be no solution to the system? That's what we want here.

So we want to get our top equation to look like the bottom equation. How do we do that?

We don't know a, so we're stuck with that part. Let's look at the second term. We have to change $3y$ into $8y$. We can't do that directly, so we'll have to divide by 3, then multiply by 8.

$$ax + 3y = -2$$
$$\frac{a}{3}x + y = \frac{-2}{3}$$
$$\frac{8a}{3}x + 8y = \frac{-16}{3}$$

Great! Now the $8y$ in this equation matches the $8y$ in the other. Therefore, the coefficients of the x's should also match. Let's set them equal and solve for a

$$\frac{8a}{3} = 5$$
$$8a = 15$$
$$a = \frac{15}{8}$$

Notice that this was really just a simple ration. The terms on the left should be proportional to each other. To wit:

$$\frac{ax}{5x} = \frac{3y}{8y}$$
$$\frac{a}{5} = \frac{3}{8}$$
$$a = \frac{15}{8}$$

13. Answer: B.

Variables in answer choices? Why not *Plug in?*

Let's pick a t. Say $t = 3$.

a is the sum of 3 and 5, so $a = 8$.

b is the sum of 3(3) and 13, or 9 and 13, so $b = 22$.

c is the sum of 2(3) and 6, or 6 and 6, so $c = 12$.

The average of 8, 22, and 12 is:

$$\frac{8 + 22 + 12}{3} = \frac{42}{3} = 14.$$

A) $t + 4$ $3 + 4$ $= 7$ ✗
B) $2t + 8$ $2(3) + 8$ $= 14$ ✓ **Choice B) it is.**
C) $3t + 12$ $3(3) + 12$ $= 21$ ✗
D) $6t + 24$ $6(3) + 24$ $= 42$ ✗

Algebra:

Translate these sentences into some equations. We want the average, which is the sum divided by how many terms there are. So we're going to need the sum of a, b, and c. Let's just add the equations.

"a is the sum of t and 5" $a = t + 5$
"b is the sum of $3t$ and 13" $b = 3t + 13$
"c is the sum of $2t$ and 6" $\underline{+\quad c = 2t + 6}$
                                   $a + b + c = 6t + 24$

There are three terms, so take that sum and divide by 3.

$$\frac{a + b + c}{3} = \frac{6t + 24}{3} = 2t + 8$$

Choice D) is an RTFQ: that's the sum, not the average. It's easy to mess up all the division here and pick A) or C) as well.

(We haven't talked about averages yet (and we won't until the Problem Solving and Data Analysis chapter) but most kids should have a basic understanding of what it means and how to find it. If not, a quick definition should be enough.)

14. Answer: A.

Plug In. Say $b = 3$.

We know a is the sum of 3 and 5, so $a = 8$.

We want the product of 3 and 5, that's **15**.

Plug $a = 8$ into the answers and see which comes out to 15.

A) $5(8 - 5) = 5(3) = 15$ ✓
B) $5(8 + 5) = 5(13) = 65$ ✗
C) $5(8) = 40$ ✗
D) $5(8) - 5 = 40 - 5 = 35$ ✗

Algebraically, this problem is all about translation:
"a is the sum of b and 5"   means $a = b + 5$.
"the product of 5 and b"   means $5b$.

We want $5b$ in terms of a. First, solve the first equation for b:
$b = a - 5$ We want $5b$, so multiply both sides by 5.
$5b = 5(a - 5)$ That's **choice A)**.

15. Answer: C.

Oh, man, this looks like it's going to be a lot of unpleasant fraction algebra.

Wait, no! Let's *Plug In!*

Say $x = 1$ and $y = 4$. We'll use those values to find a

$$a = \frac{1}{4 - 2(1)} = \frac{1}{4 - 2} = \frac{1}{2} = a.$$

Great! The question is asking for an expression showing y, which we said is 4. So let's put $x = 1$ and $a = 1/2$ into the choices and see which comes out to 4. If you're using your calculator

A) $\dfrac{1}{\frac{1}{2}} - 2 = 2 - 2 = 0$ ✗

B) $\dfrac{1}{\frac{1}{2}} - 2\left(\dfrac{1}{2}\right) = 2 - 1 = 1$ ✗

C) $\dfrac{1}{\frac{1}{2}}\left(1 + 2\left(\dfrac{1}{2}\right)\right) = 2(1 + 1) = 2(2) = 4$ ✓ **It works!**

D) $\dfrac{3(1)}{\frac{1}{2}} = 3(2) = 6$ ✗

Look at that! We turned the hardest question on the section into "$2 \times 2 = 4$"!

The algebra:

$a = \dfrac{x}{y - 2x}$ Cross multiply

$a(y - 2x) = x$ Distribute
$ay - 2ax = x$ Add $2ax$ to both sides.
$ay = x + 2ax$ Divide both sides by a

$y = \dfrac{x + 2ax}{a}$

Hmm. We've solved for y, but it still doesn't look like any of the answer choices. Let's try factoring the top.

$y = \dfrac{x(1 + 2a)}{a}$ Aha! Now just nudge the denominator left...

$y = \dfrac{x}{a}(1 + 2a)$ There it is.

Ha ha, that was terrible. Plug In is the best.

If a is the sum of t and 5, b is the sum of $3t$ and 13, and c is the sum of $2t$ and 6, what is the average of a, b, and c in terms of t ?

A) $t + 4$
B) $2t + 8$
C) $3t + 12$
D) $6t + 24$

For all real numbers a and b such that a is the sum of b and 5, which of the following expressions represents the product of b and 5 in terms of a ?

A) $5(a - 5)$
B) $5(a + 5)$
C) $5a$
D) $5a - 5$

If $a = \dfrac{x}{y - 2x}$, which of the following shows y in terms of x and a ?

A) $y = \dfrac{x}{a} - 2$

B) $y = \dfrac{x}{a} - 2a$

C) $y = \dfrac{x}{a}(1 + 2a)$

D) $y = \dfrac{3x}{a}$

STOP

Passport to Advanced Math

Phew! So we just did a lot of algebra in the last chapter. But what if we did ... *more* algebra? Would you like to do more algebra? Of course you would.

The stupidly named Passport to Advanced Math questions are basically just Fancy Algebra questions. You're going to see a lot of variables and equations just like we've already seen. The biggest difference is that this chapter will have equations and expressions that are not linear. That means you'll see some exponents, some polynomials, some quadratic equations, and tons of fun stuff like that. (You'll also see some graphing on these questions, but we'll save that for a separate chapter.)

We're going to talk a lot about algebraic methods here, but please remember that a lot of problems that seem like they need algebra can also be done with our math techniques, Plug in and Backsolve. **Don't forget about the techniques!!**

I. *F(X)* NOTATION

Look at this:

$$5^2$$

What does that mean? Duh. Obviously:

$$5^2 = 5 \times 5$$

The little "2" tells us to multiply the big number times itself. We all know that. Similarly:

$$7^2 = 7 \times 7$$
$$(-23)^2 = (-23) \times (-23)$$
$$y^2 = y \times y$$
$$\Omega^2 = \Omega \times \Omega$$
$$(\text{donkey})^2 = (\text{donkey}) \times (\text{donkey})$$

This should not be news to you. Any time you see a little "2" next to *anything*, multiply it by itself.

That's a function. It's a symbol (the "2") with a rule attached to it (multiply by self). *Everything* we do in math is a kind of function: a symbol with a rule attached to it. We can make up our own functions. But instead of using a symbol like the little 2, we'll use the letter *f*:

$$f(x) = 2x + 5$$

The *x* here is just a **placeholder**; it's a variable that stands for *any number*, an example of how to use the function. Just as the little "2" meant "multiply the number by itself", the *f* here means "multiply by 2 and add 5".

That means:	$f(2) = 2(2) + 5$
and:	$f(3) = 2(3) + 5$
therefore:	$f(18) = 2(18) + 5$
so:	$f(1979) = 2(1979) + 5$
also:	$f(y) = 2y + 5$
as well as	$f(q) = 2(q) + 5$
plus this:	$f(g(k)) = 2(g(k)) + 5$
this too:	$f(omg) = 2(omg) + 5$
ergo:	$f(\pi) = 2(\pi) + 5$
thus:	$f(x^2 + 1) = 2(x^2 + 1) + 5$
why not:	$f(\copyright) = 2(\copyright) + 5$
one more:	$f(fluffybabypandabear) = 2(fluffybabypandabear) + 5$

Get the point? "*f(x)*" doesn't mean "multiply *f* by *x*". The *f* isn't a variable; it's the name of a *function*. Whatever you see next to the *f*, stick it in for *x* in 2*x* + 5.

We can do a lot with functions, but it all comes down to **substitution:**

Take whatever you see inside the parentheses and stick it in for *x*.

Composite functions

✒ **If $f(x) = 3x + 4$ and $g(x) = x^2$ what is the value of $f(g(3))$?**

We're given two functions, $f(x)$ and $g(x)$, and we have equations for both. This may seem scary, but it works exactly the same way the previous problems did. Remember: take whatever you see inside the parentheses and stick it in for x. Here, "$g(3)$" is inside the parentheses next to f, so "$g(3)$" will go in for x in the equation for $f(x)$:

$$f(g(3)) = 3 \times g(3) + 4$$

That doesn't help: what does $g(3)$ mean? Ah, that's just a different function. We can put 3 in for x in the equation for $g(x)$:

$$g(3) = (3)^2 = 9.$$

Now we'll substitute 9 back into the first function:

$$f(g(3)) = f(9) = 3 \times 9 + 4 = 27 + 4 = \mathbf{31}$$

Note that **the order is important**: do the function inside the parentheses first. Here, g was inside the parentheses for f, so we did g first. If the question had asked for $g(f(3))$, we'd first put 3 into the equation for f, then put the result into the equation for g:

$$g(f(3)) = (f(3))^2$$
$$f(3) = 3 \times 3 + 4 = 9 + 4 = 13.$$
$$g(f(3)) = g(13)$$
$$g(13) = 13^2 \boxed{= \mathbf{169}}$$

Multiple variables

> If $f(x, y) = 2x + 3y - xy$, what is the value of $f(5,-1)$?

This function has *two* variables inside the parentheses, but it also has two variables in the equation. Whenever we see two numbers inside the parentheses, we'll make the *first* number equal to x and the *second* equal to y.

$$f(5, -1) = 2(5) + 3(-1) - (5)(-1) \qquad = 10 + (-3) - (-5) \qquad = 10 - 3 + 5 = \mathbf{12}$$

✎ If $f(x) = x^2 + 3x - 10$, then $f(10) = ?$

✎ If $f(x) = x^2 + 3x - 10$, then $f(7) = ?$

✎ If $f(x) = x^2 + 3x - 10$, then $f(-3) = ?$

✎ If $f(x) = x^2 + 3x - 10$, then $f\left(\dfrac{1}{2}\right) = ?$

✎ If $f(x) = x^2 + 3x - 10$, then $f(2x) = ?$

✎ If $k(x) = x^3 + 2x$, what is $k(-2)$?

✎ If $f(x) = 5x - 3$ and $f(a) = 12$, what is the value of a?

✎ If $f(x) = 2x + 2$, then $2f(x) + 2 = ?$

✎ If $f(x) = 7x$ and $g(x) = f(x) + 7$, what is the value of $g(10)$?

✎ If $f(x) = x^2 - 2$, what is the value of $f(f(3))$?

f(x) notation

ANSWERS:

✎ If $f(x) = x^2 + 3x - 10$, then $f(10) = $?

Answer: 120.
$f(10) = 10^2 + 3(10) - 10$
$= 100 + 30 - 10$
$= 120$

✎ If $f(x) = x^2 + 3x - 10$, then $f(7) = $?

Answer: 60.
$f(7) = 7^2 + 3(7) - 10$
$= 49 + 21 - 10$
$= 60$

✎ If $f(x) = x^2 + 3x - 10$, then $f(-3) = $?

Answer: −10.
$f(-3) = (-3)^2 + 3(-3) - 10$
$= 9 - 9 - 10$
$= -10$

✎ If $f(x) = x^2 + 3x - 10$, then $f\left(\dfrac{1}{2}\right) = $?

Answer: $-\dfrac{33}{4}$ **or −8.25.**

$f\left(\dfrac{1}{2}\right) = \left(\dfrac{1}{2}\right)^2 + 3\left(\dfrac{1}{2}\right) - 10$ Or, $f(0.5) = (0.5)^2 + 3(0.5) - 10$

$= \dfrac{1}{4} + \dfrac{3}{2} - 10$ $= 0.25 + 1.5 - 10$

$= -\dfrac{33}{4}$ $= -8.25$

✎ If $f(x) = x^2 + 3x - 10$, then $f(2x) = $?

Answer: $4x^2 + 6x - 10$.
$f(2x) = (2x)^2 + 3(2x) - 10$
$= 4x^2 + 6x - 10$

✎ If $k(x) = x^3 + 2x$, what is $k(-2)$?

Answer: −12.
Just stick −2 in for x in the equation:
$k(-2) = (-2)^3 + 2(-2)$
$= -8 + (-4)$
$= -12.$

✎ If $f(x) = 5x - 3$ and $f(a) = 12$, what is the value of a?

Answer: 3.
$f(x) = 5x - 3$
$f(a) = 5a - 3 = 12$
$5a = 15$
$a = 3$

✎ If $f(x) = 2x + 2$, then $2f(x) + 2 = $?

Answer: $4x + 6$.
$f(x) = 2x + 2$
$2f(x) + 2 \quad = 2(2x + 2) + 2$
$= 4x + 4 + 2$
$= 4x + 6$

✎ If $f(x) = 7x$ and $g(x) = f(x) + 7$, what is the value of $g(10)$?

Answer: 77.
Start with g. We want $g(10)$. So put 10 in for x in the formula for g:
$g(10) = f(10) + 7$.
We need $f(10)$. Substitute 10 for x in the formula for f:
$f(10) = 7(10) = 70$.
Now put 70 in for $f(10)$ in the first equation:
$g(10) = 70 + 7 = \mathbf{77}$.

✎ If $f(x) = x^2 - 2$, what is the value of $f(f(3))$?

Answer: 47.
$f(3) = 3^2 - 2$ $f(3) = 9 - 2$ $f(3) = 7$
Now put 7 into f and do it again.
$f(f(3)) = f(7)$ $f(7) = 7^2 - 2$ $= 49 - 2 \quad = \mathbf{47}$

Polynomials

| ANSWERS: |

$2x^2 + 2x + 5 + 4x^2 + 3x - 7 = ?$

Answer: $6x^2 + 5x - 2$.

$\underline{2x^2} + 2x + 5 \underline{+ 4x^2} + 3x - 7$ $2x^2 + 4x^2 = 6x^2$
$6x^2 + \underline{2x} + 5 \underline{+ 3x} - 7$ $2x + 3x = 5x$
$6x^2 + 5x + 5 - 7$ $5 - 7 - 2$
$\mathbf{6x^2 + 5x - 2}$

$(3x^2 - 7x + 2) - (2x^2 + 5x + 3) = ?$

Answer: $x^2 - 12x - 1$.

$(3x^2 - 7x + 2) - (2x^2 + 5x + 3)$ First, distribute the negative
$\underline{3x^2} - 7x + 2 \underline{- 2x^2} - 5x - 3$ $3x^2 - 2x^2 = 5x^2$
$x^2 \underline{- 7x} + 2 \underline{- 5x} - 3$ $-7x - 5x = -12x$
$x^2 - 12x + 2 - 3$ $2 - 3 = -1$
$\mathbf{x^2 - 12x - 1}$

$(6x^2 + 5x + 3) - 2(2x^2 - 3x - 3) = ?$

Answer: $2x^2 + 11x + 9$

$(6x^2 + 5x + 3) - 2(2x^2 - 3x - 3)$ First, distribute the -32
$\underline{6x^2} + 5x + 3 \underline{- 4x^2} + 6x + 6$ $6x^2 - 4x^2 = 2x^2$
$2x^2 + \underline{5x} + 3 \underline{+ 6x} + 6$ $5x + 6x = 11x$
$2x^2 + 11x + 3 + 6$ $3 + 6 = 9$
$\mathbf{2x^2 + 11x + 9}$

$4x^3 + 3x^2 + 2x + 1 - x^3 + 9x^2 - 11x + 8 = ?$

Answer: $3x^3 + 12x^2 - 9x + 9$

$\underline{4x^3} + 3x^2 + 2x + 1 \underline{- x^3} + 9x^2 - 11x + 8$ $4x^3 - x^3 = 3x^3$
$3x^3 + \underline{3x^2} + 2x + 1 \underline{+ 9x^2} - 11x + 8$ $3x^2 + 9x^2 = 12x^2$
$3x^3 + 12x^2 + \underline{2x} + 1 \underline{- 11x} + 8$ $2x - 11x = -9x$
$3x^3 + 12x^2 - 9x + 1 + 8$ $1 + 8 = 9$
$3x^3 + 12x^2 - 9x + 9$
(Note: you could factor out a 3 here, but you don't have to.)

$3x^2 + 8x^2y - xy^2 + 2y^2 - 6x + 4y + 4x^2 - 5x^2y +$
$xy^2 + 8y^2 - x + 10y$

Answer: $7x^2 + 3x^2y + 10y^2 - 7x + 14y$

$\underline{3x^2} + 8x^2y - xy^2 + 2y^2 - 6x + 4y \underline{+ 4x^2} - 5x^2y + xy^2 + 8y^2 - x + 10y$
          $3x^2 + 4x^2 = 7x^2$

$7x^2 \underline{+ 8x^2y} - xy^2 + 2y^2 - 6x + 4y \underline{- 5x^2y} + xy^2 + 8y^2 - x + 10y$
          $8x^2y - 5x^2y = 3x^2y$

$7x^2 + 3x^2y \underline{- xy^2} + 2y^2 - 6x + 4y \underline{+ xy^2} + 8y^2 - x + 10y$
          $- xy^2 + xy^2 = 0$

$7x^2 + 3x^2y \underline{+ 2y^2} - 6x + 4y \underline{+ 8y^2} - x + 10y$
          $2y^2 + 8y^2 = 10y^2$

$7x^2 + 3x^2y \underline{- 6x} + 4y \underline{- x} + 10y$
          $- 6x - x = -7x$

$7x^2 + 3x^2y - 7x + 4y + 10y$
          $4y + 10y = 14y$

$\mathbf{7x^2 + 3x^2y - 7x + 14y}$

II. POLYNOMIALS

1. What's a polynomial?

A **polynomial** is any mathematical expression with terms that are added or subtracted together. These terms will usually contain variables taken to different powers multiplied by a number called its **coefficient**. A polynomial containing two terms is a **binomial**.
In the following expressions, all the terms contain the same variable taken to the same power, so they can be combined directly into one term:

$$5 + 7 = 12 \qquad 5y + 7y = 12y \qquad 5x^2 + 7x^2 = 12x^2$$

But in the following expressions, the terms are all different, so they can't be combined into one term:

$$5x + 7 \qquad\qquad 5x + 7y \qquad\qquad 5x^2 + 7x + xy$$

To simplify a long polynomial with a lot of different terms, find any terms that have the same combination of variables and powers:

$x^2 + 4x + 2xy + 7x^2 - 10x + 5 + 9xy - 1$	Add the terms containing x^2.
$8x^2 + \mathbf{4x} + 2xy - \mathbf{10x} + 5 + 9xy - 1$	Subtract the terms containing x.
$8x^2 - 6x + \mathbf{2xy} + 5 + \mathbf{9xy} - 1$	Add the terms containing xy.
$8x^2 - 6x + 11xy + \mathbf{5} - \mathbf{1}$	Subtract the terms with no variables.
$8x^2 - 6x + 11xy + 4$	

TRY SOME:

✎ $2x^2 + 2x + 5 + 4x^2 + 3x - 7 = ?$

✎ $(3x^2 - 7x + 2) - (2x^2 + 5x + 3) = ?$

✎ $(6x^2 + 5x + 3) - 2(2x^2 - 3x - 3) = ?$

✎ $4x^3 + 3x^2 + 2x + 1 - x^3 + 9x^2 - 11x + 8 = ?$

✎ $3x^2 + 8x^2y - xy^2 + 2y^2 - 6x + 4y + 4x^2 - 5x^2y + xy^2 + 8y^2 - x + 10y$

---

2. FOIL

Take a look at this:

> ✏ **6(x + 5)**

Here we have a number multiplied by an entire binomial. To do this, just multiply 6 by each term inside the parentheses. We sometimes call this *distributing* the 6 inside the parentheses.

$$6(x + 5) \qquad\qquad = 6 \times x + 6 \times 5 \qquad = 6x + 30$$

Great. Sometimes we want to multiply two binomials together:

> ✏ **(x + 5)(x + 4) = ?**

Just like we did above, we want to multiply *each* term in the first binomial with *each* term in the second. To help you keep track of the terms, remember the acronym "FOIL". Multiply:

First two terms	$x \times x$
Outside terms	$x \times 4$
Inside terms	$5 \times x$
Last terms	5×4

Then add them all together and combine similar terms:

$$= x^2 + 4x + 5x + 20 \qquad = x^2 + 9x + 20$$

TRY SOME:

✏ $(x + 8)(x - 3) = ?$

✏ $(a - 7)(a - 2) = ?$

✏ $(2y + 3)(y - 4) = ?$

✏ $(x + y)^2 = ?$

✏ $(x^2 + y)(3x^2 + 2y) = ?$

Watch out for negatives! If you multiply a polynomial by a negative number, you must distribute the negative inside the parentheses.

FOIL

ANSWERS:

$(x + 8)(x - 3) = ?$

Answer: $x^2 + 5x - 24$

$(x + 8)(x - 3)$
$= x^2 - 3x + 8x - 24$
$= x^2 + 5x - 24$

$(a - 7)(a - 2) = ?$

Answer: $a^2 - 9a + 14$

$(a - 7)(a - 2)$
$= a^2 - 2a - 7a + 14$
$= a^2 - 9a + 14$

$(2y + 3)(y - 4) = ?$

Answer: $2y^2 - 5y - 12$

$(2y + 3)(y - 4)$
$= 2y^2 - 8y + 3y - 12$
$= 2y^2 - 5y - 12$

$(x + y)^2 = ?$

Answer: $x^2 + 2xy + y^2$

$= (x + y)(x + y)$
$= x^2 + xy + yx + y^2$
$= x^2 + 2xy + y^2$

$(x^2 + y)(3x^2 + 2y) = ?$

Answer: $3x^4 + 5x^2y + 2y^2$
$= (x^2)(3x^2) + (x^2)(2y) + (y)(3x^2) + y \times 2y$
$= 3x^4 + 2x^2y + 3yx^2 + 2y^2$ Note that $2x^2y$ and $3yx^2$ can be added directly.
$= 3x^4 + 5x^2y + 2y^2$

THIS PAGE INTENTIONALLY LEFT BLANK

3. Factoring

FOIL involves multiplying two binomials to get a larger polynomial. But some SAT problems might want you to go the other way. Look at this expression:

> ✐ **2x + 6**

Notice that each term in this expression is a multiple of two. We can "pull out" that two and put it off to the side:

$$2x + 6 \qquad = (2 \times x) + (2 \times 3) \qquad = 2(x + 3)$$

We call this process **factoring**. It's the opposite of distributing. In this case, 2 was a factor of each term, so we "factored out" the 2. We can do the same thing with variables:

$$x^2 - 3x \qquad = (x \times x) - (3 \times x) \qquad = x(x - 3)$$

What if we want to factor a polynomial into two binomials? Look at this expression:

> ✐ **What is the factored form of $x^2 + 7x + 12$?**

We know that there must be two binomials that multiply together to make that expression:

$$(? + ?)(? + ?)$$

The first term here, x^2, was the result of the first two terms of the binomials multiplied together. So each of the binomials must start with an x:

$$(x + ?)(x + ?)$$

The last term, 12, was the result of the last two terms of the binomials multiplied together. So we know the **product** of our last two numbers is 12. That could be 1 and 12, 2 and 6, or 3 and 4.*

The middle term, $7x$, was the result of each of the last terms multiplied by x and then added together. So we also know the **sum** of the last two numbers must be 7. What two numbers have a product of 12 and a sum of 7? Only 3 and 4 fit both requirements.

$$(x + 3)(x + 4) \qquad = x^2 + 4x + 3x + 12 \qquad = x^2 + 7x + 12$$

---

* That's assuming all terms are integers, of course. The terms might also be 24 and 0.5 if we allow decimals. But SAT problems usually stick to integers, so you don't have to worry about such madness.

This can be easier when you have answer choices:

> **12.** **Which of the following expressions is equivalent to $x^2 - 2x - 15$?**
> **A)** $(x - 2)(x + 1)$
> **B)** $(x - 3)(x + 5)$
> **C)** $(x + 3)(x - 5)$
> **D)** $(x - 3)(x - 5)$

One option here is **Backsolve**: It's often easier to FOIL than to factor, so FOIL out the answer choices and see which one equals the polynomial we want:

A)	$(x - 2)(x + 1)$	$= x^2 + x - 2x - 2$	$= x^2 - x - 2$ ✗
B)	$(x - 3)(x + 5)$	$= x^2 + 5x - 3x - 15$	$= x^2 + 2x - 15$ ✗
C)	$(x + 3)(x - 5)$	$= x^2 - 5x + 3x - 15$	$= x^2 - 2x - 15$ ✓
D)	$(x - 3)(x - 5)$	$= x^2 - 5x - 3x + 15$	$= x^2 - 8x + 15$ ✗

Even better, you could **Plug In** a number for x. Say $x = 6$.

$$(6)^2 - 2(6) - 15 \qquad = 36 - 12 - 15 \ = \mathbf{9}$$

A)	$(6 - 2)(6 + 1)$	$= (4)(7)$	$= 28$ ✗
B)	$(6 - 3)(6 + 5)$	$= (3)(11)$	$= 11$ ✗
C)	$(6 + 3)(6 - 5)$	$= (9)(1)$	$= 9$ ✓
D)	$(6 - 3)(6 - 5)$	$= (3)(1)$	$= 3$ ✗

(Note that we picked a biggish number here so that most of the choices came out positive. But if you start with $x = 0$, you can eliminate A) and D) very quickly.

Difference of Squares

Try this problem:

> ✒ $(x + y)(x - y) = ?$

Both binomials contain the same terms, except one binomial is a sum and the other is a difference. To do this, we can just FOIL as we did before:

$$(x + y)(x - y) \quad = \quad x^2 - xy + xy - y \qquad = x^2 - y^2$$

Notice that the middle terms cancelled out, so the result was just the first term squared minus the second term squared. This equation is called the **difference of squares identity**. An "identity" just means it's an equation that shows up a lot that's always true for any variables, so it's good to remember it.

THIS PAGE INTENTIONALLY LEFT BLANK

Factoring

ANSWERS:

✎ $x^2 - 2x - 8$

Answer: $(x - 4)(x + 2)$

✎ $x^2 - 14x + 24$

Answer: $(x - 2)(x - 12)$

✎ $2x^2 + 11x + 5$

Answer: $(2x + 1)(x + 5)$

✎ $9x^2 - 49$

Answer: $(3x - 7)(3x + 7)$
$9x^2$ and 49 are squares, so use the difference of squares identity.

✎ $x^4 - 16$

Answer: $(x - 2)(x + 2)(x^2 + 4)$
x^4 and 16 are squares, so use the Difference of Squares Identity.
$= (x^2 - 4)(x^2 + 4)$ Ah, look at the first term! x^2 and 4 are also both squares!
$= (x - 2)(x + 2)(x^2 + 4)$ We can't factor the last term, though.

$$x^2 - y^2 = (x + y)(x - y)$$

When you see two squares subtracted from each other, you can easily factor the expression. For example:

✎ $x^2 - 64 = ?$

Both terms here are squares, so we can immediately factor it into the sum and difference of their roots:

$$= (x + 8)(x - 8)$$

TRY SOME:

Factor the following expressions:

✎ $x^2 - 2x - 8$

✎ $x^2 - 14x + 24$

✎ $2x^2 + 11x + 5$

✎ $9x^2 - 49$

✎ $x^4 - 16$

4. Dividing polynomials

So far we've been multiplying polynomials, but we can divide polynomials, too.

$$\text{✐} \quad \frac{x+3}{x^2+x-6} = ?$$

What do we do? Remember that a fraction can be reduced when the top and bottom have a common term:

$$\frac{2}{8} = \frac{2 \times 1}{2 \times 4} = \frac{1}{4}$$

The same concept applies to polynomials. Let's factor the denominator and see if we can cross out some terms common to the top and bottom.

When factoring, our ultimate goal is canceling out terms. Don't factor blindly: *try to factor out the term that's in the numerator.* In this problem, we want to cancel out "$x + 3$", so we'll try to get "$x + 3$" on the bottom. The bottom ends in "-6": what times 3 gives -6? -2. So the other term will be "$x - 2$". Now $x + 3$ cancels out on the top and bottom:

$$\frac{x+3}{x^2+x-6} \qquad = \frac{x+3}{(x+3)(x-2)} \qquad \boxed{= \frac{1}{x-2}}$$

PLEASE NOTE: whenever a problem involves division by a binomial, there will be some values of x that are not allowed. As a rule, **you can never divide anything by zero**. Any values that make the denominator zero will not be allowed. The fancy math way of saying that is to say the expression is **undefined** for that value of x. In the problem above, the denominator is zero when $x + 3 = 0$ or when $x - 2 = 0$. So the expression is undefined when $x = -3$ and when $x = 2$.

Long division

But what if you want to divide by a polynomial that *isn't* a factor of the numerator? Can we do anything? Yes! We can use *long division!*

Let's take a refresher on how to do long division with integers. Let's try $172 \div 5$:

We're getting into some concepts that only show up on hard questions. If you have low target numbers, these concepts are probably not important to you.

1. How many times does 5 go into 17? *3 times.*

$$5\overline{)172} \quad \overset{3}{}$$

2. Multiply 3×5 to get 15. Subtract 15 from 17 to get 2.

$$\begin{array}{r} 3 \\ 5\overline{)172} \\ \underline{15} \\ 2 \end{array}$$

3. Bring down the 2 to get 22. How many times does 5 go into 22? *4 times.*

$$\begin{array}{r} 34 \\ 5\overline{)172} \\ \underline{15} \\ 22 \end{array}$$

4. Multiply 4×5 to get 20. Subtract 20 from 22 to get 2. That's as far as you can go, so your remainder is 2.

$$\begin{array}{r} 34 \\ 5\overline{)172} \\ \underline{15} \\ 22 \\ \underline{-20} \\ 2 \leftarrow R \end{array}$$

So $172 \div 5$ is 34 with a remainder of 2. But if we punch that out on the calculator we get 34.4. That's because ".4" is the same thing as 2/5:

$$\frac{172}{5} \quad = \frac{170+2}{5} \quad = \frac{170}{5} + \frac{2}{5} \quad = 34 + \frac{2}{5}$$

Basically, we split up 172 into a number that *was* divisible by 5, plus a bit that got turned into a fraction.

We can do the same thing with polynomials! Let's look at this one:

$$\frac{3x-5}{x+2} = ?$$

Here, $x + 2$ is not a factor of $3x - 5$. So let's find something that *does* have $x + 2$ as a factor.

1. Set it up as we did before. Focus on the first term. How many x's go into $3x$?

$$x+2\overline{)3x-5}$$

2. Multiply x by 3 to get $3x$.

$$x+2\overline{)3x-5} \quad \overset{3}{}$$

3. Multiply 3 by $x + 2$ and line it up.

$$x+2 \overline{)\begin{array}{r} 3 \\ 3x-5 \\ 3x+6 \end{array}}$$

4. Subtract to get a remainder of -11

$$x+2 \overline{)\begin{array}{r} 3 \\ 3x-5 \\ \underline{3x+6} \\ -11 \end{array}}$$

You don't have to do this so formally. Just think: what do I have to multiply "$x + 2$" by in order to get an answer that starts with "$3x$"? Multiply by 3! Which gets you $3x + 6$. In other words:

$$\frac{3x-5}{x+2} = \frac{(3x+6)-11}{x+2} = \frac{3x+6}{x+2} + \frac{-11}{x+2} = \frac{3(x+2)}{x+2} + \frac{-11}{x+2} \boxed{= 3 - \frac{11}{x+2}}$$

Let's try a harder one:

$$\frac{x^2+4x+5}{x+1} = ?$$

We'll start the same way:

1. Set it up as we did before. Focus on the first term. How many x's go into x^2?

$$x+1 \overline{)x^2+4x+5}$$

2. Multiply x by x to get x^2.

$$x+1 \overline{)\begin{array}{r} x \\ x^2+4x+5 \end{array}}$$

3. Multiply x by $x + 1$ and line up the result. Subtract.

$$x+1 \overline{)\begin{array}{r} x \\ x^2+4x+5 \\ \underline{x^2+x} \\ 3x \end{array}}$$

4. Bring down the "+5". How many x's go into $3x$?

$$x+1 \overline{)\begin{array}{r} x \\ x^2+4x+5 \\ \underline{x^2+x} \\ 3x+5 \end{array}}$$

5. Multiply 3 by $x + 1$ and line up the result. Subtract. Our remainder is 2.

$$x+1 \overline{)\begin{array}{r} x+3 \\ x^2+4x+5 \\ \underline{x^2+x} \\ 3x+5 \\ \underline{3x+3} \\ 2 \end{array}}$$

Like in the last one, think "what can I multiply "$x + 1$" by in order to get "$x^2 + 4x$" at the start of my polynomial. In other words:

$$\frac{x^2 + 4x + 5}{x + 1} = \frac{(x^2 + 4x + 3) + 2}{x + 1} = \frac{(x+1)(x+3) + 2}{x + 1} = \frac{(x+1)(x+3)}{x + 1} + \frac{2}{x + 1}$$

$$\boxed{= x + 3 + \frac{2}{x + 1}}$$

If all this scares you, don't worry. This kind of division is very rare on the test. Questions that do require it will usually be harder questions at the end of a section, so chances are your Target Numbers will have you skipping them anyway. (Of course, don't forget that when there are answer choices, problems like this can become super easy with Plug In.)

Divide the following expressions (assuming the denominator is not zero in all cases).

✎ $\dfrac{x}{x^2+7x}=?$

✎ $\dfrac{x+5}{x^2-25}=?$

✎ $\dfrac{x^2+6x-40}{x-4}=?$

✎ $\dfrac{2x+2}{x-1}=?$

✎ $\dfrac{x^2+5x+10}{x+2}=?$

Dividing polynomials

ANSWERS:

$\dfrac{x}{x^2 + 7x} = ?$

Answer: $\dfrac{1}{x+7}$

$= \dfrac{x}{x(x+7)}$ Cancel out an x.

$= \dfrac{1}{x+7}$

$\dfrac{x+5}{x^2-25} = ?$

Answer: $\dfrac{1}{x-5}$

$= \dfrac{x+5}{(x+5)(x-5)}$ Cancel out an $x+5$

$= \dfrac{1}{x-5}$

$\dfrac{x^2 + 6x - 40}{x-4} = ?$

Answer: $x + 10$

$= \dfrac{(x-4)(x+10)}{x-4}$ Cancel out an $x-4$

$= x + 10$

$\dfrac{2x+2}{x-1}$

Answer: $2 + \dfrac{4}{x-1}$

$x-1$ will not factor out of $2x+2$.
To get from x to $2x$ we multiply by 2: $2(x-1) = 2x-2$.
Let's factor that out of the numerator:

$\dfrac{2x+2}{x-1} \quad = \dfrac{2x-2+4}{x-1} \quad = \dfrac{2(x-1)+4}{x-1} \quad = \dfrac{2(x-1)}{x-1} + \dfrac{4}{x-1}$

$= 2 + \dfrac{4}{x-1}$

$\dfrac{x^2 + 5x + 10}{x+2}$

Answer: $x + 3 + \dfrac{4}{x+2}$

$$
\begin{array}{r}
x+3 \\
x+2\overline{\smash{)}\,x^2+5x+10} \\
\underline{x^2+2x} \\
3x+10 \\
\underline{3x+6} \\
4
\end{array}
$$

Here's the long division.

$\dfrac{x^2 + 5x + 10}{x+2} = \dfrac{(x+2)(x+3)+4}{x+2} = \dfrac{(x+2)(x+3)}{x+2} + \dfrac{4}{x+2}$

$= x + 3 + \dfrac{4}{x+2}$

THIS PAGE INTENTIONALLY LEFT BLANK

5. Quadratic equations

All the polynomial problems we've seen so far have been expressions, not equations. That means almost any value of x will make it work. But we might also see polynomials involved in *equations*, where only certain values of x will make the equation true.

Any equation in the form

$$ax^2 + bx + c = 0$$

is a **quadratic** equation—a polynomial containing one squared variable, usually set equal to zero.* So how do we solve it?

> ✎ **For what values of x does $x^2 + 7x + 12 = 0$?**

Well, we already factored this expression before, so let's do it again:

$$x^2 + 7x + 12 = (x + 3)(x + 4) = 0$$

Remember that zero has a special property: anything times zero is equal to zero. If we know $ab = 0$, then we know either a or b (or both) *must* equal zero. Since we know that $(x + 3)$ times $(x + 4)$ equals zero, we know that one or both of those terms must equal zero:

$x + 3 = 0$	or	$x + 4 = 0$
$x = -3$	**or**	$x = -4$

So our solutions are −3 and −4.[†]

Note that **you must set a quadratic equation equal to zero to solve it.**

> ✎ **For what values of x does $x^2 - 3x + 2 = 20$?**

Beware of the change in sign! We factored the expression to $x + 3$ and $x + 4$, but the solutions for x are −3 and −4.

---

* If the variable is only taken to the *second* power, why is it called *quadratic*? Doesn't "quad" mean "four"? Indeed it does. The term comes from the Latin word "quadratus", meaning "square" (as in "*x squared*"). And a square has *four* sides.

† Notice that the value of c—the number with no variable—is equal to the product of the solutions ($-3 \times -4 = 12$), and the value of b—the number next to x in the original equation—is equal to the sum of the negatives of the solutions $(3 + 4) = 12$. This is just true because of the rules of factoring that we've already seen (and because $a = 1$), but being able to recognize this fact can sometimes save you some time. (Why we take the negative of the sum but not the product? We actually can take the negatives of the terms in the product as well, it's just that −3 times −4 comes out the same as 3 times 4.)

Here we have 20 on the right side. That's no good; we want 0 there. So we'll just subtract 20 from both sides before we factor:

$$x^2 - 3x + 2 - 20 = 20 - 20$$
$$x^2 - 3x - 18 = 0$$
$$(x - 6)(x + 3) = 0$$
$$x - 6 = 0 \quad \text{or} \quad x + 3 = 0$$
$$\boxed{x = 6 \quad \text{or} \quad x = -3}$$

The Quadratic Formula

Not all quadratic equations can be happily factored. Sometimes the solutions are not integers. In your math class at school, you may have been exposed to the quadratic formula. This is a special formula you can use to find the solutions for a quadratic equation. You can use it for any quadratic equation, but it's especially useful for polynomials that can't be factored into happy integers.

For the equation $ax^2 + bx + c = 0$, the solution for x is: $\quad x = \dfrac{-b \pm \sqrt{b^2 - 4ac}}{2a}$

> ✎ **What are the solutions for $x^2 + 2x - 9 = 0$?**

The equation is in the form $ax^2 + bx + c$, where $a = 1$, $b = 2$, and $c = -9$. Let's stick 'em in the formula and see what comes out:

$$x = \frac{-b \pm \sqrt{b^2 - 4ac}}{2a} \qquad = \frac{-2 \pm \sqrt{2^2 - 4(1)(-9)}}{2(1)} \qquad = \frac{-2 \pm \sqrt{4 + 36}}{2}$$

$$= \frac{-2 \pm \sqrt{40}}{2} \qquad = \frac{-2 \pm 2\sqrt{10}}{2} \qquad = \boxed{-1 \pm \sqrt{10}}$$

That means there are two solutions: $-1 + \sqrt{10}$ and $-1 - \sqrt{10}$.

Notice that we got two solutions there. That's because of the number under the square root sign, called the **discriminant**.

$$\text{discriminant} = b^2 - 4ac$$

The formula asks you to both *add* and *subtract* the root of the discriminant. If the discriminant is positive, like 10 in the example above, the root will come out to a positive number, and you'll get two different results.

But what if the discriminant is zero? Then the root will come out to zero. Then you'll only get one result because adding zero and subtracting zero give you the same answer. What if the discriminant comes out negative? Then you'll have to take the square root of a negative, but you're not allowed to do that.* In that case there simply is no real solution. Therefore:

- If the discriminant is **positive**, you get **two solutions**.
- If the discriminant is **zero**, you get **one solution**.
- If the discriminant is **negative**, you get **no** solution.

If all this scares you, don't worry. You don't have to worry about it too much. There will be some questions that require you to know the quadratic formula. However, such questions are rare. Most of the time you should be able to do any problem involving quadratics by factoring or with Plug In and Backsolve.† Furthermore, questions that do require it will usually be harder questions at the end of a section, so chances are your Target Numbers will have you skipping it anyway.

---

* Technically you *are* allowed to do that, but you won't get *real* solutions. Only *imaginary* solutions. We'll talk more about imaginary numbers in the Additional Topics chapter.

† One way the formula can help is if you have a graphing calculator that allows programs. You can program the formula into your calculator so that you just have to input a, b, and c, and the program does the calculations for you. If you know how to do this, it can be nice and quick. But if you don't, don't worry about it. (You can also find the solutions by graphing the functions and looking where the function crosses the x-axis. We'll talk more about graphing in the next chapter.)

> What are the solutions for $x^2 - 12x = 0$?

> What are the solutions for $x^2 - 11x + 30 = 0$?

> What are the solutions for $x^2 - 7x - 8 = 0$?

> What are the solutions for $x^2 - 81 = 0$?

> What are the solutions for $x^2 - 13x = -42$?

Quadratic equations

ANSWERS:

✏ What are the solutions for $x^2 - 12x = 0$?

Answer: 0 or 12

$x(x - 12) = 0$

$x = 0$	or	$x - 12 = 0$
$x = 0$	**or**	$x = 12$

✏ What are the solutions for $x^2 - 11x + 30 = 0$?

Answer: 5 or 6

$(x - 5)(x - 6) = 0$

$x - 5 = 0$	or	$x - 6 = 0$
$x = 5$	**or**	$x = 6$

✏ What are the solutions for $x^2 - 7x - 8 = 0$?

Answer: –1 or 8

$(x + 1)(x - 8) = 0$

$x + 1 = 0$	or	$x - 8 = 0$
$x = -1$	**or**	$x = 8$

✏ What are the solutions for $x^2 - 81 = 0$?

Answer: –9 or 9

$(x + 9)(x - 9) = 0$

$x + 9 = 0$	or	$x - 9 = 0$
$x = -9$	**or**	$x = 9$

Or add 81 to both sides:

$x^2 = 81 \qquad x = \pm 9$

✏ What are the solutions for $x^2 - 13x = -42$?

Answer: 6 or 7

First, add 42 to both sides to get 0 on the right:

$x^2 - 13x + 42 = 0$ Now factor and solve.

$(x - 6)(x - 7) = 0$

$x - 6 = 0$	or	$x - 7 = 0$
$x = 6$	**or**	$x = 7$

THIS PAGE INTENTIONALLY LEFT BLANK

III. EXPONENTIAL GROWTH

We've seen lots of examples of equations that have exponents. But all the ones we've seen have had variables in the *base* of the number. In the equation $y = x^2$, x^2 is an exponential number, x is the base, and 2 is the exponent.

However, we can also make functions that have *variables in the exponents*. These are called **exponential growth functions.** They show up most frequently when you want to *apply a percent multiple times in a row.* Observe:

> ✎ **Each year the population of goats in the basement grows by 20%. If the goat population starts at 125 goats, approximately how many goats will there be after 3 years?**

Let's just do it out. After 1 year, the population will grow by 20%.

1 year:	$125 + \dfrac{20}{100} \times (125)$	That's 125 plus 20% of 125.
	$= 125 + 0.2(125)$	We can re-write this by factoring out 125.
	$= 125 \times (1 + 0.2)$	
	$= 125 \times (1.2)$	
	$= 150$	150 goats after 1 year

To find the next two years, repeat the process. The trick with questions like this is that you have to re-calculate the percent every year using the *new* total for the previous year. So when we're calculating year 2, we'll start with 150 instead of 125.

2 years:	$150 + \dfrac{20}{100} \times (150)$	
	$= 150 \times (1.2)$	
	$= 180$	That's after 2 years. One more:

3 years:	$180 \times (1.2)$	
	$= 216$	That's after 3 years.

But look what we did: to get to year *three*, we started with 125 and multiplied by 1.2 *three times*. Looking backwards from year 3:

	216	After 3 years
	$= (\mathbf{180}) \times 1.2$	That's 2 years times 1.2...
	$= ([\mathbf{150}] \times \mathbf{1.2}) \times 1.2$	which in turn was 1 year times 1.2...

$$= (\left[\mathbf{125 \times 1.2} \right] \times \mathbf{1.2}) \times 1.2 \quad \text{which in turn was the starting value times 1.2.}$$
$$= 125 \times (1.2)^3 \qquad \qquad \text{So we have the starting value times three 1.2's.}$$

If that's what we did after *three years*, we can generalize it into an equation for x years:

$$G(x) = 125 \times (1.2)^x \qquad \text{where } x \text{ is the number of years passed, and 125 is the starting}$$

value.

We can further generalize that into an equation for *any* kind of exponential growth:

$$\boxed{G(x) = a(r)^x}$$

where:

- $G(x)$ is the total quantity after growth
- a is the starting total
- r is the percent growth rate with respect to 1 (e.g. 20% growth is 1.2, while 20% decrease is 0.8)*
- x is the time passed

This may seem intimidating, but most exponential questions won't ask you to do a lot of work. More often than not, they simply ask you to understand what the parts. The more time you spend with this equation, the more you'll get to know him, maybe even love him.

---

* In most SAT problems the rate is expressed as a decimal with respect to 1 like this. But sometimes the equation may be written as $a(1 + r/100)^t$ instead. Here, with 20% growth, the equation would have $r = 20$ instead of $r = 1.2$).

THIS PAGE INTENTIONALLY LEFT BLANK

Passport to Advanced Math Exercise

1. Answer: B.
Substitute $x = -4$ into the expression:

$$\frac{(-4)^2 - 4}{-4 - 2} = \frac{16 - 4}{-6} = \frac{12}{-6} = -2$$

Some kids might notice that you can factor $x - 2$ out of the original equation:

$$\frac{x^2 - 4}{x - 2} = \frac{(x + 2)(x - 2)}{x - 2} = x + 2.$$

Substitute $x = -4$ to get $-4 + 2 = \mathbf{-2}$

But you really don't need to see that to get this problem. Anyone should be able to get this.

2. Answer: B.
$$\sqrt{x^2 + 16} - 5 = 0$$
$$\sqrt{x^2 + 16} = 5 \qquad \text{Square both sides.}$$
$$x^2 + 16 = 25$$
$$x^2 = 9$$
$$x = 3$$

You could also *Backsolve*

C) $x = 4$
$$\sqrt{4^2 + 16} - 5$$
$$= \sqrt{16 + 16} - 5$$
$$= \sqrt{32} - 5 \qquad \text{I can tell already this won't work}$$
$$= 5.65 - 5 = 0.65 \text{ ✗ No good. Should be zero. Go smaller.}$$

B) $x = 3$
$$\sqrt{3^2 + 16} - 5$$
$$= \sqrt{9 + 16} - 5$$
$$= \sqrt{25} - 5$$
$$= 5 - 5 = 0 \checkmark$$

3. Answer: B.
FOIL! Multiply the **F**irst two terms, the **O**utside terms, the **I**nside terms, and the **L**ast two, and add 'em up.
$$(x - a)(x + b) = x^2 + bx - ax - ab$$
Factor out an x in the middle two terms.
$$x^2 + (b - a)x - ab \qquad \text{That's \textbf{choice B).}}$$

You could also use *Plug In*. Just pick an a and a b.
Say $a = 3$, $b = 4$.
$$(x - 3)(x + 4) = x^2 + 4x - 3x + (-3)(4) = x^2 + x - 12.$$
Put your a and b into the choices and see which matches:

A) $x^2 - (b - a)x - ab \quad = x^2 - (4 - 3)x - 12 \quad = x^2 - x - 12$ ✗
B) $x^2 + (b - a)x - ab \quad = x^2 + (4 - 3)x - 12 \quad = x^2 + x - 12$ ✓
C) $x^2 + (a - b)x + ab \quad = x^2 + (3 - 4)x + 12 \quad = x^2 - x + 12$ ✗
D) $x^2 + (a + b)x + ab \quad = x^2 + (3 + 4)x + 12 \quad = x^2 + 7x + 12$ ✗

If you *really* don't like FOILing, you could plug in for x, too.
Say we use the same a and b and make $x = 2$.
$(2 - 3)(2 + 4) = (-1)(6) = \mathbf{-6}$. Which choice comes out to -6?

A) $x^2 - (b - a)x - ab$
$$= 2^2 - (4 - 3)2 - (3)(4) \qquad = 4 - (1)2 - 12 \qquad = -10 \text{ ✗}$$
B) $x^2 + (b - a)x - ab$
$$= 2^2 + (4 - 3)2 - (3)(4) \qquad = 4 + (1)2 - 12 \qquad = -6 \checkmark$$
C) $x^2 + (a - b)x + ab$
$$= 2^2 + (3 - 4)2 + (3)(4) \qquad = 4 + (-1)2 + 12 \qquad = 14 \text{ ✗}$$
D) $x^2 + (a + b)x + ab$
$$= 2^2 + (3 + 4)2 + (3)(4) \qquad = 4 + (7)2 + 12 \qquad = 30 \text{ ✗}$$
…but you really ought to learn to FOIL.

4. Answer: C.
FOIL! Multiply the **F**irst two terms, the **O**utside terms, the **I**nside terms, and the **L**ast two, and add 'em up.

$(4p + 3)(5p - 6)$
$= 20p^2 - 24p + 15p - 18$
$= \mathbf{20p^2 - 9p - 18}$. That's **choice C).**

You could also use *Plug In*. Let's keep it simple and say $p = 1$:
$(4 \times 1 + 3)(5 \times 1 - 6) = (4 + 3)(5 - 6) = (7)(-1) = \mathbf{-7}$. Which choice comes out to -7?

A) $20p^2 - 18 \qquad\qquad 20 - 18 \qquad\qquad = 2$ ✗
B) $20p^2 - 3p - 18 \qquad 20 - 3 - 18 \qquad = -1$ ✗
C) $20p^2 - 9p - 18 \qquad 20 - 9 - 18 \qquad = -7$ ✓
D) $20p^2 + 39p - 18 \qquad 20 + 39 - 18 \qquad = 41$ ✗

PASSPORT TO ADVANCED MATH EXERCISE

1

If $x = -4$, what is the value of $\dfrac{x^2 - 4}{x - 2}$?

A) -3
B) -2
C) 0
D) 2

2

$$\sqrt{x^2 + 16} - c = 0$$

If $x > 0$ and $c = 5$, what is the value of x?

A) 1
B) 3
C) 4
D) 5

3

Which of the following is equivalent to $(x - a)(x + b)$?

A) $x^2 - (b - a)x - ab$
B) $x^2 + (b - a)x - ab$
C) $x^2 + (a - b)x + ab$
D) $x^2 + (a + b)x + ab$

4

The expression $(4p + 3)(5p - 6)$ is equivalent to:

A) $20p^2 - 18$
B) $20p^2 - 3p - 18$
C) $20p^2 - 9p - 18$
D) $20p^2 + 39p - 18$

CONTINUE

$$(3x^4 - 2x^3 - 5) - 2(x^4 - 2x^3 + 3x^2 - 2x + 2)$$

The expression above is equivalent to which of the following expressions?

A) $x^{17} - 9$

B) $x^4 + 2x^3 - 6x^2 + 4x - 9$

C) $x^4 - 4x^3 + 3x^2 - 2x - 3$

D) $x^4 - 6x^3 + 6x^2 - 4x - 1$

$$x^2(x^2 - 10) = -9$$

Which of the following gives the solution set for x ?

A) $\{1, 3\}$

B) $\{1, 9\}$

C) $\{-3, -1, 1, 3\}$

D) $\{-9, -1, 1, 9\}$

If $x^2 \neq 16$, $\dfrac{(x+4)^2}{x^2 - 16} = ?$

A) $8x$

B) $-\dfrac{1}{4}$

C) $\dfrac{1}{x-4}$

D) $\dfrac{x+4}{x-4}$

8

If $f(x) = x^2 - 14$, then $f(x + c) = ?$

A) $x^2 + c - 14$

B) $x^2 - 14cx + c^2$

C) $x^2 + 2cx + c^2$

D) $x^2 + 2cx + c^2 - 14$

CONTINUE

5. Answer: B.

$$\left(3x^4 - 2x^3 - 5\right) - 2\left(x^4 - 2x^3 + 3x^2 - 2x + 2\right)$$

Distribute the –2. *Watch your negatives!*

$$= 3x^4 \underline{- 2x^3} - 5 - 2x^4 \underline{+ 4x^3} - 6x^2 + 4x - 4$$

Let's put similar terms next to each other.

$$= 3x^4 - 2x^4 \underline{- 2x^3 + 4x^3} - 6x^2 + 4x - 5 - 4$$

Add similar terms.

$$= x^4 + 2x^3 - 6x^2 + 4x - 9$$

RTFQs: Choice C) means they ignored the parentheses in the second half and didn't distribute.
Choice D) means they distributed positive 2 instead of –2.

Or use **Plug In**. Make $x = 2$ and compute.

$$\left(3(2)^4 - 2(2)^3 - 5\right) - 2\left(2^4 - 2(2)^3 + 3(2)^2 - 2(2) + 2\right)$$
$$= (3(16) - 2(8) - 5) - 2(16 - 2(8) + 3(4) - 4 + 2)$$
$$= 3(48 - 16 - 5) - 2(16 - 16 + 12 - 2)$$
$$= 3(9) - 2(10)$$
$$= 27 - 20$$
$$= 7$$

Now plug $x = 2$ into the answers and see which one equals 7.

A) $2^{17} - 9$ $= 131{,}063$ ✗ I think that's a bit too big.
B) $2^4 + 2(2^3) - 6(2^2) + 4(2) - 9$ $= 16 + 16 - 24 + 8 - 9$ $= 7$ ✓
C) $2^4 - 4(2^3) + 3(2^2) - 2(2) - 3$ $= 16 - 32 + 12 - 4 - 3$ $= -11$ ✗
D) $2^4 - 6(2^3) + 6(2^2) - 4(2) - 1$ $= 16 - 48 + 24 - 8 - 1$ $= -17$ ✗

Plug in can help avoid distribution errors because you'll find the value in the parentheses first. But that was kind of annoying. It's still a long string of calculations, so we need still to be careful.

However, if you want to make life *really* easy (I do!), you can try $x = 0$:

$$\left(3(0)^4 - 2(0)^3 - 5\right) - 2\left(0^4 - 2(0)^3 + 3(0)^2 - 2(0) + 2\right)$$
$$= (0 - 0 - 5) - 2(0 - 0 + 0 - 0 + 2)$$
$$= -5 - 2(2)$$
$$= -9$$

Now plug $x = 0$ into the answers and see which one equals –9. Anything with an x goes away!

A) $0^{17} - 9$ $= -9$ ✓
B) $0^4 + 2(0^3) - 6(0^2) + 4(0) - 9 = -9$ ✓
C) $0^4 - 4(0^3) + 3(0^2) - 2(0) - 3 = -3$ ✗
D) $0^4 - 6(0^3) + 6(0^2) - 4(0) - 1 = -1$ ✗

The advantage with using zero is that it's *really fast*. The disadvantage is that two choices work. Now, if you know anything at all about polynomials, it should be really obvious that A) is wrong. But not all of your students know anything at all about polynomials. Those students should eliminate C) and D), and then try a different number for x.

6. Answer: D.

Factor the denominator and cancel out any common factors.

$$\frac{(x+4)^2}{x^2 - 16} = \frac{(x+4)(x+4)}{(x+4)(x-4)} = \frac{x+4}{x-4}$$

Or **Plug In**. Let's say $x = 5$.
(We know $x^2 \neq 16$, so don't pick $x = 4$ or $x = -4$.)

$$\frac{(5+4)^2}{5^2 - 16} = \frac{81}{9} = 9$$

Now plug $x = 5$ into the answers and see which one equals 9.

A) $8(5) = 40$ ✗
B) $-\dfrac{1}{4}$ ✗
C) $\dfrac{1}{5-4} = \dfrac{1}{1} = 1$ ✗
D) $\dfrac{5+4}{5-4} = \dfrac{9}{1} = 9$ ✓

7. Answer: C.

Plug-In/Backsolve
We're going to test numbers in the equation like Plug In, but we're going to use the values in the choices like Backsolve.

All choices have $x = 1$, so don't bother with that. But only half have -1, so let's try $x = -1$

$$(-1)^2((-1)^2 - 10) = \quad (1)(1 - 10)$$
$$= (1)(-9) = -9. \; ✓ \text{ It works!}$$
Since $x = -1$ works, we can eliminate A) and B)

Now let's try $x = 3$
$$(3)^2(3^2 - 10) = \quad (9)(9 - 10)$$
$$= (9)(-1) = -9. \; ✓ \text{ It works!}$$
Since $x = 3$ works, we can eliminate D). **Choice C)** is our answer.

Algebra:

$x^2(x^2 - 10) = -9$ Distribute x^2 into the parentheses.
$x^4 - 10x^2 = -9$ Add 9 to both sides.
$x^4 - 10x^2 + 9 = 0$ Factor
$\left(x^2 - 9\right)\left(x^2 - 1\right) = 0$ *Both* terms are the difference of squares!
$(x+3)(x-3)(x-1)(x+1) = 0$ Now set each term equal to zero
$x + 3 = 0 \quad x - 3 = 0 \quad x - 1 = 0 \quad x + 1 = 0$
$x = -3 \quad\quad x = 3 \quad\quad x = 1 \quad\quad x = -1$

8. Answer: D.

$$f(x) = x^2 - 14$$
$$f(x + c) = (x + c)^2 - 14$$
$$= (x + c)(x + c) - 14$$
$$= x^2 + 2cx + c^2 - 14$$

Or, *Plug In.* Set $x = 2, c = 3$.
$$f(2 + 3) = f(5)$$
$$= 5^2 - 14$$
$$= 11$$

Now put our numbers into the choices and see which gives you 11.

A) $2^2 + 3 - 14$ $= 4 + 3 - 14$ $= -7$ ✗
B) $2^2 - 14(3)(2) + 3^2$ $= 4 - 84 + 9$ $= -71$ ✗
C) $2^2 + 2(3)(2) + 3^2$ $= 4 + 12 + 9$ $= 25$ ✗
D) $2^2 + 2(3)(2) + 3^2 - 14$ $= 4 + 12 + 9 - 14$ $= 11$ ✓

9. Answer: B.

Several ways we could do this. First, saying that $\{-3, 4\}$ is the solution set for x means that those values of x will make the equation true. Plug in either value for x into the equation and solve for k.

$$
\begin{array}{ll}
x = 4 & x = -3 \\
4^2 + k(4) - 12 = 0 & (-3)^2 + k(-3) - 12 = 0 \\
16 + 4k - 12 = 0 & 9 - 3k - 12 = 0 \\
4k + 4 = 0 & -3k - 3 = 0 \\
4k = -4 & -3k = 3 \\
\boldsymbol{k = -1} & \boldsymbol{k = -1}
\end{array}
$$

Second, we could work backwards to find the quadratic equation. If $\{-3, 4\}$, that means $x = -3$ and $x = 4$. Therefore:

$x + 3 = 0$ or $\quad x - 4 = 0$.
$(x + 3)(x - 4) = 0$
$x^2 - 4x + 3x - 12 = 0$
$x^2 - x - 12$

That equals $x^2 + k\,x - 12$. Therefore, $\boldsymbol{k = -1}$.

Third, we could use **Backsolve**. Start with choice B)

B) $k = -1$. The equation then becomes $x^2 - x - 12 = 0$.
Now put either $x = 4$ or $x = 3$ into the left side to see if it equals zero:

$$
\begin{array}{llll}
x = 4: & 4^2 - 4 - 12 & = 16 - 4 - 12 = \boldsymbol{0} \checkmark & \text{It works!} \\
x = -3: & (-3)^2 - (-3) - 12 & = 9 + 3 - 12 = \boldsymbol{0} \checkmark & \text{It works!}
\end{array}
$$

Also remember that the value of b will be equal to the sum of the negatives of the solutions. Since the solutions are -3 and 4:
$b = -4 + 3 = -1$. That's B.

10. Answer: D.

You can do this in two steps. First, do $f(-2)$. Then put the result of that through $f(x)$ again.

$$
\begin{array}{l}
f(x) = x^2 + 4 \\
f(-2) = (-2)^2 + 4 \\
f(-2) = 4 + 4 \\
f(-2) = 8
\end{array}
$$

$$
\begin{array}{ll}
f(f(-2)) & = f(8) \\
& = 8^2 + 4 \\
& = \boldsymbol{68}
\end{array}
$$

11. Answer: D.

Since FOILing is much easier than factoring, use **Backsolve**. FOIL the answer choices until you find one that matches what we started with.

A. $(2x + 9)(3x - 4)$ $\quad = 6x^2 - 8x + 27x - 36 = 6x^2 + 19x - 36$ ✘
B. $(6x - 3)(x + 12)$ $\quad = 6x^2 + 72x - 3x - 36 = 6x^2 + 69x - 36$ ✘
C. $3(2x + 3)(x - 4)$
$\quad = (6x + 9)(x - 4)$ $\quad = 6x^2 - 24x + 9x - 36 = 6x^2 - 15x - 36$ ✘
D. $3(2x - 3)(x + 4)$
$\quad = (6x - 9)(x + 4)$ $\quad = 6x^2 + 24x - 9x - 36 = \boldsymbol{6x^2 + 15x - 36}$ ✔

For choices C) and D), we also could have FOILed the polynomials first and then multiplied by 3:

C. $3(2x + 3)(x - 4)$ $\quad = 3(2x^2 - 8x + 3x - 12)$
$\quad = 3(2x^2 - 5x - 12)$ $\quad = 6x^2 - 15x - 36$ ✘
D. $3(2x - 3)(x + 4)$ $\quad = 3(2x^2 + 8x - 3x - 12)$
$\quad = 3(2x^2 + 5x - 12)$ $\quad = \boldsymbol{6x^2 + 15x - 36}$ ✔

Or, **Plug In**. Let $x = 1$. Put $x = 1$ into the original expression:
$6x^2 + 15x - 36$ $\quad = 6(1^2) + 15(1) - 36$
$\quad = 6 + 15 - 36$ $\quad = \boldsymbol{-15}$

Put $x = 1$ into the choices and see which one comes out to -15:

A. $(2(1) + 9)(3(1) - 4)$ $\quad = (11)(-1)$ $\quad = -11$ ✘
B. $(6(1) - 3)(1 + 12)$ $\quad = (3)(13)$ $\quad = 39$ ✘
C. $3(2(1) + 3)(1 - 4)$ $\quad = 3(5)(-3)$ $\quad = -45$ ✘
D. $3(2(1) - 3)(1 + 4)$ $\quad = 3(-1)(5)$ $\quad = \boldsymbol{-15}$ ✔

12. Answer: A.

This question is very easy if you know your exponential formulas. Remember, the basic equation is:
$G(x) = a(r)^x$
where a is the initial amount, and r is the rate expressed as a decimal with respect to 1.

In our question, the initial amount is $1,000, so that should go first, with no exponent. Eliminate C) and D).

The rate is 2%, which is 0.02, but we want to express it with respect to 1, so we want 1.02. Eliminate B). Our answer is **A)**

Confused? Try **Plug In**. Let's start simple and say $t = 1$, so we're calculating the amount of her deposit after 1 year.
She gets 2% of $1,000, which is $20. Add that to the $1,000 and she has **$1,020** in her account.

A) $1,000(1.02)^1 = 1,000 \times 1.02 = 1,020$ ✔
B) $1,000(0.02)^1 = 1,000 \times 0.02 = 20$ ✘
C) $1.02(1,000)^1 = 1.02 \times 1,000 = 1,020$ ✔
D) $0.02(1,000)^1 = 0.02 \times 1,000 = 20$ ✘

Two choices work, but we can eliminate B) and D).

Let's say $t = 2$. The second year, she's going to get another 2% on top of the $1,020 she got after the first year.
$0.02 \times 1020 = 20.4$. That's the interest. $1020 + 20.4 = \boldsymbol{\$1,040.4}$

A) $1,000(1.02)^2 = 1,000 \times 1.0404 = 1,040.4$ ✔
C) $1.02(1,000)^2 = 1.02 \times 1,000,000 = 1,020,000$ ✘ Whoa!

Rosie may prefer to have the account in choice C), **choice A)** is our answer.

The solution set for x for the equation $x^2 + kx - 12 = 0$ is $\{-3, 4\}$. What does k equal?

A) -7
B) -1
C) 1
D) 7

If $f(x) = x^2 + 4$, what is $f(f(-2))$?

A) 0
B) 8
C) 20
D) 68

Which of the following expressions is equivalent to $6x^2 + 15x - 36$?

A) $(2x + 9)(3x - 4)$
B) $(6x - 3)(x + 12)$
C) $3(2x + 3)(x - 4)$
D) $3(2x - 3)(x + 4)$

Rosie opens a savings account with an initial deposit of $1,000. If the account offers 2% interest compounded annually, which of the following functions f shows the amount of her deposit after t years?

A) $f(t) = 1,000(1.02)^t$
B) $f(t) = 1,000(0.02)^t$
C) $f(t) = 1.02(1,000)^t$
D) $f(t) = 0.02(1,000)^t$

CONTINUE

If $x > 2$, which of the following is equivalent to

$$\frac{1}{x+5} + \frac{1}{x-2} ?$$

A) $x^2 + 3x - 10$

B) $\dfrac{1}{2x+3}$

C) $\dfrac{1}{x^2+3x-10}$

D) $\dfrac{2x+3}{x^2+3x-10}$

Which of the following quadratic expressions has solutions $x = -8m$ and $x = 2n^2$?

A) $x^2 + (8m - 2n^2)x - 16mn^2$
B) $x^2 + (8m + 2n^2)x + 16mn^2$
C) $x^2 - (8m + 2n^2)x + 16mn^2$
D) $x^2 - (8m - 2n^2)x - 16mn^2$

In reviewing her financial history, Zoe determined that in 2005 she spent \$3,500 on food over the course of the year. She estimated that the annual amount she spent on food has increased by 5% every 3 years after 2005. If her expenses continue to grow at that rate, which of the following expressions represents her estimate of the amount she will spend on food t years after 2005?

A) $3,500(1.05)^{\frac{t}{3}}$

B) $3,500(1.05)^{3t}$

C) $3,500(0.05)^{\frac{t}{3}}$

D) $3,500(0.05)^{3t}$

STOP

13. Answer: D.

Hey look at all the variables in the choices!

Plug In

$x = 3$

$$\frac{1}{3+5} + \frac{1}{3-2} = \frac{1}{8} + \frac{1}{1} = \frac{1}{8} + \frac{8}{8} = \frac{9}{8}$$

To the choices!

A) $(3)^2 + 3(3) - 10$ $= 9 + 9 - 10 = 8$ ✗

B) $\dfrac{1}{2(3) + 3}$ $= \dfrac{1}{6+3} = \dfrac{1}{9}$ ✗

C) $\dfrac{1}{(3)^2 + 3(3) - 10}$ $= \dfrac{1}{8}$ ✗

D) $\dfrac{2(3) + 3}{(3)^2 + 3(3) - 10}$ $= \dfrac{9}{8}$ ✓

Algebra:

Multiply the binomials to get a common denominator.

$$\frac{1}{x+5} + \frac{1}{x-2} = \frac{(x-2)}{(x-2)(x+5)} + \frac{(x+5)}{(x-2)(x+5)}$$

$$= \frac{x-2+x+5}{(x-2)(x+5)}$$

$$= \frac{2x+3}{x^2 + 3x - 10}$$

A) $8^2 + [8(3) - 2(2^2)] \times 8 - 16(3)2^2$
$= 64 + [24 - 8] \times 8 - 192$
$= 64 + (16)(8) - 192$ $= 128 - 128$ $= 0$ ✓

B) $8^2 + [8(3) + 2(2^2)] \times 8 + 16(3)2^2$
$= 64 + [24 + 8] \times 8 + 192$
$= 64 + (32)(8) + 192$ $= 256 + 256$ $= 512$ ✗

C) $8^2 - [8(3) + 2(2^2)] \times 8 + 16(3)2^2$
$= 64 - [24 + 8] \times 8 + 192$
$= 64 - (32)(8) + 192$ $= 256 - 256$ $= 0$ ✓

D) $8^2 - [8(3) - 2(2^2)] \times 8 - 16(3)2^2$
$= 64 - [24 - 8] \times 8 - 192$
$= 64 - (16)(8) - 192$ $= -128 - 128$ $= -256$ ✗

Two choices work! First, eliminate B) and D). Now, plug the other solution, $x = -24$, along with $m = 3$ and $n = 2$ into choices A) and C):

A) $(-24)^2 + [8(3) - 2(2^2)] \times (-24) - 16(3)(2^2)$
$= 576 + (16)(-24) - 192$
$= 384 - 384 = 0$ ✓

C) $(-24)^2 - [8(3) + 2(2^2)] \times (-24) + 16(3)(2^2)$
$= 576 - (32)(-24) + 192$
$= 768 + 768 = 1536$ ✗

14. Answer: A.

This problem is just like question 9 above! The only difference is that the solution set here has algebraic expressions instead of numbers. We could work backwards to find the quadratic equation.

Since $x = -8m$ and $x = 2n^2$ are the *solutions* to the quadratic equation, that means:

$x = -8m$	or	$x = 2n^2$
$x + 8m = 0$	or	$x - 2n^2 = 0$.

These are the factors for our quadratic.

$(x + 8m)(x - 2n^2) = 0$

Now FOIL!

$x^2 - 2n^2 x + 8mx - 16mn^2$

Factor out an x from the middle terms.

$x^2 + (-2n^2 + 8m)x - 16mn^2$

Switch the order of the middle terms.

$x^2 + (8m - 2n^2)x - 16mn^2$

That's **choice A).**

Put another way: remember that the value of b will be equal to the sum of the negatives of the solutions. Since the solutions are $x = -8m$ and $x = 2n^2$:

$b = 8m - 2n^2$.. That's A) or D).

The value of c will be the product of the solutions.
$c = (-8m)(2n^2) = -16mn^2$. That's choice D).

Or, ***Plug In.*** Don't pick an x. Instead, say **$m = 3$** and **$n = 2$**.
Now let's find our values for x:

$x = -8m = -8(3) = $ **-24**   *or* $x = 2(x^2) = 2(2^2) = $ **8**

We'll pick 8 because it's easier to deal with.

These are the *solutions* to a quadratic expression. That means if we put these values in for x, the expression should come out to zero. So let's put $m = 3$, $n = 2$ and $x = 8$, into the choices and see which gives us zero.

15. Answer: A.

Another exponential growth question.
Let's try ***Plug in*** again.
Her food spending goes up 5% every 3 years, so let's say **$t = 3$**. If 3 years pass, then we'd expect the spending to go up 5%.
She starts at $3,500.
$0.05 \times 3{,}500 = 175$
$3{,}500 + 175 = $ **$3,675$.** Let's put $t = 3$ into the choices and look for 3675.

A) $3{,}500(1.05)^{\frac{3}{3}} = 3{,}500(1.05)^1$ $= 3{,}500(1.05)$ $= 3{,}675$ ✓

B) $3{,}500(1.05)^{3(3)} = 3{,}500(1.05)^9$ $= 3{,}500(1.55)$ $= 5{,}425$ ✗

C) $3{,}500(0.05)^{\frac{3}{3}} = 3{,}500(0.05)^1$ $= 3{,}500(0.05)$ $= 175$ ✗

D) $3{,}500(0.05)^{3(3)} = 3{,}500(0.05)^9$ $= 3{,}500(0.00)$ $= 0$ ✗

Technically choice D) comes out to 6.84×10^{-9}, but that happily rounds to zero. We can see what kind of effect we get when we use the wrong number for rate.

If you're comfortable with the exponential growth formula, you should be able to eliminate C) and D) right away. But you still may be confused between A) and B). That's when Plug In can help make sense of it for you.

THIS PAGE INTENTIONALLY LEFT BLANK

■ Graphing

Graphing questions will show up all over the test. Algebra questions, data questions, even geometry questions may involve the coordinate plane. So we're going to bring all those concepts together in one place here so we can see how they connect.

It's okay to hate graphing. We're not here to judge you.* But we are here to help you understand a few of the basic principles behind these problems. As we saw in all the other chapters, Math Test questions ask the same things over and over again, so a little bit of knowledge can go a long way.

I. THE COORDINATE PLANE

A. Getting to know the plane

This is the xy-coordinate plane (or "xy grid", or "coordinate plane" or whatever you want to call it).

A lot of you probably know your way around this guy, but here are some definitions for those who are confused:

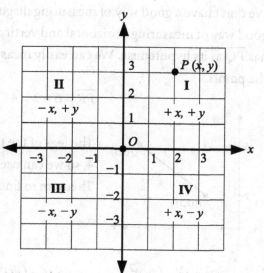

The **x-axis** is the horizontal line; it tells you the x value of a point. Values of x are positive to the right and negative to the left.

The **y-axis** is the vertical line; it tells you the y value of a point. Values of y are positive at the top and negative at the bottom.

The two axes† divide the coordinate plane into four **quadrants**, often labeled with Roman numerals. The sign of the x- and y- value of a point will determine which quadrant the point lies in.

---

* Well, maybe a little.

† Yes, the plural of "axis" is "axes". It rhymes with "taxis", not with "faxes".

Points on the graph are given as (x, y). So point P is $(2, 3)$, since it has an x value of 2 and a y value of 3. You can tell the x and y values by looking at where the point lies with respect to the axes.

The **origin** is the point where the axes cross (labeled "O" here); it has a value of $(0, 0)$.

Before we go any further, it's important to emphasize that graphs are *pictures*. Therefore, **you can use *Guesstimate* on graph problems**. In fact, you'd be astounded how many graphing problems can be done just by looking at the picture they give you. If this line looks equal to that line, then they are equal.

In fact, Guesstimate is often *easier* on coordinate geometry questions because coordinates have values you can use as references. Once you become familiar with the coordinate plane, it's easy to quickly glance at a point and see "oh, that point has a negative x and a y bigger than 7, so I can eliminate A) and D)." Don't forget Guesstimate.

Distance

If you want to find the **distance** between two points on a graph, just use **the Pythagorean Theorem**:

> ✎ **What is the distance in coordinate units between *P* (2,2) and *Q* (6,5)?**

We don't have a good way of measuring diagonal lines like that directly. But we *do* have a good way of measuring horizontal and vertical lines. Let's draw point R to make a triangle that has $\overline{PQ}$ as its hypotenuse. We can easily measure its legs because we know the coordinates of the points.

$$\overline{PR} = 6 - 2 = 4 \qquad \overline{QR} = 5 - 2 = 3$$

The legs of the triangle are 3 and 4, so we can use the Pythagorean Theorem to find the hypotenuse:*

$$3^2 + 4^2 = (PQ)^2 \qquad 9 + 16 = (PQ)^2 \qquad 25 = (PQ)^2 \qquad \mathbf{5 = PQ}$$

If you prefer, you can use **The Distance Formula**. The distance, d, between points (x_1, y_1) and (x_2, y_2) is

---

* If you don't know what the Pythagorean Theorem is, don't worry. We'll talk about it more in the Plane Geometry chapter. Some of you may be able to see right away that it's a 3-4-5 triangle.

$$d = \sqrt{(x_2 - x_1)^2 + (y_2 - y_1)^2} \qquad \text{or} \qquad d^2 = (x_2 - x_1)^2 + (y_2 - y_1)^2$$

Note that this is *exactly* the same thing we just did. **The distance formula is nothing more than the Pythagorean Theorem.** Any two points on the coordinate grid can form a right triangle: $(x_2 - x_1)$ is one leg of the triangle, $(y_2 - y_1)$ is the other leg, and the distance between the points is the hypotenuse.

Midpoint

> ✐ **What is the midpoint of (2,2) and (6,5)?**

This question asks about the same points we just looked at. To find the coordinates of the midpoint between two points, *take the average of the x's and the average of the y's.*

The average of the x-values, 2 and 6, is $\dfrac{2+6}{2} = 4$. The average of the y-values, 2 and 5, is $\dfrac{2+5}{2} = 3.5$.

So the coordinates of the midpoint are **(4, 3.5)**.

B. Graphing Functions

A graph on the coordinate plane is nothing more than **a picture of a function**.

Take the equation **$y = 2x$**. We could plug in any number we like for x and we'll get a value for y as a result. Below we have a table of x's and their respective y's, along with a graph of those points plotted on the grid.

x	y
-3	-6
-2	-4
-1	-2
0	0
1	2
2	4
3	6

We can see that the points we chose start to make a straight line. If we fill in *all* the possible x's and their corresponding y's, including all the nasty decimal numbers, that's exactly what we'd get. The graph of $y = 2x$ is a picture of *all* the possible solutions to the equation—every x paired with its corresponding y.

Rather than defining our equation as $y = 2x$, we could call it $f(x) = 2x$ and say that $y = f(x)$ in the graph. Don't get bogged down with all the different letters.

The most important thing to remember is: **If a point lies on the graph of a function, the coordinates of that point will satisfy the function's equation.** And vice versa. Even if you don't know the equation of the function, you can learn a lot just from the picture. For example:

> ✏ **The figure below shows the graph of $y = f(x)$. What is the value of $f(1)$?**

If they'd given you an equation for $f(x)$, you could find $f(1)$ by substituting "1" for "x" in the formula. No problem. But here we don't have an equation. Hmm. That's a crazy, crazy looking function. We'll never be able to write an equation for it.

But we don't need an equation because we have a graph of the function! A graph is a picture of the function. Every point on that squiggly line is a set of numbers that satisfies the equation, whatever that may be.

We want the value of $f(1)$. So we just have to find the value of y when $x = 1$. That's 3! The squiggly line crosses point $(1,3)$. When $x = 1$, $y = 3$. So $f(1) = 3$.

This is an important point, so it bears repeating:

> If the point (a, b) is on the graph of f, then $f(a) = b$.
> If $f(a) = b$, then the point (a, b) is on the graph of f.

TRY SOME:

Find these points on the graph above:

✏ $f(-1) = ?$ ✏ $f(2) = ?$

✏ $f(0) = ?$ ✏ $f(3) = ?$

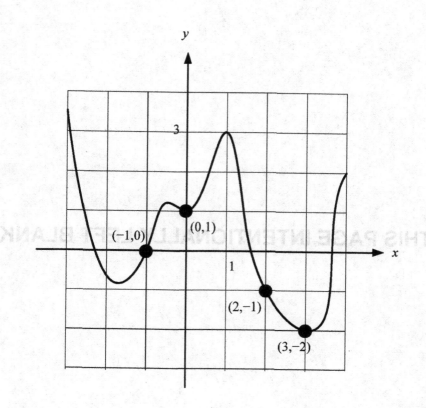

Graphing functions

ANSWERS:

✎ $f(-1) = 0$ ✎ $f(2) = -1$

✎ $f(0) = 1$ ✎ $f(3) = -2$

THIS PAGE INTENTIONALLY LEFT BLANK

A lot of people get confused by this notation, so here's a trick to help you remember. If you **draw in some parentheses**, the equation looks just like a coordinate pair. So:

$$f(1) = 3 \qquad \qquad f(x) = y$$
becomes
$$f\left((1) = 3\right) \qquad \qquad f\left((x) = y\right)$$

Intersection

This fact about points and functions has an interesting consequence: If a point on a graph is a solution to that function's equation, then **a point where two graphs intersect is a solution to *both* functions' equations.**

For example, consider these functions:

$$y = 2x + 3$$
$$y = x + 5$$

When we have two equations together like this we call it a "system of equations". Each equation has an infinite number of (x,y) pairs that make the equation true. But there's only one pair that makes both equations true at the same time: $(2,7)$.*

The graph of each of these functions is a straight line. If we draw both lines in the same plane, we can see that the two lines intersect at the point $(2,7)$. Point $(2,7)$ is the solution for the system of equations and the place where the two lines intersect.

Inequalities

Most graphs you'll see on the SAT have equations that describe them. But you can also graph *inequalities*. The graph of an inequality looks just like the graph of the corresponding equation—a line or a curve of some kind—but with a shaded region above or below the line.

For example, the figure to the right shows the graph of $y \geq 2x$. Notice that the line running through the middle looks exactly like the line for $y = 2x$ that we saw earlier, but now the region above the line is

---

* There are several ways we can solve this system algebraically. Since both have y by itself, we could set the two equations equal to each other: $2x + 3 = x + 5$, thus $x = 2$. Or we could subtract the equations directly to get $0 = x - 2$, thus $x = 2$. Then put $x = 2$ back into either equation to get $y = 7$.

shaded. That means that *all the points within the shaded region satisfy the inequality.**

For this graph, it should be easy to understand why the area above the graph is shaded. The line shows all the points where y <u>equals</u> $2x$, so all the points *above* the line have a y-value <u>greater than</u> $2x$.

But if you're not sure which region you want to shade, you can always **try some test points.** Pick a point above the graph, let's say $(0,2)$.[†] Now let's plug $x = 0$ and $y = 2$ into the inequality $y \geq 2x$ and see if it works:

$$2 \geq 2(0) \qquad\qquad 2 \geq 0 \checkmark \text{ It works!}$$

Let's check a point from the other side of the line, say $(0,-2)$, just to be sure.

$$-2 \geq 2(0) \qquad\qquad -2 \geq 0 \times \text{ That doesn't work!}$$

After trying those points, we can see we must shade the area above the graph. (Hmm… using real numbers to test an algebraic expression. Haven't we done that before? Oh yeah! That's **Plug In!**)

Note that if you want to solve for the intersection of *two* inequalities, only the region shaded by *both* graphs will be the solution.

---

* Because the inequality says y is greater than *or equal to* $2x$, the line is solid. If the inequality were $y > 2x$ without allowing them to be equal, the line would be dashed.

† Points on the axes are generally easier to test because it's easy to plug 0 into your inequality.

II. LINES

Remember when we talked about linear expressions and equations in the Heart of Algebra chapter? You don't? Jeez, it was just, like, twenty pages ago. Fine. Go back and look again, then come back here.

Okay, you're back. We said they can be drawn in the coordinate plane as lines; and we said they two unique characteristics: their rate and their starting point. We can see these characteristics in their graphs.

1. Their *rate* corresponds to **slope**:

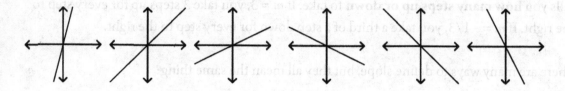

2. Their *starting point* corresponds to **y-intercept**:

These two features are all we need to uniquely define any line. These are the same features we talked about when we were writing equations for word problems about how much money you're going to earn.

Equations

We can use the slope and y-intercepts to write an equation of a line, called a "linear equation". Any line will have a corresponding equation that contains one x and one y with no exponents.* There are several different ways we can write a linear equation.

The most useful form of a linear equation is **the slope-intercept form**: $y = mx + b$. The "m" stands for the slope, the "b" stands for the y-intercept, and the "x" and "y" stand for the coordinates of any and all points on the line.

---

* Exception: an equation with *no x*, like $y = 3$, is a horizontal line. It has a slope of *zero*. Similarly, an equation with *no y*, like $x = 3$, is a vertical line. It has an *undefined* slope.

Slope

As the name implies, slope (abbreviated "m" for some reason*) is a way to measure the "steepness" of a line. Looking from left to right, a *positive* slope goes <u>up</u> and a *negative* slope goes <u>down</u>. As you can see from the examples below, the more the line goes up, the larger its positive slope; the more the line goes down, the smaller its negative slope.

$$m = 3 \qquad m = \frac{1}{3} \qquad m = 0 \qquad m = -\frac{1}{3} \qquad m = -3$$

> When the axes of a graph measure distance and time, the slope of a line gives the speed of the object.

You can think of slope like a staircase: if I take **one step to the right** along the x-axis, slope tells you **how many steps up or down** to take. If $m = 3$, you take 3 steps up for every step to the right. If $m = -1/3$, you take a third of a step down for every step to the right.

There are many ways to define slope, but they all mean the same thing:

$$\frac{\text{change in } y}{\text{change in } x} \qquad \frac{\text{rise}}{\text{run}} \qquad \frac{\Delta y}{\Delta x} \qquad \frac{y_2 - y_1}{x_2 - x_1}$$

If you know two points on a line, you can find the slope of the line. All you have to do is take the difference of the y's over the difference in the x's:

Here, $(x_1, y_1) = (1,2)$ and $(x_2, y_2) = (6,4)$

$$m = \frac{y_2 - y_1}{x_2 - x_1} = \frac{4-2}{6-1} \qquad m = \frac{2}{5}$$

Don't get bogged down by all those letters. We're just picking which point to go first and which to go second. In fact, it doesn't matter which point we use first. We could say that $(x_1, y_1) = (6,4)$ and $(x_2, y_2) = (1,2)$ and...

$$m = \frac{y_2 - y_1}{x_2 - x_1} = \frac{2-4}{1-6} = \frac{-2}{-5} = \frac{2}{5}$$

...we get the same thing.

Some things to remember when calculating slope:

✎ Make sure y is on top. We repeat: **make sure Y is on top**. You will <u>not</u> be given the

---

* No one knows how "m" became the symbol for slope. Over the years, different people in different countries have used a, k, l, p, and s for slope. Descartes, who invented "x", did not use "m". Sometimes this stuff is just random.

formula for slope. You have to remember it.

- ✎ Be consistent with the *x* and *y*. You can start with either point, but you have to start with the same point on the top and the bottom. In the example above, when we use 4 first on the top, we must use 6 first on the bottom.

- ✎ *Parallel* lines have equal slopes.

- ✎ The slopes of *perpendicular* lines are the "negative reciprocals" of one another. Take the first slope, make it negative, and flip the fraction to get the second slope.

Intercepts

An "intercept" is just the point at which the line crosses one of the axes. So the **x-intercept** is the point at which the line crosses the *x*-axis. And the **y-intercept** is the point at which the line crosses the *y*-axis.

In the figure to the right, the line has a *y*-intercept of 3, since it crosses the *y*-axis at the point $(0,3)$. The **y-intercept** always has an **x-value of zero.**

In the figure to the right, the line has an *x*-intercept of 2, since it crosses the *x*-axis at the point $(2, 0)$. The **x-intercept** always has a **y-value of zero.**

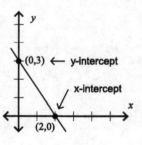

Let's see this stuff at work:

- ✎ **Line ℓ passes through the points (4,4) and (2,3) . What is the equation of line ℓ?**

To find the equation of the line, we need the *slope* and the *y-intercept*. First, since we know two points, we can find the slope.

$$m = \frac{y_2 - y_1}{x_2 - x_1} = \frac{4-3}{4-2} \qquad m = \frac{1}{2}$$

Now we know m, so our equation so far is $y = \frac{1}{2}x + b$. To find b, let's just stick one of the points

we know in for x and y. Then we can solve for b.

$$y = \frac{1}{2}x + b$$
$$3 = \frac{1}{2}(2) + b$$
$$2 = b$$

So our equation is $y = \frac{1}{2}x + 2$. The graph of the line can be seen below.

THIS PAGE INTENTIONALLY LEFT BLANK

ANSWERS:

⚟ **What is the slope of the line that passes through the points (2, 6) and (4, 1)?**

Answer: $\dfrac{-5}{2}$ or –2.5

$$\frac{1-6}{4-2}=\frac{-5}{2}$$

⚟ **What is the slope of the line represented by the equation $y = -3x + 7$**

Answer: –3

The equation is in the form $y = mx + b$.
The slope will be the value of m. That's **–3**.

⚟ **What is the slope of the line that passes through the points (−2, −3) and (−1, 5)?**

Answer: 8.

$$\frac{5-(-3)}{-1-(-2)}=\frac{5+3}{-1+2}=\frac{8}{1}=8$$

⚟ **What is the slope of the line that passes through the points (1, 8) and (3, 2)?**

Answer: –3.

$$\frac{8-2}{1-3}=\frac{6}{-2}=-3$$

⚟ **What is the slope of the line represented by the equation $2x − 6y = 7$?**

Answer: $\dfrac{1}{3}$

Convert the equation into slope-intercept form by solving for y.
$$2x - 6y = 7$$
$$-6y = -2x + 7$$
$$y = \frac{-2x+7}{-6}$$
$$y = \frac{1}{3}x - \frac{7}{6} \quad \text{The slope of this line is } \frac{1}{3}.$$

⚟ **What is the y-intercept of the line represented by the equation $ax + by = c$?**

Answer: $\dfrac{c}{b}$

Convert the equation into slope-intercept form by solving for y.
$$ax + by = c$$
$$by = -ax + c$$
$$y = \frac{-ax+c}{b}$$
$$y = \frac{-a}{b}x + \frac{c}{b} \quad \text{The } y\text{-intercept is } \frac{c}{b}.$$

⚟ **What is the equation of the line that passes through the points (−1, 2) and (1, 6)?**

Answer: $y = 2x + 4$

Slope: $m = \dfrac{6-2}{1-(-1)} = \dfrac{4}{2} = 2 = m$

Substitute one of the points into $y = 2x + b$ to solve for b. Let's do (1, 6):
$$6 = 2(1) + b$$
$$6 = 2 + b \qquad 4 = b \qquad \text{So our equation is } y = 2x + 4$$

⚟ **What are the coordinates of the $\underline{x\text{-intercept}}$ of the line $y = 4x − 10$?**

Answer: (2.5, 0)

The x-intercept will be the point where the line crosses the x-axis.
That's the point where $y = 0$.
$$0 = 4x - 10$$
$$10 = 4x \qquad 2.5 = x \qquad \text{The coordinates are } (2.5, 0).$$

⚟ **The equation of line ℓ is $y = -2x + 7$. If line k is parallel to line ℓ and passes through the point (0, 5), what is the slope of line k?**

Answer: –2

The slope of line ℓ is –2.
Parallel lines will have *equal slopes*.
So the slope of line k is also **–2**.

The point (0,5) is unnecessary information.

⚟ **The equation of line ℓ is $y = 3x + 5$. If line k is perpendicular to line ℓ and passes through the point (0, −3), what is the equation of line k?**

Answer: $y = -\dfrac{1}{3}x - 3$

The slope of a perpendicular is the *negative reciprocal*.

The slope of line ℓ is 3, so the slope of line k is $-\dfrac{1}{3}$.

The point (0, −3) *is* the y-intercept of line k.

✎ What is the slope of the line that passes through the points $(2, 6)$ and $(4, 1)$?

✎ What is the slope of the line represented by the equation $y = -3x + 7$?

✎ What is the slope of the line that passes through the points $(-2, -3)$ and $(-1, 5)$?

✎ What is the slope of the line that passes through the points $(1, 8)$ and $(3, 2)$?

✎ What is the slope of the line represented by the equation $2x - 6y = 7$?

✎ What is the y-intercept of the line represented by the equation $ax + by = c$?

✎ What is the equation of the line that passes through the points $(-1, 2)$ and $(1, 6)$?

✎ What are the coordinates of the <u>x-intercept</u> of the line $y = 4x - 10$?

✎ The equation of line ℓ is $y = -2x + 7$. If line k is parallel to line ℓ and passes through the point $(0, 5)$, what is the slope of line k?

✎ The equation of line ℓ is $y = 3x + 5$. If line k is perpendicular to line ℓ and passes through the point $(0, -3)$, what is the equation of line k?

III. PARABOLAS

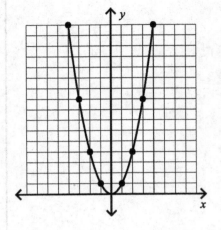

A **parabola** is the graph of a *quadratic function*—that is, an equation containing the square of x and a y with no exponent. Shown here is the graph of $y = x^2$. You can see that the marked points fit the equation: the y value of each point is the square of the x value:

x	−4	−3	−2	−1	0	1	2	3	4
y	16	9	4	1	0	1	4	9	16

The standard form of an equation of a parabola is

$$y = ax^2 + bx + c$$

where a, b, and c are constants.* For $y = x^2$, $a = 1$, $b = 0$, and $c = 0$.

Some of you may recognize this form as what's called a "quadratic equation". Some of you may also know that there is a complicated formula (the "quadratic formula") that you can use to solve quadratic equations. Hmm. Did we talk about those already?

Let's take a look at the different parts of the parabola and how they relate to the equation. The figure below shows the graph of the function $y = x^2 - 6x + 8$.

Intercepts

The **y-intercept** is determined by the value of c, the number by itself with no variable in the formula shown above. In our equation, $y = x^2 - 6x + 8$, $c = 8$, so the y-intercept is $(0, 8)$.

Just like in a straight line, the y-intercept is the value of y when $x = 0$. Because c is the only term in the equation that doesn't come with an x next to it, if $x = 0$, all that's left is c.[†]

---

*   Constants are numbers that don't change at all *within a given equation*. You can stick in any numbers you want for x and y and it'll still be the same equation. If you change the values of a, b, or c, it's no longer considered the same equation.

†   Don't be confused by the fact that c is the y-intercept for parabolas, while b is the y-intercept for lines. The letters are entirely arbitrary. We could call them p and q for all it matters. Heck, we don't even have to put it last; we could say $y = b + xm$. What does matter is that it's the number that stands by itself. In each case, the y-intercept is the number that doesn't have an x next to it.

The **x-intercepts** are the **zeroes** or **solutions** to the equation. That is, they are the values of x when $y = 0$. These are the numbers you get when you factor the quadratic. Here, our equation can be factored into $y = (x - 2)(x - 4)$, so the x-intercepts are $(2, 0)$ and $(4, 0)$.

NOTE: the factored form of the equation shows the *negative* value of the solutions. That is, if the function can be factored into

$$y = (x + m)(x + n)$$

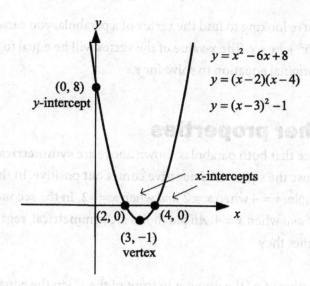

$$y = x^2 - 6x + 8$$
$$y = (x - 2)(x - 4)$$
$$y = (x - 3)^2 - 1$$

then the solutions are $-m$ and $-n$, and the x-intercepts will be $(-m, 0)$ and $(-n, 0)$. *

Previously, we talked about *quadratic equations*. There, we had an equation equal to zero instead of equal to y: there were only one or two values of x that solved the equation. Here, we have a function: we can stick in any value for x and get out a y. A quadratic equation is a quadratic function in which $y = 0$. An x-intercept is a point on the graph where $y = 0$. So you can quickly find the solutions to a quadratic equation by looking at its graph and finding the places where it crosses the x-axis.

NOTE: not all quadratic equations have solutions. If an equation has no solution, the parabola will not cross the x-axis.

Vertex

The **vertex** is the point at the very bottom of the curve (or the very top, if the curve points down). This point is also called the **maximum** or **minimum** of the curve. You can actually rewrite a quadratic function into another form: $y - h = j(x - k)^2$ where (h,k) is the vertex of the parabola.[†]

---

* Strictly speaking, this is only true because there's no coefficient before the x's here. To find the intercepts, set each factor equal to zero and solve for x. If our equation factored into $(5x + 1)(3x - 2)$, the x-intercepts would be $-1/5$ and $2/3$. But you probably won't see this on the SAT.

† You can convert a function into this format using a process called "completing the square", which you may have heard about in your math class. If you have, great. If not, don't worry about it. You likely won't need to do it on the SAT.

If you're looking to find the vertex of a parabola, you can do that from the equation $y = ax^2 + bx + c$. The x-value of the vertex will be equal to $\frac{-b}{2a}$. Then put that x value back in the original equation to solve for y.

Other properties

Notice that both parabolas shown above are **symmetrical**. That's because the square of a negative comes out positive. In the first example: $y = 4$ when $x = 2$ *and* when $x = -2$. In the second, $y = 0$ when $x = 2$ *and* when $x = 4$. *All* parabolas are symmetrical, regardless of whether they

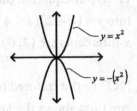

The value of **a** (the number in front of the x^2) in the equation $y = ax^2 + bx + c$ will tell you which direction the parabola will point. If *a* is *positive*, the parabola will point <u>up</u>. If *a* is *negative*, the parabola will point <u>down</u>.

TRY SOME:

✍ **What is the y-intercept of the graph of $y = 3x^2 - 39x - 24$?**

✍ **What is the y-intercept of the graph of $y = (x - 2)(x + 7)$?**

✍ **What is the y-intercept of the graph of $y = (x - 3)^2$?**

✍ **What are the x-intercepts of the graph of $y = (x + 7)(x - 8)$?**

✍ **What are the x-intercepts of the graph of $y = x^2 + x - 20$?**

Parabolas

ANSWERS:

➤ **What is the y-intercept of the graph of $y = 3x^2 - 39x - 24$?**

Answer: (0, −24)

The y-intercept is value of c, the number that doesn't have a variable next to it. Here, it's **−24**.
So the point is **(0, −24)**

➤ **What is the y-intercept of the graph of $y = (x - 2)(x + 7)$?**

Answer: (0, −14)

FOIL it out to find the value of c.
$$(x - 2)(x + 7) = x^2 + 7x - 2x - 14$$
$$= x^2 + 5x - 14$$
$c = -14$ so the intercept is **(0, −14)**

➤ **What is the y-intercept of the graph of $y = (x - 3)^2$?**

Answer: (0, 9)

FOIL it out to find the value of c.
$$(x - 3)(x - 3) = x^2 - 3x - 3x + 9$$
$$= x^2 - 6x + 9$$
$c = -9$ so the intercept is **(0,9)**

➤ **What are the x-intercepts of the graph of $y = (x + 7)(x - 8)$?**

Answer: (−7, 0) and(8, 0)

It's already factored, so just set the factors each equal to zero:
$x + 7 = 0$ $x - 8 = 0$
$x = -7$ $x = 8$
So the x-intercepts are **(−7, 0)** and **(8, 0)**

➤ **What are the x-intercepts of the graph of $y = x^2 + x - 20$?**

Answer: (−5, 0) and (4, 0)

Factor the equation and set it equal to zero:
$x^2 + x - 20 = (x + 5)(x - 4)$
$x + 5 = 0$ $x - 4 = 0$
$x = -5$ $x = 4$
So the x-intercepts are **(−5, 0)** and **(4, 0)**

THIS PAGE INTENTIONALLY LEFT BLANK

IV. CIRCLES

Sometimes you may want to graph circles on the *xy*-coordinate plane. The equation of a circle is defined as:

$$(x-a)^2 + (y-b)^2 = r^2$$

where *r* is the radius, and (a, b) is the center of the circle. If the circle is centered on the origin $(0,0)$, the "– *a*" and "– *b*" won't be there. For the grand majority of circle graphing questions, all you need to know is this equation, **SO LEARN IT!** Let's look at an example:

> ✐ **A circle in the standard (*x*,*y*) coordinate plane has center (3,2) and radius 5 coordinate units. What is the equation of the circle?**

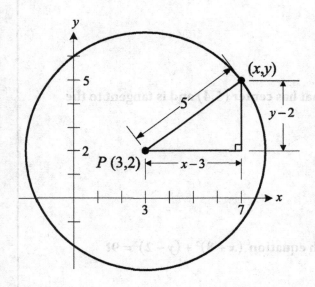

Using the formula above, we know the equation will be $(x-3)^2 + (y-2)^2 = 25$

Does the form of this equation look familiar? It should. **It's the Pythagorean Theorem again!**

Think about it: what *is* a circle? A circle is defined as the set of all points that are a certain distance (the radius) from a single point (the center). In this case, the curve will define all points that are a distance of 5 away from the point (3,2). How do we find the distance between points? With **the distance formula**:

$$d^2 = (x_2 - x_1)^2 + (y_2 - y_1)^2$$

Here, (x_1, y_1) is the center of the circle, (3,2) and (x_2, y_2) is the general point (x, y). That just means (x,y) refers to any point that's on the actual circle. So the distance between (3,2) and any point on the circle is 5.

TRY SOME:

☞ **What is an equation of a circle that has center $(2,1)$ and radius 6 coordinate units?**

☞ **What is an equation of a circle that has center $(-4,0)$ and radius 5 coordinate units?**

☞ **What is an equation of a circle that has center $(5,4)$ and is tangent to the x-axis?**

☞ **What is the center of a circle with equation $(x+8)^2+(y-2)^2=9$?**

☞ **What is the radius of a circle with equation $(x-1)^2+(y+2)^2=7$?**

Circles

ANSWERS:

✐ What is an equation of a circle that has center (2,1) and radius 6 coordinate units?

Answer: $(x - 2)^2 + (y - 1)^2 = 36$

$(x - a)^2 + (y - b)^2 = r^2$
$(x - 2)^2 + (y - 1)^2 = 36$

✐ What is an equation of a circle that has center (−4,0) and radius 5 coordinate units?

Answer: $(x + 4)^2 + y^2 = 25$

$(x - a)^2 + (y - b)^2 = r^2$
$(x - (-4))^2 + (y - 0)^2 = 5^2$
$(x + 4)^2 + y^2 = 25$

✐ What is an equation of a circle that has center (5,4) and is tangent to the x-axis?

Answer: $(x - 5)^2 + (y - 4)^2 = 16$

Draw it! We know the center, but we don't know radius.
Since the circle is tangent to the x-axis, the point (5,0) is on the circle.
The radius is the distance from (5, 4) to (5,0). **$r = 4$.**
Now use the formula for a circle.
$(x - h)^2 + (y - k)^2 = r^2$
$(x - 5)^2 + (y - 4)^2 = 16$
It's really easy to mix up the 5 and the 4. Drawing helps.

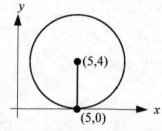

✐ What is the center of a circle with equation $(x + 8)^2 + (y - 2)^2 = 9$?

Answer: (–8, 2)

Remember the circle formula: $(x - a)^2 + (y - b)^2 = r^2$
The center is (a, b) so the center here is **(–8, 2)**

✐ What is the radius of a circle with equation $(x - 1)^2 + (y + 2)^2 = 7$?

Answer: $\sqrt{7}$

Remember the circle formula: $(x - a)^2 + (y - b)^2 = r^2$
Here, $r^2 = 7$, so **$r = \sqrt{7}$**

THIS PAGE INTENTIONALLY LEFT BLANK

V. TRANSFORMATION OF FUNCTIONS

Here are some examples of how functions can move depending on what you do to them:

- For any $f(x)$, the graph of $f(x) + c$ is the graph of $f(x)$ shifted c places UP.
- For any $f(x)$, the graph of $f(x) - c$ is the graph of $f(x)$ shifted c places DOWN.

Subtracting a number from the end means you'll lower the y value by that number, so the graph will shift down. Adding will increase the y value, so the graph will shift up. This is true of all functions, no matter what the equation looks like.

Okay, this next one is a bit weird, so bear with us.

- For any $f(x)$, the graph of $f(x + c)$ is the graph of $f(x)$ shifted c places to the LEFT.
- For any $f(x)$, the graph of $f(x - c)$ is the graph of $f(x)$ shifted c places to the RIGHT.

Before, we were adding to or subtracting from the *end* of the function. Here, we're adding or subtracting from *inside* the parentheses. Think of the space *inside* the parentheses as *Bizarro World*: adding to the x moves the graph toward the negatives, subtracting from the x moves the graph toward the positives.

If you have a graphing calculator, you can try this out yourself. Type these equations into "Y="

$$Y_1 = (x)^2 \qquad Y_2 = (x+1)^2$$

You can see that the graph of the second equation looks just like that of the first equation, but shifted to the left by one space.*

This can be confusing, and it isn't really that important, so if you're still confused, just move on. But if you're curious and really must know why this is true, let's explain. Take a look at these:

---

* We've already seen this rule at work in the vertex form of a parabola. The graph of $y = (x - 3)^2 - 1$ is the graph of $y = x^2$ shifted right 3 spaces and down 1 space. That's why the vertex moves from (0,0) to (3, –1).

Man, that's a funny-looking function. We certainly don't know the equation for it. But no matter what the original equation for $f(x)$ is, we know that $f(x + 2)$ will make the graph shift 2 places *to the left*.

To understand, let's look at some points.

x	$f(x)$	point	$f(x+2)$	point
$x = 0$	$f(0) = 2$	$(0,2)$	$f(0 + 2) = f(2)$	$(0,1)$
$x = 2$	$f(2) = 1$	$(2,1)$	$f(2 + 2) = f(4)$	$(2,5)$
$x = 4$	$f(4) = 5$	$(4,5)$	$f(4 + 2) = f(6)$	$(4,3)$

When x is 0 in $f(x + 2)$, the y value will be the same as $f(2)$ in the first graph, which is 1. So $f(0+2) = 1$, so the graph will touch $(0,1)$. When $x = 0$, $y = 1$.

When x is 2 in $f(x + 2)$, the y value will be the same as $f(4)$ in the first graph, which is 5. So $f(2 + 2) = 4$, so the graph will touch $(2,5)$. When $x = 2$, $y = 5$.

So every point in $f(x + 2)$ takes its y value from the point two spaces to the right. That means $f(x + 2)$ is two spaces to the left of $f(x)$.

THIS PAGE INTENTIONALLY LEFT BLANK

Graphing Exercise

1. Answer: C.

Only B) and C) have positive slopes.
Only C) and D) have negative y-intercepts.
Only C) has both.

3. Answer: C.

Plug In might help keep things straight here.
Say $a = 4$ and $b = 3$.

The x-value of M is now negative: -4
The y-value of M remains the same: 3
So point M is $(-4, 3)$ or $(-a, b)$

2. Answer: C.

Draw it! It won't be perfect, but try to be close. Clearly all these choices are very similar, so we want to make sure we don't make any careless mistakes.

Now ***Guesstimate***: The line goes *down*, so the slope must be negative; eliminate A) and B).

Slope is the change in y over the change in x.

$$\frac{2-0}{-3-0} = -\frac{2}{3}$$

4. Answer: A.

Put the equation of the line in $y = mx + b$ form to find the slope.

$$3y + 6x = 8$$
$$3y = -6x + 8$$
$$y = -\frac{6}{3}x + \frac{8}{3}$$
$$y = -2x + \frac{8}{3}$$

Any line parallel to this one will have the same slope. This line's slope is -2, so the parallel line will also have a slope of **-2.**

GRAPHING EXERCISE

1

Which of the following could be the graph of a line with a positive slope and a negative *y*-intercept?

A)

B)

C)

D)

2

What is the slope of a line that passes through the origin and the point (–3, 2)?

A) $\dfrac{3}{2}$

B) $\dfrac{2}{3}$

C) $-\dfrac{2}{3}$

D) $-\dfrac{3}{2}$

3

In the figure above, $\overline{MN}$ is parallel to the *x*-axis. If $ML = LN$, what are the coordinates of point *M*?

A) (b, a)

B) $(a, -b)$

C) $(-a, b)$

D) $(-a, -b)$

4

What is the slope of a line that is parallel to the line represented by the equation $3y + 6x = 8$?

A) -2

B) $-\dfrac{1}{2}$

C) $\dfrac{1}{2}$

D) 2

CONTINUE

Which of the following could be the graph of the function f, shown above?

A) $f(x) = x^2 - 2x - 1$

B) $f(x) = x^2 - x - 1$

C) $f(x) = x^2 + 2x + 1$

D) $f(x) = x^2 + 2x - 2$

The graph of $y = ax^2 + bx + c$ in the standard (x,y) coordinate plane is shown above. When $y = 0$, which of the following best describes the real solution set for x?

A) 2 negative solutions
B) 1 positive and 1 negative solution
C) 1 positive solution only
D) 1 negative solution only

A circle in the standard (x,y) coordinate plane has center $(5, -7)$ and radius 3 coordinate units. Which of the following is an equation of the circle?

A) $(x+5)^2 + (y-7)^2 = 3$

B) $(x+5)^2 + (y-7)^2 = 9$

C) $(x-5)^2 + (y+7)^2 = 3$

D) $(x-5)^2 + (y+7)^2 = 9$

8

In the xy-plane, the graph of $y = (x-6)^2$ intersects with the graph of $y = 16$ at two points. What are the x-values of the points of intersection?

A) -10 and 10
B) 2 and 10
C) 4 and -6
D) 10 and 24

CONTINUE

5. Answer: C.

According to the picture, the *y*-intercept is 1. So in the equation, the number without an *x*—the "*c*" value—will be 1. Only choice C) works.

That's it! It's just that easy!

7. Answer: B.

Remember what we said in the parabola section: *the real solutions to the quadratic equation correspond to the x-intercepts of the parabola.* Because the solutions to the quadratic equation are the *x*-values when $y = 0$.

Where does $y = 0$ for the graph in this picture? It does so twice (eliminate C and D), once on the left part of the *x*-axis and once on the right part. Therefore, it has **1 positive and 1 negative solution.**

6. Answer: D.

Remember the equation for a circle:
$(x - a)^2 + (y - b)^2 = r^2$, where (a,b) is the center and *r* is the radius.
In this problem, $(a,b) = (5, -7)$ and $r = 3$,
so the equation is $(x - 5)^2 + (y + 7)^2 = 9$

All the wrong choices mix up the values in the equation, so you can see why it's important to memorize it.

8. Answer: B.
Backsolve
Let's start with C)

C) 4 and −6

Okay, now what?
The question asks for the *x*-values of the intersection of the graphs. One graph is $y = 16$. It has no *x*, so we can't stick them in there. The other should come out equal to 16 with our number.

$x = 4$
$y = (4 - 6)^2 = (-2)^2 = 4$ ✘ Nope.
Didn't even have to check the other one. Once the first one fails, the choice is out.

Where shall we go now? B) perhaps?

B) **2 and 10**

$x = 2$
$y = (2 - 6)^2 = (-4)^2 = 16$ ✓
$x = 10$
$y = (10 - 6)^2 = (4)^2 = 16$ ✓   They both work!

Frontsolve:
Set the equations equal to each other:

$(x - 6)^2 = 16$ Square root both sides
$x - 6 = \pm 4$ Don't forget the negative solution!
$\quad\quad\quad x - 6 = 4 \quad\quad\quad\quad x - 6 = -4$
$\quad\quad\quad\quad x = 10 \quad\quad\quad\quad\quad x = 2$

9. Answer: A.

The best way to understand the graph of a line is to have its equation in slope-intercept form ($y = mx + b$).

$$x + 2y - 6 = 0$$
$$2y = -x + 6$$
$$y = -\frac{1}{2}x + \frac{6}{2}$$
$$y = -\frac{1}{2}x + 3$$

The slope of the line is $-\frac{1}{2}$. We know we want a negative slope, so the line should point *down*. Eliminate B) and C).

Not that that matters, though. The y-intercept of this line is 3, and the only graph with a y-intercept of 3 is **choice A)**.

Foolishness: kids who choose B) likely looked at the original equation and thought the y-intercept was −6.

10. Answer: D.

To find the slope of AC, we need two points on AC. We know point A is (0, 6), so we just need point C.

We haven't done area yet, but we can still manage. We'll have to know the formula for the area of a triangle, but they give that to us in the front of the section (flip the Geometry chapter to see).

Triangle ABC has an area of 15 and a height of 6 (that's AO). So let's find the base:

$$15 = \frac{1}{2}b(6) \qquad\qquad 15 = 3b \qquad b = 5 = BC$$

We're talking about triangle ABC; its base is BC.

$BC = 5$, $OB = 3$, so $OC = 8$. So point C is (8, 0).

Now we have two points, so we can find the slope of AC:

$$\frac{6-0}{0-8} = \frac{6}{-8} = -\frac{3}{4}$$

Foolishness:
Choice A) is the slope of AB.
Choice B) means you thought $OC = 5$. Guesstimate can help sort out these lengths.

11. Answer: B.

To write the equation of this line, we need the slope and the y-intercept. Fortunately, one of the points given is the point (0, 2), which is the y-intercept (b). Now find the slope:

$$m = \frac{y_2 - y_1}{x_2 - x_1} = \frac{(-1) - (2)}{3 - 0} = \frac{-3}{3} = -1 \,.$$

Now plug $m = -1$ and $b = 2$ into the equation $y = mx + b$ to get $y = -x + 2$.

Or, ***Plug In.*** We have two points, so those points must be solutions to the equation.
Start with (0,2). Put $x = 0$ into the choices and see which gives you $y = 2$. Eliminate A) and D).
Now try (3,−1). Put $x = 3$ into the remaining choices and see which gives you −1. Eliminate C).

	$(x,y) = (0,2)$	$(x,y) = (3,-1)$
A)	$(-3)(0) + 6 = 6$ ✗	
B)	$(-1)(0) + 2 = 2$ ✓	$-3 + 2 = -1$ ✓
C)	$0 + 2 = 2$ ✓	$3 + 2 = 5$ ✗
D)	$2(0) - 2 = -2$ ✗	

Which of the following is the graph of the equation $x + 2y - 6 = 0$ in the standard (x,y) coordinate plane?

A)

B)

C)

D)

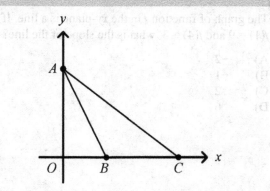

In the xy plane above, the area of $\triangle ABC$ is 15, the length of $\overline{OB}$ is 3 and the coordinates of point A are $(0, 6)$. What is the slope of segment $\overline{AC}$?

A) -2

B) $-\dfrac{6}{5}$

C) $-\dfrac{5}{6}$

D) $-\dfrac{3}{4}$

The points $(0,2)$ and $(3,-1)$ lie on a straight line in the standard (x,y) coordinate plane. What is the slope-intercept equation of the line?

A) $y = -3x + 6$
B) $y = -x + 2$
C) $y = x + 2$
D) $y = 2x - 2$

CONTINUE

The graph of function *f* in the *xy*-plane is a line. If *f*(1) = 9 and *f*(4) = 3, what is the slope of the line?

A)   −2
B)   −1
C)   2
D)   6

In the *xy*-coordinate plane, the distance between point *A* (7,7) and point *B* (1, *k*) is 10. Which of the following is a possible value of *k*?

A)   −3
B)   −1
C)   1
D)   8

Note: Figure not drawn to scale.

In the figure above, if line *ℓ* has a slope of 3, what is the *y*-intercept of *ℓ* ?

A)   −7
B)   −8
C)   −9
D)   −10

The function *y* = *f*(*x*), defined for the interval −3 ≤ *x* ≤ 4, is shown in the graph above. For how many values of *x* does *f*(*x*) = −1?

A)   One
B)   Two
C)   Three
D)   More than three

STOP

12. Answer: A.

We know $f(1) = 9$ and $f(4) = 3$. That means the line contains the points $(1, 9)$ and $(4, 3)$. Find the slope!

$$\frac{9-3}{1-4} = \frac{6}{-3} = -2$$

Roughly sketching the points helps eliminate careless mistakes. Here, we can easily see we have a negative slope, so we can eliminate C) and D) right away (That's *Guesstimate!*)

This kind of elimination is important, because the *only* reason people miss slope questions is that they mix up the points. It's *incredibly* easy to make a sign mistake here. Guesstimate helps eliminate careless errors.

13. Answer: D.

Even though the graph isn't to scale, we can still tell that point $(2, -4)$ is on line ℓ.

We know the slope is 3, so we can use $y = mx + b$ to find the y-intercept:

$-4 = 3(2) + b$
$-4 = 6 + b$
$-10 = b$

Some people might prefer a more visual way of figuring this out. Since the slope is 3, every time you go right one space, you go up three spaces. Conversely, every time you go left one space, you go down three spaces. So you can start at $(2, -4)$ and count back to the y-intercept.

Go left one and down 3, you get $(1, -7)$
Go left one and down 3, you get $(0, -10)$. That's the y-intercept!

14. Answer: B.

As always, if there's no picture, draw one. Plot point A, $(7, 7)$. We know the x-value of point B is 1, but we don't know if k is greater or less than 7. Let's pick one. Let's say it's bigger than 7.

Let's draw a triangle! We know the distance $AB = 10$. We know the difference of the x-values is $7 - 1 = 6$. So we can use the Pythagorean theorem to find the third side:

$6^2 + b^2 = 10^2$
…
$b = 8$

(Some might be able to see that's a 6-8-10 triangle)

Note: Figure not drawn to scale

That means that the y-value of B is 8 more than the y-value of A.
$k = 7 + 8$ $k = 15$.

Wait, 15 isn't a choice. Ahh, we said earlier that B might also be *below* A.
$k = 7 - 8$ $k = -1$.

It's worth mentioning that when we draw our own pictures, they won't be to scale. If we had drawn point B below point A instead of above it, we wouldn't know whether to put the point above or below the x-axis. If anything, we probably would have put it above the x-axis, because we wouldn't have realized that k was going to come out to be negative.

Note: Figure not drawn to scale

It's easy to get confused, but it doesn't matter. This is just a stupid sketch. No one's grading you on your crude not-to-scale drawing. In fact, you don't have to draw in the x-axis at all. Just recognize that your poorly drawn picture is not to scale. It's a just a guide.

15. Answer: D.

This can be confusing if you're still not comfortable with the $f(x)$ format, but it's really much easier than it looks. Remember that the value of $f(x)$ corresponds with the value of y on the graph. So the question is really just asking:

"How many points on the curve have a y-value of -1?"

That's easy! Count them! We don't need to know the x-values of the points—we just want to know how many there are. There are **three**.

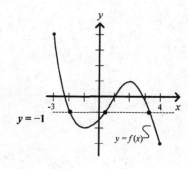

THIS PAGE INTENTIONALLY LEFT BLANK

Problem Solving and Data Analysis

We're almost at the end. Problem Solving and Data Analysis is the last category of math questions for which you will get a subscore, and the one with the least dumb name.* Here you'll find a collection of different concepts that are united by a connection to the real world.

Most of the math we've been doing has been *pure math*. That means we've been dealing with equations that apply to numbers in the abstract or the principles of how numbers work. But the SAT also has a lot of *statistics*. This is the realm of *applied math*, working with the real world of real things. And the real world contains *data*, when you've got a lot of different numbers that you have to make sense of.

You will see a total of 17 Problem Solving and Data Analysis questions on the SAT, about the same number as the other two main categories. However, note that these questions are different from the other categories in that **they only appear on section 4, the Calculator OK section.** The other question types all appear on both sections. If you hate data questions, this is good news. It means that you'll have an entire section with none of these questions. *And* it means you'll always get to use your calculator on them. Of course, the flip side is that section 4 is going to seem like it's heavy on data questions because they'll make up almost half the section.

---

* It is still a little bit dumb, mind you. After all, every question on the Math test involves some kind of problem solving. And it's too long (though not as bad as "Evidence-based Reading and Writing").

I. PROPORTIONS

Do you remember the chapter called Math Fundamentals? Right after Techniques, right before Heart of Algebra? That chapter was *chock full* of concepts that the SAT classifies as Problem Solving and Data Analysis concepts. That includes:

- Ratios
- Rates and unit conversion
- Percentages

All these concepts are different kinds of **proportions**. Basically almost any concept involving fractions strictly speaking belongs in this chapter. We decided to talk about them early because they have relevance to some of the concepts we talk about in the algebra chapters. Since we talked about them there, we're not going to talk about them here. Feel free to flip back and review those sections, though, as they might show up on some practice problems later on.

If you're itching for some fraction work, though, don't worry. We've got some concepts coming up in a few pages—*averages* and *probability*—that are loaded with fraction work.

II. FIGURES

Many data analysis problems will arrange data into some sort of graphical representation, be it a table, line graph, or something else. Over half of the Problem Solving and Data Representation questions will contain a figure of some kind. So let's get to know these figures.

1. Tables

Tables are the most common way of presenting data on the SAT. In general, the test will have about as many tables as all other figures combined. You probably have some experience with tables already. Heck, we've seen a bunch of them in this book already. Most of them are straightforward. Just match up the rows and the columns to find a value:

Trees in Springfield Gardens

Species	Tree Condition			
	Good	Fair	Poor	Total
Pin oak	23	7	2	32
Horse chestnut	17	10	8	35
Bald cypress	3	4	13	20
Total	43	21	23	87

> ✒ **Based on the table above, how many horse chestnut trees in Springfield Gardens are in fair condition?**

To find out, find the "Horse chestnut" row and see where it crosses the "Fair" column:

Species	Tree Condition			
	Good	**Fair**	Poor	Total
Pin oak	23	7	2	32
Horse chestnut	17	**10**	8	35
Bald cypress	3	4	13	20
Total	43	21	23	87

There are 10 fair horse chestnuts.

Subtotals

As we can see here, tables with multiple rows and columns like this will often show **subtotals** at the end of a row or column. In our example above, there are a total of six different groups: three types of trees (in the rows) and three types of conditions (in the columns). Each row or column shows the total of all the items in that category at the end.

For pin oak trees, there are 23 in Good condition, 7 in Fair condition, and 2 in Poor condition. Add them up to get 23 + 7 + 2 = 32 total pin oak trees.

The box in the very bottom right, then, is the total of the totals: it shows the total number of all trees in all conditions. Notice that it's both the sum of the column totals and the sum of the row totals, since you'll get the same number of total trees no matter how you count.

$$
\begin{array}{ll}
32 & \text{Pin oak} \\
35 & \text{Horse chestnut} \\
+\,20 & \text{Bald cypress} \\
\hline
87 & \text{Total trees}
\end{array}
\qquad
\begin{array}{ll}
43 & \text{Good trees} \\
21 & \text{Fair trees} \\
+\,23 & \text{Poor trees} \\
\hline
87 & \text{Total trees}
\end{array}
$$

Approximation

Sometimes tables will come with crazy ugly numbers:

Population of New Shelbyville in 2010

Gender	Age in years			Total
	18–34	35–54	55 or older	
Male	11,922	35,106	14,807	61,835
Female	24,012	14,765	15,289	54,066
Total	35,934	49,871	30,096	115,901

10. **According to the table above, approximately what fraction of residents 55 or older are female?**

A) 1/3

B) 1/2

C) 2/3

D) 3/4

"Phew," you think. "With all those crazy numbers, good thing I'm allowed to use my calculator." WAIT, STOP! Don't. Don't do that. Look at our choices. These are all basic fractions, not crazy fractions. Let's do some **rounding.**

We're talking about 55+ residents, so let's look at that column and **round** to the nearest thousand:

Gender	55 or older	Rounded
Male	14,807	**15,000**
Female	15,289	**15,000**
Total	30,096	**30,000**

Aha! There are about 30,000 people 55 or older, and about 15,000 of them are female. That's about **one half**.

Grouping

So far we've been dealing with only one table cell at a time. But sometimes we might have to combine parts of the table. Look at this one, still about the same table of residents of New Shelbyville:

11. **According to the table above, approximately what fraction of residents 35 or older are female?**

    A) 1/2
    B) 2/4
    C) 3/8
    D) 3/10

This time it's asking about residents who are 35 or older. That encompasses *two* columns: "35–54" and "55 and older". So we'll have to deal with both those columns together:

Gender	Age in years			Total
	18–34	**35–54**	**55 or older**	
Male	11,922	**35,106**	**14,807**	61,835
Female	24,012	**14,765**	**15,289**	54,066
Total	35,934	**49,871**	**30,096**	115,901

Let's focus on those two columns and round them:

Gender	35–54	55 or older
Male	35,000	15,000
Female	15,000	15,000
Total	50,000	30,000

We want the number of *women* in these two columns as a fraction of the *total* for these two columns.

> Total women: 15,000 + 15,000 = 30,000
> Total residents: 50,000 + 30,000 = 80,000

So the fraction of women would be 30 ÷ 80 = **3/8**.

Frequency tables

Take a look at this table:

Number of goats owned	Number of students
0	8
1	14
2	22
3	45
4	11
Total	100

> ✏ **A survey asked 100 students in school how many goats they own at home. The results are shown in the table above.**

This is a **frequency table**. The study counted 100 students and asked how many goats they have at home. Every student had somewhere from 0 to 4 goats. This table shows how many students fall into each of the ownership categories. That is:

- ✏ There were 8 students who had 0 goats.
- ✏ There were 14 students who had 1 goat each.
- ✏ There were 22 students who had 2 goats each.

Et cetera. This is a convenient way to organize data when you have a lot of the same values over and over again. Instead of writing "3 goats" forty-five times, you can summarize it in this table.

2. Coordinate Planes

We just spent a ton of time talking about the coordinate plane in the Graphing chapter, so you should have a decent sense of how it works by now. But all those questions dealt with *functions*, lines or curves that describe an equation. But you can also use the plane to map *data*.

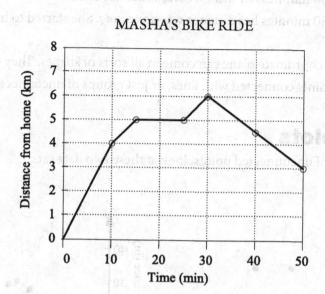

MASHA'S BIKE RIDE

The graph shown above looks a lot like the kinds of graphs we've seen before, but the line looks different. It's jagged and blocky. We're used to seeing single straight lines or smooth curves. This graph instead shows a relationship that changes as it progresses. There's no single equation that describes the line shown, but the figure itself behaves the same way all graphs do. We can look up points by matching up the *x* and *y* axes, and we can see whether the line increases, decreases, or stays the same.

This graph describes a trip Masha takes on her bike. We can see:

- She starts at home (time = 0, distance from home = 0)
- After 10 minutes she's 4 km away from home.
- After 15 minutes, she's 5 km away.
- She stays 5 km away for the next 10 minutes.
- After 30 minutes, she's 6 km away.
- At 40 minutes, she's 4.5 km away. She's starting to come back home.
- After 50 minutes, she's 3 km away.

All of this just involves looking at the picture and matching up the axes.

We can also see the various relationships in the data:

- From 0 to 15 minutes her distance is *increasing*. Note that it increases at a higher rate from 0 to 10 than from 10 to 15. We can tell because the first part has a steeper line—that is, a *greater slope*.
- From 15 to 25 minutes her distance *stays the same*. She probably took a break. Maybe stopped for a donut. Gotta have donuts if you're on a bike ride.
- From 25 to 30 minutes her distance was *increasing* again.
- From 30 to 50 minutes her distance was *decreasing*. She started to head back home.

Graphs using the *xy*-coordinate plane can come in all sorts of shapes. They can be jagged lines, wiggly lines, points connected with lines, or just groups of unconnected points.

3. Scatterplots

Speaking of groups of unconnected points, look at these two data sets:

These graphs are called **scatterplots**. All that means is that the graph shows points representing data that we collected. If you have data with two characteristics, you can put those characteristics on some axes and show that data on a plane as a jumble of points.

In each of these graphs above, we measured the height of some trees. Each point here represents one tree. In the graph on the left, we matched each tree's height with the number of cicadas we found in it. In the graph on the right, we matched each tree's height with the circumference of its trunk.

Notice a difference? The graph on the left has points that seem randomly scattered around the graph. The graph on the right, however, has points that seem to make a straight line. In fact, we can try to draw that line.*

---

* We don't have to draw it by hand; there are mathematically rigorous ways of calculating this line. But on the SAT you won't have to draw them at all. If you care about a trend line, it will probably already be on the figure.

The graph here has a **trend line** or **line of best fit**. That's a line that closely approximates the behavior of the points. The line doesn't exactly describe their behavior—you can see that not all the points are on the line. But it comes close.

Why would we want a line? First, in order to see that there is a strong relationship between our variables. You can see the line has a *positive slope*. That means that as tree height increases, trunk circumference likewise increases. Makes sense.

Of course, we saw that positive relationship without the line. Having the line there, however, allows us to make a **prediction**. There's a trend in the rate at which the circumference grows. The slope of the line tells us how many inches of circumference a tree expects to gain for every meter of height it gains. We can use that to find the expected circumference for any given height.

That may sound fancy, but what we mean is to just look at the line and find new points.

> ✎ **According to the line of best fit, a tree that is 60 m tall can be predicted to have what trunk circumference?**

Let's just find the 60 on the *x*-axis, follow it up to the line, and look up the value of trunk circumference on the *y*-axis:

So a tree with a height of 60 m will have a circumference of 40 inches, right?
NO. A tree with a height of 60 m will **probably** have a circumference of **about** 40 inches. Remember that not all points lie exactly on the line. They're all pretty close, so we can be

confident that the circumference should be pretty close to 40.* But we don't know *for sure* that it will be *exactly* 40 in.†

In contrast, the first data set we saw showed no relationship between tree height and number of cicadas. For example, one tree that was 40 m tall had around 7 cicadas, while another was also 40 m tall but had 14 cicadas. So we can't make any predictions at all. A tree that's 60 m tall might have 5 cicadas, might have 20. We don't know.

Mind you, we could draw a line of best fit for any collection of data. It's just that when the points are closer to the line the relationship is stronger, and therefore we can be more confident in our predictions.

Of course, an increasing linear relationship is only one possible relationship. Here are some more:

---

* There are different ways for measuring how confident we are in our projection, based on how well the points fit the line. But you don't have to worry about such calculations on the SAT.

† And that's to say nothing of *outliers*. No matter how good our predictions are, there are sometimes some weirdos that just buck whatever trend you have. This may be for good reason. For example, you may find a 60-m-tall tree with a circumference of 80 in, because it used to be 120 m tall but lost half its height in a storm. Or it might just be a freakishly fat tree. There are lots of reasons why things may not turn out as we expect. Life is a rich tapestry.

4. Bar Graphs

Bar graphs work basically the same way as the *xy*-coordinate plane.* You have two axes and you match up the data. Let's try one. Let's say we leave home and stop every 10 km to count how many goats we see:

Each bar corresponds to a different distance from home, matched up to a number of goats. Just like our scatterplot, but with bars instead of points. In fact, you can often represent the same data several different ways. Here's the same data as a table and as a scatterplot:

Distance from home (km)	Number of goats
10	10
20	25
30	30
40	35

With a bar graph you've got a little bit more leeway with what to do with the *x*-axis. You could make it a value just like we did above. Or you could make the bars different labels for different groups:

---

* Some people reserve the word "bar graph" for graphs where the bar stretch horizontally, and call these graphs that have vertical graphs "column graphs". The SAT does not care what you call them.

III. STATISTICS

All right, we talked about figures. Now let's talk about some numbers. What can we do with all this data we have?

Averages

There's a fancy word in statistics called *centrality* or *central tendency*, which means the value at the *center* of a group of numbers. That is, one number that best represents a whole set of numbers. There are several different ways to find the center. Two in particular are of interest to us on the SAT: *mean* and *median*.

Arithmetic Mean

This is what we usually mean when we say "average". Find the average by taking the **sum of the numbers** divided by the **number of terms**.

> ✏ **What is the average (arithmetic mean) of 7, 18, 4, 9 and 2?**

The sum is $7 + 18 + 4 + 9 + 2 = 40$.
There are 5 terms, so the average is $40 \div 5 = \textbf{8}$.

Median

The median is the **middle** number, *when you put the terms in order*.

> ✏ **What is the median of 7, 18, 4, 9 and 2?**

Write them in order, you get 2, 4, 7, 9, 18. The one in the middle is 7, so the median is **7**.

Note that the value of the median doesn't change if you make the highest term higher or the lowest term lower. For example, if we changed the sequence above to 2, 4, 7, 9, 157, the median would still be 7.

If there are an *even* number of terms, such that there is no one number in the middle, the median is **the average of the two middle numbers**.

> ✏ **What is the median of 9, 2, 7, 8, 4 and 18?**

Write them in order and you get 2, 4, 7, 8, 9, 18. The two middle numbers are 7 and 8, so the median is **7.5**.

*You must put the terms **in numerical order** before finding the median.*

What's the difference?

We just took the same set of five numbers and got two different centers: the mean is 8 and the median is 7. What's the difference between median and mean? Why bother having different calculations like this? The difference is that *the median is not affected by extreme values*, while mean is. This may be important.

Let's say you're in a book club with some people from your neighborhood. Let's look at the median and mean net worth for everyone in your book club:*

Net worth of book club members	
Median	$0.00
Mean	$46,428,571.43

Huh. That's weird. There seems to be a discrepancy between the median and mean. You know what? Let's look at the individual values for the people in the book club to try to figure out the cause:

Member	Net Worth	Member	Net Worth
You	$0.00	Jamelle	$0.00
Molly	$0.00	Audrey	$0.00
Nihal	$0.00	Ariel	$0.00
Jeanne	$0.00	Colleen	$0.00
Yehuda	$0.00	Isabelle	$0.00
Gary	$0.00	Michael Jordan	$650,000,000.00
Steve	$0.00	Bob	$0.00

Did you catch it? Most of the members of the book club are high school kids who have no jobs, assets, or money, so they're all worth nothing. Except for NBA Hall-of-Famer Michael Jordan, who is also in the book club for some reason and is worth $650 million. In this case, using the mean doesn't actually give you an accurate picture of the group as a whole, because one member is skewing the average by so much. But the median only uses the term in the middle and is totally unaffected by how far away the endpoints are.

That doesn't mean that median is always better, of course. We use mean a lot! In cases that aren't as extreme as this, we often do want to account for all the values, including the ones at the top and bottom. There's no one answer for which is "better"; it depends on what you're trying to figure out.

---

* "Net worth" is basically a fancy term for the value of everything you own.

Using the Sum

Let's take a closer look at arithmetic mean (which we'll just call "average" from here on out). We all know pretty well how to take the average of a list of numbers they give us. If you're given a list of numbers, just add them all up and divide by how many there are.

But on SAT questions sometimes *we don't know what the individual numbers are.* Let's look at one:

> The average of 5 numbers is 15. If the average of 3 of those numbers is 19, what is the average of the other two numbers?

It looks like we don't have enough information. Since we don't know the terms, we can't add them up. What do we do **?**

Ah, we know more than we think. Let's look again at the definition of average:

$$\text{Average} = \frac{\text{Sum of terms}}{\text{How many terms}}$$

If we multiply both sides of this equation by the number of terms, we get:

(How many terms) × (Average) = Sum of the terms

This equation is very important. Even if we don't know the *individual* numbers, we can still work directly with their sum. In our problem, we know we have 5 numbers that have an average of 15, so their sum *must* be 5 × 15 = 75. Regardless of what the individual numbers are, they must have a sum of 75, or else they wouldn't have an average of 19.

We can fill out a chart to help us organize this information:

How many terms	Average	Sum of terms	
5	15	75	5 numbers with an average of 15, so their sum is 5(15) = 75
− 3	19	− 57	3 numbers with an average of 19, so their sum is 3(19) = 57
2		18	There are **2** numbers we don't know, so their sum must be **18**.

Once we know that those two numbers have a sum of 18, we can find the average:

$$\text{Average} = \frac{\text{Sum of terms}}{\text{How many terms}} = \frac{18}{2} = 9$$

But again, you only need to do this when you don't know the individual terms involved. If you're given a list of numbers, just add them up and divide by how many there are.

Other calculations

Mode

The **mode** is the number that occurs most frequently.

> ✎ **What is the mode of 5, 2, 7, 2 and 9?**

Each number occurs once, except for 2, which occurs twice. So the mode is **2**.

Standard deviation

Standard deviation measures how far the data collectively strays from the mean. The more spread out the values are, the larger the standard deviation.

Let's look at two sets of data.

> **Class 1: {1, 2, 3, 3, 3, 3, 3, 3, 4, 5}**
> **Class 2: {1, 1, 2, 2, 3, 3, 4, 4, 5, 5}**

> ✎ **Mr. Lundqvist has two math classes, each with 10 students. He asked each student how many pets they own. The two sets above show the results. Which class has a larger standard deviation?**

For both these sets, the average is 3. Both classes had students with as few as 1 pet and as many as 5 pets. But for class 1, most students were clustered around the average, whereas for class 2, the data was evenly distributed across the values (each value had 2 students). Since class 2 was *more spread out*, **class 2** will have a *larger standard deviation*.

Would you like to see this data as a frequency table? No? Too bad, here it is:

Number of pets		1	2	3	4	5
Frequency	Class 1	1	1	6	1	1
	Class 2	2	2	2	2	2

Calculating standard deviation can start to get *very* complex very quickly—we're dipping our toe into the pool of Crazy Math here. But on the SAT, you will only need to know what the term means. Now let us never speak of it again.

$$\{\,4, 6, 9, 17, 24\,\}$$

✒ What is the average (arithmetic mean) of the numbers in the set above?

✒ A set contains 3 consecutive integers that have a sum of 78. What is the median of the set?

✒ The 12 trees in John's backyard have an average height of 135 inches. If 7 of the trees have an average height of 100 inches, what is the average height of the other 5 trees?

The next two questions refer to the following information:

A survey asked 30 people how many floors their house has. Results are shown in the graph below.

✒ What is the median number of floors for these houses?

✒ What is the mean number of floors for these houses (round your answer to the nearest tenth) ?

Averages

{ 4, 6, 9, 17, 24 }

✍ **What is the average (arithmetic mean) of the numbers in the set above?**

Answer: 12.

Average = sum of terms ÷ number of terms
Sum of terms = 4 + 6 + 9 + 17 + 24 = 60
Number of terms = 5
60 ÷ 5 = **12**

✍ **A set contains 3 consecutive integers that have a sum of 78. What is the median of the set?**

Answer: 26.

3 integers with a sum of 78 have an average of 78 ÷ 3 = 26.
The numbers are consecutive, and their average is in the middle, so our numbers are 25, 26, and 27.
The median is the middle number, so the median is 26.

If we had answer choices, this would be a good Backsolve. (In fact, we saw a question just like this in the Backsolve Drill.)

✍ **The 12 trees in John's backyard have an average height of 135 inches. If 7 of the trees have an average height of 100 inches, what is the average height of the other 5 trees?**

Answer: 184.

	How many?	Average		Sum
	12	135		1620
−	7	100	−	700
	5			920

920 ÷ 5 = **184**

✍ **What is the median number of floors for these houses?**

Answer: 2

We know there are 30 people. That means the median value will be the one between the 15th and 16th value.

The graph represents a list of repeated numbers and tells you how many of each there are. If we wrote out the data as a list, it would look like:
{1,1,1,1,1,1,1,1,2,2,2,2,2,2,2,2,2,2,3,3,3,3,4,4,5,5,5,5,5,5}

Let's get the values from the graph and start a running tab, starting from the bottom, and see when we hit the 15th value.

8 houses have 1 floor.
10 houses have 2 floors. That's 8 + 10 = 18 so far.
STOP! We're already past the median. The 15th and 16th values were both **2.**

✍ **What is the mean number of floors for these houses (round your answer to the nearest tenth) ?**

Answer: 2.6

To find the average, we'll need to find the total number of floors divided by the total number of houses.
To find the total floors, **multiply** each value for number of floors by its frequency of houses.

$1 \times 8 = 8$
$2 \times 10 = 20$
$3 \times 4 = 12$
$4 \times 2 = 8$
$5 \times 6 = \underline{30}$
78 total floors

We know there were 30 houses:
78 ÷ 30 = **2.6**

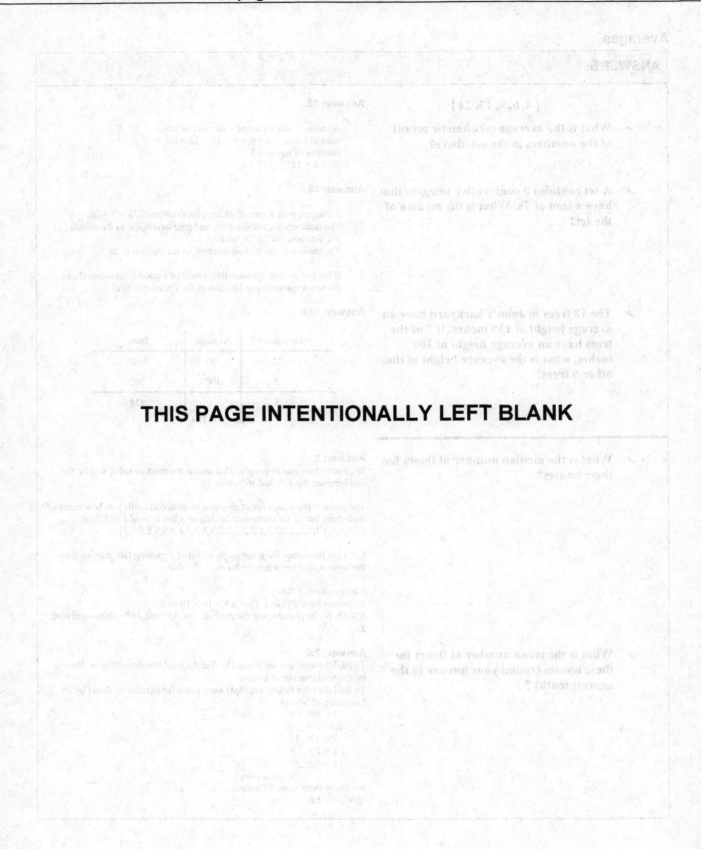

THIS PAGE INTENTIONALLY LEFT BLANK

Probability

"Probability" means exactly what it sounds like: how "probable" is this event. The probability of an event is defined as:

$$\frac{\text{number of "winners"}}{\text{total possible events}}$$

If the probability of winning the lottery is "one in a million", that just means there's *one* winning number out of *a million* possible numbers. Since probabilities are just glorified fractions, you can think of probability as basically **the same thing as a percentage**. People talk this way all the time; when the weatherman says there's a 60% chance of rain, that's the same thing as a probability of 3/5. So most probability questions just boil down to: what **part of the whole** is the thing you're looking for?

> ✐ **A certain jar with 32 marbles contains only red marbles and blue marbles. If the jar contains 8 red marbles, what is the probability that a marble chosen from the jar will be blue?**

We're looking for the probability of choosing a blue marble. So all we have to find is:

$$\frac{\text{number of blue marbles}}{\text{total number of marbles}} = \frac{\text{blue}}{32}$$

We know there are 32 total marbles, so 32 will go on the bottom. We don't know how many blue marbles there are, but we do know there are 8 red marbles, and there are only red and blue marbles. So if we subtract the red from the total, we'll be left with the blue.

$$\frac{32-8}{32} = \frac{24}{32} = \frac{3}{4}$$

We're done! The probability of choosing a blue marble is 3/4.

Note that instead of solving for the blue marbles, we could've found the probability of choosing a red marble and subtracted from 1.

$$\frac{\text{red}}{\text{total}} = \frac{8}{32} = \frac{1}{4}$$

There's a 1/4 chance of picking a red marble...

$$1 - \frac{1}{4} = \frac{3}{4}$$

...so there's a 3/4 chance of picking a blue marble.

We can see from this that *the probabilities of all events surrounding a given problem must add up to 1*. Just like all percents of a whole add up to 100%, all probabilities add up to 1.

Probability questions on the SAT often get involve getting data from tables. That means you'll have to find and group data just like we saw earlier when we were discussing tables. In fact, questions we saw like this:

> **10. According to the table above, approximately what fraction of residents 55 or older are female?**

...could just as easily have been phrased like this:

> **10. According to the table above, what is the probability that a randomly selected resident 55 or older will be female?**

Because *probability and fractions are one and the same.*

THIS PAGE INTENTIONALLY LEFT BLANK

Probability

ANSWERS:

If a 15-year-old is chose at random, what is the probability that he or she got 7 hours of sleep?

Answer: 9/26
There are 26 total 15-year-olds.
9 of them got 7 hours of sleep.
So it's **9/26**

If a student who got 7 hours of sleep is chosen at random, what is the probability that he or she is 15 years old?

Answer: 3/7
There are 21 total students who got 7 hours of sleep.
9 of them are 15 years old.
So it's 9/21 = **3/7**

What is the probability that a student who is 16 or older got 6 hours of sleep?

Answer: 7/22
Students who are 16 *or older* include 16 year olds and 17 year olds.
There are 20 16-yr-olds and 24 17-yr-olds. 20 + 24 = 44 total.

10 16-yr-olds and 4 17-yr-olds got 7 hours of sleep. 10 + 4 = 14.
So it's 14/44 = **7/22**

What is the probability that a student in the 11th grade class is 15 years old?

Answer: 13/35
There are 70 total students in 11th grade.
There are 26 15-year-olds in 11th grade.
So it's 26/70 = **13/35**

What is the probability that a student in the 11th grade class got 7 hours of sleep?

Answer: 3/10
There are 70 total students in 11th grade.
There are 21 total students who got 7 hours of sleep .
So it's 21/70 = **3/10**

If a student is chosen at random, what is the probability he or she is a 15-year-old who got 7 hours of sleep or a 17-year-old who got 8 hours?

Answer: 12/35
There are 70 total students in 11th grade.
Of those, 9 are 15-yr-olds who got 7 hours of sleep, and 15 are 17-yr-olds who got 8 hours of sleep.
9 + 15 = 24 students fit our requirements.
So it's 24/70 = 12/35

What is the probability that someone in the class is 16 years old and got 8 hours of sleep?

Answer: 3/70
There are 70 total students in 11th grade.
There are 3 total students who both are 16 years old and got 8 hours of sleep.
So it's **3/70**

What is the probability that someone in the class is 16 years old and got at least 7 hours of sleep?

Answer: 1/7
There are 70 total students in 11th grade.
There are 7 students who are 16 and got 7 hours of sleep.
There are 3 students who are 16 and got 8 hours of sleep.
7 + 3 = 10.
So it's 10/70 = **1/7**

What is the probability that someone in the class is 16 or younger and got less than 7 hours of sleep?

Answer: 8/35
There are 70 total students in 11th grade.
The only value less than 7 hours of sleep is 6 hours of sleep.
There are 10 students who are 16 and got 6 hours of sleep.
There are 6 students who are 15 and got 6 hours of sleep.
10 + 6 = 16.
So it's 16/70 = **8/35**

If a student who got 7 hours of sleep or less is selected at random, what is the probability that he or she is 16 or younger?

Answer: 32/41
There are 21 students who got 7 hours of sleep.
There are 20 students who got 6 hours of sleep.
21 + 20 = 41 total students.
Of those students:
   6 are 15 and got 6 hours
   10 are 16 and got 6 hours
   9 are 15 and got 7 hours
   7 are 16 and got 7 hours.
6 + 10 + 9 + 7 = 32.
So it's **32/41**

The following questions all refer to the table below.

Hours of Sleep for 11th Grade Students at Cromwell High School

Age	Hours of sleep			Total
	6	7	8	
15	6	9	11	26
16	10	7	3	20
17	4	5	15	24
Total	20	21	29	70

A survey asked all 70 students in the 11th grade class of Cromwell High School how many hours of sleep they got the previous evening. The results are shown in the table above.

- If a 15-year-old is chosen at random, what is the probability that he or she got 7 hours of sleep?

- If a student who got 7 hours of sleep is chosen at random, what is the probability that he or she is 15 years old?

- What is the probability that a student who is 16 or older got 6 hours of sleep?

- What is the probability that a student in the 11th grade class is 15 years old?

- What is the probability that a student in the 11th grade class got 7 hours of sleep?

- If a student is chosen at random, what is the probability he or she is a 15-year-old who got 7 hours of sleep or a 17-year-old who got 8 hours of sleep?

- What is the probability that someone in the class is 16 years old and got 8 hours of sleep?

- What is the probability that someone in the class is 16 years old and got at least 7 hours of sleep?

- What is the probability that someone in the class is 16 or younger and got less than 7 hours of sleep?

- If a student who got 7 hours of sleep or less is selected at random, what is the probability that he or she is 16 or younger?

Sampling and Projection

One of the main reasons people collect data is to get a *sample*. Most of the time, I can't count everything. There are too many things! If I have a question about the world, I can't get total knowledge of everything. But I can learn about a small portion of the world and assume that the rest of the world is similar.

We see this all the time with polling. Let's look at some data:

Survey Responses:
Do you support Proposition 409?

	Total
Yes	60
No	26
Unsure	14
Total	100

✎ **The table above shows the results of a survey of 100 residents of Hartsville. Respondents were asked whether they support Proposition 409. If the city of Hartsville has approximately 20,000 residents, roughly how many total residents can be expected to support Proposition 409?**

We can see from the results that 60 people out of the 100 who responded said yes, they support the proposition. That's 60%. So we could expect that 60% of the whole population supports the proposition. So

$$20,000 \times (0.60) = \textbf{12,000} \text{ residents would support the proposition.}$$

A projection is **another kind of proportion**. We take a small sample we take to be representative of the whole group. We can then project that ratio onto the entire group. If 3/5 of the sample would vote yes, then 3/5 of the whole city will probably vote yes.

Most SAT questions about projection will work that way. However, we had a big assumption here: *how do we know that the whole group will behave like the sample?* We have to be sure that our sample is **representative** of the whole town. That is, that it behaves the same way the whole town behaves.

First of all, **sample size** will make a difference. The more people you ask, the more reliable your sample is. I mean, if this was the result of my survey:

	Total
Yes	2
No	0
Unsure	0
Total	2

I can't use this data to project that 100% of the town will vote yes. I only asked two people! This is not a representative sample of the entire town. There are probably a wider range of opinions than these two people have.

That doesn't mean we need a *huge* sample to be accurate. A 100-person sample is a perfectly fine sample size for our city. But there may be other problems.

Secondly, we can look for **bias**. Let's get more information about Proposition 409:

> **Proposition 409 is a bill to use taxpayer money to install fancy plush seats at Hartsville Stadium, home of the Hartsville Hounds football team.**

Huh. That's an odd bill. And tell me more about this survey we gave. Where was this survey given exactly?

> **100 Hartsville residents were surveyed as they were leaving a Hartsville Hounds game.**

Aha! So *all* the people who responded to the survey had just been to a football game. So these people are likely to be football fans. That's important because the proposition is *about football*. People who don't care about football are probably less likely to support using taxpayer money for football. And those people were less likely to take this survey. So this survey is *biased* towards people who would vote yes. So it's *not* a representative sample.

If you want a sample to be representative of a large group, then it has to be varied in the same way the group is. It should be a **random** survey. If all people in the sample share a particular trait, it could be biased toward that trait.

The last thing to keep in mind about sampling is that everything we do is an **estimate**. Even if we're certain our sample is large and unbiased, we can't know definitively how all 20,000 residents are going to vote. We can only get close to knowing how they're *likely* to vote. This is just like when we were talking about trend lines in scatterplot graphs: the trend line is a kind of projection that tells us *likely* values. That doesn't mean that it's useless and we can't know anything about anything. We can still be confident in our projection. We can even be *very* confident in our projection. But we won't be absolutely certain.

Note that everything we're talking about here is just a brief glimpse into the world of sampling and projection. A quick internet search will show you that the math behind this sort of thing can get very complicated very quickly.* There are ways you can calculate how confident you are in your projections, ways you can make adjustments to correct for bias, and more.

I assure you, you will not have to know any of that. Statistical questions on the SAT tend to be very direct, only testing you on whether you understand the underlying concepts, not asking you to do excessive computation. Really, most projection questions on the SAT are just glorified ratios.

---

* But be warned that if you google "sampling" you may get a lot of results about the Beastie Boys.

THIS PAGE INTENTIONALLY LEFT BLANK

Problem Solving and Data Analysis Exercise

1.   Answer: A.
Just look to see which direction the line is going over every interval. If it goes up and *only* goes up, it's our answer.

A)   10:00 – 12:00: **only up**
B)   12:00 – 2:00: up, then constant
C)   2:00 – 4:00: down, then up
D)   4:00 – 6:00: only down.

3.   Answer: B.
We know that 32.8% of the sample liked the Fightin' Sand Crabs. We can project that same percentage to the whole group of 425.

It wants us to approximate, so let's just divide 425 by 3.

$425 \div 3 = 141.67$

Choice B), 140 is close enough for me.

Note that the fact that there were 70 people in the sample was irrelevant to us. That might be useful information if, say, it told us how many people in the sample preferred the mascot. But it gave us the percentage directly, so we could just use that.

2.   Answer: C.
4 of 100 will win, so 96 of 100 will not win.

$$\frac{96}{100} = \frac{24}{25}$$

RTFQ: B). That's the probability Dave will win.
A) and D) mean you didn't notice there are *four* winners.

PROBLEM SOLVING AND DATA ANALYSIS EXERCISE

1

The figure above shows the change in temperature in degrees Fahrenheit over the course of a certain day. In which of the following intervals is the temperature strictly increasing?

A) Between 10:00 AM and 12:00 PM
B) Between 12:00 PM and 2:00 PM
C) Between 2:00 PM and 4:00 PM
D) Between 4:00 PM and 6:00 PM

2

Four randomly chosen employees at Dave's company will win large cash prizes. If there are 100 employees at the company, what is the probability that Dave will <u>not</u> win?

A) $\dfrac{1}{100}$

B) $\dfrac{1}{25}$

C) $\dfrac{24}{25}$

D) $\dfrac{99}{100}$

3

Mr. Gordon surveyed a random sample of students in Seabreeze High School to determine what their new school mascot should be. Of the 70 students he surveyed, 32.8% preferred the mascot to be the Fightin' Sand Crabs. Based on this information, about how many students in the entire 425-person class would be expected to prefer the mascot to be the Fightin' Sand Crabs?

A) 130
B) 140
C) 150
D) 160

CONTINUE

4

Which of the following scatterplots best shows a strong negative linear association between x and y?

A)

B)

C)

D)

	Pronunciation		
Gender	Two syllables	Three syllables	Total
Male	8	6	14
Female	5	11	16
Total	13	17	30

Bob asked some of his coworkers how they pronounce the word "caramel". Some pronounced it with two syllables (CAR-mul), while other pronounced it with three syllables (CARE-ah-mell). The results are shown in the table.

5

According to the results, what is the ratio of men who pronounce the word with three syllables to women who pronounce it with two syllables?

A) $\frac{6}{5}$

B) $\frac{6}{11}$

C) $\frac{8}{5}$

D) $\frac{8}{11}$

6

Approximately what percent of the women who responded pronounce the word with three syllables?

A) 31%
B) 36%
C) 65%
D) 69%

CONTINUE

4. **Answer: D.**

We want a "linear association". That means the points should (roughly) look like a straight line. Eliminate A) and C).

A "negative association" meant that as x increases, y decreases. So we want a graph that goes *down*. Eliminate B).

Choice D) it is.

5. **Answer: A.**

There are 6 men who use three syllables.
There are 5 women who use two syllables.
That's a ratio of **6/5**.

This is purely a matter of looking up numbers. Lots of ways you can mess up:

Choice B) is three-syllable men to three-syllable women.
Choice C) is two-syllable men to two-syllable women.
Choice D) is two-syllable men to three-syllable women.

6. **Answer: D.**

It asks, "what percent **of the women**…" That means we want the women who use three syllables *as a percent of the total number of women*.
There are a total of 16 women.
11 women use three syllables.

$$\frac{11}{16} = 0.6875 = \mathbf{69\%}$$

Again, there are many ways to pick the wrong numbers:

Choice A) is two-syllable women out of all women. (5/16)
Choice B) is three-syllable women out of all people (11/30)
Choice C) is three-syllable women out of all three-syllable people (11/17)

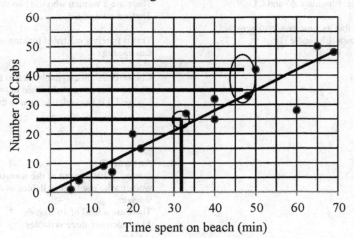

Crabs Caught on North Beach

7. **Answer: C.**

    Find 25 on the crab axis and see where it crosses the trend line.
    Go down from that point to the time axis and find the value.

    It should take about **35 minutes**.

    (There's something very pleasing about the phrase "the crab axis".)

8. **Answer: B.**

    Find 50 minutes on the x-axis and find the point mentioned in the
    question. It's at about 42 crabs.

    Staying on 50 minutes, find the corresponding point on the line of
    best fit. It's at about 35 crabs.

    $42 - 25 =$ **7 crabs over.**

    You can do a lot of *Guesstimate* here as well. Try to determine the
    length of the segment from that point straight down to the line of
    best fit. We know the grid lines are in intervals of 5. It's more than
    one square away, but less than two squares away. 7 is our best
    option.

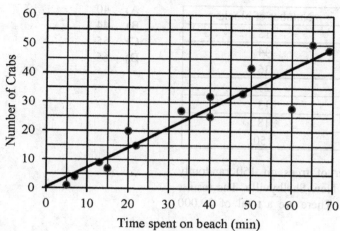

Crabs Caught on North Beach

Carla made 15 trips to North Beach to try to catch crabs she found on the beach. The scatterplot above shows the amount of time she spent on each trip to the beach with the number of crabs she found on that trip.

7

According to the line of best fit in the scatterplot above, which of the following best approximates the amount of time it would take to find 25 crabs ?

A) 18 min
B) 30 min
C) 35 min
D) 40 min

8

On the trip that took 50 minutes, Carla actually caught about how many crabs more than the number predicted by the line of best fit?

A) 5
B) 7
C) 10
D) 12

CONTINUE

Number of trees	Number of blocks
0	18
1	44
2	36
3	21
4	13
5	18
Total	150

A survey counted the number of trees on 150 randomly selected blocks in the town of New Shelbyville. The results are shown in the table above. There are a total of 20,000 blocks in New Shelbyville.

9

What is the median number of trees per city block in the survey?

A) 1
B) 2
C) 3
D) 4

10

Based on the survey data, which of the following is the closest to the expected total number of blocks that have at least one tree?

A) 8,800
B) 16,400
C) 17,600
D) 42,800

11

The average (arithmetic mean) of $a, b, c, d, e, f,$ and g is 50. If the average of a, b and c is 30, what is the average of $d, e, f,$ and g?

A) 40
B) 44
C) 55
D) 65

CONTINUE

9.   Answer: B.

Like we did in the drill earlier, let's find the median by going through each number of trees and starting a running total of the number of blocks .

We know there are 150 total blocks. $150 \div 2 = 75$, so the median value should be between the 75th and 76th terms.

Trees	Blocks	Total so far
0	18	18
1	44	62
2	36	**98 STOP**

The 75th and 76th blocks must both have 2 trees. So our median is **2**.

10.   Answer: C.

Rather than dealing with the blocks that *have* trees, let's focus on the blocks that have *no* trees, and subtract from the total.

There were 18 blocks with 0 trees, out of a total of 150 blocks.

$$\frac{18}{150} = .12 = 12\%$$

So 12% of the blocks had no trees.
That means $100 - 12 = 88\%$ of the blocks had one or more trees.

We know there are 20,000 total blocks.

$$20,000\left(\frac{88}{100}\right) = \textbf{17,600 blocks have trees.}$$

11.   Answer: D.

Let's work directly off the sum.

How many?	Average	Sum
7	50	350
− 3	30	− 90
4		**260**

$260 \div 4 = \textbf{65}$

If you prefer, you can see this algebraically:

$$\frac{a+b+c+d+e+f+g}{7} = 50 \rightarrow \qquad a+b+c+d+e+f+g = 350$$

$$\frac{a+b+c}{3} = 30 \rightarrow \qquad\qquad\qquad\quad a+b+c = 90$$

$$\text{Subtract!} \qquad\qquad\qquad \overline{\quad d+e+f+g = 260\quad}$$

$$\frac{d+e+f+g}{4} = \frac{260}{4} = \textbf{65}$$

12. **Answer: D.**

Like we did in question 10 above, this will be easier if we focus on the kids who had *no* sick days, and subtract from the whole group.

There were a total of 600 kids.
There were 198 kids who had no sick days.
That's *almost* 200, so let's call it 200.

$\frac{200}{600} = \frac{1}{3}$. So a third of the kids had no sick days. That's 33%.

That means *two*-thirds took one or more sick days. That's **67%**.

Choice A) is the percent of kids who took 3-4 sick days.
Choice B) is the percent of kids who took no sick days.
Choice C) is the percent of kids who took 1-2 sick days.

13. **Answer: A.**

There were a total of 150 12th graders.
There were 27 12th graders who took 3-4 sick days.
There were 3 12th graders who took 5 or more sick days.
So there were a total of 30 12th graders who took 3 or more sick days.

$\frac{30}{150} = \frac{1}{5}$

Choice B) is the probability a 12th grader took 5 or more sick days.
Choice C) is the probability a 12th grader took 3-4 sick days.
Choice D) is the probability a 12th grader took 1 or more sick days.

14. **Answer: C.**

First, let's find the likelihood that a 10th grader took no sick days:
There are 74 such 10th graders out of 150 total.
$74 \div 150 = 0.49$

Next, let's find the likelihood that an 11th grader took 3 or more sick days.
There are 38 11th graders who took 3-4 sick days.
There are 0 11th graders who took 5 or more sick days.
That's a total of 38 out of 150 11th graders.
$38 \div 150 = 0.25$

We want to know the likelihood of the 10th grader is how many times more than the likelihood of the 11th grader.

You can probably already tell that 0.49 is almost 0.5, which is **about twice as likely**. Closest choice is clearly **choice C).**

Or you could divide: $0.49 \div 0.25 = 1.96$.

You could also divide $74 \div 38$ directly. That answer will be slightly lower, 1.94, because we approximated before in order to get 0.49 and 0.25.

Choice A) means you used 11th graders for both numbers (27/38)
Choice D) means you used 10th graders for both numbers (74/19)

15. **Answer: C.**
Plug In.
Pick 15 consecutive numbers:

1, 2, 3, 4, 5, 6, 7, **8**, 9, 10, 11, 12, 13, 14, 15

The median is the term in the middle, so the median is 8.

Now go through all the choices, perform the operation in question and see which one changes the median.

A) Decreasing the smallest number by 5
   −4, 2, 3, 4, 5, 6, 7, **8**, 9, 10, 11, 12, 13, 14, 15
   1 became −4. The median is still 8.

B) Decreasing the largest number by 5
   1, 2, 3, 4, 5, 6, 7, **8**, 9, 10, 10, 11, 12, 13, 14
   15 became 10. The median is still 8.

C) **Increasing the smallest number by 8**
   2, 3, 4, 5, 6, 7, 8, **9**, 9, 10, 11, 12, 13, 14, 15
   1 became 9. **The median is now 9.**

D) Increasing the largest number by 8
   1, 2, 3, 4, 5, 6, 7, **8**, 9, 10, 11, 12, 13, 14, 23
   15 became 23. The median is still 8.

The median is the middle number. That means it separates the top half of the terms from the bottom half of the terms. In this case, there are seven numbers above the median and seven numbers below the median.

In our original list, the median was 8. In order for the median to change, one of the numbers has to "switch sides"—that is, a number less than 8 must become greater than 8 or vice versa. In all the wrong choices, the number that gets changed doesn't change enough to switch to the other side.

Questions 12-14 refer to the following information

A survey studied 150 randomly selected students in each grade level across all 6 high schools in New Shelbyville. The survey gathered data about how many days during the 2014-2015 school year they missed school due to illness. The results are shown in the table below.

Sick Days Taken by Students in New Shelbyville High School, 2014-2015					
Grade	0	1-2	3-4	5+	Total
9	46	81	21	2	150
10	74	57	18	1	150
11	27	85	38	0	150
12	51	69	27	3	150
Total	198	292	104	6	600

12

Which of the following is closest to the percent of students who took at least 1 sick day?

A) 17%
B) 33%
C) 50%
D) 67%

13

Based on the data shown, what is the probability that a 12ᵗʰ grader took 3 or more sick days?

A) $\frac{1}{5}$

B) $\frac{1}{50}$

C) $\frac{9}{50}$

D) $\frac{33}{50}$

14

Based on the survey data, how many times more likely is it for a 10ᵗʰ grader to have taken no sick days than it is for an 11ᵗʰ grader to have taken 3 or more sick days? (Round the answer to the nearest hundredth.)

A) 0.72
B) 1.38
C) 1.96
D) 3.77

15

There are 15 consecutive numbers in a list. Which of the following operations would change the value of the median?

A) Decreasing the smallest number by 5
B) Decreasing the largest number by 5
C) Increasing the smallest number by 8
D) Increasing the largest number by 8

STOP

© A-List Education

STOP

SAT Math | Problem Solving and Data Analysis   405

■ Additional Topics in Math

The smallest portion of the SAT is called Additional Topics in Math. This involves a few different concepts, but mostly it means one thing: **GEOMETRY**. Geometry is a love-it-or-hate-it world. Some students can't get enough of it. Some students freeze up and wet themselves at the very thought of it. You're going to have to do some geometry on the SAT.

But luckily, not that much! There are only **6 questions** on the test categorized as Additional Topics in Math, and usually at least one of them isn't on Geometry, so we're really only talking about 5 questions out of 58—that's less than 10 percent of the test.

We're going to show you a few simple rules and not much else. Any other theorems or rules that you may have heard about are only true *because of* the stuff in this chapter. For the most part, the basic rules really are all you need. But if you do need a more complicated rule, you can figure it out from the basic rules.

Of course, if you haven't had a rigorous geometry class in school, you need to learn the basic rules really, really well. But don't worry. All you need is the stuff in this chapter. Learn it, and you're good to go on every geometry question on the SAT.

Seriously, this is a tiny part of the test. Don't spend time here. Go back to Algebra.

I. INTRODUCTORY REMARKS

A few quick remarks before we get started:

A. Techniques

Don't forget about **Guesstimate**. If you see a question with a picture, *before you do anything else*, check that it's to scale, guess the value they're asking for, and then eliminate any implausible choices.

In this chapter we're going to be talking about a lot of straight math content (rules and formulas). But that doesn't mean you should forget about the techniques. And not just Guesstimate, either. You can use Plug In and Backsolve on geometry problems, too. So stay alert.

B. Not sure of a formula?

We're going to talk about a lot of little rules and formulas throughout this lecture. However, you don't even *really* have to know a lot of them. They **tell you** many of the facts and formulas you'll need. On the first page of every math section, you'll see this:

$A = \pi r^2$ $A = \ell w$ $A = \frac{1}{2} bh$ $c^2 = a^2 + b^2$ Special Right Triangles

$C = 2\pi r$

$V = \ell w h$ $V = \pi r^2 h$ $V = \frac{4}{3} \pi r^3$ $V = \frac{1}{3} \pi r^2 h$ $V = \frac{1}{3} \ell w h$

The number of degrees of arc in a circle is 360.
The number of radians of arc in a circle is 2π.
The sum of the measures in degrees of the angles of a triangle is 180.

It's astounding how little math you actually have to know on this test.

Obviously, you'll work a lot more quickly if you know all this stuff by heart. But if you're ever unsure of a formula, take a few seconds to check the front. Better safe than sorry.

C. General Strategy for Geometry

While the number of rules you need on the test is relatively small, it may still seem burdensome to you. I mean, how do you know which rule to use on which question? Where do you even begin?

Just like we said in the very first math chapter, there are two questions to ask yourself:

1. What do I *want*?   **2. What do I *know*?**

The goal of every geometry problem is to connect these two questions, to play with what you *know* in order to get what you *want*.

Take a look at this problem:

9.   In the figure below, a circle is tangent to two sides of a 12 by 6 rectangle. What is the area of the circle?

A) 6π
B) 9π
C) 12π
D) 36π

1.   **What do we want?** The area of the circle.

The formula for the area of a circle $A = \pi r^2$. To find the area, we'll need the radius of the circle (or the diameter, which is just double the radius).

2.   **What do we know?** The length of the rectangle is 12 and the width is 6.

So the real key to this problem is: *how can I use the length or width of the rectangle to find the radius or diameter of the circle?*

Aha! The width of the rectangle is equal to the diameter of the circle! How can I tell? By Guesstimate! Don't worry about the weird "tangent" stuff: they *look* equal.

The width of the rectangle is 6, so the diameter of the circle is 6. So the radius is 3, and the area of the circle is 9π, which is **choice C).***

The point here is that *you should never be absolutely stuck on a geometry question.* There's always *something* that you know, something that you can figure out. Don't be scared of the figures, just put down what you know and try to connect it to what you want.

If a geometry problem doesn't already have a picture, DRAW A PICTURE! It doesn't have to be perfect; even a rough sketch can help you understand the problem and catch careless mistakes.

---

*   Note that we could also use Guesstimate to get the area of the circle directly. The rectangle is 12 by 6, so its area is 72. The circle looks like a bit less than half the rectangle, so its area should be a bit less than 36. All the answers are in terms of π, so we'll multiply the choices by 3.14 (or use the "π" button if your calculator has one) and see which is closest. C) and D) are more than 36. A) is 18.84, and B) is 28.27. B) is closest. Bam.

II. ANGLES

There are five things you have to know about angles.

1. A straight line equals 180°.

2. A triangle equals 180°.

3. An isosceles triangle has two equal sides and two equal angles.

4. Vertical Angles are equal.

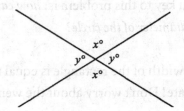

If we know that $\angle BAC = \angle ACB$, then we know $AB = BC$.

When straight lines cross, angles across from each other are equal to each other.

5. Parallel lines with a transversal produce a bunch of equal angles.

When a third line (a "transversal") cuts through two parallel lines, eight angles are formed. The four at the top are collectively the same as the four at the bottom.

Basically, we've got two types of angles: big ones and little ones. All the big ones are equal, and all the little ones are equal. <u>Any</u> of the big ones (*a, d, e, h*) plus <u>any</u> of the little ones (*b, c, f, g*) equals 180°.

Of course, there are other rules that exist about angles, but they're only true *because of* these rules. For example, take a look at this problem:

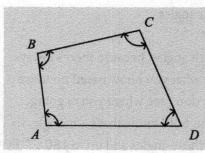

What is the sum of the marked angles in quadrilateral *ABCD* shown to the left?

What? They don't tell us anything about this thing! Whatever shall we do? *

Fear not. We didn't learn any rules about angles of quadrilaterals. But we *do* know that a triangle has 180°. Let's split this guy up into triangles!

The quadrilateral is made up of two triangles. Each triangle has 180°. So the quadrilateral has $2 \times 180 = \mathbf{360°}$. That's it. We're done!

Some of you may have already known that the angles of any quadrilateral add up to 360°. But we can do this with any shape. Draw triangles using only the shape's existing vertices. We can see that a pentagon contains 3 triangles, so its angles add up to:

$3 \times 180 = 540°.$

And a hexagon contains 4 triangles, so its angles add up to

$4 \times 180 = 720°.$ †

Our point is not to get you to memorize the number of degrees in every polygon. The point is that you don't have to memorize a bunch of rules like that. Just know the five basic angle rules

---

* If we had answer choices, this would be a great Guesstimate problem.

† If you're interested here's the formula: the angles a polygon with *n* sides will add up to $(n-2)180$ degrees.

    That's because $n-2$ is the number of triangles you can draw in the shape. When drawing triangles, remember to only connect points in the polygon—don't use the center of the shape as a triangle's vertex.

and you can figure out anything else you need to know about angles.

You should never be totally stuck on a problem that deals with angles, because there's always *something* you know. More often than not, just putting down what you know based on these rules will lead you to what you're trying to find—even if you don't see where you're going with it. "Okay, I really don't know how to find what they want, but I know that's a triangle, so its angles add up to 180. And I know that's a straight line, so those angles add up to 180…" Et cetera. Just play with these rules and see where it takes you.

And remember: **when in doubt, draw triangles**.

THIS PAGE INTENTIONALLY LEFT BLANK

Angle Drill

8. Answer: B.

Guesstimate: The two together are bigger than 25 (eliminate A) and smaller than 180 (eliminate D).

$a + b + 65 = 180$

$a + b = \mathbf{115}$

Note that it doesn't matter what the individual angles are since we're asked for the sum.

9. Answer: B.

Guesstimate: x looks smaller than y, so it's smaller than 50 (eliminate D).

$y = 50$, so the unmarked angle next to it is 130.

$130 + x + x = 180$.

$2x = 50$ $x = \mathbf{25}$

14. Answer: B.

Guesstimate: y alone is around 60, so $y - z$ has to be less than 60. Eliminate C) and D). (If you've got a good eye, you can eliminate A), too.)

We know $x = 115$, so $y = \mathbf{65}$ because of parallel line rules. This is easier to see if you ignore line k.

Since $y = 65$, and line k is perpendicular to m, $z = \mathbf{25}$.

$y - z = 65 - 25 = \mathbf{40}$.

This question is a good demonstration of a basic rule of angle questions: *Put down what you know.* If you can find the value of an angle, do it. You may stumble upon what you're looking for without realizing it.

Choice A) is an RTFQ: That's z.
Choice C) is an RTFQ: That's y.

ANGLE DRILL

In the figure above, what is the value of $a + b$?

A)   25
B)   115
C)   125
D)   295

In the figure above, if $y = 50$, then $x =$

A)   20
B)   25
C)   30
D)   50

In the figure above, line k is perpendicular to line ℓ and lines ℓ and m are parallel. If $x = 115$, what is the value of $y - z$?

A)   25
B)   40
C)   65
D)   90

In the figure above, $p =$

A) 115
B) 120
C) 125
D) 130

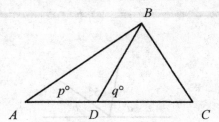

Note: Figure not drawn to scale

In $\triangle ABC$ above, $AB = BC$ and $\overline{BD}$ bisects $\angle ABC$. If $q = 4p$, what is the measure of $\angle ABC$?

A) 22.5°
B) 45°
C) 90°
D) 135°

STOP

22. Answer: C.

Guesstimate might eliminate A), if you've got a good eye (look at the (undrawn) angle that's supplemental to *p*). But most kids can't guess that well.

There are two triangles here. Let's start with the big one.

The top angle is 70. $180 - 70 = 110$. So the other two large angles add up to 110. Those two large angles are split up into four small angles. We know two of them are 25 and 30.

$110 - 25 - 30 = \mathbf{55}$.
So the two small unmarked angles together are 55.

(We don't know how that 55 is split between the two unmarked angles. To make things easier, you could *Plug In* here, say they're also 25 and 30.)

Now let's look at the small triangle. The two unmarked angles plus *p* make 180.
$55 + p = 180$ $\mathbf{p = 125}$.
Backsolve also works here. Put the choices in for *p* and find the two unmarked angles. Then add all other known angles to see if the big triangle comes out to 180°.

30. Answer: D.

It's not to scale, so we can't Guesstimate. But *Backsolve* makes it better.

C) 90°. That's the whole top angle, *ABC*.
1. *BD* bisects the top angle, so each smaller top angle is 45.
2. $AB = BC$, so triangle *ABC* is isosceles. Therefore, $\angle A = \angle C = p$.
3. The whole triangle is 180, and the top is 90.
$180 - 90 = 90$.
$90 \div 2 = 45 = \angle A = \angle C = p$.
4. $\angle BDC = q = 4p = 4(45) = \mathbf{180} = q$.
✱ Way too big.
AC is a straight line, so those two angles at point *D* together make 180°. The three angles in triangle *BCD* should add up to 180 as well.

It may not be obvious which way to go. Pick one.

D) $135° = \angle ABC$
$135 \div 2 = 67.5$, so each top angle is 67.5°.
$180 - 135 = 45$. $45 \div 2 = 22.5° = p$
$q = 4p = 4(22.5) = \mathbf{90} = q$ ✓
Could this work? Let's see: we know all the angles of $\triangle BCD$, so let's add them up:
$67.5 + 22.5 + 90 = 180$. ✓ It works!

The key to this problem is that as a rule, *q* **must be 90**. In an isosceles triangle, a segment that bisects the angle between the equal sides *must* be perpendicular to the opposite side. Try it yourself: draw any isosceles triangle (to scale) and bisect the top angle. You'll make a right angle at the bottom line.

"Wait," some of you are saying. "That's a new rule. You said before that we only need those 5 rules, not other complicated rules." Well, that's true. We *didn't* need to know this rule. They wanted us to know it, but we got the problem just fine by using Backsolve with the small rules. Praise be to Backsolve!

THIS PAGE INTENTIONALLY LEFT BLANK

III. PERIMETER, AREA & VOLUME

Let's start with a few definitions and formulas. Note that this is *all* you need to know for the SAT about perimeter, area, and volume. If you want to find the area or volume of a shape that isn't listed here (like a pentagon), either:

A) you can find it by using some combination of the shapes listed here, **or**

B) you don't actually need that area (you only *think* you do).

A. Perimeter

The perimeter of any figure is the sum of the lengths of all the outside edges. Okay? Okay.

2. Area

$$A = \frac{1}{2}bh \qquad A = bh \qquad A = \ell w \qquad A = s^2$$

AREA:

Triangle: $A = \frac{1}{2}bh$

Rectangle: $A = \ell w$

Square: $A = s^2$

Parallelogram: $A = bh$

Some notes:

- In a triangle, the *base* is just whatever side happens to be lying flat on the ground. The *height* is a line from the topmost point of the triangle extending perpendicular to the base. Sometimes that's just a side of the triangle, sometimes it's inside the triangle, sometimes it's outside the triangle. All three of the following triangles have identical areas, because they have the same base and height:

- The formulas for squares and rectangles say the same thing. A square is just a rectangle with equal sides, so $s = \ell = w$.

- Notice that the area of a triangle is half the area of a rectangle. Imagine cutting a rectangle in half along the diagonal; you'd get two right triangles. And for each triangle, the base and height are equal to the length and width of the original

📝 You can also use triangles to find the area of other shapes. The area of a parallelogram is base times height (that's the *height; not* the side). You can see this by drawing in two triangles, as we do below. Again, we use the rules we know to figure out the rules we don't.

$A = bh$

$A = 2 \times \left(\frac{1}{2} bh \right)$

Shaded Area Problems

Shaded area problems are best done by **subtraction**. Find the area of the whole figure and take away what you don't need.

Take a look at this one:

> 📝 In the figure below, a small square is inside a larger square. What is the area of the shaded region?

Note: Figure not drawn to scale.

It may be tempting to try to find the area directly by dividing up the shaded region into four rectangles. But we can't find those areas because we don't know all of their dimensions. Plus it's kind of tedious.

Instead, let's just find the area of the **whole** square and subtract the area of the **unshaded** square. Whatever's left will be the area of the shaded region.

$$A_{whole} = s^2 = 8^2 = 64$$
$$A_{unshaded} = 5^2 = 25$$
$$A_{shaded} = A_{whole} - A_{unshaded}$$
$$= 64 - 25 \boxed{= 39}$$

C. Surface Area

We find the "surface area" by finding the *area* of the *surface.** That means we have to find the areas of all the shapes on the outside of the box. A box is made up of a bunch of rectangles; we'll find the area of the rectangles and add them all up. That's it.

This box has dimensions 12, 8, and 5. To find the surface area, we'll take the areas of all the rectangles on the outside and add them up.

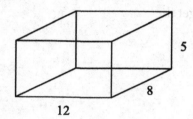

We can see that there are three types of rectangles in this box:

$A_1 = 12 \times 8 = 96$
$A_2 = 12 \times 5 = 60$
$A_3 = 8 \times 5 = 40$

BUT, each of these sides shows up *twice* in the box (top and bottom, front and back, side and side.)

$$SA = 2(A_1 + A_2 + A_3)$$
$$SA = 2(96 + 60 + 40) = 2(196)$$
$$\mathbf{SA = 392}$$

Again, a cube is just a special type of box. Since it's made up of 6 squares, we'll just find the area of one face and multiply by 6. This square has edges of length 4.

$$SA = 6(A_\square)$$
$$SA = 6(s^2) = 6(4^2) = 6(16)$$
$$\mathbf{SA = 96}$$

---

*   Brilliant.

VOLUME:

Box: $V = \ell wh$

Cylinder: $V = \pi r^2 h$

Cone: $V = \dfrac{1}{3}\pi r^2 h$

Sphere: $V = \dfrac{4}{3}\pi r^3$

Rectangular

Pyramid: $V = \dfrac{1}{3}\ell wh$

D. Volume

$V = \ell wh$ $V = \pi r^2 h$ $V = \dfrac{4}{3}\pi r^3$ $V = \dfrac{1}{3}\pi r^2 h$ $V = \dfrac{1}{3}\ell wh$

✒ Just as the area of a rectangle is found by multiplying its two dimensions, the volume of a box is found by multiplying its three dimensions.*

✒ Just as a square is a rectangle with equal sides, a cube is a box with equal sides.

✒ Notice that the volume of a cylinder works under the same principle as the volume of a box. For a box, the base is a rectangle, so its area is length times width; get the volume by multiplying that by the height. For a cylinder, the base is a circle, so its area is pr^2; get the volume by multiplying that by the height.

$V = (\ell w) \times h$ $V = (\pi r^2) \times h$

---

* In a sense, it doesn't really matter which side you call length, width, or height, since the volume comes out the same no matter what ($1 \times 2 \times 3 = 2 \times 3 \times 1$), but there are some conventions about what to call them. In a rectangle, the length is usually the longer side and the width is the shorter one. In a box, the height will always be the side that goes *up*, away from the face lying flat on the ground. Thus if the box is, say, a tank filled with water, the height will correspond to the *depth* of the water.

THIS PAGE INTENTIONALLY LEFT BLANK

Perimeter, Area, Volume Drill

2.   Answer: D.

$w = 3$. The width is one foot less than the length. So 3 is one less than the length. So the length is 4. $\ell = 3 + 1 = 4$.

$A = \ell w = 4(3) = \mathbf{12}$.

Choice A) is an RTFQ: thinking that the length is 1 less than the width.

18. Answer: C.

Two ways to go about this:

First:
The volume of the original block is $15 \times 21 \times 24 = 7560$.
The volume of the small cube is $3 \times 3 \times 3 = 27$.
$7560 \div 27 = \mathbf{280\ small\ cubes}$.

Or:
The 15-inch side of the big block can fit **5** small cubes ($15 \div 3 = 5$)
The 21-inch side of the big block can fit **7** small cubes ($21 \div 3 = 7$)
The 24-inch side of the big block can fit **8** small cubes ($24 \div 3 = 8$)

So the big block has 5 cubes going along one side, 7 along another, and 8 along the last.

$5 \times 7 \times 8 = \mathbf{280\ small\ cubes}$.

21. Answer: B.

Add up the sides and set it equal to 48:

$x + (x + 4) + (x - 4) = 48$
$3x = 48$
$x = 16$

The three sides of the triangle are 16, 20, and 12.
How do we know which sides are the base and height of the triangle? The hypotenuse has to be the longest side—that's 20. So the base and height are 12 and 16. (It's also a 3-4-5 triangle multiplied by 4!)

$A = \frac{1}{2}bh = \frac{1}{2}(16)(12) = \mathbf{96}$.

2

The width of a rectangular quilt is 1 foot less than its length. If the width of the quilt is 3 feet, what is the area of the quilt in square feet?

A)   6
B)   7
C)   10
D)   12

18

Orestes has a rectangular block of cheese with dimensions 15 inches by 21 inches by 24 inches. If he cuts this block entirely into cubes with a side of length 3, how many such cubes are produced?

A)   27
B)   96
C)   280
D)   480

21

What is the area of a right triangle whose sides are x, $x + 4$, and $x - 4$ and whose perimeter is 48?

A)   48
B)   96
C)   144
D)   192

CONTINUE

Note: Figure not drawn to scale.

In △ABC above, the area of the shaded region is given

by $\frac{\pi b h}{9}$. If the area of the shaded region is 6π, what is

the area, to the nearest whole number, of the unshaded

regions of △ABC?

A) 5
B) 8
C) 19
D) 27

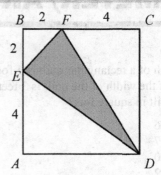

In the figure above, △EFD is an isosceles triangle inscribed in a square of side 6. What is the area of the shaded region?

[For a change of pace, here's a grid-in. No choices. Deal with it.]

Grid in your answer:

STOP

24. Answer: B.

Weird question. Start by asking: what are we looking for? *The area of the unshaded regions.*

Well, we can find that by *subtraction:* take the whole triangle and subtract the shaded circle.

The problem tells us the shaded circle has an area of 6π. It *also* tells us that the shaded region is $\frac{\pi bh}{9}$. So let's set that equal to 6π and see what happens:

$$\frac{\pi bh}{9} = 6\pi \qquad\qquad \frac{bh}{9} = 6 \qquad\qquad bh = 54.$$

Aha! The area of the triangle is $A = \frac{1}{2}bh$. Substitute for bh.

$$A = \frac{1}{2}bh = \frac{1}{2}(54) = 27.$$

Wait! Don't pick D)! This is the area of the *triangle*. We want to *unshaded region*. RTFQ!

The unshaded region will be the triangle minus the circle: $27 - 6\pi = 8.15$

Choice B): 8 is closest.

36. Answer: 10.

Remember: Shaded area problems are best done by *subtraction*.

The *whole* figure is a square with side 6. $A_{square} = 6^2 = 36$.

The *unshaded* regions are three triangles:

$$A_{AED} = \frac{1}{2}(6)4 = 12$$

$$A_{FCD} = \frac{1}{2}(6)4 = 12$$

$$A_{BEF} = \frac{1}{2}(2)2 = 2$$

So, to find the shaded area, take the square and subtract the three unshaded triangles.
$36 - 12 - 12 - 2 = \mathbf{10}$.

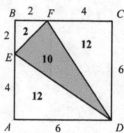

It's tempting to try to find the shaded area directly because it's a triangle and we know the formula for the area of a triangle. But that's actually really hard to do here. We can find the base, *EF*, easily enough by using the Pythagorean Theorem on triangle *BEF*. But where's the height of the shaded region? It's *not FD* or *ED*: those are the sides of the triangle, and neither makes a right angle with the base. So to get the height, we'd have to draw a line from point *D* to the midpoint of *EF*. Ugh. How do we find that? Don't. Use subtraction. It's much, much easier.

THIS PAGE INTENTIONALLY LEFT BLANK

IV. CIRCLES

Circles are a wee bit different from other shapes, so they get their own section.

A. Definitions

Some fun circle facts:*

- A circle has **360°**. In the figure to the right, angles surrounding point *O* will add up to 360°.†

- The **diameter** of a circle is a line segment from one end of the circle the other, passing through the center. In the figure, *AB* is a diameter. The diameter by definition is the longest segment you can draw through a circle.

- The **radius** of a circle is a line segment from the center to the end of a circle. The radius is half of the diameter. In the figure, *OA*, *OB*, and *OC* are all radii. All radii of a circle are equal.

- A **chord** is *any* line segment from one end of the circle to the other. The longest chord in a circle is a diameter.

Almost everything we do with a circle requires knowing its radius (or diameter, which is just double the radius). If you're given a circle and you don't know its radius, before you do anything else **try to find the radius**. You'll probably need it, even if you don't yet know why.

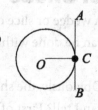

- When a line is **tangent** to a circle, that means it touches the circle at exactly one point. In the figure to the right, segment *AB* is tangent to circle *O* at point *C*. Note that a tangent line is always perpendicular to the radius of the circle at the point of intersection. Here, radius *OC* is perpendicular to segment *AB*.

- When one shape is **inscribed** inside another shape, that means it fits exactly within the larger shape,

A circle inscribed in a square   *A square inscribed in a circle*

Circles are named for their center points, so this circle is circle O. A lot of circles are named "O". Can you guess why?

---

* Well, not that fun.

† Actually, we can already figure this out from our angle rules. The diameter is a straight line, so the angles above it add up to 180° and the angles below it add up to 180°. Put them together and you've got 360°.

© A-List Education

SAT Math | Additional Topics   421

touching its edges at one point on each side.* If you encounter a question involving circles and inscribed shapes, the radius or diameter of the circle likely corresponds with a key element of the other shape. In the first figure to the right, the circle's diameter is the same length as the side of the square. In the second, the diameter is the same as the diagonal of the square.

CIRCLE FORMULAS:
$C = \pi d = 2\pi r$
$A = \pi r^2$

B. Formulas

✎ The perimeter of a circle is called its *circumference* (**C**). The circumference is equal to the diameter times π, which is the same as two times the radius times π (since the diameter equals two radii).

✎ Note that the distance a wheel travels in one revolution is equal to the circumference of the circle.

✎ The *area* of a circle is equal to the radius squared times π.

✎ π (pronounced "pi") stands for a special number whose value is approximately 3.14. For most SAT problems, you don't have to calculate the number; you can just leave it as the symbol π.

In the circle shown here, the radius is 3, so

$$C = 2\pi r$$
$$C = 2\pi (3)$$
$$\boxed{C = 6\pi}$$

$$A = \pi r^2$$
$$A = \pi \left(3^2\right)$$
$$\boxed{A = 9\pi}$$

C. Slices

A wedge or slice of a circle is nothing more than a *part* of a circle. Problems dealing with them can be done with simple ratios. Take a look at this circle:

Obviously, the shaded section is one fourth of the circle. How can I tell? First of all, because it *looks* like a fourth of the circle (Guesstimate!)

That central angle, $\angle AOB$, is 90°. 90 is one fourth of 360. So that central angle is one fourth of the whole angle (360).

---

* The opposite of inscribed is *circumscribed*. To say that a circle is inscribed within a square means the same thing as saying the square is circumscribed about the circle.

Let's say the circle has a radius of 10. So its area is 100π. The area of the slice is one fourth of that: 25π.

If the circle has a radius of 10, its circumference is 20π. The length of minor arc AB is one fourth of it: 5π.

This is pretty easy to see. Since that slice is one fourth of the circle, everything about that slice is one fourth of the corresponding characteristic of the circle: the angle is one fourth of 360, the area is one fourth of the circle's area, and the arc length is one fourth of the circumference.

$$\frac{1}{4} = \frac{90°}{360°} = \frac{25\pi}{100\pi} = \frac{5\pi}{20\pi}$$

This is true of *all* slices. The slice shown to the left is 1/60 of the circle, so that angle is 1/60 of 360°, the arc is 1/60 of the circumference, and the area of the slice is 1/60 of the whole area.

So if you know any one thing about a slice, you can figure out what fraction of the circle it is. Once you know what fraction of the circle it is, you can find anything else about that slice.

You can set up any such problem with a series of ratios:

$$\frac{\text{part}}{\text{whole}} = \frac{\text{angle}}{360°} = \frac{A_{\text{slice}}}{A_O} = \frac{\text{arc}}{C}$$

CIRCLE DRILL

8

If the radius of a circle is doubled, by what factor does the circle's area increase?

A) 2
B) 4
C) 6
D) 8

14

Through how many degrees does the hour hand of a clock turn from 4:00 pm to 8:00 pm of the same day?

A) 20
B) 40
C) 80
D) 120

20

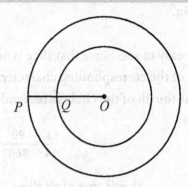

In the figure above, two circles have their centers at point O, with radii OP and OQ. If $OQ = 4$ and $PQ = 2$, what is the ratio of the circumference of the smaller circle to the circumference of the larger circle?

A) 1:3
B) 1:2
C) 2:3
D) 3:5

CONTINUE

Circle Drill

8.   Answer: B.

Plug In! Say *r* = **3**.   So *A* = 9π.
If we double the radius, *r* = 6.   Now *A* = 36π.

The area went from 9π to 36π.
It increased **by a factor of 4**.

20.   Answer: C.

Smaller circle: *r* = *OQ* = 4, so *C* = 8π.
Larger circle: *r* = *OP* = **6**, so *C* = 12π. Careful!

8π:12π = **2:3**

RTFQ is B): that's just taking the ratio of *OQ* : *PQ*.

14.   Answer: D.

If you can draw a clock half-decently (or if there's one in the room), you can use *Guesstimate* to eliminate A) and B), if not also C).

This is just a simple ratio. The hand moved 4 hours. There are 12 hours in a day. There are 360° in a circle.

$$\frac{x°}{360°} = \frac{4hr}{12hr} \qquad x = 120.$$

24. Answer: C.

Plug In helps here, though it can still be a bit rough. Try *s* = **4**. As before, to find the shaded area, we'll subtract the *unshaded* from the *whole*.

The whole is a square; the area of the square is **16**.

The unshaded are semicircles; the two semicircles are identical, so together they make a circle.

The *diameter* of the circle would be 4, so the radius is 2.
$A = \pi r^2 = 4\pi$.
So the shaded area is **16 − 4π**, which is about **3.43**.
(You don't have to be this precise with the decimals.)

Let's plug in *s* = 4 to the answers:

A) $4^2 - \pi 4^2 = 16 - 16\pi = -34.27$ ✗

B) $\dfrac{4^2 - \pi 4^2}{4} = \dfrac{16 - 16\pi}{4} = 4 - 4\pi = -8.57$ ✗

C) $4^2\left(1 - \dfrac{\pi}{4}\right) = 16 - \dfrac{16\pi}{4} = 16 - 4\pi = 3.43$ ✓

D) $4^2\left(1 - \dfrac{\pi}{16}\right) = 16 - \dfrac{16\pi}{16} = 16 - \pi = 12.86$ ✗

Algebra:
$A_{square} = s^2$

$A_{circle} = \pi r^2 = \pi\left(\dfrac{s}{2}\right)^2 = \dfrac{\pi s^2}{4}$

$A_{shaded} = s^2 - \dfrac{\pi s^2}{4} = s^2\left(1 - \dfrac{\pi}{4}\right)$

Lots of ways to mess up this algebra. Choice A) makes *s* the radius of the circle. Choice B) improperly applies the denominator to the square's area.

29. Answer: D.

A weird question. The question asks which of these three items, if we knew them, would be enough information to find the area of the circle.

Well, the formula for area is $A = \pi r^2$. So we need the radius to find the area. Similarly, if we have the diameter, we can find the radius, thus we can find the area.

So the question is: which of these three choices can give us the radius or diameter of the circle?

(We can test each option via *Plug In*.)

I.   Perimeter   Yes!   **Eliminate B).**
The perimeter of a square is 4 times the side. The side of the square is the diameter of the circle.

If we know $P = 24$, we know $s = 6$, therefore $r = 3$, therefore $A_O = 9\pi$

II. Area   Yes!   **Eliminate A).**
The area of a square is the side squared. The side of the square is the diameter of the circle.

If we know $A = 36$, we know $s = 6$, therefore $r = 3$, therefore $A_O = 9\pi$

III. Diagonal   Yes!   **Eliminate C).**
This one's tougher. The diagonal of the square *is not* the diameter of the circle, so we can't use it to *directly* find the diameter. This leads many students to pick D).

But look: The diagonal is *the hypotenuse of an isosceles right triangle*, a 45-45-90 triangle! If we know the hypotenuse, we can divide by $\sqrt{2}$ to get the leg of the triangle. The leg of the triangle is the side of the square, which is the diameter of the circle, which we can use to find the area.

If we know $BD = 6\sqrt{2}$, we know $s = 6$, therefore $r = 3$, therefore $A_O = 9\pi$

So any of the three would be sufficient, **choice D)** is our answer.

In the figure above $ABCD$ is a square with sides of length s and AD and BC are both diameters of semicircles inscribed in square $ABCD$. What, in terms of s, is the area of the shaded region?

A) $s^2 - \pi s^2$

B) $\dfrac{s^2 - \pi s^2}{4}$

C) $s^2\left(1 - \dfrac{\pi}{4}\right)$

D) $s^2\left(1 - \dfrac{\pi}{16}\right)$

The circle in the figure above with center O is inscribed in square $ABCD$. Which of the following measures for the figure would be sufficient by itself to determine the area of the circle?

I. The perimeter of square $ABCD$
II. The area of square $ABCD$
III. The length of diagonal BD

A) I only
B) III only
C) I and II only
D) I, II, and III

STOP

V. TRIANGLES

Triangles are the key to a lot of SAT questions. In fact, if you're confronted with an odd shape you don't understand, try drawing in a triangle. Triangles are your best friend. Trust us.

1. Similar Triangles

If all the angles of one triangle are equal to all the corresponding angles of a second triangle, then they are *similar triangles*. That means that all their sides are in the same ratio with each other.

Here, $\triangle ABC$ has all the same angles as $\triangle DEF$, so they are similar triangles. $AB = 7$ and $DE = 14$, so DE is double AB. Since the triangles are similar, each side of $\triangle DEF$ will be double the corresponding side of $\triangle ABC$. So $EF = 2(10) = 20$, and $DF = 2(12) = 24$.

When dealing with similar triangles, it's important to keep track of which side is which. AB will be proportional to DE because each of them is across from the "z" angle.

Similar triangles don't have to be next to each other. Often these questions will feature *a triangle inside of a triangle.* In the figure to the left, if DE is parallel to BC, then $\angle ADE = \angle ABC$. Therefore $\triangle ABC$ is similar to $\triangle ADE$ because all of their corresponding angles are equal.

2. The Pythagorean Theorem

The Pythagorean Theorem is a way to find the third side of **a right triangle.***

$$a^2 + b^2 = c^2$$

The sum of the squares of the legs of a right triangle is equal to the square of the hypotenuse.

> A *right triangle* is a triangle with a right angle (a 90° angle). The side opposite the right angle is called the *hypotenuse*. The two sides next to the right angle are called *legs*.

By the way, if you forget the Pythagorean Theorem, look at the front of any math section: *they give it to you.* You don't even have to actually know it! Things will obviously go more swiftly if you know it by heart (and many of you probably do), but even if you're *slightly* unsure about it, check the front. Better safe than sorry.

Try this one:

> ✎ **If a right triangle has legs of length 3 and 4, what is the length of the hypotenuse?**

$3^2 + 4^2 = x^2$

$9 + 16 = x^2$

$25 = x^2$

$5 = x$

Some of you may have recognized the triangle in the problem above. It's a "Pythagorean Triple". Because the Pythagorean Theorem has all those "squares" in it, most right triangles don't have integer values for all the sides. So the triangles that *do* have all integers show up a lot. The 3-4-5 is a common one. If you see a triangle that has legs of length 3 and 4, you know immediately that the hypotenuse must be 5.

Be on the lookout for multiples of the 3-4-5, as well. For example, a 6-8-10 triangle is just a 3-4-5 triangle with each side multiplied by two. They're **similar triangles**: they have the same side ratios with different values.

---

* The theorem is named for the Greek philosopher Pythagoras and his cult, the Pythagoreans, but the fundamentals of the theorem were known hundreds of years before him by the Babylonians, Indians, and Chinese among others. There is little evidence that he or his followers ever proved the theorem. Why it was named for him, we have no idea. The Pythagoreans did a lot of important work in mathematics, but they also thought eating beans was sinful.

3. Special Right Triangles

The similar triangle rule tells us that triangles with the same set of angles will have the same ratio of dimensions. There are two particular sets of angles that show up more frequently than others.

The Isosceles Right Triangle (45-45-90)

An *isosceles* right triangle has two legs of equal length, and two 45° angles.* The dimensions of these triangles are always in the same proportion:

If you can't remember these dimensions, **look in the front of the section.** They *tell* you the dimensions. You don't even have to remember them! They're written in the front!

$$a^2 + b^2 = c^2$$
$$x^2 + x^2 = c^2$$
$$2x^2 = c^2$$
$$\sqrt{2x^2} = \sqrt{c^2}$$
$$(\sqrt{2})x = c$$

This means that if you know the length of a leg of the triangle, you can immediately find the hypotenuse—it's just the leg multiplied by $\sqrt{2}$.

Why do we know all these triangles have the same dimensions? They all have the same angles, so they're **similar triangles!**

Notice that we know all of these triangles are 45-45-90 even though they didn't tell us the angles are 45°. That's because we know each has two equal sides—and that alone is enough to make them isosceles.

The 30-60-90 Triangle

Any triangle with angles of 30°, 60°, and 90° will always have the same dimensions.

It's the same concept as the 45-45-90 triangle: if I know just a few things about the triangle, I can just fill in all the values for the rest of the triangle without doing a lot of calculations or bothering with the

---

* Plus a 90° angle. Thus "right triangle".

Pythagorean Theorem.* They all have the same angles, so they're **similar triangles!**

Remembering these triangles

It can be tough to remember all these dimensions. The 45-45-90 is a bit easier since two of the sides are the same. But in the 30-60-90 since each side has a different value and it's easy to mix up where everything goes. Here's a tip for remembering which angle and which length goes where:

- ✏ The 45-45-90 triangle is **half a square**. The diagonal of the square cuts two right angles into 45° angles. The two x's are the sides of the square and the hypotenuse is the diagonal.

- ✏ The 30-60-90 triangle is **half an equilateral triangle**. A line divides one of the 60° angles into two 30° angles, and then cuts the opposite side in half as well.

But again, if you're not sure where to put everything—*check the front of the section*. They *give* you this. You don't have to remember it.

Sometimes, it may not be obvious that a triangle in a problem is 30-60-90 or 45-45-90. But notice that these triangles involve two **happy magic numbers**: $\sqrt{2}$ and $\sqrt{3}$. These numbers don't show up very often in other situations. In fact, they rarely show up in other situations. So if you're doing a problem and notice $\sqrt{3}$ in the answer choices, there's a pretty good chance that there's a 30-60-90 triangle in the problem. The same goes for $\sqrt{2}$; if you see it in the answers, there's a good chance there's a 45-45-90 triangle in the problem. Of course, this isn't *always* true. But if you're stuck on a problem, look for these happy magic numbers. They could help you spot something you would have missed otherwise.[†]

---

* You could prove these dimensions with the Pythagorean Theorem the same way we did above with the 45-45-90 triangle. We didn't, because we don't feel like it and we don't think any of you care. But if you do, go ahead, knock yourself out.

[†] $\sqrt{2}$ is certainly a magic number. It was the first "irrational number" — a decimal that can't be expressed as a fraction. It was first discovered by Hippasus of Metapontum, a Pythagorean mathematician. He was at sea when he discovered it, and some of his Pythagorean shipmates were so angered and offended by the idea of an irrational number, they threw him overboard and drowned him. The Pythagoreans were nuts. If you know any Pythagoreans, don't mention $\sqrt{2}$ to them.

TRIANGLE DRILL

What is the area of a square that has a diagonal of length $3\sqrt{2}$?

A) 3
B) 4
C) 9
D) 18

Triangle ABC is similar to triangle XYZ. $AB = 6$, $BC = 12$, and $AC = 15$. If the shortest side of $\triangle XYZ$ is 10, what is the perimeter of $\triangle XYZ$?

A) 22
B) 35
C) 55
D) 66

Mariano lives 12 miles due south of school and Nancy lives 16 miles due west of school. If Chris walks in a straight line from Nancy's house to Mariano's house, what is the distance, in miles, that he will have walked?

A) 16
B) 20
C) 25
D) 28

CONTINUE

Triangle Drill

6. Answer: C.

The diagonal of a square makes two 45-45-90 triangles. So the side is 3, the area is 9.

15. Answer: B.

Draw the picture. You get a right triangle with legs 16 and 12. You could use the Pythagorean Theorem to find the third side:

$$12^2 + 16^2 = x^2$$
$$144 + 256 = x^2$$
$$400 = x^2$$
$$20 = x$$

Or, you could notice that this is just a 3-4-5 triangle multiplied by a factor of 4:

$$3(4) = 12 \qquad 4(4) = 16 \qquad 5(4) = \mathbf{20}$$

17. Answer: C.

Draw it! Sketch out $\triangle ABC$ and write down the known sides. Sketch out $\triangle XYZ$, making it a similar shape to $\triangle ABC$. The *shortest* side is 10. In our drawing, that's XY.

(It doesn't *really* matter which way you label the points X, Y, and Z. All that matters is that you make the shortest side 10. If you draw it differently so that YZ is the shortest side, then make $YZ = 10$.)

All corresponding sides of the triangles will be in the same ratio, so we can find the other two sides:

$$\frac{10}{6} = \frac{YZ}{12} \qquad 120 = 6(YZ) \qquad YZ = 20$$
$$\frac{10}{6} = \frac{XZ}{15} \qquad 150 = 6(XZ) \qquad 25 = XZ$$

Now just add up the sides to get the perimeter:
$$P_{XYZ} = 10 + 20 + 25 = \mathbf{55}.$$

Actually, you don't really have to find all the sides of $\triangle XYZ$. You could set up a proportion of the perimeter to the shortest side:
For $\triangle XYZ$, we're looking for the perimeter, and the shortest side is 10.
For $\triangle ABC$, the perimeter is 6 + 12 + 15 = 33, and the shortest side is 6. Therefore:

$$\frac{\text{Perimeter}}{\text{shortest}} = \frac{33}{6} = \frac{P}{10}$$
$$330 = 6P$$
$$\frac{330}{6} = P = \mathbf{55}$$

RTFQ: Choice A. You get A if you make $XZ = 10$. $\triangle ABC$ has a side that's a multiple of 5 ($AC = 15$). Since 10 is also a multiple of 5, it's tempting to match up 10 with AC. But AC is the *longest* side of $\triangle ABC$ and 10 is the *shortest* side of $\triangle XYZ$.

27. **Answer: C.**

This is a tough guy, but let's just take it one step at a time. Put down what you know and see what the consequences are.

1. $\angle ABC = 150$ and $\angle DBC = 90$, so $\angle ABD = 60$.
2. Therefore $\triangle ABD$ is 30-60-90 and $\angle ADB = 30$.
3. BD bisects $\angle ADC$ so $\angle BDC = 30$ too. So $\triangle BDC$ is also 30-60-90.

NOTE: This does *not* mean the two triangles are *identical*. This is where most kids go wrong.

Now we can use the 30-60-90 rules to fill in the other sides.

Let's look at $\triangle BDC$: We know $BC = 8$, so $BD = 8\sqrt{3}$ and $DC = 16$.

We can do the same thing for $\triangle ABD$. HOWEVER: Notice that the $8\sqrt{3}$ is opposite the **90°** angle, so it is the "**2x**" side of the 30-60-90 triangle. (Feel free to refer back to the dimensions on the previous page if you get confused.) The side opposite the 30° angle, AB, will be half $8\sqrt{3}$, or $4\sqrt{3}$.

The side opposite the 60° angle, AD, will be AB times $\sqrt{3}$.
$$AD = 4\sqrt{3} \times \sqrt{3} = 4 \times 3 = 12$$

So the perimeter of the quadrilateral is
$$12 + 16 + 8 + 4\sqrt{3} = 36 + 4\sqrt{3}$$
Choice C).

Choice D) is an RTFQ: we don't count the middle line, BD, in the perimeter of the quadrilateral.

A good way to think about these 30-60-90 dimensions is to associate each side with its opposite angle. This question can be confusing because the same line is opposite the 60° in one triangle and opposite the 90° side in the other triangle. As a result, in the top triangle, a "$\sqrt{3}$" is used in the "2x" side.

When using the chart at the front of the section: in $\triangle BCD$, $x = 8$, but in $\triangle ABD$, $x = 4\sqrt{3}$.

30. **Answer: D.**

When in doubt, *draw triangles*.

We want AB. If we draw in line AC, we make a right triangle, $\triangle ABC$. Any time you have two sides of a right triangle, you can find the third.

We know $BC = 2$. If we can find CA, we can use the Pythagorean Theorem to get BA.

So how do we find CA? Ah! There's another triangle in the base of the cube. Look at this aerial view of the square on the bottom of the cube:

Triangle CDA is a 45-45-90 triangle. So $CA = 2\sqrt{2}$.
CA and BC are legs in a right triangle, in which BA is the hypotenuse.

$$(2)^2 + \left(2\sqrt{2}\right)^2 = x^2$$
$$4 + 4(2) = x^2$$
$$12 = x^2$$
$$x = \sqrt{12}$$

$\sqrt{12}$ isn't a choice here, but we can use our calculators to see that's **3.464**. Then we can punch out all the choices and see which one comes to 3.464. That's **Choice D) $2\sqrt{3}$**

(If you like, you can convert $\sqrt{12}$ to our answer choice by looking for a square in the factors of the number under the radical. Here, 4 is a factor of 12, so $\sqrt{12} = \sqrt{4 \times 3} = 2 \times \sqrt{3}$. But if you get confused by that, you can always use your calculator to double-check your answer.)

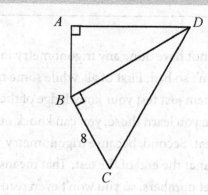

In quadrilateral *ABCD* above, ∠*ABC* = 150° and $\overline{BD}$ bisects ∠*ADC*. What is the perimeter of *ABCD*?

A) $24+8\sqrt{3}$

B) $32+8\sqrt{3}$

C) $36+4\sqrt{3}$

D) $36+12\sqrt{3}$

The figure above shows a cube with edges of length 2. What is the length of diagonal *AB*?

A) $\sqrt{2}$

B) $2\sqrt{2}$

C) $\sqrt{6}$

D) $2\sqrt{3}$

STOP

VI. TRIGONOMETRY

Trigonometry can be a scary topic. Some of you may not have done any trigonometry in school yet, so this will all be new. But trigonometry isn't so bad. First of all, while some trig questions do involve some tricky concepts, most of them just test your knowledge of the definitions of the basic trigonometric functions. Once you learn those, you can knock out most trigonometry questions without breaking a sweat. Second, because trigonometry questions are difficult for students, they tend to appear at the end of the test. That means that a lot of trigonometry questions will be past your target numbers, so you won't even read them at all.

Basic Functions

What is trigonometry and why do we need it? It all begins with right triangles.

Remember when we were talking about 45-45-90 triangles? We said that every triangle whose angles measure 45°, 45°, and 90° have dimensions in the same proportion, $1:1:\sqrt{2}$.

The same was true of the 30-60-90 triangle. Every triangle whose angles measure 30°, 60°, and 90° have sides in the ratio $1:\sqrt{3}:2$. We call triangles like this *similar triangles*—if their angles are all the same measure, their sides will be in the same ratio.

Rather than looking at the ratio of all three sides at the same time, it's easier to look at two sides at a time. If a right triangle has a 45° angle, the ratio of the side opposite the angle to the side next to it will be 1:1. If a right triangle has a 60° angle, the ratio of the side across from it to the hypotenuse will be $\sqrt{3}$:2.

These ratios are the whole point of trigonometry. There are three basic trigonometry functions: **sine**, **cosine**, and **tangent** (abbreviated "sin", "cos", and "tan"). These functions do exactly what we just did: they take the ratios of the sides of a right triangle in relation to a specific angle.

Here are the definitions for these functions:

For any given angle of a triangle:

- the **SINE** of the angle is equal to the length of the **opposite** side over the length of the **hypotenuse**.

$$\sin \theta = \frac{Opposite}{Hypotenuse} = \frac{y}{r}$$

- the **COSINE** of the angle is the length of the **adjacent** side over the **hypotenuse**.

$$\cos \theta = \frac{Adjacent}{Hypotenuse} = \frac{x}{r}$$

- the **TANGENT** of the angle is the length of the **opposite** side over the **adjacent**.

$$\tan \theta = \frac{Opposite}{Adjacent} = \frac{y}{x}$$

The symbol "θ" is the Greek letter "theta". It's often used to describe angles in trigonometry problems. Note that these functions only work with *right triangles*—triangles that contain a right angle.

MEMORIZE THESE DEFINITIONS. Many trigonometry questions require nothing more than knowing these three definitions. You can remember these ratios via the acronym **SohCahToa** :

> **S**ine = **O**pposite over **H**ypotenuse
> **C**osine = **A**djacent over **H**ypotenuse
> **T**angent = **O**pposite over **A**djacent

Calculating the ratios

Let's look at an example:

- In △*ABC* to the right, what is the value of sin *A*?

We know that sine is equal to the opposite side over the hypotenuse. The side opposite angle *A* is 4, but we don't know the hypotenuse. We can use the Pythagorean Theorem to find it, or we can see that it's a 3-4-5 triangle, so the hypotenuse is 5. Therefore, $\sin A = \frac{4}{5}$.

In fact, once we have all the lengths of the sides, it's easy to find all the ratios:*

$$\sin A = \frac{4}{5} \qquad \cos A = \frac{3}{5} \qquad \tan A = \frac{4}{3} \qquad \sin B = \frac{3}{5} \qquad \cos B = \frac{4}{5} \qquad \tan B = \frac{3}{4}$$

Let's try one that has answer choices:

17.   If $0° < x < 90°$ and $\tan x = \frac{5}{8}$, what is $\cos x$?

A) $\dfrac{5}{\sqrt{89}}$

B) $\dfrac{\sqrt{89}}{8}$

C) $\dfrac{8}{\sqrt{89}}$

D) $\dfrac{8}{5}$

This question doesn't give us a figure, so **we should draw one**. It doesn't have to be to scale, just draw a triangle and call one angle x.

Tangent is *opposite* over *adjacent*, so the side opposite x is 5 and the side next to x is 8.

We want $\cos x$: that's *adjacent* over *hypotenuse*. We know that the adjacent side is 8, but we don't know the hypotenuse. We could use the Pythagorean Theorem to find it. But look—all the answer choices contain combinations of 5, 8, and $\sqrt{89}$. So the hypotenuse *must* be $\sqrt{89}$. We don't have to do out the work. Nice!

The side adjacent to x is 8, the hypotenuse is $\sqrt{89}$, so $\cos x$ is $\dfrac{8}{\sqrt{89}}$. That's **choice C)**.

---

* Notice that $\sin A = \cos B$, and $\cos A = \sin B$. That's because the side that's opposite one angle is adjacent to the other.

THIS PAGE INTENTIONALLY LEFT BLANK

Basic functions

ANSWER::

Use the Pythagorean Theorem to find the third side:

$$7^2 + (BC)^2 = 25^2$$
$$49 + (BC)^2 = 625$$
$$(BC)^2 = 576$$
$$BC = 24$$

☞ $\sin(\angle A) = \dfrac{24}{25}$

☞ $\tan(\angle B) = \dfrac{7}{24}$

☞ $\cos(\angle B) = \dfrac{24}{25}$

☞ $\sin (\angle A) = ?$

☞ $\tan (\angle B) = ?$

☞ $\cos (\angle B) = ?$

Reciprocal functions

The three basic functions show three ratios of sides of a right triangle. But those are not the only combinations of sides. We could also flip the fractions to get the *reciprocal functions*. These are called **cosecant** (csc), **secant** (sec), and **cotangent** (cot).

COSECANT: $\csc \theta = \dfrac{1}{\sin \theta} = \dfrac{Hypotenuse}{Opposite} = \dfrac{r}{y}$

SECANT: $\sec \theta = \dfrac{1}{\cos \theta} = \dfrac{Hypotenuse}{Adjacent} = \dfrac{r}{x}$

COTANGENT: $\cot \theta = \dfrac{1}{\tan \theta} = \dfrac{Adjacent}{Opposite} = \dfrac{x}{y}$

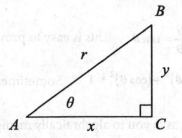

It's easy to mix these up because the "co-"s don't match: *cosecant* is the reciprocal of *sine*, and *secant* is the reciprocal of *cosine*.

The reciprocal functions don't show up nearly as much as the basic functions, but you will see them occasionally, so it's still important to learn them.

Inverse functions

So far we've been solving for lengths or the ratios of lengths. But what if we want to solve for the angles?

We can solve that directly for x by using **inverse sine** (abbreviated $\sin^{-1}$). This is *not* the same thing as the reciprocal functions mentioned above. It's purely a way to solve an equation like this for the angle. It asks "the sine of what angle comes to 0.529?" You can solve this by punching it out on your calculator:*

$$\sin x = 0.529 \qquad\qquad x = \sin^{-1}(0.529) \qquad\qquad x \approx 32.$$

All trigonometric functions have inverse functions like this, which you can use to solve for an angle.

Neither the reciprocal functions nor the inverse functions are likely to show up often on the SAT. But it's worth knowing that they're there.

Identities

Identities are equations that show up frequently (like the "difference of squares" identity) so that you can memorize their forms and do the algebra quickly.

There are a *lot* of rules and identities related to trigonometry functions. They can get complicated and hard to remember. However, there are two identities that you should remember:

- $\dfrac{\sin\theta}{\cos\theta} = \tan\theta$ This is easy to prove: $\left(\dfrac{opp}{hyp}\right) \div \left(\dfrac{adj}{hyp}\right) = \left(\dfrac{opp}{hyp}\right) \times \left(\dfrac{hyp}{adj}\right) = \dfrac{opp}{adj} = \tan$

- $(\sin\theta)^2 + (\cos\theta)^2 = 1$ Sometimes this is written "$\sin^2\theta + \cos^2\theta = 1$"

If a question asks you to algebraically manipulate an expression that contains a trig function, chances are you'll need one of these identities.

Radians

Any time you do any trig functions on your calculator, be sure to check whether your calculator is set to radians or degrees.

There are two different scales for measuring angles: degrees and **radians**. Radians are a different way of measuring angles instead of degrees, used mostly in problems involving trigonometry. It's like the difference between miles and kilometers. You can convert degrees to radians using this formula:

$$2\pi \text{ radians} = 360°$$

---

*   Just make sure that your calculator is set to degrees, not radians. We'll talk more about radians in a minute.

Degrees:	90°	180°	270°	360°
Radians:	$\dfrac{\pi}{2}$	π	$\dfrac{3\pi}{2}$	2π

Remember when we said that every part of the slice of a circle was proportional to every other part? That's the idea with radians. Imagine an angle as a slice of a circle with radius 1. The measure in radians is the arc length of the slice. 360° is 2π radians because 2π is the circumference of the whole circle. Similarly, π radians is half the circumference and 180° is the angle of a semicircle, etc.

For example, in the circle to the right, the central angle of arc AB measures 90°, which is equivalent to $\pi/2$ radians. We can see that the slice is one-fourth of the circle. The radius is 1, so the circumference is 2π, and the arc length is $2\pi \div 4$ or $\pi/2$. The measure in radians is equivalent to the arc length of a slice of a circle with radius 1.

TRIGONOMETRY DRILL

10

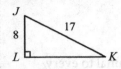

In $\triangle JKL$ shown above, $JK = 17$ and $JL = 8$. What is $\cos K$?

A) $\dfrac{8}{15}$

B) $\dfrac{8}{17}$

C) $\dfrac{15}{17}$

D) $\dfrac{17}{15}$

20

Note: Figure not drawn to scale.

In $\triangle DEF$ above, $\tan x = \dfrac{\sqrt{3}}{1}$. What is the measure, in radians, of x?

A) $\dfrac{p}{6}$

B) $\dfrac{p}{4}$

C) $\dfrac{p}{3}$

D) $\dfrac{2p}{3}$

14

In $\triangle DEF$ above, $\sin F = \dfrac{5}{9}$. Which of the following expressions equals $\sin D$?

A) $\dfrac{\sqrt{56}}{9}$

B) $\dfrac{\sqrt{106}}{9}$

C) $\dfrac{\sqrt{56}}{5}$

D) $\dfrac{\sqrt{106}}{5}$

CONTINUE

Trigonometry Drill

10. Answer: C.

Some students might immediately recognize this as an 8–15–17 triangle, a Pythagorean Triple, so the missing side is 15. But most will probably have to use the Pythagorean Theorem.

Wait, wait! Not so fast. All the ratios in the answers contain the numbers 8, 15, or 17. So that missing side *has* to be 15. We don't have to do it out!

We want the cosine of $\angle K$. Cosine is adjacent over hypotenuse.

The side adjacent to K is 15, the hypotenuse is 17, so $\cos K = \dfrac{15}{17}$.

14. Answer: A.

We know $\sin F = \dfrac{5}{9}$. Sine is opposite over hypotenuse. Therefore, the opposite side is 5 and the adjacent side is 9.* Unlike in question 21 above, the choices here give two different options for what the third side might be, so we will have to actually do the Pythagorean Theorem. Drat.

$$5^2 + (FE)^2 = 9^2$$
$$25 + (FE)^2 = 81$$
$$(FE)^2 = 56$$
$$FE = \sqrt{56}$$

So the sides are 5, $\sqrt{56}$, and 9.

We want $\sin D$, that's the opposite, FE, over the hypotenuse, FD, or $\dfrac{\sqrt{56}}{9}$.

Students who got $\sqrt{106}$ did the theorem in the wrong order. That would be the *hypotenuse* if the *legs* were 5 and 9.

20. Answer: C.

We're given $\tan x = \dfrac{\sqrt{3}}{1}$. Tangent is opposite over adjacent. So let's make the opposite side = $\sqrt{3}$ and the adjacent = 1.

Note: Figure not drawn to scale.

We can tell from the presence of $\sqrt{3}$ that this is going to be a 30-60-90 triangle. We see x is opposite the $\sqrt{3}$, so $x = 60$.

Don't be fooled by the picture! It looks more like x will be 30, but it's *not drawn to scale!* Use the dimensions at the front of the section if you can't remember them.

Okay, so x is 60, but that's degrees. We want *radians*. Converting is just a simple ratio:

$$\frac{2\pi \text{ rad}}{360°} = \frac{x \text{ rad}}{60°}$$
$$\frac{60(2\pi)}{360} = x$$
$$\frac{\pi}{3} = x$$

---

* Technically, we don't actually *know* the sides are 5 and 9, we only know their *ratio* is 5:9. The sides could be 10 and 18. In the end, it won't matter since the question is asking for $\sin D$, which is another ratio. If the sides were multiples of 5 and 9 by some factor, that factor would be cancelled out when we take the second sine. So saying the sides are 5 and 9 is actually a form of *Plug In!*

25. Answer: A.

Plug In!

Let's say this is a **3–4–5 triangle**.
That means $b = 3$ and $a = 4$, and the
unlabeled hypotenuse is 5.
We want $\cos A$.

That would be $\dfrac{3}{5}$.

Put $a = 4$ and $b = 3$ into the choices and see which gives you $\dfrac{3}{5}$

A) $\dfrac{b}{\sqrt{a^2+b^2}} = \dfrac{3}{\sqrt{4^2+3^2}} = \dfrac{3}{\sqrt{16+9}} = \dfrac{3}{\sqrt{25}} = \dfrac{3}{5}$ ✓

B) $\dfrac{a}{\sqrt{a^2+b^2}} \qquad\qquad = \dfrac{4}{5}$ ✗

C) $\dfrac{b}{\sqrt{a^2-b^2}} = \dfrac{3}{\sqrt{4^2-3^2}} = \dfrac{3}{\sqrt{16-9}} = \dfrac{3}{\sqrt{7}}$ ✗

D) $\dfrac{a}{\sqrt{a^2-b^2}} \qquad\qquad = \dfrac{4}{\sqrt{7}}$ ✗

Once you figure out that $\sqrt{4^2+3^2} = 5$ and $\sqrt{4^2-3^2} = \sqrt{7}$ the
rest of the choices go by much more quickly.

Plug in here isn't really much different from the algebra. This
problem is just like all the others we've been doing—a
combination of the Pythagorean Theorem and the trig function
definitions. But biggest danger on a question like this is
carelessness, and having real numbers can help students keep track
of their work and be more certain of their answers.

As in question 28, students who picked a choice containing
$\sqrt{a^2-b^2}$ mixed up the terms in the theorem.

38. Answer: 4/5 or 0.8

There's no figure, so let's draw one. We know:
1. ABC is a right triangle.
2. Angle C is the right angle.
3. $\sin A = 3/5$. Let's use that to *Plug In.*
   Sine is opposite over hypotenuse, so
   let's say the opposite side is 3 and the
   hypotenuse is 5.
4. That would make it a 3-4-5 triangle, so
   the third side is 4.

Great, there's our triangle.

We know the other triangle, DEF, is similar, so it will also be a
version of the 3-4-5, though not in those dimensions. We know one
of the sides, DE, is 12, but we don't know yet whether that
corresponds with the 3, the 4, or the 5.

We do know that $\cos B = \sin D$.
We can look at the figure we already drew and see that $\cos B = 3/5$.
Therefore $\sin D = 3/5$. But we already knew $\sin A = 3/5$. So point
D must correspond with point A.

We don't yet know enough to actually draw all of DEF but we do
know enough to solve the problem. If D corresponds to A, then
$\cos D = \cos A$. We can see from our drawing that $\cos A = 4/5$, so
$\cos D = 4/5$

The problem told us that $DE = 12$, so we could
draw the rest of the figure if you like. Let's
make E the right angle so that DE is the leg that
corresponds with the "4" side. That would make
the other sides 9 and 15 by proportion.

Technically, we don't know that E is the right angle. F could be the
right angle and DE could be the hypotenuse. That would just mean
that the legs would come out to weird decimals ($DF = 9.6$ and $EF
= 7.2$). But since trig functions are ratios, we'd still get the same
answer either way.

Triangle $\triangle ABC$ shown above has legs of length a and b, as shown. In terms of a and b, what is the value of $\cos A$?

A) $\dfrac{b}{\sqrt{a^2+b^2}}$

B) $\dfrac{a}{\sqrt{a^2+b^2}}$

C) $\dfrac{b}{\sqrt{a^2-b^2}}$

D) $\dfrac{a}{\sqrt{a^2-b^2}}$

In triangle ABC, angle C is 90° and sin $\angle A$ is 3/5. Triangle DEF is similar to triangle ABC, where cos B = sin D, and DE = 12. What is the value of cos D ?

Grid in your answer:

STOP

VII. IMAGINARY AND COMPLEX NUMBERS

This is the one concept in this section that has nothing to do with Geometry, but somehow they get lumped together into the Additional Topics category. You will not see many questions involving imaginary numbers on the SAT, but they may pop up every now and then.

You know how sometimes a problem will start by saying "For all real numbers"? Why do they say that? Are there any numbers that aren't real?

Yes there are! **Imaginary numbers** are numbers that contain i, defined as $i = \sqrt{-1}$. Questions involving imaginary numbers often give the definition as $i^2 = -1$, but that's the same thing. Usually you're not allowed to take the square root of a negative, which is why numbers that do so are called "imaginary". But don't be scared by the name! You can manipulate i just like you do any variable.

Most imaginary numbers on the SAT involve **complex numbers**. A complex number is a polynomial in the form $a + bi$, a real number plus or minus an imaginary number.* Let's look at an example:

> ✐ **(3 + 2i)(5 + 3i) = ?**

Complex numbers work like any other polynomial and can be multiplied using FOIL:

$$(3+2i)(5+3i) = 3(5) + 9i + 10i + 6i^2 \qquad = 15 + 19i + 6i^2$$

We're not done. Remember that $i^2 = -1$, so we can substitute -1 in the last term:

$$= 15 + 19i + 6(-1) \qquad \boxed{= 9 + 19i}$$

Occasionally you may be asked about higher powers of i. If you multiply i by itself a bunch of times, you'll see that the powers of i show a repeating pattern:

$$i^1 = \sqrt{-1} = i \qquad i^2 = \sqrt{-1} \times \sqrt{-1} = -1 \qquad i^3 = i^2 \times i = -1 \times i = -i \qquad i^4 = i^3 \times i = (-i) \times i = -i^2 = 1$$

$$i^5 = i^4 \times i = i \qquad i^6 = i^5 \times i = i \times i = -1 \qquad i^7 = i^6 \times i = -1 \times i = -i \qquad i^8 = i^7 \times i = (-i) \times i = -i^2 = 1$$

$$\text{etc}\ldots$$

---

* Actually, all real numbers are technically also complex numbers. Every number in this book can be written as $a + bi$, it's just that most of the time $b = 0$.

THIS PAGE INTENTIONALLY LEFT BLANK

Imaginary and Complex Numbers

ANSWERS:

✒ **What is the value of i^{18} ?**

Answer: −1

The number i taken to a power that's a multiple of 4 will equal 1.
Therefore, $i^{16} = 1$.
Therefore, $i^{17} = 1 \times i = i$
Therefore, $i^{18} = i \times i = i^2 = -1$

If you remember that $i^2 = -1$, you could also rewrite i^{18} as:
$$\left(i^2\right)^9 = \left(-1\right)^9 = -1$$
Since −1 is being taken to an *odd* power, it will come out negative.

✒ **$(5 + 8i)(4 − 6i) = ?$**

Answer: 68 + 2i
$= 20 - 30i + 32i - 48i^2$
$= 20 - 30i + 32i - 48(-1)$
$= 20 + 2i + 48$
$= 68 + 2i$

✒ **$(-2 − 7i)(2 + 3i) = ?$**

Answer: 17 − 20i
$= -4 - 6i - 14i - 21i^2$
$= -4 - 6i - 14i - 21(-1)$
$= -4 - 20i + 21$
$= 17 - 20i$

✒ **$(3 − 2i)(3 − 2i) = ?$**

Answer: 5 − 12i
$= 9 - 6i - 6i + 4i^2$
$= 9 - 6i - 6i + 4(-1)$
$= 9 - 12i - 4$
$= 5 - 12i$

✒ **$(4 + 3i)(4 − 3i) = ?$**

Answer: 25   Difference of squares!
$= 16 - 9i^2$
$= 16 - 9(-1)$
$= 16 + 9$
$= 25$.

✒ What is the value of i^{18} ?

✒ $(5 + 8i)(4 - 6i) = ?$

✒ $(-2 - 7i)(2 + 3i) = ?$

✒ $(3 - 2i)(3 - 2i) = ?$

✒ $(4 + 3i)(4 - 3i) = ?$

ADDITIONAL TOPICS IN MATH EXERCISE

In the figure above, if line k is parallel to line ℓ, the sum of which of the following pairs of angles must equal 180°?

A) a and c
B) b and d
C) c and d
D) e and f

A rectangle has a perimeter of 200 and a width of 40. What is the length of the rectangle?

A) 50
B) 60
C) 70
D) 80

How many more degrees of arc are there in $\frac{1}{3}$ of a circle than in $\frac{1}{4}$ of a circle?

A) 20°
B) 25°
C) 30°
D) 35°

In $\triangle ABC$ above, what is the length of AC?

A) 5

B) $5\sqrt{3}$

C) $10\sqrt{3}$

D) 20

CONTINUE

Additional Topics in Math Exercise

1. Answer: B.
All the small angles are equal: a, c, and d.
All the big angles are equal: b, e, and f.
To add up to 180°, we need one small angle and one large angle.

A) a and c are both small.
B)   b and d are one of each!
C) c and d are both small.
D) e and f are both big.

If it helps, you can **Plug In** here. Just come up with a number for a.
Say, **50**. So b will be $180 - 50 = 130$.

So $a = c = d = 50$, and $b = e = f = 130$. Put those numbers into the
choices and see which gives you 180:

A) a and c $50 + 50 = 100$ ✗
B)   b and d   130 + 50 = 180 ✓
C) c and d $50 + 50 = 100$ ✗
D) e and f $130 + 130 = 260$ ✗

3. Answer: C.
$(1/3)360 = 120°$
$(1/4)360 = 90°$
     30 more degrees

2. Answer: B.
$P = 2\ell + 2w$
$200 = 2\ell + 2(40)$
$120 = 2\ell$
$60 = \ell$

4. Answer: A.
Guesstimate! Compare AC to the side we know. $AB = 10$, and AC
is smaller than AB, so $AC < 10$. Choices D), and E) are out right
away. Choice B) is $5\sqrt{3}$, or about 8.66. That's too big. It's got to
be **choice A), 5.**

Or you could notice it's a 30-60-90 triangle, so the side opposite
the 30 will be half the side opposite the 90. But it's easy to mix up
the dimensions, and Guesstimate is an excellent way to double-
check. The only one that makes sense is **5**.

5. Answer: D.

Area of a triangle is $\frac{1}{2}bh$. Two ways we could go:

1. Draw in the height of the triangle; you'll split it up into two 45-45-90 triangles with legs of 5. So the whole triangle has $h = 5$, $b = 10$.

$A = \frac{1}{2}(5)10 = \mathbf{25}$.

2. The big triangle is *already* a 45-45-90 triangle, but watch out: The *leg* is $5\sqrt{2}$. So the base and height are each $5\sqrt{2}$. (This is easier to see if you rotate the triangle).

$A = \frac{1}{2}(5\sqrt{2})5\sqrt{2} = \frac{1}{2}(25)2 = \mathbf{25}$.

6. Answer: B.

If $\sin x = 5/13$, we can **Plug In** values for the lengths.
We know sin is *opposite over hypotenuse*, so let's say the opposite, AC is 5 and the hypotenuse, AB, is 13.
That means that the adjacent side, BC, must be 12. We can tell that by doing the Pythagorean Theorem, by knowing the 5-12-13 triplet, or just by looking at the choices and seeing lots of 12's.

We want cos x: that's *adjacent over hypotenuse*.
The adjacent is BC: that's 12.
The hypotenuse is AB: that's still 13.

So $\cos x = \dfrac{\mathbf{12}}{\mathbf{13}}$

[Note we don't actually know that AC and AB are 5 and 13 respectively, only that the ratio of their sides is 5 to 13. They could be 10 and 26 or 50 and 130 for all we know. But it doesn't matter what their actual measures are because we want cosine, which is also a ratio. So no matter what we choose for length, the answer will reduce to 12/13.]

7. Answer: C.

Shaded area problems are done with subtraction. We'll find the square and subtract the triangles.

The square has sides of 12, so the area of the square is 144. So the shaded area will be a bit less than 144. Therefore, *Guesstimate* eliminates A) (too big). While we're at it, we'll eliminate D), too: 72 is half of 144, and the shaded area is more than half the square.

Since all the points are midpoints, the legs of the triangles are each 6.

Area of each triangle $= A = \frac{1}{2}(6)6 = 18$.

$144 - 18 - 18 = \mathbf{108}$.

8. Answer: D.

The small triangle APQ is similar to the big triangle ABC. We know this because their corresponding angles are equal: both have right angles and share angle A (two equal angles means the third is equal as well: 180 – 90 – angle A.)

So they're similar. That means all sides are in the same ratio. Since P and Q are midpoints, AP and AQ are each half of AB and AC respectively. So PQ is half of BC as well.

The question asks for the area of ABC, so we need the base, BC, and the height, AB.

$h = AB = 2AP = 2(5) = 10$
$b = BC = 2PQ = 2(3) = 6$

$A = \frac{1}{2}(6)10 = \mathbf{30}$

Choice A) is an RTFQ: that's the area of the small triangle, APQ.

(Note also that although each side of the big one is double the corresponding side of the little one, the *area* of the big triangle is *four times* the little one.)

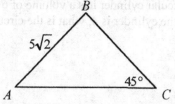

5

In the figure above, $AB = BC$. What is the area of $\triangle ABC$?

A) 10
B) 15
C) 20
D) 25

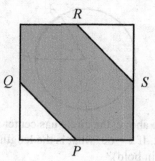

In the figure above, P, Q, R, and S are midpoints of the sides of the square. If the square has sides of length 12, what is the area of the shaded region?

A) 144
B) 126
C) 108
D) 72

Note: Figure not drawn to scale.

In $\triangle JKL$, $\sin x = \dfrac{5}{13}$, then $\cos x = ?$

A) $\dfrac{5}{12}$

B) $\dfrac{12}{13}$

C) $\dfrac{12}{5}$

D) $\dfrac{13}{5}$

In the figure above, P is the midpoint of $\overline{AB}$ and Q is the midpoint of $\overline{AC}$. If $\overline{AP}$ is 5 and $\overline{PQ}$ is 3, what is the area of $\triangle ABC$?

A) 7.5
B) 8
C) 15
D) 30

CONTINUE

In the figure above, the circle has center O and has a radius of 12. If $x = 60$, what is the length of minor arc AB (shown in bold)?

A) 4π
B) 6π
C) 12π
D) 24π

For $\triangle TUV$ above, what is $\cos \angle T$?

A) $\dfrac{7}{11}$

B) $\dfrac{11}{7}$

C) $\dfrac{\sqrt{72}}{7}$

D) $\dfrac{\sqrt{72}}{11}$

A right circular cylinder has a volume of 64π. If the height of the cylinder is 4, what is the circumference of the base?

A) 8π
B) 12π
C) 16π
D) 20π

Which of the following is equivalent to $(i + 1)^2$?

(Note: $i = \sqrt{-1}$)

A) 0
B) $2i$
C) $2i + 2$
D) $2i - 2$

CONTINUE

9. Answer: A.

$$\frac{60°}{360°} = \frac{\text{arc}}{C}$$

$$\frac{1}{6} = \frac{\text{arc}}{24\pi}$$

$$\frac{24\pi}{6} = \text{arc}$$

$$\mathbf{4\pi = arc}$$

10. Answer: D.

Glancing at the choices, we see that the only numbers are 7, 11, and $\sqrt{72}$. So the unmarked side, TV, must be $\sqrt{72}$.

We want $\cos T$, that's adjacent over hypotenuse. The adjacent side, TV, is $\sqrt{72}$. The hypotenuse, TU, is 11. So $\cos T = \dfrac{\sqrt{72}}{\mathbf{11}}$

11. Answer: A.

$V = \pi r^2 h$. Don't know it? *Look it up!* It's given to you in the front of the section.

$64\pi = \pi r^2\, 4$

$16 = r^2 \qquad \mathbf{r = 4}$

We want the circumference of the base. $C = 2\pi r = 2\pi 4 = \mathbf{8\pi}$. Choice C) is RTFQ: That's the *area* of the base.

12. Answer: B.

FOIL!

$(i + 1)^2 = (i + 1)(i + 1)$

$= i^2 + i + i + 1$

$= i^2 + 2i + 1 \qquad$ But remember: $i^2 = -1$

$= -1 + 2i + 1$

$\mathbf{= 2i}$

13. **Answer: B.**

To find the circumference, we'll need the radius or the diameter. So how can we use the side of the square to find the diameter of the circle?

Of course! The diagonal of the square is equal to the diameter of the circle. (Remember our motto: when in doubt, draw triangles.) To find the diagonal, we'll use the Pythagorean Theorem:

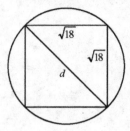

$$\left(\sqrt{18}\right)^2 + \left(\sqrt{18}\right)^2 = d^2$$
$$18 + 18 = d^2$$
$$36 = d^2$$
$$6 = d$$

$$C = \pi d = \mathbf{6\pi}.$$

14. **Answer: D.**

Variables in the answer choices? ***Plug In!*** Let's say $x = 70$. The picture is to scale, so we'll pick something close to what it looks like. (Don't pick 60. If you do, A) and D) will both work.) Now we'll just fill in angle values till we get to y; just like we did in question 16 above.

Since $AP = PR$, triangle APR is isosceles.
Since $x = 70$, $\angle PRA$ also is 70. So $\angle APR = 40$.

This part can be tricky: Since PQ is parallel to AC, we know $\angle PRA = \angle RPQ = 70$. The trick is to look for the "Z" shape—the armpits of the "Z" will be equal.
(Some call them "alternate interior angles". I call them "armpits".)

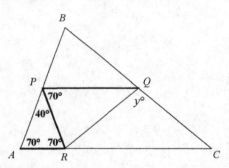

So $\angle RPQ = 70$. We know $PQ = QR$, so $\angle PRQ$ is also 70. That means $\angle PQR = 180 - 70 - 70 = 40$.

$\angle APR$, $\angle RPQ$, and $\angle BPQ$ make a straight line, so their sum is 180. $\angle APR = 40$ and $\angle RPQ = 70$, so $\angle BPQ = 180 - 40 - 70 = 70$.

Since $BQ = PQ$, $\angle PBQ$ is also 70 and $\angle BQP$ is also 40.

$\angle BQP$, $\angle PQR$, and $\angle RQC$ make a straight line, so their sum is 180. $\angle BQP = 40$ and $\angle PQR = 40$, so $\angle RQC = 180 - 40 - 40 = 100 = y$.
There. We've got y.

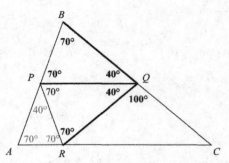

(Notice we could also figure out that the last two unmarked angles are each 40, but now that we have y, we don't care anymore, and we can stop.)

Okay. So when $x = 70$, $y = 100$. Let's put 70 into the choices and see which gives us 100.

A) $180 - 2(70) = 180 - 140 = 40$ ✗
B) $180 - 4(70) = 180 - 280 = -100$ ✗
C) $2(70) - 180 = 140 - 180 = -40$ ✗
D) $4(70) - 180 = 280 - 180 = \mathbf{100}$ ✓

Simply a great Plug In problem. With Plug In, it's just filling in the blanks.

15. **Answer: C.**

We can see that the question wants us to get i out of the denominator of the fractions. The question is: *how?*

Since $i = \sqrt{-1}$, we would be back to real numbers if we could square the i. But we can't just square it by itself because it's part of the polynomial "$4 - 2i$". If we try to square the i, we'll have to square the whole binomial. And if we do that, we'll get a middle term that still has an i in it:
$(4 - 2i)^2 = 4^2 - 2(4)(2i) + (2i)^2 = 16 - 16i - 4$.
See? Still got an i up in there.

What if instead of squaring the binomial, we used ***the Difference of Squares***? That way, we'll have no middle term!

$$\frac{(5 - 7i)(4 - 2i)}{(4 + 2i)(4 - 2i)}$$

$$= \frac{20 - 10i - 28i + 14i^2}{4^2 - (2i)^2}$$

$$= \frac{20 - 38i - 14}{16 - (-4)}$$

$$= \frac{6 - 38i}{20} \qquad \text{Cancel out a 2.}$$

$$= \frac{3 - 19i}{10} \qquad \text{Split it up into two fractions.}$$

$$= \frac{3}{10} - \frac{19i}{10} \qquad \text{Hey look! It's \textbf{choice C}.}$$

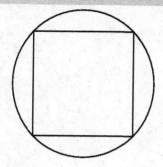

13

In the figure above, a square with side of length $\sqrt{18}$ is inscribed in a circle. What is the circumference of the circle?

A) 3π
B) 6π
C) 9π
D) 18π

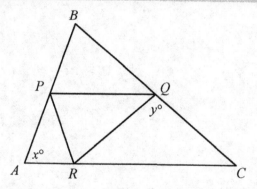

In the figure above, $BQ = PQ = RQ$ and $AP = PR$. If $\overline{PQ}$ is parallel to $\overline{AC}$, what is y in terms of x?

A) $180 - 2x$
B) $180 - 4x$
C) $2x - 180$
D) $4x - 180$

Which of the following complex numbers is equivalent

to $\dfrac{5-7i}{4+2i}$? (Note: $i = \sqrt{-1}$)

A) $\dfrac{5}{4} - \dfrac{7i}{2}$

B) $\dfrac{5}{4} + \dfrac{7i}{2}$

C) $\dfrac{3}{10} - \dfrac{19i}{10}$

D) $\dfrac{3}{10} + \dfrac{19i}{10}$

STOP

STOP

THE ESSAY

◼ THE ESSAY

The essay can be scary. It's quite intimidating to write a coherent essay in 50 minutes, especially to write about something you've never read before. As with every other section, timing is important. And as with every other section, practice will help you get used to it. And as with the rest of the test, you don't have to have any *actual knowledge* to do well.

There is one big thing that makes this section different: **the Essay is optional**. It's the only section that you don't *have* to take. It will always be the last section of the test. There will be a break after the four main sections are over, at which time you're welcome to get the heck out of there if you want.*

In this chapter, we'll take a look at the format of the Writing test, what it takes to write a good essay, and some tips for making your writing sparkle.†

I. ABOUT THE TEST

Should I take it?

In some ways, the essay is the least important section because it's optional. Some colleges don't even look at it. For many of you, your time would probably be better spent working on the other sections.

On the other hand, some colleges *do* require the Essay with any SAT scores you send. If you know which colleges you're interested in, you can check to see if they require it. The College Board's website has some lists of different colleges' essay policies, or you can ask the colleges directly. Most schools consider it optional—they're happy to consider your score if you have one, but it's not necessary. But some schools will require it, particularly top-tier schools.

In short, it's probably a good idea to take the Essay, but don't sweat it too much. Make sure your other scores are where you want them to be before you worry about the Essay.

---

* You can't wait until the last minute to decide if you want to take it; you have to specify whether you want to take the Essay when you register for the SAT. There is an extra fee for taking the Essay.

† Disclaimer: essay may not literally sparkle.

Format

You'll have **50 minutes** for your essay and may use up to four pages. But you won't just be writing—the Essay section also wants you to do some reading. You'll be presented with a **source text**, a fancy term for an essay that someone else has already written. By now this kind of essay will be familiar to you from the Reading Test. In fact, the source text will look and feel just like the passages you have already learned to read. And what you've already learned from the Reading chapters of this book will help lead to your success on the Essay. (You do remember the Reading chapters, don't you?)

The source texts might be from almost any subject area—history, science, literature, politics, and so on. But don't worry: just like on the Reading passages, you don't have to *know* anything ahead of time. The passages are written for general audiences and are meant to persuade readers to a particular point of view.

Every test will begin with this introduction before the passage:

As you read the passage below, consider how [the author] uses

- evidence, such as facts or examples, to support claims.
- reasoning to develop ideas and to connect claims and evidence.
- stylistic or persuasive elements, such as word choice or appeals to emotion, to add power to the ideas expressed.

And every test will have a version of this text after the passage:

Write an essay in which you explain how [the author] builds an argument to persuade [his or her] audience that [the author's claim]. In your essay, analyze how [the author] uses one or more of the features listed in the box above (or features of your own choice) to strengthen the logic and persuasiveness of [his or her] argument. Be sure that your analysis focuses on the most relevant features of the passage. Your essay should not explain whether you agree with [the author's] claims, but rather explain how [the author] builds an argument to persuade [his or her] audience.

The good news is that every essay will have the same format and ask you to do the same thing; the only thing that varies will be the passage itself. That means you know ahead of time exactly what you're in for. If you have a good sense of how to effectively analyze a passage ahead of time, you'll find the task goes much more quickly.

Scoring

You don't receive a single score for the Essay but three separate scores. Your essay will be read and scored by two different Official SAT Essay Readers (or OSATERS as we've decided to call them). They'll be evaluating your essay in three areas—Reading, Analysis, and Writing— and giving you a score from 1 to 4 in each area. Your final score in each area will be the sum of the score given to you by each reader in that area.

In the unlikely event that the OSATERs disagree by more than one point within a single area, your essay will go to a third reader for adjudication. So, for example, you could get a 2 in Reading from one OSATER and a 3 from the other (for a total score of 5), but you can't get a 2 and a 4. However, the readers are free to give you widely different scores in different areas. So it's perfectly fine for one OSATER to give you a 4 in Writing but a 1 in Analysis.

Let's see what they're looking for in each of these sections.

- **Reading**: This is pretty straightforward. They want to know how well you understood the source text. Since the OSATERs can't peer into your mind (yet), you'll have to make it clear in your essay that you understood the text by giving a fair representation of the author's point of view, as well as appropriate quotations and paraphrases.

- **Analysis**: Here the readers will want to see how well you can evaluate the argument made by the author of the source text. You must go beyond understanding *what* the author says and analyze *how* he or she tries to persuade the reader to his or her point of view.

- **Writing**: The readers want to see that you know how to write. You must give a clear thesis, organize your thoughts and present them in a way that naturally moves from one idea to the next. You should use varied sentence structure, and generally demonstrate good command of English, just like you do in your English essays in school.

Timing

How long should you spend reading and analyzing and how long writing? It is *very* important not to skimp on your understanding of the passage and analysis of it; it's two-thirds of what you will be graded on. You should spend a *minimum* of 15 minutes reading, taking notes, and outlining. That will leave you with 35 minutes to write, which should be plenty of time. The flip side is that you don't want to spend too much time reading. You should save a *minimum* of 20 minutes to write the actual essay. That means if 30 minutes have passed and you still haven't started writing, you need to start right now.

But as with every section on the test, the best way to prepare is to **time yourself**. Do a practice essay at your own leisure, whatever pace feels right to you, and take note of how long it takes you to read, prepare, then write. Then think about what you did: did you end up with enough time to write? Did you spend enough time reading to understand the passage? Experiment with your timing until you find something that works.

II. READING

Before you begin writing your own essay you must read and analyze the source text. There are two absolutely crucial things you must get from this text: the central thesis and the ways in which the author tries to convince you of his or her central thesis. Actually, that's *all* you have to get from it. Once you're sure you understand the point and how the author makes that point you're ready to move on to writing.

Central Thesis = Main Idea

The central thesis of the passage is the point that the author is trying to make, the thing he or she is trying to persuade you to believe. Good news: you've already learned how to find this. In the Reading chapter we called it the *main idea* of the passage. It's no less important here. You can't do anything else until you've identified the main idea. Luckily, the source texts won't be too tricky with main ideas; they won't be the kind you have to go hunting for.

Getting main ideas is important for several reasons. First, the main idea for the passage as a whole is the author's central thesis, the thing that he or she is trying to argue for. That's important because it's crucial to your understanding of the passage, and you want to let the OSATERs know you got the central thesis. Second, finding main ideas for individual paragraphs help you make sense of the development of the passage. It helps you follow how the author moves from one strategy to the next. It produces a nice little outline so you can find information quickly. You've got at least 15 minutes to read and plan, so you have plenty of time to write them down. There's no excuse to not write down your main ideas.

Let's take a look at a sample passage and work on getting main ideas:

READING DRILL: MAIN IDEAS

Below find a full sample essay prompt. Read the passage and find the main idea for each paragraph.

Adapted from Murray J. Siskind, "Bloomberg's Bike Lanes Go Too Far", *New York Herald*, 2012

1   In 1997 New York's Department of Transportation issued a "Bicycle Master Plan". This plan had many good elements, among them building bicycle-only "greenways" in city parks and along underused waterside areas. A much more controversial part of the plan was to enormously increase the amount of roadway given over to bicycle-only traffic, the notorious "bike lanes". Since then, under Mayor Michael Bloomberg the reach of bike lanes has doubled to now over 400 miles. The increased infrastructure for recreational bicycling has been a boon to the city, but introducing bicycles to the city's vehicular roadways has caused several serious problems.

MAIN IDEA:

2   Bloomberg was in many ways a visionary mayor, looking for ideas to improve life in New York not only locally, but worldwide. The unprecedented increase in bicycle infrastructure was based upon similar initiatives in cities like Copenhagen, Denmark, and Portland, Oregon. But New York is a unique metropolis, and comparisons to these two cities are doomed to fail.

MAIN IDEA:

3   Bloomberg's Commissioner of Transportation, Janette Sadik-Khan, acknowledges that "several of my ideas were inspired by what I saw in Copenhagen." One wonders how she failed to notice the great differences between a city of 600,000 and one with a metropolitan area population of 14 million. The former is a typical European city with a center made for pedestrians; the business of such cities is conducted on their peripheries. Not so in New York, which is dependent upon vehicular traffic, as anyone who has experienced midtown on a weekday will attest. Bikes in Copenhagen have been a common sight for more than a hundred years; the bike fad in New York is of very recent vintage.

MAIN IDEA:

4   Portland is no better point of comparison than Copenhagen is. Portland is a lovely city, but its residents have priorities that differ greatly from those of New Yorkers, who place a premium on time and getting business done. No useful analogies can be drawn between the two cities because of differences of scale. Portland's GDP of $164 billion pales next to New York's $1.5 trillion. Crucially, New York's population density is seven times that of Portland, yet Portland has eleven times the roadway per capita that New York has. What has worked for Portland simply will not work for New York: the latter is just too densely populated. Nor are Portland's roads much like New York's. Some Manhattan streets were designed in the 17th Century and are too narrow to accommodate both vehicular and bicycle traffic.

MAIN IDEA:

5   While Bloomberg and Sadik-Khan have trumpeted what they believe to be progress, enthusiasm for the project seems restricted to a very small, albeit vocal, constituency. The Department of Transportation trots out study after study about the expanding use of bike lanes but such use will always be insignificant in comparison to the vehicular use of roadways. Count for yourself the number of bikes and the number of cars on the road to judge just how small the bike lane constituency must be. If that is inadequately scientific for you then take the word of John Pucher, a professor of Urban Planning at Rutgers University. Pucher has estimated that the city's claims about the increase in bicycle use are exaggerated by as much as 100%.

MAIN IDEA:

6   While the city's numbers may be exaggerated there are without a doubt more cyclists on city streets today. These are people who are not—as drivers must be—trained and licensed. Imagine the outcry if a city were to suddenly unleash on the streets thousands of truck drivers who had never before been behind the wheel. One can already notice that bicyclists frequently feel they don't need to follow the same traffic rules that drivers do, as they zip through stoplights and go the wrong way down one-way streets

MAIN IDEA:

7   Finally, such an increase in bicycles causes greatly decreased safety for all citizens, regardless of their mode of transportation. Passenger and commercial vehicular traffic have been forced into increasingly narrow stretches of roadway; pedestrians must now contend with two forms of traffic and—worse—have had their lines of sight reduced at crossings. It's little wonder that accidents between motor vehicles and bicycles have increased by 22% since the Bicycle Master Plan was accepted and will increase dramatically as more road space is given to bicycles, further frustrating already-beleaguered drivers. Accidents involving bikes and pedestrians are similarly on the increase.

MAIN IDEA:

8   Bicycles are wonderful for recreation but not for the transportation of people and goods. The latter should be New York's priority and it's no wonder that lawsuits have been filed to stop the expansion of bike lanes and several community boards have already requested that lanes in their neighborhoods be removed.

MAIN IDEA:

Write an essay in which you explain how Murray J. Siskind builds an argument to persuade his audience that New York City should not build bicycle lanes. In your essay, analyze how Siskind uses one or more of the features listed in the box above (or features of your own choice) to strengthen the logic and persuasiveness of his argument. Be sure that your analysis focuses on the most relevant features of the passage.

Your essay should not explain whether you agree with Siskind's claims, but rather explain how Siskind builds an argument to persuade his audience.

By now, after having done the Reading chapters, you're probably a pro at finding main ideas. No doubt you figured out here that the author thinks that *bike lanes are bad*. In fact, **the essay prompt will *tell you* the main idea of the passage in the box at the end**. Here, "that New York City should not build bicycle lanes."

Even though the overall main idea is given to you, getting the main ideas for individual paragraphs will go a long way toward helping you organize your essay. Remember, a third of your grade will be based on how well you read the passage, so you must be sure that you understand what the author is saying.

Argument

The more challenging part of analyzing the source text will be in identifying all the ways the author tries to convince the reader of this central thesis. This is called *the argument*. Finding main ideas tell us *what* the author says. But we also must figure out *how* he says it. That means analyzing his *argument*.

By "argument" we do not mean a disagreement or a fight . If your brother yells that it's your turn to feed the dog and you shout *"IS NOT!"*, neither of you has made an argument. An argument is a series of statements meant to *persuade* the reader to accept a point (the central thesis). There are a few methods of persuasion that you should focus on.

Evidence

Evidence generally means *facts*. If you point to the dog-feeding schedule on the refrigerator and your brother's name appears under today's date, that's evidence. Some evidence is better than other evidence. Saying "Mom says so" may not be the best evidence, but it's also a kind of evidence. Yelling *"IS NOT!"* is not evidence at all.

Reasoning

Facts aren't quite enough. To persuade someone, we need to connect those facts to action. You can present your brother that you fed the dog yesterday, but that fact alone doesn't mean anything. Maybe you *always* feed the dog. If you add that you take turns feeding the dog, *therefore* it is his turn to feed the dog, that's reasoning.

Style

Sometimes evidence and reasoning aren't enough and some *rhetoric* is needed to help persuade people of your point of view. Maybe reminding your brother of the importance of cooperation and fair play will help. Maybe you can bring up times when you helped him in the past, and appeal to his sense of family and camaraderie.

Okay, so most of the arguments you are faced with in the source text may not be so simple as this one, but your analyses of them will always come down to understanding and evaluating these three elements: evidence, reasoning, and style. And that's exactly what the Readers will be looking for.

Let's take a look at that same source text again. Now that we have the main ideas, it's time to look for how the author uses evidence, reasoning, and style to make his point.

READING DRILL: STRATEGIES

Read through the passage again, this time taking note of any examples of the author's use of **Evidence**, **Reasoning**, *or* **Style**. *You can also underline or circle sentences in the passage itself and mark with an* **E**, **R**, *or* **S**. *Note that paragraphs do not necessarily contain examples of all three.*

1　In 1997 New York's Department of Transportation issued a "Bicycle Master Plan". This plan had many good elements, among them building bicycle-only "greenways" in city parks and along underused waterside areas. A much more controversial part of the plan was to enormously increase the amount of roadway given over to bicycle-only traffic, the notorious "bike lanes". Since then, under Mayor Michael Bloomberg the reach of bike lanes has doubled to now over 400 miles. The increased infrastructure for recreational bicycling has been a boon to the city, but introducing bicycles to the city's vehicular roadways has caused several serious problems.

Evidence:

Reasoning:

Style:

2　Bloomberg was in many ways a visionary mayor, looking for ideas to improve life in New York not only locally, but worldwide. The unprecedented increase in bicycle infrastructure was based upon similar initiatives in cities like Copenhagen, Denmark, and Portland, Oregon. But New York is a unique metropolis, and comparisons to these two cities are doomed to fail.

Evidence:

Reasoning:

Style:

3　Bloomberg's Commissioner of Transportation, Janette Sadik-Khan, acknowledges that "several of my ideas were inspired by what I saw in Copenhagen." One wonders how she failed to notice the great differences between a city of 600,000 and one with a metropolitan area population of 14 million. The former is a typical European city with a center made for pedestrians; the business of such cities is conducted on their peripheries. Not so in New York, which is dependent upon vehicular traffic, as anyone who has experienced midtown on a weekday will attest. Bikes in Copenhagen have been a common sight for more than a hundred years; the bike fad in New York is of very recent vintage.

Evidence:

Reasoning:

Style:

4　Portland is no better point of comparison than Copenhagen is. Portland is a lovely city, but its residents have priorities that differ greatly from those of New Yorkers, who place a premium on time and getting business done. No useful analogies can be drawn between the two cities because of differences of scale. Portland's GDP of $164 billion pales next to New York's $1.5 trillion. Crucially, New York's population density is seven times that of Portland, yet Portland has eleven times the roadway per capita that New York has. What has worked for Portland simply will not work for New York: the latter is just too densely populated. Nor are Portland's roads much like New York's. Some Manhattan streets were designed in the 17th Century and are too narrow to accommodate both vehicular and bicycle traffic.

Evidence:

Reasoning:

Style:

---

5 While Bloomberg and Sadik-Khan have trumpeted what they believe to be progress, enthusiasm for the project seems restricted to a very small, albeit vocal, constituency. The Department of Transportation trots out study after study about the expanding use of bike lanes but such use will always be insignificant in comparison to the vehicular use of roadways. Count for yourself the number of bikes and the number of cars on the road to judge just how small the bike lane constituency must be. If that is inadequately scientific for you then take the word of John Pucher, a professor of Urban Planning at Rutgers University. Pucher has estimated that the city's claims about the increase in bicycle use are exaggerated by as much as 100%.	**Evidence:** **Reasoning:** **Style:**
6 While the city's numbers may be exaggerated there are without a doubt more cyclists on city streets today. These are people who are not—as drivers must be—trained and licensed. Imagine the outcry if a city were to suddenly unleash on the streets thousands of truck drivers who had never before been behind the wheel. One can already notice that bicyclists frequently feel they don't need to follow the same traffic rules that drivers do, as they zip through stoplights and go the wrong way down one-way streets	**Evidence:** **Reasoning:** **Style:**
7 Finally, such an increase in bicycles causes greatly decreased safety for all citizens, regardless of their mode of transportation. Passenger and commercial vehicular traffic have been forced into increasingly narrow stretches of roadway; pedestrians must now contend with two forms of traffic and—worse—have had their lines of sight reduced at crossings. It's little wonder that accidents between motor vehicles and bicycles have increased by 22% since the Bicycle Master Plan was accepted and will increase dramatically as more road space is given to bicycles, further frustrating already-beleaguered drivers. Accidents involving bikes and pedestrians are similarly on the increase.	**Evidence:** **Reasoning:** **Style:**
8 Bicycles are wonderful for recreation but not for the transportation of people and goods. The latter should be New York's priority and it's no wonder that lawsuits have been filed to stop the expansion of bike lanes and several community boards have already requested that lanes in their neighborhoods be removed.	**Evidence:** **Reasoning:** **Style:**

What did you find? There's a lot you could list under each area, and you may have found much more than we list here, but some things shouldn't have gotten past you:

Evidence

- Bike lanes have doubled to over 400 miles.
- Accidents between motor vehicles and bicycles have increased by 22%.
- Prof. Pucher says the city's claims about bicycle use are exaggerated.

Reasoning

- The loss of road space creates danger.
- Portland and New York are too different to form effective comparisons.
- Bicyclists are unlicensed and so more dangerous than drivers.

Style

- Inflammatory word choice: Part of the plan is *controversial*; The bike paths are *notorious*; Drivers are *already-beleaguered*.
- Direct address to the reader: "Count for yourself the number of bikes and the number of cars"
- Hypothetical thought experiment: We're asked to imagine what it would be like if unlicensed truck drivers were suddenly driving on the roads

There is more you could have found. You don't have to mention every strategy the author uses, but you must find *some* points to discuss, and certainly focus on the ones that are most prominent in the passage.

We've separated finding main ideas and finding the argument into two exercises, but you don't have to read the source text twice. You can find elements of evidence, reasoning, and style at the same time you identify the thesis. Of course, you may want to go back and read parts of it while you are gathering your thoughts and even once you have started your essay.

III. ANALYSIS

Okay, we've identified different strategies to show *how* the author made his argument. But simply pointing them out is not enough. If we just list his tactics, we're not actually analyzing the passage, we're *describing* it. This is not a book report. We want to *evaluate the passage's effectiveness*.

"Wait a minute," you ask. "Didn't the prompt specifically say that I shouldn't write about whether I agree with the author." That's true, but that's not what we mean here. Saying an argument is effective does not automatically mean you agree with the conclusion, and agreeing with a conclusion does not mean the argument is effective.

For example, here's a claim:

> ✏ **We should get donuts.**

I like where this is going. Continue. What's your argument?

> ✗ **We should get donuts because they're good for you.**

Okay, well, I do want donuts, but I know that's not true. And now you've got me thinking about my diet and I feel guilty for wanting donuts. Try again.

> ✗ **We should get donuts because Dave wanted to come over and he likes donuts.**

Ugh, Dave? But Dave's a jerk. I don't want to see Dave. If getting donuts will make Dave come over, then I don't want donuts. Try again.

> ✗ *I WANT DONUTS RIGHT NOW!*

Are you five? Stop yelling at me!

> ✓ **We should get donuts because we've worked hard on this project and deserve a treat.**

Yes! I do deserve a treat! Great. I love this argument. Much better.

In your essay, **we don't care whether you agree with the author's claim.** But we do care whether the author made a good case for the claim. That means we have to make connections between the different tactics he or she uses.

Evaluating the argument

Identifying the author's tactics is a necessary first step, but we also want to discuss how the author weaves together all the choices he or she made. *Why* does the author make those choices? How does this piece of evidence relate to that piece of reasoning. Why is the passage structured the way it's structured, and what effect does it have on the reader?

For the bicycle passage, here are some questions you can ask:

- Why does the author begin by saying good things about the "Bicycle Master Plan"?
- Why does the author spend so much time talking about Copenhagen and Portland?
- How does his argument transition from paragraph 5 to paragraph 6? From paragraph 6 to paragraph 7?

IV. WRITING

A second thesis

We spent some time discussing the thesis of the passage, but remember: *your* essay needs a thesis, too. Before you start writing, you need to come up with one and say it clearly right at the beginning.

Remember that your job isn't to agree or disagree with the author; it's to *analyze* the author's argument. Your thesis should mention what the author's claim is and how he makes it.

So your thesis should *not* be:

> ✗ **I agree with Siskind that bicycle lanes are a bad idea.**

That's an opinion, not an analysis. We care about Siskind, not you. How about this:

> ✗ **Siskind makes a strong case against bicycle lanes.**

This is better, but still not enough. Be more specific. How about this:

> ✓ **Siskind effectively argues against bicycle lanes by citing statistics, pointing out flaws in Bloomberg's argument, and appealing to the reader's common sense.**

Perfect. Now we know exactly what you're going to say in your essay.

Outline

This is absolutely crucial. You *must* outline.

A lot of students don't bother much with planning the organization of their essays, but it's *incredibly* important. **You must write an outline before you begin.**

It's one thing to have brilliant ideas swimming around in your head; it's another to be able to communicate them to your readers. These essays are not little short stories—they're *arguments*. As such, you must pay close attention to how you present your case. An outline takes very little time and will help the actual writing process go much more quickly and coherently. You must write an outline. You must write an outline.

You cannot outline without notes. You should be underlining parts of the text and taking notes while you read. After you do that you can organize what you've found. It's important to

It's perfectly fine to argue that the essay makes a bad argument. That's not the same thing as disagreeing with the author's conclusion.

You must write an outline

have *written down* the central thesis and some points for each of the three areas of evidence, reasoning, and style. Some texts may be heavy on evidence and light on style. It doesn't matter how much you have, just make sure you have something for all three areas.

You don't have to invent each outline from scratch. You can use this sample outline and simply fill in each item from your notes as appropriate.

I.   **Intro: the two theses.** Provide a short summary of the source text with a *clear statement of its central thesis*, along with *your thesis* about the passage. This introductory paragraph is important. It sets the tone for the rest of the essay by letting us know that you understand the passage and where you're going with it. You don't have to go into a lot of details—those will come out in the following paragraphs.

II. **Evidence:** What evidence does the author provide? Do you feel the evidence is sufficient? Does is seem reliable?

III. **Reasoning:** What reasoning does the author use to persuade the reader? If we accept the evidence do we have to accept his central thesis? If not, you must say *why not*.

IV. **Style:** Does the author write in a style that makes the reader think, *yeah, this guy is on to something*! Or does it add little to the evidence and reasoning?

V.   **Conclusion:** This can be brief, but you should restate your thesis with a summary of the previous paragraphs.

This outline is just a suggestion. You don't have to present them in this order; you can write about the three elements in any order you feel is appropriate. You don't even have to mention all three categories. If the passage is long on style and short on evidence, focus your discussion more on style. (Of course, if you feel its lack of evidence hurts the argument, feel free to bring that up.)

You also don't have to delineate between Evidence, Reasoning, and Style like this. Another option is to talk about the contents of the passage in the order that the author presents it:

I.   **Intro: the two theses.**

II. **First tactic:** Describe the first tactic that the author uses in his or her argument, discussing any evidence, reasoning, or style within it.

III. **Second tactic:** Describe the second tactic the author uses.

IV. **Third tactic:** Describe the third tactic the author uses.

V. Conclusion.

There's no one right way to do an outline; you can make your decision based on the contents of the particular passage you're analyzing. If the passage is neatly divided into Evidence, Reasoning, and Style, then order your essay that way. If it isn't, but does have discrete sections where it discusses different aspects of the topic, use the chronological outline. All that matters here is that you organize your thoughts into different units with concrete ideas.

OUTLINE EXERCISE

Using your notes from the previous exercises, write an outline for your essay about the bicycle lane passage.

I. Intro

    Passage Thesis: _____

    Your Thesis: _____

II. **Topic:**_____

    Evidence: _____

    _____

    _____

III. **Topic:**_____

    Evidence: _____

    _____

    _____

IV. **Topic:**_____

    Evidence: _____

    _____

    _____

IV. **Conclusion:** _____

    _____

Paragraphs

So what do you say in these paragraphs?

No matter what outline style you choose, each paragraph should begin with a **clear topic sentence**. This will be the main idea of *your* paragraph. That topic tells us what this paragraph will be about.

Following that, you must give **evidence** for whatever claim you made in your topic. If you topic is about the author's use of style, tell us *what* that style is and *where* he used it.

Quoting

You spent a long time taking notes and identifying different elements of the passage. Obviously you'll want to bring those up in your essay. But don't just say "the author cited some statistics" or "the author used a rhetorical question"—**quote the passage**. The use of direct quotes will strengthen your essay by giving evidence to your claims. It's something that's specifically mentioned in the scoring rubric and something that the OSATERs will be actively looking for.

Don't quote too much. Don't just quote a whole paragraph and move on. That's just plagiarism. Make sure you *talk about* the quote. What is the quote? What kind of tactic is it an example of? How does it strengthen the author's case?

Language

It's very difficult to improve your actual writing style. It can be done, but it takes lots of practice and revision. Improving your reading, analysis, organization or development is a much more effective way of improving your essay score than trying to improve your language. Nevertheless, there are some things to keep in mind about the way you write.

Vocabulary

Using sophisticated vocabulary can certainly improve your writing. Just be sure to use vocabulary *appropriately*. Using a difficult word can backfire if you use it in a way that shows you don't know what it means or you don't know its proper usage. Using a hard word incorrectly is worse than using an easy word correctly.

More important than vocabulary is *concrete language*. This means being *specific* in everything you say. Give us details, give us examples, give us concrete words, not abstract ideas. Say *exactly* what you mean.

Using concrete language is directly related to what we've already been preaching. One of the biggest problems that students have on their essays is that they don't know the difference between *saying* something and *proving* it. You can't assume that your reader will automatically understand why your examples support your point. You've got to *prove* it explicitly.

Sentences

If all your sentences sound the same, your writing becomes dull. Varying your sentence structure can help break up the monotony and make you sound like a big shot. What does that mean? Glad you asked.

There are three different types of sentences (get ready, I'm about to use Fancy Grammatical Terms™):

1. **Simple** Sentence has only one clause.

   - I like cats.
   - My science partner smells like onions.

2. **Compound** Sentence has two or more independent clauses stuck together.

   - I like cats, but John does not.
   - My science partner smells like onions, and his clothes are dirty.

3. **Complex** Sentence has an independent clause and a *subordinate* clause (a clause of lesser importance).

   - Although I like cats, John apparently does not.
   - My science partner, who sits next to me every day in Biology class, smells like onions.

Many students only write in simple and compound sentences. To shake things up, try to throw at least one complex sentence into your essay. Just make a point of using a sentence with the word "although". That's all you need.

Grammar

Believe it or not, your grammatical competence is probably the *least* important element of The Essay. The Essay is intended to be a first draft. That means it doesn't have to be totally polished. They know that you only have 50 minutes for this bad boy, so you've got some leeway. They're not looking for Shakespeare here. You can make spelling and grammatical errors and still get a perfect score. Your argument is more important than your grammar. That said, your mistakes should be within the limits of reason. Every little mistake adds up.

Your essay doesn't have to be neat. You can cross words out or insert whole sentences with asterisks and arrows pointing here and there. But stay in the box—any text outside the box around the page will not be read.

A few scattered here and there are okay, but if you consistently butcher every sentence you write, it won't matter how good your analysis is—no one will be able to understand what you're saying. So while grammar shouldn't be your *main* concern on The Essay, you should try to cut down on errors whenever possible.

We've already discussed pretty much all of the major rules of grammar, so we don't have to go over them all again.* Just know that all the grammatical rules we've talked about so far apply to you too.

One way to avoid grammatical problems is to **reread your work**. When you've got a time limit, you write quickly, so it's incredibly easy to lose track of what you've already written. In fact, many of the grammatical mistakes students make on the essay arise because they *literally forgot* what they had just written. Obviously, timing is an issue on the essay, so if you don't have time to re-read, that's okay. But giving your essay another read once you've finished can help you spot errors and clean things up a bit.

---

* Well, we *shouldn't* have to go over them again.

SAMPLE PASSAGE

Adapted from Peter Mitchell, *The Language Death Crisis*, 2005.

1   On October 7, 1992, Tevfik Esenc died peacefully in his sleep at the age of 88, and with him died an entire language. His gravestone memorializes him as "the last person able to speak the language they called Ubykh". Imagine if this were to happen to your language, if all the vocabulary, the sounds and poetry, the intricate grammars of English simply died quietly overnight. The phenomenon called language death. It is a global catastrophe that unfortunately is all too common.

2   How does this happen? When people hear the term "language death", they often think of "dead languages", imagining lost civilizations, and ruins filled with broken stone pillars. True, there are thousands of ancient languages no longer in use, but most didn't simply vanish—they evolved into other languages over the course of hundreds of years. Latin didn't "die"; it turned into French, Italian, and other Romance languages.

3   Language death, however, is a different phenomenon. It's happening now and it happens suddenly, sometimes over the course of just a few generations. The death of a language does not even require the death of the culture that speaks it. A language dies from disuse, when another language becomes dominant in the area, and the speakers of the indigenous language shift to the dominant language. The Ubykh language may be dead, but the Ubykh people live on, their native language having been supplanted by Turkish.

4   But even though the community survives the death of its language, the culture nonetheless suffers. Every language is a repository of its people's history. Not only the traditional myths and stories, but the very words themselves are the heritage of the people, their bloodline and connection to the past. Without a language of its own, a community is robbed of its identity, particularly if the native language has been supplanted by that of an oppressor.

5   Preserving a language is not without barriers, though. When a community abandons its language, there is often good reason to do so—sometimes it even can mean the difference between life and death. In areas of extreme poverty, speaking the dominant language can mean better economic opportunities, a greater income, or a better life. In imperialist colonies or war-torn regions, a group in power will sometimes prohibit the use of indigenous languages, sometimes even under penalty of death. The United States is not immune to such practices. In the late 19th and early 20th centuries, the government helped fund Native American boarding schools that were set up to "civilize" Native American children with the goal of assimilating them into American society. This kind of assimilation meant forbidding children from using their native languages.

6   Some sociolinguists estimate that a language dies every two weeks. This means that, of the 6,000 languages that are currently spoken throughout the world, half will be extinct within a century. These numbers can be mind-boggling to Americans—especially the idea that there are 6,000 languages in the world. Most of us are only familiar with the most commonly spoken languages—English, Spanish, Chinese Mandarin, etc. But more than half the world's known languages have fewer than 10,000 speakers, and one quarter have fewer than 1,000. With populations that small, it's easy for languages to slip away without fanfare.

7   Once a language begins to fade from use, is there anything that can be done? One way to preserve a dying language is through documentation. At a minimum, it ensures that future generations can continue to study its sounds and structures. Occasionally, documentation can even allow a dead language to be resurrected. Hebrew had fallen out of everyday use around the time of the late Roman Empire, kept alive only by religious scholars. A revival in the nineteenth century brought it back, and it is now spoken by 15 million people worldwide, over 1500 years after its original displacement. Several studies of Ubykh were published before the death of poor Tevfik. Perhaps it too will be revived in a few hundred years.

Write an essay in which you explain how Mitchell builds an argument to persuade his audience that language death is a global crisis. In your essay, analyze how Mitchell uses one or more of the features listed in the box above (or features of your own choice) to strengthen the logic and persuasiveness of his argument. Be sure that your analysis focuses on the most relevant features of the passage.

Your essay should not explain whether you agree with Mitchell's claims, but rather explain how he builds an argument to persuade his audience.

SAMPLE ESSAY NOTES

APPENDICES

Appendix A: Writing Drills   475

Appendix B: Math Drills   481

Appendix C: Summaries   513

Performance Logs   519

Verb Agreement Drill

1. *Lynn*, ~~one of my best friends~~, [**IS** / are] taking me to New Hampshire this weekend.

    Ignore the phrase separated by commas.

2. Despite the often unbearable heat, *residents* ~~of Houston~~ [**STAY** / stays] in the city during the summer.

    Ignore the prepositional phrase.

3. *The staff* ~~of pastry chefs~~ [**IS** / are] working around the clock due to the holiday rush.

    Ignore the prepositional phrase.

4. *Pizza*, ~~originally introduced to the U.S. by Italian immigrants~~, [**HAS** / have] become a thoroughly American fast food.

    Ignore the phrase separated by commas.

5. For someone new to New York, *the process* ~~(of looking)~~ ~~(at apartments to rent)~~ [**IS** / are] often daunting.

    Ignore the two prepositional phrases.

6. *Nightmares* ~~(about his student's performance)~~ ~~(on the national exam)~~ [has / **HAVE**] plagued the tutor every night this week.

    Ignore the two prepositional phrases.

7. *Each individual animal* ~~(in the exhibit)~~ ~~(, including all the gulls, the seals, and the penguins,)~~ [**WAS** / were] prescribed a unique, specialized diet according to its particular needs.

    Ignore the phrase separated by commas and the prepositional phrase.

8. ~~(Out of the cracks)~~ ~~(in the cobblestones)~~ [grow / **GROWS**] *a tangle* ~~(of weeds and wildflowers)~~.

    The subject is after the verb. Ignore the two prepositional phrases at the beginning (and the prepositional phrase at the end).

9. Ever since the movie was released, there [has / **HAVE**] been *many rumors* about the co-stars' off-screen relationship.

    "There" is not a subject—it's a sign that the subject will come after the verb.

10. Oprah Winfrey's *business ventures* ~~(, which include television shows, charities, a book club, and a magazine,)~~ [has / **HAVE**] made her the most influential woman in the world.

    Ignore the phrase separated by commas.

■ Appendix A
Writing Drills

VERB AGREEMENT DRILL

Circle the verb form that appropriately agrees with its subject.

1. Lynn, one of my best friends, [**is** / **are**] taking me to New Hampshire this weekend.

2. Despite the often unbearable heat, residents of Houston [**stay** / **stays**] in the city during the summer.

3. The staff of pastry chefs [**is** / **are**] working around the clock due to the holiday rush.

4. Pizza, originally introduced to the U.S. by Italian immigrants, [**has** / **have**] become a thoroughly American fast food.

5. For someone new to New York, the process of looking at apartments to rent [**is** / **are**] often daunting.

6. Nightmares about his student's performance on the national exam [**has** / **have**] plagued the tutor every night this week.

7. Each individual animal in the exhibit, including all the gulls, the seals, and the penguins, [**was** / **were**] prescribed a unique, specialized diet according to its particular needs.

8. Out of the cracks in the cobblestones [**grow** / **grows**] a tangle of weeds and wildflowers.

9. Ever since the movie was released, there [**has** / **have**] been many rumors about the co-stars' off-screen relationship.

10. Oprah Winfrey's business ventures, which include television shows, charities, a book club, and a magazine, [**has** / **have**] made her the most influential woman in the world.

VERB TENSE DRILL

Circle the verb form that is in the appropriate tense.

1. After Daniel left for college, his mother [**converts** / **converted**] his bedroom into a workout room.

2. Alexandra [**sees** / **saw**] all twenty-three of her cousins whenever she goes back home for her family reunion.

3. Charles Lindbergh was catapulted to international fame when he successfully [**flies** / **flew**] from New York to Paris in 1927, the first non-stop transatlantic flight in history.

4. I always pay my rent as soon as I [**received** / **receive**] the bill.

5. Every year there is a new trend in fantasy fiction: last year it was vampires, this year it is zombies, and next year it [**is** / **will be**] something else.

6. In 1291, the communities of Uri, Schwyz, and Nidwalden [**have allied** / **allied**] themselves to form the Old Swiss Confederacy, the precursor to modern Switzerland.

7. Despite growing up close to the beach, Marjorie had never [**swam** / **swum**] in the ocean until she went to Greece.

8. Although treatments and techniques in medicine [**evolved** / **have evolved**] a great deal over the last few centuries, the fundamental needs of patients for care and comfort remain the same.

9. When I was in high school I thought I knew everything, but I [**learned** / **have learned**] a lot since I started college last year.

10. Since 2005, when Lance Armstrong announced his initial retirement, he [**rode** / **has ridden**] in many bicycle races, including the 2009 Tour de France.

Verb Tense Drill

1. *After* Daniel *left* for college, his mother [converts / **CONVERTED**] his bedroom into a workout room.

   Use the simple past for a specific past event.

2. Alexandra [**SEES** / saw] all twenty-three of her cousins *whenever* she *goes* back home for her family reunion.

   The verb "goes" is present, and "whenever" tells us the two verbs occur at the same time. So "sees" should be present, too.

3. Charles Lindbergh *was* catapulted to international fame when he successfully [flies / **FLEW**] from New York to Paris *in 1927*, the first non-stop transatlantic flight in history.

   We're talking about a specific past event in 1927, so we want the simple past "flew".

4. I always *pay* my rent *as soon as* I [received / **RECEIVE**] the bill.

   The verb "pay" is present and "as soon as" tells us the two verbs occur at the same time. So "receive" should be present, too.

5. Every year there is a new trend in fantasy fiction: last year it was vampires, this year it is zombies, and *next year* it [is / **WILL BE**] something else.

   The phrase "next year" tells us we want the future "will be".

6. *In 1291*, the communities of Uri, Schwyz, and Nidwalden [have allied / **ALLIED**] themselves to form the Old Swiss Confederacy, the precursor to modern Switzerland.

   "In 1291" tells us we're talking about a specific past event, so we want the simple past "allied".

7. Despite growing up close to the beach, Marjorie *had* never [swam / **SWUM**] in the ocean until she went to Greece.

   The verb "swim" is irregular. Since the verb here is a two-word form with "had", we need the past participle "swum". The form "swam" is the simple past, which we could use if we didn't have the "had". (Actually, in this sentence we really ought to use the past perfect "had swum" because the verb refers to a time *before* Marjorie "went to Greece." The past perfect is used for the past of the past.)

8. Although treatments and techniques in medicine [evolved / **HAVE EVOLVED**] a great deal *over the last few centuries*, the fundamental needs of patients for care and comfort remain the same.

   The phrase "over the last few centuries" tell us that we're talking about a *span* of time, not just a specific event. The present perfect "have evolved" is used for time periods starting in the past and *stretching up to the present*.

9. When I was in high school I thought I knew everything, but I [learned / **HAVE LEARNED**] a lot *since I started college last year*

   The phrase "since I started college last year" tells us I learned this stuff over a stretch of time from last year to the present.

10. *Since 2005*, when Lance Armstrong announced his initial retirement, he [rode / **HAS RIDDEN**] in many bike races, including the 2009 Tour de France.

    The phrase "*since 2005*" tells us that we're talking about a *span* of time, not just a specific event. The present perfect "has ridden" is used for time periods starting in the past and *stretching up to the present*.

    Don't be fooled by the simple past "announced"—that's something that occurred *in* 2005. But the riding occurs from 2005 to the present.

Pronoun Agreement Drill

1. _Susan and Molly_ never enjoyed playing Scrabble until [she / **THEY**] started studying vocabulary.

   While it's theoretically possible that only one of them studied vocabulary, we can't use "she" because we wouldn't know which girl the pronoun refers to.

2. If _one_ speeds on the highway, [you / **ONE**] may get pulled over by the police.

   Generic pronoun shift.

3. Though [**IT** / they] may not be very social, _the house rabbit_ makes an excellent pet.

   The antecedent, "the house rabbit", is singular.

4. _Reality television_, which has given rise to a new type of celebrity, makes up a huge share of the market due to [**ITS** / their] relatively low production costs.

   The antecedent, "reality television", is singular.

5. _The coach_ informed his players that [**HE** / they] would be retiring at the end of the season.

   The antecedent, "the coach", is singular. Structurally speaking, "they" could refer to the plural "players". But it would not make sense for the coach to tell the players that _they_ were retiring. This is a good example of the importance of using your common sense of the context when determining the antecedent.

6. A huge number of _zombies_ approached the school, but we were not intimidated; [it was / **THEY WERE**] clumsy, stupid, and easy to evade.

   The antecedent, "zombies", is plural. Note that it's okay for the antecedent to be within a prepositional phrase. Who's clumsy? It's not the number, it's the zombies.

7. _Representatives_ on the city-wide planning committee will need to get the support of [his or her / **THEIR**] constituents in order to approve the construction of a new park.

   Who has constituents? _Representatives_. That's plural, so we need the plural pronoun, "their".

8. _Every teenage girl_ argues with [**HER** / their] mother occasionally, but I used to fight with my mother every day.

   "Every teenage girl" is a _singular_ antecedent, so we need the singular pronoun "her".

9. Although [**IT** / they] had already played for four hours, _the ukulele band_ played four encores to thunderous applause at the end of its sold-out concert.

   The antecedent, "the ukulele band", is _singular_, so we the singular pronoun "it". And look: there's an "its" later in the sentence, too, also referring to the band. That's a big clue!

10. As recent graduates, _we_ knew that the US debt crisis, though not as severe as that of other countries, would negatively impact [their / **OUR**] ability to get good jobs right out of college.

    Generic pronoun shift. The sentence starts in the first person with "we", so it must continue to use "we". Who has an ability to get jobs. The recent graduates do, certainly. But that's _us_.

PRONOUN AGREEMENT DRILL

Circle the pronoun that appropriately agrees with its antecedent.

1. Susan and Molly never enjoyed playing Scrabble until [she / they] started studying vocabulary.

2. If one speeds on the highway, [you / one] may get pulled over by the police.

3. Though [it / they] may not be very social, the house rabbit makes an excellent pet.

4. Reality television, which has given rise to a new type of celebrity, makes up a huge share of the market due to [its / their] relatively low production costs.

5. The coach informed his players that [he / they] would be retiring at the end of the season.

6. A huge number of zombies approached the school, but we were not intimidated; [it was / they were] clumsy, stupid, and easy to evade.

7. Representatives on the city-wide planning committee will need to get the support of [his or her / their] constituents in order to approve the construction of a new park.

8. Every teenage girl argues with [her / their] mother occasionally, but I used to fight with my mother every day.

9. Although [it / they] had already played for four hours, the ukulele band played four encores to thunderous applause at the end of its sold-out concert.

10. As recent graduates, we knew that the US debt crisis, though not as severe as that of other countries, would negatively impact [their / our] ability to get good jobs right out of college.

FRAGMENT DRILL

Determine whether each sentence is a complete sentence or a sentence fragment. If it is a fragment, write a corrected version below. If it is a complete sentence, circle the subject and verb of each independent clause.

1. On a trip to the mountains, Klaus and his daughters learning the basics of rock climbing.

2. "Spork", an example of a portmanteau, a blend of two words that are merged to form a new word.

3. Poems about war and conquest, which seem violent to today's reader, were considered romantic in the eighteenth century.

4. The five-year-old's playhouse, equipped with a kitchen, bathroom, and lounging area, which cost $10,000 to build.

5. Striving toward sustainable coexistence with the environment, permaculture, which is an approach to architectural and landscape design based on patterns that occur in nature.

6. Searching for the highest ratio of cookie dough to ice cream, Josie sampled every brand at the grocery store and determined that none of them had enough cookie dough.

7. The United States Flag Code lays out the official guidelines for the use of the American flag, many of which are routinely ignored; for example, prohibiting printing the American flag on clothing, bedding, or napkins.

8. The term "Siamese twins", popularized by the famous pair of conjoined twins, Chang and Eng Bunker, who traveled with the P. T. Barnum Circus in the late nineteenth century, but is now considered offensive.

9. His aunt, who was a physician herself and knew how difficult it was to see people in pain, warned him not to go into pediatrics if he couldn't bear to see children suffer.

10. A native of New York City, Theodore Roosevelt, who made his permanent home on Long Island at Sagamore Hill, which became known as the "Summer White House" during the seven summers he spent there as President.

Fragment Drill

1. Fragment.
Needs a verb to go with the subject "Klaus and his daughters".

Possible correction:
On a trip to the mountains, Klaus and his daughters **learned** the basics of rock climbing

2. Fragment.
It seems like "Spork" will be the subject, but there's no verb to go with it.

"Spork", [an example of a portmanteau,] [a blend of two words that are merged to form a new word.]

(The final phrase "a blend... word" is a modifier that contains a dependent clause "that are ...word.")

Possible correction:
"Spork" **is** an example of a portmanteau, a blend of two words that are merged to form a new word.

3. Complete sentence.
The core sentence is "Poems ... were considered".
Poems about war and conquest, [which seem violent to today's reader,] **were considered** romantic in the eighteenth century.

4. Fragment.
It seems like "The five-year-old's playhouse" will be the subject, but there's no verb to go with it.
The five-year-old's playhouse, [equipped with a kitchen, bathroom, and lounging area,] [which cost $10,000 to build.]

Possible correction:
The five-year-old's **playhouse**, [equipped with a kitchen, bathroom, and lounging area,] **cost** $10,000 to build.

5. Fragment.
There's no verb to go with "permaculture":
[Striving toward sustainable coexistence with the environment,] permaculture, [which is an approach to architectural and landscape design based on patterns that occur in nature.]

Possible correction:
[Striving toward sustainable coexistence with the environment,] **permaculture is** an approach to architectural and landscape design based on patterns that occur in nature.

6. Complete sentence.
The core sentence has two coordinated verbs: "Josie sampled... and determined"
[Searching for the highest ratio of cookie dough to ice cream,] **Josie sampled** every brand at the grocery store **and determined** that none of them had enough cookie dough.

7. Fragment.
The first half is fine and has an independent clause: "The US Flag Code *lays*". However, we also must have a complete sentence after the semicolon. Here, we have no subject or main verb after the semicolon.

Possible correction:
... ignored; for example, **it prohibits** printing the American flag on clothing, bedding, or napkins.

[You could also remove the semicolon and attach the last phrase with a comma, treating it as a modifier. But if you do that, you might want to do something with the "for example" for stylistic reasons. You could replace it with "such as". Lots of options here. Don't worry about it too much. Just make sure everyone sees that you can't have a fragment after a semicolon.]

8. Fragment.
There's no main verb to go with the subject "The term 'Siamese twins'"
The term "Siamese twins", [popularized by the famous pair of conjoined twins,] [Chang and Eng Bunker,] [who traveled with the P. T. Barnum Circus in the late nineteenth century,] [but is now considered offensive.]

[Note that we do have a verb, "is (now) considered" in the last phrase. But that verb is hidden behind a "but". Like "and", if "but" is followed by a verb alone, that verb must be the second of a pair of two verbs. So we need another verb before that.]

Possible solution:
The term "Siamese twins" was popularized by the famous pair of conjoined twins, Chang and Eng Bunker, [who traveled with the P. T. Barnum Circus in the late nineteenth century,] **but is now considered** offensive.

Note that in our correction we now have two coordinated verbs. "The term ... was popularized... but is now considered"

9. Complete sentence.
The core sentence is "his aunt...warned him".
His aunt, [who was a physician herself and knew how difficult it was to see people in pain,] **warned** him not to go into pediatrics [if he couldn't bear to see children suffer].

10. Fragment.
There's no main verb to go with "Theodore Roosevelt".
[A native of New York City,] Theodore Roosevelt, [who made his permanent home on Long Island at Sagamore Hill,] [which became known as the "Summer White House" during the seven summers he spent there as President].

Possible solution:
[A native of New York City,] **Theodore Roosevelt made** his permanent home on Long Island at Sagamore Hill, [which became known as the "Summer White House" during the seven summers he spent there as President].

Run-On Drill

1. Run-on.
Two independent clauses are "Travis told…" and "we should go…", joined only with a comma:

[**Travis told** me about a new skate park on the east side of town], [**we should go** there tomorrow.]

We could correct it by swapping the comma with a semicolon or inserting an "and" after the comma.

2. Not a run-on.
There is one main clause with two coordinated verbs:

Lucy's team had a substantial lead at halftime but **wound up** losing by just one point.

3. Run-on.
Two independent clauses joined only with a comma:

[**Veterinarians must be** familiar with the anatomy of many different species] , [**doctors** only **have to be** familiar with humans.]

If you want to connect them with a conjunction, you should use a *contrast* conjunction. However, the best correction here is probably just a semicolon. The parallelism of the clauses implies a contrast, so the contrast connector isn't strictly necessary.

4. Run-on.
[**People tend** to think of democracy in monolithic terms], [**they are** unaware that it can take many different forms].

We could correct it with a semicolon or by inserting a conjunction, possibly "but". We could also correct it by striking "they are" to make the final phrase a modifier: "unaware that it can take many different forms."

5. Not a run-on.
The two clauses are properly joined by "because".

[*Because* **his boss refused** to listen to any of his ideas for improving the business,] [**Manny decided** to leave and start his own company.]

6. Not a run-on.
The two clauses are properly joined by "but".

[**Our family has** a tradition of going camping every June to celebrate the beginning of summer vacation,] [*but* last year **we had** to cancel the trip because my father broke his leg.]

7. Run-on.
The first two clauses are properly joined by "although". But the last clause is joined with a comma alone.

[*Although* **Sophie** often **read** Grimm's fairy tales as a child] , [**she** always **found** Greek myths much more compelling] , [**she preferred** the gods and goddesses to the witches and princesses.]

8. Not a run-on.
Ignore the two opening modifiers and the dependent clause in the middle.

[During the Second Punic War,] [fought between the Roman Republic and Carthage,] [**Hannibal marched** his army, [which notably included 37 war elephants,] across the Alps] ; [his shrewd war **tactics** eventually **enabled** him to defeat the Romans.]

We have two independent clauses, but they are properly joined by a semicolon.

9. Run-on.
Two independent clauses joined with a comma and "however". Remember that "however" is not a conjunction and cannot be used to connect clauses.

[With the success of "The Wizard of Oz" in 1939,] [**Judy Garland became** a role-model to little girls across America] , [*however* **little was known** of her troubles with drugs and alcohol.]

The best correction is probably to replace the comma with a semicolon (and add a comma after "however"). Or you could replace "however" with "but".

10. Run-on.
The first two clauses are properly joined by "even though". But the last clause is joined with a comma alone. Don't be distracted by the pointless "in fact". That's not a conjunction, so we can't use it to connect the clauses.

[*Even though* gold medal winner **Thomas Hicks was given** a strychnine injection during the 1904 Olympic marathon] , [**he was** not disqualified for doping] , [in fact, at the time **this procedure was believed** to be necessary to survive the demanding race.]

The best solution is probably to replace the comma before "in fact" with a semicolon.

RUN ON DRILL

Identify which of the following sentences are run-ons. Circle the subject and verb of each independent clause, and circle the connection between the clauses (either the punctuation or the words used to connect the clauses). If it is a run-on, write a suggestion for how to fix it.

1. Travis told me about a new skate park on the east side of town, we should go there tomorrow.

2. Lucy's team had a substantial lead at halftime but wound up losing by just one point.

3. Veterinarians must be familiar with the anatomy of many different species, doctors only have to be familiar with that of humans.

4. People tend to think of democracy in monolithic terms, they are unaware that it can take many different forms.

5. Because his boss refused to listen to any of his ideas for improving the business, Manny decided to leave and start his own company.

6. Our family has a tradition of going camping every June to celebrate the beginning of summer vacation, but last year we had to cancel the trip because my father broke his leg.

7. Although Sophie often read Grimm's fairy tales as a child, she always found Greek myths much more compelling, she preferred the gods and goddesses to the witches and princesses.

8. During the Second Punic War, fought between the Roman Republic and Carthage, Hannibal marched his army, which notably included 37 war elephants, across the Alps; his shrewd war tactics eventually enabled him to defeat the Romans.

9. With the success of "The Wizard of Oz" in 1939, Judy Garland became a role model to little girls across America, however little was known of her troubles with drugs and alcohol.

10. Even though gold medal winner Thomas Hicks was given a strychnine injection during the 1904 Olympic marathon, he was not disqualified for doping, in fact, at the time this procedure was believed to be necessary in order to survive the demanding race.

Plug In Drill

NOTE: Since this drill is intended for practicing techniques, algebraic solutions will not be shown here.

1. Answer: C.
Say $a = 4$.
$4 + 3b = 10$
$3b = 6$
$b = 2$

$2a + 6b$
$= 2(4) + 6(2)$
$= 8 + 12$
$= 20$.   That's **choice C.**

You can do this problem very quickly if you notice that $2a + 6b$ is double $a + 3b$, so it will be double 10, or 20. But if you don't notice that, you won't have any idea what to do. Plug in gives you an alternative. Also, even if you do notice it, this is a nice easy problem to practice Plug In.

3. Answer: D.
Pick a t. Say $t = 2$.

$x = 3t - 1 = 3(2) - 1 = 6 - 1 = 5 = x$
$y = t + 4 = 2 + 4 = 6 = y$

Put $y = 6$ into the choices and see which comes out to 5.

A) $6 - 4 = 2$ ✗
B) $3(6) + 3 = 18 + 3 = 21$ ✗
C) $3(6) - 5 = 18 - 5 = 13$ ✗
D) $3(6) - 13 = 18 - 13 = 5$ ✓

2. Answer: C.
It's easier to start with y. Say $y = 5$.
Now read the question again:
"The number x is 3 less than 2 times the number y."
Now instead of y, we have 5. Work backwards through the sentence.
2 times 5 is 10.
3 less than 10 is 7. So $x = 7$.

Now put $x = 7$ into the answers and see which comes out to 5.

A) $2(7) - 3$ $= 14 - 3$ $= 11$ ✗

B) $3(7) + 2$ $= 21 + 2$ $= 23$ ✗

C) $\dfrac{7 + 3}{2}$ $= \dfrac{10}{2}$ $= 5$ ✓

D) $\dfrac{7 - 3}{2}$ $= \dfrac{4}{2}$ $= 2$ ✗

4. Answer: D.
We know rectangle A is a square, so Plug In for its dimensions. Say the square has $s = 6$.

Rectangle B has double the length and half the width. That means the length of B is **12** and the width of B is **3**.

The perimeter of $A = 4 \times 6 = 24$.
The perimeter of $B = 12 + 3 + 12 + 3 = 24 + 6 = 30$.

Ratio of P(A):P(B) = 24:30 = **4:5.** That's **choice D).**

Appendix B
Math Drills

PLUG IN DRILL

1

If $a + 3b = 10$, what is the value of $2a + 6b = ?$

A) 12
B) 15
C) 20
D) 30

2

The number x is 3 less than 2 times the number y. Which of the following expressions gives y in terms of x?

A) $2x - 3$

B) $3x + 2$

C) $\dfrac{x+3}{2}$

D) $\dfrac{x-3}{2}$

3

If $x = 3t - 1$ and $y = t + 4$, what is x in terms of y?

A) $y - 4$
B) $3y + 3$
C) $3y - 5$
D) $3y - 13$

4

Note: Figure not drawn to scale.

The length of rectangle B is double that of rectangle A, and the width of rectangle B is half that of rectangle A. If rectangle A is a square, what is the ratio of the perimeter of A to the perimeter of B?

A) 1:2
B) 1:4
C) 2:3
D) 4:5

5

Three people are eating a box of cookies. Caroline ate half the number of cookies that Sherwyn did, and Sherwyn ate 4 times as many as Laura. What fraction of the cookies did Sherwyn eat?

Grid in your answer:

6

If $z = x - 3$ and $z = y + 5$, which of the following *must* be true?

A) $x > y$
B) $x < y$
C) $z < 0$
D) $z > 0$

7

A certain two-digit number, n, has a units digit that is three times the tens digit. Which of the following *must* be true?

A) $n > 20$
B) $n < 40$
C) n is odd
D) n is even

8

Sujit has only white shirts and red shirts. He has four times as many white shirts as red shirts. What percent of his shirts are red?

A) 20%
B) 25%
C) 75%
D) 80%

9

Note: Figure not drawn to scale.

In the figure above, what is z in terms of x and y?

A) $3y + x$
B) $4y - x$
C) $180 - 2y - x$
D) $180 - 3y - x$

10

Veerle is selling waffles for x dollars each. If her expenses totaled y dollars, which of the following expressions represents the number of waffles she must sell in order to make a profit of $100? (Profit equals total sales minus expenses.)

A) $\dfrac{100 + y}{x}$

B) $\dfrac{100 - y}{x}$

C) $\dfrac{100 + x}{y}$

D) $100x - y$

5. Answer: 4/7 or .571
Say that **Laura ate 4 cookies.**
Sherwyn ate 4 times as many as Laura,
so **Sherwyn ate 16 cookies.**
Caroline ate half as many as Sherwyn,
so **Caroline ate 8 cookies.**

That's a total of $4 + 16 + 8 = 28$ cookies.
We want to know what fraction of the cookies Sherwyn ate.

That's $\dfrac{16}{28} = \dfrac{4}{7}$ **of the cookies.**

6. Answer: A.
You can start with any of the three variables. Let's say $z = 8$.
$z = x - 3$
$8 = x - 3$ $11 = x$
$z = y + 5$
$8 = y + 5$ $3 = y$

Let's check all our answers and see which ones are true.
Remember: we want the choice that **must** be true, so be sure to check **all** choices.

A) $x > y$ $11 > 3$ ✓ It works!
B) $x < y$ $11 < 3$ ✗
C) $z < 0$ $8 < 0$ ✗
D) $z > 0$ $8 > 0$ ✓ It works!

A) and D) both work, but we can eliminate B) and C).

Let's test the remaining two choices. Since D) says that z must be positive, let's try a negative z and see if it works. If it does, we can eliminate D).
$z = -2$
$-2 = x - 3$ $-2 = y + 5$
$x = 1$ $y = -7$

A) $x > y$ $1 > -7$ ✓ **It works! Choice A) is our answer.**
D) $z > 0$ $-2 > 0$ ✗ It fails!

7. Answer: B.
Let's try a bunch of different numbers.
We know the units digit is three times the tens digit. Start picking numbers for the *tens* digit and multiply by 3 to get the units digit.
We know digits must be positive integers, so let's start with 1:

tens	units	n
1	3	13
2	6	26
3	9	39
4	12✗	That won't work!

The units digit can't be 12 because 12 is a two-digit number!
So our only possible values for n are **13, 26, and 39.**
Let's put those into the choices and see which *must* be true for all possible values of n: 13, 26, and 39.

A) $n > 20$ ✗   No: $13 < 20$.
B) $n < 40$ ✓   Yes! 13, 26, and 39 are all less than 40.
C) n is odd ✗   No: 26 is even.
D) n is even ✗   No: 13 and 39 are odd.

RTFQ: A), if you mix up the units and tens places.

8. Answer: A.
Say that Sujit has **10 red shirts.**
We know he has 4 times as many white shirts, so he has **40 white shirts.**
That means he has $10 + 40 = 50$ total shirts. What percent of his shirts are red?

$\dfrac{10}{50} = \dfrac{20}{100} = 0.20 = \mathbf{20\%}$

Since we're dealing with percents, it may be tempting to plug in 100 total shirts and then figure out how many red and white there are, but that's actually a bit tricky. It's much better to plug in for the red shirts here.
Choice B) is the Fool's Gold here, if you fixate on the 1:4 ratio and think that *one-fourth* of the shirts (or 25%) are red. But that's the ratio of red to white. The percent is the ratio of red to the total. That's much easier to see when you plug in for the red shirts.

9. Answer: C.
Pick an x. Say $x = 30$.
Hmm. That doesn't tell us much.
Let's pick a y, too. Say $y = 40$.
That means $3y = 3(40) = 120$.

We know the angle next to 120°
will be $180 - 120 = 60°$.

Note: Figure not drawn to scale.

We know the angles in the small triangle on the right add up to 180°, so the rightmost angle $= 180 - 40 - 60 = 80$.

We know the angles in the big triangle add up to 180, so
$30 + 80 + z = 180$
$z = 70.$

Note: Figure not drawn to scale.

Put $x = 30$ and $y = 40$ into the answers and see what gives you 70.

A) $3(40) + 30$ $= 120 + 30$ $= 150$ ✗
B) $4(40) - 30$ $= 160 - 30$ $= 130$ ✗
C) $180 - 2(40) - 30$ $= 180 - 80 - 30$ $= \mathbf{70}$ ✓
D) $180 - 3(40) - 30$ $= 180 - 120 - 30$ $= 30$ ✗

You can do this algebraically by following exactly the same steps but with variables instead of numbers. But you're much more likely to make a careless mistake that way.

10. Answer: A.
Pick separate numbers for x and y. Say $x = 5$ and $y = 20$.
Now let's read the problem with our numbers:

Waffles cost $5 each.
Veerle's expenses totaled $20.
She wants a profit of $100.
Profit = sales – expenses
So she needs to make $120 in sales.
$120 in sales, $5 each waffle: $120 \div 5 = $ **24 waffles.**

She needs to sell 24 waffles to make a $100 profit. Put $x = 5$ and $y = 20$ into the choices and see which comes out to 24:

A) $\dfrac{100 + 20}{5}$ $= \dfrac{120}{5}$ $= \mathbf{24}$ ✓
B) $\dfrac{100 - 20}{5}$ $= \dfrac{80}{5}$ $= 16$ ✗
C) $\dfrac{100 + 5}{20}$ $= \dfrac{105}{20}$ $= 5.25$ ✗
D) $100(5) - 20$ $= 500 - 20$ $= 480$ ✗

It's very easy to get confused here, but using real number makes it easier to catch your mistakes. For example, you might subtract profit minus expenses to get sales, and get choice B). But if you think about what the numbers mean, you know she's got to sell *more than* $100 if she's going to make $100 profit.

Backsolve Drill

NOTE: Since this drill is intended for practicing techniques, algebraic solutions will not be shown here.

1.   Answer: A.

C) $9 = xy$.

$18 - 9^2 = 18 - 81 = -63$ ✗   Should be 2.

It may not be obvious if you want a bigger or smaller number for xy. If you're not sure, don't waste time thinking about it. Just pick one. Keep trying answer choices till you find one that works.

B) $3 = xy$

$18 - 3^2 = 18 - 9 = 9$ ✗   Getting closer

A) $-4 = xy$

$18 - (-4)^2 = 18 - 16 = 2$ ✓   **Bingo.**

2.   Answer: B.

B)   **2 minutes.**
Put $t = 2$ into the given equation and see if it comes out to 50,000.

$k(t) = 3125 \times 2^{2t}$

$k(2) = 3125 \times 2^{2 \times 2}$

$k(2) = 3125 \times 2^4$

$k(2) = 3125 \times 16 = \mathbf{50,000}$ ✓   **It works!**

Choice D) means you thought the exponent was t. It's $2t$.

3.   Answer: A.

C) $6 = $ height.
The width is twice the height, so $w = 12$.
The length is twice the width, so $\ell = 24$.

$V = \ell w h$

$= 24 \times 12 \times 6$

$= 1,728$ ✗   Way too big.

B) $4 = h$
So $w = 8$, and $\ell = 16$.

$V = 16 \times 8 \times 4$

$= 512$ ✗   Getting closer.

A) $2 = h$
So $w = 4$, and $\ell = 8$.

$V = 8 \times 4 \times 2$

$= 64$ ✓   It works!

4.   Answer: D.

B)   72 total pies.

Half the pies were blueberry, so $72 \div 2$	$= 36$ blueberry pies.
One third were raspberry, so $72 \div 3$	$= 24$ raspberry pies.
And 21 were pecan.	$= 21$ pecan pies.
The total should still come to 72.	$= 81$ total pies ✗

Again, it may not be clear which direction to go. Pick one.

C)   108 total pies

Half the pies were blueberry, so $108 \div 2$	$= 54$ blueberry pies.
One third were raspberry, so $108 \div 3$	$= 36$ raspberry pies.
And 21 were pecan.	$= 21$ pecan pies.
The total should still come to 108.	$= 111$ total pies ✗

The totals are getting closer together, so we're going in the right direction.

D)   126 total pies

Half the pies were blueberry, so $126 \div 2$	$= 63$ blueberry pies.
One third were raspberry, so $126 \div 3$	$= 42$ raspberry pies.
And 21 were pecan.	$= 21$ pecan pies.
The total should still come to 126.	$= \mathbf{126}$ **total pies** ✓

5.   Answer: C.

B) $5 = c$.
That means we add 5 to each term to get the next term.
We know the sixth term is 28, so let's subtract 5 and work our way backwards.

Term	6th	5th	4th	3rd	2nd	1st
Value	28	23	18	13	8 ✓	3 ✗

We know that the 2nd term is supposed to be positive and the 1st term is supposed to be negative. This doesn't work.

3 was too big, so let's go to a *bigger c*. That way we'll be subtracting more and getting smaller terms. (If kids don't see this and want to go the wrong way, fine, let them.)

C) $6 = c$.

Term	6th	5th	4th	3rd	2nd	1st
Value	28	22	16	10	4 ✓	–2 ✓

It works!

BACKSOLVE DRILL

1

If $18 - (xy)^2 = 2$, which of the following could be the value of xy?

A)   −4
B)   3
C)   9
D)   16

3

The length of a certain rectangular box is twice the width, and the width of the box is twice the height. If the volume of the box is 64 cubic inches, what is its height, in inches?

A)   2
B)   4
C)   6
D)   8

2

The number of koalas, k, in a certain colony can be predicted according to the function $k(t) = 3125 \times 2^{2t}$, where t represents the number of minutes after the start of the observation. After how many minutes will the population reach 50,000 koalas?

A)   1
B)   2
C)   3
D)   4

4

Emily's Bakery made some pies for a party. Half of the pies were blueberry, one third were raspberry, and the remaining 21 were pecan. How many total pies did the bakery make for the party?

A)   63
B)   72
C)   108
D)   126

Each term of a certain sequence is formed by adding a positive integer, c, to the term immediately before it. The first term in the sequence is negative and the second term is positive. If the sixth term is 28, what is the value of c?

A) 4
B) 5
C) 6
D) 7

If $x^2 - 6x \leq -8$, which of the following is a possible value of x?

A) −5
B) −3
C) 0
D) 3

If the measures of the angles of a triangle are in a 1:3:5 ratio, what is the measure of the largest angle?

A) 40°
B) 60°
C) 80°
D) 100°

One number is 5 less than half of another number. If the sum of the two numbers is 34, what is the greater of the two numbers?

A) 8
B) 13
C) 26
D) 39

Of the 68 students in tenth grade, 31 students take Dutch, 45 students take Polish, and 5 students take neither language. How many students take both Polish and Dutch?

A) 11
B) 13
C) 18
D) 23

There are three integers, x, y, and z, such that $x < y < z$. The median of the three numbers is equal to three times their average (arithmetic mean). If $z = 10$, what is the least possible value of y?

A) −10
B) −9
C) −3
D)   3

6.   Answer: D.

B) $x = -3$.

$$x^2 - 6x \le -8$$
$$(-3)^2 - 6(-3) \le -8$$
$$9 - (-18) \le -8$$
$$9 + 18 \le -8$$
$$27 \le -8 \;\textbf{✗}\qquad\qquad \text{Too big.}$$

C) $x = 0$.

$$(0)^2 - 6(0) \le -8$$
$$0 - 0 \le -8$$
$$0 \le -8 \;\textbf{✗}\qquad\qquad \text{Still too big, but closer.}$$

D) $x = 3$.

$$(3)^2 - 6(3) \le -8$$
$$9 - 18 \le -8$$
$$\mathbf{-9 \le -8}\;\textbf{✓}\qquad\qquad \textbf{It works!}$$

7.   Answer: D.

B)   60. That's the *largest* angle.
The three angles are in a 1:3:5 ratio. Let's find the other two.

$$\frac{\text{largest}}{\text{smallest}} = \frac{5}{1} = \frac{60}{s}\qquad s = 12$$

$$\frac{\text{largest}}{\text{middle}} = \frac{5}{3} = \frac{60}{m}\qquad m = 36$$

(There are a bunch of other ways you can use this ratio to find the other angles. Whatever works best for you.)
The three angles make a triangle, so they should add up to 180.
$12 + 36 + 60 = 108$ **✗**   Too small.

C)   80 is the largest angle.

$$\frac{\text{largest}}{\text{smallest}} = \frac{5}{1} = \frac{80}{s}\qquad s = 16$$

$$\frac{\text{largest}}{\text{middle}} = \frac{5}{3} = \frac{80}{m}\qquad m = 48$$

$16 + 48 + 80 = 144$ **✗**   Still too small, but closer.

D)   **100 is the largest angle.**

$$\frac{\text{largest}}{\text{smallest}} = \frac{5}{1} = \frac{100}{s}\qquad s = 20$$

$$\frac{\text{largest}}{\text{middle}} = \frac{5}{3} = \frac{100}{m}\qquad m = 60$$

$20 + 60 + 100 = \mathbf{180}$ **✓**   **It works!**

8.   Answer: C.

B)   13 is the greater number.
"One number is 5 less than half of another number"
Half of 13 is 6.5.   (We can already tell this won't work.)
5 less than 6.5 is **1.5**. The other number is 1.5.
$13 + 1.5 = 14.5$ **✗**   The sum of the numbers should be 34.

C)   **26 is the greater number.**
Half of 26 is 13.
5 less than 13 is **8**. The other number is 8.
$26 + 8 = \mathbf{34}$ **✓**   **It works!**

9.   Answer: B.

B)   13 students take both Polish and Dutch.

31 take Dutch − 13 take both	= 18 take Dutch only.
45 take Polish − 13 take both	= 32 take Polish only.
	13 take both
	5 take neither
	68 total students ✓

Here's a Venn diagram to help keep it straight:

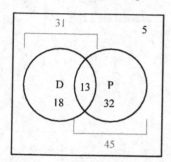

The "5" outside the circles represent the students who take neither class. Some students might like to ignore those 5. Subtract those 5 first to get $68 - 5 = 63$ students who took at least one language.

10.   Answer: B.
Tough one.
Since we want the *least possible* value, start with the smallest number in the list. That's A).

A) $-10 = y$.
We already know $z = 10$.
We know $x < y < z$, so $x < -10 < 10$.
We know the median of the three numbers is equal to three times the average.
We know y is the middle number, so *−10 is the median*.
That's three times the average, so the average is $\frac{-10}{3}$. Let's use that to find x.

$$\frac{x + y + z}{3} = \frac{-10}{3}$$
$$\frac{x - 10 + 10}{3} = \frac{-10}{3}$$
$$\frac{x}{3} = \frac{-10}{3}$$
$$x = -10. \;\textbf{✗}$$

Why not? Because now our three numbers are −10, −10, and 10.
But we know $x < y$.

B) $-9 = y$.
z is still 10, so $x < -9 < 10$. The median is now −9.

That means the average is $\frac{-9}{3} = -3$.

$$\frac{x - 9 + 10}{3} = -3$$
$$x - 9 + 10 = -9$$
$$x + 1 = -9$$
$$x = \mathbf{-10} \;\textbf{✓} \text{ It works! Our numbers are −10, −9, and 10.}$$

Wait, that's the same thing we got in A). Didn't we say $x = -10$ didn't work?
It didn't work when $y = -10$. But now $y = -9$, so $x < y < z$.

Fraction Drill

1. Answer: $\frac{13}{3}$ or $4\frac{1}{3}$.

$\frac{7}{2}+\frac{5}{6}$ Lowest common denominator is 6.

$=\frac{21}{6}+\frac{5}{6}$ Add the numerators.

$=\frac{26}{6}$ Cancel out a 2.

$=\frac{13}{3}$

2. Answer: $\frac{23}{24}$.

$\frac{13}{8}-\frac{2}{3}$ Lowest common denominator is 24.

$=\frac{39}{24}-\frac{16}{24}$ Subtract the numerators.

$=\frac{23}{24}$

3. Answer: $\frac{1}{2}$.

$\frac{3}{4}\times\frac{2}{3}$ Cancel out the 3's

$=\frac{1}{4}\times\frac{2}{1}$ Cancel out a 2.

$=\frac{1}{2}\times\frac{1}{1}$

$=\frac{1}{2}$

4. Answer: $\frac{8}{3}$ or $2\frac{2}{3}$.

$\frac{4}{5}\div\frac{3}{10}$ Flip the second fraction and multiply.

$=\frac{4}{5}\times\frac{10}{3}$ Cancel out a 5.

$=\frac{4}{1}\times\frac{2}{3}$ Multiply across the top and bottom.

$=\frac{8}{3}$

5. Answer: $\frac{3}{4}$.

$\frac{1}{2}\left(\frac{8}{9}+\frac{11}{18}\right)$ Start inside the parentheses. The LCD is 18.

$=\frac{1}{2}\left(\frac{16}{18}+\frac{11}{18}\right)$ Now add the numerators.

$=\frac{1}{2}\left(\frac{27}{18}\right)$ Cancel out a 9.

$=\frac{1}{2}\left(\frac{3}{2}\right)$ Multiply across the top and bottom.

$=\frac{3}{4}$

You could also distribute first.

$\frac{1}{2}\left(\frac{8}{9}+\frac{11}{18}\right)$ Multiply the terms in the parentheses by $\frac{1}{2}$

$=\frac{1}{2}\left(\frac{8}{9}\right)+\frac{1}{2}\left(\frac{11}{18}\right)$ Multiply the denominators by 2.

$=\frac{8}{18}+\frac{11}{36}$ Now the LCD is 36.

$=\frac{16}{36}+\frac{11}{36}$ Add the numerators.

$=\frac{27}{36}$ Cancel out a 9.

$=\frac{3}{4}$

6. Answer: $\frac{15}{56}$.

$\frac{1}{3}\times\frac{5}{8}\times\frac{9}{7}$ Cancel out a 3.

$=\frac{1}{1}\times\frac{5}{8}\times\frac{3}{7}$ Multiply across the top and bottom.

$=\frac{15}{56}$

FRACTION DRILL

_____ **1.** $\dfrac{7}{2} + \dfrac{5}{6} =$

_____ **2.** $\dfrac{13}{8} - \dfrac{2}{3} =$

_____ **3.** $\dfrac{3}{4} \times \dfrac{2}{3} =$

_____ **4.** $\dfrac{4}{5} \div \dfrac{3}{10} =$

_____ **5.** $\dfrac{1}{2}\left(\dfrac{8}{9} + \dfrac{11}{18}\right) =$

_____ **6.** $\dfrac{1}{3} \times \dfrac{5}{8} \times \dfrac{9}{7} =$

_____ 7. $\dfrac{\dfrac{2}{3}+\dfrac{3}{5}}{\dfrac{1}{3}} =$

_____ 9. Steve is trying to plan his monthly budget. He plans to use one fourth of his income on rent, one fourth on shoes, one sixth on hair products, and the rest on food. What fraction of his income is left to spend on food?

_____ 8. Bruiser is planning his budget. Daddy Woods gives him an allowance of $200 a month. If he spends one half of his allowance on candy, one quarter on ice cream, and one fifth on dental care, what fraction of his allowance did he spend?

_____ 10. Sweetie and Cutie are making horse treats for the annual pony show. They have a recipe that calls for: $1\dfrac{1}{2}$ cups of oats, $\dfrac{3}{4}$ cup of apples, $2\dfrac{1}{4}$ cups of hay, and $\dfrac{1}{2}$ cup of carrots. After mixing all the ingredients together, carrots make up what fraction of the mix?

7. **Answer:** $\frac{19}{5}$ or $3\frac{4}{5}$.

$$\frac{\frac{2}{3}+\frac{3}{5}}{\frac{1}{3}}$$ Re-write horizontally.

$$=\left(\frac{2}{3}+\frac{3}{5}\right)\div\frac{1}{3}$$ Flip the second fraction and multiply.

$$=\left(\frac{2}{3}+\frac{3}{5}\right)\times\frac{3}{1}$$ The LCD in the parentheses is 15.

$$=\left(\frac{10}{15}+\frac{9}{15}\right)\times\frac{3}{1}$$ Add the numerators in the parentheses.

$$=\left(\frac{19}{15}\right)\times\frac{3}{1}$$ Cancel out a 3.

$$=\left(\frac{19}{5}\right)\times\frac{1}{1}=\frac{19}{5}$$

Again, you could distribute into the parentheses first, if you prefer.

$$=\left(\frac{2}{3}+\frac{3}{5}\right)\times\frac{3}{1}$$ Multiply each term by $\frac{3}{1}$.

$$=\left(\frac{2}{3}\right)\frac{3}{1}+\left(\frac{3}{5}\right)\frac{3}{1}$$ Simplify & multiply across.

$$=\frac{2}{1}+\frac{9}{5}$$ The LCD is 5.

$$=\frac{10}{5}+\frac{9}{5}$$ Add the numerators.

$$=\frac{19}{5}$$

8. **Answer:** $\frac{19}{20}$.

Start with $200.

One half was spent on candy: $\frac{1}{2}(200)=\$100$

One quarter on ice cream: $\frac{1}{4}(200)=\$50$

One fifth on dental care: $\frac{1}{5}(200)=\$40$

How much did he spend in all: $=\$190$

He started with $200, so the fraction he spent is:

$$\frac{190}{200}=\frac{19}{20}.$$

You could also add the fractions directly:

$$\frac{1}{2}+\frac{1}{4}+\frac{1}{5}=\frac{3}{4}+\frac{1}{5}=\frac{15}{20}+\frac{4}{20}=\frac{19}{20}$$

9. **Answer:** $\frac{1}{3}$.

Two options here. You could add the fractions together:

$$\frac{1}{4}+\frac{1}{4}+\frac{1}{6}$$ LCD is 12.

$$\frac{3}{12}+\frac{3}{12}+\frac{2}{12}$$ Add the numerators.

$$=\frac{8}{12}$$ Cancel out a 4.

$$=\frac{2}{3}$$ Don't stop!

You're not done! That's how much he *spent*. We want the fraction that he *has left*. To find that, subtract from 1.

$$1-\frac{2}{3}=\frac{3}{3}-\frac{2}{3}=\frac{1}{3}$$

Or, you could **Plug In**. Say his income is **$600**.

He spends one fourth on rent:	$150 on rent.
He spends one fourth on shoes:	$150 on shoes.
He spends one sixth on hair:	$100 on hair.
In total, she spends:	$400 total.

He started with $600. So he has $600 – $400 = $200 remaining.

$$\frac{200}{600}=\frac{2}{6}=\frac{1}{3}$$

10. **Answer:** $\frac{1}{10}$.

It's easy to get confused here, so be careful.

We want to know what fraction of the mix are carrots.

We know they use $\frac{1}{2}$ cup of carrots in the mix. So we need to figure out the total number of cups in the mix.

$1\frac{1}{2}$ cup oats, $\frac{3}{4}$ cup apples, $2\frac{1}{4}$ cup hay, and $\frac{1}{2}$ cup carrots.

$$\frac{3}{2}+\frac{3}{4}+\frac{9}{4}+\frac{1}{2}$$ LCD is 4.

$$\frac{6}{4}+\frac{3}{4}+\frac{9}{4}+\frac{2}{4}$$ Add the numerators.

$$\frac{20}{4}$$ Cancel out a 4.

5 cups total. They use $\frac{1}{2}$ cup of carrots in the mix:

$$\frac{\frac{1}{2}}{5}=\frac{1}{2}\div\frac{5}{1}=\frac{1}{2}\times\frac{1}{5}=\frac{1}{10}$$

Ratio Drill

1. Answer: 3:2.

$$\frac{24 \text{ boys}}{16 \text{ girls}}$$ Cancel out an 8.

$$= \frac{3}{2}$$

2. Answer: 20.

$$\frac{x \text{ filling}}{12 \text{ crust}} = \frac{5 \text{ filling}}{3 \text{ crust}}$$

$$3x = 60$$

$$x = \textbf{20 cups of filling}$$

Or you can see that $12 = 3 \times 4$, thus $x = 5 \times 4 = \textbf{20}$.

3. Answer: 25.

$$\frac{x \text{ sodas}}{20 \text{ hot dogs}} = \frac{5 \text{ sodas}}{4 \text{ hot dogs}}$$

$$4x = 100$$

$$x = \textbf{25 sodas}$$

Or you can see that $20 = 4 \times 5$, thus $x = 5 \times 5 = \textbf{25}$.

4. Answer: 12.

$$\frac{x \text{ llamas}}{28 \text{ animals}} = \frac{3 \text{ llamas}}{4 \text{ goats}}$$ ✗ We want animals on the bottom.

$$\frac{x \text{ llamas}}{28 \text{ animals}} = \frac{3 \text{ llamas}}{7 \text{ animals}}$$

$$7x = 84$$

$$x = \textbf{12 llamas}$$

Or you can see that $28 = 7 \times 4$, thus $x = 3 \times 4 = \textbf{12}$.

5. Answer: 15.

$$\frac{x \text{ magazines}}{40 \text{ items}} = \frac{5 \text{ books}}{3 \text{ magazines}}$$ ✗ Units don't match!

$$\frac{x \text{ magazines}}{40 \text{ items}} = \frac{3 \text{ magazines}}{8 \text{ items}}$$

$$8x = 120$$

$$x = \textbf{15 magazines}$$

Or you can see that $40 = 8 \times 5$, thus $x = 3 \times 5 = \textbf{15}$.

6. Answer: 16.

$$\frac{x}{y} = \frac{6}{9} = \frac{x}{24}$$

$$144 = 9x$$

$$\textbf{16} = x$$

RATIO DRILL

_____1. In Jackson Middle School's 8th grade class, there are 24 boys and 16 girls. What is the ratio of boys to girls in the class? (Remember to simplify!)

_____4. At Pablo's Perfect Petting Zoo, Pablo keeps llamas and goats. There are 3 llamas for every 4 goats. If there are 28 animals, how many llamas does Pablo have?

_____2. A certain recipe for apple pie calls for 3 cups of crust for every 5 cups of filling. If you use 12 cups of crust, how many cups of filling do you need?

_____5. Bob's Bookstore stocks books and magazines in a 5 to 3 ratio. If this week Bob stocked 40 total items, how many magazines did he stock?

_____3. For every 4 hot dogs he eats, Fat Sal drinks 5 Big Sip soda pops. If Fat Sal ate 20 hot dogs on Tuesday, how many sodas did he drink?

_____6. If x is directly proportional to y and $x = 6$ when $y = 9$, what is x when $y = 24$?

_____ 7. Terry's truck has a 20-gallon gas tank. On a full tank, Terry can drive 375 miles. How many tankfuls of gas would Terry need to drive from Boston to Seattle (3000 miles)?

_____ 9. Steve's Grocery Delivery Truck delivers groceries to Sam's Little Grocery Store, and each shipment contains meat, dairy, and produce in a 1:5:10 ratio by weight. If this week's delivery weighs 480 pounds, how many pounds of dairy does it contain?

_____ 8. 20% of the employees at a company are single, childless, and lonely. Of the rest, half are married with children, and half are married without children. What is the ratio of employees with children to employees without children?

_____ 10. A certain type of cotton gin working at a constant rate will separate 3 bushels of cotton in 2 hours. If 3 of these cotton gins work simultaneously, how long, in hours, will it take them to separate 36 bushels of cotton?

7.   Answer: 8.

Two routes here.

First, use the gallons:miles ratio we're given.

$$\frac{x \text{ gallons}}{3000 \text{ miles}} = \frac{20 \text{ gallons}}{375 \text{ miles}}$$

$375x = 60{,}000$
$x = 160$ gallons.

Now how many tanks are 160 gallons?
$160 \div 20 =$ **8 tanks**

Or: ignore gallons of gas altogether and find the tanks directly.
We know *one tank* takes us 375 miles.

$$\frac{x \text{ tanks}}{3000 \text{ miles}} = \frac{1 \text{ tank}}{375 \text{ miles}}$$

$375x = 3000$
$x =$ **8 tanks**

9.   Answer: 150.

We want the dairy for 480 total pounds.
We know the ratio of meat:dairy:produce is 1:5:10.
The dairy part is 5, the total is $10 + 5 + 1 = 16$.

$$\frac{x \text{ dairy}}{480 \text{ total}} = \frac{5 \text{ dairy}}{16 \text{ total}}$$

$16x = 2400$
$x =$ **150 lbs.**

8.   Answer: 2:3.

Plug In!
We're dealing with percents, so say there are **100 people** in the company.

20 % are single, so 20 employees are single with no children.
The remaining 80 are married.
Of those 80, half have children, half do not.
So 40 employees are married with children,
and 40 employees are married with no children.

40 have children.
20 singles and 40 marrieds = 60 have no children.

The ratio of children to no children
= 40:60
= 4: 6
= **2: 3**

10.   Answer: 8.

We know we have 3 gins working on 36 bushels.
We know they all work at the same rate and all finish at the same time. So those 36 bushels will be evenly spread out among the 3 gins. So each individual gin will do $36 \div 3 = 12$ bushels.

Now set up the ratio using one gin:

$$\frac{x \text{ hrs}}{12 \text{ bushels}} = \frac{2 \text{ hrs}}{3 \text{ bushels}}$$

$3x = 24$
$x =$ **8 hours**

That first step might have been confusing for some kids. It might be easier to understand once we've finished the calculation above.

If it takes 2 hours for 3 bushels, clearly it will take one gin 8 hours to do 12 bushels.

If you have 3 gins working at the same time, *each* of them will do 12 bushels in that same 8-hr period. So the three of them will together do 36 bushels.

Percent Drill

1. Answer: 27.

$$n = \frac{60}{100} \times 45$$ Reduce the fraction by 20.

$$n = \frac{3}{5} \times 45$$ Cancel out a 5.

$$n = 3 \times 9$$

$$n = 27$$

4. Answer: 320.

$$16 = \frac{5}{100} \times n$$ Reduce the fraction by 5.

$$16 = \frac{1}{20} \times n$$ Multiply both sides by 20.

$$16 \times 20 = n$$

$$320 = n$$

2. Answer: 75.

$$15 = \frac{20}{100} \times n$$ Reduce the fraction by 20.

$$15 = \frac{1}{5} \times n$$ Multiply both sides by 5.

$$15 \times 5 = n$$

$$75 = n$$

5. Answer: 300.

$$69 = \frac{23}{100} \times n$$ Multiply both sides by 100 and divide by 23 simultaneously

$$(69) \times \left(\frac{100}{23}\right) = n$$ Cancel out a 23.

$$3 \times 100 = n$$

$$300 = n$$

3. Answer: 60.

$$45 = \frac{n}{100} \times 75$$ Cancel out a 25.

$$45 = \frac{n}{4} \times 3$$ Divide both sides by 3.

$$15 = \frac{n}{4}$$ Multiply both sides by 4.

$$60 = n$$

6. Answer: 18.

$$n = \frac{50}{100} \times \frac{15}{100} \times 240$$ Reduce the first fraction by 50.

$$n = \frac{1}{2} \times \frac{15}{100} \times 240$$ Reduce the second fraction by 5.

$$n = \frac{1}{2} \times \frac{3}{20} \times 240$$ Cancel out a 2.

$$n = \frac{1}{1} \times \frac{3}{20} \times 120$$ Cancel out a 20.

$$n = \frac{1}{1} \times \frac{3}{1} \times 6$$

$$n = 18$$

PERCENT DRILL

_____ 1.   What is 60 percent of 45?

_____ 4.   16 is 5% of what number?

_____ 2.   15 is 20% of what number?

_____ 5.   69 is 23% of what number?

_____ 3.   45 is what percent of 75?

_____ 6.   What is 50% of 15% of 240?

_____ 7. What is $\frac{1}{2}$ percent of 160?

_____ 9. Timmy earns a 5% commission on every vehicle he sells at Lenny's Lemon Lot. On Friday, he sold a car for $450, a truck for $1,300 and a scooter for $200. How much money in dollars did Timmy earn in commissions on Friday?

_____ 8. Holden goes out to dinner at Salinger's Saloon, and his bill is $36 without a tip. What will his total cost in dollars be if he pays his bill with a 15% tip?

_____ 10. In February, Rosie's Flower shop sold 300 bouquets of roses for $40 each, 250 bunches of tulips for $30 each, and 44 wedding centerpieces at $125 each. In March, Rosie advertised a special St. Patty's Day clover arrangement, and the shop made a total of $30,000 in sales. What was the percent increase in her sales from February to March?

7. **Answer: $\dfrac{4}{5}$ or 0.8.**

Be careful!

$$n = \dfrac{\dfrac{1}{2}}{100} \times 160 \qquad \text{Cancel out a 20.}$$

$$n = \dfrac{\dfrac{1}{2}}{5} \times 8 \qquad \text{Dividing by 5 means multiplying by } \dfrac{1}{5}.$$

$$n = \left(\dfrac{1}{2}\right)\left(\dfrac{1}{5}\right) \times 8 \qquad \text{Multiply the fractions.}$$

$$n = \dfrac{1}{10} \times 8 \qquad \text{Cancel out a 2.}$$

$$n = \dfrac{4}{5}$$

You might be better off using your calculator here:

$$n = \dfrac{\dfrac{1}{2}}{100} \times 160$$

$$n = \dfrac{0.5}{100} \times 160$$

$$n = 0.005 \times 160$$

$$\mathbf{n = 0.8}$$

8. **Answer: $41.40.**

What is 15% of 36?
$0.15 \times 36 = $5.40.$ Now add that to the original bill.
$$36 + $5.40 = \mathbf{\$41.40}$$

You could also do this in one step by taking 115% of 36:

$$n = \dfrac{115}{100} \times 36$$

$$n = 1.15 \times 36$$

$$\mathbf{n = \$41.40}$$

9. **Answer: $97.50.**

Total sales: $450 + $1300 + $200 = $1950.
What is 5% of $1,950?
$0.05 \times 1950 = \mathbf{\$97.50}$

You could also take the percents first and then add.

0.05×450	= $22.50
0.05×1300	= $65.00
0.05×200	= $10.00
Total commissions	**= $97.50**

10. **Answer: 20%.**

First find the total sales for February.

300 roses	× $40 each	= $12,000
250 tulips	× $30 each	= $7,500
44 centerpieces	× $125 each	= $5,500
Total sales		= $25,000

In March, the total sales were $30,000.
The amount of the change is what percent of the original?
The change is $5,000. The original is $25,000.

$$\dfrac{5000}{25000} = \dfrac{20}{100} = 0.20 = \mathbf{20\%}$$

Exponent Drill

1. Answer: $8x^5$.

$$\left(4x^2\right)\left(2x^3\right)$$

$$= 8x^{2+3}$$

$$= 8x^5$$

2. Answer: $4x^2$.

$$\frac{12x^4}{3x^2}$$

$$= 4x^{4-2}$$

$$= 4x^2$$

3. Answer: $27x^6$.

$$\left(3x^2\right)^3$$

$$= (3)^3 \times \left(x^2\right)^3$$

$$= 27x^{2\times 3}$$

$$= 27x^6$$

4. Answer: $3x^3$.

$$\frac{15x^{10}}{5x^5 x^2}$$

$$= \frac{15x^{10}}{5x^5 x^2}$$

$$= \frac{3x^{10}}{x^7}$$

$$= 3x^{10-7}$$

$$= 3x^3$$

5. Answer: $5x^{-2}$ or $\dfrac{5}{x^2}$.

$$\left(5x^2\right)\left(x^{-4}\right)$$

$$= 5x^{2+(-4)}$$

$$= 5x^{-2}$$

OR:

$$= \frac{5x^2}{x^4}$$

$$= \frac{5}{x^2}$$

6. Answer: $3x^2$.

$$\left(9x^4\right)^{\frac{1}{2}}$$

$$= (9)^{\frac{1}{2}}\left(x^4\right)^{\frac{1}{2}}$$

$$= \sqrt{9}\left(x^{4\times \frac{1}{2}}\right)$$

$$= 3x^2$$

7. Answer: 2^{7x}.

Put the two terms into the same base by substituting $8 = 2^3$

$$\left(2^x\right)\left(8^{2x}\right)$$

$$= \left(2^x\right)\left(2^3\right)^{2x}$$

$$= \left(2^x\right)\left(2^{3\times 2x}\right)$$

$$= \left(2^x\right)\left(2^{6x}\right)$$

$$= 2^{x+6x}$$

$$= 2^{7x}$$

8. Answer: $14x^6$.

$$\left(2x^2\right)^3 + 3x\left(2x^5\right)$$

$$= (2)^3\left(x^2\right)^3 + 6x^{1+5}$$

$$= 8x^{2\times 3} + 6x^6$$

$$= 8x^6 + 6x^6$$

$$= 14x^6$$

9. Answer: $5x$.

$$\left(\frac{(5x)\left(5x^3\right)}{x^2}\right)^{\frac{1}{2}}$$ Combine the terms in the numerator.

$$= \left(\frac{25x^4}{x^2}\right)^{\frac{1}{2}}$$ Combine the x's.

$$= \left(25x^2\right)^{\frac{1}{2}}$$

$$= \sqrt{25x^2}$$

$$= 5x$$

10. Answer: $20x$.

$$\frac{10x^2\left(\dfrac{4x^5}{2x^3} + 6x^2\right)}{4x^3}$$ Simplify the fraction inside the parentheses.

$$= \frac{10x^2\left(2x^2 + 6x^2\right)}{4x^3}$$ Add the terms in the parentheses.

$$= \frac{10x^2\left(8x^2\right)}{4x^3}$$ Multiply the terms in the numerator.

$$= \frac{80x^4}{4x^3}$$ Divide.

$$= 20x$$

EXPONENT DRILL

Simplify the following expressions:

_____ 1. $\left(4x^2\right)\left(2x^3\right)=$

_____ 2. $\dfrac{12x^4}{3x^2}=$

_____ 3. $\left(3x^2\right)^3=$

_____ 4. $\dfrac{15x^{10}}{5x^5x^2}=$

_____ 5. $\left(5x^2\right)\left(x^{-4}\right)=$

_____ 6. $\left(9x^4\right)^{\frac{1}{2}}=$

_____ 7. $\left(2^x\right)\left(8^{2x}\right)=$

_____ 8. $\left(2x^2\right)^3+3x\left(2x^5\right)=$

_____ 9. $\left(\dfrac{(5x)\left(5x^3\right)}{x^2}\right)^{\frac{1}{2}}=$

_____ 10. $\dfrac{10x^2\left(\dfrac{4x^5}{2x^3}+6x^2\right)}{4x^3}=$

ONE-VARIABLE ALGEBRA DRILL

Solve the following equations for <u>all</u> possible solutions.

_____ **1.** $\quad 5x + 3 = 18$

_____ **2.** $\quad 4x - 55 + 3x = 2x$

_____ **3.** $\quad 13 - 3z = 15z + 4$

_____ **4.** $\quad \dfrac{5}{x} = \dfrac{2}{3}$

_____ **5.** $\quad x + 4 > \dfrac{x}{5}$

_____ **6.** $\quad (p + 4)^2 = 36 \text{ and } p > 0$

_____ **7.** $\quad x^2 - x = 0$

_____ **8.** $\quad \dfrac{r}{8} = \dfrac{2}{r}$

_____ **9.** $\quad \sqrt{x + 4} = 9$

_____ **10.** $\quad \dfrac{2(q + 8.5)}{9} = \dfrac{5q + 5}{10}$

One-variable Algebra Drill

1. Answer: 3.

$5x + 3 = 18$
$5x = 15$
$x = 3$

2. Answer: 11.

$4x - 55 + 3x = 2x$
$7x - 55 = 2x$
$-55 = -5x$
$11 = x$

3. Answer: $\dfrac{1}{2}$ **or 0.5**

$13 - 3z = 15z + 4$
$13 = 18z + 4$
$9 = 18z$
$\dfrac{1}{2} = z = 0.5$

4. Answer: $\dfrac{15}{2}$ **or 7.5**

$\dfrac{5}{x} = \dfrac{2}{3}$
$15 = 2x$
$\dfrac{15}{2} = x = 7.5$

5. Answer: $x > -5$

$x + 4 > \dfrac{x}{5}$
$5x + 20 > x$
$20 > -4x$ Watch the sign!
$-5 < x$

You can avoid the sign flip if you try to avoid getting a negative coefficient for x.

$5x + 20 > x$
$4x + 20 > 0$
$4x > -20$
$x > -5$

Note that we want *all* possible solutions in this drill, not a particular possible value of x, so students must answer $x > 5$.

6. Answer: 2.

Don't FOIL it out. Just take the square root of both sides.

$(p + 4)^2 = 36$
$p + 4 = 6$ or $p + 4 = -6$
$p = 2$ $p = -10$ ✗ We know $p > 0$.

7. Answer: 0 or 1.

$x^2 - x = 0$ Factor out an x.
$x(x - 1) = 0$
$x = 0$ or $x - 1 = 0$
                $x = 1$

8. Answer: 4 or –4.

$\dfrac{r}{8} = \dfrac{2}{r}$ Cross multiply.
$r^2 = 16$ Square root both sides.
$r = 4$ or   **$r = -4$**

9. Answer: 77.

$\sqrt{x + 4} = 9$ Square both sides.
$x + 4 = 81$
$x = 77$

10. Answer: 5.

$\dfrac{2(q + 8.5)}{9} = \dfrac{5q + 5}{10}$

$\dfrac{2q + 17}{9} = \dfrac{5(q + 1)}{10}$

$\dfrac{2q + 17}{9} = \dfrac{q + 1}{2}$

$2(2q + 17) = 9(q + 1)$
$4q + 34 = 9q + 9$
$34 = 5q + 9$
$25 = 5q$
$5 = q$

Multi-variable Algebra Drill

1. **Answer:** $x = \dfrac{y-6}{5}$.

$y = 5x + 6$
$y - 6 = 5x$

$\dfrac{y-6}{5} = x$

2. **Answer:** $m = 4n + 27$.

$\dfrac{m-15}{4} = n + 3$

$m - 15 = 4(n + 3)$
$m - 15 = 4n + 12$
$m = 4n + 27$

3. **Answer:** -20.
Set the two equations equal to each other.
$z = 10 + 2x \qquad\qquad z = x - 5$

$10 + 2x = x - 5$
$10 + x = -5$
$x = -15.$ Don't stop! We want z.

$z = x - 5$
$z = -15 - 5$
$z = -20$

4. **Answer:** $x = 23 - 5y$.
Solve the second equation for t.
$y = 2 - t$
$y + t = 2$
$t = 2 - y$

Now substitute that for t in the first equation.
$x = 5t + 13.$
$x = 5(2 - y) + 13$
$x = 10 - 5y + 13$
$x = 23 - 5y$

5. **Answer:** $u = \dfrac{3v + 8}{4}$.

Substitute the first equation into the second for t.
$t = 4u - 24 \qquad\qquad 3v - t = 16$

$3v - (4u - 24) = 16$ Watch the parentheses!
$3v - 4u + 24 = 16$ Now solve for u.
$3v + 24 = 16 + 4u$
$3v + 8 = 4u$

$\dfrac{3v + 8}{4} = u$

6. **Answer:** $j = n + 4$.
Take them one at a time.
$j = k + 1$ Let's get rid of that k.

$k + 2 = m$ Solve for k.
$k = m - 2$ Stick this in the first equation.

$j = (m - 2) + 1$
$j = m - 1$ Now let's get rid of the m.
$m - 5 = n$ Solve for m.
$m = n + 5$ Stick this in the first equation for m.

$j = (n + 5) - 1$
$j = n + 4$

MULTI-VARIABLE ALGEBRA DRILL

_____ **1.** If $y = 5x + 6$, then what is x in terms of y?

_____ **4.** If $x = 5t + 13$ and $y = 2 - t$, then what is x in terms of y?

_____ **2.** If $\dfrac{m - 15}{4} = n + 3$, then what is m in terms of n?

_____ **5.** If $t = 4u - 24$ and $3v - t = 16$, then what is u in terms of v?

_____ **3.** If $z = 10 + 2x$ and $z = x - 5$, then $z = ?$

_____ **6.** If $j = k + 1$, $k + 2 = m$, and $m - 5 = n$, then what is j in terms of n?

_____ 7. If $2x + 3y = 31$ and $x - 2y = 5$, then what is the value of y?

_____ 9. If $z = 3x^2$ and $x = y + 5$, then what is z in terms of y?

_____ 8. If $3a + b = 12$ and $\dfrac{2a + 2b}{3} = 12$, then what are the values of a and b?

_____ 10. If $a = bc$, $d = b - 5$, and $c = d - 3$, then what is a in terms of d?

7. Answer: 3.
Solve the second equation for x.
$x - 2y = 5$
$x = 5 + 2y$ Stick that in the first equation.

$2x + 3y = 31$
$2(5 + 2y) + 3y = 31$
$10 + 4y + 3y = 31$
$10 + 7y = 31$
$7y = 21$
$y = 3$

You could also solve them more directly. Multiply the second
equation by -2 and add the equations:
$$
\begin{array}{rcr}
2x + 3y = & & 31 \\
-2x + 4y = & & -10 \\
\hline
7y = & & 21 \\
y = & & 3
\end{array}
$$

9. Answer: $z = 3y^2 + 30y + 75$
Substitute the second equation into the first for x.
$z = 3x^2$
$x = y + 5$
$z = 3(y + 5)^2$
$z = 3(y + 5)(y + 5)$
$z = 3(y^2 + 10y + 25)$
$z = 3y^2 + 30y + 75$

8. Answer: $a = -3$, $b = 21$.
Solve the first equation for b.
$3a + b = 12$
$b = 12 - 3a$ Stick this in the second equation for b.

$\dfrac{2a + 2b}{3} = 12$

$\dfrac{2a + 2(12 - 3a)}{3} = 12$

$\dfrac{2a + 24 - 6a}{3} = 12$

$\dfrac{24 - 4a}{3} = 12$

$24 - 4a = 36$
$-4a = 12$
$a = -3$ We're not done. We need b, too.

$3a + b = 12$
$3(-3) + b = 12$
$-9 + b = 12$
$b = 21$

10. Answer: $a = d^2 + 2d - 15$
$d = b - 5$ Solve for b.
$d + 5 = b$ Substitute this into the first equation for b.

We already have an expression for c:
$c = d - 3$ Substitute this into the first equation for c.

$a = bc$
$a = (d + 5)(d - 3)$ Now FOIL.
$a = d^2 + 2d - 15$

F(x) Drill

1. Answer: 22.

$f(5) = 6(5) - 8$

$f(5) = 30 - 8$

$f(5) = 22$

2. Answer: –26.

$f(-3) = 6(-3) - 8$

$f(-3) = -18 - 8$

$f(-3) = -26$

3. Answer: –6.

$f\left(\dfrac{1}{3}\right) = 6\left(\dfrac{1}{3}\right) - 8$

$f\left(\dfrac{1}{3}\right) = 2 - 8$

$f\left(\dfrac{1}{3}\right) = -6$

4. Answer: $12a - 8$.

$f(2a) = 6(2a) - 8$

$f(2a) = 12a - 8$

5. Answer: 52.

$f(3) = w$

$f(3) = 6(3) - 8 = w$

$18 - 8 = w$

$10 = w$

$f(10) = 6(10) - 8$

$f(10) = 60 - 8$

$f(10) = 52$

6. Answer: 9.

$f(c) = 46$

$f(c) = 6c - 8 = 46$

$6c = 54$

$c = 9$

7. Answer: 2.

$2f(d) - 4 = 4$

$2(6d - 8) - 4 = 4$

$12d - 16 - 4 = 4$

$12d - 20 = 4$

$12d = 24$

$d = 2$

Or you could solve for $f(d)$ first:

$2f(d) - 4 = 4$

$2f(d) = 8$

$f(d) = 4$

$6d - 8 = 4$

$6d = 12$

$d = 2$

8. Answer: 5.

$f(z - 2) = 10$

$6(z - 2) - 8 = 10$

$6z - 12 - 8 = 10$

$6z - 20 = 10$

$6z = 30$

$z = 5$

9. Answer: 56.

$g(8) = 8^2 - 8$

$g(8) = 64 - 8$

$g(8) = 56$

10. Answer: 12.

$g(-3) = (-3)^2 - (-3)$

$g(-3) = 9 + 3$

$g(-3) = 12$

F(x) DRILL

© A-List Education

Questions 1 to 20 refer to the following functions:

Let $f(x) = 6x - 8$

Let $g(x) = x^2 - x$

_____ 1. $f(5) =$

_____ 2. $f(-3) =$

_____ 3. $f\left(\dfrac{1}{3}\right) =$

_____ 4. $f(2a) =$

_____ 5.   If $f(3) = w$, what is the value of $f(w)$?

_____ 6.   If $f(c) = 46$, what is the value of c ?

_____ 7.   If $2f(d) - 4 = 4$, what is the value of d ?

_____ 8.   If $f(z - 2) = 10$, what is the value of z ?

_____ 9. $g(8) =$

_____ 10. $g(-3) =$

_____ 11. $g\left(\dfrac{1}{2}\right) =$

_____ 12. $g\left(-2x^2\right)=$

_____ 13. $g(x + 4) =$

_____ 14. $3g(5) =$

_____ 15. If $g(q) = 0$, what are the two possible values of q?

_____ 16. If $g(4) = v$, what is the value of $f(v)$?

_____ 17. If $f(-1) = k - 8$, what is the value of $g(k)$?

_____ 18. If $g(3) = 4t$, what is the value of $f(t)$?

_____ 19. If $f(2.5) = m$, what is the value of $g\left(\sqrt{m}\right)$?

_____ 20. If $g(-8) = f(-8) + s$, what is the value of s?

11. **Answer:** $-\dfrac{1}{4}$.

$$g\left(\dfrac{1}{2}\right) = \left(\dfrac{1}{2}\right)^2 - \left(\dfrac{1}{2}\right)$$

$$g\left(\dfrac{1}{2}\right) = \left(\dfrac{1}{4}\right) - \left(\dfrac{1}{2}\right)$$

$$g\left(\dfrac{1}{2}\right) = -\dfrac{1}{4}$$

12. **Answer:** $4x^4 + 2x^2$.

$$g\left(-2x^2\right) = \left(-2x^2\right)^2 - \left(-2x^2\right)$$

$$g\left(-2x^2\right) = 4x^4 + 2x^2$$

13. **Answer:** $x^2 + 7x + 12$.

$$g(x+4) = (x+4)^2 - (x+4)$$

$$g(x+4) = (x+4)(x+4) - x - 4$$

$$g(x+4) = x^2 + 8x + 16 - x - 4$$

$$g(x+4) = x^2 + 7x + 12$$

14. **Answer:** 60.

$$3g(5) = 3\left(5^2 - 5\right)$$

$$3g(5) = 3(25 - 5)$$

$$3g(5) = 3(20)$$

$$3g(5) = \mathbf{60}$$

15. **Answer:** 0 or 1.

$$g(q) = 0$$

$$q^2 - q = 0$$

$$q(q-1) = 0$$

$$\mathbf{q = 0} \qquad \text{or} \qquad q - 1 = 0$$

$$\qquad\qquad\qquad\qquad q = 1$$

16. **Answer:** 64.

$$g(4) = v$$

$$4^2 - 4 = v$$

$$16 - 4 = v$$

$$12 = v$$

$$f(v) = f(12) = 6(12) - 8$$

$$= 72 - 8$$

$$= \mathbf{64}$$

17. **Answer:** 42.

$$f(-1) = k - 8$$

$$6(-1) - 8 = k - 8$$

$$-6 - 8 = k - 8$$

$$-6 = k$$

$$g(-6) = (-6)^2 - (-6)$$

$$= 36 + 6$$

$$= \mathbf{42}$$

18. **Answer:** 1.

$$g(3) = 4t$$

$$3^2 - 3 = 4t$$

$$9 - 3 = 4t$$

$$6 = 4t$$

$$\dfrac{3}{2} = t$$

$$f\left(\dfrac{3}{2}\right) = 6\left(\dfrac{3}{2}\right) - 8$$

$$= 9 - 8$$

$$= \mathbf{1}$$

19. **Answer:** $7 - \sqrt{7}$.

$$f(2.5) = 6(2.5) - 8 = m$$

$$15 - 8 = m$$

$$7 = m$$

$$g\left(\sqrt{m}\right) = g\left(\sqrt{7}\right) = \left(\sqrt{7}\right)^2 - \sqrt{7}$$

$$= 7 - \sqrt{7}$$

20. **Answer:** 128.

$$g(-8) = f(-8) + s$$

$$(-8)^2 - (-8) = 6(-8) - 8 + s$$

$$64 + 8 = -48 - 8 + s$$

$$72 = -56 + s$$

$$\mathbf{128} = s$$

Polynomial Drill

1. **Answer:** $5x^3 + 2x^2 - 6x - 7$.
Combine like terms:

$$\frac{2x^3 + 5x^2 \quad -7x \quad +4 \quad +3x^3 - 3x^2 + x - 11}{}$$
$$5x^3 + 5x^2 \quad -7x \quad +4 \qquad\qquad -3x^2 + x - 11$$
$$5x^3 + 2x^2 \quad \underline{-7x} \quad +4 \qquad\qquad \underline{+x} - 11$$
$$5x^3 + 2x^2 \quad -6x \quad \underline{+4} \qquad\qquad\qquad \underline{-11}$$
$$5x^3 + 2x^2 \quad -6x \quad -7$$

2. **Answer:** $-10x^3 - 6x^2 + 7x + 11$
First, distribute the negative across the parentheses:

$$(-9x^3 + 3x + 5) - (x^3 + 6x^2 - 4x - 6)$$
$$-9x^3 + 3x + 5 - x^3 - 6x^2 + 4x + 6$$

Now combine like terms:

$$\frac{-9x^3 + 3x + 5 \quad -x^3 - 6x^2 + 4x + 6}{}$$
$$-10x^3 + 3x + 5 \qquad\qquad -6x^2 + 4x + 6$$
$$-10x^3 - 6x^2 + \underline{3x} + 5 \qquad\qquad \underline{+4x} + 6$$
$$-10x^3 - 6x^2 + 7x \quad \underline{+5} \qquad\qquad \underline{+6}$$
$$-10x^3 - 6x^2 + 7x \quad +11$$

3. **Answer:** $x^2 + 7x + 12$
FOIL:
$$(x + 3)(x + 4)$$
$$x^2 + 4x + 3x + 12$$
$$x^2 + 7x + 12$$

4. **Answer:** $x^2 - 4x - 5$
FOIL:
$$(x - 5)(x + 1)$$
$$x^2 + x - 5x - 5$$
$$x^2 - 4x - 5$$

5. **Answer:** $15x^2 - 26x + 8$
FOIL:
$$(3x - 4)(5x - 2)$$
$$15x^2 - 6x - 20x + 8$$
$$15x^2 - 26x + 8$$

POLYNOMIAL DRILL

Simplify the following expressions:

_____ **1.** $\quad 2x^3 + 5x^2 - 7x + 4 + 3x^3 - 3x^2 + x - 11 = ?$

Answer: _____

_____ **2.** $\quad (-9x^3 + 3x + 5) - (x^3 + 6x^2 - 4x - 6) = ?$

Answer: _____

Multiply the following expressions:

_____ **3.** $\quad (x + 3)(x + 4) = ?$

Answer: _____

_____ **4.** $\quad (x - 5)(x + 1) = ?$

Answer: _____

_____ **5.** $\quad (3x - 4)(5x - 2) = ?$

Answer: _____

Factor the following expressions:

_____ **6.** $x^2 - x - 2 = ?$

Answer: _____

Simplify the following expression (when x is defined):

_____ **9.** $\dfrac{x^2 - 3x - 10}{x + 2} = ?$

Answer: _____

_____ **7.** $x^2 - 8x + 12 = ?$

Answer: _____

_____ **10.**   What are the solutions for
             $x^2 + 14x + 48 = 0$?

Answer: _____

_____ **8.** $x^2 - 16 = ?$

Answer: _____

6. **Answer: $(x-2)(x+1)$**

Factoring is the reverse of FOIL, so we want to turn this into the product of two binomials.

In the expression $x^2 - x - 2$, the last term, -2, will be the product of the numbers in the binomials, and the coefficient of the middle term, $-x$, will be the sum.

Start with the last term. The two numbers in the binomials will have a product of -2.
What are the factors of -2?
Either -2×1 or 2×-1.
The middle term is $-x$, so our terms must add up to -1.

$$-2 + 1 = -1 \checkmark \qquad 2 + (-1) = 1 \text{ ✗}$$

So our factors are $(x-2)(x+1)$

7. **Answer: $(x-6)(x-2)$**

The last term, 12, is positive, but the middle term, $-8x$, is negative. That means that in our binomials, *both* last numbers will be negative. Their sum will be negative but their product will be positive.
What are the negative factors of 12?

Factors	Sum
$-12, -1$	$-12 - 1 = -13$ ✗
$-6, -2$	**$-6 - 2 = -8$** $\checkmark$
$-3, -4$	$-3 - 4 = -7$ ✗

So our factors are $(x-6)(x-2)$

8. **Answer: $(x+4)(x-4)$**

It's the difference of squares!

9. **Answer: $x - 5$**

Let's try to factor the numerator, using the denominator as one of the factors.

$$x^2 - 3x - 10 = (x+a)(x+2)$$

The numerator has a last term of -10 and the denominator has a last term of 2.

$$2 \times a = -10$$
$$a = -5$$

So:

$$\frac{x^2 - 3x - 10}{x+2} = \frac{(x-5)(x+2)}{x+2} \qquad \text{The } (x+2)\text{'s cancel out.}$$
$$= x - 5$$

10. **Answer: $x = -6$ and $x = -8$**

To find the solution of a quadratic equation, first factor it.

$$x^2 + 14x + 48 = 0$$

We want two numbers whose product is 48 and whose sum is 14:

$$(x+6)(x+8) = 0 \qquad \text{Don't stop!}$$
$$x + 6 = 0 \quad \text{or} \quad x + 8 = 0$$
$$\mathbf{x = -6} \quad \textbf{or} \quad \mathbf{x = -8}$$

Solve Directly for Expressions

1. Answer: 64.
Double the first equation to get $6x - 20$.

$$3x - 10 = 32$$
$$6x - 20 = 64$$

4. Answer: 46.
Use the identity $(x + y)^2 = x^2 + y^2 + 2xy$

$$(x + y)^2 = x^2 + y^2 + 2xy$$
$$x^2 + y^2 = 36 \qquad xy = 5$$
$$(x + y)^2 = 36 + 2(5)$$
$$(x + y)^2 = 36 + 10$$
$$(x + y)^2 = \mathbf{46}$$

2. Answer: 23.
Add the equations to get $5x + 3y$.

$$
\begin{array}{r}
2x + 5y = 11 \\
+ \quad 3x - 2y = 12 \\
\hline
5x + 3y = 23
\end{array}
$$

5. Answer: 18.
FOIL the equation:
$(3x - 3)(3x + 3) = 9$ It's the difference of squares identity.
$9x^2 - 9 = 9$ Add 9 to both sides.
$9x^2 = \mathbf{18}$ Stop! That's what we're looking for.

3. Answer: 24.
Add all three equations together.

$$
\begin{array}{r}
a + b \qquad = 9 \\
b + c = 22 \\
+ \quad a \qquad + c = 17 \\
\hline
2a + 2b + 2c = 48 \\
a + b + c = 24
\end{array}
$$

Now divide by 2.

SOLVE DIRECTLY FOR EXPRESSIONS

_____ **1.** If $3x - 10 = 32$, then $6x - 20 = ?$

_____ **2.** If $2x + 5y = 11$ and $3x - 2y = 12$, what is the value of $5x + 3y$?

$$a + b = 9$$
$$b + c = 22$$
$$a + c = 17$$

_____ **3.** Given the equations above, what is the value of the sum of a, b, and c?

_____ **4.** If $x^2 + y^2 = 36$ and $xy = 5$, what is the value of $(x + y)^2$?

_____ **5.** If $(3x - 3)(3x + 3) = 9$, what is the value of $9x^2$?

_____ **6.** If $(x + y)(x - y) = 4$, what is the value of $(2x + 2y)(2x - 2y)$?

_____ **7.** If $\dfrac{x^2 y}{2x} = 2$ and $x \neq 0$, what is the value of xy ?

_____ **8.** If $a^2 + b^2 = c + 5$, $ab = c - 5$, and $c > 0$, what is $(a + b)^2$ in terms of c ?

_____ **9.** If $\dfrac{a + 2b}{b} = \dfrac{8}{3}$ and $b \neq 0$, what is the value of $\dfrac{a}{b}$?

_____ **10.** If $b = a + 3c$ and $a + 2b + 3c = 12$, $b = $?

6. Answer: 16.

It's tempting to say that the expression we want is just double the given equation, thus it's $2 \times 4 = 8$.

But the expression is actually **four times** the given equation.

$(2x + 2y)$ is double $(x + y)$ AND

$(2x - 2y)$ is double $(x - y)$

$$(2x + 2y)(2x - 2y)$$
$$= 2(x + y) \times 2(x - y)$$
$$= 4 \times (x + y)(x - y)$$
$$= 4 \times 4 = \mathbf{16.}$$

This may be easier to see if you FOIL out the terms.

$(x + y)(x - y) = 4$	Use the difference of squares identity.
$x^2 + y^2 = 4$	

$(2x + 2y)(2x - 2y)$	Again, the difference of squares
$= 4x^2 + 4y^2$	Factor out a 4.
$= 4 \times (x^2 + y^2)$	Substitute $x^2 + y^2 = 4$.
$= 4 \times 4$	
$= \mathbf{16}$	

7. Answer: 4.

We want xy. The fraction *almost* has xy in the numerator, but it has one x too many. But we can cancel out an x.

$\dfrac{x^2 y}{2x} = 2$	There's an x on the top and bottom.
$\dfrac{xy}{2} = 2$	Multiply by 2.
$xy = 4$	

8. Answer: 3c − 5.

The identity tells us that $(a + b)^2 = a^2 + b^2 + 2ab$.

Substitute the equations into this expression.

$$(a + b)^2 = a^2 + b^2 + 2ab$$
$$a^2 + b^2 = c + 5 \qquad ab = c - 5$$
$$(a + b)^2 = (c + 5) + 2(c - 5)$$
$$(a + b)^2 = c + 5 + 2c - 10$$
$$(a + b)^2 = \mathbf{3c - 5}$$

9. Answer: $\dfrac{2}{3}$.

We want $\dfrac{a}{b}$. Let's try to play with the given equation to get that.

$\dfrac{a + 2b}{b} = \dfrac{8}{3}$	Split the left side into two fractions.
$\dfrac{a}{b} + \dfrac{2b}{b} = \dfrac{8}{3}$	Cancel out the b's in the second fraction.
$\dfrac{a}{b} + 2 = \dfrac{8}{3}$	Subtract 2.
$\dfrac{a}{b} = \dfrac{8}{3} - 2$	
$\dfrac{a}{b} = \dfrac{8}{3} - \dfrac{6}{3}$	
$\dfrac{a}{b} = \dfrac{2}{3}$	

10. Answer: 4.

We know $b = a + 3c$. Let's look at the other equation and look for similarities.

$a + 2b + 3c = 12$	Switch the order of terms
$a + 3c + 2b = 12$	Hey, we know $a + 3c = b$! Substitute!
$b + 2b = 12$	
$3b = 12$	
$b = 4$	

Graphing Drill

Since you're going to have to look up a lot of points, it may help to write the numbers along the axes to make the lookup go more quickly.

1. Answer: 4.
The point (–4, 4) is on the graph of f.
$f(-4) = 4$

2. Answer: 8.
The point (5, 1) is on the graph of f.
$f(5) = 1$
$f(5) + 7 = 8$

3. Answer: –6.
The point (3, –1) is on the graph of f.
$f(3) = -1$

$4f(3) - 2 = 4(-1) - 2$
$= -4 - 2$
$= -6$

4. Answer: –6 or –2.
$f(b) = 5$, so we want to find a point on the graph of f with a y-value of 5.
There are two such points: (–6, 5) and (–2, 5)
So $b = -6$ or $b = -2$.

It may be difficult to see that (–2, 5) is on the graph of f. Clearly the graph touches $y = 5$ somewhere around there, but it's a bit hard to tell. That's okay, though, because we only need one possible value for b, and $b = -6$ clearly works.

5. Answer: 0.
The point (1, 0) is on the graph of f.
$f(1) = 0$
Therefore $k = 0$

6. Answer: $1 < x < 4$
Look at the picture.
The graph of f crosses the x-axis at (1, 0) and again at (4, 0). All y-values between those points are negative, and all values on either side of that range are positive.
So f is negative when $1 < x < 4$

7. Answer: 3.
Draw a line across $y = 4$ and see how many places it crosses the graph of f.

It crosses **three times**. So there are 3 values of $f(x)$ that equal 4.

Note that we're not asked to actually *find* those values of x. We can see the points (–4, 4) and (–1, 4) fairly easily, but the third point is somewhere around (–5.8, 4) or so. Just because it doesn't come out to an integer I can easily find doesn't mean there isn't a solution for $f(x) = 4$ there.

8. Answer: C.
The point (4, 0) is on the graph of f, so $f(4) = 0$.
$f(p) = 0$. What other values of x give a y-value of 0?
(Hint: the graph has a y-value of 0 at the place where it crosses the x-axis.)
When $x = 1$. **That's choice C).**

You could also do some *Backsolve* and find the y-values for each of the x-values in the choices.

A) $f(-4) = 4$ ✗
B) $f(0) = 2$ ✗
C) $f(1) = 0$ ✓
D) $f(3) = 1$ ✗

9. Answer: 4.
Don't freak out because $g(x)$ doesn't appear in the picture. This is pure substitution. We want $g(1)$, so plug in 1 for x:

$g(x) = f(x - 2)$
$g(1) = f(1 - 2)$
$g(1) = f(-1)$.   Aha! Now we just need to find $f(-1)$.

The point (–1, 4) is on the graph of f.
$f(-1) = 4$

10. Answer: 7.
Again, just substitute. Plug in –2 for x:
$h(x) = f(2x) + 3$
$h(-2) = f(2(-2)) + 3$
$= f(-4) + 3$ According to the graph, $f(-4) = 4$
$= 4 + 3$
$= 7$

GRAPHING DRILL

Questions 1 through 10 refer to the figure below:

The function f graphed above is defined for −6 < x < 6.

_____ **1.** What is the value of $f(-4)$?

_____ **2.** What is the value of $f(5) + 7$?

_____ **3.** What is the value of $4f(3) - 2$?

_____ **4.** If $f(b) = 5$, what is one possible value of b?

_____ **5.** If $f(1) = k$, what is the value of k?

_____ **6.** For what values of x is $f(x)$ negative?

_____ **7.** For how many different values of x does $f(x) = 4$?

_____ **8.** If $f(p) = f(4)$, which of the following could be p?

    A)   −4
    B)   0
    C)   1
    D)   3

_____ **9.** If $g(x) = f(x - 2)$, what is the value of $g(1)$?

_____ **10.** If $h(x) = f(2x) + 3$, what is the value of $h(-2)$

Questions 11 through 20 refer to the figure below:

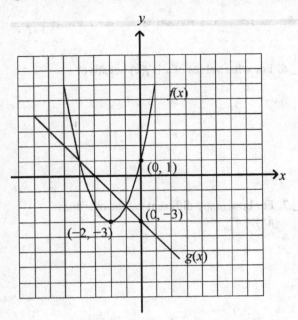

_____ 11. What is the value of $f(-3)$?

_____ 12. What is the value of $f(1) + g(-5)$?

_____ 13. What is the value of $f(-2) - g(2)$?

_____ 14. If $f(a) = 1$, what could be the value of a?

_____ 15. If $f(-4) = -k$, what is the value of $g(k)$?

_____ 16. If $g(0) = m$, what is the value of $f(m) + 6$?

_____ 17. What is the slope of the graph of $g(x)$?

_____ 18. If $f(r) = -3$, what is the value of $g(r)$?

_____ 19. What are all values of x between -7 and 2 for which $f(x) \leq g(x)$?

_____ 20. Which of the following could be the equation of the graph of $f(x)$?

A) $f(x) = -x^2 - 4x + 1$

B) $f(x) = x^2 + 4x + 1$

C) $f(x) = x^2 - 2x + 3$

D) $f(x) = x^2 - 6x + 7$

11. **Answer: –2.**
The point $(-3, -2)$ is on the graph of f.
$f(-3) = -2$

12. **Answer: 8.**
The point $(1, 6)$ is on the graph of f.
$f(1) = 6$
The point $(-5, 2)$ is on the graph of g.
$g(-5) = 2$

$f(1) + g(-5) = 6 + 2 = \mathbf{8}$

13. **Answer: 2.**
The point $(-2, -3)$ is on the graph of f.
$f(-2) = -3$
The point $(2, -5)$ is on the graph of g.
$g(2) = -5$

$f(-2) - g(2) = -3 - (-5)$
$= -3 + 5$
$= \mathbf{2}$

14. **Answer: –4 or 0.**
$f(a) = 1$, so we want to find a point on the graph of f with a y-value of 1.
There are two such points: $(-4, 1)$ and $(0, 1)$
So $a = -4$ or $a = 0$.

15. **Answer: –2.**
The point $(-4, 1)$ is on the graph of f.
$f(-4) = 1 = -k$
$-1 = k$.

$g(k) = g(-1)$.
The point $(-1, -2)$ is on the graph of g.
$g(-1) = -2$

16. **Answer: 4.**
The point $(0, -3)$ is on the graph of g. $g(0) = -3$.
$g(0) = m = -3$.

$f(m) = f(-3)$
The point $(-3, -2)$ is on the graph of f.
$f(-3) = -2$.
$f(m) + 6 = f(-3) + 6$
$= -2 + 6$
$= \mathbf{4}$

17. **Answer: –1.**
Pick two points on g: say, $(0, -3)$ and $(1, -4)$.

Slope $= \dfrac{y_2 - y_1}{x_2 - x_1}$

$= \dfrac{-4 - (-3)}{1 - 0}$

$= \dfrac{-4 + 3}{1}$

$= \mathbf{-1}$

Students who have a good intuitive understanding of slope can figure it out just by looking at the picture.
As you go from point to point along g, every time you go right one step, you go down one step. That's a slope of **–1.**

18. **Answer: –1.**
$f(r) = -3$, so we want to find a point on the graph of f with a y-value of -3.
There is only one: $(-2, -3)$. Therefore, $r = -2$.

$g(r) = g(-2)$.
The point $(-2, -1)$ is on the graph of g.
$g(-2) = \mathbf{-1}$.

19. **Answer: $-4 \leq x \leq -1$.**
-7 and 2 are just the edges of the graph we have, so that doesn't tell us anything new.

We want to know when $f(x) \leq g(x)$. That's where the line for g falls **above** the parabola for f.

20. **Answer: B.**
Equations for a parabola like $f(x)$ take the form
$f(x) = ax^2 + bx + c$
We know two things about that equation:
1. The sign of a tells us whether the parabola opens up or down.
2. The value of c is the y-intercept of the parabola.

We know $f(x)$ crosses the y-axis at $(0, 1)$, so its y-intercept is 1. That means that in the equation for $f(x)$, the value of c, the number that doesn't have an x next to it, must be 1.
Eliminate C) and D).

We also know that the parabola opens *upwards*. That means that a, the number next to x^2, must be *positive*. **Eliminate A).**

Our answer must be **choice B).**

You could *Plug In* here. Pick a point on the graph of f. Put the x-value in each of the answer choices and eliminate any that don't give you the correct y-value.

Say $x = 1$. The point $(1,6)$ is on the graph of f, so $f(1) = 6$.
Which choices work? Only B).

A)	$f(1) = -1^2 - 4(1) + 1$	$-1 - 4 + 1$	-4 ✗	
B)	$f(1) = 1^2 + 4(1) + 1$	$1 + 4 + 1$	**6** ✓	**It works!**
C)	$f(1) = 1^2 - 2(1) + 3$	$1 - 2 + 3$	2 ✗	
D)	$f(1) = 1^2 - 6(1) + 7$	$1 - 6 + 7$	2 ✗	

If you have a graphing calculator, you can *Backsolve*. Graph the given equations on your calculator and see which one matches the graph shown.

Average Drill

1. Answer: 25.

How many?	Average	Sum of the terms
5	16	80
− 3	10	− 30
2		50

$$50 \div 2 = \textbf{25}$$

2. Answer: 170.

How many?	Average	Sum of the terms
9	74	666
− 8	62	− 496
1		170

$$170 \div 1 = \textbf{170}$$

3. Answer: 30.

The long way:

$$\frac{5+13+x}{3} = 15$$

$$18 + x = 45$$

$x = 27$ Don't stop! We're not done yet.

$$\frac{10+26+2x}{3}$$

$$= \frac{36+2(27)}{3}$$

$$= \frac{36+54}{3}$$

$$= \frac{90}{3}$$

$$= \textbf{30}$$

OR, the short way:
Notice that 10, 26, and 2x are all double 5, 13, x.
Since each of the terms is doubled, the average will also be doubled.
$15 \times 2 = \textbf{30}$.

4. Answer: 24.

The median is the middle number, so the middle number will be 29.

But wait: we have six numbers, so there is no middle number. If there are an even number of terms, the median will be the average of the two middle terms.

$$\underline{}\quad\underline{}\quad\underline{}\quad\overset{29}{\underline{}}\quad\underline{}\quad\underline{}$$
1   2   3   4   5   6

We also know that all the numbers are consecutive even numbers, meaning that each number is 2 away from the one next to it. The two numbers in the middle must be the even numbers on either side of 29: 28 and 30.

$$\underline{}\quad\underline{}\quad\underset{3}{\underline{28}}\;\;{}_{29}\;\;\underset{4}{\underline{30}}\quad\underline{}\quad\underline{}$$
1   2   3   4   5   6

Now just fill out the rest of the numbers:

$$\underset{1}{\underline{24}}\quad\underset{2}{\underline{26}}\quad\underset{3}{\underline{28}}\;\;{}_{29}\;\;\underset{4}{\underline{30}}\quad\underset{5}{\underline{32}}\quad\underset{6}{\underline{34}}$$

We want the least number. That's **24**.

5. Answer: 300.

Here the "average" is given as "pages per week". That means that the *sum of the terms* will correspond to the *number of pages read* and the *number of terms* will correspond to the number of weeks.

$$\text{Average} = \frac{\text{Sum of terms}}{\text{How many}} = \frac{\text{Pages}}{\text{Week}}$$

How many?	Average	Sum of the terms
6		1200
− 4	150	− 600
2		600

$$600 \div 2 = \textbf{300}.$$

She has 600 pages left to go over the last two weeks. That's an average of 300 per week.

AVERAGE DRILL

_____ 1. There are five numbers whose average is 16. The average of three of the numbers is 10. What is the average of the remaining two numbers?

_____ 2. A certain block on 105th Street has 8 buildings with an average height of 62 feet. After a new building is constructed on a formerly empty lot, the average height of all 9 buildings is now 74 feet. What is the height, in feet, of the new building?

_____ 3. The average of 5, 13, and x is 15. What is the average of 10, 26, and $2x$?

_____ 4. What is the least of six consecutive even integers whose median is 29?

_____ 5. Jenny has six weeks to read a 1,200-page book for a book report. She reads an average of 150 pages per week for the first four weeks. How many pages per week must Jenny read over the last two weeks in order to finish the book?

Number of students	Grade
7	70
5	100
4	90
2	80
1	50
1	60

The table above shows the grades for 20 students who took Monday's geography test in Ms. Frizzle's class. The test was scored on a range from 0 to 100.

_____ 6. What was the mode of the scores on the test?

_____ 7. What was the average (arithmetic mean) score on the test?

_____ 8. What was the median score on the test?

_____ 9. Five students were absent on the day of the test so their grades were not included in the table. When they took the test on Tuesday, they each received a score of 100. What is the new average score for all 25 students in the class?

_____ 10. What is the new median score for all 25 students in the class?

6. **Answer: 70.**

The mode is the term that appears the most frequently.
The grades are actually ordered by frequency in the table, with the most frequent ones at the top.

7 students got a grade of **70**. That's the mode.

7. **Answer: 81.**

The average will be the sum of all scores divided by the number of students.

Don't just take the average of the listed grades: in most cases there were multiple students who got that grade. You have to add up *all* the total points.

You can do that pretty easily directly on the table. Make a new column for the total points. Multiply the grade by the number of students who got that grade to get the total. Then add them all up to get the total for the class:

Number of students	Grade	Total points
7	70	490
5	100	500
4	90	360
2	80	160
1	50	50
1	60	60
20		**1620**

$1620 \div 20 = \mathbf{81}$

8. **Answer: 80.**

The median is the middle number *when all the terms are in order.* Again, don't just look at the table. You've got to put all the terms in order and find the middle number.

Term	1	2	3	4	5	6	7	8	9	10
Grade	50	60	70	70	70	70	70	70	70	80
Term	11	12	13	14	15	16	17	18	19	20
Grade	80	90	90	90	90	100	100	100	100	100

Since there are an even amount of terms, the median will be the average of the two middle terms. That's the 10th and the 11th.

Both the 10th and the 11th are **80**, so that's the median.

(Note that you don't have to literally write them all out. You could just count. It's easier to count down: The 5 highest terms are 100. The next 4 terms are 90. That's already 9 terms. The next two will be the 10th and 11th. Both are **80**.)

9. **Answer: 84.8.**

Don't start from scratch! Use the information we've already seen.

Before, we had 20 students with a total of 1620 points.

We're taking the same data from the table and adding 5 students.
We now have 25 students.
The 5 new students each got a score of 100.
We're adding a total of $5 \times 100 = 500$ points
Our new total is $1620 + 500 = 2120$ points.

	Students	Total points
Original	20	1620
Added	5	500
New total	25	2120

The new average is $2120 \div 25 = \mathbf{84.8}$

Seems kinda fishy, doesn't it? They all were absent and then all five of them get 100's the next day? I think there might have been some foul play involved.

10. **Answer: 90.**

Now that there are 25 students, the median will be the 13th term.

Count them out again:

Term	1	2	3	4	5	6	7	8	9	10	11	12
Grade	50	60	70	70	70	70	70	70	70	80	80	90
Term						13						
Grade						90						
Term	14	15	16	17	18	19	20	21	22	23	24	25
Grade	90	90	100	100	100	100	100	100	100	100	100	100

The new median is **90**.

Angle Drill

1. Answer: 35.
The two angles make a straight line, so their sum is 180°.
$145 + x = 180$
$x = 180 - 145$
$x = 35$

2. Answer: 100.
Since $AB = BC$, the triangle is isosceles and $\angle A = \angle C$.
That means $\angle C = 40$.

The angles in a triangle add up to 180°.
$40 + 40 + x = 180$.
$80 + x = 180$
$x = 100$

3. Answer: 125.
Looking at the bottom four angles, each angle next to the 55° angle will make 180° with it. Each is $180 - 55 = 125$. The angle opposite is a vertical angle, so it is also 55°.

Because $\ell \parallel k$, the four angles at the top will equal their corresponding angles at the bottom. If you like, you can look for the "alternate interior angles"—the angles in the armpits of the Z shape will be equal. Or you can just Guesstimate.

So $x = 125$.

Remember the rules of parallel lines with a transversal: all the big angles are equal, all the little angles are equal, and any big plus any little will equal 180°.

4. Answer: 18.
It's a rectangle, so each of its angles will be 90°.
That means the triangles are right triangles.

The angles of the triangle add up to 180°.
$90 + 72 + x = 180$
$162 + x = 180$
$x = 18$

Or, notice that the sides of a rectangle are parallel. Therefore, alternate interior angles will be equal. That means the angle next to x will be 72°,

The angles in the rectangle are each 90°.
$x + 72 = 90$
$x = 18$

5. Answer: 120.
The angles of the triangle add up to 180°, so the unmarked angle is
$180 - 65 - 55 = 60$.

That angle makes a straight line with x, so they add up to 180°:
$180 - 60 = x$
$120 = x$

6. Answer: 90.
Start with $\triangle ABC$. We know $AB = AC$, so the triangle is isosceles and $\angle ABC = \angle BCA$. Call them each y.
The angles of the triangle add up to 180°, so:
$40 + y + y = 180$
$40 + 2y = 180$
$2y = 140$
$y = 70$.

$\angle BCA$ and $\angle ECD$ are vertical angles, so they are equal. Therefore $\angle ECD = 70$.
The angles of $\triangle CDE$ add up to 180°, so:
$70 + 20 + x = 180$
$90 + x = 180$
$x = 90$

ANGLE DRILL

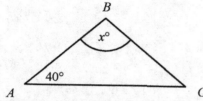

_____ **1.** What is the value of *x*?

_____ **2.** In the figure above, $AB = BC$. What is the value of *x*?

_____ **3.** In the figure above, lines ℓ and k are parallel. What is the value of *x*?

_____ **4.** The figure above shows a rectangle. What is the value of *x*?

_____ **5.** What is the value of *x*?

6. In the figure above, $AB = AC$. What is the value of x?

9. In the figure above, $ABCDE$ is a regular pentagon. What is the value of x?

7. In the figure above, $ABCD$ is a parallelogram. What is the value of x?

10. In the figure above, $BCDG$ is a rectangle and $AF \parallel BE$. If C and F lie on a straight line and $\angle GFE = 115°$, what is the value of x?

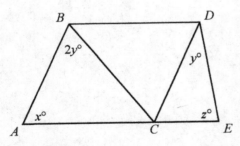

8. In the figure above, $AB \parallel CD$ and $BD \parallel AE$. If $x = 65$ and $y = 35$, what is the value of z?

7. Answer: 25.
The long way:
∠BCD makes a straight line with a 145° angle, so
∠BCD = 180 − 145 = 35°.

The angles of △DBC add up to 180°, so
∠BDC = 180 − 120 − 35
∠BDC = 25°.

ABCD is a parallelogram, so AB ∥ DC. That means ∠ABD and ∠BDC are alternate interior angles. Therefore, they are equal. So **x = 25.**

The faster, harder-to-see way:
As we said, AB ∥ DC. That means that BC is also a transversal intersecting parallel lines, so the 145° angle and ∠ABC are also alternate interior angles.

Therefore:
x + 120 = 145
x = 25

8. Answer: 80.
Write the angles you know into the figure.
The angles of △ABC add up to 180°, so
∠BCA = 180 − 70 − 65 = 45.

BD ∥ AE, so ∠CBD and ∠BCA are alternate interior angles.
So ∠CBD = 45°
AB ∥ CD, so ∠ABC and ∠BCD are alternate interior angles.
So ∠CBD = 70°

AE is a straight line, so ∠ACB, ∠BCD, and ∠DCE make a straight line. Therefore, they add up to 180°
So ∠DCE = 180 − 45 − 70 = 65.
The angles of △CDE add up to 180°:
65 + 35 + z = 180
100 + z = 180
z = 80

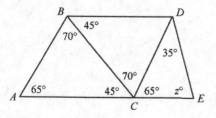

9. Answer: 108.
Several ways to go here.

First, we can split the pentagon into triangles. Be sure to only use the existing angles as vertices of your triangles.
You can get **three triangles.**

Each triangle has 180°, so three triangles would have 3 × 180 = 540°.

The pentagon has 5 angles that add up to 540°. Therefore, each one is 540 ÷ 5 = **108°**

Alternatively, you could split the pentagon up from the middle. This is a bit more intuitive for most kids. This gives you 5 triangles. However, notice that these triangles have an additional 5 angles in the middle that aren't part of the pentagon. So when we add up the angles, we have to subtract those middle angles.

Luckily, those 5 middle angles make a circle, so we know they add up to 360°.

5 × 180 = 900.
900 − 360 = 540.
We still get 540° for the sum of the pentagon's angles.

10. Answer: 60.
Super-fast way that's tough to notice: ACF is a triangle!
We know ∠BAG = 35 and ∠GFE = 115, so ∠BCE = 30.
BCDG is a rectangle, so 30 + x = 90, **x = 60.**

Slightly longer method:
We know BCDG is a rectangle, so ∠ABG = 90°
△ABG is a right triangle, so ∠AGB = 180 − 90 − 35 = 55.

AF is a straight line and ∠BGE is a right angle, so
∠EGF = 180 − 55 − 90 = 35.

We know that ∠GFE = 115, and △GFE is a triangle, so
∠GEF = 30°.
FC is a straight line, GD is a straight line, so ∠GEF and ∠CED are vertical angles. Therefore ∠CED = 30.
△CED adds up to 180, ∠CDE = 90, so **x = 60.**

There are other routes you could take, too. Just start filling in angles until you get to x.

Perimeter, Area, Volume Drill

1. Answer: 3.

Perimeter is the sum of the lengths of the sides.

$P = \ell + \ell + w + w$

$P = 2\ell + 2w$

$20 = 2(7) + 2x$

$20 = 14 + 2x$

$6 = 2x$

$\mathbf{3 = x}$

2. Answer: 22.

Area of a rectangle $= \ell w$

$30 = 5\ell$

$6 = \ell$

$P = 2\ell + 2w$

$P = 2(6) + 2(5)$

$P = 12 + 10$

$\mathbf{P = 22}$

3. Answer: 18.

Area of a triangle $= \dfrac{1}{2}bh$

$A = \dfrac{1}{2}(9)(4)$

$A = \dfrac{1}{2}(36)$

$\mathbf{A = 18}$

4. Answer: 24.

Area of a triangle $= \dfrac{1}{2}bh$. We know the base is 6, but we don't know the height. Use the Pythagorean Theorem to find it.

$a^2 + b^2 = c^2$

$h^2 + 6^2 = 10^2$

$h^2 + 36 = 100$

$h^2 = 64$

$h = 8$.

(You could also notice that it's a 6-8-10 triangle—double a 3-4-5 triangle.)

$A = \dfrac{1}{2}bh$

$A = \dfrac{1}{2}(6)(8)$

$A = 3(8)$

$\mathbf{A = 24}$

5. Answer: $16\sqrt{3}$.

Area of a triangle $= \dfrac{1}{2}bh$. We know the base, AC, is 8, but we don't know the height, BD.

It's an equilateral triangle with side of length 8.
Each of its angles are 60° and ED makes 90° angle with AC.
Therefore, $\angle ABD$ and $\angle DBC$ are each 30°.
Therefore, the two smaller triangles are
30-60-90 triangles.
$AD = DC = 4$ and $BD = 4\sqrt{3}$

$A = \dfrac{1}{2}(8)(4\sqrt{3})$

$A = 4(4\sqrt{3})$

$\mathbf{A = 16\sqrt{3}}$

PERIMETER, AREA, VOLUME DRILL

7

x

_____ **1.** The rectangle shown above has a perimeter of 20. What is the value of x?

5

_____ **2.** The rectangle shown above has an area of 30. What is the perimeter of the rectangle?

4

9

_____ **3.** What is the area of the triangle shown above?

10

6

_____ **4.** What is the area of the triangle shown above?

B

8

A   D   C

_____ **5.** In the figure above $\triangle ABC$ is equilateral and $BD \perp AC$. What is the area of $\triangle ABC$?

_____ 6. In the figure above, *ABCD* is a rectangle and *E* is the midpoint of *DC*. What is the area of the shaded region?

_____ 7. What is the volume of a right circular cylinder with radius 3 and height 7?

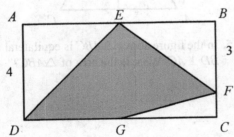

_____ 8. In the figure above, *ABCD* is a rectangle. *E* is the midpoint of *AB* and *G* is the midpoint of *DC*. If *AB* = 8, what is the area of the shaded region?

_____ 9. A rectangular box has dimensions of 3 centimeters by 5 centimeters by 7 centimeters. What is the surface area, in square centimeters, of the box?

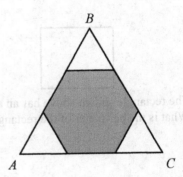

_____ 10. In the figure above, △*ABC* is an equilateral triangle with area 18 and the shaded region is a regular hexagon. What is the area of the shaded hexagon?

6.   Answer: 10.

Two methods here:

First, you can find the area of a shaded region by subtraction.
E is the midpoint of DC, so $DE = 5$ and $EC = 5$.

$$A_{rect} = \ell w = 4 \times 10 = 40$$

$$A_{ADE} = \frac{1}{2}bh = \frac{1}{2}(5)(4) = 10$$

$$A_{ABC} = \frac{1}{2}bh = \frac{1}{2}(10)(4) = 20$$

$$A_{shaded} = A_{rect} - A_{ADE} - A_{ABC}$$
$$= 40 - 10 - 20$$
$$= 10$$

Alternatively, you can actually find the area of the triangle directly.
The base of $\triangle AEC$ is EC.
The height of $\triangle AEC$ is AD.

$$A_{AEC} = \frac{1}{2}bh = \frac{1}{2}(5)(4) = \textbf{10}$$

7.   Answer: 63π.

$$V = \pi r^2 h$$
$$V = \pi(3)^2 7$$
$$V = \pi \times 9 \times 7$$
$$\textbf{V = 63}\pi$$

8.   Answer: 16.

E is the midpoint of AB, and $AB = 8$. Therefore $AE = EB = 4$.
G is the midpoint of DC, and $DC = 8$. Therefore $DG = GC = 4$.
$AD = BC = 4$, and $BF = 3$, so $FC = 1$.

Find the shaded area by subtraction:

$$A_{rect} = \ell w = 8 \times 4 = 32.$$

$$A_{ADE} = \frac{1}{2}bh = \frac{1}{2}(4)(4) = 8$$

$$A_{EBF} = \frac{1}{2}bh = \frac{1}{2}(4)(3) = 6$$

$$A_{GFC} = \frac{1}{2}bh = \frac{1}{2}(4)(1) = 2$$

$$A_{shaded} = A_{rect} - A_{ADE} - A_{EBF} - A_{GFC}$$
$$= 32 - 8 - 6 - 2$$
$$= \textbf{16}.$$

Shortcut:
You can tell (via Guesstimate) that the shaded area will be half of the area of the rectangle.
Why? The shaded area is equal to the three unshaded triangles put together.

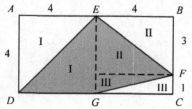

9.   Answer: 142.

The surface area is the sum of the areas of the faces of the box.

The first face is 3×5	$A = 15$
The second face is 5×7	$A = 35$
The third face is 7×3	$A = 21$

But there are *two* of each type of face: top and bottom, front and back, left and right.

$$SA = 2(15) + 2(35) + 2(21)$$
$$SA = 30 + 70 + 42$$
$$\textbf{SA = 142}$$

10.   Answer: 12.

Don't worry about the base and height of the triangles.
Don't worry about the formula for the area of a hexagon.

Instead, draw in the diagonals of the shaded hexagon:

The shaded area is made up of 6 equilateral triangles, each equal to the small unshaded triangles.

(We could prove that rigorously, but it's really, really obvious that they're all equal. So we don't have to.)

Those 6 triangles plus the 3 unshaded triangles make a total of 9 small triangles in the figure.
The area of the whole figure is 18.
So each small triangle has an area of $18 \div 9 = 2$.

We want the area of the hexagon. It's made up of 6 small triangles.
$6 \times 2 = \textbf{12}$

Circle Drill

1.   Answer: 9π.

The area of a circle is πr^2.

$r = 3$.

$A = \pi(3)^2$

$A = 9\pi$

2.   Answer: 14π.

The circumference of a circle is $2\pi r$ or πd.

$r = 7$

$C = 2\pi(7)$

$C = 14\pi$

3.   Answer: 25π.

The area of a circle is πr^2.

$d = 10$.   Therefore, $r = 5$.

$A = \pi(5)^2$

$A = 25\pi$

4.   Answer: 18π.

The area of a circle is πr^2.

$r = 6$.

$A = \pi(6)^2$

$A = 36\pi$

But we have a *semicircle*. That's half the circle.

$36\pi \div 2 = 18\pi$

5.   Answer: 64π.

The circumference of a circle is $2\pi r$.

$16\pi = 2\pi r$

$8 = r$

The area of a circle is πr^2.

$A = \pi(8)^2$

$A = 64\pi$

6.   Answer: 36π.

The side of the square is equal to the diameter of the circle.

The side is 12, so $d = 12$.

The area of a circle is πr^2.

$r = 6$.

$A = \pi(6)^2$

$A = 36\pi$

CIRCLE DRILL

_____ 1. What is the area of a circle with radius 3?

_____ 4. What is the area of a semicircle with radius 6?

_____ 2. What is the circumference of a circle with radius 7?

_____ 5. What is the area of a circle with circumference of 16π?

_____ 3. What is the area of a circle with diameter 10?

_____ 6. The figure above shows a circle inscribed within a square. If the square has a side of length 12, what is the area of the circle?

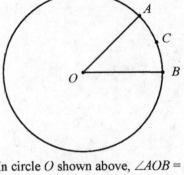

_____ 7. The figure above is composed of two small circles and one large semicircle. *AB* is a diameter of the large circle, and *AO* and *OB* are diameters of the two small circles. If the radius of the large circle is 6, what is the total length of the darkened edge of the figure?

_____ 9. In circle *O* shown above, $\angle AOB = 45°$ and the length of arc $ACB = \frac{3}{2}\pi$. What is the radius of the circle?

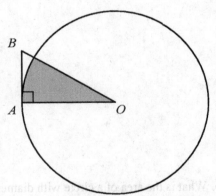

_____ 8. In the figure above, point *A* is the center of the large circle and the two circles are tangent at point *B*. If *AB* = 20, what is the area of the shaded region?

_____ 10. In the figure above, $\angle BOA = 30°$ and *OB* = 8. What is the area of the shaded region?

7. **Answer: 12π.**

Let's break the darkened edge into three parts: arc AB, arc AO, and arc OB.

Each arc is a semicircle with length equal to half a circumference. The circumference of a circle is $2\pi r$ or πd.

The large circle has a radius of 6. Its diameter $= AB = 12$.
$C = 12\pi$
arc $AB = 6\pi$

The small circles have diameters AO and OB.
Each is equal to a radius of the large circle, so each is 6.
$C = 6\pi$
arc $AO =$ arc $OB = 3\pi$

The dark edge $=$ arc $AB +$ arc $AO +$ arc OB
$= 6\pi + 3\pi + 3\pi$
$= \mathbf{12\pi}$

8. **Answer: 300π.**

$AB = 20$. That's the radius of the large circle.
$A = \pi(20)^2$
$A = 400\pi$

$AB = 20$. That's the diameter of the small circle, so $r = 10$.
$A = \pi(10)^2$
$A = 100\pi$

Shaded area $=$ whole $-$ unshaded
$= 400\pi - 100\pi$
$= \mathbf{300\pi}$

9. **Answer: 6.**

The angle is 45°. So that slice is $\dfrac{45}{360} = \dfrac{1}{8}$ of the circle.

The length of the arc is $\dfrac{3}{2}\pi$. That's $\dfrac{1}{8}$ of the circumference.

$8 \times \left(\dfrac{3}{2}\pi\right) = 12\pi = C$

Don't stop! We want the *radius*.

$C = 2\pi r = 12\pi$
$\mathbf{r = 6}$

You could also set this up as a more rigorous ratio, if you prefer:

$$\dfrac{45}{360} = \dfrac{\frac{3}{2}\pi}{C}$$

10. **Answer: 4π.**

We want the area of the slice. We can find it by taking a fraction of the area of the circle. But we don't know the area of the circle. We could figure out the area of the circle if we had the radius. But we don't have the radius.
The radius is NOT 8. $OB = 8$, but OB is not a radius. Notice that point B does not lie on the circle.

OA is a radius—A is on the circle and O is the center. But how can we find OA?

OA is in a triangle. What do we know about the triangle? We know one angle is 30° and another is 90°.

Aha! **It's a 30-60-90 triangle.**
The side opposite the 90° angle is 8, the side opposite the 30° angle is 4, and the side opposite the 60° angle is $4\sqrt{3} = OA$. That's the radius.

Now we can find the area of the circle.
$A = \pi r^2$
$A = \pi\left(4\sqrt{3}\right)^2$
$A = \pi(16)(3)$
$A = 48\pi$

That's the area of the circle. Now we need the area of the slice.
$\angle BOA = 30°$. So that slice is $\dfrac{30}{360} = \dfrac{1}{12}$ of the circle.

$48\pi\left(\dfrac{1}{12}\right) = \mathbf{4\pi}$

Triangle Drill

1. Answer: 25.

Pythagorean Theorem:

$a^2 + b^2 = c^2$

$15^2 + 20^2 = x^2$

$225 + 400 = x^2$

$625 = x^2$

$\mathbf{25 = x}$

OR, notice that this is a 3-4-5 triangle multiplied by a factor of 5:

$3 \times 5 = 15$

$4 \times 5 = 20$

$5 \times 5 = \mathbf{25}$

2. Answer: $\sqrt{97}$.

Pythagorean Theorem:

$a^2 + b^2 = c^2$

$4^2 + 9^2 = x^2$

$16 + 81 = x^2$

$97 = x^2$

$\sqrt{97} = x$

3. Answer: $3\sqrt{2}$.

Since the whole figure is a square, the triangle is an isosceles right triangle.

Therefore, the hypotenuse will be the leg times $\sqrt{2}$.

The leg is 3, so the hypotenuse is $\mathbf{3\sqrt{2}}$.

4. Answer: $3\sqrt{3}$.

Remember the dimensions of the 30-60-90 triangle.

The leg opposite the 30° will be half the hypotenuse.

The other leg will be that leg times $\sqrt{3}$.

Here the hypotenuse is 6, so $x = \mathbf{3\sqrt{3}}$.

5. Answer: 8.

Remember the dimensions of the 30-60-90 triangle.

The leg opposite the 30° will be half the hypotenuse. That leg is 4, so $x = \mathbf{8}$.

TRIANGLE DRILL

_____ **1.** What is the value of x?

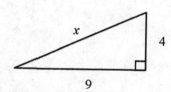

_____ **2.** What is the value of x?

_____ **3.** The figure above shows a square. What is the value of x?

_____ **4.** What is the value of x?

_____ **5.** What is the value of x?

6. In the figure above, $AC \parallel DE$. If $AB = 9$, what is the value of CE?

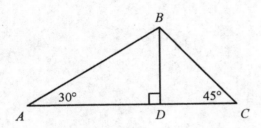

7. In the figure above, if $BC = 5\sqrt{2}$, what is the value of AB?

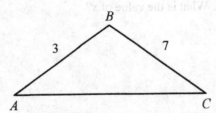

Note: Figure not drawn to scale.

8. In the figure above, BC is the largest side of the triangle. If $\triangle ABC$ is not isosceles, what is one possible value for the length of AC?

9. In the figure above, $ABCD$ is a square, $BD = 12\sqrt{2}$ and $BE = 13$. What is the length of DE?

10. What is the length of BC?

6. Answer: 4.

Since $AC \parallel DE$, $\triangle ACB$ and $\triangle DEB$ are similar triangles. That means corresponding sides will be proportional with each other.

$$\frac{DB}{AB} = \frac{EB}{CB}$$

$$\frac{6}{9} = \frac{8}{CB}$$

$6 \times CB = 72$

$CB = 12$.

$CB = CE + EB$

$12 = CE + 8$

$4 = CE$

Note that we actually could have set up the proportion with CE and AD, even though they aren't sides of the triangle. We know $AD = 3$.

$$\frac{DB}{AD} = \frac{EB}{CE}$$

$$\frac{6}{3} = \frac{8}{CE}$$

$6 \times CE = 24$

$CE = 4$

7. Answer: 10.

$\triangle BCD$ is an isosceles right triangle. The hypotenuse, BC, is $5\sqrt{2}$, so the legs, BD and DC, are each 5.

$\triangle BDA$ is a 30-60-90 triangle. The side opposite the 30° is 5, so the hypotenuse, AB, will be double 5, so **$AB = 10$**.

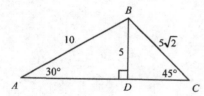

8. Answer: 4 < AC < 7 (any value).

The third side of a triangle must be greater than the difference of the other two sides. Therefore, AC must be greater than $7 - 3 = 4$.

The third side of a triangle must be less than the sum of the other two sides. Therefore, AC must be less than $7 + 3 = 10$.

However, we also know BC is the longest side, so AC must be less than 7. So **4 < AC < 7.**

Note the question asks for any possible value in that range, so pick one you like. **But not the endpoints.** The third side cannot be *equal* to 4 or 7.

We could also find a particular possible value, rather than finding the range. How? We know that BC is the greatest side, so let's say it's the **hypotenuse of a right triangle**. It's clearly not drawn that way, but it's not to scale, so I can make it any triangle I like.

We know one of the legs, AB, is 3. We can use the Pythagorean Theorem to find the other leg.

$a^2 + b^2 = c^2$

$3^2 + AC^2 = 7^2$

$9 + AC^2 = 49$

$AC^2 = 40$

$AC = \sqrt{40} = 2\sqrt{10}$ That's about **6.32**, well within our range.

9. Answer: 7.

Because $ABCD$ is a square, $\triangle BDC$ is an isosceles right triangle. Since $BD = 12\sqrt{2}$, BC and DC are each 12.

$\triangle BEC$ is a right triangle. The hypotenuse, BE, is 13, and one leg, BC, is 12. So we can use the Pythagorean Theorem to find the third side.

$EC^2 + BC^2 = BE^2$

$EC^2 + 12^2 = 13^2$

$EC^2 + 144 = 169$

$EC^2 = 25$

$EC = 5$.

Don't stop! We want DE.

$DC = DE + EC$

$12 = DE + 5$

$7 = DE$

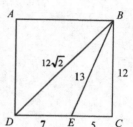

10. Answer: $\sqrt{37}$.

$\triangle ABD$ is a 30-60-90 triangle. The leg opposite the 30° angle is 2, so the leg opposite the 60° angle will be $2\sqrt{3}$.

$\triangle BDC$ is a right triangle with legs $2\sqrt{3}$ and 5. Use the Pythagorean Theorem to find the hypotenuse.

$BD^2 + DC^2 = BC^2$

$\left(2\sqrt{3}\right)^2 + 5^2 = BC^2$

$(4)(3) + 25 = BC^2$

$12 + 25 = BC^2$

$37 = BC^2$

$\sqrt{37} = BC$

THIS PAGE INTENTIONALLY LEFT BLANK

Appendix C
Summaries

Reading Summary

READING TECHNIQUES
The Passage
- Read quickly and get the **main ideas** of the passage, paragraph by paragraph.
- To find the main idea, ask: **what's it about?**
- If you can't find the main idea, read the **first and last sentences** of the paragraph.
- Don't spend too much time. Don't overanalyze. If you're not sure, **move on**.

The Question
- Read the question, **ignore the choices**.
- When there's a line reference, **go back to the passage** and read the line.
- **Read the whole sentence**, not just the line referred to.
- If that line is unclear, read the **sentence before** or the **sentence after**.
- Try to answer the question with what you just learned. That's your **anticipation**.
- If you can't anticipate, go to the choices to **eliminate**.

The Choices
- If you find a choice that matches your anticipation, pick it.
- If you don't find a match or if you don't have an anticipation, **look for wrong choices**. You can eliminate even if you don't understand the passage or question.
- **Work quickly**. If you're not sure about a choice, skip it and come back later.
- Eliminate choices that are **random**, **false**, or **irrelevant**.
- As you eliminate, **cross out** words that make a choice wrong.
- No matter what, *guess one*. **Never leave blanks.**

READING QUESTION TYPES
Explicit Questions
- These questions ask what the passage literally said. If there's a line reference, go back to the passage and anticipate. If not, use your main ideas to help you find it.

Vocab-in-context Questions
- Don't just define the word. Anticipate for these just like for Explicit questions. Use the context of the sentence to anticipate the meaning of the word.

Evidence Questions
- These questions ask you to find a line reference to justify your answer to the previous question.
- It's often helpful to do Evidence questions together with the questions they refer to:
  - Go back to the passage and check the line references.
  - See if the lines answer the previous question.

Main Idea Questions
- If a question asks about a full paragraph or the entire passage, use your main ideas as your anticipation.

Inferential Questions
- These questions ask about things that the passage doesn't literally say, but that must be true based on what the passage does say.
- While sometimes they are easy to anticipate for, Inferential questions are often more likely to be solved by elimination than by anticipation because the answer isn't literally stated in the passage.

Strategy Questions
- These questions ask why the author wrote the passage the way that he or she did. The answers often discuss the author's rhetorical strategies.

Tone Questions
- These questions often come down to whether the author has a positive, negative, or neutral attitude towards the subject.

Data Questions
- Some Data questions will ask you to lookup values that appear on the figure.
- Some Data questions will ask you to understand the meaning of the values in the figure.

Double Passages
- Do the passages separately.
  - Read the passage 1 and do the questions about passage 2.
  - Then read passage 2 and do the questions about passage 2 and the questions about both passages.

Writing Summary

CONVENTIONS OF USAGE

Verbs

- The verb must **agree** in number with the subject.
  - Ask: who is performing the action?
  - Ignore interrupting phrases and prepositional phrases.
  - One verb can have multiple subjects; one subject can have multiple verbs.
- The verb must be in the appropriate **tense**.
  - Look for **time words** or **other verbs** in the sentence or nearby sentences.
  - Watch for special tenses: present perfect, past perfect, and "would".
- **Irregular** verbs may have special forms.
- Don't confuse active and **passive** voice.
  - In a passive verb, the subject does not perform the action.
  - In general, if you know who the actor is, don't use the passive.

Pronouns

- A pronoun must **agree** in number with its antecedent.
  - Ask: what does the pronoun refer to?
  - Watch for **vague pronouns** and **mystery pronouns**, when the antecedent is unclear or missing.
  - Be consistent with **generic pronouns**.
  - Sometimes **nouns** must agree with each other, too.
- A pronoun's **case** is determined by its role in the sentence.
  - Subjects and objects use different forms.
  - Use **reflexive pronouns** when subject and object refer to the same person.
  - Don't confuse **contractions** and **possessive** pronouns.
- **Relative** pronouns (like *who, which,* or *that*) behave similarly to regular pronouns.
  - Their verbs agree with the antecedent of the relative pronoun.
  - Relatives have cases, like regular pronouns.
  - *Who* is for people, *which* is for non-people.

Other Issues

- **Adjectives** describe nouns. **Adverbs** describe all other words.
- **Comparatives** compare two things, **superlatives** compare three or more.
- When making a **comparison**, you must compare similar *concepts*, not just similar forms.
- Make sure to use the correct **prepositions**.
- Your choice of preposition may affect the form of the **verb** that follows.
- Beware of commonly confused words:
  - Use "would **have**", not "would of".
  - Use "**than**" for comparisons, not "then".

SENTENCE STRUCTURE

Definitions

- An **independent clause** can stand by itself as a sentence. It must have a subject and main verb.
- A **dependent clause** cannot stand by itself as a sentence.
- A **relative clause** is a dependent clause with a relative pronoun that describes a single word in the sentence.
- A **modifier** is a phrase with no main verb that modifies something in the sentence.

Fragments

- Every sentence must have **at least one independent clause** with a subject and verb.
- Fix a fragment by:
  - Turning a *partial verb* into a **main verb.**
  - Removing unnecessary connectors or relative pronouns.
  - **Joining it** to another sentence by *removing the period.*

Run-on Sentences

- **Don't** connect independent clauses with a **comma alone**, or with **no connection** at all.
- Fix a run-on by:
  - Separating the clauses with a **period**.
  - Using a **comma** with a **conjunction**.
  - Making one of the independent clauses a **dependent clause or modifier**.

Modifiers

- A modifier at the *beginning of a sentence* must describe the *subject of the main clause* (the word right after the comma) or else it's a dangling **modifier**.
- A modifier at *the end of a sentence* may describe:
  - the **subject**, if there's a *comma*.
  - the **word next to it**, if there's *no comma*.
- *Prepositional phrases* must be **placed right after** the words they describe.

Parallelism

- Use **parallel forms** for **parallel ideas.** Any words or phrases joined with the word "**and**" must be in parallel forms.
- Don't use "and" if the forms **aren't parallel.**

CONVENTIONS OF PUNCTUATION

DO use commas:
- between **independent clauses** with a conjunction.
- around **parenthetical phrases**.
- in a list of **three or more**.
- with **coordinate adjectives**.
- before a **direct quote**.
- around **sentence adverbs**.

DON'T use commas:
- between **subject and verb**.
- between **verb and object**.
- before **infinitives**.
- before or in the middle of **prepositional phrases**.
- with a **two part list** (two nouns or verbs with a conjunction).
- with a **"that"** clause.
- before **restrictive** clauses.

Apostrophes
- **Plurals** usually take -s.
- **Possessives** take -'s.
- **Plural possessives** take -s'.
- **Contractions** use apostrophes for missing letters.
- **Pronouns** take *contraction* apostrophes but **not** *possessive* apostrophes.

Other marks
- A **semicolon** separates *independent clauses* (interchangeable with a period).
- A **colon** *strongly* connects phrases.
- A **dash** connects independent clauses or parenthetical phrases.
- Don't mix up **sentence-final marks**: *periods, question marks,* and *exclamation points.*

EXPRESSION OF IDEAS

Effective Language Use
- Be **concise**. Avoid *redundant* or *wordy* choices.
- Be **specific**. Avoid *vague* choices and vague *pronouns*.
- Choose **the right word**. Make sure it has the right *meaning* and *tone*.

Organization
- Choose the right **transition word** to connect *similar or contrasting* sentences.
- Choose the right **transition phrase** to connect the *topics* of adjacent sentences.
- An **introductory or concluding sentence** should state the *main idea* of the paragraph.
- Find the right **sentence order** by looking at references within the sentences.

Development
- Does a choice **fulfill the writer's goal**? Focus on the *stated goal*, not your opinion.
- Should the writer **add or delete** a sentence? Look out for *irrelevant* choices.
- If the writer deleted a phrase, what **would the essay lose**? Find the *meaning* of the phrase and how it *relates* to the paragraph.
- Is the sentence true according to a **data figure**?

Mathematics Summary

MATH TECHNIQUES
General Strategies
- Before you do anything else, **circle the question** you're being asked.
- **Show your work** for every question. Don't do math in your head.
- If a picture is drawn to scale, **Guesstimate!**. Get a **rough guess** of what the value should be based on the picture. Eliminate choices that are obviously too big or too small.

Common Mistakes
- **RTFQ**: make sure you answer the question you're being asked!
- **Fool's Gold**: if a choice seems too easy for a hard question, it's probably wrong.

Target Numbers
- Don't do all the questions! **Guess on the last ones**.
- If you take **more time per question**, you'll cut down on carelessness and are more likely to get them right.
- It's not that those questions are too hard for you. It's about doing **fewer questions**, but doing them **more accurately**.

Plug In
- **Pick a number** for the variable.
- Do the problem with that number and get a number for an answer.
- Put the number you chose into the choices and see which gives you the same answer.
- Check all choices. If more than one works, pick a different number.
- Sometimes you have to plug in for more than one variable. Sometimes plugging in for one gives you the value of another.
- Sometimes there are implicit variables—there are no variables with letters, but there is an unnamed value you don't know.
- If a question asks about a **relationship**, try Plug In. That often means **variables in the answer choices**.

Backsolve
- **Start with choice C)**. Assume that's the answer.
- That's the answer to the question. Put that number through the information given to see if it all matches.
- If it matches, that's your answer. If it doesn't, pick another one.
- If C) fails, often you can tell whether you want a higher or lower number. If you can't, just pick one.
- If a question is asking for a **value**, try Backsolve. That usually means there are **numbers in the answer choices**.

MATH FUNDAMENTALS
- Know some basic **definitions** of numbers: integer, factor, multiple, prime number, remainder, positive/negative, even/odd, prime factor.
- Know how to add, subtract, multiply, and divide **fractions**.
- Solve **ratios** by cross multiplying. Make sure units match across the equals sign.
- Convert **rates and units** by multiplying fractions and cancelling out like terms
- A **percent** is a ratio out of 100. Know how to manipulate percents and percent change.
- Know the rules of combining **exponents**:
  - To multiply exponentials, *add* exponents.
  - To divide exponentials, *subtract* exponents.
  - To raise an exponent to another exponent, *multiply* the exponents.
- The **absolute value** of a term is its value without its sign— that is, *make it positive.*

HEART OF ALGEBRA
- Solve an algebraic equation by getting the **variable by itself**. Move terms around by doing the opposite of any function.
- Understand how to **write equations** based on sentences. Recognize the parts of a **linear equation**.
- When you have **multiple equations** you may:
  - Solve one equation for a variable and *substitute* into the other equation.
  - Solve a *system* of equations by adding or subtracting to eliminate on variable
  - If the question asks for an expression, try to solve directly for the expression.
- **Inequalities** can be manipulated just like equations. Remember to flip the inequality sign if you multiply or divide by a negative.

PASSPORT TO ADVANCED MATH
F(x) notation
- For equations using the "$f(x)$" notation, the value **inside the parentheses** tells you the value of x.
- **Plug that value in** for x. If $f(x) = 2x + 5$, then $f(4) = 2(4) + 5$

Polynomials
- **Simplify** polynomials by combining terms with the same exponential terms.
- To multiply binomials, use **FOIL**: Multiply the First terms, the Outside terms, the Inside terms, and the Last terms.
- The reverse of FOILing is **factoring**. Know how to split a polynomial into its constituent factors.
- Recognize the **difference of squares**:
  $(x + y)(x - y) = x^2 - y^2$

- You can **divide** polynomials by canceling out a factor from the top and bottom.
- Find the solutions to a **quadratic equation** by:
  - Factoring and setting the terms equal to zero
  - Using the quadratic formula.
- Know the equation for **exponential growth**.

GRAPHING

- Know how to read a **coordinate plane**. The x-axis is horizontal, and the y-axis is vertical.
- A **graph of a function** is a picture of its solutions. Saying "$f(3) = 4$" means that the point $(3, 4)$ appears on the graph of $f(x)$.
- The **slope** of a line is the change in y over the change in x.
- The **equation of a line** can be written $y = mx + b$, where m is the slope and b is the y-intercept.
- A **parabola** can be written with the equation $y = ax^2 + bx + c$, where c is the y-intercept.
- The x-intercepts of a parabola are the solutions to its quadratic equation.
- A **circle** can be described by the equation $(x - a)^2 + (y - b)^2 = r^2$, where (a, b) is the center and r is the radius.

PROBLEM SOLVING AND DATA ANALYSIS

- Be familiar with **data representations**: tables, coordinate planes, scatterplots, bar graphs.
  - Be ready to *approximate* when necessary
  - *Scatterplots* may have a line of best fit that shows the relationship between points and predicts other points
- Know how to compute **averages**.
  - *Mean* is the sum over the number of terms.
  - *Median* is the number in the middle when written in order.
  - Average problems can often be solved via the **sum** instead of the terms. The average times the number of terms equals the sum.
- **Probability** is the number of *winning events* divided by the *total possible events*. The probabilities of all events associated with a problem must *add up to 1*.
- A **sample** is when a survey gathers a small group of data to represent a larger group.
  - You can *project* values for the large group with a simple ratio.
  - Be sure that your sample is *random* and *unbiased*.

ADDITIONAL TOPICS IN MATH
General strategies

- Use **Guesstimate** whenever possible. Try it on *every question with a figure*.
- Need a formula? **Look it up!** There's a bunch of them given at the beginning of the section.

Angles

- A **straight line** equals 180°.
- A **triangle** equals 180°.
- An **isosceles triangle** has two equal sides and two equal angles.
- **Vertical angles** are equal.
- **Parallel lines** with a transversal produces two kinds of angles: big ones and little ones.

Perimeter, Area, Volume

- The **perimeter** of a figure is the sum of the lengths of the sides.
- Know some formulas for **area**: triangle = $(1/2)bh$; rectangle = ℓw; square = s^2
- **Shaded area** problems can best be done by subtraction: find the area of the whole figure and subtract the part you don't need.
- **Surface area** is the sum of the areas of the faces of an object.
- Know some formulas for **volume**: box = ℓwh; cube = s^3; cylinder = $\pi r^2 h$

Circles

- A circle's center has 360°.
- The **diameter** goes from end to end of a circle, passing through the center.
- The **radius** goes from the center to the end. The radius is half a diameter.
- The **area** of a circle is πr^2.
- The **circumference** of a circle is $2\pi r$.
- A **slice** of a circle is a fraction of the circle. Everything about that slice is the same fraction: angle, area, and arc length.

Triangles

- Any two triangles with the same three angles are **similar**. The lengths of their corresponding sides are in the same ratio with each other.
- In a right triangle, **the Pythagorean theorem** says $a^2 + b^2 = c^2$, where a and b are legs and c is the hypotenuse.
- A **45-45-90** triangle has dimensions $x, x, x\sqrt{2}$.
- A **30-60-90** triangle has dimensions $x, x\sqrt{3}, 2x$.

Trigonometry

- The trigonometric functions are the ratios of various sides of a right triangle.
  - **Sine** of an angle is the opposite side over the hypotenuse.
  - **Cosine** is the adjacent side over the hypotenuse.
  - **Tangent** is the opposite over the adjacent.
- Learn the **reciprocal functions**: *sec, cos, cot*
- The **inverse functions** allow you to solve trigonometric equations.
- Learn some identities.
  - sin / cos = tan
  - $\sin^2 + \cos^2 = 1$
- Convert **radians** to degrees with the formula 360 degrees = 2π radians.

Essay Summary

Format

- The Essay is **optional**.
- You will receive a 600-700 word persuasive passage.
- You must read the passage and write a 1-4 page essay analyzing how the author makes his or her argument.
- You are not expected to agree or disagree with the author, but you must discuss how the argument is presented and why.

Scoring

- You will get three scores, 2 to 8 each, in the each of these areas: *Reading*, *Analysis*, and *Writing*.
- Essay will be graded by two readers. Each reader will give a score from 1 to 4 in three areas. Your score will be the sum of the two scores in each area.
- Scores cannot differ by more than 1 point within an area.

Reading

- Identify the **central thesis** of the passage. That's the same as the main idea.
- Find the **main ideas** of each paragraph.
- Take notes and **write things down**.
- Identify the author's use of
  - **Evidence**: facts and figures.
  - **Reasoning**: connecting facts into an argument
  - **Style**: rhetorical devices and persuasive language.

Analysis

- Don't just summarize the argument, evaluate how it is effective.
- Connect the author's strategies and show how they relate to each other.
- Explain why the author presents the argument the way he or she does.

Writing

- Make an **outline** of your essay:
  - *Introduction*: include the author's central thesis and your thesis.
  - *First tactic*
  - *Second tactic*
  - *Third tactic*
  - *Conclusion*
- For each tactic you discuss, give **evidence** from the passage. Quote directly when appropriate.
- Include sophisticated **vocabulary** whenever possible.
- Make sure you use **concrete language** whenever possible.
- Use **complex sentences** with a varied structure.
- Watch out for **grammatical mistakes** (like those we discussed in the other chapters).

Appendix D
Answer Keys

READING

READING TECHNIQUES

Main Idea Drill

See main reading section for discussion of Main Ideas.

Anticipation Drill

See main reading section of this manual for discussion of Anticipations.

Elimination Drill

1. C
2. C
3. A
4. D
5. A
6. B
7. A
8. D
9. B
10. D

Leavitt questions

1. D
2. A
3. B
4. C
5. C
6. B
7. C
8. C
9. D
10. C
11. A

READING QUESTION TYPES

Explicit Questions

1. A
2. B

Vocab in Context Questions

3. A
4. D

Evidence Questions

5. C
6. D

Main Idea Questions

7. C
8. C

Inferential Questions

9. C
10. D

Strategy Questions

10. B
11. A

Tone Questions

13. D
14. C

Tone Questions

15. C
16. C

Double Passage Questions

17. A
18. B
19. C
20. C

Reading Passage Exercise

Passage I: Fiction

1. D
2. C
3. A
4. D
5. C
6. B
7. D
8. D
9. B
10. A

Passage II: Social Science/ History

11. A
12. D
13. C
14. C
15. C
16. D
17. C
18. D
19. D
20. B
21. B

Passage III: Science

22. D
23. C
24. A
25. C
26. B
27. B
28. B
29. C
30. A
31. D

WRITING

CONVENTIONS OF USAGE

Verb mini-drills

Agreement

- have
- was
- is
- come
- was

Tense

- slept
- will be felt
- brings
- cooked
- would buy

Verb Drill

1. B
2. B
3. C
4. D
5. C
6. A
7. B
8. A
9. C
10. D
11. B
12. C
13. D
14. B
15. D

Pronoun mini-drills

Agreement

- their
- we
- they
- it
- their

Case

- its
- You're
- their
- me
- their

Relatives

- who are
- who's
- who
- whose
- who

Pronoun Drill

1. B
2. D
3. A
4. B
5. D
6. D
7. A
8. B
9. C
10. B
11. B
12. D
13. D
14. A
15. C

Conventions of Usage Exercise

1. A
2. B
3. C
4. C
5. A
6. D
7. A
8. D
9. C
10. C
11. B

SENTENCE STRUCTURE

Fragment Drill

1. Complete Sentence
2. Fragment
3. Complete Sentence
4. Fragment
5. Fragment
6. Fragment
7. Fragment
8. Complete Sentence
9. Fragment
10. Fragment
11. Fragment
12. Complete Sentence
13. Fragment
14. Fragment
15. Complete Sentence

Run-On Drill

1. C
2. B
3. C
4. D
5. D
6. B
7. A
8. C
9. C
10. B
11. B
12. D
13. D
14. A
15. B

Sentence Structure Exercise

1. A
2. D
3. B
4. C
5. A
6. C
7. D
8. B
9. A
10. B
11. D

CONVENTIONS OF PUNCTUATION

Comma Drill

1. D
2. A
3. C
4. C
5. A
6. D
7. D
8. C
9. B
10. B
11. A

Punctuation Exercise

1. C
2. C
3. A
4. D
5. D
6. B
7. D
8. C
9. C
10. D
11. B

EXPRESSION OF IDEAS

Expression of Ideas Exercise

1. D
2. D
3. A
4. B
5. C
6. A
7. D
8. D
9. A
10. D
11. D

MATH

MATH TECHNIQUES

Plug In Drill

8. D
12. C
14. B
17. B
18. B
21. D
23. C
24. D
29. C
30. B

Backsolve Drill

5. A
8. D
11. A
14. B
15. A
17. D
20. D
23. C
26. C
27. B

Big Technique Exercise

1. A. Plug In
2. A. Plug In
3. D. Backsolve
4. D. Backsolve
5. C. Plug In
6. C. Plug In
7. A. Backsolve
8. B. Backsolve
9. C. Plug In
10. B. Backsolve
11. A. Plug In
12. C. Guesstimate or Plug In
13. D. Plug In
14. A. Backsolve
15. B. Plug In

MATH FUNDAMENTALS

Number Concepts and Definitions

- 9
- I and III
- 11
- 10
- −1

Fractions

- $\dfrac{55}{12}$ or $4\dfrac{7}{12}$
- $\dfrac{7}{6}$ or $1\dfrac{1}{6}$
- $\dfrac{19}{10}$ or $1\dfrac{9}{10}$
- $\dfrac{4}{5}$
- $\dfrac{15}{2}$ or $7\dfrac{1}{2}$

Ratios

- 3
- 27
- 88
- 35
- 31.5

Rates

- 1,500
- 120
- 25
- 60
- 450

Percentages

- 21
- 125
- 60
- 9
- 10

Exponents

- a^{11}
- 3
- x^2
- $-7x^2$
- 1/3
- $-8x^6$
- 39
- $30x^7y^5$
- $a^{27}bc^{16}$
- $-10x^2y^6$

Absolute Value

- 6
- 6
- −11
- 8 or −4
- 12 or −34

Math Fundamentals Exercise

1. A
2. D
3. D
4. C
5. A
6. C
7. C
8. D
9. C
10. B
11. B
12. A
13. A
14. C
15. C

HEART OF ALGEBRA

Evaluating an expression

- −1
- 51
- 29
- 1,210
- −10

Solving an equation

- 9
- 12
- −2
- 11/3
- 1/2
- −20
- 24/13
- $a = \dfrac{P}{5} - 8$
- $x = \dfrac{3}{2}y + 9$
- $b = \dfrac{cde}{a}$

Writing equations

- 2.5
- 2
- 120
- 0.15
- 250

Multiple equations

- $24x - 7$
- 1/3
- 22
- (3,3)
- (7,−2)
- (13,6)
- 7
- 11
- 19
- 18

Inequalities

- $x < 2$
- $x < -6$
- $x < -2$
- $x > -10$
- $x \ge -7$

Heart of Algebra Exercise

1. D
2. C
3. C
4. C
5. C
6. B
7. C
8. C
9. B
10. D
11. A
12. D
13. B
14. A
15. C

PASSPORT TO ADVANCED MATH

F(x) notation

- 120
- 60
- −10
- −33/4 or −8.25
- $4x^2 + 6x - 10$
- −12
- 3
- $4x + 6$
- 77
- 47

Polynomials

- $6x^2 + 5x - 2$
- $x^2 - 12x - 1$
- $2x^2 + 11x + 9$
- $3x^3 + 12x^2 - 9x + 9$
- $7x^2 + 3x^2y + 10y^2 - 7x + 14y$

FOIL

- $x^2 + 5x - 24$
- $a^2 - 9a + 14$
- $2y^2 - 5y - 12$
- $x^2 + 2xy + y^2$
- $3x^4 + 5x^2y + 2y^2$

Factoring

- $(x - 4)(x + 2)$
- $(x - 2)(x - 12)$
- $(2x + 1)(x + 5)$
- $(3x - 7)(3x + 7)$
- $(x - 2)(x + 2)(x^2 + 4)$

Dividing polynomials

- $\dfrac{1}{x + 7}$
- $\dfrac{1}{x - 5}$
- $x + 10$
- $2 + \dfrac{4}{x - 1}$
- $x + 3 + \dfrac{4}{x + 2}$

Quadratic equations

- 0 or 12
- 5 or 6
- −1 or 8
- −9 or 9
- 6 or 7

Passport to Advanced Math Exercise

1. B
2. B
3. B
4. C
5. B
6. D
7. C
8. D
9. B
10. D
11. D
12. A
13. D
14. A
15. A

GRAPHING

Graphing Functions

- $f(-1) = 0$
- $f(0) = 1$
- $f(2) = -1$
- $f(3) = -2$

Lines

- −5/2 or −2.5
- −3
- 8
- −3
- 1/3
- c/b
- $y = 2x + 4$
- (2.5, 0)
- −2
- $y = -\dfrac{1}{3}x - 3$

Parabolas

- (0, −24)
- (0, −14)
- (0, 9)
- (−7, 0) and (8, 0)
- (−5, 0) and (4, 0)

Circles

- $(x - 2)^2 + (y - 1)^2 = 36$
- $(x + 4)^2 + y^2 = 25$
- $(x - 5)^2 + (y - 4)^2 = 16$
- (−8, 2)
- $\sqrt{7}$

Graphing Exercise

1. C
2. C
3. C
4. A
5. C
6. D
7. B
8. B
9. A
10. D
11. B
12. A
13. D
14. B
15. D

PROBLEM SOLVING AND DATA ANALYSIS

Averages

- 12
- 26
- 184
- 2
- 2.6

Probability

- 9/26
- 3/7
- 7/22
- 13/35
- 3/10
- 12/35
- 3/70
- 1/7
- 8/35
- 32/41

Problem Solving and Data Analysis Exercise

1. A
2. C
3. B
4. D
5. A
6. D
7. C
8. B
9. B
10. C
11. D
12. D
13. A
14. C
15. C

ADDITIONAL TOPICS IN MATH

Angle Drill

8. B
9. B
14. B
22. C
30. D

Perimeter, Area, Volume Drill

2. D
18. C
21. B
24. B
36. 10

Circle Drill

8. B
14. D
20. C
24. C
29. D

Triangle Drill

6. C
15. B
17. C
27. C
30. D

Trigonometry functions

- 24/25
- 7/24
- 24/25

Trigonometry Drill

10. C
14. A
20. C
25. A
38. 4/5 or 0.8

Imaginary and complex numbers

- −1
- $68 + 2i$
- $17 - 20i$
- $5 - 12i$
- 25

Additional Topics in Math Exercise

1. B
2. B
3. C
4. A
5. C
6. B
7. C
8. D
9. A
10. D
11. A
12. B
13. B
14. D
15. C

APPENDIX A: Writing drills

WRITING

Verb Agreement Drill

1. is
2. stay
3. is
4. has
5. is
6. have
7. was
8. grows
9. have
10. have

Verb Tense Drill

1. converted
2. sees
3. flew
4. receive
5. will be
6. allied
7. swum
8. have evolved
9. have learned
10. has ridden

Pronoun Agreement Drill

1. they
2. one
3. it
4. its
5. he
6. they were
7. their
8. her
9. it
10. our

Fragment Drill

1. Fragment
2. Fragment
3. Complete sentence
4. Fragment
5. Fragment
6. Complete sentence
7. Fragment
8. Fragment
9. Complete sentence
10. Fragment

Run-On Drill

1. Run-on
2. Not a run-on
3. Run-on
4. Run-on
5. Not a run-on
6. Not a run-on
7. Run-on
8. Not a run-on
9. Run-on
10. Run-on

APPENDIX B: Math drills

Plug In Drill

1. C
2. C
3. D
4. D
5. 4/7 or .571
6. A
7. B
8. A
9. C
10. A

Backsolve Drill

1. A
2. B
3. A
4. D
5. C
6. D
7. D
8. C
9. B
10. B

Fraction Drill

1. $\frac{13}{3}$ or $4\frac{1}{3}$
2. $\frac{23}{24}$
3. $\frac{1}{2}$
4. $\frac{8}{3}$ or $2\frac{2}{3}$
5. $\frac{3}{4}$
6. $\frac{15}{56}$
7. $\frac{19}{5}$ or $3\frac{4}{5}$
8. $\frac{19}{20}$
9. $\frac{1}{3}$
10. $\frac{1}{10}$

Ratio Drill

1. 3:2
2. 20
3. 25
4. 12
5. 15
6. 16
7. 8
8. 2:3
9. 150
10. 8

Percent Drill

1. 27
2. 75
3. 60
4. 320
5. 300
6. 18
7. 4/5 or 0.8
8. $41.40
9. $97.50
10. 20%

Exponent Drill

1. $8x^5$
2. $4x^2$
3. $27x^6$
4. $3x^3$
5. $5x^{-2}$ or $5/x^2$
6. $3x^2$
7. $2x^{7x}$
8. $14x^6$
9. $5x$
10. $20x$

One-variable Algebra Drill

1. 3
2. 11
3. 1/2 or 0.5
4. 15/2 or 7.5
5. $x > -5$
6. 2
7. 0 or 1
8. 4 or -4
9. 77
10. 5

Multi-variable Algebra Drill

1. $x = \dfrac{y-6}{5}$
2. $m = 4n + 27$
3. -20
4. $x = 23 - 5y$
5. $u = \dfrac{3v+8}{4}$
6. $j = n + 4$
7. 3
8. $a = -3, b = 21$
9. $z = 3y^2 + 30y + 75$
10. $a = d^2 + 2d - 15$

F(x) Drill

1. 22
2. -26
3. -6
4. $12a - 8$
5. 52
6. 9
7. 2
8. 5
9. 56
10. 12
11. $-(1/4)$
12. $4x^4 + 2x^2$
13. $x^2 + 7x + 12$
14. 60
15. 0 or 1
16. 64
17. 42
18. 1
19. $7 - \sqrt{7}$
20. 128

Polynomial Drill

1. $5x^3 + 2x^2 - 6x - 7$
2. $-10x^3 - 6x^2 + 7x + 11$
3. $x^2 + 7x + 12$
4. $x^2 - 4x - 5$
5. $15x^2 - 26x + 8$
6. $(x-2)(x+1)$
7. $(x-6)(x-2)$
8. $(x-4)(x+4)$
9. $x - 5$
10. $x = -6$ and $x = -8$

Solve Directly for Expressions

1. 64
2. 23
3. 24
4. 46
5. 18
6. 16
7. 4
8. $3c - 5$
9. $2/3$
10. 4

Graphing Drill

1. 4
2. 8
3. -6
4. -6 or -2
5. 0
6. $1 < x < 4$
7. 3
8. C
9. 4
10. 7
11. -2
12. 8
13. 2
14. -4 or 0
15. -2
16. 4
17. -1
18. -1
19. $-4 \le x \le -1$
20. B

Average Drill

1. 25
2. 170
3. 30
4. 24
5. 300
6. 70
7. 81
8. 80
9. 84.8
10. 90

Angle Drill

1. 35
2. 100
3. 125
4. 18
5. 120
6. 90
7. 25
8. 80
9. 108
10. 60

Perimeter, Area, Volume Drill

1. 3
2. 22
3. 18
4. 24
5. $16\sqrt{3}$
6. 10
7. 63π
8. 16
9. 142
10. 12

Circle Drill

1. 9π
2. 14π
3. 25π
4. 18π
5. 64π
6. 36π
7. 12π
8. 300π
9. 6
10. 4π

Triangle Drill

1. 25
2. $\sqrt{97}$
3. $3\sqrt{2}$
4. $3\sqrt{3}$
5. 8
6. 4
7. 10
8. $4 < AC < 7$ (any value)
9. 7
10. $\sqrt{37}$

■ PERFORMANCE LOGS

READING

Reading Techniques

Main Idea Drill _____

Anticipation Drill _____

Elimination Drill _____

Reading Exercise 1 _____

_____

Reading Question Types

Explicit Questions _____

Vocab-in-context Questions _____

Evidence Questions _____

Main Idea Questions _____

Inferential Questions _____

Strategy Questions _____

Tone Questions _____

Data Questions _____

Double Passages _____

Reading Exercise 2 _____

_____

WRITING

Conventions of Usage

Verb Agreement_____

Verb Tense_____

Verb Drill_____

Pronoun Agreement_____

Pronoun Case _____

Relative Pronouns _____

Pronoun Drill _____

Conventions of Usage Exercise _____

_____

Sentence Structure

Fragment Drill _____

Run-on Drill _____

Sentence Structure Exercise _____

_____

Punctuation

Comma Drill _____

Punctuation Exercise _____

_____

Rhetorical Skills

Rhetorical Skills Exercise _____

_____

Appendix A

Verb Agreement Drill _____

Pronoun Agreement Drill _____

Verb Tense Drill _____

Fragment Drill _____

Run-On Drill _____

MATHEMATICS

Techniques

Plug In Drill _____

Backsolve Drill _____

Big Technique Exercise _____

_____

Math Fundamentals

Number Concepts & Definitions _____

Fractions _____

Ratios _____

Rates and Units _____

Percentages _____

Exponents _____

Absolute Value _____

Math Fundamentals Exercise _____

_____

Heart of Algebra

Evaluating an expression _____

Solving an equation _____

Writing an equation _____

Multiple equations _____

Inequalities _____

Heart of Algebra Exercise _____

_____

Passport to Advanced Math

$F(x)$ notation _____

Combining polynomials _____

FOIL _____

Factoring _____

Dividing polynomials _____

Quadratic equations _____

Passport to Advanced Math Exercise _____

_____

Graphing

Graphing Functions _____

Lines _____

Circles _____

Graphing Exercise _____

_____

Problem Solving and Data Analysis

Averages _____

Probability _____

Problem Solving and Data Analysis Exercise

_____

Additional Topics in Math

Angle Drill _____

Perimeter, Area, Volume Drill _____

Circle Drill _____

Triangle Drill _____

Trigonometry functions _____

Trigonometry Drill _____

Imaginary and Complex Numbers _____

Additional Topics in Math Exercise _____

_____

Appendix B

Plug In Drill _____

Backsolve Drill _____

Fraction Drill _____

Ratio Drill _____

Percent Drill _____

Exponent Drill _____

One-variable Algebra Drill _____

Multi-variable Algebra Drill _____

$F(x)$ Drill _____

Polynomial Drill _____

Solve Directly for Expressions _____

Graphing Drill _____

Average Drill _____

Angle Drill _____

Perimeter, Area, Volume Drill _____

Circle Drill _____

Triangle Drill _____

NOTES:

NOTES:

A-LIST EDUCATION PRODUCTS & SERVICES

✔ Test Preparation & Advising

Our test prep program takes a unique approach matching each student's learning style and motivation with the right educator.

- In-person or online tutoring for the SSAT, SAT, ACT, GRE, LSAT, MCAT & more

- Full support for elementary, university, and graduate school application process

- Academic support, time management, and study skills development

✔ Direct Instruction

A-List provides direct instruction services to schools and institutions. Our class offerings can focus on any of the following subjects:

- ACT/SAT
- State Exams
- Core Skills
- College Readiness Programming

✔ Professional Development

Our professional development programs equip instructors with the resources to effectively integrate ACT/SAT content into existing curricula or to run a stand-alone test prep course. Offerings include:

- ACT/SAT Test Prep
- ACT/SAT Integrated Curriculum
- ACT/SAT Comparison
- Customized Academic Workshops

> " *We have been using A-List since 2012 and are very happy with our results. A-List has trained our teachers how to integrate SAT/ACT skills and use A-List materials in their classrooms. Our school SAT mean this year is 1211 compared to our district mean of 962. Overall, 97% of our students meet the SAT ELA benchmark, 89% of our students meet the SAT Math benchmark, and 95% of our students are above the district mean. Thank you!"*

— Kevin F., Principal, Manhattan Hunter Science High School, New York

Learn more at www.alisteducation.com

The ACT/SAT Book of Knowledge

A-List's core text contains all the test taking skills and content necessary to conquer the ACT or SAT.

✔ **The Book of Knowledge SAT**
Everything you need for the SAT

✔ **The Book of Knowledge SAT Student Solutions**
Detailed explanations for the SAT book

✔ **The Book of Knowledge SAT Teacher Manual**
All of the regular book alongside explanations

✔ **The Book of Knowledge ACT**
Everything you need for the ACT

✔ **The Book of Knowledge ACT Student Solutions**
Detailed explanations for the ACT book

✔ **The Book of Knowledge ACT Teacher Manual**
All of the regular book alongside explanations

Visit www.alisteducation.com/bookstore to shop A-List's products!

ACT & SAT in The Classroom Series

This series reveals how the content of the ACT & SAT closely align with state standards. Teachers learn how to integrate test prep into an existing curriculum. Books are available for ACT ELA, ACT Math, SAT ELA, and SAT Math.

Online Test Content & Assessment Portal

The portal is a low-cost, automated, rapid solution for ACT & SAT scoring and analysis. Data allows teachers to steer instruction and address crucial topics. Features include:

- Test grading and analysis
- Downloadable lesson plans, quizzes, and drills
- Slides featuring explanations for every question in The Book of Knowledge

ACT & SAT Instructional Videos

Watch A-List's educators discuss every concept and question found in The Book of Knowledge.

- Advice from trainers with thousands of hours of classroom experience
- Highly engaging videos followed by assessments that ensure retention

Vocab Videos Online System + Workbook

Vocab Videos uses short videos to illustrate the meanings of 500 high-value high school vocabulary words.

- Quizzes and worksheets for each episode
- Multimedia flashcard maker
- Photo & video uploading (for students to create their own!)

